北京2020统计年鉴

Beijing Statistical Yearbook

北京市统计局
国家统计局北京调查总队 编
Beijing Municipal Bureau of Statistics
NBS Survey Office in Beijing

中国统计出版社
China Statistics Press

图书在版编目（CIP）数据

北京统计年鉴. 2020 = Beijing Statistical Yearbook 2020：汉英对照 / 北京市统计局，国家统计局北京调查总队编. ——北京：中国统计出版社，2020.9
ISBN 978－7－5037－9247－2

Ⅰ.①北… Ⅱ.①北… ②国… Ⅲ.①统计资料－北京－2020－年鉴－汉、英 Ⅳ.①C832.1－54

中国版本图书馆CIP数据核字（2020）第162393号

北京统计年鉴-2020

作　　者/北京市统计局　国家统计局北京调查总队
责任编辑/李　冲
封面设计/高　立
出版发行/中国统计出版社
通信地址/北京市丰台区西三环南路甲6号　　邮政编码/100073
电　　话/邮购（010）63376909　　书店（010）68783171
网　　址/http://www.zgtjcbs.com
印　　刷/河北鑫兆源印刷有限公司
经　　销/新华书店
开　　本/880mmx1230mm　1/16
字　　数/1200千字
印　　张/39.25印张　彩插/1.5印张
版　　别/2020年9月第1版
版　　次/2020年9月第1次印刷
定　　价/350.00元

本书附同版本CD-ROM一张，光盘内容以书面文字为准。
如有印装差错，由本社发行部调换。

2019年的北京
BEIJING IN 2019

83.5
第三产业增加值占地区生产总值比重（%）
Add Value of Tertiary Industry as % of GDP (%)

35371.3
地区生产总值（亿元）
Gross Domestic Product (100 million yuan)

5817.1
一般公共预算收入（亿元）
General Public Budget Revenue (100 million yuan)

164220
人均地区生产总值（元）
Per Capita Gross Domestic Product (yuan)

2233.6
研究与试验发展(R&D)经费内部支出(亿元)
Internal R&D Expenditures (100 million yuan)

281752
社会劳动生产率（元/人）
Overall Labor Productivity (yuan / person)

67756
全市居民人均可支配收入（元）
Per Capita Disposable Income of Residents of the Whole City (yuan)

102.3
居民消费价格指数（上年=100）
Consumer Price index (preceding year = 100)

2019年的北京
BEIJING IN 2019

2153.6
常住人口（万人）
Permanent Population
(10000 persons)

1312
常住人口密度（人/平方公里）
Permanent Population Density
(person/sq.km)

152
街道办事处（个）
Sub-district (unit)

38
建制乡（个）
Designated Township (unit)

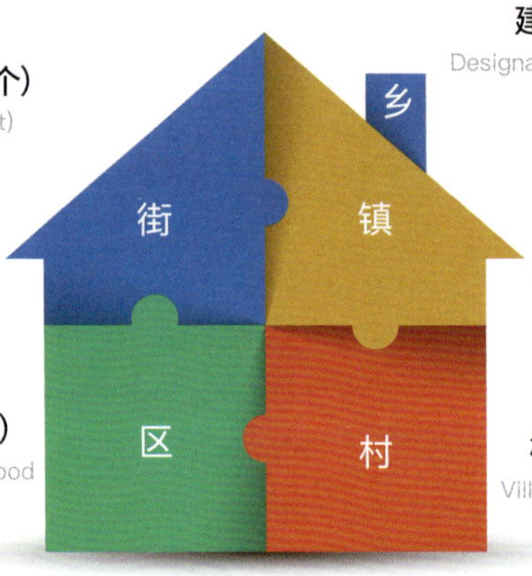

143
建制镇（个）
Designated Town (unit)

3231
社区居委会（个）
Community Neighborhood
Committee (unit)

3891
村民委员会（个）
Villagers' Committee (unit)

22366
公路里程（公里）
Highway Mileage (km)

63928
全市集中供热面积（万平方米）
Centralized Heating Area in Beijing
(10000 sq.m)

699
轨道交通运营线路长度（公里）
Length of Operating Rail Transit Lines
(km)

1877422
天然气供气总量（万立方米）
Supply Volume of Natural Gas
(10000 cu.m)

598.9
自来水综合生产能力（万立方米/日）
Gereral Production Capacity of Tap Water
(10000 cu.m/day)

27632
公共电汽车运营线路长度（公里）
Length of Operating Buses and
Trolley Buses Lines (km)

1166.4
全社会用电量（亿千瓦时）
Electricity Consumption
(100 million kWh)

636.5
机动车保有量（万辆）
Possession of Motor Vehicles
(10000 units)

6.31

研究与试验发展经费内部支出相当于地区生产总值比例（%）

Internal R&D Expenditures as % of GDP (%)

132

万人发明专利拥有量（件）

Invention Patent Ownership per 10000 persons (unit)

5695.3

技术合同成交总额（亿元）

Total Volume of Transaction of Technical Contracts (100 million yuan)

5.55

每千常住人口医院床位数(张)

Number of Ward Beds per 1000 Permanent Population (unit)

5.38

每千常住人口执业(助理)医师数(人)

Number of Certified (Assistant) Doctors per 1000 Permanent Population (person)

13.8

平均每一专任教师负担小学生数(人)

Average Number of Students in Primary School Instructed by a Full-time Teacher (person)

8.0

每十万常住人口幼儿园数(个)

Number of Kindergartens per 100000 Permanent Population (unit)

0.85

每十万常住人口博物馆数(个)

Number of Museums per 100000 Permanent Population (unit)

6.17

每十万常住人口公共图书馆书刊文献外借册次(万册次)

Volume-times of Borrowed Books, Magazines and Documents of Public Libraries per 100000 Permanent Population (10000 volume-times)

42.0

$PM_{2.5}$年平均浓度(微克/立方米)

Annual Average Concentration of $PM_{2.5}$ (μg/cu.m)

114.0

人均水资源(立方米)

Per Capita Water Resource (cu.m)

16.4

人均公园绿地面积（平方米）

Per Capita Park Green Area (sq.m)

48.5

城市绿化覆盖率(%)

Urban Green Coverage (%)

每日创造
Daily Production

159372.6
一般公共预算收入
(万元)
General Public Budget Revenue
(10000 yuan)

202964.1
一般公共预算支出
(万元)
General Public Budget Expenditure
(10000 yuan)

11813.5
发电量
(万千瓦时)
Electricity Generated
(10000 kWh)

4493
汽车生产量
(辆)
Output of Motor Vehicles
(vehicle)

229406
移动电话机生产量
(台)
Output of Mobile Telephones
(set)

3894.0
实际利用外商直接投资额
(万美元)
Actual Use of Foreign Direct Investment
(USD 10000)

12879
显示器生产量
(台)
Output of Display Devices
(set)

969076.7
地区生产总值(万元)
Gross Domestic Product
(10000 yuan)

3115.1
第一产业(万元)
Primary Industry
(10000 yuan)

156578.1
第二产业(万元)
Secondary Industry
(10000 yuan)

809383.6
第三产业(万元)
Tertiary Industry
(10000 yuan)

643967.1
地区进口总值
(万元)
Total Imports of Local Enterprises
(10000 yuan)

858.5
公共电汽车客运量
(万人次)
Passenger Traffic of Buses and Trolley Buses
(10000 person-times)

141708.9
地区出口总值
(万元)
Total Exports of Local Enterprises
(10000 yuan)

1085.6
轨道交通客运量
(万人)
Passenger Traffic of Rail Transit
(10000 person-times)

160717.8
国内旅游收入
(万元)
Revenue from Domestic Tourism
(10000 yuan)

1421.9
国际旅游收入
(万美元)
Revenue from Inbound Tourism
(USD 10000)

25.3
民航客运量
(万人次)
Passenger Traffic of Civil Aviation
(10000 person-times)

131.9
公路客运量
(万人次)
Passenger Traffic of Highway
(10000 person-times)

40.4
铁路客运量
(万人次)
Passenger Traffic of Railway
(10000 person-times)

每日生活
Daily Life

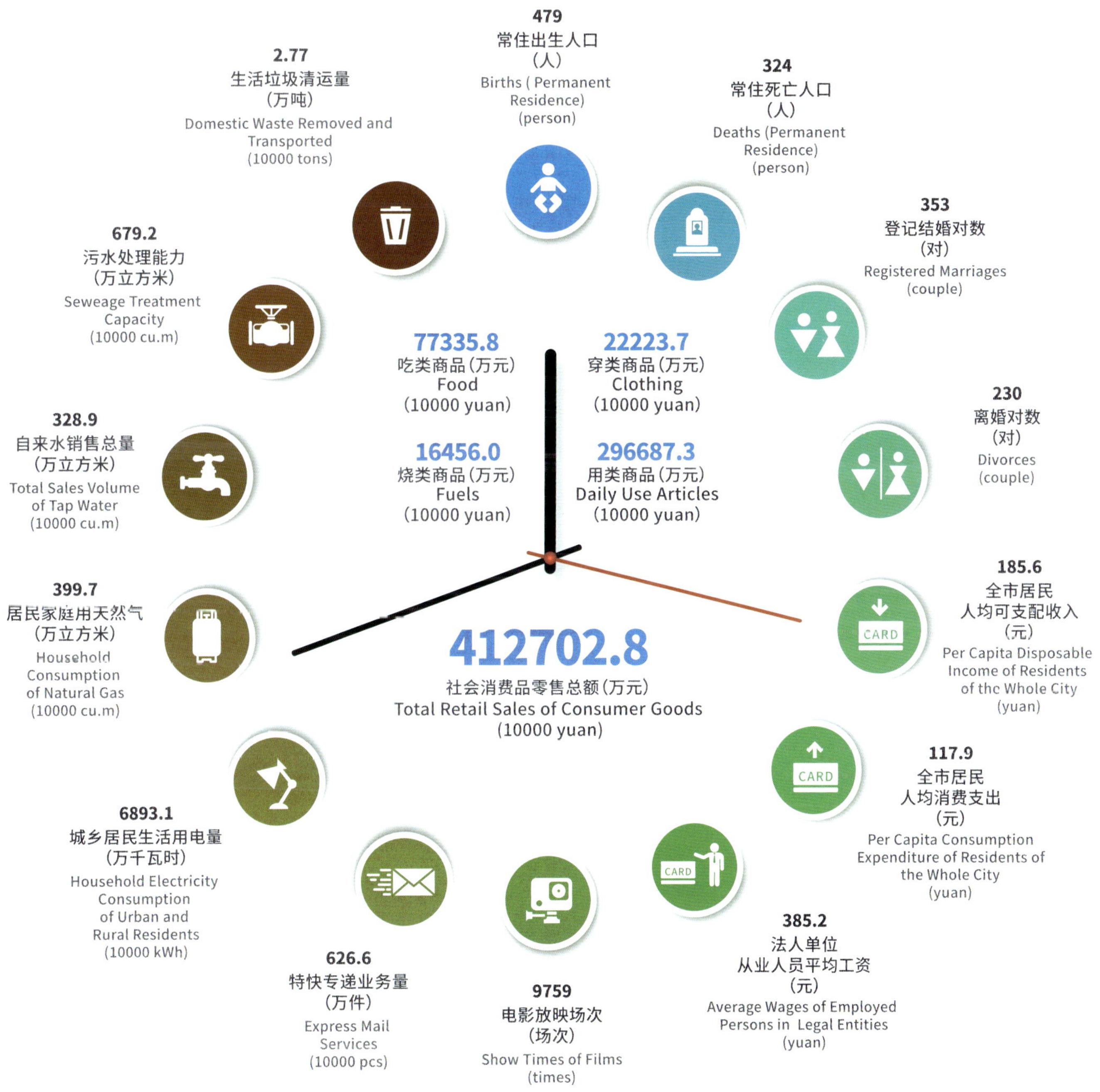

2019

地区生产总值（亿元）
Gross Domestic Product (100 million yuan)

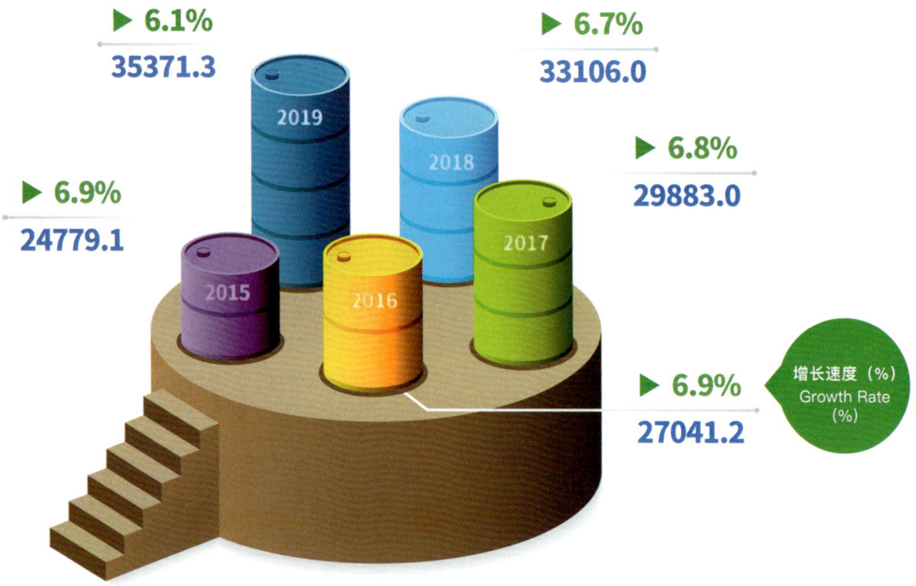

人均地区生产总值（元）
Per Capita Gross Domestic Product (yuan)

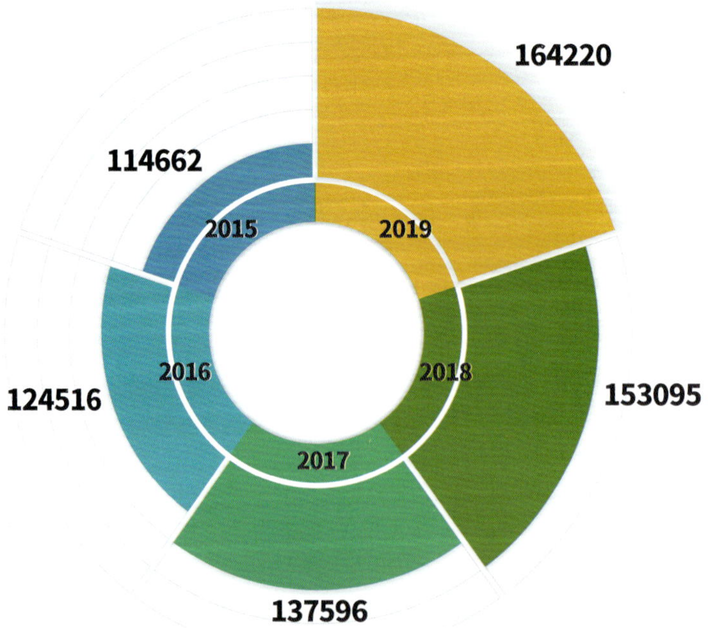

一般公共预算收入（亿元）
General Public Budget Revenue（100 million yuan）

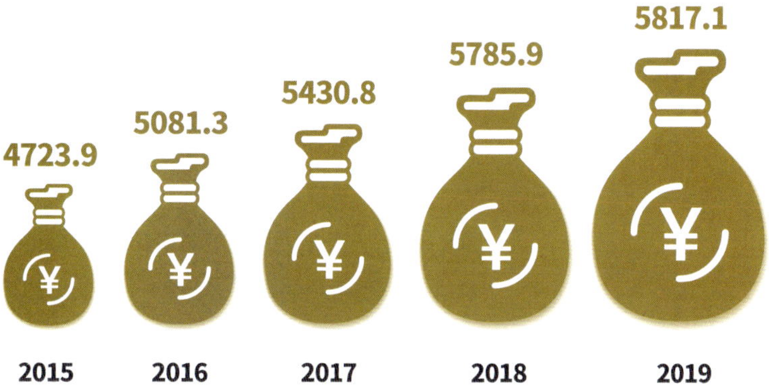

一般公共预算支出（亿元）
General Public Budget Expenditure (100 million yuan)

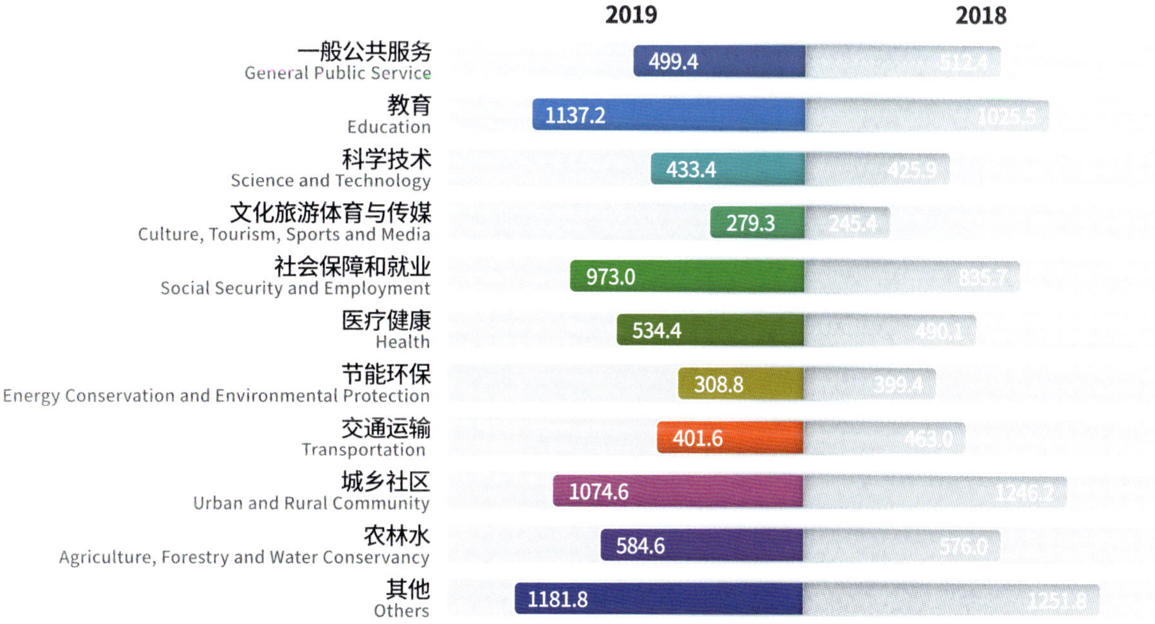

常住人口（万人）
Permanent Population (10000 persons)

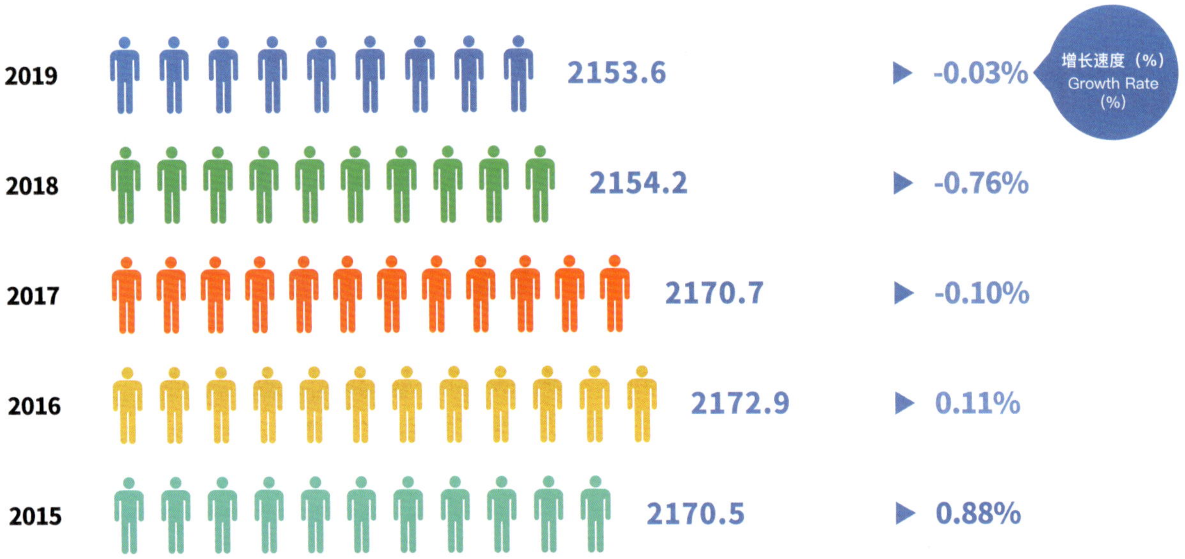

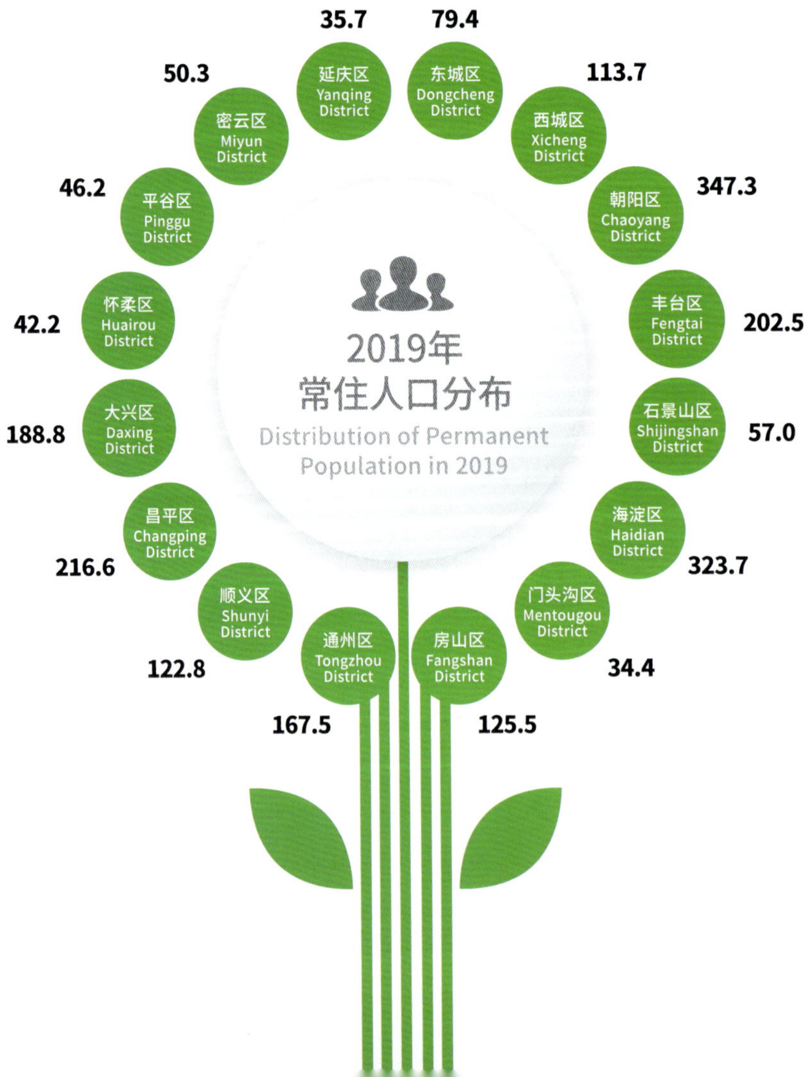

从业人员（万人）
Employed Persons (10000 persons)

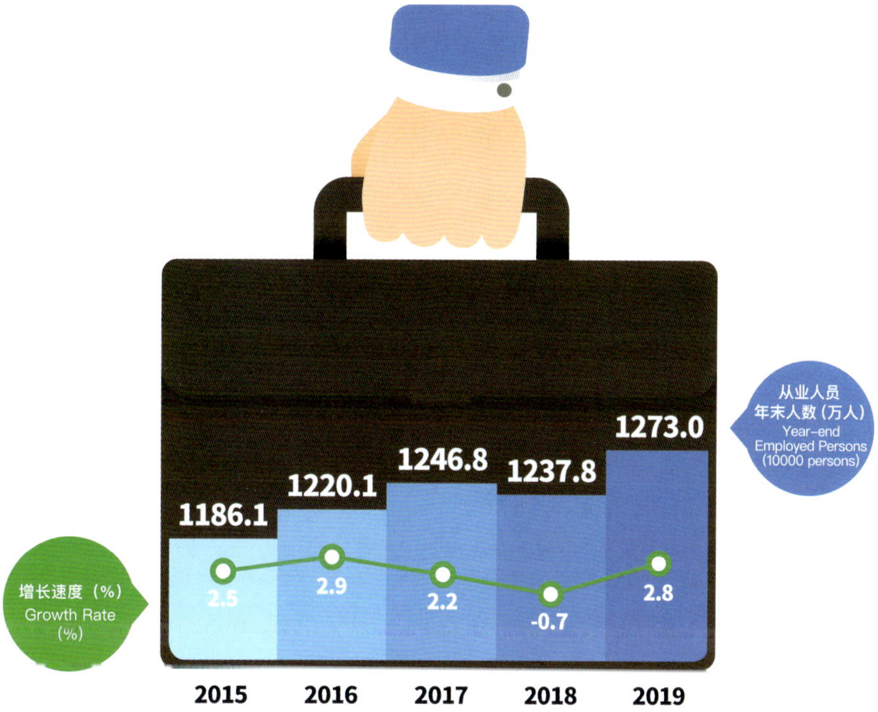

法人单位从业人员平均工资（元）
Average Wages of Employed Persons in Legal Entities (yuan)

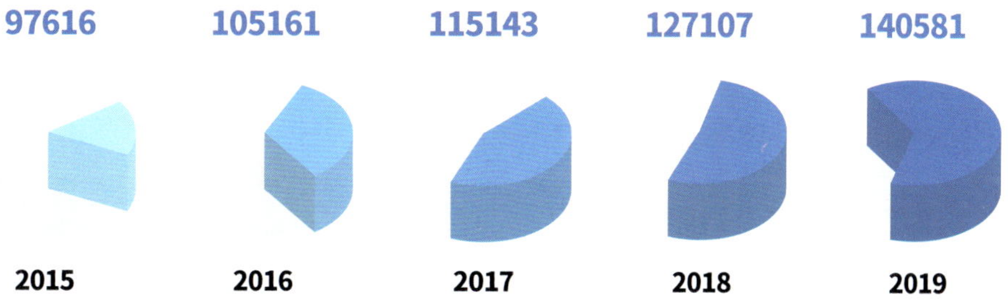

价格指数(上年=100)
Price Index (preceding year=100)

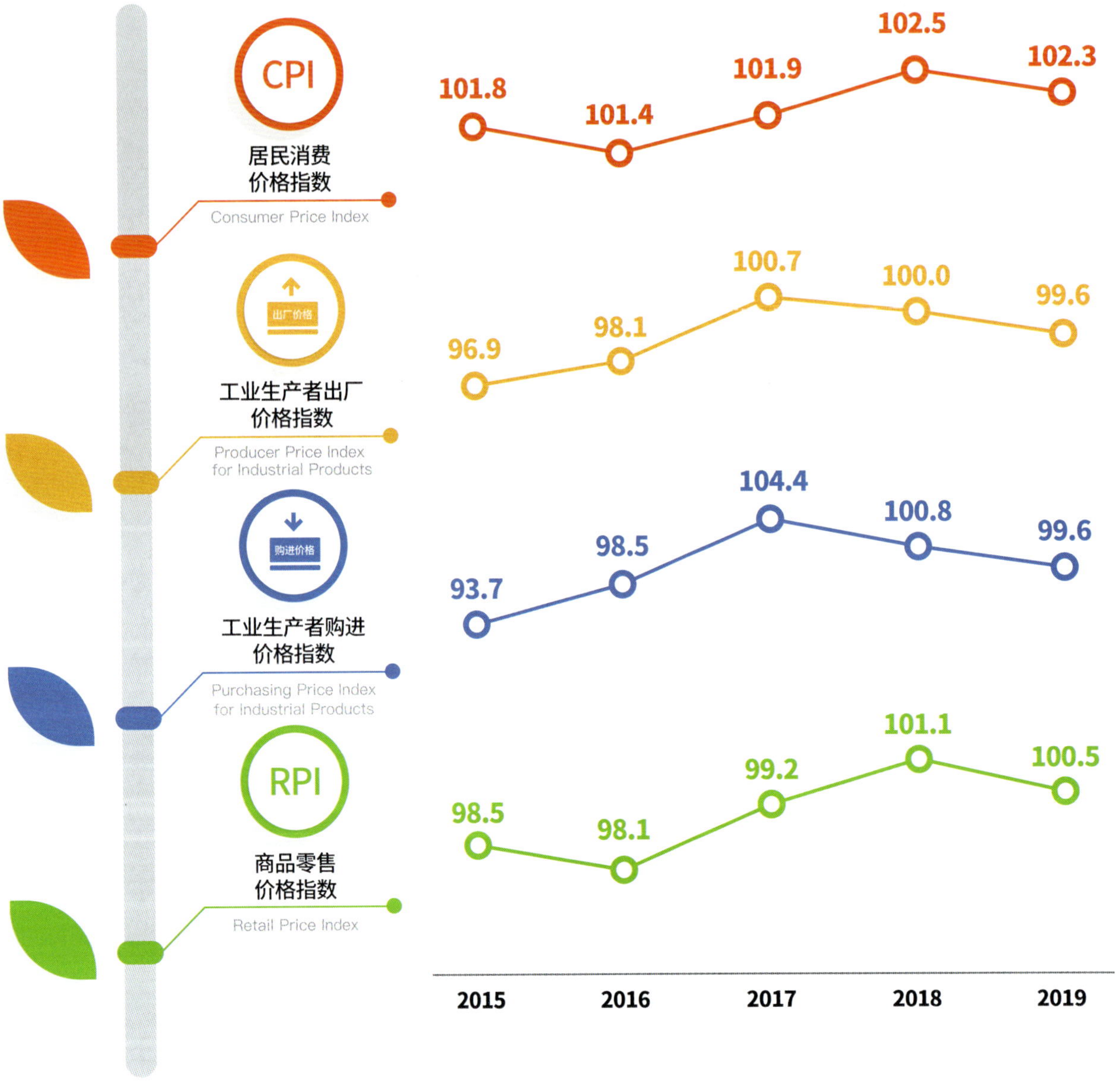

居民人均可支配收入（元）
Per Capita Disposable Income of the Residents (yuan)

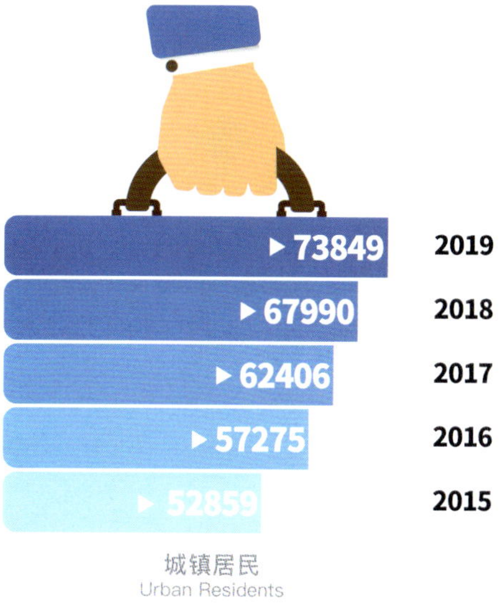

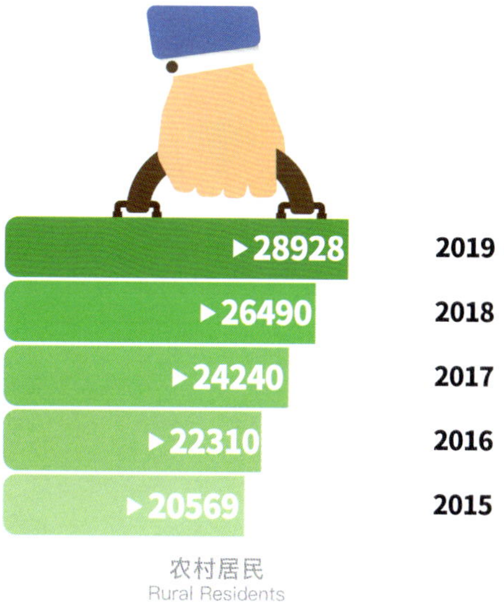

居民人均消费支出（元）
Per Capita Consumption Expenditure of the Residents (yuan)

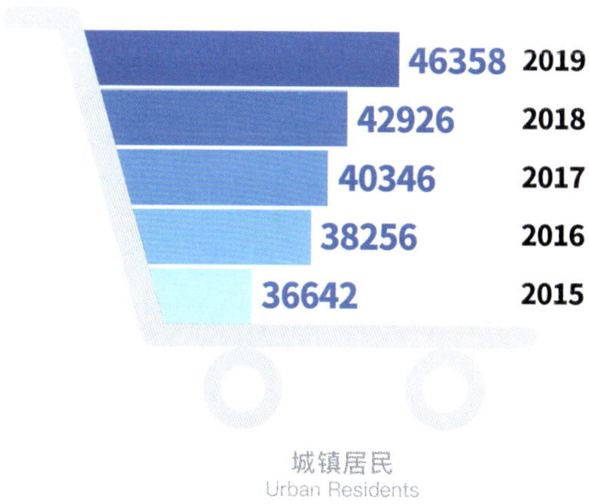

三次产业增加值结构（%）
Structure of Added Value of Three Industries (%)

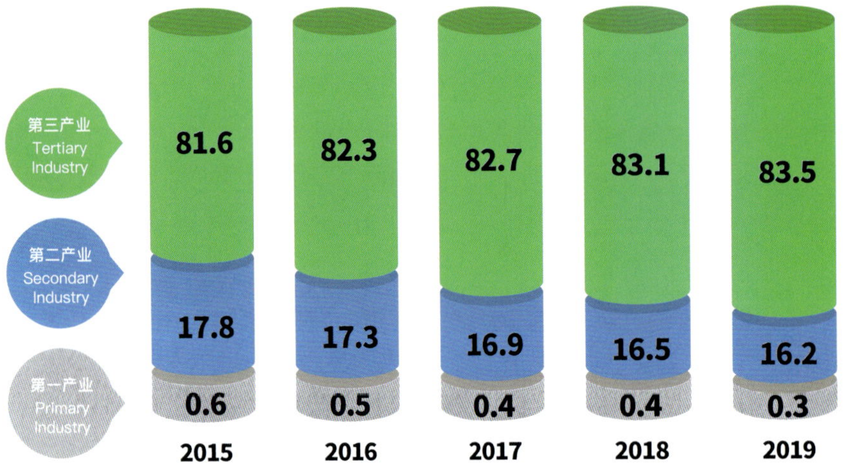

部分新兴产业增加值（亿元）
Added Value of Some Emerging Industries (100 million yuan)

固定资产投资增长速度（%）
Growth Rate of Investment In Fixed Assets（%）

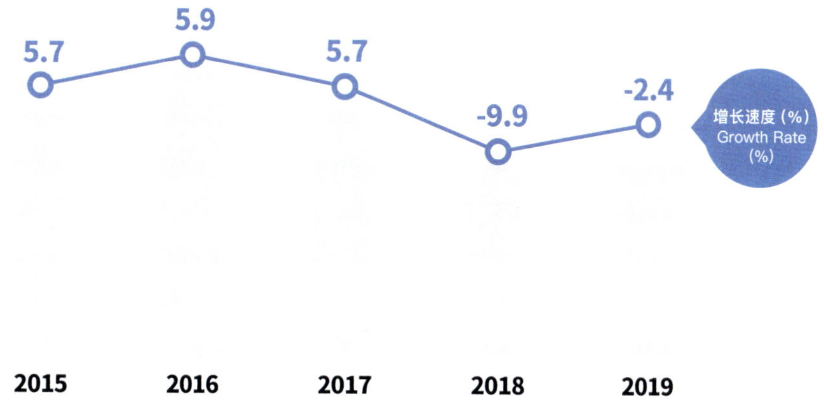

注：2018年及以前为全社会口径，2019年为不含农户口径。
Note: In and before 2018, the data on fixed asset investment were those of full coverage. The data for 2019 were those that excluding rural households.

社会消费品零售总额（亿元）
Total Retail Sales of Consumer Goods (100 million yuan)

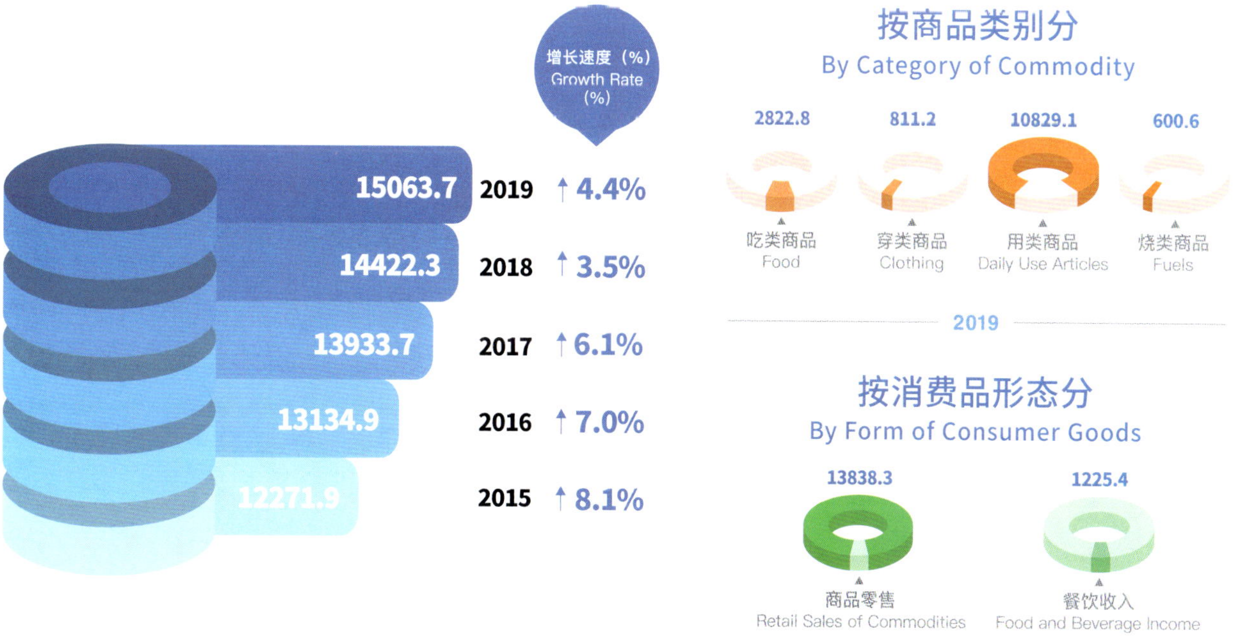

进出口总值（亿元）
Total Value of Imports and Exports (100 million yuan)

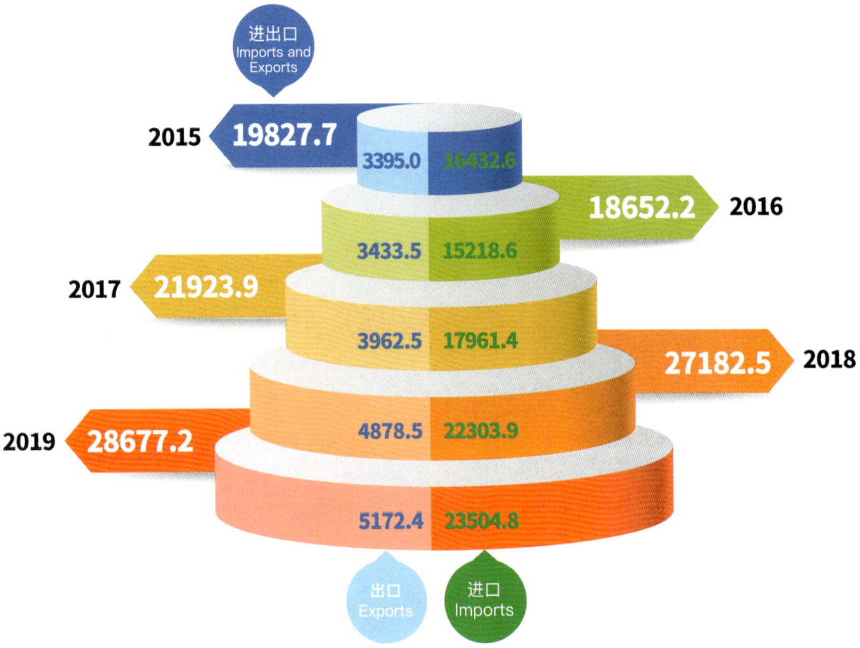

服务贸易总额（亿美元）
Total Value of Service Trade (USD 100 million)

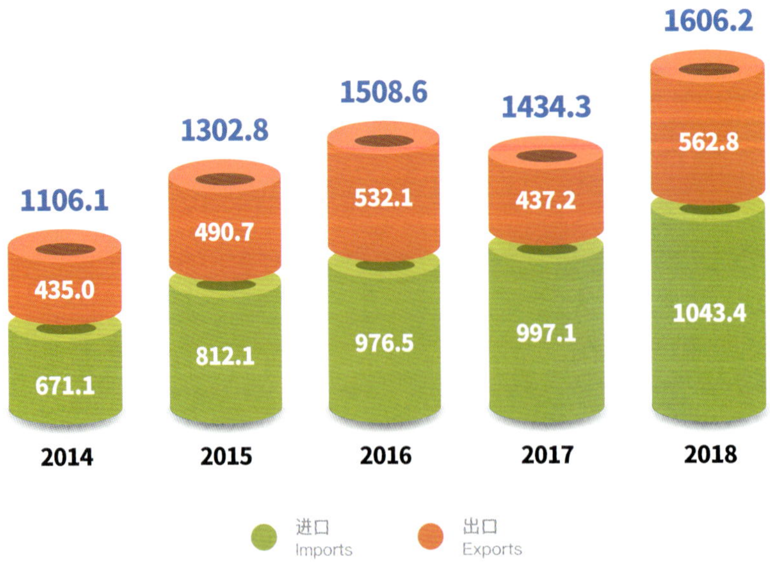

实际利用外商直接投资额（亿美元）
Actal Use of Foreign Direct Investment (USD 100 million)

对外经济合作完成营业额（亿美元）
Turnover in Foreign Economic Cooperation (USD 100 million)

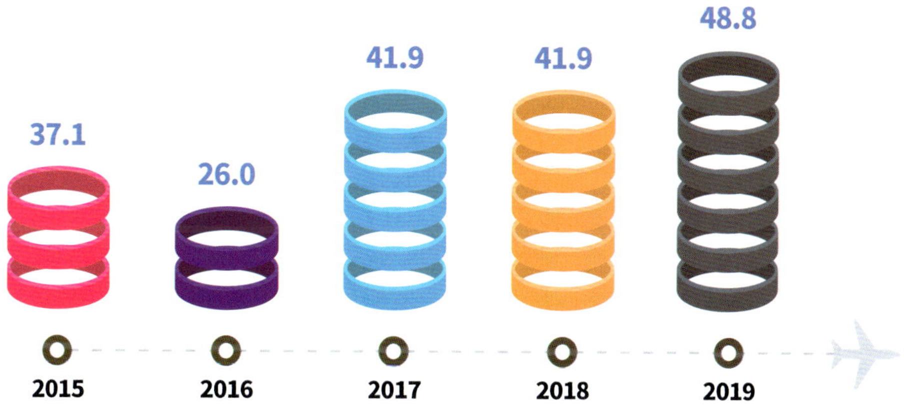

万元地区生产总值能耗（吨标准煤）
Energy Consumption per 10000 Yuan of GDP (ton of SCE)

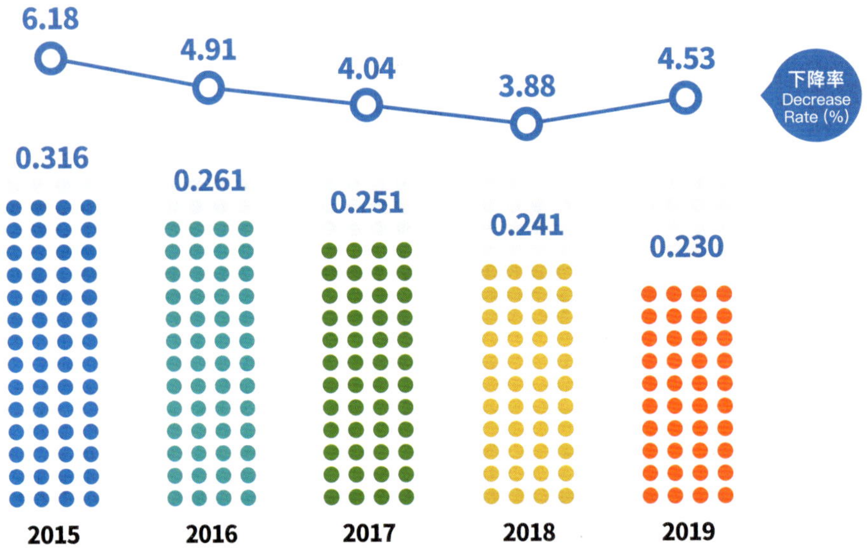

万元地区生产总值水耗（立方米）
Water Consumption per 10000 Yuan of GDP (cu.m)

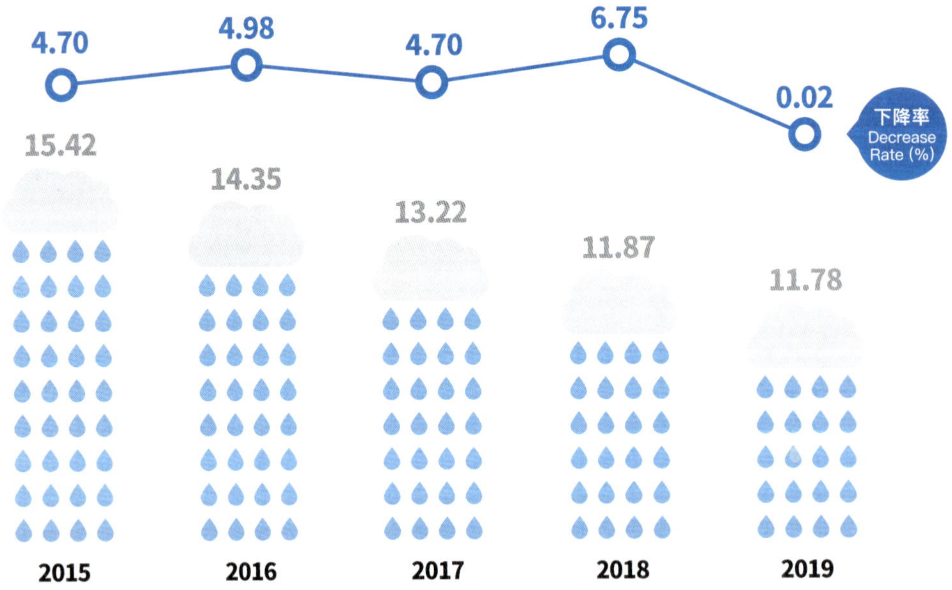

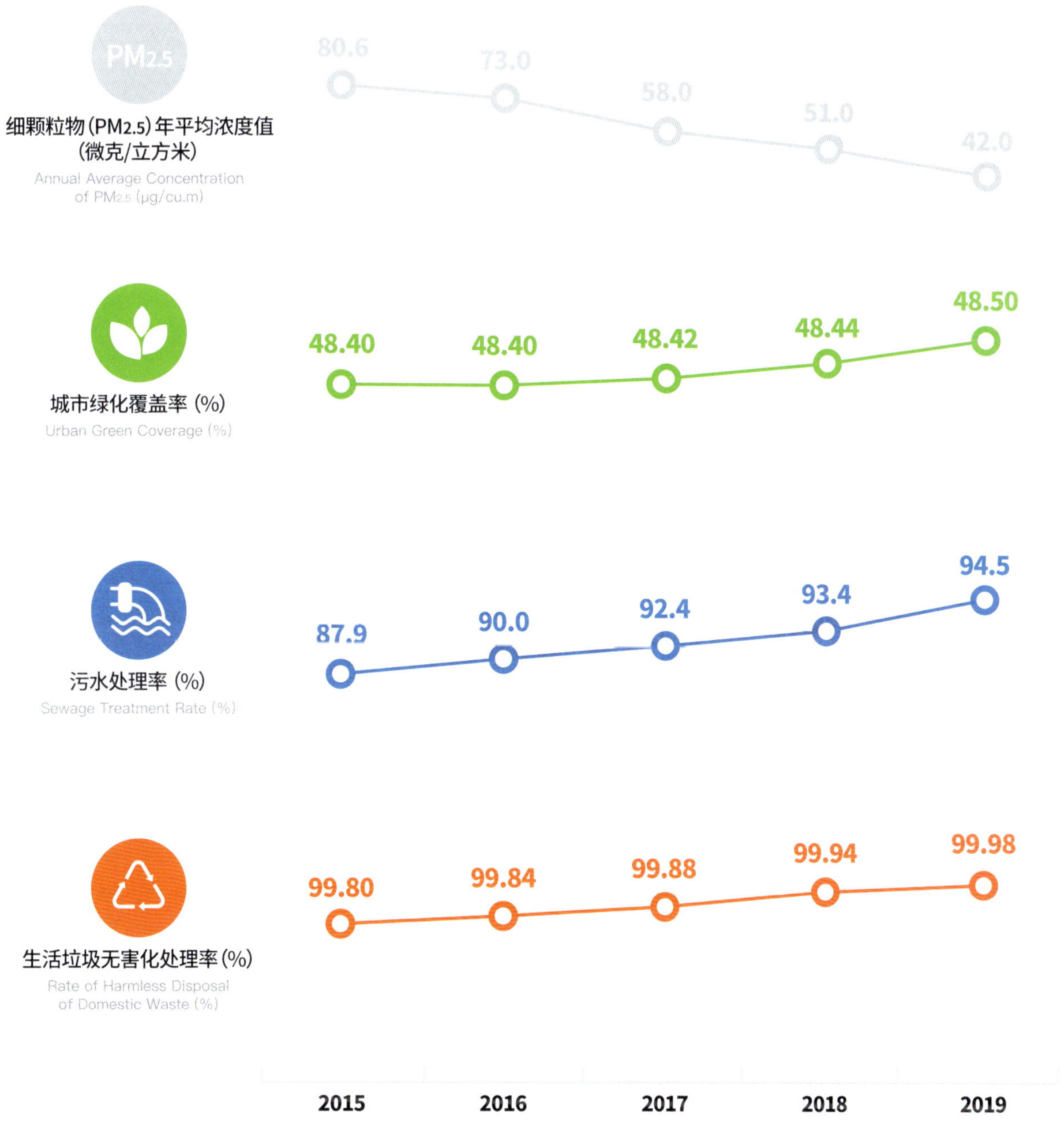
PM2.5
细颗粒物(PM2.5)年平均浓度值(微克/立方米)
Annual Average Concentration of PM2.5 (μg/cu.m)
80.6
73.0
58.0
51.0
42.0
城市绿化覆盖率 (%)
Urban Green Coverage (%)
48.40
48.40
48.42
48.44
48.50
污水处理率 (%)
Sewage Treatment Rate (%)
87.9
90.0
92.4
93.4
94.5
生活垃圾无害化处理率(%)
Rate of Harmless Disposal of Domestic Waste (%)
99.80
99.84
99.88
99.94
99.98
2015
2016
2017
2018
2019

研究与试验发展（R&D）经费内部支出（亿元）
Internal R&D Expenditures (100 million yuan)

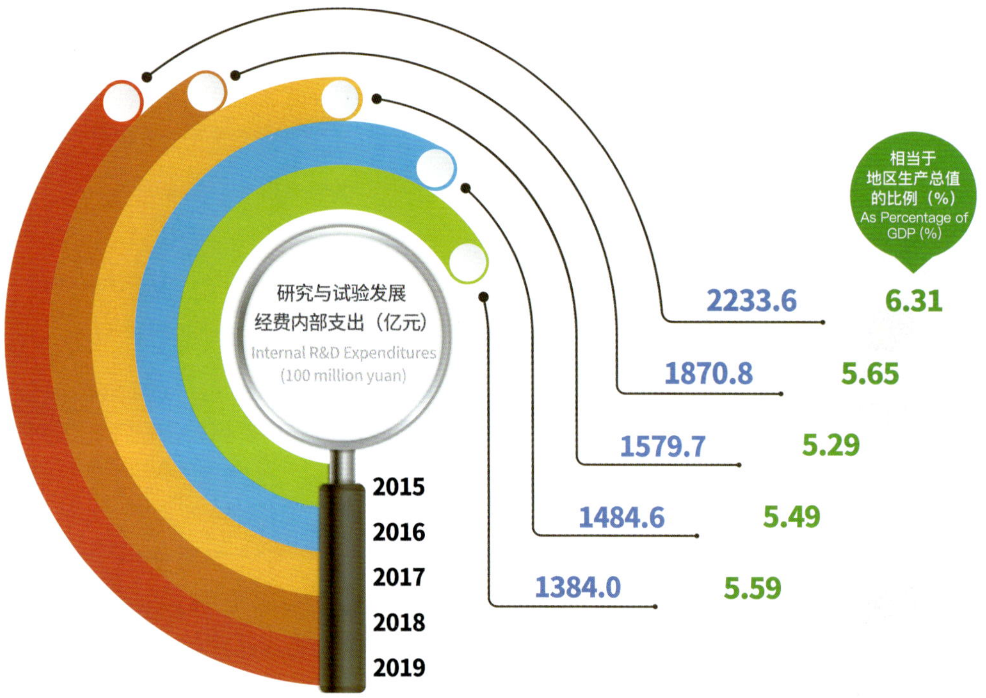

技术合同成交总额（亿元）
Total Volume of Transaction of Technical Contracts (100 million yuan)

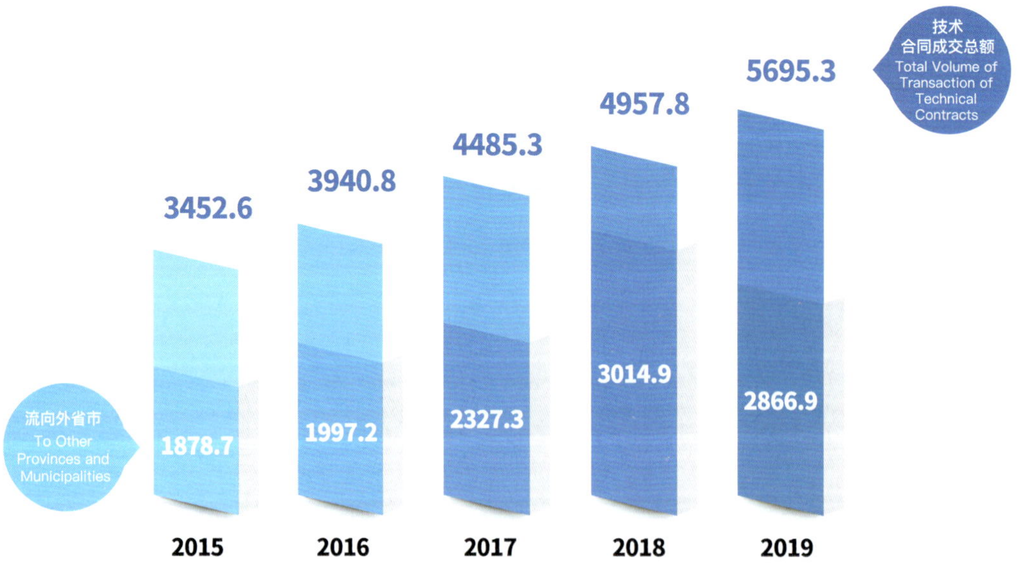

专利和发明专利授权量（件）
Patent and Invention Patent Granted (unit)

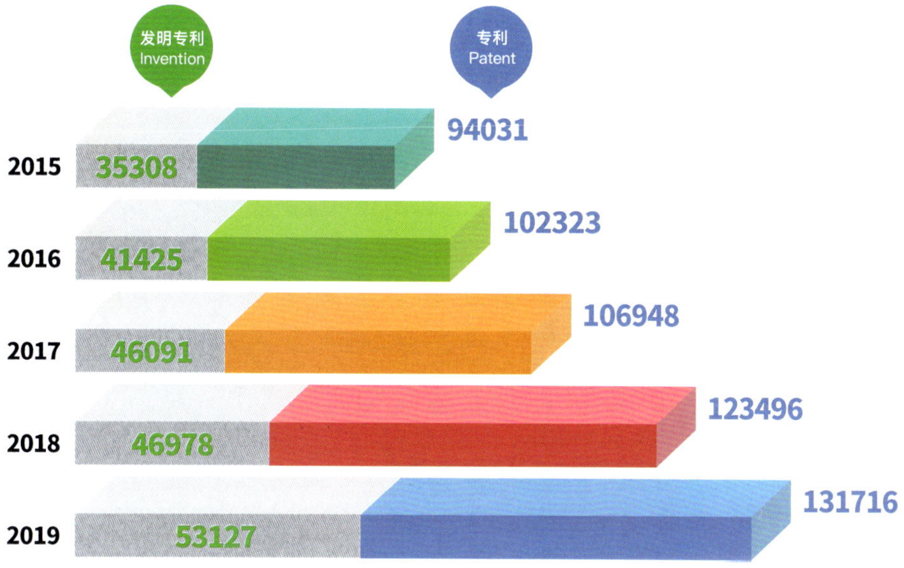

中关村国家自主创新示范区企业收入（亿元）
Revenue of Enterprises in Zhongguancun National Independent Innovation Demonstration Zone (100 million yuan)

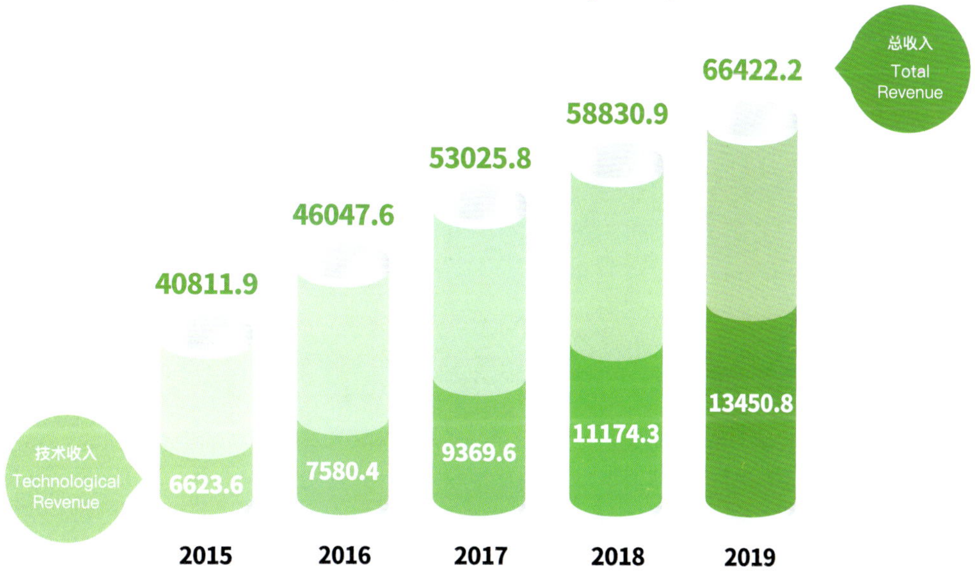

教育
Education

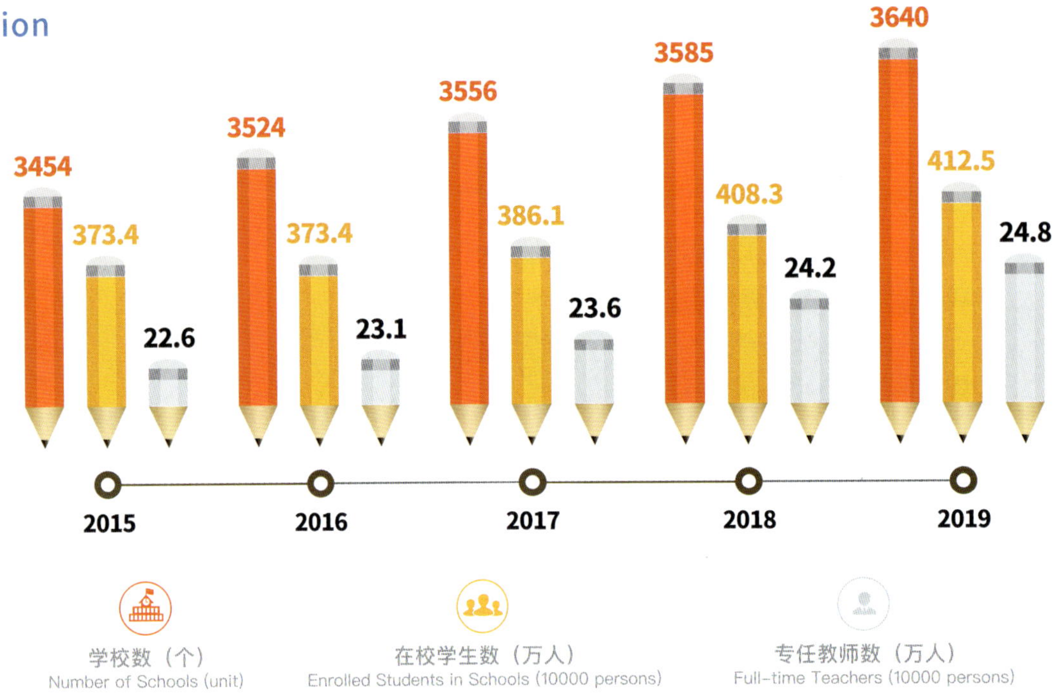

卫生
Health Care

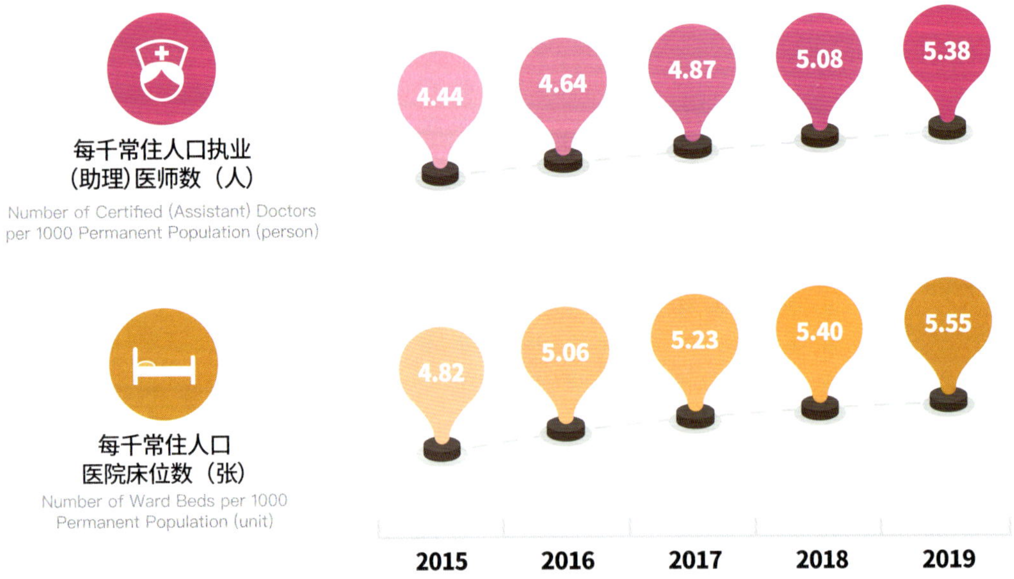

文化
Culture

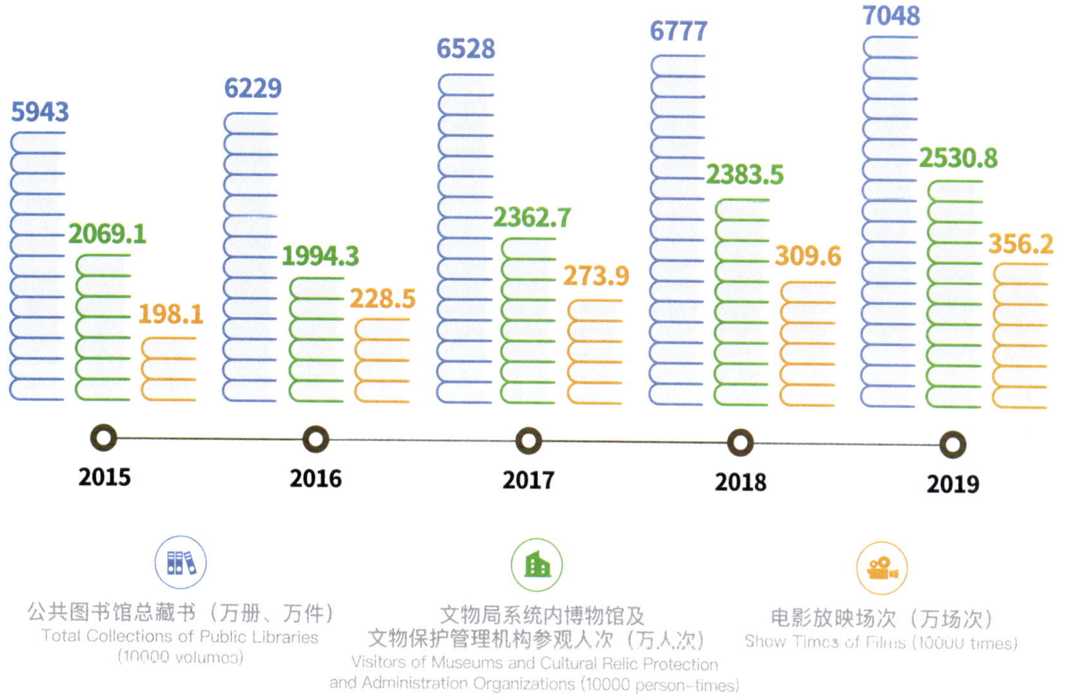

交通
Traffic

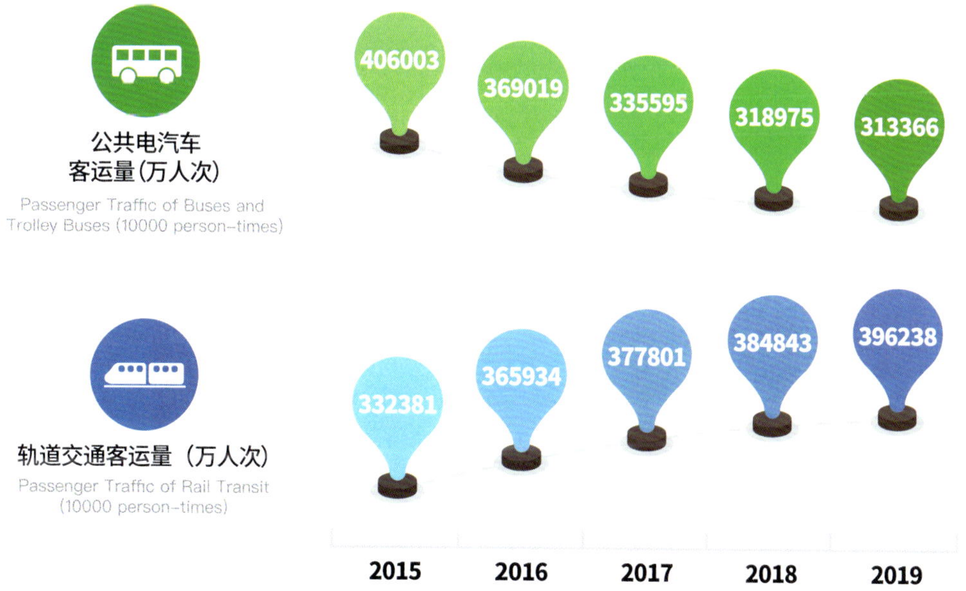

社会保障
Social Security

2019	2200
2018	2120
2017	2000
2016	1890
2015	1720

职工最低工资（元/月）
Minimum Wages of Employed Persons (yuan/month)

2019	1706
2018	1536
2017	1292
2016	1212
2015	1122

失业保险金最低标准（元/月）
Minimum Unemployment Insurance (yuan/month)

2019	1100
2018	1000
2017	900
2016	800
2015	710

城乡居民最低生活保障标准（元/月）
Minimum Subsistence Allowance for Urban and Rural Residents (yuan/month)

注：2017年及以前"城乡最低生活保障标准"数据为"城市居民最低生活保障标准"数据。
Note: Data on minimum subsistence allowance for urban and rural residents of 2017 and before refer to the data of minimum subsistence allowance for urban residents.

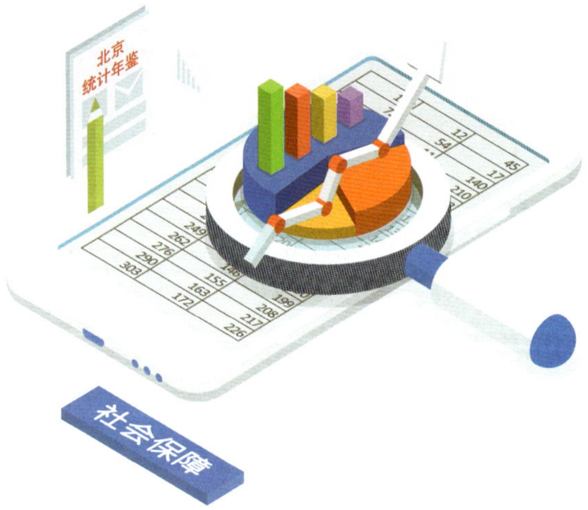

2019	1651.6
2018	1591.5
2017	1514.3
2016	1459.1
2015	1424.2

参加企业职工基本养老保险人数（万人）
Enterprise Employed Persons Participating in Basic Pension Insurance (10000 persons)

2019	1682.5
2018	1628.9
2017	1569.2
2016	1517.6
2015	1475.7

参加职工基本医疗保险人数（万人）
Staff and Workers Participating in Basic Medical Care Insurance (10000 persons)

《北京统计年鉴—2020》
编辑委员会及编辑工作人员

编委会

编辑工作人员

使用指南

《北京统计年鉴》是一部按年连续出版的大型统计资料书，通过大量的统计数据记录北京市一年来经济社会发展变化情况，是国内外各界人士了解北京、认识北京的重要资料工具书。

一、关于框架结构

（一）总体结构

本年鉴整体框架保持稳定，彩页部分以图文并茂的形式反映北京市主要经济社会指标发展变化趋势；统计表是年鉴的主体内容，主要包括综合，国民经济核算，人口与就业，价格指数，人民生活，财政与税收，能源、资源和环境，城市公用事业，固定资产投资和房地产开发，对外经济贸易，农业及农村经济，工业，建筑业，第三产业，交通运输邮电业，批发和零售业、住宿和餐饮业，旅游业，金融业，科技，教育，卫生及社会服务，文化和体育，公共管理、社会保障和社会组织，开发区等 24 个章节，从多领域、多行业反映北京市经济和社会发展情况。

（二）章节结构

章节内结构：每一章节由简要说明、统计表和主要统计指标解释三部分组成。其中，简要说明在每一章节首页，主要介绍该章节的主要内容、统计范围、指标口径和历史数据调整方法；统计指标解释在每章节尾页，主要对本章节内所涉及的主要指标、计算方法等做简要解释。

统计表排列：每一章节从反映该领域主要情况出发编排统计表内容。统计表的排列顺序一般先是主要指标历史数据表，后为当年数据表。

二、关于使用方法

（一）年份

按照惯例，书名中标注的年份为出版年份，年鉴中最新数据为上一年数据。例如，《北京统计年鉴 2020》表示该年鉴为 2020 年出版，年鉴中最新数据年份截至 2019 年。

统计表名中的“年份”主要有三种标识方法，分别代表三种含义：一是“表格名称（****-****年）”表示表内所列数据是包含了这两个年份之间的各年资料；二是统计表名中未显示年份，表示表内所列数据为当年和上年两年数据；三是“表格名称（****年）”表示表内所列数据仅为某一年资料。

（二）符号

统计表中常见符号如下：

：表示总计中的其中项；有“#”号的分组指标表示总计的部分项目，无“#”号的分组指标则表示其中项之和等于总计。

‖ ：宾栏中的“‖”为分组符号，代表某个指标存在几种分组数据。

… ：表示该数据不足该表最小计量单位数。

空格：表示该项指标数据不详或没有数据。

*** ：在可能根据数据识别或者推断单个统计调查对象身份时，予以屏蔽处理，以“***”表示。

（三）数据

1.本年鉴各章节均包含历史数据表和当年数据表两部分。历史数据表中的历史数据原则上可以连续使用，部分历史数据有调整的，应以最新出版的年鉴为准，使用时需留意简要说明、表下注释中对制度方法、口径范围等变化情况的说明。当年数据表中如指标的口径范围、计算方法以及与上年度数据相比变化较大时，会在表下注释中进行说明。

2.根据北京市第四次全国经济普查结果，在《北京统计年鉴 2020》中，对地区生产总值、能源、房地产、工业、建筑业、服务业、批发和零售业、研究与试验发展（R&D）情况等相关领域 2018 年数据进行补充，并对相关历史数据进行了修订。

3.与 2019 年版统计年鉴相比，对部分章节内容进行调整，将文化产业相关内容移至文化和体育章节；在国民经济核算中补充修订后的 2001 年以来分行业增加值历史数据，在能源、资源和环境中增加平均每万元地区生产总值天然气消费量历史数据和分行业规模以上工业用水量情况，在对外经济贸易中增加服务贸易历史数据，在科技中增加 PCT 国际专利申请量、国内专利及发明专利有效量、万人发明专利拥有量等历史数据，在教育中增加教育经费历史数据，在文化和体育章节中增加了文化产业增加值、规模以上文化产业经营情况历史数据，在公共管理、社会保障和社会组织中，补充检察机关办理案件情况历史数据等。

（四）电子光盘

《北京统计年鉴》配有电子光盘，包括中文和英文两种语言的版本，辅助用户对数据进行加工处理。

（五）本年鉴中部分数据合计数或相对数由于单位取舍不同而产生的计算误差，均未作机械调整。

USER GUIDE

Beijing Statistical Yearbook is a large statistical book published continuously on a chronological basis. With a great deal of statistical data, this Yearbook gives a reflection of the economic and social development and changes in Beijing over the past year. It serves as an important reference book for domestic and foreign personnel in all circles to understand and know Beijing.

I. Framework Structure

(I) Overall Structure

The overall structure of *Beijing Statistical Yearbook* remains stable. In color pages, the development and changing trends of main economic and social indicators of Beijing have been presented with both illustration and pictures; statistical tables are the main part of this Yearbook, mainly including 24 chapters, i.e. General Survey; National Accounts; Population and Employment; Price Index; People's Living Conditions; Government Finance and Tax Revenues; Energy, Resources and Environment; Public Utilities; Total Investment in Fixed Assets and Real Estate Development; Foreign Economic Relations and Trade; Agriculture and Rural Economy; Industry; Construction; Tertiary Industry; Transport, Post and Telecommunication Services; Wholesale and Retail Trade, Accommodation and Restaurants; Tourism; Finance; Science and Technology; Education; Health Care and Social Services; Culture and Sports; Public Management, Social Security and Social Organizations; and Development Zones, reflecting the economic and social development situation across the city through multiple fields and industries.

(II) Structure of Chapters

Internal structure of chapters in this Yearbook: Each chapter is composed of the Brief Introduction, Statistical Tables and Explanatory Notes to Main Statistical Indicators. Thereinto, Brief Introduction appears on the first page of each chapter, mainly introducing the main content, statistical scope, indicator standards, method of adjustment to historical data in each chapter; Explanatory Notes to Statistical Indicators come on the last page of each chapter, mainly giving a brief explanation to the main indicators and calculation method, etc. involved in the chapter.

Arrangement of statistical tables: In each chapter, statistical tables are arranged for the purpose of reflecting the main conditions in the field. Generally speaking, main indicators historical data tables come before current year data tables.

II. How to Use

(I) Years

Conventionally, the year indicated in the title of the book is the year of publication. The latest data indicated in this Yearbook are data in the previous years. For example, this book is titled *2020 Beijing Statistical Yearbook*, which means it will be published in 2020 while the latest data in the book is by the end of 2019.

"Years" in the statistical tables are marked in three ways, each indicating a different meaning. Firstly, the statistical table is named "****** (AAAA- BBBB)", which refers to that the data listed in the table are those from the year of AAAA to BBBB; Secondly, the statistical table contains no years, indicating that the data listed in the table are those of current year and last year; Thirdly, the statistical table is named "****** (AAAA)", indicating that the data listed in the table are those of the year of AAAA.

(II) Symbols

Symbols in statistical tables include:

#: means that the item is included in the total. Grouped indicators marked with "#" are part of the total, while those without "#" mean that sum of included items equals to the total.

||: grouping symbol, means that there are multiple ways of grouping the indicators.

…: means that the figure is less than the minimum measurement unit of the table.

Blank: means that the figure is unknown or unavailable.

: When it is possible to identify or infer the identity of the individual statistical respondent based on the data, it shall be shielded and indicated with "".

(III) Data

1. Each chapter in this Yearbook consists of two parts: historical data tables and current year data tables. In principle, historical data that are shown in the historical data tables can be used continuously; for some historical data that have been adjusted, please refer to the latest yearbook; When using the data, it is necessary to refer to the Brief Introduction and the explanations on the change in method system, standards and scope in the Notes under the statistical tables. In the current year data tables, if the standards and scope, calculation method for the corresponding indicators, and certain data greatly differ from that of the previous year, they shall be explained in the Notes under the statistical tables.

2. In the *2020 Beijing Statistical Yearbook*, the data of 2018 on gross domestic product, energy, real estate, industry, construction, services, wholesale and retail trade, research and experimental development (R&D) and other relevant fields have been supplemented, and the relevant historical data have been revised according to the results of the fourth national economic census in Beijing.

3. Compared with the *2019 Beijing Statistical Yearbook*, adjustments have been made to the content of some chapters. Content related to the cultural industry has been moved to the Culture and Sports chapter. Revised historical data since 2001 on added value by sector are supplemented in the National Accounts part; historical data on natural gas consumption per RMB 10,000 of GDP and data on water used by industry above designated size by sector are added in the Energy, Resources and Environment part; historical data on trade in services are added in the Foreign Economic Relations and Trade part; historical data on PCT international patent applications, domestic patents in force and invention patents in force, and invention patent ownership per 10,000 persons, etc. are added in the Science and Technology part; historical data on educational funds are added in the Education part; historical data on added value of cultural industry and on the operation of cultural industry enterprises above designated size are added in the Culture and Sports part; and historical data on cases handled by procuratorial organs are supplemented in the Public Management, Social Security and Social Organization part.

(IV) Electronic CD-ROM

Beijing Statistical Yearbook is provided with a CD-ROM, which contains Chinese and English versions of this Yearbook. The CD-ROM helps users in working with and processing the data.

(V) The sum of some statistics or some relative numbers in this Yearbook might have certain calculation errors because of the choice of different units of measurement. All the statistics have not undergone mechanical adjustment.

目　录

Contents

一、综合

GENERAL SURVEY

二、国民经济核算
NATIONAL ACCOUNTS

三、人口与就业
POPULATION AND EMPLOYMENT

四、价格指数
PRICE INDEX

五、人民生活
PEOPLE'S LIVING CONDITIONS

六、财政与税收
GOVERNMENT FINANCE AND TAX REVENUES

七、能源、资源和环境
ENERGY, RESOURCES AND ENVIRONMENT

八、城市公用事业
PUBLIC UTILITIES

九、固定资产投资和房地产开发
INVESTMENT IN FIXED ASSETS AND REAL ESTATE DEVELOPMENT

十、对外经济贸易
FOREIGN ECONOMIC RELATIONS AND TRADE

十一、农业及农村经济
AGRICULTURE AND RURAL ECONOMY

十二、工业
INDUSTRY

十三、建筑业
CONSTRUCTION

十四、第三产业
TERTIARY INDUSTRY

十五、交通运输邮电业
TRANSPORT，POST AND TELECOMMUNICATON SERVICES

十六、批发和零售业、住宿和餐饮业
WHOLESALE AND RETAIL TRADE，ACCOMMODATION AND RESTAURANTS

十七、旅游业

TOURISM

十八、金融业
FINANCE

十九、科技
SCIENCE AND TECHNOLOGY

二十、教育
EDUCATION

二十一、卫生及社会服务
HEALTH CARE AND SOCIAL SERVICES

二十二、文化和体育
CULTURE AND SPORTS

二十三、公共管理、社会保障和社会组织
PUBLIC MANAGEMENT,SOCIAL SECURITY AND SOCIAL ORGANIZATION

二十四、开发区
DEVELOPMENT ZONES

01

北京统计年鉴2020　BEIJING STATISTICAL YEARBOOK

综 合
GENERAL SURVEY

简要说明

一、主要内容

本章资料包括北京市行政区划，全市社会经济发展的主要指标以及“十三五”时期监测指标，法人及产业活动单位数，私营个体、非公经济、中小微型企业基本情况等。

二、有关统计标准的变化说明

（一）《国民经济行业分类》（GB/T 4754-2002）与原（GB/T 4754-94）的主要框架结构变化：

1.增加的门类：(1)信息传输、计算机服务和软件业；(2)租赁和商务服务业；(3)住宿和餐饮业；(4)水利、环境和公共设施管理业；(5)教育；(6)国际组织。

2.名称或范围进行调整的门类：(1)农、林、牧、渔业；(2)采矿业；(3)制造业；(4)交通运输、仓储和邮政业；(5)批发和零售业；(6)金融业；(7)科学研究、技术服务和地质勘查业；(8)居民服务和其他服务业；(9)卫生、社会保障和社会福利业；(10)文化、体育和娱乐业；(11)公共管理和社会组织。

3.取消的门类：(1)地质勘查、水利管理；(2)其他行业。

（二）《国民经济行业分类》（GB/T 4754-2011）与原（GB/T 4754-2002）的主要框架结构变化：

1.门类名称调整：(1)“电力、燃气及水的生产和供应业”更名为“电力、热力、燃气及水生产和供应业”；(2)“信息传输、计算机服务和软件业”更名为“信息传输、软件和信息技术服务业”；(3)“科学研究、技术服务和地质勘查业”更名为“科学研究和技术服务业”；(4)“居民服务和其他服务业”更名为“居民服务、修理和其他服务业”；(5)“卫生、社会保障和社会福利业”更名为“卫生和社会工作”；(6)“公共管理和社会组织”更名为“公共管理、社会保障和社会组织”。

2.门类位次调整：(1)“批发和零售业”调至“交通运输、仓储和邮政业”之前；(2)“住宿和餐饮业”调至“交通运输、仓储和邮政业”之后。

3.门类范围调整：(1)农、林、牧、渔业；(2)制造业；(3)交通运输、仓储和邮政业；(4)信息传输、软件和信息技术服务业；(5)金融业；(6)租赁和商务服务业；(7)科学研究和技术服务业；(8)居民服务、修理和其他服务业；(9)教育；(10)卫生和社会工作；(11)文化、体育和娱乐业；(12)公共管理、社会保障和社会组织。

（三）《国民经济行业分类》（GB/T 4754-2017）与原（GB/T 4754-2011）的门类名称和门类位次无调整。

Brief Introduction

I. Main Content

Statistics in this chapter mainly show the basic information of administrative divisions of Beijing, main indicators for social and economic development of the city, and monitoring indicators for the 13th Five-Year Plan, number of corporate and industrial entities, non-public economy, small-, medium- and micro-sized enterprises, etc.

II. Adjustment to Historical Statistics According to New Industrial Standards

(I) Changes to the main framework of the *Classification and Codes of National Economic Sectors* (GB/T 4754-2002) as compared with the previous version (GB/T 4754-94):

1. Sectors added: (1) information transmission, computer service and software; (2) renting and leasing activities and business services; (3) accommodation and restaurants; (4) management of water conservancy, environment and public facilities; (5) education; (6) international organizations.

2. Sectors with name or range changed: (1) agriculture, forestry, animal production and hunting, fishing; (2) mining and quarrying; (3) manufacturing; (4) transport, storage and post; (5) wholesale and retail trade; (6) finance; (7) scientific research, technical service, geological prospecting; (8) resident service and other service; (9) health care, social security, and social welfare; (10) culture, sports and recreation; (11) public administration and social organizations.

3. Sectors cancelled: (1) geological prospecting, water conservancy management; (2) other sectors.

(II) Compared with the previous (GB/T 4754-2002) version, the *Classification of National Economic Sectors* (GB/T 4754-2011) mainly involves the following framework changes:

1. Changes to the name of category: (1) The "electric power, gas and water production and supply" is renamed "production and distribution of electricity, heating power, gas and water"; (2) the "information transmission, computer service and software" is renamed "information transmission, software and information technology services"; (3) the "scientific research, technical service and geological prospecting" is renamed "scientific research and development, technical services"; (4) the "resident service and other service" is renamed "resident services, repair and other services"; (5) the "health, social security and social welfare" is renamed "health care and social works"; (6) "public administration and social organization" is renamed "public administration, social security and social organizations".

2. Changes to the order of categories: (1) the "wholesale and retail trade" is put before the "transport, storage and post"; (2) the "accommodation and restaurants" is put after the "transport, storage and post".

3. Changes to the scope of category: (1) agriculture, forestry, animal production and hunting, fishing; (2) manufacturing; (3) transport, storage and post; (4) information transmission, software and information technology services; (5) finance; (6) renting and leasing activities and business services; (7) scientific research and development, technical service; (8) resident services, repair and other services; (9) education; (10) health care and social works; (11) culture, sports and entertainment; (12) public administration, social security and social organizations.

(III) Compared with the previous (GB/T 4754-2011) version, no adjustment has been made in the name of categories and the order of categories in the *Classification of National Economic Sectors* (GB/T 4754-2017) version.

1-1 行政区划(2019年)
ADMINISTRATIVE DIVISIONS (2019)

单位：个 (unit)

地 区	District	街道办事处 Sub-district	建制镇 Designated Town	建制乡 Designated Township	社区居委会 Community Neighborhood Committee	村民委员会 Villagers' Committee
全 市	**Total**	**152**	**143**	**38**	**3231**	**3891**
东城区	Dongcheng District	17			177	
西城区	Xicheng District	15			259	
朝阳区	Chaoyang District	24		19	492	144
丰台区	Fengtai District	16	2	3	337	57
石景山区	Shijingshan District	9			150	
海淀区	Haidian District	22	7		581	67
门头沟区	Mentougou District	4	9		123	178
房山区	Fangshan District	8	14	6	160	459
通州区	Tongzhou District	6	10	1	130	470
顺义区	Shunyi District	6	19		135	426
昌平区	Changping District	8	14		238	301
大兴区	Daxing District	8	14		233	527
怀柔区	Huairou District	2	12	2	35	284
平谷区	Pinggu District	2	14	2	41	272
密云区	Miyun District	2	17	1	93	330
延庆区	Yanqing District	3	11	4	47	376

资料来源：中共北京市委社会工作委员会北京市民政局。
Source: Social Work Committee of Beijing Municipal Committee of the Communist Party of China Beijing Municipal Civil Affairs Bureau.

1-2 主要经济指标增长速度(1979—2019年)

单位：%

年　份 Year	地区生产总值比上年增长 YoY Growth Rate of Gross Domestic Product	农林牧渔业总产值比上年增长 YoY Growth Rate of Gross Output Value of Agriculture, Forestry, Animal Production and Hunting, Fishing	规模以上工业总产值比上年增长 YoY Growth Rate of Gross Output Value of Industrial Enterprises Above Designated Size	固定资产投资比上年增长 YoY Growth Rate of Fixed Asset Investment	社会消费品零售总额比上年增长 YoY Growth Rate of Retail Sales of Consumer Goods
1979	9.7	7.0		17.3	20.6
1980	11.8	16.3		25.3	17.8
1981	-0.5	4.2		10.2	12.6
1982	7.4	12.8		5.5	6.6
1983	16.4	16.7		32.9	14.6
1984	17.4	13.3		29.2	22.5
1985	8.7	16.7	17.4	41.8	27.0
1986	8.0	8.5	3.8	13.0	15.3
1987	9.6	22.4	15.2	28.2	21.9
1988	12.8	52.9	27.9	19.7	35.5
1989	4.4	14.8	21.6	-14.4	15.2
1990	5.2	16.2	3.8	28.5	17.1
1991	9.9	9.0	16.7	7.1	18.3
1992	11.3	10.5	17.8	38.5	23.2
1993	12.3	18.8	35.7	54.3	22.4
1994	13.7	43.7	35.1	58.1	26.4
1995	12.0	13.9	-5.3	29.7	24.9
1996	9.8	2.7	6.5	4.2	12.5
1997	10.2	0.9	14.4	9.6	14.7
1998	9.6	2.5	7.0	20.2	14.5
1999	11.0	3.3	12.1	1.3	10.7
2000	12.0	4.4	30.2	10.8	10.7
2001	11.8	7.2	15.1	18.0	11.2
2002	11.8	5.6	10.7	18.5	10.3
2003	11.1	5.2	21.8	18.9	15.4
2004	13.3	4.5	30.0	17.2	15.7
2005	12.3	1.9	21.2	11.8	11.7
2006	12.8	0.4	18.2	19.3	14.0
2007	14.4	13.4	17.5	17.6	17.3
2008	9.0	11.6	7.9	-3.0	22.1
2009	10.0	3.6	6.0	26.2	16.8
2010	10.4	4.1	24.1	13.1	18.5
2011	8.1	10.7	5.9	13.3	14.6
2012	7.7	9.0	7.5	9.3	13.3
2013	7.7	6.6	11.4	8.8	10.0
2014	7.4	-0.4	6.2	7.5	9.4
2015	6.9	-12.3	-5.4	5.7	8.1
2016	6.9	-8.2	3.7	5.9	7.0
2017	6.8	-8.8	4.5	5.7	6.1
2018	6.7	-3.7	4.4	-9.9	3.5
2019	6.1	-5.1	3.6	-2.4	4.4

注：1．地区生产总值增长速度按可比口径计算。
2．农林牧渔业总产值、规模以上工业总产值、固定资产投资、社会消费品零售总额增长速度按现价计算。
3．2018年及以前，固定资产投资数据为全社会口径，2019年为不含农户口径，下同。
4．进出口总值增长速度为以美元计价的进出口总值增长速度，以人民币计价，2019年进出口总值增长5.5%。

YOY GROWTH RATE OF MAIN INDICATORS (1979-2019)

(%)

进出口总值比上年增长 YoY Growth Rate of Gross Value of Imports & Exports	居民消费价格指数(上年=100) Consumer Price Index (Previous year=100)	城镇居民人均可支配收入 Per-capita Disposable Income of Urban Households		农村居民人均可支配收入 Per-capita Net Income of Rural Households	
		比上年名义增长 Nominal Growth Rate as Compared with That in the Last year	比上年实际增长 Real Growth Rate as Compared with That in the Last year	比上年名义增长 Normal Growth Rate as Compared with That in the Last year	比上年实际增长 Real Growth Rate as Compared with That in the Last year
	101.8	13.6	11.6	11.2	9.2
	106.0	20.8	14.0	16.2	9.6
	101.3	10.7	9.3	20.7	19.2
	101.8	1.1	-0.7	23.4	21.2
	100.5	5.2	4.7	20.1	19.5
16.3	102.2	17.5	15.0	27.9	25.2
-8.6	117.6	30.8	11.2	16.7	-0.8
-6.0	106.8	17.6	10.1	6.2	-0.6
-12.7	108.6	10.7	1.9	11.3	2.5
11.9	120.4	21.6	1.0	16.0	-3.7
-4.3	117.2	11.1	-5.2	15.8	-1.2
-17.4	105.4	19.1	13.0	5.4	-0.04
2.5	111.9	14.1	2.0	9.7	-2.0
3.1	109.9	17.8	7.2	10.5	0.6
11.7	119.0	38.8	16.6	19.8	0.7
3.5	124.9	43.4	14.8	27.5	2.1
28.2	117.3	22.6	4.5	34.3	14.5
-20.8	111.6	17.6	5.4	10.5	-1.0
3.7	105.3	6.6	1.2	2.8	-2.4
0.4	102.4	9.3	6.7	7.4	4.9
12.6	100.6	9.2	8.5	6.4	5.8
43.8	103.5	13.6	9.8	8.4	4.7
4.2	103.1	12.7	9.3	8.6	5.3
2.0	98.2	8.5	10.5	6.9	8.9
30.5	100.2	12.2	12.0	3.2	3.0
38.1	101.0	13.5	12.4	9.6	8.5
32.7	101.5	13.8	12.1	18.4	16.7
25.9	100.9	14.1	13.1	12.0	11.0
22.1	102.4	10.9	8.3	13.4	10.7
40.8	105.1	13.3	7.8	12.3	6.9
-20.9	98.5	9.0	10.7	8.9	10.6
40.4	102.4	9.6	7.0	13.0	10.4
29.1	105.6	13.2	7.2	11.1	5.2
4.8	103.3	10.8	7.3	11.8	8.2
5.4	103.3	10.6	7.1	11.3	7.7
-3.4	101.6	8.9	7.2	10.3	8.6
-23.1	101.8	8.9	7.0	9.0	7.1
-11.6	101.4	8.4	6.9	8.5	7.0
14.6	101.9	9.0	7.0	8.7	6.7
27.4	102.5	8.9	6.2	9.3	6.6
0.9	102.3	8.6	6.2	9.2	6.7

Note: a) The Growth Rate of Gross Domestic Product shall be calculated based on a comparable caliber.

b) The Growth Rate of Gross Output Value of Agriculture, Forestry, Animal Production and Hunting, Fishing, Gross Output Value of Industrial Enterprises Above Designated Size, Fixed Asset Investment and Retail Sales of Consumer Goods shall be calculated based on the current price.

c) In and before 2018, the data on fixed asset investment were those of full coverage. The data for 2019 were those that excluding rural households, the same below.

d) The Growth Rate of Gross Value of Imports & Exports shall be the growth rate of gross value of imports & exports calculated in USD. Calculated in RMB, the growth rate of gross value of imports & exports is 5.5% in 2019.

1-3 主要年份国民经济和社会发展总量与速度指标

项目		Item		1990	1995
人口与就业		**Population and Employment**			
年末全市常住人口	(万人)	Year-end Permanent Population	(10000 persons)	1086.0	1251.1
#城镇人口		Urban Population		798.0	946.2
年末户籍人口	(万人)	Year-end Registered Population	(10000 persons)	1032.2	1070.3
从业人员年末人数	(万人)	Year-end Employed Persons	(10000 persons)	627.1	665.3
城镇单位在岗职工平均工资	(元)	Average Wages of Fully Employed Staff and Workers in Urban Entities	(yuan)	2653	8144
年末实有城镇登记失业人员	(万人)	Registered Unemployed Persons in Urban Areas at Year End	(10000 persons)	1.67	2.19
国民经济核算		**National Accounts**			
地区生产总值	(亿元)	Gross Domestic Product	(100 million yuan)	500.8	1516.2
人均地区生产总值	(元)	Per Capita Gross Domestic Product	(yuan)	4635	12762
价格指数(上年=100)		**Price Indices (Preceding Year=100)**			
居民消费价格指数		Consumer Price Index		105.4	117.3
工业生产者出厂价格指数		Producer Price Index for Industrial Products		107.9	107.3
人民生活		**People's Living Conditions**			
全市居民人均可支配收入	(元)	Per Capita Disposable Income of Households of the Whole City	(yuan)	1741	5501
全市居民人均消费支出	(元)	Per Capita Living Expenditures of Households of the Whole City	(yuan)	1469	4366
财 政		**Government Finance**			
一般公共预算收入	(亿元)	General Public Budget Revenue	(100 million yuan)		
一般公共预算支出	(亿元)	General Public Budget Expenditure	(100 million yuan)		
能源、资源和环境		**Energy, Resources and Environment**			
能源消费总量	(万吨标准煤)	Total Energy Consumption	(10000 tons of SCE)	2709.7	3533.3
水资源总量	(亿立方米)	Total Volume of Water Resource	(100 million cu.m)	36.9	30.3
城市绿化覆盖率	(%)	Urban Green Coverage	(%)	28.0	32.7
城市公用事业		**Public Utilities**			
全社会用电量	(亿千瓦时)	Electricity Consumption	(100 million kWh)	150.5	222.6
自来水销售总量	(亿立方米)	Total Sales Volume of Tap Water	(100 million cu.m)	5.3	6.8
居民燃气用户	(万户)	Households Gas Users	(10000 households)	176.1	219.8
公共交通客运量	(亿人次)	Passengers Traffic of Public Transport	(100 million person-times)	33.5	37.2
污水处理率	(%)	Sewage Treatment Rate	(%)	7.3	19.4

注：1. 地区生产总值绝对值按现价计算，指数按可比价格计算。历史数据根据北京市第四次全国经济普查结果进行了修订，2019年为初步核算数据，下同。
2. 全市居民人均可支配收入及人均消费支出绝对值按现价计算，指数按可比价格计算。
3. 全社会用电量来源于北京市电力公司，2000年以前工业用电量不包含输配损失和发电企业自产自用电量。
4. 城镇单位在岗职工平均工资2000年及以前数据为职工口径，职工包括在岗职工和不在岗职工；从2001年开始，调整为在岗职工的指标；2007年及以前城镇单位在岗职工工资包括乡及乡以上独立核算法人单位，不包括乡镇企业、私营单位和个体工商户；2008年及以后包括乡镇企业。

AGGREGATE INDICATORS AND SPEED INDICATORS ON NATIONAL ECONOMIC AND SOCIAL DEVELOPMENT IN KEY YEARS

总量指标 Aggregate Indicator						速度指标(%) Speed Indicator (%) 指 数(2019年为以下各年) Index (2019 as Percentage of the Following Year)						
2000	2005	2010	2015	2018	2019	1990	1995	2000	2005	2010	2015	2018
1363.6	1538.0	1961.9	2170.5	2154.2	2153.6	198.3	172.1	157.9	140.0	109.8	99.2	99.97
1057.4	1286.1	1686.4	1877.7	1863.4	1865.0	233.7	197.1	176.4	145.0	110.6	99.3	100.1
1107.5	1180.7	1257.8	1345.2	1375.8	1397.4	135.4	130.6	126.2	118.4	111.1	103.9	101.6
619.3	878.0	1031.6	1186.1	1237.8	1273.0	203.0	191.3	205.6	145.0	123.4	107.3	102.8
15726	34191	65683	113073	149843	173205	6528.6	2126.8	1101.4	506.6	263.7	153.2	115.6
3.32	10.57	7.73	9.16	10.24	9.35	559.9	426.9	281.6	88.5	121.0	102.1	91.3
3277.8	7149.8	14964.0	24779.1	33106.0	35371.3	1620.5	926.5	562.0	318.0	186.2	129.3	106.1
25014	47182	78307	114662	153095	164220	812.8	511.3	342.0	223.8	165.1	129.6	106.5
103.5	101.5	102.4	101.8	102.5	102.3							
102.5	101.3	102.2	96.9	100.0	99.6							
9230	16853	29228	48458	62361	67756	1007.2	683.4	510.4	290.7	183.6	129.0	106.3
7644	13289	21834	33803	39843	43038	758.0	547.0	391.4	234.2	156.1	117.5	105.6
345.0	919.2	2353.9	4723.9	5785.9	5817.1			1686.1	632.8	247.1	123.1	100.5
443.0	1058.3	2717.3	5737.7	7471.4	7408.2			1672.3	700.0	272.6	129.1	99.2
4144.0	5049.8	6359.5	6802.8	7269.8	7360.3	271.6	208.3	177.6	145.8	115.7	108.2	101.2
16.9	23.2	23.1	26.8	35.5	24.6	66.6	81.1	145.3	105.9	106.3	91.6	69.3
36.5	42.0	45.0	48.4	48.4	48.5							
384.4	570.5	809.9	952.7	1142.4	1166.4	775.1	524.0	303.4	204.4	144.0	122.4	102.1
7.5	7.2	8.9	10.4	11.6	12.0	227.7	176.9	159.3	167.7	134.6	115.5	103.6
291.9	462.6	634.2	885.7	926.4	873.2	495.9	397.3	299.2	188.8	137.7	98.6	94.3
40.7	51.8	69.0	73.8	70.4	71.0							
39.4	62.4	81.0	87.9	93.4	94.5							

Note: a) Absolute values on GDP are calculated at current prices, and the indices are calculated at comparable prices. The related historical data on GDP have been revised according to the results of the fourth national economic census in Beijing;the GDP data for 2019 were the preliminary accounting data, the same below.

b) The absolute values of the per capital disposable income and the per capital living expenditures of households of the whole city are calculated at current prices, and the indices are calculated at comparable prices.

c) Figures on electricity consumption are provided by State Grid Beijing Electric Power Company. Before 2000, electricity consumption by industry excluded transmission and distribution losses and electricity generated and consumed by power generating enterprises.

d) Figures on average wages of fully employed staff and workers in urban entities in and before 2000 referred to that of staff and workers which included both fully employed staff and workers, and employees that are not on the job. Since 2001, the figures were adjusted to that of fully employed staff and workers. In and before 2007, figures on wages of fully employed staff and workers in urban entities had been kept separate accounts at and above the township level, excluding township enterprises, private entities and self-employed operators; in and after 2008, such figures have included township enterprises.

1-3 续表 1

项　目		Item		1990	1995
固定资产投资		**Investment In Fixed Assets**			
全社会固定资产投资	(亿元)	Total Investment In Fixed Assets	(100 million yuan)	179.2	841.5
#基础设施投资		Infrastructure Investment		31.6	156.1
#房地产开发投资		Investment in Real Estate Development		22.5	352.8
对外经济贸易		**Foreign Economic Relations and Trade**			
北京地区进出口总值	(亿美元)	Total Value of Imports and Exports	(USD 100 million)	236.4	370.4
北京地区进出口总值	(亿元)	Total Value of Imports and Exports	(100 million yuan)		3108.2
实际利用外商直接投资额	(亿美元)	Paid-in Foreign Investment	(USD 100 million)	2.8	14.0
农　业		**Agriculture**			
农林牧渔业总产值(现价)	(亿元)	Gross Output Value of Agriculture, Forestry, Animal Production and Hunting, Fishing (at current prices)	(100 million yuan)	70.2	164.4
工　业		**Industry**			
规模以上工业总产值	(亿元)	Gross Output Value of Industry Above Designated Size	(100 million yuan)	625.9	1493.3
规模以上工业主要经济指标		Main Economic Indicators for Industrial Above Designated Size			
资产总计	(亿元)	Total Asset	(100 million yuan)	498.3	2582.6
负债总额	(亿元)	Total Liability	(100 million yuan)		1528.8
营业收入	(亿元)	Businesses Income	(100 million yuan)		
利润总额	(亿元)	Total Profit	(100 million yuan)	48.9	85.3
建 筑 业		**Construction**			
建筑业总产值	(亿元)	Gross Output Value	(100 million yuan)	94.7	426.6
建筑业企业年末从业人员	(万人)	Year-end Employed Persons	(10000 persons)	60.2	82.6
交通运输邮电业		**Transport, Post and Telecommunication Services**			
运　输		**Transport**			
货物周转量	(亿吨公里)	Total Freight Turnover	(100 million ton-km)	268.8	323.1
旅客周转量	(亿人公里)	Total Passenger Turnover	(100 million passenger-km)	119.8	207.7
邮　电		**Post and Telecommunication Services**			
邮电业务总量	(亿元)	Business Volume of Post and Telecommunications	(100 million yuan)	11.9	56.1
固定电话用户	(万户)	Fixed Telephone Subscribers	(10000 subscribers)	33.3	150.5
移动电话用户	(万户)	Mobile Telephone Subscribers	(10000 subscribers)	0.3	16.9
批发和零售业、住宿和餐饮业		**Wholesale and Retail Trade, Accommodation and Restaurants**			
社会消费品零售总额	(亿元)	Total Retail Sales of Consumer Goods	(100 million yuan)	345.1	971.8
旅游业		**Tourism**			
入境游客人数	(万人次)	Inbound Tourists	(10000 persons)	100.0	207.0
国内游客人数	(万人次)	Domestic Tourists	(10000 persons)		6320
国际旅游收入	(亿美元)	Revenue from Inbound Tourism	(USD 100 million)	6.6	21.8
国内旅游收入	(亿元)	Revenue from Domestic Tourism	(100 million yuan)		352.6

注：1．从2011年起，根据国家统计局相关规定，固定资产投资起点由50万元调整至500万元。
　　2．工业总产值按现价计算。
　　3．邮电业务总量2000年及以前按1990年不变价格计算，2001—2010年按2000年不变价格计算，2011—2015年按2010年不变价格计算，2018年和2019年邮政业务量按2010不变价计算、电信业务量按2015年不变价格计算。
　　4．2006年至2019年社会消费品零售总额数据根据北京市第四次全国经济普查结果进行了修订。

1-3 Continued 1

总量指标 Aggregate Indicator						速度指标(%) Speed Indicator (%)						
						指 数(2019年为以下各年) Index (2019 as Percentage of the Following Year)						
2000	2005	2010	2015	2018	2019	1990	1995	2000	2005	2010	2015	2018
1297.4	2827.2	5493.5	7990.9									
351.9	610.7	1403.5	2174.5									
522.1	1525.0	2901.1	4226.3									
494.0	1255.1	3016.6	3194.2	4124.3	4162.8	1760.5	1124.0	842.7	331.7	138.0	130.3	100.9
4090.1	10331.9	20478.2	19827.7	27182.5	28677.2		922.6	701.1	277.6	140.0	144.6	105.5
24.6	35.3	63.6	130.0	173.1	142.1	5131.9	1013.2	578.2	403.0	223.3	109.4	82.1
188.6	239.3	328.0	368.2	296.8	281.7	401.3	171.4	149.4	117.7	85.9	76.5	94.9
2842.0	6946.2	13699.8	17449.6	19669.0	20386.1	3257.1	1365.2	717.3	293.5	148.8	116.8	103.6
4612.7	12829.8	22750.6	38609.8	49321.5	52222.0	10480.0	2022.1	1132.1	407.0	229.5	135.3	105.9
2676.4	4706.7	11548.1	18102.4	22270.2	21974.5		1437.4	821.0	466.9	190.3	121.4	98.7
		14807.1	19256.1	22348.1	23419.1					158.2	121.6	104.8
127.1	413.5	1028.3	1597.7	1647.0	1710.3	3494.8	2005.2	1345.7	413.6	166.3	107.0	103.8
812.5	1894.0	5196.0	8436.7	10939.8	11999.4	12671.0	2812.8	1476.8	633.5	230.9	142.2	109.7
56.6	67.2	59.9	59.0	53.4	55.5	92.2	67.2	98.1	82.6	92.7	94.0	103.9
299.6	457.7	513.7	623.7	780.7	900.8	335.1	278.8	300.6	196.8	175.4	144.4	115.4
314.0	838.1	1399.5	1747.7	2220.0	2291.8	1913.1	1103.4	729.9	273.5	163.8	131.1	103.2
214.7	413.0	1108.9	991.2	1861.0	2759.6							
451.2	943.5	885.6	784.7	614.5	555.4	1668.1	369.0	123.1	58.9	62.7	70.8	90.4
347.2	1459.8	2129.8	4051.6	4008.8	4019.7	1339900.0	23785.2	1157.7	275.4	188.7	99.2	100.3
1760.3	3221.4	7273.0	12271.9	14422.3	15063.7	4365.0	1550.0	855.7	467.6	207.1	122.7	104.4
282.1	362.9	490.1	420.0	400.4	376.9	376.9	182.1	133.6	103.9	76.9	89.7	94.1
10186	12500	17900	26859	30693	31833		503.7	312.5	254.7	177.8	118.5	103.7
27.7	36.2	50.4	46.1	55.2	51.9	789.9	237.9	187.5	143.4	102.9	112.7	94.1
683.0	1300	2425.1	4320.0	5556.2	5866.2		1663.7	858.9	451.2	241.9	135.8	105.6

Note: a) From 2011, the starting point of fixed asset investment is changed from RMB 500,000 to RMB 5 million according to relevant regulations of National Bureau of Statistics.

b) Gross output value is calculated at current prices.

c) Business volume of post and telecommunications service in and before 2000 was calculated at 1990's constant prices; that of 2001-2010 was calculated at 2000's constant prices; that of 2011-2015 was calculated at 2010's constant prices; business volume of post service of 2018 and 2019 was calculated at 2010's constant prices, and that of telecommunications service was calculated at 2015's constant prices.

d) Historical Date of Retail Sales of Consumer Goods were revised according to the forth national economic census in Beijing.

1-3 续表 2

项　目		Item		1990	1995
金融业		**Finance**			
金融机构(含外资)本外币存款余额	(亿元)	Deposits of Financial Institutions (Including Foreign Institutions)	(100 million yuan)		
金融机构(含外资)本外币贷款余额	(亿元)	Loans of Financial Institutions (Including Foreign Institutions)	(100 million yuan)		
原保险保费收入	(亿元)	Premiums Revenue	(100 million yuan)		
证券市场交易额	(亿元)	Trading Volume of Stock Market	(100 million yuan)		
科　技		**Science and Technology**			
研究与试验发展经费内部支出	(亿元)	Internal R&D Expenditures	(100 million yuan)		
技术合同成交总额	(亿元)	Total Volume of Transaction of Technological Contracts Concluded	(100 million yuan)	20.3	41.2
专利授权量	(件)	Patents Granted	(unit)	2268	4025
教　育		**Education**			
在校学生数	(万人)	Students Enrollment	(10000 persons)		238.0
专任教师数	(万人)	Full-time Teachers	(10000 persons)		17.7
卫生及社会服务		**Health Care and Social Services**			
卫生		Health Care			
医疗卫生机构个数	(个)	Medical and Health Institutions	(unit)	4953	4955
医疗机构实有床位数	(万张)	Beds in Medical Institutions	(10000 beds)	5.9	6.7
医疗卫生技术人员数	(万人)	Medical Technical Personnel	(10000 persons)	11.2	11.6
#执业(助理)医师		Certified (Assistant) Doctors		5.1	5.4
注册护士		Registered Nurses		3.5	3.7
婚姻		Marriage and Divorce			
登记结婚对数	(万对)	Number of Registered Marriages	(10000 couples)	9.3	8.6
离婚对数	(万对)	Number of Registered Divorces	(10000 couples)	1.5	2.0
文化		**Culture**			
公共图书馆总藏数	(万册、万件)	Collection of Public Libraries	(10000 volumes)	2205	2629
博物馆及其他文物保护机构	(个)	Museums and Other Cultural Relic Protection and Administration Organizations	(unit)		51
电影放映场次	(万场次)	Show Times of Films	(10000 times)	20.7	9.2
社会保障		**Social Security**			
参加企业职工基本养老保险人数	(万人)	Enterprise Employed Persons Participating in Basic Pension Insurance	(10000 persons)		261.1
参加职工基本医疗保险人数	(万人)	Staff and Workers Participating in Basic Medical Care Insurance	(10000 persons)		

注：1. 离婚对数包括在民政部门登记的对数和经法院调离和判离的对数。
2. 2010年及以前，卫生机构个数不含村卫生室及驻京部队医院情况。2011年开始，包含村卫生室情况。2012年开始，卫生机构个数、卫生技术人员数含驻京部队医院，床位数不包含驻京部队医院。
3. “博物馆及其他文物保护机构”数据为北京市文物局系统内数据。
4. 按照国家知识产权局相关要求，2017年起对专利相关数据的统计范围进行调整。

1-3 Continued 2

总量指标 Aggregate Indicator						速度指标(%) Speed Indicator (%)						
						指 数(2019年为以下各年) Index (2019 as Percentage of the Following Year)						
2000	2005	2010	2015	2018	2019	1990	1995	2000	2005	2010	2015	2018
11526.0	28969.9	66584.6	128573.0	157092.2	171062.3			1484.1	590.5	256.9	133.0	108.9
6407.9	15335.5	36479.6	58559.4	70483.7	76875.6			1199.7	501.3	210.7	131.3	109.1
93.4	498.2	966.5	1403.9	1793.3	2076.5			2222.1	416.8	214.9	147.9	115.8
14727.2	12930.0	129495.2	918064.8	911465.7	946425.6			6426.4	7319.6	730.9	103.1	103.8
155.7	379.5	821.8	1384.0	1870.8	2233.6			1434.5	588.5	271.8	161.4	119.4
140.3	434.4	1579.5	3452.6	4957.8	5695.3	28097.2	13833.6	4059.7	1311.1	360.6	165.0	114.9
5905	10100	33511	94031	123496	131716	5807.6	3272.4	2230.6	1304.1	393.1	140.1	106.7
229.9	226.4	330.0	373.4	408.3	412.5		173.3	179.4	182.2	125.0	110.5	101.0
16.7	17.5	20.7	22.6	24.2	24.8		140.6	148.6	142.2	120.2	109.8	102.7
6176	7536	9511	10425	11100	11340	229.0	228.9	183.6	150.5	119.2	108.8	102.2
7.1	7.9	9.3	11.2	12.4	12.7	215.3	189.9	178.4	160.8	136.9	113.9	102.9
11.6	12.0	17.1	25.7	28.2	29.7	266.3	256.3	257.3	247.4	173.7	115.9	105.5
5.2	5.1	6.6	9.6	10.9	11.6	227.3	213.9	224.5	227.4	175.0	120.0	105.8
4.0	4.3	6.7	11.4	12.4	13.1	379.9	357.6	329.1	306.1	195.1	114.9	106.3
8.0	9.7	13.8	16.6	13.8	12.9	138.7	150.8	160.8	133.0	93.4	77.7	93.6
2.7	3.4	4.4	8.2	7.4	8.4	569.8	416.8	315.7	245.4	191.1	102.2	113.0
3020	3626	4613	5943	6777	7048	319.6	268.1	233.4	194.4	152.8	118.6	104.0
53	73	79	77	78	78		152.9	147.2	106.8	98.7	101.3	100.0
12.2	22.6	74.3	198.1	309.6	356.2	1720.6	3871.4	2919.4	1576.0	479.4	179.8	115.0
391.6	520.0	982.5	1424.2	1591.5	1651.6		632.6	421.8	317.6	168.1	116.0	103.8
	574.8	1063.7	1475.7	1628.9	1682.5				292.7	158.2	114.0	103.3

Note: a) Number of registered divorces includes those registered with civil affair authorities and those mediated and ruled in courts.

b) In and before 2010, figures on health centers were emerged with other health institutions such as community health service centers (stations). From 2011, health care institutions included village health centers. From 2012, figures of health care institutions and health care technical personnel have included military hospitals in Beijing, but beds are exclusive.

c) Figures of museums and other cultural relic protection and administration organizations were the one under the jurisdiction of Beijing Municipal Administration of Cultural Heritage.

d) According to relevant requirements of the State Intellectural Property Office,the statistical range of patent-related data was adjusted since 2017.

1-4 主要年份国民经济和社会发展结构指标
STRUCTURAL INDICATORS ON NATIONAL ECONOMIC AND SOCIAL DEVELOPMENT IN KEY YEARS

单位：% (%)

项目	Item	1990	1995	2000	2005	2010	2015	2019
人口与就业	**Population and Employment**							
常住人口	**Permanent Population**							
按性别分	By Sex							
男	Male	50.2	50.1	52.1	50.6	51.6	51.3	50.8
女	Female	49.8	49.9	47.9	49.4	48.4	48.7	49.2
按城乡分	By Urban Area and Rural Area							
城 镇	Urban	73.5	75.6	77.5	83.6	86.0	86.5	86.6
乡 村	Rural	26.5	24.4	22.5	16.4	14.0	13.5	13.4
就 业	**Employment**							
从业人员年末人数	Year-end Employed Persons							
第一产业	Primary Industry	14.5	10.6	11.8	7.1	6.0	4.2	3.3
第二产业	Secondary Industry	44.9	40.7	33.6	26.3	19.6	17.0	13.6
第三产业	Tertiary Industry	40.6	48.7	54.6	66.6	74.4	78.8	83.1
国民经济核算	**National Accounts**							
地区生产总值	Gross Domestic Product							
第一产业	Primary Industry	8.7	4.8	2.4	1.2	0.8	0.6	0.3
第二产业	Secondary Industry	52.3	42.1	31.2	26.7	21.6	17.8	16.2
第三产业	Tertiary Industry	39.0	53.1	66.4	72.1	77.6	81.6	83.5
人民生活	**People's Living Conditions**							
城镇居民人均消费支出	Per Capita Consumption Expenditure of Urban Residents							
#食品烟酒	Food, Tobacco and Liquor	54.2	48.5	35.8	29.4	26.8	22.1	19.3
衣 着	Clothing	14.7	15.1	8.7	8.1	8.5	7.2	5.2
医疗保健	Health Care and Medical Services	1.4	2.9	7.0	9.8	6.4	6.5	8.6
交通通信	Transport and Communication	1.5	4.7	7.0	13.1	13.7	13.3	11.3
教育文化娱乐	Education, Cultural and Entertainment	11.6	10.2	14.8	14.7	11.5	11.0	10.2
农村居民人均消费支出	Per Capita Consumption Expenditure of Rural Residents							
#食品烟酒	Food, Tobacco and Liquor	50.7	49.6	37.5	30.3	26.6	27.7	25.3
衣 着	Clothing	9.5	10.9	7.0	6.4	5.9	6.3	5.5
医疗保健	Health Care and Medical Services	3.8	4.8	7.3	9.4	8.4	8.4	10.3
交通通信	Transport and Communication	1.7	4.1	7.0	11.9	11.7	13.5	15.5
教育文化娱乐	Education, Cultural and Entertainment	6.6	10.6	13.6	12.9	7.5	7.2	7.3
财 政	**Government Finance**							
一般公共预算收入	General Public Budget Revenue							
#增值税	Value Added Tax			13.3	10.6	8.9	15.2	31.3
个人所得税	Private Income Tax			16.3	9.2	9.1	10.1	9.4
企业所得税	Corporate Income Tax			16.8	17.9	21.8	21.7	21.1

1-4 续表 1 Continued 1

单位：% (%)

项 目	Item	1990	1995	2000	2005	2010	2015	2019
能源消费总量	**Energy Consumption**							
第一产业	Primary Industry	3.9	3.4	2.5	1.7	1.5	1.2	0.8
第二产业	Secondary Industry	63.5	65.9	58.5	46.8	37.2	28.0	25.1
第三产业	Tertiary Industry	19.0	17.9	26.1	35.1	41.7	48.7	51.1
生活消费	Living Consumption	13.6	12.8	12.9	16.4	19.5	22.1	23.0
投 资	**Investment**							
固定资产投资资金来源	Source of Capital for Investment in Fixed Assets							
中央预算资金	Central Budgetary Appropriation	25.3	7.7	7.4	2.8	1.2	1.7	1.7
国内贷款	Domestic Loans	16.7	13.4	26.0	23.2	26.6	22.2	23.1
利用外资	Foreign Investment	11.2	20.5	3.6	1.6	0.5	0.1	0.04
债券、自筹和其他资金	Securities, Fundraising and Other Investment	46.8	58.5	63.0	72.4	71.6	76.0	75.2
对外经济贸易	**Foreign Economic Relations and Trade**							
海关出口商品(以美元计价)	Commodities Exported at Customs (Calculated in USD)							
#一般贸易	General Trade		70.6	65.9	54.5	45.0	54.8	76.3
加工贸易	Processing Trade		21.3	29.6	39.6	42.1	28.0	6.3
海关进口商品(以美元计价)	Commodities Imported at Customs (Calculated in USD)							
#一般贸易	General Trade		84.4	87.3	85.2	88.7	85.7	86.9
加工贸易	Processing Trade		5.2	3.5	8.2	5.9	7.7	5.4
农 业	**Agriculture**							
农林牧渔业产值	Output Value of Agriculture, Forestry, Animal Production and Hunting, Fishing							
农 业	Agriculture	55.6	52.8	46.7	38.0	47.0	42.0	36.3
林 业	Forestry	1.3	1.7	2.8	5.2	5.1	15.6	41.0
牧 业	Animal Production and Hunting	39.8	41.8	46.4	50.5	42.6	36.9	17.5
渔 业	Fishing	3.3	3.7	4.1	3.6	3.5	3.2	1.9
农林牧渔专业及辅助性活动	Professional and Supporting Activities of Agriculture, Forestry, Animal Production and Hunting, Fishing				2.7	1.8	2.3	3.2
工 业	**Industry**							
规模以上工业总产值	Gross Output Value of Industry Above Designated Size							
#医药制造业	Manufacture of Medicines	1.8	1.5	2.1	1.9	2.7	4.2	6.0
汽车制造业	Manufacture of Motor Vehicles	7.8	11.6	3.9	11.8	15.9	22.3	19.4
计算机、通信和其他电子设备制造业	Manufacture of Computer, Communication Equipment and Other Electronic Equipment	6.0	10.4	32.9	25.6	16.3	12.1	12.8
电力、热力的生产和供应业	Production and Distribution of Electricity and Heating Power	2.6	2.8	2.9	8.6	15.5	23.4	26.9
建筑业	**Construction**							
建筑业总产值	Gross Output Value of Construction							
房屋建筑业	Construction of Buildings						51.3	51.7
土木工程建筑业	Civil Engineering Construction						32.7	34.2
建筑安装业	Construction Installation						7.9	7.0
建筑装饰和其他建筑业	Building Decoration and Other Construction						8.1	7.2
交通运输业	**Transport**							
货运量(按运输方式分)	Freight Traffic (By Means of Transportation)							
铁 路	Railway	11.4	9.2	8.5	6.1	6.6	4.3	1.6
公 路	Road	87.5	90.4	91.2	92.4	85.1	82.0	81.7
民 航	Civil Aviation	0.04	0.05	0.11	0.24	0.55	0.68	0.61
管 道	Pipeline	1.0	0.3	0.2	1.2	7.7	13.0	16.1

注：1.2017年，原“国家预算内资金”调整为“中央预算资金”。

2.根据《国民经济行业分类》(GB/T 4754—2017)标准，将原“农林牧渔服务业”调整为“农林牧渔专业及辅助性活动”。

Note: a) In 2017, the original State Budgets was renamed Central Budgetary Fund.

b) According to the standards in the Classification of National Economic Sectors (GB/T 4754-2017), the original Service Activities for Agriculture, Forestry, Animal Husbandry and Fishing is Adjusted into Professional and Supporting Activities of Agriculture, Forestry, Animal Production and Hunting, Fishing.

1-4 续表 2 Continued 2

单位：% (%)

项　　目	Item	1990	1995	2000	2005	2010	2015	2019
客运量(按运输方式分)	Passenger (By Means of Transportation)							
铁　路	Railway	50.4	45.1	24.2	9.5	6.3	18.3	20.5
公　路	Road	46.7	47.7	70.7	85.3	89.7	71.4	66.7
民　航	Civil Aviation	2.9	7.2	5.1	5.2	4.0	10.3	12.8
消　费	**Consumption**							
社会消费品零售总额	Total Retail Sales of Consumer Goods							
吃类商品	Food	39.6	41.8	26.1	24.9	20.9	18.1	18.7
穿类商品	Clothing	13.2	14.3	9.2	8.4	7.6	6.1	5.4
用类商品	Daily Use Articles	44.8	42.0	59.7	59.0	64.9	71.4	71.9
烧类商品	Fuels	2.3	1.9	5.0	7.7	6.6	4.5	4.0
入境旅游	**Inbound Tourism**							
接待海外旅游人数	Inbound Tourist							
外国人	Foreigners	63.8	80.4	84.4	85.9	86.0	85.1	85.1
港澳台同胞	Compatriots from Hong Kong, Macao and Taiwan	34.7	17.5	15.6	14.1	14.0	14.9	14.9
科　技	**Science and Technology**							
研究与试验发展(R&D)	Full-time Equivalents of							
人员折合全时当量	R&D Professionals							
基础研究	Basic Research				12.9	15.2	16.8	20.2
应用研究	Applied Research				29.8	27.1	25.1	29.5
试验发展	Experimental Development				57.3	57.7	58.1	50.3
研究与试验发展(R&D)	Internal							
经费内部支出	R&D Expentures							
基础研究	Basic Research				10.1	11.6	13.8	15.9
应用研究	Applied Research				27.8	26.4	23.0	25.2
试验发展	Experimental Development				53.1	62.0	63.2	58.8
教　育	**Education**							
在校学生	Students Enrollment							
#普通本专科	Regular Undergraduates and College Students		7.7	12.3	23.7	17.5	15.9	14.2
中等教育	Secondary Education		35.1	42.3	37.9	22.1	15.7	13.0
小学教育	Primary Education		42.3	32.3	21.8	19.8	22.8	22.8
专任教师	Full-time Teachers							
#高等教育	Higher Education	24.6	22.7	22.2	32.7	35.9	30.3	28.7
中等教育	Secondary Education	38.3	38.6	40.5	33.6	29.1	32.0	31.8
小学教育	Primary Education	36.7	37.9	36.8	25.3	23.9	22.1	22.5
卫　生	**Health Care**							
卫生技术人员	Medical Personnel							
#执业(助理)医师	Certified (Assistant) Doctors	45.6	46.7	44.6	42.4	38.6	37.6	38.9
注册护士	Registered Nurses	31.0	31.7	34.5	35.7	39.3	44.6	44.2

1-5 国民经济和社会发展主要比例和效益指标

MAIN INDICATORS ON PROPORTIONS AND EFFICIENCY IN NATIONAL ECONOMIC AND SOCIAL DEVELOPMENT

项 目		Item		2019	2018
人口与就业		**Population and Employment**			
出生率(常住人口)	(‰)	Birth Rate (Permanent Population)	(‰)	8.12	8.24
死亡率(常住人口)	(‰)	Death Rate (Permanent Population)	(‰)	5.49	5.58
自然增长率(常住人口)	(‰)	Natural Growth Rate (Permanent Population)	(‰)	2.63	2.66
少儿抚养比(常住人口)	(%)	Child-age Dependency Rate (Permanent Population)	(%)	13.49	13.44
老年抚养比(常住人口)	(%)	Old-age Dependency Rate (Permanent Population)	(%)	14.64	14.32
城镇登记失业率	(%)	Registered Unemployment Rate in Urban Areas	(%)	1.30	1.40
国民经济核算		**National Accounts**			
人均地区生产总值	(元)	Per Capita Gross Domestic Product	(yuan)	164220	153095
社会劳动生产率	(元/人)	Overall Labor Productivity	(yuan/person)	281752	266494
第一产业		Primary Industry		25897	25594
第二产业		Secondary Industry		322211	292110
第三产业		Tertiary Industry		285674	272980
人民生活		**People's Living Conditions**			
城镇与农村居民收入比例（以农村居民人均可支配收入为1）		Ratio of Urban Residents' Income to Rural Residents' Income (Per capita Disposable Income of Rural Residents = 1)		2.55	2.57
能源消费		**Energy Consumption**			
能源消费弹性系数		Energy Consumption Elasticity Coefficient		0.21	0.38
电力消费弹性系数		Electricity Consumption Elasticity Coefficient		0.35	1.06
万元地区生产总值能耗（可比价）	(吨标准煤)	Energy Consumption per 10000 yuan of GDP (Comparable Price)	(ton of SCE)	0.230	0.241
万元地区生产总值水耗（现价）	(立方米)	Water Consumption per 10000 yuan of GDP (Current Price)	(cu.m)	11.78	11.87
对外经济贸易		**Foreign Economic Relations and Trade**			
进出口总值与地区生产总值之比(按人民币计算)	(%)	Ratio of Total Value of Imports and Exports to Gross Domestic Product (calculated in RMB)	(%)	81.07	82.11
工业		**Industry**			
资产负债率	(%)	Asset-liability Ratio	(%)	42.08	45.15
流动资产周转率	(次)	Turnover Rate of Working Capital	(time)	1.23	1.19
成本费用利润率	(%)	Ratio of Profits to Total Industrial Cost	(%)	7.74	7.82
建筑业		**Construction**			
产值竣工率	(%)	Rate of Buildings Completed (by Output Value)	(%)	43.5	40.9
面积竣工率	(%)	Rate of Buildings Completed (by Floor Space)	(%)	11.9	13.6
邮电通信业		**Post and Communications**			
移动电话普及率	(户/百人)	Penetration Rate of Mobile Phone	(sets/100 persons)	186.7	186.1
固定电话主线普及率	(线/百人)	Penetration Rate of Main Line of Fixed Telephone	(line/100 persons)	25.8	28.5
科 技		**Science and Technology**			
研究与试验发展经费内部支出相当于地区生产总值比例	(%)	Internal R&D Expenditures as % of GDP	(%)	6.31	5.65
教 育		**Education**			
平均每一专任教师负担学生数		Average Number of Students Instructed by a Full-time Teacher			
#普通中学	(人)	Ordinary Secondary Education	(person)	8.2	7.9
小学学校	(人)	Primary Education	(person)	13.8	13.9
文 化		**Culture**			
每万人拥有公共图书馆	(个)	Public Libraries per 10,000 persons	(library)	0.01	0.01
每万人拥有博物馆	(个)	Museums per 10,000 persons	(museum)	0.08	0.08
卫 生		**Health Care**			
平均每千常住人口医院床位数	(张)	Ward Beds per 1000 Permanent Population on Average	(unit)	5.55	5.40
平均每千常住人口拥有执业(助理)医师数	(人)	Certified (Assistant) Doctors per 1000 Permanent Population on Average	(person)	5.38	5.08

1-6 北京一日
A DAY IN BEIJING

项目		Item		2019	2018
每日创造		**Daily Production**			
地区生产总值	(万元/日)	Gross Domestic Product	(10000 yuan/day)	969076.7	907013.7
第一产业		Primary Industry		3115.1	3304.1
第二产业		Secondary Industry		156578.1	150065.8
第三产业		Tertiary Industry		809383.6	753646.6
一般公共预算收入	(万元/日)	General Public Budget Revenue	(10000 yuan/day)	159372.6	158518.3
一般公共预算支出	(万元/日)	General Public Budget Expenditure	(10000 yuan/day)	202964.0	204696.8
发电量	(万千瓦时/日)	Electricity Generated	(10000 kWh/day)	11813.5	11980.8
汽车生产量	(辆/日)	Output of Motor Vehicles	(vehicle/day)	4493	4471
移动电话机生产量	(台/日)	Output of Mobile Telephones	(set/day)	229406	231452
显示器生产量	(台/日)	Output of Display Devices	(set/day)	12879	11132
公共电汽车客运量	(万人次/日)	Passenger Traffic of Buses and Trolley Buses	(10000 person-times/day)	858.5	873.9
轨道交通客运量	(万人次/日)	Passenger Traffic of Rail Transit	(10000 person-times/day)	1085.6	1054.4
铁路客运量	(万人次/日)	Passenger Traffic of Railway	(10000 person-times/day)	40.4	39.1
公路客运量	(万人次/日)	Passenger Traffic of Road	(10000 person-times/day)	131.9	121.0
民航客运量	(万人次/日)	Passenger Traffic of Civil Aviation	(10000 person-times/day)	25.3	25.0
旅游外汇收入	(万美元/日)	Foreign Exchange Earning from Tourism	(USD 10000/day)	1421.9	1511.2
国内旅游收入	(万元/日)	Domestic Tourism Earnings	(10000 yuan/day)	160717.8	152223.8
地区出口总值	(万元/日)	Total Exports of Local Enterprises	(10000 yuan/day)	141708.9	133658.7
地区进口总值	(万元/日)	Total Imports of Local Enterprises	(10000 yuan/day)	643967.1	611066.7
实际利用外商直接投资额	(万美元/日)	Paid-in Foreign Investment	(USD 10000/day)	3894.0	4742.7
每日生活		**Daily Life**			
社会消费品零售总额	(万元/日)	Total Retail Sales of Consumer Goods	(10000 yuan/day)	412702.8	395131.3
吃类商品		Food		77335.8	71864.6
穿类商品		Clothing		22223.7	22392.6
用类商品		Daily Use Articles		296687.3	283284.4
烧类商品		Fuels		16456.0	17591.1
常住出生人口	(人/日)	Births (Permanent Residence)	(person/day)	479	488
常住死亡人口	(人/日)	Deaths (Permanent Residence)	(person/day)	324	331
登记结婚对数	(对/日)	Registered Marriages	(couple/day)	353	378
离婚对数	(对/日)	Divorces	(couple/day)	230	204
全市居民人均可支配收入	(元/日)	Per Capita Disposable Income of Residents of the Whole City	(yuan/day)	185.6	170.9
全市居民人均消费支出	(元/日)	Per Capita Consumption Expenditure of Reside of the Whole City	(yuan/day)	117.9	109.2
法人单位从业人员平均工资	(元/日)	Average Wages of Employed Persons in Legal Entities	(yuan/day)	385.2	348.2
电影放映场次	(场次/日)	Show Times of Fimls	(times/day)	9759	8482
特快专递业务量	(万件/日)	Express Mail Services	(10000 pcs/day)	626.6	605.1
城乡居民生活用电量	(万千瓦时/日)	Household Electricity Consumption of Urban and Rural Residents	(10000 kWh/day)	6893.1	7023.5
居民家庭用天然气	(万立方米/日)	Household Consumption of Natural Gas	(10000 cu.m/day)	399.7	386.5
自来水销售总量	(万立方米/日)	Total Sales Volume of Tap Water	(10000 cu.m/day)	328.9	317.4
污水处理能力	(万立方米/日)	Seweage Treatment Capacity	(10000 cu.m/day)	679.2	670.6
生活垃圾清运量	(万吨/日)	Domestic Waste Removed and Transported	(10000 tons/day)	2.77	2.67

注：离婚对数包括在民政部门登记的对数和经法院调离和判离的对数。
Note: Divorces include those registered with civil affair authorities and those mediated and ruled in courts.

1-7 “十三五”时期经济社会发展主要监测指标
MAIN MONITORING INDICATORS OF SOCIAL AND ECONOMIC DEVELOPMENT IN THE THIRTEENTH FIVE-YEAR PLAN PERIOD

项 目	Item	“十三五”时期监测发展目标	Target in the 13th Five-year Plan	2019
常住人口规模 (万人)	Permanent Population (10000 persons)	<2300	<2300	2153.6
地区生产总值年均增速 (%)	Average Annual Growth Rate of GDP (%)	年均增长6.5%	average annual growth of 6.5%	【6.6】
第三产业增加值占地区生产总值比重 (%)	Added Value of Tertiary Industry as % of GDP (%)	>80%	>80%	83.5
一般公共预算收入年均增速 (%)	Average Annual Growth Rate of General Public Budget Revenue (%)	年均增长>6.5%	average annual growth > 6.5%	【5.3】
全市居民人均可支配收入年均实际增速 (%)	Average Annual Real Growth Rate of Per Capita Disposable Income of Residents of the Whole City (%)	与经济增长同步	keeping pace with economic growth	【6.6】
用水总量 (亿立方米)	Total Volume of Water Consumed (100 million Cu.m)	<43	<43	41.7
细颗粒物($PM_{2.5}$)年均浓度值 (微克/立方米)	Average Annual Concentration of $PM_{2.5}$ (μg/cu.m)	达到国家要求	meeting the national requirements	42.0
森林覆盖率 (%)	Forest Coverage Rate (%)	44.0	44.0	44.0
生活垃圾无害化处理率 (%)	Rate of Harmless Disposal (%)	>99.8%	>99.8%	99.98
全市污水处理率 (%)	Sewage Treatment Rate (%)	>95%	>95%	94.5
城镇登记失业率 (%)	Urban Registered Unemployment Rate (%)	控制在4%以内	under 4%	1.30
重点食品安全监测抽检合格率 (%)	Up-to-standard Rate of Key Foods Security (%)	达到98%以上	Over 98%	98.89
药品抽验合格率 (%)	Up-to-standard Rate of Drug Spot Checks (%)	达到99%以上	Over 99%	100.0
全社会研究与试验发展经费支出占地区生产总值的比例 (%)	R&D Expenditure as % of GDP (%)	6%左右	6% or so	6.31
万元地区生产总值水耗累计降低 (%)	Decrease of Water Consumption per 10000 yuan of GDP (%)	累计降低15%	Cumulative decrease by 15%	15.58
万元地区生产总值能耗累计降低 (%)	Decrease of Energy Consumption per 10000 yuan of GDP (%)	达到国家要求	meeting the national requirements	16.27
服务贸易总额 (亿美元)	Total Service Trade (USD 100 million)	达到2000亿美元	Reaching USD 200 billion	
社会劳动生产率 (万元/人)	Overall Labor Productivity (10000 yuan/person)	达到23	Reaching 23	24.4

注：1.【】内数值为“十三五”以来年均增速。
2. 2019年服务贸易总额为10646.9亿元。

Note: a) Figures in [ ] refer to the average annual growth rate since the 13th five-year plan period.
b) The total service trade in 2019 was RMB 1.06469 trillion.

1-8 四次经济普查法人单位基本情况

项目	Item	法人单位数(个) Total Number of Legal Entities (unit)			
		2004	2008	2013	2018
合 计	**Total**	**220947**	**267890**	**630545**	**988619**
按登记注册类型分	**By Registration Type**				
内 资	Domestically-Invested Enterprises	213857	258238	617359	973887
国 有	State-owned Enterprises	20722	15672	22094	17953
集 体	Collectively-owned Enterprises	15879	9936	13845	15366
股份合作	Joint-equity Cooperative Enterprises	22180	10666	14456	6005
联 营	Associated Enterprises	614	403	1363	350
有限责任公司	Limited Liability Companies	31480	49555	149881	76162
股份有限公司	Companies Limited by Shares	3798	4602	5011	4475
私 营	Private Enterprises	110531	161288	390809	835891
其 他	Others	8653	6116	19900	17685
港澳台商投资	Hong Kong, Macao and Taiwan-invested	2257	2986	4960	5511
外商投资	Foreign-invested Enterprises	4833	6666	8226	9221
按隶属关系分	**By Affiliation**				
中 央	Central	10484	8728	9747	8732
地 方	Local	210463	259162	620798	979887
按行业分	**By Sector**				
农、林、牧、渔业	Agriculture, Forestry, Animal Production and Hunting, Fishing				413
采矿业	Mining and Quarrying	564	142	127	78
制造业	Manufacturing	30870	28786	33055	25684
电力、热力、燃气及水生产和供应业	Production and Distribution of Electricity, Heating Power, Gas and Water	271	359	638	1193
建筑业	Construction	5878	9164	18486	35130
批发和零售业	Wholesale and Retail Trade	65084	85054	190704	273395
交通运输、仓储和邮政业	Transport, Storage and Post	3889	6022	14290	19176
住宿和餐饮业	Accommodation and Restaurants	8705	10695	16323	34458
信息传输、软件和信息技术服务业	Information Transmission, Software and Information Technology Services	11611	15776	47602	77152
金融业	Finance	672	1025	3811	12796
房地产业	Real Estate	8782	10955	17805	26885
租赁和商务服务业	Renting and Leasing Activities and Business Services	32527	45003	134926	184764
科学研究和技术服务业	Scientific Research and Development, Technical Services	13828	20451	71206	154187
水利、环境和公共设施管理业	Management of Water Conservancy, Environment and Public Facilities	1476	1719	3964	7346
居民服务、修理和其他服务业	Resident Services, Repair and Other Services	13001	10239	18735	36756
教 育	Education	5423	6242	11145	21236
卫生和社会工作	Health Care and Social Works	1745	2270	3810	6607
文化、体育和娱乐业	Culture, Sports and Entertainment	5856	7369	26784	53885
公共管理、社会保障和社会组织	Pulic Administration,Social Security and Social Organizations	10765	6619	17134	17478

注：1.本表2004年、2008年行业划分执行《国民经济行业分类》(GB/T4754—2002)标准，2013年执行《国民经济行业分类》(GB/T4754—2011)标准，2018年执行《国民经济行业分类》(GB/T4754—2017)标准。
2.2018年，资产总计、收入总计、企业利润、年末从业人员合计数中包括铁路部门数据，分组数据不含。

BASIC STATISTICS FOR LEGAL ENTITIES IN THE FOURTH ECONOMIC CENSUS

资产总计(亿元) Total Assets (100 million yuan)				收入总计 (亿元) Total Income (100 million yuan)			
2004	2008	2013	2018	2004	2008	2013	2018
216316.9	**646673.0**	**1220785.2**	**2119561.6**	**30942.0**	**66702.8**	**140828.4**	**199152.1**
206314.5	623894.6	1166922.3	1985481.9	25986.1	52376.6	114828.6	162106.2
92836.4	280476.4	318572.3	828238.3	7729.4	11678.0	16652.3	24528.0
1711.4	1468.7	2684.0	5463.1	665.0	682.7	614.3	677.1
2953.8	625.6	1098.2	1359.5	387.2	310.8	446.6	322.6
130.8	101.9	107.7	62.6	63.0	29.5	45.6	14.7
45133.1	111630.9	225521.5	432145.1	8661.3	21588.4	62577.8	81395.9
58244.2	219733.8	587253.5	585069.2	4634.1	10644.3	18133.4	20911.1
4951.7	9085.3	29471.4	130690.4	3769.7	7155.3	15808.7	33206.9
353.2	772.2	2213.7	2453.5	76.4	287.7	550.0	1049.8
3558.1	7515.9	16959.1	38758.3	1110.0	3722.8	6725.3	15675.8
6444.2	15262.4	36903.9	56531.1	3845.8	10603.3	19274.5	20542.2
168110.5	532422.7	918654.6	1551884.8	13037.9	26806.7	58770.4	72168.2
48206.4	114250.3	302130.6	528886.5	17904.1	39896.0	82058.0	126156.0
			28.0				5.6
69.0	433.1	2927.1	3983.7	152.7	384.6	1419.2	553.3
6531.1	9981.8	17827.4	26713.7	5259.5	9703.6	14565.1	17012.0
6851.8	7317.3	13204.4	21867.4	813.1	1780.8	4070.5	5759.3
3199.9	7283.4	18021.1	35232.6	2083.4	4140.5	10244.9	15415.5
8103.0	17832.9	40399.0	62339.8	9636.2	24305.8	55353.5	66771.0
2494.3	4999.9	15176.9	54752.4	751.0	2378.1	4878.5	6396.0
777.7	1204.6	2048.6	2559.2	361.4	662.0	1020.8	1412.3
8734.8	11120.3	28206.2	55834.3	1347.0	2953.3	5719.9	13749.1
141269.9	474100.4	873336.5	1486292.5	4117.1	6199.0	16762.4	24901.7
10016.4	20042.3	47129.9	96972.5	1760.1	2518.3	4964.0	6526.8
19440.6	74670.8	117957.3	194326.7	1203.5	3575.7	10240.0	12313.4
2932.3	9569.2	24304.6	43862.1	1132.9	3785.8	6722.1	11717.8
714.0	929.3	2870.9	5839.4	88.9	216.5	413.9	1093.7
822.7	252.7	897.7	1075.3	266.8	137.5	316.2	535.0
1120.8	1990.3	3710.9	6591.7	490.1	852.0	692.0	2913.4
464.6	741.9	1338.2	2513.1	323.4	621.0	1146.7	2526.6
1083.2	1747.0	4367.3	9011.1	446.6	826.8	1360.7	2653.1
1690.9	2455.8	7061.4	9765.9	708.2	1661.5	938.0	6896.5

Note: a) In 2004 and 2008, the sectors in this table were classified in accordance with the standards in the Classification of National Economic Sectors (GB/T4754-2002); in 2013, the classification was carried out in accordance with the standards in the Classification of National Economic Sectors (GB/T4754-2011); and in 2018, the classification was carried out in accordance with the standards in the Classification National Economic Sectors (GB/T4754-2017).

b) In 2018, the data on total assets, total income, enterprise profits and year-end total number of persons employed included that of the railway sector; however, the grouped data did not cover the data of the railway sector.

1-8 续表 Continued

项 目	Item	企业利润(亿元) Profit of Enterprises (100 million yuan)				年末从业人员(万人) Employed Persons (100 million yuan)			
		2004	2008	2013	2018	2004	2008	2013	2018
合 计	**Total**	**1989.0**	**5488.1**	**20566.8**	**24842.9**	**705.2**	**816.9**	**1111.3**	**1361.0**
按登记注册类型分	**By Registration Type**								
内 资	Domestially-Invested Enterprises	1460.7	4602.9	17673.4	19658.5	639.3	704.7	965.1	1199.4
国 有	State-owned Enterprises	806.5	1332.1	2880.4	4161.7	195.2	195.0	194.9	178.8
集 体	Collectively-owned Enterprises	23.2	14.7	18.5	-19.4	43.6	26.5	21.7	16.7
股份合作	Joint-equity Cooperative Enterprises	26.2	6.8	6.6	7.8	28.6	14.0	12.2	5.9
联 营	Associated Enterprises	1.2	-0.9	-0.4	0.3	2.4	1.3	1.1	0.5
有限责任公司	Limited Liability Companies	393.4	1536.3	8916.4	9953.8	155.2	221.1	331.1	343.2
股份有限公司	Companies Limited by Shares	134.6	1630.4	5645.9	5682.8	39.3	62.4	80.8	92.1
私 营	Private Enterprises	75.6	65.2	191.9	-139.9	162.4	170.6	300.6	537.5
其 他	Others	0.1	18.4	14.1	11.4	12.7	13.9	22.6	24.5
港澳台商投资	Hong Kong, Macao and Taiwan-invested	188.0	113.1	649.4	910.8	20.4	39.0	55.1	73.6
外商投资	Foreign-invested Enterprises	340.2	772.1	2244.0	3915.5	45.4	73.2	91.2	79.7
按隶属关系分	**By Affiliation**								
中 央	Central	1083.5	3475.3	14647.9	16544.0	134.6	168.3	178.3	185.4
地 方	Local	905.5	2012.8	5918.9	7940.8	570.5	648.6	933.1	1167.2
按行业分	**By Sector**								
农、林、牧、渔业	Agriculture, Forestry, Animal Production and Hunting, Fishing				-0.4				0.2
采矿业	Mining and Quarrying	16.8	44.9	18.6	-69.9	4.1	5.1	6.9	3.6
制造业	Manufacturing	268.7	301.8	860.4	1095.6	148.8	134.7	138.5	96.8
电力、热力、燃气及水生产和供应业	Production and Distribution of Electricity, Heating Power, Gas and Water	104.3	192.6	377.5	535.5	7.8	6.7	9.3	10.8
建筑业	Construction	46.9	87.7	436.5	498.0	69.7	54.7	65.5	96.5
批发和零售业	Wholesale and Retail Trade	221.7	726.5	1026.1	1456.0	83.2	94.3	147.8	161.4
交通运输、仓储和邮政业	Transport, Storage and Post	76.0	-3.3	275.2	776.3	43.0	69.5	68.6	71.5
住宿和餐饮业	Accommodation and Restaurants	-0.3	7.1	-24.2	20.2	38.4	44.9	50.6	56.3
信息传输、软件和信息技术服务业	Information Transmission, Software and Information Technology Services	550.3	651.4	1830.7	2998.0	28.5	46.6	93.0	138.9
金融业	Finance	237.6	1356.6	10964.5	12027.4	15.0	25.1	43.3	80.6
房地产业	Real Estate	126.2	316.2	819.7	899.4	31.9	41.0	56.4	73.0
租赁和商务服务业	Renting and Leasing Activities and Business Services	244.8	1484.9	3192.2	4318.9	63.8	95.9	141.7	187.2
科学研究和技术服务业	Scientific Research and Development, Technical Services	58.4	280.0	668.8	291.6	38.9	56.4	95.2	140.4
水利、环境和公共设施管理业	Management of Water Conservancy, Environment and Public Facilities	-0.3	5.2	21.2	9.0	7.5	9.3	12.9	18.4
居民服务、修理和其他服务业	Resident Services, Repair and Other Services	15.1	6.2	-1.0	-22.0	19.6	14.1	21.5	30.6
教 育	Education	-0.8	0.5	11.2	-26.1	38.7	43.1	53.1	67.1
卫生和社会工作	Health Care and Social Works	-0.3	0.5	0.5	-35.3	16.0	20.0	27.8	36.4
文化、体育和娱乐业	Culture, Sports and Entertainment	23.8	29.4	89.0	70.6	16.2	18.6	27.6	37.5
公共管理、社会保障和社会组织	Pulic Administration,Social Security and Social Organizations					34.1	36.6	51.8	54.1

1-9 规模(限额)以上法人单位基本情况(2019年)
NUMBER OF LEGAL ENTITIES ABOVE DESIGNATED SIZE(2019)

单位：个 (unit)

项目	Item	法人单位数合计 Total Number of Legal Entities	单产业法人 Single-industry Legal Entities	多产业法人 Multi-industry Legal Entities
合计	**Total**	**46505**	**36913**	**9592**
按登记注册类型分	**By Registration Type**			
内资	Domestically-invested Enterprises	42624	34425	8199
国有	State-owned Enterprises	4396	4034	362
集体	Collectively-owned Enterprises	475	419	56
股份合作	Joint-equity Cooperative Enterprises	303	251	52
联营	Associated Enterprises	25	21	4
有限责任公司	Limited Liability Companies	15179	11513	3666
股份有限公司	Companies Limited by Shares	1575	942	633
私营	Private Enterprises	20180	16762	3418
其他	Others	491	483	8
港澳台商投资	Hong Kong, Macao and Taiwan-invested Enterprises	1596	1024	572
与港澳台商合资经营	Joint Ventures	439	297	142
与港澳台商合作经营	Cooperative Enterprises	72	56	16
港澳台商独资	Solely-funded Enterprises	1048	652	396
港澳台商投资股份有限公司	Companies Limited by Shares	21	10	11
其他港澳台商投资	Others	16	9	7
外商投资	Foreign-invested Enterprises	2285	1464	821
中外合资经营	Joint Ventures	671	464	207
中外合作经营	Cooperative Enterprises	55	46	9
外资企业	Solely-funded Enterprises	1503	918	585
外商投资股份有限公司	Companies Limited by Shares	40	25	15
其他外商投资	Others	16	11	5
按隶属关系分	**By Affiliation**			
中央	Central	4080	3208	872
地方	Local	42425	33705	8720
按机构类型分	**By Organization Type**			
企业	Enterprises	42232	32828	9404
事业单位	Institutions	3410	3245	165
机关	Government Agencies and Organizations	3	2	1
社会团体	Social Organizations	304	292	12
其他机构	Others	556	546	10

1−10 国民经济各行业规模(限额)以上法人单位情况(2019年)
NUMBER OF LEGAL ENTITIES IN DIFFERENT SECTORS OF THE NATIONAL ECONOMY ABOVE DESIGNATED SIZE (2019)

单位：个 (unit)

行业	Sector	法人单位数 合计 Total Number of Legal Entities	单产业法人 Single-industry Legal Entities	多产业法人 Multi-industry Legal Entities
合计	**Total**	**46505**	**36913**	**9592**
农、林、牧、渔业	**Agriculture, Forestry, Animal Production and Hunting, Fishing**			
采矿业	**Mining and Quarrying**	**15**	**7**	**8**
煤炭开采和洗选业	Mining and Washing of Coal	1	1	
石油和天然气开采业	Extraction of Petroleum and Natural Gas	3		3
黑色金属矿采选业	Mining of Ferrous Metal Ores	5	4	1
有色金属矿采选业	Mining of Non-Ferrous Metal Ores			
非金属矿采选业	Mining and Processing of Nonmetal Ores	1	1	
开采专业及辅助性活动	Mining Support Service Activities	5	1	4
其他采矿业	Mining of Other Ores			
制造业	**Manufacturing**	**2917**	**2170**	**747**
农副食品加工业	Processing of Food from Agricultural Products	107	69	38
食品制造业	Manufacture of Foods	118	78	40
酒、饮料和精制茶制造业	Manufacture of Wine, Beverage and Refined Tea	39	27	12
烟草制品业	Manufacture of Cigarettes and Tobacco	1	1	
纺织业	Manufacture of Textile	12	10	2
纺织服装、服饰业	Manufacture of Textile, Wearing Apparel and Ornament	84	51	33
皮革、毛皮、羽毛及其制品和制鞋业	Manufacture of Leather, Fur, Feather and Its Products, and Footwear	8	7	1
木材加工和木、竹、藤、棕、草制品业	Processing of Timbers, Manufacture of Wood, Bamboo, Rattan, Palm and Straw Products	8	8	
家具制造业	Manufacture of Furniture	40	27	13
造纸和纸制品业	Manufacture of Paper and Paper Products	36	31	5
印刷和记录媒介复制业	Printing, Reproduction of Recording Media	95	88	7
文教、工美、体育和娱乐用品制造业	Manufacture of Articles for Culture, Education, Artwork, Sport and Entertainment Activities	29	21	8
石油、煤炭及其他燃料加工业	Processing of Petroleum, Coal and Other Fuels	16	13	3
化学原料和化学制品制造业	Manufacture of Chemical Raw Materials and Chemical Products	147	114	33
医药制造业	Manufacture of Medicines	235	175	60
化学纤维制造业	Manufacture of Chemical Fibres	2	1	1
橡胶和塑料制品业	Manufacture of Rubber and Plastics Products	73	59	14
非金属矿物制品业	Manufacture of Non-metallic Mineral Products	188	138	50
黑色金属冶炼和压延加工业	Manufacture and Pressing of Ferrous Metals	7	6	1

注：行业划分执行《国民经济行业分类》(GB/T 4754—2017)标准。

Note: Sectors in this table are classified in accordance with the Standard for Industrial Classification for National Economic Activities (GB/T 4754-2017).

1-10 续表 1 Continued 1

单位：个 (unit)

行业	Sector	法人单位数 合计 Total Number of Legal Entities	单产业法人 Single-industry Legal Entities	多产业法人 Multi-industry Legal Entities
有色金属冶炼和压延加工业	Manufacture and Processing of Non-ferrous Metals	23	21	2
金属制品业	Manufacture of Fabricated Metal Products	157	126	31
通用设备制造业	Manufacture of General-Purpose Machinery	212	159	53
专用设备制造业	Manufacture of Special-Purpose Machinery	310	221	89
汽车制造业	Manufacture of Motor Vehicles	210	169	41
铁路、船舶、航空航天和其他运输设备制造业	Manufacture of Railway Locomotives, Building of Ships and Boats, Manufacture of Air and Spacecrafts and Other Transportation Equipments	65	46	19
电气机械和器材制造业	Manufacture of Electrical Machinery and Equipment	220	164	56
计算机、通信和其他电子设备制造业	Manufacture of Computers, Communication Equipment and Other Electronic Equipment	270	192	78
仪器仪表制造业	Manufacture of Measuring Instrument and Meter	172	122	50
其他制造业	Other Manufacturing	10	10	
废弃资源综合利用业	Waste Rrecycling and Recovery	7	7	
金属制品、机械和设备修理业	Repair of Fabricated Metal Products, Machinery and Equipmen	16	9	7
电力、热力、燃气及水生产和供应业	**Production and Distribution of Electricity, Heating Power, Gas and Water**	**155**	**120**	**35**
电力、热力生产和供应业	Production and Supply of Electric Power and Heat Power	98	81	17
燃气生产和供应业	Production and Distribution of Gas	26	17	9
水的生产和供应业	Production and Distribution of Water	31	22	9
建筑业	**Construction**	**3030**	**2233**	**797**
房屋建筑业	Construction of Building	585	346	239
土木工程建筑业	Civil Engineering Construction	639	450	189
建筑安装业	Construction Installation	719	551	168
建筑装饰、装修和其他建筑业	Building Decoration, Finishing and Other Construction	1087	886	201
批发和零售业	**Wholesale and Retail Trade**	**9921**	**8085**	**1836**
批发业	Wholesale	7419	6389	1030
零售业	Retail Trade	2502	1696	806
交通运输、仓储和邮政业	**Transport, Storage and Post**	**1050**	**776**	**274**
铁路运输业	Transport via Railway	16	8	8
道路运输业	Transport via Road	518	422	96
水上运输业	Water Transport	3	2	1
航空运输业	Air Transport	33	17	16
管道运输业	Transport via Pipeline	2	1	1
多式联运和运输代理业	Multimodal Transport and Transport Agent Service	322	201	121
装卸搬运和仓储业	Loading, Unloading, Portage and Storage	111	95	16
邮政业	Post	45	30	15
住宿和餐饮业	**Accommodation and Restaurants**	**3329**	**2551**	**778**
住宿业	Accommodation	1253	1057	196
餐饮业	Restaurants	2076	1494	582
信息传输、软件和信息技术服务业	**Information Transmission, Software and Information Technology Services**	**3923**	**2868**	**1055**
电信、广播电视和卫星传输服务	Telecommunications, Broadcasting, Television and Satellite Transmission Services	289	207	82
互联网和相关服务	Internet and Related Services	715	556	159
软件和信息技术服务业	Software and Information Technology Services	2919	2105	814

1-10 续表 2 Continued 2

单位：个 (unit)

行业	Sector	法人单位数 合计 Total Number of Legal Entities	单产业法人 Single-industry Legal Entities	多产业法人 Multi-industry Legal Entities
金融业	**Finance**	**2345**	**1872**	**473**
货币金融服务	Monetary Financial Services	771	659	112
资本市场服务	Capital Market Services	748	657	91
保险业	Insurance	584	361	223
其他金融业	Other Financial Services	242	195	47
房地产业	**Real Estate**	**3760**	**2985**	**775**
租赁和商务服务业	**Renting and Leasing Activities and Business Services**	**6062**	**4870**	**1192**
租赁业	Renting and Leasing Activities	177	133	44
商务服务业	Business Services	5885	4737	1148
科学研究和技术服务业	**Scientific Research and Development, Technical Services**	**3780**	**2841**	**939**
研究和试验发展	Research and Experimental Development	571	507	64
专业技术服务业	Professional Technique Services	1793	1205	588
科技推广和应用服务业	Technique Generalization and Application Services	1416	1129	287
水利、环境和公共设施管理业	**Management of Water Conservancy, Environment and Public Facilities**	**670**	**556**	**114**
水利管理业	Management of Water Conservancy	47	41	6
生态保护和环境治理业	Ecological Protection and Environmental Control	96	73	23
公共设施管理业	Management of Public Facilities	512	431	81
土地管理业	Management of Land	15	11	4
居民服务、修理和其他服务业	**Resident Services, Repair and Other Services**	**612**	**496**	**116**
居民服务业	Resident Services	199	142	57
机动车、电子产品和日用产品修理业	Repair of Motor Vehicles, Electronics and Household Appliances	188	155	33
其他服务业	Other Services	225	199	26
教　育	**Education**	**1888**	**1715**	**173**
卫生和社会工作	**Health Care and Social Works**	**864**	**758**	**106**
卫　生	Health Care	782	680	102
社会工作	Social Work Activities	82	78	4
文化、体育和娱乐业	**Culture, Sports and Entertainment**	**1794**	**1632**	**162**
新闻和出版业	Journalism and Publishing	496	446	50
广播、电视、电影和录音制作业	Radio Broadcasting, Television, Movies and Sound Recording	483	441	42
文化艺术业	Cultures and Arts	320	306	14
体　育	Sports Activities	206	178	28
娱乐业	Entertainments	289	261	28
公共管理、社会保障和社会组织	**Public Administration, Social Security and Social Organizations**	**390**	**378**	**12**
中国共产党机关	Organs of Communist Party of China			
国家机构	Organs of State	7	7	
人民政协、民主党派	Peole's Political Consultative Conference and Democratic Parties			
社会保障	Social Security	7	7	
群众团体、社会团体和其他成员组织	Mass Communities, Social Organizations and Other Membership Organizations	376	364	12
基层群众自治组织及其他组织	Grass Roots Self-Government Organization and Other Organizations			
国际组织	**International Organizations**			

1-11 规模(限额)以上企业法人单位情况(2019年)
NUMBER OF CORPORATE ENTERPRISES ABOVE DESIGNATED SIZE (2019)

单位：个 (unit)

项 目	Item	法人单位合计 Total Number of Legal Entities	项 目	Item	法人单位合计 Total Number of Legal Entities
合 计	**Total**	**42232**	与港澳台商合资经营	Joint Ventures	439
按成立时间分	**By Establishment Time**		与港澳台商合作经营	Cooperative Enterprises	72
1949年以前	Before 1949	25	港澳台商独资	Solely-funded Enterprises	1047
1950-1965	From 1950 to 1965	208	港澳台商投资股份有限公司	Companies Limited by Shares	21
1966-1979	From 1966 to 1979	130	其他港澳台商投资	Others	16
1980-1989	From 1980 to 1989	1251	外商投资企业	Foreign-invested Enterprises	2282
1990年以后	After 1990	40618	中外合资经营	Joint Ventures	671
按登记注册类型分	**By Registration Type**		中外合作经营	Cooperative Enterprises	54
内资企业	Domestically-invested Enterprises	38355	外资企业	Solely-funded Enterprises	1501
国有企业	State-owned Enterprises	811	外商投资股份有限公司	Companies Limited by Shares	40
集体企业	Collectively-owned Enterprises	422	其他外商投资	Other	16
股份合作企业	Joint-equity Cooperative Enterprises	303	**按控股情况分**	**By Share Holding Status**	
联营企业	Associated Enterprises	24	国有控股	State-owned Enterprises	7364
有限责任公司	Limited Liability Companies	15172	集体控股	Collectively-controlled Enterprises	1291
股份有限公司	Companies Limited by Shares	1575	私人控股	Privately-controlled Enterprises	29325
私营企业	Private Enterprises	20040	港澳台商控股	Hong Kong, Macao and Taiwan-controlled Enterprises	1447
其他内资企业	Other Domestically-invested Enterprises	8	外商控股	Foreign-controlled Enterprises	2054
港澳台商投资企业	Hong Kong, Macao and Taiwan-invested Enterprises	1595	其 他	Others	751

1-12 全市私营个体经济基本情况
STATISTICS FOR PRIVATE AND INDIVIDUAL ECONOMY

单位：万元 (10000 yuan)

项 目	Item	私营 Private 2019	2018	2019年为2018年% 2019 as % of 2018	个体 Individual 2019	2018	2019年为2018年% 2019 as % of 2018
登记注册*	**Registered at Administration**						
户 数 (户)	Number of Business Entities (unit)	1464755	1475462	99.3	441197	488966	90.2
注册资本	Registered Capital	1841715805	1686995658	109.2	1906483	1990360	95.8
税收情况	**Taxes**						
税收收入合计	Total Tax Revenue	15335469	12604613	121.7	3225628	3818957	84.5

注：*为期末时点数。
资料来源：北京市市场监督管理局、国家税务总局北京市税务局。
Note: Figures with * indicate the accumulative figures at end of the year.
Source: Beijing Municipal Administration of Market Supervision,Beijing Municipal Tax Service of State Taxation Administration.

1—13 规模以上非公经济主要指标(2018年)
MAIN INDICATORS OF NON-PUBLIC SECTORS OF THE ECONOMY ABOVE DESIGNATED SIZE (2018)

项　目	Item	单位数 (个) Number of Enterprises (unit)	收入合计 (亿元) Total Income (100 million yuan)	利润总额 (亿元) Total Profits (100 million yuan)	从业人员平均人数 (万人) Average Number of Persons Employed (10000 persons)
合　计	**Total**	**26706**	**67531.8**	**6015.9**	**442.0**
按登记注册类型分	**Grouped by Registration Type**				
内　资	Domestic-funded	23406	38842.2	1965.5	326.3
港澳台商投资	Hong Kong, Macao and Taiwan-funded	1336	13694.8	772.7	55.3
外商投资	Foreign-funded	1964	14994.7	3277.7	60.4
按规模分	**Grouped by Size**				
#大型企业	Large-sized Enterprises	1159	29839.4	3798.7	170.0
中小微型企业	Mini-, Small-, Medium-sized Enterprises	22750	33462.6	1155.2	231.1
中　型	Medium Size	5957	19076.8	863.2	129.5
小　型	Small Size	13326	11975.9	376.0	94.6
微　型	Mini Size	3467	2409.9	-84.0	7.0
按行业分	**Grouped by Sector**				
#制造业	Manufacturing	2333	8913.6	571.6	49.0
建筑业	Construction	2436	2793.3	36.6	32.6
批发和零售业	Wholesale and Retail Trade	5672	28013.2	831.6	52.9
交通运输、仓储和邮政业	Transport, Storage and Post	709	1627.4	63.5	21.1
住宿和餐饮业	Accommodation and Restaurants	1644	807.5	38.2	29.0
信息传输、软件和信息技术服务业	Information Transmission, Software and Information Technology Services	3046	9680.8	2481.1	75.3
金融业	Finance	1569	2780.0	1005.0	20.7
房地产业	Real Estate	2114	2593.4	292.1	32.4
租赁和商务服务业	Renting and Leasing Activities and Business Services	3457	5975.4	451.9	68.6
科学研究和技术服务业	Scientific Research and Development, Technical Services	1874	2158.0	140.2	25.6
水利、环境和公共设施管理业	Management of Water Conservancy, Environment and Public Facilities	204	236.5	15.9	2.6
居民服务、修理和其他服务业	Resident Services, Repair and Other Services	359	167.8	-1.9	9.2
教　育	Education	350	475.1	12.6	12.8
卫生和社会工作	Health Care and Social Works	236	210.7	…	4.3
文化、体育和娱乐业	Culture, Sports and Entertainment	537	351.7	41.0	3.9
公共管理和社会组织	Public Administration, Social Security and Social Organizations	122	306.0		0.5

注：1. 本表不包含个体经营户数据。
2. 按规模分组中，各类型非公经济是指执行企业会计制度的非公企业数据，不包含执行事业会计制度的非公单位数据，因此，规模分组合计数不等于其他分组合计数。
3. 行业划分执行《国民经济行业分类》(GB/T 4754—2017)标准。
4. 利润总额中，金融业为营业利润数据；从业人员平均人数中，金融业为从业人员期末人数。
5. 2018年，全市非公经济实现增加值13448.4亿元，其中第二产业增加值2018.0亿元，第三产业增加值11430.4亿元。

Note: a) Data of the self-employed are not included in this table.
b) In the group by size, figures of various types of non-public sectors in the economy are those of non-public enterprises implementing enterprise accounting system, excluding those of non-public entities implementing public institution accounting system. Therefore,total amounts in the group by size are not equal to total amounts of other groups.
c) The sectors in this table are classified in accordance with the Standard in the Classification of National Economic Sectors (GB/T4754-2017).
d) In the Total Profits, the data of finance referred to the operating profit data, and in the Average Number of Persons Employed, the data of finance referred to the period-end number of employed persons.
e) In 2018, non-public sectors of the economy in Beijing achieved added value of RMB 1344.84 billion, of which the added value in the secondary industry reached RMB 201.8 billion and that in the tertiary industry hit RMB 1143.04 billion.

1-14 规模以上非公经济主要指标(2019年)
MAIN INDICATORS OF NON-PUBLIC SECTORS OF THE ECONOMY ABOVE DESIGNATED SIZE (2019)

项 目	Item	单位数 (个) Number of Enterprises (unit)	收入合计 (亿元) Total Income (100 million yuan)	利润总额 (亿元) Total Profits (100 million yuan)	应交税金合计 (亿元) Taxes Payable (100 million yuan)	从业人员平均人数 (万人) Average Number of Persons Employed (10000 persons)
合 计	**Total**	**34390**	**78643.6**	**5055.7**	**2497.9**	**467.1**
按登记注册类型分	**Grouped by Registration Type**					
内 资	Domestic-funded	30746	47057.0	1800.6	1450.8	350.5
港澳台商投资	Hong Kong, Macao and Taiwan-funded	1512	16003.0	884.6	387.2	57.2
外商投资	Foreign-funded	2132	15583.6	2370.5	659.9	59.5
按规模分	**Grouped by Size**					
#大型企业	Large-sized Enterprises	1235	33534.8	2866.2	940.5	169.5
中小微型企业	Mini-, Small-, Mediume-sized Enterprises	29131	39685.5	930.5	1229.7	235.6
中 型	Medium Size	6515	21863.1	599.5	752.2	132.2
小 型	Small Size	16974	14721.0	395.1	416.4	97.7
微 型	Mini Size	5642	3101.4	-64.2	61.1	5.6
按行业分	**Grouped by Sector**					
#制造业	Manufacturing	2397	9027.2	675.1	352.2	45.6
建筑业	Construction	2512	2879.7	29.8	77.7	30.1
批发和零售业	Wholesale and Retail Trade	8489	32946.0	860.3	546.8	58.0
交通运输、仓储和邮政业	Transport, Storage and Post	824	2069.5	27.3	31.3	16.8
住宿和餐饮业	Accommodation and Restaurants	2724	972.3	29.7	26.5	31.9
信息传输、软件和信息技术服务业	Information Transmission,Software and Information Technology Services	3428	12335.9	1412.2	485.2	81.3
金融业	Finance	1573	3559.1	1201.5	205.5	23.8
房地产业	Real Estate	2271	2869.8	128.4	404.5	33.7
租赁和商务服务业	Renting and Leasing Activities and Business Services	5019	6778.0	442.4	192.5	76.7
科学研究和技术服务业	Scientific Research and Development, Technical Services	2159	2488.4	156.4	99.5	27.8
水利、环境和公共设施管理业	Management of Water Conservancy, Environment and Public Facilities	247	255.5	11.8	10.9	3.1
居民服务、修理和其他服务业	Resident Services, Repair and Other Services	511	231.9	2.9	9.6	10.0
教 育	Education	450	650.7	8.3	23.2	16.4
卫生和社会工作	Health Care and Social Works	316	273.7	-1.7	3.6	5.1
文化、体育和娱乐业	Culture, Sports and Entertainment	915	534.5	23.9	19.0	4.7
公共管理和社会组织	Pulic Administration, Social Security and Social Organizations	180	302.0		0.7	0.4

注：1. 本表不包含个体经营户数据。
2. 按规模分组中，各类型非公经济是指执行企业会计制度的非公企业数据，不包含执行事业会计制度的非公单位数据，因此，规模分组合计数不等于其他分组合计数。
3. 行业划分执行《国民经济行业分类》(GB/T 4754-2017)标准。

Note: a) Data of the self-employed are not included in this table.
b) In the group by size, figures of various types of non-public sectors in the economy are those of non-public enterprises implementing enterprise accounting system, excluding those of non-public entities implementing public institution accounting system. Therefore, total amounts in the group by size are not equal to total amounts of other groups.
c) The sectors in this table are classified in accordance with the Standard in the Classification of National Economic Sectors(GB/T4754-2017).

1－15 规模以上中小微企业主要指标(2018年)

MAIN INDICATORS OF MICRO- SMALL- AND MEDIUM-SIZED ENTERPRISES ABOVE DESIGNATED SIZE (2018)

项 目	Item	单位数 (个) Number of Enter-prises (unit)	收入合计 (亿元) Total Income (100 million yuan)	利润总额 (亿元) Total Profits (100 million yuan)	应交税金合计 (亿元) Taxes Payable (100 million yuan)	从业人员平均人数 (万人) Average Number of Persons Employed (10000 persons)
合 计	**Total**	**29158**	**58024.5**	**3810.0**	**2008.0**	**314.1**
按规模分	**Grouped by Size**					
中 型	Medium Size	8480	37577.8	2164.6	1380.0	186.2
小 型	Small Size	16376	16539.0	1078.4	550.5	118.3
微 型	Mini Size	4302	3907.7	567.0	77.5	9.6
按登记注册类型分	**Grouped by Registration Type**					
内 资	Domestic-funded	26452	49813.0	3310.1	1636.4	276.6
港澳台商投资	Hong Kong, Macao and Taiwan-funded	1071	3137.5	75.0	124.6	16.4
外商投资	Foreign-funded	1635	5074.0	424.9	247.1	21.1
按行业分	**Grouped by Sector**					
#制造业	Manufacturing	2849	7578.8	570.7	399.0	50.8
建筑业	Construction	2787	2673.7	52.8	92.1	34.8
批发和零售业	Wholesale and Retail Trade	6619	28114.0	519.7	462.4	33.9
交通运输、仓储和邮政业	Transport, Storage and Post	887	1574.4	51.7	9.0	13.6
住宿和餐饮业	Accommodation and Restaurants	2043	500.8	4.9	20.8	16.7
信息传输、软件和信息技术服务业	Information Transmission,Software and Information Technology Services	3095	4675.7	771.3	149.9	36.3
房地产业	Real Estate	2560	2622.2	410.6	384.3	23.8
租赁和商务服务业	Renting and Leasing Activities and Business Services	4181	6062.0	993.7	273.6	68.0
科学研究和技术服务业	Scientific Research and Development, Technical Services	2309	2341.5	206.5	107.1	20.0
水利、环境和公共设施管理业	Management of Water Conservancy, Environment and Public Facilities	331	329.4	25.5	17.0	2.8
居民服务、修理和其他服务业	Resident Services, Repair and Other Services	336	111.7	4.9	6.4	3.4
卫生和社会工作	Health Care and Social Works	7	1.8	-0.4	…	0.1
文化、体育和娱乐业	Culture, Sports and Entertainment	1021	913.9	129.4	45.2	7.4

注：1. 本表中的企业规模划型标准执行《统计上大中小微型企业划分办法(2017)》。按照国家统计局要求，铁路运输业、教育、卫生、房地产租赁经营、金融业不划分规模，因此中小微数据不含这五个行业数据。
2. 行业划分执行《国民经济行业分类》(GB/T 4754—2017)标准。
3. 2018年，全市中小微企业实现增加值9654.6亿元，其中第二产业增加值1969.5亿元，第三产业增加值7685.1亿元。

Note: a) In this table, enterprise size is identified in accordance with the provisions stated in the Statistical Division Standards of Micro-, Small-, Medium- and Large-sized Enterprises . According to requirements of National Bureau of Statistics, size division is unnecessary in sectors of railway transportation,education, health care, real estate rent and operation, finance,so no data related to the five sectors is included in the table.

b)The sectors in this table are classified in accordance with the Standard in the Classification of National Economic Sectors(GB/T4754-2017).

c)In 2018, micro-, small- and medium-sized enterprises above designated size in Beijing achieved added value of RMB 965.46 billion, of which added value in the secondary industry reached RMB 196.95 billion and above designated size that in the tertiary industry reached RMB 768.51 billion.

1-16 规模以上中小微企业主要指标(2019年)
MAIN INDICATORS OF MICRO- SMALL- AND MEDIUM-SIZED ENTERPRISES ABOVE DESIGNATED SIZE (2019)

项 目	Item	单位数 (个) Number of Enterprises (unit)	收入合计 (亿元) Total Income (100 million yuan)	利润总额 (亿元) Total Profits (100 million yuan)	应交税金合计 (亿元) Taxes Payable (100 million yuan)	从业人员平均人数 (万人) Average Number of Persons Employed (10000 persons)
合 计	**Total**	**35788**	**64929.1**	**3582.3**	**2005.9**	**315.6**
按规模分	**Grouped by Size**					
中 型	Medium Size	9029	40791.0	2030.8	1302.9	186.4
小 型	Small Size	20192	19719.9	963.8	614.6	121.3
微 型	Mini Size	6567	4418.2	587.7	88.4	7.8
按登记注册类型分	**Grouped by Registration Type**					
内 资	Domestic-funded	32792	55491.5	2925.1	1643.6	277.3
港澳台商投资	Hong Kong, Macao and Taiwan-funded	1216	3850.8	115.7	128.4	16.3
外商投资	Foreign-funded	1780	5586.7	541.5	233.8	22.0
按行业分	**Grouped by Sector**					
#制造业	Manufacturing	2827	7544.9	669.3	366.7	47.3
建筑业	Construction	2664	2530.9	55.8	80.1	19.0
批发和零售业	Wholesale and Retail Trade	9349	31610.8	559.6	446.4	38.5
交通运输、仓储和邮政业	Transport, Storage and Post	977	1556.4	71.4	19.8	12.7
住宿和餐饮业	Accommodation and Restaurants	3034	617.9	5.2	22.6	17.8
信息传输、软件和信息技术服务业	Information Transmission,Software and Information Technology Services	3434	6184.2	546.2	173.1	38.0
房地产业	Real Estate	2450	2478.1	185.8	371.2	23.1
租赁和商务服务业	Renting and Leasing Activities and Business Services	5691	7325.6	1016.7	299.4	78.7
科学研究和技术服务业	Scientific Research and Development, Technical Services	2893	2728.3	235.1	114.8	22.2
水利、环境和公共设施管理业	Management of Water Conservancy, Environment and Public Facilities	375	399.5	27.7	16.6	3.1
居民服务、修理和其他服务业	Resident Services, Repair and Other Services	487	148.2	5.2	7.5	4.2
卫生和社会工作	Health Care and Social Works	16	4.0	-1.0	0.1	0.1
文化、体育和娱乐业	Culture, Sports and Entertainment	1437	1231.9	147.1	49.5	8.1

注：1. 本表中的企业规模划型标准执行《统计上大中小微型企业划分办法(2017)》。按照国家统计局要求，铁路运输业、教育、卫生、房地产租赁经营、金融业不划分规模，因此中小微数据不含这五个行业数据。
2. 行业划分执行《国民经济行业分类》(GB/T 4754—2017)标准。

Note: a) In this table, enterprise size is identified in accordance with the provisions stated in the Statistical Division Standards of Micro-, Small-, Medium- and Large-sized Enterprises . According to requirements of National Bureau of Statistics, size division is unnecessary in sectors of railway transportation,education, health care, real estate rent and operation, finance,so no data related to the five sectors is included in the table.
b)The sectors in this table are classified in accordance with the Standard in the Classification of National Economic Sectors(GB/T4754-2017).

主要统计指标解释

法人单位 指有权拥有资产、承担负债，并独立从事社会经济活动（或与其他单位进行交易）的组织。法人单位应同时具备以下条件：(1) 依法成立，有自己的名称、组织机构和场所，能够独立承担民事责任；(2) 独立拥有（或授权使用）资产或者经费，承担负债，有权与其他单位签订合同；(3) 具有包括资产负债表在内的账户，或者能够根据需要编制账户。

单产业法人 指仅包含一个产业活动单位的法人单位，该法人单位同时也是一个产业活动单位。

多产业法人 指由两个及以上产业活动单位组成的法人单位，这些产业活动单位接受法人单位的管理和控制。

登记注册类型 企业法人或企业产业活动单位的登记注册类型，按其在工商行政管理机关登记注册的类型填写。如企业登记注册类型发生变化，但未及时到工商部门变更登记，企业应根据变化后的实际情况填写。其他法人和产业活动单位的登记注册类型，按其主要经费来源和管理方式，根据实际情况，比照《企业登记注册类型与代码》填写。

国有企业 指企业全部资产归国家所有，并按《中华人民共和国企业法人登记管理条例》规定登记注册的非公司制的经济组织。不包括有限责任公司中的国有独资公司。

集体企业 指企业资产归集体所有，并按《中华人民共和国企业法人登记管理条例》规定登记注册的经济组织。

股份合作企业 指以合作制为基础，由企业职工共同出资入股，吸收一定比例的社会资产投资组建，实行自主经营，自负盈亏，共同劳动，民主管理，按劳分配与按股分红相结合的一种集体经济组织。

联营企业 指两个及两个以上相同或不同所有制性质的企业法人或事业单位法人，按自愿、平等、互利的原则，共同投资组成的经济组织称为联营企业。联营企业包括国有联营企业、集体联营企业、国有与集体联营企业和其他联营企业。

有限责任公司 指根据《中华人民共和国公司登记管理条例》规定登记注册，由两个以上，五十个以下的股东共同出资，每个股东以其所认缴的出资额对公司承担有限责任，公司以其全部资产对其债务承担责任的经济组织。有限责任公司包括国有独资公司、其他有限责任公司。

私营企业 指由自然人投资设立或由自然人控股，以雇佣劳动为基础的营利性经济组织。包括按照《公司法》、《合伙企业法》、《私营企业暂行条例》、《个人独资企业法》规定登记注册的私营独资企业、私营合伙企业、私营有限责任公司、私营股份有限公司和个人独资企业。

其他企业 指上述类型之外的其他内资经济组织。

港澳台商投资企业 指港澳台地区投资者依照中华人民共和国有关涉外经济的法律、法规成立的企业，包括与港澳台商合资经营企业、与港澳台商合作经营企业、港澳台商独资经营企业、港澳台商投资股份有限公司、其他港澳台商投资企业。

外商投资企业 指外国企业或外国人依照中华人民共和国有关涉外经济的法律、法规成立的企业，包括中外合资经营企业、中外合作经营企业、外资企业、外商投资股份有限公司、其他外商投资企业。

非公经济 指资产由我国私人控股、港澳台商控股、外商控股的“非公有控股”的企业法人单位，以及主要经费来源于私人、港澳台资和外资的非企业法人单位和个体工商户。其中，私人、港澳台及外商控股是指由其绝对控股和相对控股的经济成分。

Explanatory Notes on Main Statistical Indicators

Legal Entity refers to any organization that has the right to own assets and bear liabilities, and conducts social and economic activities independently (or conducts transactions with other entities). A business entity shall meet all of such conditions as: (1) established in accordance with law, having its own name, organization and site, capable of assuming civil responsibilities independently; (2) independently owning and using (or using under authorization) assets or outlays, assuming liabilities, having the right to sign contracts with other entities; (3) maintaining accounts including balance sheet, or capable of preparing accounts as needed.

Single-industry Legal Entity refers any business entity conducting only one industrial activity. Such business entity is also an industrial activity entity.

Multi-industry Legal Entity refers to any business entity composed of two or more industrial activity entities which are managed and controlled by the business entity.

Registration Type of an enterprise as legal person or as industrial activity entity shall be completed according to the type registered at the administration for industry and commerce. In the event of any change in registration type, and no registration alteration is made with administration for industry and commerce in good time, the registration type shall be completed according to the actual situation. Registration type for other legal persons and industrial activity entities shall be completed according to the main source of outlays and management manner, pursuant to the actual conditions, and by referring to the *Type of Enterprise Registration and Code*.

State-owned Enterprise refers to non-corporation economic organizations where the entire assets are owned by the state and which have registered in accordance with the *Regulation of the People's Republic of China on the Management of Registration of Corporate Enterprises*, excluding solely state-funded corporations in limited liability companies.

Collectively-owned Enterprise refer to economic organizations where the assets are owned collectively and which have registered in accordance with the *Regulation of the People's Republic of China on the Management of Registration of Corporate Enterprises*.

Joint-equity Cooperative Enterprise refers to a form of collective economic organizations based on cooperative system, where capitals come mainly from employees as their shares, with certain proportion of capital from the public, where production is organized on the basis of independent operation, independent accounting for profits and losses, joint work, democratic management, and where the distribution system integrates distribution according to work with distribution according to capital share.

Associated Enterprise refers to organizations established by two or more corporate legal persons or institutional legal persons of the same or different ownership, through joint investment on the basis of equality, voluntary participation and mutual benefits. They include state-owned associated enterprises, collectively-owned associated enterprises, state-collective associated enterprises and other associated enterprises.

Limited Liability Company refers to organizations established with investment from 2-50 shareholders and registered in accordance with the *Regulation of the People's Republic of China on the Management of Registration of Corporations*, each shareholder bearing limited liability to the corporation depending on its share of investment, and the corporation bearing liability to its debt to the maximum of its total assets. Limited liability companies include solely state-funded limited liability companies and other limited liability companies.

Private Enterprise refers to profit-making organizations established by natural persons or controlled by natural persons using employed labor. Private enterprises include solely private-funded enterprises, private partnership enterprises, private limited liability companies, private companies limited by shares, and private-funded enterprises registered in accordance with provisions in the *Corporation Law*, *Partnership Enterprises Law*, *Interim Regulations on Private Enterprises* and *Sole Proprietorship Enterprise Law*.

Other Enterprise refers to domestically funded organizations other than those mentioned above.

Hong Kong, Macao and Taiwan-invested Enterprise refers to enterprises established by investors from Hong Kong, Macao and Taiwan in accordance with laws and rules of the People's Republic of China on foreign-related businesses. They include joint ventures with investors from Hong Kong, Macao and Taiwan, cooperative enterprises with investors from Hong Kong, Macao and Taiwan, enterprises wholly funded by investors from Hong Kong, Macao and Taiwan, companies limited by shares and funded by investors from Hong Kong, Macao and Taiwan, and other enterprises funded by investors from Hong Kong, Macao and Taiwan.

Foreign-invested Enterprise refers to enterprises

established by foreign enterprises or foreigners in accordance with laws and regulations of the People's Republic of China on foreign-related businesses. They include Sino-foreign joint ventures, Sino-foreign cooperative enterprises, foreign wholly-funded enterprises, foreign-funded companies limited by shares, and other foreign-funded enterprises.

Non-public Economy means enterprises as business entities whose shares are controlled by "non-public entities" and whose assets are controlled by individuals, investors from Hong Kong, Macao and Taiwan, and foreign investors, along with enterprises not as business entities and self-employed operators whose main funds are from individuals, investors from Hong Kong, Macao and Taiwan, and foreign investors. Here, enterprises controlled by individuals, investors from Hong Kong, Macao and Taiwan, and foreign investors mean economic sectors with absolute or relative control by such companies.

02

国民经济核算
NATIONAL ACCOUNTS

简要说明

一、主要内容

本章资料包括历年北京市地区生产总值、部分新兴产业增加值、各行业增加值、三次产业及三大需求贡献率、居民消费水平、社会劳动生产率等资料。

二、统计调查方法说明

地区生产总值是统计部门根据统计资料、会计资料和部门财务资料采用不同方法核算的数据。

三、关于历史数据调整的问题

按照国家统计局部署，2016 年开始实施地区研发支出核算方法改革，将研发支出未计入地区生产总值部分进行补充核算，并对历史数据进行了修订。

2018 年数据为北京市第四次全国经济普查数据，并根据普查结果对历史数据进行了修订。

2019 年的地区生产总值为初步统计数据，待最终核实数据确定后将在次年年鉴中进行更新。

四、有关统计标准的变化说明

（一）关于行业划分标准。本章行业划分执行《国民经济行业分类》（GB/T 4754—2017）标准。

（二）关于三次产业划分。三次产业分类依据国家统计局 2018 年修订的《三次产业划分规定（2012）》。第一产业是指农、林、牧、渔业（不含农、林、牧、渔专业及辅助性活动）。第二产业是指采矿业（不含开采专业及辅助性活动），制造业（不含金属制品、机械和设备修理业），电力、热力、燃气及水生产和供应业，建筑业。第三产业即服务业，是指除第一产业、第二产业以外的其他行业。

本章三次产业的分类均执行调整后的划分规定。

Brief Introduction

I. Main Content

Statistics in this chapter include the GDP of Beijing, added value of some emerging sectors, added value of different sectors, contribution rate of three industries and three demands, residents' consumption level and social labor productivity in previous years.

II. Statistical Survey Methods

The GDP of Beijing is calculated by the statistics department using different measures according to statistical data, accounting data and financial data of sectors.

Ⅲ. Adjustment to Historical Statistics

In accordance with the deployment of the National Bureau of Statistics of the People's Republic of China (NBS), the reform of calculation method of regional R&D expenditure has been implemented since 2016, according to which supplementary accounting was carried out on the part of R&D expenditure not included in GDP data, and historical data were revised.

The data for 2018 were collected from the fourth national economic census in Beijing, and historical data were revised according to the census results.

The GDP data for 2019 were the preliminary statistical data and shall be updated in the yearbook of the following year after the final data verification and confirmation.

IV. Explanation on Changes of Statistical Standards

(I) Standard for Classification of Sectors.The standards in the *Classification of National Economic Sectors* (GB/T 4754-2017) have been implemented.

(II) Classification of Three Industries. The classification of three industries is based on the Regulations on Three Industries Classification (2012) revised by the National Bureau of Statistics in 2018. The primary industry refers to agriculture, forestry, animal production and hunting, fishing (excluding professional and support activities for agriculture, forestry, animal husbandry and fishing). The secondary industry refers to mining and quarrying (excluding professional and support activities for mining), manufacturing (excluding repair of fabricated metal products, machinery and equipment), production and distribution of electricity, heating power, gas and water and construction. The tertiary industry refers to others excluding the primary and secondary industries.

The classification of three industries since 1978 as mentioned in this chapter has all been subject to the classification provisions after adjustment.

2-1 地区生产总值(1978–2019年)
GROSS DOMESTIC PRODUCT (1978-2019)

单位：亿元 (100 million yuan)

年份 Year	地区生产总值 Gross Domestic Product	按产业分 By Three Industies			按行业分 By Sector		人均地区生产总值(元) Per Capita Gross Domestic Product (yuan)	人均地区生产总值(美元) Per Capita Gross Domestic Product (USD)
		第一产业 Primary Industry	第二产业 Secondary Industry	第三产业 Tertiary Industry	#工业 Industry	#建筑业 Construction		
1978	108.8	5.6	77.2	26.0	70.2	7.2	1257	797
1979	120.1	5.2	85.0	29.9	77.4	7.8	1358	908
1980	139.1	6.1	95.6	37.4	86.9	8.9	1544	1009
1981	139.2	6.6	92.3	40.3	82.7	9.8	1526	895
1982	154.9	10.2	99.6	45.1	89.3	10.5	1671	883
1983	183.1	12.7	112.5	57.9	98.8	13.9	1943	983
1984	216.6	14.7	130.5	71.4	114.0	16.7	2262	972
1985	257.1	17.7	153.5	85.9	130.7	23.0	2643	900
1986	284.9	19.0	165.6	100.3	141.2	24.6	2836	821
1987	326.8	24.2	182.2	120.4	154.5	28.1	3150	846
1988	410.2	36.9	220.9	152.4	189.5	31.8	3892	1046
1989	456.0	38.3	251.8	165.9	212.8	39.4	4269	1134
1990	500.8	43.7	262.0	195.1	219.3	43.1	4635	969
1991	598.9	45.5	290.5	262.9	255.6	35.9	5494	1032
1992	710.2	48.7	343.4	318.1	291.3	53.2	6468	1173
1993	888.9	53.2	416.3	419.4	336.5	81.2	8030	1393
1994	1149.8	66.8	512.7	570.3	413.4	100.9	10280	1193
1995	1516.2	72.2	638.3	805.7	520.7	119.8	12762	1529
1996	1819.4	75.0	709.2	1035.2	570.0	141.6	14495	1743
1997	2118.1	77.2	774.8	1266.2	627.6	149.7	16949	2045
1998	2439.1	77.9	834.1	1527.1	661.5	175.1	19625	2371
1999	2759.8	78.4	900.0	1781.5	713.3	189.5	22054	2664
2000	3277.8	79.3	1023.7	2174.9	831.0	196.6	25014	3022
2001	3861.5	80.8	1127.2	2653.6	920.2	212.3	28097	3395
2002	4525.7	82.4	1235.1	3208.2	999.6	239.7	32231	3894
2003	5267.2	84.1	1456.4	3726.7	1195.1	276.1	36583	4420
2004	6252.5	85.4	1773.7	4393.4	1483.2	308.9	42402	5123
2005	7149.8	86.9	1907.4	5155.5	1600.5	326.8	47182	5760
2006	8387.0	87.2	2072.1	6227.7	1713.8	379.4	53438	6703
2007	10425.5	99.4	2413.4	7912.8	1989.1	448.5	63629	8368
2008	11813.1	111.4	2526.7	9175.1	2030.8	520.4	68541	9869
2009	12900.9	116.8	2736.4	10047.7	2182.6	580.3	71059	10402
2010	14964.0	122.8	3233.1	11608.1	2607.5	656.9	78307	11568
2011	17188.8	134.5	3563.3	13491.0	2859.6	738.1	86365	13371
2012	19024.7	148.4	3856.0	15020.3	3090.1	803.0	93078	14745
2013	21134.6	159.8	4168.3	16806.5	3336.6	872.0	101023	16313
2014	22926.0	159.2	4433.0	18333.9	3522.8	952.7	107472	17495
2015	24779.1	140.4	4419.8	20218.9	3458.9	1002.6	114662	18409
2016	27041.2	129.8	4665.8	22245.7	3635.5	1074.5	124516	18746
2017	29883.0	121.9	5049.4	24711.7	3885.9	1210.9	137596	20379
2018	33106.0	120.6	5477.4	27508.1	4139.9	1387.8	153095	23135
2019	35371.3	113.7	5715.1	29542.5	4241.1	1513.7	164220	23805

注：1.本表数据按当年价格计算。
2.人均地区生产总值按年平均常住人口计算。
3.本表历史数据根据北京市第四次全国经济普查结果进行了修订，下同。

Note: a) Figures in this table are calculated at current year's prices.
b) Per capita GDP is calculated at average permanent population.
c) Historical figures in this table have been revised according to the results of the fourth national economic census in Beijing, the same below.

2-2 地区生产总值指数(上年=100)(1978−2019年)
INDICES OF GROSS DOMESTIC PRODUCT (PRECEDING YEAR=100) (1978-2019)

单位：% (%)

年份 Year	地区生产总值 Gross Domestic Product	按产业分 By Three Industies			按行业分 By Sector		人均地区生产总值 Per Capita Gross Domestic Product
		第一产业 Primary Industry	第二产业 Secondary Industry	第三产业 Tertiary Industry	#工业 Industry	#建筑业 Construction	
1978	110.5	109.0	116.5	97.7	112.4	153.0	109.1
1979	109.7	105.0	109.1	113.2	110.1	108.4	107.4
1980	111.8	109.3	109.6	118.5	110.1	110.3	109.8
1981	99.5	109.2	96.3	106.0	95.3	106.4	98.3
1982	107.4	113.4	105.8	109.9	105.8	106.1	105.6
1983	116.4	107.5	113.6	124.2	111.5	132.3	114.5
1984	117.4	106.8	116.1	121.8	115.7	118.8	115.6
1985	108.7	106.3	111.0	104.4	109.1	124.7	106.9
1986	108.0	100.1	104.8	115.7	105.0	103.7	104.6
1987	109.6	113.4	105.6	116.7	105.5	106.3	106.1
1988	112.8	111.2	112.1	114.1	113.0	106.5	111.0
1989	104.4	101.1	108.9	97.3	108.4	112.2	103.1
1990	105.2	103.3	101.1	113.3	101.9	95.6	104.0
1991	109.9	103.7	107.5	114.5	112.6	81.6	108.9
1992	111.3	103.1	111.8	112.3	109.6	126.4	110.5
1993	112.3	103.2	112.8	113.3	110.2	128.8	111.4
1994	113.7	102.8	113.9	115.4	113.2	117.3	112.5
1995	112.0	92.0	107.4	120.7	107.3	107.8	105.4
1996	109.8	96.8	106.3	115.2	106.0	107.5	103.9
1997	110.2	103.0	107.7	113.4	108.2	105.3	110.7
1998	109.6	101.1	109.3	110.6	108.3	114.3	110.2
1999	111.0	102.5	111.7	111.0	112.4	108.3	110.2
2000	112.0	103.2	111.1	113.5	112.8	102.4	107.0
2001	111.8	103.6	109.0	113.4	109.0	106.7	106.6
2002	111.8	103.0	107.8	113.9	107.1	111.1	109.4
2003	111.1	98.5	110.2	111.9	111.4	110.7	108.4
2004	113.3	99.6	115.4	112.8	117.8	105.4	110.6
2005	112.3	98.4	109.7	113.8	110.4	106.6	109.3
2006	112.8	100.8	109.9	114.1	108.7	115.8	108.9
2007	114.4	102.0	111.9	115.5	112.1	111.0	109.6
2008	109.0	101.6	100.3	112.1	99.6	103.7	103.6
2009	110.0	104.6	110.0	110.1	108.2	118.3	104.5
2010	110.4	98.4	113.4	109.6	114.6	108.6	104.9
2011	108.1	100.9	106.6	108.6	107.5	102.9	103.8
2012	107.7	103.2	106.8	108.0	106.1	109.4	104.9
2013	107.7	103.0	107.7	107.8	107.3	109.4	105.3
2014	107.4	100.0	106.8	107.6	105.9	110.3	105.3
2015	106.9	89.2	102.8	108.2	100.2	112.4	105.5
2016	106.9	91.3	105.3	107.4	104.5	108.1	106.4
2017	106.8	95.2	104.2	107.4	105.0	101.7	106.8
2018	106.7	98.0	103.9	107.3	104.0	103.5	107.2
2019	106.1	97.5	104.5	106.4	103.0	108.0	106.5

注：本表数据按不变价格计算。
Note: Statistics in this table are calculated at constant prices.

2-3 地区生产总值指数(1978年=100)(1978-2019年)
INDICES OF GROSS DOMESTIC PRODUCT (YEAR OF 1978=100) (1978-2019)

单位：% (%)

年份 Year	地区生产总值 Gross Domestic Product	按产业分 By Three Industies 第一产业 Primary Industry	第二产业 Secondary Industry	第三产业 Tertiary Industry	按行业分 By Sector #工业 Industry	#建筑业 Construction	人均地区生产总值 Per Capita Gross Domestic Product
1978	100.0	100.0	100.0	100.0	100.0	100.0	100.0
1979	109.7	105.0	109.1	113.2	110.1	108.4	107.4
1980	122.6	114.8	119.6	134.1	121.2	119.6	117.9
1981	122.0	125.4	115.2	142.1	115.5	127.3	115.9
1982	131.0	142.2	121.9	156.2	122.2	135.1	122.4
1983	152.5	152.9	138.5	194.0	136.3	178.7	140.1
1984	179.0	163.3	160.8	236.3	157.7	212.3	162.0
1985	194.6	173.6	178.5	246.7	172.1	264.7	173.2
1986	210.2	173.8	187.1	285.4	180.7	274.5	181.2
1987	230.4	197.1	197.6	333.1	190.6	291.8	192.3
1988	259.9	219.2	221.5	380.1	215.4	310.8	213.5
1989	271.3	221.6	241.2	369.8	233.5	348.7	220.1
1990	285.4	228.9	243.9	419.0	237.9	333.4	228.9
1991	313.7	237.4	262.2	479.8	267.9	272.1	249.3
1992	349.1	244.8	293.1	538.8	293.6	343.9	275.5
1993	392.0	252.6	330.6	610.5	323.5	442.9	306.9
1994	445.7	259.7	376.6	704.5	366.2	519.5	345.3
1995	499.2	238.9	404.5	850.3	392.9	560.0	363.9
1996	548.1	231.3	430.0	979.5	416.5	602.0	378.1
1997	604.0	238.2	463.1	1110.8	450.7	633.9	418.6
1998	662.0	240.8	506.2	1228.5	488.1	724.5	461.3
1999	734.8	246.8	565.4	1363.6	548.6	784.6	508.4
2000	823.0	254.7	628.2	1547.7	618.8	803.4	544.0
2001	920.1	263.9	684.7	1755.1	674.5	857.2	579.9
2002	1028.7	271.8	738.1	1999.1	722.4	952.3	634.4
2003	1142.9	267.7	813.4	2237.0	804.8	1054.2	687.7
2004	1294.9	266.6	938.7	2523.3	948.1	1111.1	760.6
2005	1454.2	262.3	1029.8	2871.5	1046.7	1184.4	831.3
2006	1640.3	264.4	1131.8	3276.4	1137.8	1371.5	905.3
2007	1876.5	269.7	1266.5	3784.2	1275.5	1522.4	992.2
2008	2045.4	274.0	1270.3	4242.1	1270.4	1578.7	1027.9
2009	2249.9	286.6	1397.3	4670.6	1374.6	1867.6	1074.2
2010	2483.9	282.0	1584.5	5119.0	1575.3	2028.2	1126.8
2011	2685.1	284.5	1689.1	5559.2	1693.4	2087.0	1169.6
2012	2891.9	293.6	1804.0	6003.9	1796.7	2283.2	1226.9
2013	3114.6	302.4	1942.9	6472.2	1927.9	2497.8	1291.9
2014	3345.1	302.4	2075.0	6964.1	2041.6	2755.1	1360.4
2015	3575.9	269.7	2133.1	7535.2	2045.7	3096.7	1435.2
2016	3822.6	246.2	2246.2	8092.8	2137.8	3347.5	1527.1
2017	4082.5	234.4	2340.5	8691.7	2244.7	3404.4	1630.9
2018	4356.0	229.7	2431.8	9326.2	2334.5	3523.6	1748.3
2019	4621.7	224.0	2541.2	9923.1	2404.5	3805.5	1861.9

注：本表数据按不变价格计算。
Note: Statistics in this table are calculated at constant prices.

2-4 地区生产总值指数(2000年=100)(2000—2019年)
INDICES OF GROSS DOMESTIC PRODUCT (YEAR OF 2000=100) (2000-2019)

单位：% (%)

年份 Year	地区生产总值 Gross Domestic Product	按产业分 By Three Industies 第一产业 Primary Industry	第二产业 Secondary Industry	第三产业 Tertiary Industry	按行业分 By Sector #工业 Industry	#建筑业 Construction	人均地区生产总值 Per Capita Gross Domestic Product
2000	100.0	100.0	100.0	100.0	100.0	100.0	100.0
2001	111.8	103.6	109.0	113.4	109.0	106.7	106.6
2002	125.0	106.7	118.8	129.2	116.7	118.5	116.6
2003	138.9	105.1	129.5	144.6	130.0	131.2	126.4
2004	157.4	104.7	141.2	163.1	153.1	138.3	139.8
2005	176.8	103.0	153.9	185.6	169.0	147.4	152.8
2006	199.4	103.8	167.8	211.8	183.7	170.7	166.4
2007	228.1	105.9	182.9	244.6	205.9	189.5	182.4
2008	248.6	107.6	199.4	274.2	205.1	196.5	189.0
2009	273.5	112.5	217.3	301.9	221.9	232.5	197.5
2010	301.9	110.7	236.9	330.9	254.3	252.5	207.2
2011	326.4	111.7	258.2	359.4	273.4	259.8	215.1
2012	351.5	115.3	281.4	388.2	290.1	284.2	225.6
2013	378.6	118.8	306.7	418.5	311.3	310.9	237.6
2014	406.6	118.8	334.3	450.3	329.7	342.9	250.2
2015	434.7	106.0	364.4	487.2	330.4	385.4	264.0
2016	464.7	96.8	397.2	523.3	345.3	416.6	280.9
2017	496.3	92.2	432.9	562.0	362.6	423.7	300.0
2018	529.6	90.4	471.9	603.0	377.1	438.5	321.6
2019	561.9	88.1	514.4	641.6	388.4	473.6	342.5

注：本表数据按不变价格计算。
Note: Statistics in this table are calculated at constant prices.

2-5 地区生产总值构成(1978-2019年)
COMPOSITION OF GROSS DOMESTIC PRODUCT (1978-2019)

单位：% (%)

年 份 Year	地区生产总值 Gross Domestic Product	按产业分 By Three Industies			按行业分 By Sector	
		第一产业 Primary Industry	第二产业 Secondary Industry	第三产业 Tertiary Industry	#工业 Industry	#建筑业 Construction
1978	100.0	5.1	71.0	23.9	64.5	6.6
1979	100.0	4.3	70.8	24.9	64.4	6.5
1980	100.0	4.4	68.7	26.9	62.5	6.4
1981	100.0	4.7	66.3	29.0	59.4	7.0
1982	100.0	6.6	64.3	29.1	57.7	6.8
1983	100.0	6.9	61.4	31.6	54.0	7.6
1984	100.0	6.8	60.2	33.0	52.6	7.7
1985	100.0	6.9	59.7	33.4	50.8	8.9
1986	100.0	6.7	58.1	35.2	49.6	8.6
1987	100.0	7.4	55.8	36.8	47.3	8.6
1988	100.0	9.0	53.9	37.2	46.2	7.8
1989	100.0	8.4	55.2	36.4	46.7	8.6
1990	100.0	8.7	52.3	39.0	43.8	8.6
1991	100.0	7.6	48.5	43.9	42.7	6.0
1992	100.0	6.9	48.4	44.8	41.0	7.5
1993	100.0	6.0	46.8	47.2	37.9	9.1
1994	100.0	5.8	44.6	49.6	36.0	8.8
1995	100.0	4.8	42.1	53.1	34.3	7.9
1996	100.0	4.1	39.0	56.9	31.3	7.8
1997	100.0	3.6	36.6	59.8	29.6	7.1
1998	100.0	3.2	34.2	62.6	27.1	7.2
1999	100.0	2.8	32.6	64.6	25.8	6.9
2000	100.0	2.4	31.2	66.4	25.4	6.0
2001	100.0	2.1	29.2	68.7	23.8	5.5
2002	100.0	1.8	27.3	70.9	22.1	5.3
2003	100.0	1.6	27.7	70.8	22.7	5.2
2004	100.0	1.4	28.4	70.3	23.7	4.9
2005	100.0	1.2	26.7	72.1	22.4	4.6
2006	100.0	1.0	24.7	74.3	20.4	4.5
2007	100.0	1.0	23.1	75.9	19.1	4.3
2008	100.0	0.9	21.4	77.7	17.2	4.4
2009	100.0	0.9	21.2	77.9	16.9	4.5
2010	100.0	0.8	21.6	77.6	17.4	4.4
2011	100.0	0.8	20.7	78.5	16.6	4.3
2012	100.0	0.8	20.3	79.0	16.2	4.2
2013	100.0	0.8	19.7	79.5	15.8	4.1
2014	100.0	0.7	19.3	80.0	15.4	4.2
2015	100.0	0.6	17.8	81.6	14.0	4.0
2016	100.0	0.5	17.3	82.3	13.4	4.0
2017	100.0	0.4	16.9	82.7	13.0	4.1
2018	100.0	0.4	16.5	83.1	12.5	4.2
2019	100.0	0.3	16.2	83.5	12.0	4.3

注：本表数据按当年价格计算。
Note: Figures in this table are calculated at current year's prices.

2–6 三次产业贡献率(1982–2019年)
CONTRIBUTION RATE OF THREE INDUSTRIES TO THE INCREASE OF GDP (1982-2019)

单位：%

(%)

年 份 Year	地区生产总值 Gross Domestic Product	第一产业 Primary Industry	第二产业 Secondary Industry	第三产业 Tertiary Industry	#工 业 Industry	#建筑业 Construction
1982	100.0	8.7	52.8	38.4	47.2	5.6
1983	100.0	2.3	54.6	43.1	41.3	13.2
1984	100.0	1.8	59.2	39.0	51.0	8.2
1985	100.0	3.1	80.6	16.3	58.5	22.1
1986	100.0	0.1	39.0	61.0	34.8	4.1
1987	100.0	5.4	36.8	57.8	31.2	5.6
1988	100.0	3.5	57.5	39.0	53.3	4.2
1989	100.0	1.0	121.1	-22.1	99.6	21.5
1990	100.0	2.4	12.8	84.8	19.8	-7.0
1991	100.0	3.3	39.8	56.9	55.8	-16.0
1992	100.0	2.2	53.6	44.1	37.9	14.9
1993	100.0	2.0	53.7	44.4	36.7	17.0
1994	100.0	1.5	52.3	46.3	41.7	10.5
1995	100.0	-4.3	31.9	72.2	26.3	5.6
1996	100.0	-1.7	31.7	70.0	25.5	6.3
1997	100.0	1.3	36.3	62.4	32.1	4.2
1998	100.0	0.5	45.5	54.0	34.0	11.6
1999	100.0	0.9	49.7	49.4	43.6	6.1
2000	100.0	1.0	43.4	55.6	41.9	1.5
2001	100.0	0.7	23.8	75.5	19.4	3.4
2002	100.0	0.6	20.2	79.2	14.8	5.4
2003	100.0	-0.3	27.0	73.3	24.4	5.5
2004	100.0	…	33.7	66.4	31.7	2.3
2005	100.0	-0.2	23.3	76.9	20.8	2.8
2006	100.0	0.1	20.7	79.2	15.2	5.7
2007	100.0	0.2	21.5	78.3	18.2	3.6
2008	100.0	0.2	0.8	99.0	-1.0	1.8
2009	100.0	0.4	23.4	76.2	15.8	7.9
2010	100.0	-0.1	30.2	70.0	26.6	3.9
2011	100.0	0.1	17.6	82.3	16.3	1.6
2012	100.0	0.3	18.7	81.0	13.8	5.1
2013	100.0	0.3	21.0	78.7	16.1	5.2
2014	100.0		19.4	80.6	13.5	6.0
2015	100.0	-1.0	8.5	92.6	0.5	7.9
2016	100.0	-0.7	13.8	86.9	9.2	4.7
2017	100.0	-0.3	10.8	89.5	9.9	1.0
2018	100.0	-0.1	10.0	90.2	8.0	2.1
2019	100.0	-0.2	12.4	87.8	6.5	5.0

注：1. 本表数据按不变价格计算。
2. 产业贡献率指各产业增加值增量与地区生产总值增量之比。

Note: a) Statistics in this table are calculated at constant prices.
b) Share of the contributions of the three industries to the increase of the GDP refers to the proportion of the increment of the value-added of each industry to the increment of GDP.

2-7 按行业分地区生产总值(2001-2019年)

单位：亿元

项　　目	Item	2001	2002	2003	2004	2005	2006
地区生产总值	**Gross Domestic Product**	**3861.5**	**4525.7**	**5267.2**	**6252.5**	**7149.8**	**8387.0**
按产业分	**By Three Industies**						
第一产业	Primary Industry	80.8	82.4	84.1	85.4	86.9	87.2
第二产业	Secondary Industry	1127.2	1235.1	1456.4	1773.7	1907.4	2072.1
第三产业	Tertiary Industry	2653.6	3208.2	3726.7	4393.4	5155.5	6227.7
按行业分	**By Sector**						
农、林、牧、渔业	Agriculture, Forestry, Animal Production and Hunting, Fishing	81.8	82.9	84.6	87.4	88.7	88.8
工业	Industry	920.2	999.6	1195.1	1483.2	1600.5	1713.8
建筑业	Construction	212.3	239.7	276.1	308.9	326.8	379.4
批发和零售业	Wholesale and Retail Trade	442.8	485.3	542.4	607.9	718.9	894.9
交通运输、仓储和邮政业	Transport, Storage and Post	227.6	249.2	271.1	303.4	333.9	373.5
住宿和餐饮业	Accommodation and Restaurants	103.3	130.5	121.0	172.9	190.8	230.2
信息传输、软件和信息技术服务业	Information Transmission, Software and Information Technology Services	233.0	309.3	415.9	492.8	637.4	751.0
金融业	Finance	519.7	600.8	683.9	755.9	879.9	1036.1
房地产业	Real Estate	233.6	346.3	402.3	508.7	573.4	775.0
租赁和商务服务业	Renting and Leasing Activities and Business Services	146.4	230.1	250.4	294.6	379.9	474.4
科学研究和技术服务业	Scientific Research and Development, Technical Services	195.2	230.4	273.1	305.3	373.3	459.7
水利、环境和公共设施管理业	Management of Water Conservancy, Environment and Public Facilities	27.3	29.8	33.6	37.5	43.5	50.9
居民服务、修理和其他服务业	Resident Services, Repair and Other Services	45.5	59.4	70.0	85.7	85.5	91.7
教　育	Education	160.8	174.5	225.7	288.5	312.9	347.3
卫生和社会工作	Health Care and Social Works	73.6	80.8	96.2	115.3	127.5	152.7
文化、体育和娱乐业	Culture, Sports and Entertainment	101.6	117.6	132.2	148.5	174.9	195.2
公共管理、社会保障和社会组织	Pulic Administration,Social Security and Social Organizations	137.0	159.8	193.8	256.2	302.0	372.6
国际组织	International Organizations						

注：本表数据按当年价格计算。

GROSS DOMESTIC PRODUCT BY SECTOR(2001-2019)

(100 million yuan)

2007	2008	2009	2010	2011	2012	2013	2014	2015	2016	2017	2018	2019
10425.5	**11813.1**	**12900.9**	**14964.0**	**17188.8**	**19024.7**	**21134.6**	**22926.0**	**24779.1**	**27041.2**	**29883.0**	**33106.0**	**35371.3**
99.4	111.4	116.8	122.8	134.5	148.4	159.8	159.2	140.4	129.8	121.9	120.6	113.7
2413.4	2526.7	2736.4	3233.1	3563.3	3856.0	4168.3	4433.0	4419.8	4665.8	5049.4	5477.4	5715.1
7912.8	9175.1	10047.7	11608.1	13491.0	15020.3	16806.5	18333.9	20218.9	22245.7	24711.7	27508.1	29542.5
101.3	112.8	118.3	124.6	136.5	150.4	162.0	161.5	142.8	132.2	124.3	122.6	116.2
1989.1	2030.8	2182.6	2607.5	2859.6	3090.1	3336.6	3522.8	3458.9	3635.5	3885.9	4139.9	4241.1
448.5	520.4	580.3	656.9	738.1	803.0	872.0	952.7	1002.6	1074.5	1210.9	1387.8	1513.7
1155.1	1502.0	1606.6	1995.4	2256.9	2356.3	2483.2	2579.0	2506.7	2544.3	2703.7	2824.1	2856.9
412.5	408.4	449.2	570.4	637.3	635.5	670.6	724.8	739.8	790.8	901.0	1015.9	1025.3
265.0	297.7	285.7	346.3	380.6	408.8	413.1	404.4	441.7	447.0	470.4	515.3	540.4
959.7	1117.6	1165.3	1314.1	1611.7	1758.8	2015.8	2283.0	2600.0	3003.9	3508.2	4290.1	4783.9
1410.2	1648.5	1744.4	2038.1	2421.6	2783.2	3247.5	3736.8	4365.5	4784.7	5299.6	5951.3	6544.8
999.6	1037.8	1319.1	1261.4	1358.2	1588.1	1731.5	1745.2	1899.2	2241.2	2420.5	2481.5	2620.8
679.4	836.1	886.2	1055.7	1285.5	1488.1	1746.9	1917.2	1987.1	2079.7	2226.4	2421.0	2583.9
591.8	720.3	808.2	940.2	1106.6	1245.9	1442.0	1628.9	1765.4	1980.0	2260.5	2578.3	2826.4
57.7	66.1	75.5	85.2	97.9	115.5	138.7	159.6	211.2	239.2	269.2	287.0	327.8
90.5	83.0	82.3	111.0	125.6	139.9	158.5	177.4	163.3	184.3	201.1	220.8	233.7
406.7	451.0	498.0	594.5	694.4	788.0	886.0	1000.1	1119.3	1263.9	1459.0	1603.4	1768.9
181.9	211.1	240.7	290.0	355.9	417.6	481.0	547.0	675.5	750.2	835.0	938.1	1025.2
236.3	262.4	275.4	313.9	361.6	430.1	482.4	508.1	568.5	612.7	657.4	728.1	745.7
440.2	507.0	583.1	658.9	760.7	825.6	866.8	877.6	1131.7	1277.1	1450.1	1600.9	1616.7

Note: Figures in this table are calculated at current year's prices.

2-8 按行业分地区生产总值指数(上年=100)(2001-2019年)

单位：%

项　　目	Item	2001	2002	2003	2004	2005
地区生产总值	**Gross Domestic Product**	**111.8**	**111.8**	**111.1**	**113.3**	**112.3**
按产业分	**By Three Industies**					
第一产业	Primary Industry	103.6	103.0	98.5	99.6	98.4
第二产业	Secondary Industry	109.0	107.8	110.2	115.4	109.7
第三产业	Tertiary Industry	113.4	113.9	111.9	112.8	113.8
按行业分	**By Sector**					
农、林、牧、渔业	Agriculture, Forestry, Animal Production and Hunting, Fishing	103.7	102.7	98.9	99.4	98.1
工业	Industry	109.0	107.1	111.4	117.8	110.4
建筑业	Construction	106.7	111.1	110.7	105.4	106.6
批发和零售业	Wholesale and Retail Trade	112.5	109.2	111.3	111.1	117.8
交通运输、仓储和邮政业	Transport, Storage and Post	102.5	102.8	102.6	106.4	104.6
住宿和餐饮业	Accommodation and Restaurants	109.3	117.5	90.9	135.8	107.2
信息传输、软件和信息技术服务业	Information Transmission,Software and Information Technology Services	113.5	119.8	124.4	112.0	121.8
金融业	Finance	113.4	112.1	110.9	106.0	113.3
房地产业	Real Estate	132.4	131.6	111.9	119.3	109.3
租赁和商务服务业	Renting and Leasing Activities and Business Services	106.7	132.6	103.5	109.5	122.0
科学研究和技术服务业	Scientific Research and Development, Technical Services	127.6	113.2	112.2	108.6	115.3
水利、环境和公共设施管理业	Management of Water Conservancy, Environment and Public Facilities	95.2	102.5	104.3	104.2	113.5
居民服务、修理和其他服务业	Resident Services, Repair and Other Services	103.2	112.2	109.0	114.4	97.8
教　育	Education	125.6	109.7	128.1	124.5	107.6
卫生和社会工作	Health Care and Social Works	116.2	106.8	112.6	116.2	111.8
文化、体育和娱乐业	Culture, Sports and Entertainment	104.5	107.8	106.9	107.8	115.6
公共管理、社会保障和社会组织	Pulic Administration,Social Security and Social Organizations	107.0	109.9	114.1	125.9	115.4
国际组织	International Organizations					

注：本表数据按可比价格计算。

INDICES OF GROSS DOMESFIC PRODUCT BY SECTOR (PRECEDING YEAR=100) (2001-2019)

(%)

2006	2007	2008	2009	2010	2011	2012	2013	2014	2015	2016	2017	2018	2019
112.8	**114.4**	**109.0**	**110.0**	**110.4**	**108.1**	**107.7**	**107.7**	**107.4**	**106.9**	**106.9**	**106.8**	**106.7**	**106.1**
100.8	102.0	101.6	104.6	98.4	100.9	103.2	103.0	100.0	89.2	91.3	95.2	98.0	97.5
109.9	111.9	100.3	110.0	113.4	106.6	106.8	107.7	106.8	102.8	105.3	104.2	103.9	104.5
114.1	115.5	112.1	110.1	109.6	108.6	108.0	107.8	107.6	108.2	107.4	107.4	107.3	106.4
100.6	102.2	101.1	104.6	98.6	100.9	103.2	103.0	100.1	89.4	91.5	95.3	97.7	97.5
108.7	112.1	99.6	108.2	114.6	107.5	106.1	107.3	105.9	100.2	104.5	105.0	104.0	103.0
115.8	111.0	103.7	118.3	108.6	102.9	109.4	109.4	110.3	112.4	108.1	101.7	103.5	108.0
118.1	122.5	125.4	109.3	121.5	109.2	103.7	105.3	105.4	98.4	103.0	107.0	100.8	101.6
106.2	106.7	102.8	101.5	111.1	104.7	105.3	105.6	105.7	102.8	105.4	110.9	105.9	102.2
115.8	108.0	98.3	97.0	115.7	102.7	99.7	97.2	99.5	100.5	100.5	102.3	102.2	100.3
111.6	116.8	115.4	104.9	109.8	123.0	106.9	108.9	112.2	111.9	112.3	113.5	119.0	112.0
111.1	121.9	108.0	106.7	109.4	108.1	112.5	112.5	113.2	118.4	109.3	107.7	107.6	109.5
123.1	106.3	95.7	123.2	86.8	94.3	114.5	103.1	98.8	105.2	106.7	99.5	100.8	106.9
117.6	124.3	123.6	111.8	111.4	118.4	109.5	109.9	106.5	98.5	101.8	103.7	103.7	103.8
115.5	118.5	119.1	118.8	108.6	107.6	107.8	111.5	110.3	112.4	108.6	109.8	108.9	106.5
110.7	104.8	115.1	120.4	105.6	106.0	106.9	106.7	112.8	113.6	109.3	110.7	103.8	111.3
101.0	92.3	92.1	104.5	126.1	112.9	104.4	103.6	113.5	102.5	109.7	103.4	104.4	102.6
106.9	111.6	110.3	109.4	111.2	103.7	106.0	106.3	110.4	111.8	108.8	108.6	106.8	108.4
113.7	109.2	114.4	114.1	112.7	108.5	108.7	112.1	111.4	114.3	107.7	108.1	109.2	106.8
107.9	109.9	113.7	107.5	106.6	106.4	109.4	106.3	102.2	103.7	106.9	102.8	106.0	101.6
118.5	111.4	110.0	112.5	107.5	103.8	104.8	103.9	99.2	110.3	109.1	108.8	107.5	97.4

Note: Figures in this table are calculated at current year's prices.

2-9 部分新兴产业增加值（2016–2019年）
ADDED VALUE OF SOME EMERGING INDUSTRIES（2016-2019）

单位：亿元 (100 million yuan)

项　目	Item	2016	2017	2018	2019
地区生产总值	**Gross Domestic Product**	**27041.2**	**29883.0**	**33106.0**	**35371.3**
#新经济	New Economy	9226.5	10366.0	11875.5	12765.8
#战略性新兴产业	Strategic Emerging Industry	5654.7	6619.8	7831.5	8405.5
#高技术产业	High-tech Industry	5888.8	6834.5	7996.0	8630.0
#生产性服务业	Producer Service Industry	13032.2	14549.2	16449.9	
#生活性服务业	Consumer Service Industry	6205.3	6839.0	7475.9	

注：本表数据按当年价格计算。
Note: Data in the table is calculated based on price in current year.

2-10 收入法地区生产总值(1978-2018年)
GROSS DOMESTIC PRODUCT BY INCOME APPROACH (1978-2018)

单位：亿元 (100 million yuan)

年 份 Year	地区生产总值 Gross Domestic Product	劳动者报酬 Compensation for Labors	生产税净额 Net Taxes on Production	固定资产折旧 Depreciation of Fixed Assets	营业盈余 Operating Surplus
1978	108.8	37.1	16.5	11.5	43.7
1979	120.1	42.0	18.3	13.4	46.4
1980	139.1	48.9	21.0	15.4	53.8
1981	139.2	52.9	22.0	16.9	47.4
1982	154.9	57.4	23.2	17.7	56.6
1983	183.1	66.0	26.8	20.7	69.6
1984	216.6	79.1	31.8	25.4	80.3
1985	257.1	95.5	39.0	30.3	92.3
1986	284.9	107.8	43.4	34.9	98.8
1987	326.8	125.4	48.0	40.9	112.5
1988	410.2	153.9	59.7	49.9	146.7
1989	456.0	179.3	66.5	57.1	153.1
1990	500.8	207.3	72.9	62.1	158.5
1991	598.9	254.2	86.4	75.7	182.6
1992	710.2	327.1	103.4	87.5	192.2
1993	888.9	410.5	132.5	106.2	239.7
1994	1149.8	537.7	170.5	135.5	306.1
1995	1516.2	683.8	230.1	187.2	415.2
1996	1819.4	801.3	270.4	244.8	502.9
1997	2118.1	927.6	310.0	284.3	596.2
1998	2439.1	1062.4	351.8	336.9	688.0
1999	2759.8	1194.8	402.1	397.7	765.3
2000	3277.8	1395.3	484.2	496.4	901.9
2001	3861.5	1617.3	579.2	607.6	1057.5
2002	4525.7	1893.5	684.5	748.2	1199.5
2003	5267.2	2231.4	800.3	875.8	1359.6
2004	6252.5	2695.3	932.1	1047.9	1577.2
2005	7149.8	3218.7	1036.5	1206.6	1688.0
2006	8387.0	3697.8	1218.1	1405.7	2065.5
2007	10425.5	4402.4	1521.8	1730.6	2770.8
2008	11813.1	5815.8	1934.1	1935.7	2127.5
2009	12900.9	6388.1	1974.3	2036.4	2502.0
2010	14964.0	7228.3	2194.9	2325.7	3215.1
2011	17188.8	8337.7	2537.6	2596.5	3717.0
2012	19024.7	9505.1	2865.8	2794.4	3859.4
2013	21134.6	10703.8	3131.2	2972.1	4327.6
2014	22926.0	11679.6	3165.4	3099.8	4981.2
2015	24779.1	13435.5	3259.5	3454.9	4629.2
2016	27041.2	14518.9	3405.4	3526.5	5590.4
2017	29883.0	16141.0	3542.6	3911.5	6287.9
2018	33106.0	18011.8	3568.1	4430.8	7095.3

注：本表数据按当年价格计算。
Note: Figures in this table are calculated at current year's prices.

2-11 支出法地区生产总值(1978-2018年)
GROSS DOMESTIC PRODUCT BY EXPENDITURE APPROACH (1978-2018)

单位：亿元 (100 million yuan)

年份 Year	地区生产总值 Gross Domestic Product	最终消费支出 Final Consumption Expenditure	居民消费 Households Consumption	政府消费 Government Consumption	资本形成总额 Gross Capital Formation	固定资本形成总额 Completed Fixed Assets	存货增加 Changes in Inventories	货物和服务净流出 Net Outflow of Goods and Services	最终消费率(消费率)(%) Final Consumption Rate (%)	资本形成率(投资率)(%) Capital Formation Rate (%)
1978	108.8	53.0	28.6	24.4	31.7	24.9	6.8	24.1	48.7	29.1
1979	120.1	55.4	31.5	23.9	37.0	29.1	7.9	27.7	46.1	30.8
1980	139.1	57.3	39.6	17.7	45.1	36.5	8.6	36.7	41.2	32.4
1981	139.2	61.8	44.2	17.6	50.5	40.2	10.3	26.9	44.4	36.3
1982	154.9	68.6	48.8	19.8	51.8	42.3	9.5	34.5	44.3	33.4
1983	183.1	77.6	54.6	23.0	62.9	56.1	6.8	42.6	42.4	34.4
1984	216.6	96.5	64.8	31.7	84.7	72.5	12.2	35.4	44.6	39.1
1985	257.1	127.1	88.7	38.4	150.6	102.7	47.9	-20.6	49.4	58.6
1986	284.9	161.1	109.9	51.2	178.8	116.0	62.8	-55.0	56.5	62.8
1987	326.8	181.5	124.3	57.2	201.2	148.6	52.6	-55.9	55.5	61.6
1988	410.2	222.6	161.9	60.7	251.1	177.7	73.4	-63.5	54.3	61.2
1989	456.0	244.0	176.1	67.9	271.5	151.9	119.6	-59.5	53.5	59.5
1990	500.8	269.7	194.1	75.6	296.5	195.0	101.5	-65.4	53.9	59.2
1991	598.9	302.6	225.7	76.9	327.3	208.8	118.5	-31.0	50.5	54.7
1992	710.2	342.2	261.2	81.0	415.5	289.2	126.3	-47.4	48.2	58.5
1993	888.9	446.7	355.5	91.2	537.3	446.1	91.2	-95.1	50.3	60.4
1994	1149.8	616.3	505.5	110.8	792.6	705.2	87.4	-259.1	53.6	68.9
1995	1516.2	848.4	675.1	173.2	1045.0	914.6	130.5	-377.2	56.0	68.9
1996	1819.4	1016.2	819.1	197.1	1074.9	981.5	93.4	-271.6	55.8	59.1
1997	2118.1	1207.5	998.9	208.7	1287.7	1080.5	207.2	-377.1	57.0	60.8
1998	2439.1	1318.0	1075.2	242.8	1439.3	1313.0	126.3	-318.3	54.0	59.0
1999	2759.8	1496.7	1184.5	312.2	1624.7	1334.9	289.9	-361.7	54.2	58.9
2000	3277.8	1654.4	1288.8	365.6	1836.0	1512.9	323.1	-212.6	50.5	56.0
2001	3861.5	1889.8	1417.4	472.4	2095.8	1728.3	367.4	-124.0	48.9	54.3
2002	4525.7	2279.3	1738.4	540.9	2541.8	2117.1	424.7	-295.4	50.4	56.2
2003	5267.2	2615.8	1977.5	638.3	2989.9	2635.0	354.9	-338.5	49.7	56.8
2004	6252.5	3054.4	2260.3	794.1	3478.3	3086.1	392.2	-280.3	48.9	55.6
2005	7149.8	3432.6	2521.1	911.5	3955.5	3494.8	460.7	-238.3	48.0	55.3
2006	8387.0	4112.5	2982.5	1130.1	4365.9	3880.8	485.1	-91.4	49.0	52.1
2007	10425.5	5087.3	3566.9	1520.4	4996.9	4428.7	568.2	341.3	48.8	47.9
2008	11813.1	6045.3	4137.3	1908.0	5335.7	4461.5	874.2	432.1	51.2	45.2
2009	12900.9	6991.8	4784.4	2207.4	5681.6	4910.1	771.5	227.5	54.2	44.0
2010	14964.0	8048.2	5634.1	2414.1	6873.2	5956.4	916.8	42.6	53.8	45.9
2011	17188.8	9501.3	6552.8	2948.4	7631.9	6670.1	961.8	55.6	55.3	44.4
2012	19024.7	10716.0	7364.0	3352.0	8508.4	7866.5	641.9	-199.6	56.3	44.7
2013	21134.6	12249.5	8424.8	3824.7	9218.1	8642.2	575.9	-333.0	58.0	43.6
2014	22926.0	13519.8	9174.6	4345.3	9633.4	8954.2	679.3	-227.3	59.0	42.0
2015	24779.1	14745.9	10071.6	4674.3	9910.8	9225.8	685.0	122.4	59.5	40.0
2016	27041.2	16056.4	10923.8	5132.6	10690.2	9951.8	738.4	294.6	59.4	39.5
2017	29883.0	17782.7	11971.2	5811.4	11784.3	10766.3	1018.0	316.1	59.5	39.4
2018	33106.0	20012.7	13284.0	6728.7	12527.8	11488.2	1039.7	565.5	60.5	37.8

注：本表数据按当年价格计算。

Note: Data in the table is calculated based on price in current year.

2-12 支出法地区生产总值
GROSS DOMESTIC PRODUCT BY EXPENDITURE APPROACH

单位：亿元 (100 million yuan)

项 目	Item	2018	2017	指数(2017=100) Index(2017=100)
地区生产总值	**Gross Domestic Product**	**33106.0**	**29883.0**	**106.7**
最终消费支出	**Final Consumption Expenditure**	**20012.7**	**17782.7**	**107.8**
居民消费	Households Consumption	13284.0	11971.2	105.9
城镇居民	Urban Resident	12388.9	11169.6	105.8
农村居民	Rural Resident	895.1	801.6	107.9
政府消费	Government Consumption	6728.7	5811.4	111.5
资本形成总额	**Gross Capital Formation**	**12527.8**	**11784.3**	**102.3**
固定资本形成总额	Completed Fixed Asset	11488.2	10766.3	102.5
存货增加	Changes in Inventories	1039.7	1018.0	100.0
货物和服务净流出	**Net Outflow of Goods and Services**	**565.5**	**316.1**	**254.4**

注：本表总量数据按当年价格计算，指数按不变价格计算。
Note: Absolute values are calculated at current prices, whereas Indices are calculated at constant prices.

2-13 三大需求贡献率(1982-2018年)
CONTRIBUTION RATE OF THREE DEMANDS TO THE INCREASE OF GDP (1982-2018)

单位：% (%)

年份 Year	最终消费支出 Final Consumption Expenditure	资本形成总额 Gross Capital Formation	货物和服务净流出 Net Outflow of Goods and Services
1982	52.8	5.9	41.3
1983	18.3	44.6	37.1
1984	53.1	69.1	-22.2
1985	115.4	337.5	-352.9
1986	154.5	51.1	-105.5
1987	33.8	69.0	-2.8
1988	46.7	-10.8	64.1
1989	86.9	180.5	-167.4
1990	165.0	128.7	-193.7
1991	61.5	42.9	-4.4
1992	18.2	83.8	-1.9
1993	41.0	73.3	-14.2
1994	54.0	106.8	-60.8
1995	69.3	42.2	-11.5
1996	50.2	-25.2	75.1
1997	87.1	108.1	-95.1
1998	19.8	41.3	39.0
1999	56.1	68.9	-25.0
2000	30.5	46.2	23.2
2001	33.9	45.6	20.5
2002	72.2	68.9	-41.1
2003	40.0	69.4	-9.3
2004	39.7	43.5	16.8
2005	33.3	49.3	17.5
2006	63.0	27.6	9.4
2007	60.6	26.8	12.6
2008	87.4	10.1	2.5
2009	78.9	43.4	-22.3
2010	61.7	55.7	-17.4
2011	79.6	16.9	3.5
2012	72.7	50.9	-23.6
2013	66.3	43.4	-9.7
2014	73.4	25.0	1.5
2015	65.7	26.4	7.9
2016	60.4	31.3	8.2
2017	63.9	38.9	-2.8
2018	69.4	13.3	17.3

注：1．三大需求指支出法地区生产总值的三大构成项目，即最终消费支出、资本形成总额、货物和服务净流出。
2．贡献率指三大需求增量与支出法地区生产总值增量之比。
3．本表数据按不变价格计算。

Note: a) Three demands of GDP by expenditure method are final consumption expenditure, gross capital formation and net outflow of goods and services.
b) Contribution rate of the three demands to GDP growth refers to the proportion of the increment of the each component of GDP by expenditure method to the increment of GDP.
c) Figures in this table are calculated at constant prices.

2–14 居民消费水平(1978–2018年)
HOUSEHOLDS CONSUMPTION LEVEL (1978-2018)

年 份 Year	居民消费水平(元) Level(yuan)			城乡消费水平对比(农村居民=1) Uban/Rural Consumption Ratio(Rural Households=1)	指数(1978年=100) Index(1978=100)			指数(上年=100) Index(Preceding=100)		
	全 市 All Households	城镇居民 Urban Households	农村居民 Rural Households		全 市 All Households	城镇居民 Urban Households	农村居民 Rural Households	全 市 All Households	城镇居民 Urban Households	农村居民 Rural Households
1978	330	451	185	2.4	100.0	100.0	100.0	112.3	110.1	122.6
1979	356	464	221	2.1	117.5	114.5	120.8	117.5	114.5	120.8
1980	440	562	280	2.0	147.6	140.0	159.0	125.6	122.1	131.5
1981	485	590	338	1.7	160.3	144.8	189.4	108.6	103.6	119.2
1982	526	622	384	1.6	170.6	149.7	211.2	106.4	103.4	111.5
1983	579	674	432	1.6	175.4	151.2	222.6	102.8	101.0	105.4
1984	677	789	494	1.6	201.4	173.9	250.4	114.8	115.0	112.5
1985	912	1101	585	1.9	263.2	235.3	289.2	130.7	135.3	115.5
1986	1094	1284	749	1.7	312.9	272.0	365.8	118.9	115.6	126.5
1987	1198	1391	827	1.7	316.7	272.0	375.3	101.2	100.0	102.6
1988	1536	1779	1046	1.7	367.7	313.3	435.7	116.1	115.2	116.1
1989	1648	1874	1169	1.6	398.2	337.1	472.7	108.3	107.6	108.5
1990	1797	2045	1186	1.7	466.7	393.4	527.5	117.2	116.7	111.6
1991	2071	2330	1345	1.7	528.3	440.2	587.1	113.2	111.9	111.3
1992	2379	2701	1458	1.9	554.7	466.2	583.6	105.0	105.9	99.4
1993	3211	3749	1637	2.3	620.7	530.1	589.4	111.9	113.7	101.0
1994	4520	5321	2120	2.5	719.4	620.2	631.8	115.9	117.0	107.2
1995	5682	6520	3113	2.1	776.2	659.3	739.2	107.9	106.3	117.0
1996	6525	7508	3437	2.2	817.3	696.9	744.4	105.3	105.7	100.7
1997	7993	9341	3659	2.6	1001.2	866.9	795.0	122.5	124.4	106.8
1998	8652	10097	3900	2.6	1031.2	892.9	801.4	103.0	103.0	100.8
1999	9466	11032	4196	2.6	1123.0	970.6	860.7	108.9	108.7	107.4
2000	9835	11445	4314	2.7	1137.6	981.3	866.7	101.3	101.1	100.7
2001	10313	11903	4740	2.5	1147.8	981.3	923.0	100.9	100.0	106.5
2002	12380	14404	5073	2.8	1345.2	1159.9	961.8	117.2	118.2	104.2
2003	13734	15992	5336	3.0	1419.2	1223.7	964.7	105.5	105.5	100.3
2004	15328	17820	5786	3.1	1522.8	1309.4	1012.0	107.3	107.0	104.9
2005	16636	18877	6693	2.8	1591.3	1336.9	1120.3	104.5	102.1	110.7
2006	19003	21173	7613	2.8	1771.1	1459.9	1241.3	111.3	109.2	110.8
2007	21769	24103	9124	2.6	1930.5	1581.1	1411.4	109.0	108.3	113.7
2008	24005	26435	10548	2.5	2063.7	1680.7	1573.7	106.9	106.3	111.5
2009	26353	28871	12125	2.4	2247.4	1821.9	1773.6	108.9	108.4	112.7
2010	29483	32171	13642	2.4	2429.4	1962.2	1933.2	108.1	107.7	109.0
2011	32924	35991	13927	2.6	2582.5	2089.7	1873.3	106.3	106.5	96.9
2012	36028	39396	14963	2.6	2755.5	2227.6	2000.7	106.7	106.6	106.8
2013	40270	43653	19048	2.3	2937.4	2356.8	2378.8	106.6	105.8	118.9
2014	43008	46491	20965	2.2	3099.0	2477.0	2592.9	105.5	105.1	109.0
2015	46604	50327	22841	2.2	3303.5	2638.0	2766.6	106.6	106.5	106.7
2016	50301	54236	25057	2.2	3508.3	2798.9	2974.1	106.2	106.1	107.5
2017	55121	59473	27294	2.2	3708.3	2958.4	3140.6	105.7	105.7	105.6
2018	61429	66251	30601	2.2	3945.6	3144.8	3401.3	106.4	106.3	108.3

注：本表居民消费水平数据按当年价格计算，指数按不变价格计算。

Note: Fingers of households comsumption level are calculated at current prices, whereas Indices are calculated at constant prices.

2-15 社会劳动生产率(1978-2019年)
OVERALL LABOR PRODUCTIVITY (1978-2019)

单位：元/人 (yuan/person)

年 份 Year	社会劳动生产率 Overall Labor Productivity	第一产业 Primary Industry	第二产业 Secondary Industry	第三产业 Tertiary Industry
1978	2504	444	4484	1911
1979	2626	421	4556	2033
1980	2914	510	4750	2391
1981	2795	561	4316	2420
1982	2959	878	4437	2467
1983	3368	1094	4799	2998
1984	3909	1287	5347	3646
1985	4580	1671	6040	4268
1986	5002	1932	6331	4783
1987	5669	2569	6917	5501
1988	7046	4084	8309	6745
1989	7742	4270	9432	7140
1990	8203	4810	9564	7941
1991	9498	5014	10351	10145
1992	11068	5556	12236	11637
1993	13921	7111	14841	14808
1994	17798	9666	18590	18940
1995	22807	10036	23501	25077
1996	27453	10479	26708	31789
1997	32190	10757	29930	38674
1998	38170	10928	34495	46851
1999	44485	10733	40704	54598
2000	52958	10753	48241	65302
2001	61874	11212	53157	78046
2002	69194	11879	54745	89352
2003	76198	12910	63171	94215
2004	80294	13749	77352	90158
2005	82556	14049	82234	90091
2006	93308	14232	90784	102203
2007	111958	16399	106434	122898
2008	122823	17977	116034	134512
2009	130364	18653	134467	138876
2010	147436	19877	160731	154363
2011	163602	22330	168915	173084
2012	174779	25491	178603	184434
2013	188005	28362	196850	196326
2014	199556	29530	210697	207269
2015	211534	27339	215236	221046
2016	224760	25984	236960	232634
2017	242274	24770	261755	249274
2018	266494	25594	292110	272980
2019	281752	25897	322211	285674

注：1.本表数据按当年价格计算。
2.社会劳动生产率为地区生产总值（增加值）与从业人员平均人数之比。

Note: a) Figures in this table are calculated at current year's prices.
b) Overall Labor productivity refers to the ratio of Gross Domestic Product (the value added) and the average number of practitioners.

主要统计指标解释

国内（地区）生产总值 是按市场价格计算的地区生产总值的简称。它是一个地区所有常住单位在一定时期内生产活动的最终成果。地区生产总值有三种表现形式，即价值形态、收入形态和产品形态。从价值形态看，它是所有常住单位在一定时期内所生产的全部货物和服务价值与同期投入的全部非固定资产货物和服务价值的差额，即所有常住单位的增加值之和；从收入形态看，它是所有常住单位在一定时期内创造的各项收入之和，包括劳动者报酬、生产税净额、固定资产折旧和营业盈余；从产品形态看，它是所有常住单位在一定时期内最终使用的货物和服务价值与货物和服务净出口（净流出）价值之和。在实际核算中，地区生产总值有三种计算方法，即生产法、收入法和支出法。三种方法分别从不同的方面反映地区生产总值及其构成。

最终消费率(消费率) 通常指一定时期内最终消费支出占国内（地区）生产总值的比重，一般按现行价格计算。

$$\text{最终消费率（消费率）}=\frac{\text{最终消费支出}}{\text{国内（地区）生产总值}}\times 100\%$$

资本形成率(投资率) 通常指一定时期内资本形成总额占国内（地区）生产总值的比重，一般按现行价格计算。

$$\text{资本形成率（投资率）}=\frac{\text{资本形成总额}}{\text{国内（地区）生产总值}}\times 100\%$$

部分新兴产业统计划分标准：

1. 新经济 新经济是指经济发展新常态下，由科技创新和技术进步所催生的符合未来发展方向、推动发展动能接续转换的新型经济形态。包括高技术产业、战略性新兴产业所有活动，科技服务业、旅游及相关产业、健康服务业、文化创意及相关产业等各产业中符合新经济特征的活动，以及互联网金融，电子商务，众创、众包、众扶、众筹等活动内容，共涉及《国民经济行业分类》(GB/T 4754-2011）中16个行业门类、471个行业小类。

2. 战略性新兴产业 战略性新兴产业是以重大技术突破和重大发展需求为基础，对经济社会全局和长远发展具有重大引领带动作用，知识技术密集、物质资源消耗少、成长潜力大、综合效益好的产业，包括：新一代信息技术产业、高端装备制造产业、新材料产业、生物产业、新能源汽车产业、新能源产业、节能环保产业、数字创意产业、相关服务业等9大领域。战略性新兴产业是以《国民经济行业分类》（GB/T 4754-2017）为基础，对其中符合“战略性新兴产业”特征的有关活动进行再分类。

3. 高技术产业 高技术产业包括高技术制造业和高技术服务业。高技术制造业是指国民经济行业中 R&D 投入强度相对高的制造行业，包括：医药制造，航空、航天器及设备制造，电子及通信设备制造，计算机及办公设备制造，医疗仪器设备及仪器仪表制造，信息化学品制造等 6 大类。高技术服务业是采用高技术手段为社会提供服务活动的集合，包括信息服务、电子商务服务、检验检测服务、专业技术服务业的高技术服务、研发与设计服务、科技成果转化服务、知识产权及相关法律服务、环境监测及治理服务和其他高技术服务等 9 大类。高技术产业标准以《国民经济行业分类》（GB/T 4754-2017）为基础，根据高技术产业的特性，结合我国的实际情况制定。

4. 生产性服务业 生产性服务业指为生产活动提供的研发设计与其他技术服务，货物运输、通用航空生产、仓储和邮政快递服务，信息服务，金融服务，节能与环保服务，生产性租赁服务，商务服务，人力资源管理与职业教育培训服务，批发与贸易经纪代理服务，生产性支持服务。生产性服务业标准是以《国民经济行业分类》(GB/T 4754-2017）为基础，是对国民经济行业分类中符合生产性服务业特征有关活动的再分类。

5. 生活性服务业 生活性服务业是指满足居民最终消费需求的服务活动。分类范围包括十二大领域：居民和家庭服务，健康服务，养老服务，旅游游览和娱乐服务，体育服务，文化服务，居民零售和互联网销售服务，居民出行服务，住宿餐饮服务，教育培训服务，居民住房服务，其他生活性服务等。生活性服务业标准是以《国民经济行业分类》(GB/T 4754-2017）为基础，是对国民经济行业分类中符合生活性服务业特征有关活动的再分类。

Explanatory Notes on Main Statistical Indicators

Gross Domestic (Regional) Product is the abbreviation of gross regional product calculated at market prices. It represents the final results of all resident units in an area from their productive activities over a given period of time. It is expressed in three different perspectives respectively, namely value, income, and product. From the value perspective, it refers to the total value of all goods and services produced by all resident units during a certain period of time, minus the total value of input of goods and services of the nature of non-fixed assets; in other words, it is the sum of added value of all resident units. From the income perspective, it is the sum of incomes created by all resident units during a certain period of time, including compensation for labors, net taxes on production, depreciation of fixed assets and operating surplus. From the product perspective, it refers to the value of all goods and services for final demand by all resident units plus the net exports (net outflow) value of goods and services during a given period of time. In actual national accounting, gross regional product is calculated in three methods, namely production method, income method and expenditure method, which reflect the gross regional product and its composition from different angles.

Final Consumption Rate (Consumption Rate) It usually refers to the proportion of final consumption in GDP (GRP) within a certain period, and is generally calculated at current price.

Final Consumption Rate (Consumption Rate) = Final Consumption / GDP (GRP) × 100%

Capital Formation Rate (Investment Rate) It usually refers to the proportion of total capital formation in GDP (GRP) within a certain period, and is generally calculated at current price.

Capital Formation Rate (Investment Rate) = Total Capital Formation / GDP (GRP) ×100%

Standards for the Statistical Classification of Some Emerging Industries:

1. New Economy New economy refers to a new type of economy under the new normal of economic development brought about by scientific and technological innovation and technological progress that is in line with the future development direction and can promote the shift in driving forces for development. It includes all activities in the high-tech industry and strategic emerging industries, the activities in the science and technology service industry, tourism and related industries, healthcare industry, cultural creative and related industries that are in line with the characteristics of new economy, together with the Internet finance, e-commerce, crowd innovation, crowd sourcing, crowd support, crowd funding and other activities. The new economy involves 471 categories in 16 classes in the *Classification of National Economic Sectors (GB/T 4754-2011)*.

2. Strategic Emerging Industries Strategic emerging industries refer to the industries that are based on major technological breakthroughs and major development needs, play important leading and driving role in the overall economic and social situation and in the long-term development, are knowledge and technology intensive, consume little material resources, with great growth potential and good comprehensive benefits. The strategic emerging industries include 9 major areas which are respectively the new generation of information and technology industry, high-end equipment manufacture industry, new material industry, bioindustry, new-energy automobile industry, new energy industry, energy conservation and environmental protection industry, digital creative industry and related services industry. The strategic emerging industries are the re-classification of related activities that are in line with the characteristics of strategic emerging industries based on the *Classification of National Economic Sectors (GB/T 4754-2017)*.

3. High-tech Industry High-tech industry includes high-tech manufacturing industry and high-tech service industry. High-tech manufacturing industry refers to the manufacturing industry with relatively high intensity of R&D input among the national economic sectors. It includes 6 major categories which are respectively manufacture of medicines, manufacture of aircrafts and spacecrafts, manufacture of electronic and communication equipment, manufacture of computers and office equipment, manufacture of medical equipment and appliance and measuring instrument and meter, and manufacture of information chemical products. High-tech service industry means the collection of services provided to the society by adopting high-tech means. It includes 9 categories which are respectively information services, e-commerce services, inspection and testing services, high-tech service in professional technique services, R&D and design services, services for transformation of scientific and technological achievements, intellectual property right and related legal services, environmental monitoring and governance services, and other high-tech services. The standards for high-tech industry are formulated on the basis of the *Classification of National Economic Sectors (GB/T 4754-2017)*, depending on the characteristics of the high-tech industry and upon combining with the actual situation in China.

4. Producer Service Industry Producer service industry refers to the R&D and design and other technology services, cargo transportation, general aviation production, storage and express mail services, information services, financial services, human resource management and vocational education and training services, wholesale and trading agency services, and the productive support services provided for production activities. The standards for producer service industry are based on the *Classification of National Economic Sectors (GB/T 4754-2017)*. It is the re-classification of related activities that are in line with the characteristics of producer service industry in the national economic sectors.

5. Consumer Service Industry Consumer service industry refers to the service activities to meet the final consumption demands of residents. The scope of classification covers 12 areas which are respectively resident and household services, healthcare services, pension services, tourism, sightseeing and entertainment services, sport services, cultural services, resident retail and Internet sales services, resident trip services, accommodation and restaurants services, education and training services, resident housing services, and other consumer-oriented services, etc. The standards for consumer service industry are based on the *Classification of National Economic Sectors (GB/T 4754-2017)*. It is the re-classification of related activities that are in line with the characteristics of consumer service industry in the national economic sectors.

03

北京统计年鉴2020　　BEIJING STATISTICAL YEARBOOK

人口与就业
POPULATION AND EMPLOYMENT

简要说明

一、主要内容

人口部分包括历年北京市常住人口和户籍人口的分组资料、新中国成立以来已开展的六次人口普查数据、1990 年以后的人口变动情况抽样调查数据。

就业部分包括北京市三次产业从业人员情况、法人单位从业人员及平均工资情况、城镇单位在岗职工人数及工资的分组情况、城镇登记失业情况等。

二、统计调查方法说明

（一）关于人口数据。1953 年、1964 年、1982 年、1990 年、2000 年和 2010 年分别进行了六次人口普查，1987 年、1995 年、2005 年、2015 年进行了 1%人口抽样调查，从 1982 年开始进行人口变动抽样调查。

（二）关于劳动工资数据。城镇非私营单位采用全面调查方法，城镇私营单位采用抽样调查方法。

三、有关统计标准的变化说明

（一）关于行业划分。2011 年以前执行《国民经济行业分类》（GB/T 4754-2002）标准，2012-2017 年执行《国民经济行业分类》（GB/T 4754-2011）标准，2018 年起执行《国民经济行业分类》（GB/T 4754-2017）标准。

（二）关于三次产业划分。2003 年，根据《国民经济行业分类》（GB/T 4754—2002），国家统计局印发了《国家统计局关于印发〈三次产业划分规定〉的通知》（国统字〔2003〕14 号）。2012 年，根据国家质检总局和国家标准委颁布的《国民经济行业分类》（GB/T 4754—2011），国家统计局对 2003 年《三次产业划分规定》进行了修订。主要在以下方面作出调整：一是将门类“农、林、牧、渔业”中的“农、林、牧、渔服务业”，“采矿业”中的“开采辅助活动”，“制造业”中的“金属制品、机械和设备修理业”等三个大类一并调整到第三产业。调整后，第一产业为 4 个大类；第二产业为 2 个门类和 36 个大类；第三产业为 15 个门类和 3 个大类。二是明确第三产业即为服务业。

本章 2012 年及以后三次产业的分类执行调整后的划分规定。

四、“城镇人口”和“乡村人口”口径变化情况

本章中 1978-1989 年“城镇人口”和“乡村人口”数据为户籍管理统计中的“非农业人口”和“农业人口”口径；1990-1999 年根据 1990 年、2000 年两次人口普查数据进行调整；2000 年为国家统计局 1999 年发布的《关于统计上划分城乡的规定(试行)》中的“城镇人口”和“乡村人口”口径，2001-2005 年为该口径的推算数；2006-2008 年为国家统计局 2006 年发布的《关于统计上划分城乡的暂行规定》中的“城镇人口”和“乡村人口”口径的推算数；2009 年及以后国家统计局每年对《统计用区划代码和城乡分类代码》进行更新维护，至此，2009 年及以后“城镇人口”和“乡村人口”的划分均按当年的城乡分类标准进行推算。

Brief Introduction

I. Main Content

Population statistics in this chapter include classified data for permanent population and registered population in Beijing in previous years, statistics of population in Beijing from six national population censuses since the founding of the People's Republic of China, and statistics of sample survey on population changes after 1990.

Employment statistics in this chapter include information on employed persons in three industries in Beijing, employees and average wages in business entities, classified statistics for the number and wage of fully employed staff and workers in urban entities, and registered unemployment in urban areas.

II. Statistical Survey Methods

(I) Data on Population. Six population censuses were conducted respectively in 1953, 1964, 1982, 1990, 2000 and 2010; 1% population sample surveys were conducted respectively in 1987, 1995, 2005 and 2015; and sample surveys on population changes have been conducted since 1982.

(II) Data on Employment Wage. Urban non-private entities adopt comprehensive survey method and urban private entities adopt sample survey method.

III. Changes in Relevant Statistical Standards

(I) Classification of Sectors. The standards in the *Classification of National Economic Sectors* (GB/T 4754-2002) were implemented before 2011. The standards in the *Classification of National Economic Sectors* (GB/T 4754-2011) were implemented from 2012 to 2017. The standards in the *Classification of National Economic Sectors* (GB/T 4754-2017) are implemented since 2018.

(II) Classification of Three Industries. According to the *Classification of National Economic Sectors* (GB/T 4754-2002), the National Bureau of Statistics issued the *Notice of the National Bureau of Statistics on the Issuance of the 'Regulations on Three Industries Classification'* (G.T.Z. [2003] No. 14) in 2003. According to the *Classification of National Economic Sectors* (GB/T 4754-2011) promulgated by the General Administration of Quality Supervision, Inspection and Quarantine of the People's Republic of China and the Standardization Administration of the People's Republic of China, the National Bureau of Statistics revised the *Regulations on Three Industries Classification* of 2003 version in 2012. Adjustments were mainly made in the following aspects: Firstly, the service activities for agriculture, forestry, animal husbandry and fishing in the category of agriculture, forestry, animal production and hunting, fishing, the mining support service activities in the category of mining and quarrying, and the repair of fabricated metal products, machinery and equipment in the category of manufacturing were adjusted to the tertiary industry. After adjustment, the primary industry fell into 4 categories; the secondary industry fell into 2 classes and 36 categories; and the tertiary industry fell into 15 classes and 3 categories. Secondly, the tertiary industry was defined as the service industry.

The classification of thee industries since 2012 as mentioned in this chapter has all been subject to the classification provisions after adjustment.

IV. Changes in the Terms of Urban Population and Rural Population

The data on urban population and rural population for the period from 1978 to 1989 as mentioned in this chapter refer to the non-agricultural population and agricultural population in the household registration statistics; the data had been adjusted from 1990 to 1999 in accordance with the data on two population censes which were conducted respectively in 1990 and 2000; that of 2000 referred to the urban population and rural population in the *Regulations on the Statistical Division of Rural and Urban Areas (Trial)* issued by the National Bureau of Statistics in 1999; the data of 2001 to 2005 were estimated on the same basis; the data of 2006 to 2008 were the estimated figures of the urban population and rural population in the *Provisional Regulations on the Statistical Division of Rural and Urban Areas* issued by the National Bureau of Statistics in 2006; the National Bureau of Statistics of China has carried on update and maintenance of the *Division Codes and Urban-rural Classification Codes for Statistical Use* since 2009; so far, the division of urban population and rural population in and after 2009 had all been estimated and calculated in accordance with the urban-rural classification standards for each year.

3-1 六次人口普查人口基本情况
BASIC STATISTICS ON POPULATION CENSUS

项　　目	Item	1953	1964	1982	1990	2000	2010
常住人口 (万人)	**Permanent Population (10000 persons)**	**276.8**	**759.7**	**923.1**	**1081.9**	**1356.9**	**1961.2**
按性别分	**By Sex**						
男	Male	159.8	391.1	467.1	559.3	707.4	1012.6
女	Female	117.0	368.6	456.0	522.6	649.5	948.6
性别比(女=100)	Sex Ratio (Female=100)	136.5	106.1	102.4	107.0	108.9	106.8
按城乡分	**By Urban Area and Rural Area**						
城镇人口	Urban Population	205.8	425.8	597.0	794.5	1052.2	1685.9
乡村人口	Rural Population	71.0	333.9	326.1	287.4	304.7	275.3
家庭户规模 (人/户)	**Average Family Size (person/household)**			**3.7**	**3.2**	**2.9**	**2.5**
各年龄组人口比重 (%)	**Composition by Age Group (%)**						
0-14	Age 0-14	30.1	41.5	22.4	20.2	13.6	8.6
15-59	Age 15-59	64.3	51.9	69.1	69.7	73.9	78.9
60岁及以上	Age 60 and Above	5.6	6.6	8.5	10.1	12.5	12.5
#65岁及以上	Age 65 and Above	3.3	4.1	5.6	6.3	8.4	8.7
总抚养比 (%)	**Gross Dependency Ratio (%)**	**50.2**	**83.8**	**38.9**	**36.1**	**28.2**	**20.9**
老年抚养比	Old-age Dependency Ratio	5.0	7.5	7.8	8.6	10.8	10.5
少儿抚养比	Child Dependency Ratio	45.2	76.3	31.1	27.5	17.4	10.4
民族人口	**Population by Ethnic Group**						
汉　族 (万人)	Han Chinese (10000 persons)	260.0	731.2	890.8	1040.5	1298.4	1881.1
占常住人口比重 (%)	Percentage in Permanent Population (%)	93.9	96.2	96.5	96.2	95.7	95.9
少数民族 (万人)	Ethnic Minority (10000 persons)	16.8	28.5	32.3	41.4	58.5	80.1
占常住人口比重 (%)	Percentage in Permanent Population (%)	6.1	3.8	3.5	3.8	4.3	4.1
每十万人口拥有的各种受教育程度人口 (人)	**Population with Various Education Attainment Per 100000 Persons (person)**						
大专及以上	Junior College and Above		4359	4866	9300	16839	31499
高中和中专	Senior Secondary/Secondary Technical School		4513	17646	18978	23165	21220
初　中	Junior Secondary School		11768	29086	30551	34380	31396
小　学	Primary School		31883	26197	22579	16963	9956
文盲人口及文盲率	**Illiterate Population and Illiteracy Rate**						
文盲人口 (万人)	Illiterate Population (10000 persons)		168.9	114.7	94.3	57.8	33.3
文盲率 (%)	Illiteracy Rate (%)		34.2	16.0	10.9	4.9	1.9
平均受教育年限 (年)	**Average Education Years (year)**		**5.3**	**7.8**	**8.6**	**10.0**	**11.5**
平均预期寿命 (岁)	**Average Life Expectancy (year old)**			**71.9**	**72.9**	**76.1**	**80.2**

注：1. 1964年的文盲人口数为12周岁及以上文盲和半文盲人口，1982年、1990年、2000年、2010年的文盲人口数为15周岁及以上文盲和半文盲人口。文盲率是指15周岁及以上人口中，文盲人口和半文盲人口所占比重。

2. 本表常住人口与表3-2相同的年份数据不同，是因为本表数据为普查时点数，表3-2为年末时点数。1953年普查时点为7月1日零时；1964年普查时点为7月1日零时；1982年普查时点为7月1日零时；1990年普查时点为7月1日零时；2000年普查时点为11月1日零时；2010年普查时点为11月1日零时。

Note: a) Statistics on illiterate population covered the illiterate and semi-illiterate people at 12 and above in 1964, and those at 15 and above in 1982, 1990, 2000, and 2010. Illiteracy rate means the share of illiterate and semi-illiterate people in the population at 15 and above.

b) This table has the same indicators but different figures from 3-2, because this table uses the data at the time point of the census, while 3-2 uses the year end as the time point. The time point of the census in 1953 was 12 o'clock midnight, July 1st; the time point in 1964 was 12 o'clock midnight, July 1st; the time point in 1982 was 12 o'clock midnight, July 1st; the time point in 1990 was 12 o'clock midnight,July 1st; the time point in 2000 was 12 o'clock midnight, November 1st; the time point in 2010 was 12 o'clock midnight, November 1st.

3-2 常住人口(1978-2019年)
PERMANENT POPULATION (1978-2019)

年份 Year	常住人口(万人) Permanent Population (10000 persons)	#常住外来人口 Permanent Migrant Population	按性别分 By Sex		按城乡分 By Urban Area and Rural Area		常住人口密度(人/平方公里) Permanent Population Density (person/sq.km)	常住人口出生率(‰) Birth Rate (‰)	常住人口死亡率(‰) Death Rate (‰)	常住人口自然增长率(‰) Natural Growth Rate (‰)
			男 Male	女 Female	城镇人口 Urban Population	乡村人口 Rural Population				
1978	871.5	21.8	443.2	428.3	479.0	392.5	519	12.93	6.12	6.81
1979	897.1	26.5	454.6	442.5	510.3	386.8	534	13.67	5.92	7.75
1980	904.3	18.6	457.8	446.5	521.1	383.2	538	15.56	6.30	9.26
1981	919.2	18.4	465.9	453.3	533.3	385.9	547	16.93	6.02	10.91
1982	935.0	17.2	474.0	461.0	544.0	391.0	556	20.04	5.68	14.36
1983	950.0	16.8	483.0	467.0	557.0	393.0	565	15.63	5.49	10.14
1984	965.0	19.8	491.0	474.0	570.0	395.0	574	16.74	5.53	11.21
1985	981.0	23.1	500.0	481.0	586.0	395.0	584	15.45	5.75	9.70
1986	1028.0	56.8	524.0	504.0	621.0	407.0	612	15.82	4.47	11.35
1987	1047.0	59.0	525.0	522.0	637.0	410.0	623	17.29	5.40	11.89
1988	1061.0	59.8	534.0	527.0	650.0	411.0	631	14.43	5.08	9.35
1989	1075.0	53.9	538.0	537.0	664.0	411.0	640	12.84	5.35	7.49
1990	1086.0	53.8	545.0	541.0	798.0	288.0	646	13.04	5.81	7.23
1991	1094.0	54.5	547.0	547.0	808.0	286.0	651	8.03	5.82	2.21
1992	1102.0	57.1	554.0	548.0	819.0	283.0	656	9.22	6.11	3.11
1993	1112.0	60.8	559.0	553.0	831.0	281.0	662	9.35	6.16	3.19
1994	1125.0	63.2	564.0	561.0	846.0	279.0	669	8.96	5.76	3.20
1995	1251.1	180.8	627.0	624.1	946.2	304.9	744	7.92	5.12	2.80
1996	1259.4	181.7	639.0	620.4	957.9	301.5	749	8.02	5.34	2.68
1997	1240.0	154.5	628.7	611.3	948.3	291.7	738	7.91	6.02	1.89
1998	1245.6	154.1	630.6	615.0	957.7	287.9	741	6.00	5.30	0.70
1999	1257.2	157.4	636.4	620.8	971.7	285.5	748	6.50	5.60	0.90
2000	1363.6	256.1	710.9	652.7	1057.4	306.2	811	6.20	5.30	0.90
2001	1385.1	262.8	722.1	663.0	1081.2	303.9	824	6.10	5.30	0.80
2002	1423.2	286.9	743.1	680.1	1118.0	305.2	847	6.60	5.73	0.87
2003	1456.4	307.6	761.2	695.2	1151.3	305.1	867	5.06	5.15	-0.09
2004	1492.7	329.8	779.9	712.8	1187.2	305.5	910	6.13	5.39	0.74
2005	1538.0	357.3	778.7	759.3	1286.1	251.9	937	6.29	5.20	1.09
2006	1601.0	403.4	817.6	783.4	1350.2	250.8	976	6.22	4.94	1.28
2007	1676.0	462.7	850.8	825.2	1416.2	259.8	1021	8.16	4.83	3.33
2008	1771.0	541.1	900.2	870.8	1503.6	267.4	1079	7.89	4.59	3.30
2009	1860.0	614.2	949.8	910.2	1581.1	278.9	1133	7.66	4.33	3.33
2010	1961.9	704.7	1013.0	948.9	1686.4	275.5	1196	7.27	4.29	2.98
2011	2018.6	742.2	1040.7	977.9	1740.7	277.9	1230	8.29	4.27	4.02
2012	2069.3	773.8	1068.1	1001.2	1783.7	285.6	1261	9.05	4.31	4.74
2013	2114.8	802.7	1090.7	1024.1	1825.1	289.7	1289	8.93	4.52	4.41
2014	2151.6	818.7	1106.5	1045.1	1859.0	292.6	1311	9.75	4.92	4.83
2015	2170.5	822.6	1113.4	1057.1	1877.7	292.8	1323	7.96	4.95	3.01
2016	2172.9	807.5	1112.7	1060.2	1879.6	293.3	1324	9.32	5.20	4.12
2017	2170.7	794.3	1107.4	1063.3	1876.6	294.1	1323	9.06	5.30	3.76
2018	2154.2	764.6	1095.6	1058.6	1863.4	290.8	1313	8.24	5.58	2.66
2019	2153.6	745.6	1094.0	1059.6	1865.0	288.6	1312	8.12	5.49	2.63

注：1978-1981年为户籍统计数，含暂住人口；1982-1989年数据根据1982年、1990年两次人口普查数据进行了修订；1990年为第四次人口普查推算数，1990年以后数据为人口变动情况抽样调查推算数，其中1995年、2005年、2015年为1%人口抽样调查推算数；2000年为第五次人口普查快速汇总推算数；2010年为第六次人口普查推算数。2006-2009年常住人口、出生率、死亡率等数据根据2010年人口普查数据进行了修订。

Note: Statistics for 1978-1981 were figures of registered residents, including temporary residents; statistics for 1982-1989 were adjusted from population censuses in 1982 and 1990; data for 1990 were estimated from the fourth population census; data after 1990 were estimated from sample surveys on population changes; data for 1995,2005 and 2015 were estimated from sample surveys on 1% of the population; data for 2000 were estimated from fast summarizing of the fifth population census; data for 2010 were estimated from the sixth population census. Data of permanent population, birth rate and death rate, etc. from 2006 to 2009 were adjusted from population census in 2010.

3–3 常住人口总量及人口密度(按地区分)(2019年)
TOTAL NUMBER AND DENSITY OF PERMANENT POPULATION (BY DISTRICT) (2019)

地区	District	常住人口(万人) Permanent Population (10000 persons)	#常住外来人口 Permanent Migrant Population	城镇人口 Urban Population	乡村人口 Rural Population	常住人口密度(人/平方公里) Permanent Population Density (person/sq.km)
全　　市	**Total**	**2153.6**	**745.6**	**1865**	**288.6**	**1312**
东城区	Dongcheng District	79.4	15.4	79.4		18968
西城区	Xicheng District	113.7	21.0	113.7		22501
朝阳区	Chaoyang District	347.3	149.1	347.0	0.3	7632
丰台区	Fengtai District	202.5	64.1	202.1	0.4	6622
石景山区	Shijingshan District	57.0	13.7	57.0		6760
海淀区	Haidian District	323.7	123.7	320.3	3.4	7515
门头沟区	Mentougou District	34.4	5.7	30.8	3.6	237
房山区	Fangshan District	125.5	30.8	94.4	31.1	631
通州区	Tongzhou District	167.5	64.6	118.0	49.5	1848
顺义区	Shunyi District	122.8	48.0	71.0	51.8	1204
昌平区	Changping District	216.6	105.1	182.4	34.2	1612
大兴区	Daxing District	188.8	77.1	139.9	48.9	1822
怀柔区	Huairou District	42.2	10.2	30.1	12.1	199
平谷区	Pinggu District	46.2	4.7	27.1	19.1	486
密云区	Miyun District	50.3	7.9	30.5	19.8	226
延庆区	Yanqing District	35.7	4.5	21.3	14.4	179

注：本表数据为人口抽样调查推算数据，为年末数。
Note: Figures in this table are estimated figures from sample survey on population in the end of year.

3-4 常住人口自然变动(按地区分)(2019年)
NATURAL CHANGE OF PERMANENT POPULATION (BY DISTRICT) (2019)

地 区	District	出生人数 (人) Number of Births (person)	死亡人数 (人) Number of Deaths (person)	自然增加人数 (人) Natural Increase of Population (person)	出生率 (‰) Birth Rate (‰)	死亡率 (‰) Death Rate (‰)	自然增长率 (‰) Natural Growth Rate (‰)
全 市	**Total**	**174941**	**118323**	**56618**	**8.12**	**5.49**	**2.63**
东城区	Dongcheng District	6193	6173	20	7.66	7.64	0.02
西城区	Xicheng District	8516	7090	1426	7.35	6.12	1.23
朝阳区	Chaoyang District	31018	21226	9792	8.76	6.00	2.76
丰台区	Fengtai District	13905	11163	2742	6.73	5.41	1.32
石景山区	Shijingshan District	4281	3630	651	7.38	6.26	1.12
海淀区	Haidian District	25689	15324	10365	7.79	4.65	3.14
门头沟区	Mentougou District	2456	2294	162	7.27	6.79	0.48
房山区	Fangshan District	11285	6963	4322	9.23	5.70	3.53
通州区	Tongzhou District	14581	8710	5871	8.96	5.35	3.61
顺义区	Shunyi District	10105	8699	1406	8.43	7.26	1.17
昌平区	Changping Ddistrict	15268	8042	7226	7.14	3.76	3.38
大兴区	Daxing District	17185	8486	8699	9.33	4.61	4.72
怀柔区	Huairou District	3296	2416	880	7.89	5.78	2.11
平谷区	Pinggu District	4051	3358	693	8.83	7.32	1.51
密云区	Miyun District	4212	2687	1525	8.44	5.38	3.06
延庆区	Yanqing District	2900	2062	838	8.22	5.84	2.38

注：本表数据为人口抽样调查推算数据。
Note: Figures in this table are estimated figures from the sample survey on population.

3-5 常住人口年龄构成(2019年)
PERMANENT POPULATION BY AGE COMPOSITION (2019)

年龄组 Age Group	常住人口数(万人) Permanent Population (10000 persons)	比 重(%) Percentage (%)
合 计 Total	**2153.6**	**100.0**
0-4	87.5	4.1
5-9	81.3	3.8
10-14	57.9	2.7
15-19	44.1	2.0
20-24	137.3	6.4
25-29	243.2	11.3
30-34	237.6	11.0
35-39	212.4	9.9
40-44	165.1	7.6
45-49	183.0	8.5
50-54	182.8	8.5
55-59	150.1	7.0
60-64	125.3	5.8
65-69	84.7	3.9
70-74	58.7	2.7
75-79	42.2	2.0
80-84	34.0	1.6
85岁及以上 85 and above	26.4	1.2

注：本表数据为人口抽样调查推算数据，为年末数。
Note: Figures in this table are estimated figures from the sample survey on population in the end of year.

3-6 常住人口受教育程度(2019年)
EDUCATION ATTAINMENT OF PERMANENT POPULATION (2019)

单位：人 (person)

项 目	Item	调查人口合计 Total	男 Male	女 Female
6岁及以上人口	**Population at 6 and above**	**405159**	**202738**	**202421**
#小 学	Primary School	46554	21149	25405
初 中	Junior Secondary School	106002	56608	49394
普通高中	Senior Secondary School	59850	30137	29713
中 职	Vocational School	26157	13698	12459
大学专科	Junior College	57107	28514	28593
大学本科	4-year Unversity Education	79526	39418	40108
研究生	Postgraduate	22520	11272	11248

注：本表数据为人口抽样调查样本数据。
Note: Figures in this table are sample figures from the sample survey on population.

3-7 常住人口家庭户规模(2019年)
FAMILY SIZE OF PERMANENT POPULATION (2019)

地 区	Area	调查家庭总户数(户) Total Number of Households (household)	家庭户规模所占比重(%) Percentage of Various Sized Family (%)				
			一人户 One Person	二人户 Two Persons	三人户 Three Persons	四人户 Four Persons	五人及以上户 Five Persons and above
全 市	**Total**	**159859**	**23.6**	**31.6**	**25.1**	**10.5**	**9.2**
城 镇	Urban	129726	23.2	31.5	26.6	10.5	8.2
乡 村	Rural	30133	25.1	32.1	18.6	10.6	13.6

注：本表数据为人口抽样调查样本数据。
Note: Figures in this table are sample figures from the sample survey on population.

3-8 户籍人口(1978-2019年)
REGISTERED POPULATION (1978-2019)

单位：万人 (10000 persons)

年份 Year	户籍户数(万户) Registered Households (10000 households)	户籍人口 Registered Population	#60岁及以上人口 Population at 60 and above	按性别分 By Sex 男 Male	女 Female	按户籍性质分 By Type of Household Register 非农业户 Non-Agricultural	农业户 Agricultural	户籍人口出生人数 Births of Registered Population	户籍人口死亡人数 Deaths of Registered Population	户籍人口自然增加人数 Natural Increase of Registered Population
1978	205.5	849.7		432.1	417.5	467.0	382.6	10.9	5.2	5.7
1979	214.6	870.6		441.1	429.4	495.2	375.4	11.8	5.1	6.7
1980	223.2	885.7		448.4	437.3	510.4	375.3	13.7	5.5	8.2
1981	234.8	900.8		456.6	444.2	522.6	378.2	15.1	5.4	9.7
1982	245.0	917.8		465.5	452.3	534.0	383.8	18.2	5.2	13.1
1983	255.1	933.2		474.7	458.5	547.1	386.0	14.5	5.1	9.4
1984	263.1	945.2		481.2	464.0	558.1	387.0	13.2	5.1	8.1
1985	274.1	957.9		488.0	469.9	572.5	385.4	11.8	5.2	6.6
1986	284.6	971.2		495.5	475.7	586.8	384.4	12.9	5.2	7.8
1987	299.4	988.0		504.1	483.9	601.0	387.0	16.9	5.3	11.6
1988	310.8	1001.2		510.4	490.8	614.3	387.0	15.3	5.5	9.8
1989	322.5	1021.1		520.3	500.8	630.6	390.5	19.0	5.7	13.3
1990	335.0	1032.2		525.3	507.0	640.2	392.1	14.0	6.3	7.7
1991	343.1	1039.5		528.5	511.1	648.4	391.2	9.2	5.7	3.5
1992	349.3	1044.9		530.8	514.1	656.3	388.6	8.3	6.2	2.2
1993	354.6	1051.2		533.9	517.3	668.7	382.5	7.9	6.3	1.6
1994	360.3	1061.8		538.9	522.8	683.8	377.9	8.5	6.3	2.2
1995	365.7	1070.3		543.0	527.3	696.9	373.5	8.5	6.2	2.3
1996	370.9	1077.7		546.8	530.9	709.7	368.0	7.8	6.7	1.2
1997	375.7	1085.5		550.4	535.1	722.7	362.9	7.6	6.7	0.9
1998	383.4	1091.5		552.6	538.9	733.6	357.8	6.7	7.5	-0.8
1999	390.3	1099.8		556.7	543.1	747.2	352.6	6.3	6.2	0.1
2000	397.9	1107.5		560.1	547.4	760.7	346.8	7.2	7.8	-0.5
2001	405.3	1122.3		567.3	555.0	780.2	342.2	6.0	5.3	0.7
2002	416.3	1136.3		574.7	561.6	806.9	329.4	6.0	5.2	0.8
2003	427.6	1148.8		581.0	567.9	830.8	318.0	4.5	5.8	-1.3
2004	439.8	1162.9		587.2	575.7	854.7	308.2	6.6	6.2	0.4
2005	451.7	1180.7		596.0	584.7	880.2	300.5	7.5	7.0	0.5
2006	463.7	1197.6		604.2	593.4	905.4	292.2	7.7	5.1	2.6
2007	473.0	1213.3	210.3	612.0	601.3	929.0	284.3	9.9	5.2	4.8
2008	481.2	1229.9	218.6	620.0	609.9	950.7	279.2	10.6	5.1	5.5
2009	488.7	1245.8	228.7	627.5	618.9	971.9	273.9	10.9	6.2	4.7
2010	496.1	1257.8	237.2	632.8	625.0	989.5	268.3	10.2	9.1	1.1
2011	503.1	1277.9	250.5	642.4	635.6	1013.8	264.2	12.5	5.3	7.2
2012	509.2	1297.5	266.1	651.7	645.8	1039.3	258.2	14.5	5.7	8.8
2013	516.2	1316.3	283.2	660.4	655.9	1065.0	251.4	13.6	5.7	7.9
2014	522.6	1333.4	301.0	668.3	665.1	1089.8	243.6	17.2	7.6	9.6
2015	529.2	1345.2	318.0	673.3	671.9	1111.3	233.8	12.3	7.3	4.9
2016	538.2	1362.9	334.4	681.5	681.4	1132.0	230.9	20.5	8.9	11.6
2017	543.1	1359.2	336.4	676.8	682.4	1131.7	227.5	18.6	26.5	-7.9
2018	548.8	1375.8	352.3	684.2	691.6	1152.3	223.5	15.7	10.1	5.6
2019	554.4	1397.4	371.1	694.7	702.7	1176.3	221.2	15.3	4.9	10.4

资料来源：北京市公安局。
Source: Beijing Municipal Bureau of Public Security.

3-9 户籍人口年龄构成(2019年)
AGE COMPOSITION OF REGISTERED POPULATION (2019)

年龄组 Age Group	户籍人口(人) Registered Population (persons)			占人口比重(%) Percentage (%)		
	合计 Total	男 Male	女 Female	合计 Total	男 Male	女 Female
合 计 Total	**13974221**	**6946923**	**7027298**	**100.0**	**49.7**	**50.3**
0–4	768416	397101	371315	5.5	2.8	2.7
5–9	710936	367140	343796	5.1	2.6	2.5
10–14	484053	249894	234159	3.5	1.8	1.7
15–19	418992	212770	206222	3.0	1.5	1.5
20–24	595486	298135	297351	4.3	2.1	2.1
25–29	744302	375622	368680	5.3	2.7	2.6
30–34	1166087	583586	582501	8.3	4.2	4.2
35–39	1208949	604663	604286	8.7	4.3	4.3
40–44	866704	439470	427234	6.2	3.1	3.1
45–49	1029762	513364	516398	7.4	3.7	3.7
50–54	1020356	510776	509580	7.3	3.7	3.6
55–59	1249138	631344	617794	8.9	4.5	4.4
60–64	1148976	565117	583859	8.2	4.0	4.2
65–69	957399	461271	496128	6.9	3.3	3.6
70–74	556821	264031	292790	4.0	1.9	2.1
75–79	383097	172734	210363	2.7	1.2	1.5
80–84	356114	159572	196542	2.5	1.1	1.4
85–89	206181	94830	111351	1.5	0.7	0.8
90岁及以上 90 and above	102452	45503	56949	0.7	0.3	0.4

资料来源：北京市公安局。
Source: Beijing Municipal Bureau of Public Security.

3-10 户籍人口变动情况
CHANGES OF REGISTERED POPULATION

单位：人 (person)

项　　目	Item	2019	2018
自然变动	**Natural Changes**		
自然增加	Natural Increase	103981	55927
非农业人口	Non-agricultural Population	104175	64126
农业人口	Agricultural Population	-194	-8199
出　生	Births	153133	156625
非农业人口	Non-agricultural Population	137873	140388
农业人口	Agricultural Population	15260	16237
死　亡	Deaths	49152	100698
非农业人口	Non-agricultural Population	33698	76262
农业人口	Agricultural Population	15454	24436
机械变动	**Non-natural Changes**		
机械增加	Non-natural Increase	112270	110493
非农业人口	Non-agricultural Population	104922	104226
农业人口	Agricultural Population	7348	6267
市外迁入	Inflow	190152	194206
非农业人口	Non-agricultural Population	181982	186561
农业人口	Agricultural Population	8170	7645
迁往市外	Outflow	77882	83713
非农业人口	Non-agricultural Population	77060	82335
农业人口	Agricultural Population	822	1378

资料来源：北京市公安局。
Source: Beijing Municipal Bureau of Public Security.

3-11 三次产业从业人员年末人数及构成(1978-2019年)
EMPLOYED PERSONS IN THREE INDUSTRIES AND THEIR COMPOSITION (1978-2019)

年 份 Year	从业人员年末人数(万人) Year-end Employed Persons (10000 persons)				构 成(%) (合计=100) Composition (%) (Total=100)		
		第一产业 Primary Industry	第二产业 Secondary Industry	第三产业 Tertiary Industry	第一产业 Primary Industry	第二产业 Secondary Industry	第三产业 Tertiary Industry
1978	444.1	125.9	177.9	140.3	28.3	40.1	31.6
1979	470.5	121.4	195.2	153.9	25.8	41.5	32.7
1980	484.2	118.0	207.3	158.9	24.4	42.8	32.8
1981	511.7	117.2	220.4	174.1	22.9	43.1	34.0
1982	535.2	115.1	228.6	191.5	21.5	42.7	35.8
1983	552.0	117.1	240.2	194.7	21.2	43.5	35.3
1984	556.2	111.3	247.9	197.0	20.0	44.6	35.4
1985	566.5	100.6	260.4	205.5	17.7	46.0	36.3
1986	572.7	96.1	262.7	213.9	16.8	45.9	37.3
1987	580.2	92.3	264.1	223.8	15.9	45.5	38.6
1988	584.1	88.4	267.6	228.1	15.1	45.8	39.1
1989	593.9	91.0	266.3	236.6	15.3	44.9	39.8
1990	627.1	90.7	281.6	254.8	14.5	44.9	40.6
1991	634.0	90.8	279.7	263.5	14.3	44.1	41.6
1992	649.3	84.5	281.6	283.2	13.0	43.4	43.6
1993	627.8	65.1	279.4	283.3	10.4	44.5	45.1
1994	664.3	73.2	272.2	318.9	11.0	41.0	48.0
1995	665.3	70.6	271.0	323.7	10.6	40.7	48.7
1996	660.2	72.5	260.1	327.6	11.0	39.4	49.6
1997	655.8	71.0	257.6	327.2	10.8	39.2	50.0
1998	622.2	71.5	226.0	324.7	11.5	36.3	52.2
1999	618.6	74.5	216.2	327.9	12.1	34.9	53.0
2000	619.3	72.9	208.2	338.2	11.8	33.6	54.6
2001	628.9	71.2	215.9	341.8	11.3	34.3	54.4
2002	679.2	67.6	235.3	376.3	10.0	34.6	55.4
2003	703.3	62.7	225.8	414.8	8.9	32.1	59.0
2004	854.1	61.5	232.8	559.8	7.2	27.3	65.5
2005	878.0	62.2	231.1	584.7	7.1	26.3	66.6
2006	919.7	60.3	225.4	634.0	6.6	24.5	68.9
2007	942.7	60.9	228.1	653.7	6.5	24.2	69.3
2008	980.9	63.0	207.4	710.5	6.4	21.2	72.4
2009	998.3	62.2	199.6	736.5	6.2	20.0	73.8
2010	1031.6	61.4	202.7	767.5	6.0	19.6	74.4
2011	1069.7	59.1	219.2	791.4	5.5	20.5	74.0
2012	1107.3	57.3	212.6	837.4	5.2	19.2	75.6
2013	1141.0	55.4	210.9	874.7	4.8	18.5	76.7
2014	1156.7	52.4	209.9	894.4	4.5	18.2	77.3
2015	1186.1	50.3	200.8	935.0	4.2	17.0	78.8
2016	1220.1	49.6	193.0	977.5	4.1	15.8	80.1
2017	1246.8	48.8	192.8	1005.2	3.9	15.5	80.6
2018	1237.8	45.4	182.2	1010.2	3.7	14.7	81.6
2019	1273.0	42.4	172.5	1058.1	3.3	13.6	83.1

注：2010年及以前，劳务派遣人员按照“谁发工资谁统计”的原则进行统计。2011年以后，劳务派遣人员按照“谁用工谁统计”的原则进行统计。

Note:In 2010 and before, dispatched personnel of labor service were calculated by wage payers. After 2011, dispatched personnel of labor service were calculated by employers.

3-12 按登记注册类型分从业人员年末人数(1978-2019年)
YEAR-END EMPLOYED PERSONS BY TYPE OF REGISTRATION (1978-2019)

单位：万人 (10000 persons)

年 份 Year	合 计 Total	#城 镇 Urban	#国有单位 State-owned Enterprises	#集体单位 Collectively-owned Enterprises	#联营单位 Associated Enterprises	#有限责任公司 Limited Liability Companies	#股份有限公司 Companies Limited by Shares	#外商投资 Foreign-invested	#港澳台商投资 Hong Kong, Macao and Taiwan-invested	#私 营 Private Enterprises	#个 体 Individual Economy
1978	444.1	291.6	240.9	50.7							
1979	470.5	311.9	254.2	57.8							
1980	484.2	326.8	269.4	57.1							0.3
1981	511.7	345.2	283.1	61.3							
1982	535.2	361.1	293.0	67.1							
1983	552.0	373.8	303.4	68.5							
1984	556.2	377.6	302.5	71.6				1.3			
1985	566.5	392.6	308.1	72.6				1.6			2.5
1986	572.7	400.5	324.4	71.1				2.4			2.6
1987	580.2	408.3	331.8	70.7				2.8			3.1
1988	584.1	413.9	336.4	69.9	0.2			3.4			3.5
1989	593.9	424.0	343.8	67.4	3.4			3.7			5.6
1990	627.1	461.2	357.9	86.8	5.1			4.6			6.3
1991	634.0	477.2	367.8	89.0	0.5			7.7	0.2		7.2
1992	649.3	490.6	371.5	90.5	0.4			11.4	0.2		14.0
1993	627.8	481.4	362.3	79.7	2.8			11.0	6.4		14.0
1994	664.3	492.7	363.5	73.3	3.5			15.0	9.4		20.9
1995	665.3	492.7	358.2	72.1	3.7			17.4	10.0		21.9
1996	660.2	495.7	355.1	68.6	3.4			20.7	10.1		22.9
1997	655.8	498.7	354.7	68.5	3.2			21.2	10.2		21.2
1998	622.2	463.2	308.1	51.0	5.2	13.7	10.8	21.2	13.1		20.1
1999	618.6	456.1	287.6	49.7	4.8	24.0	12.2	20.6	13.5		23.7
2000	619.3	456.3	266.2	48.3	4.0	34.2	14.0	23.8	14.2		24.4
2001	628.9	464.2	246.3	45.8	4.1	50.6	17.3	22.4	12.9		24.8
2002	679.2	513.6	224.8	36.8	4.1	85.0	27.1	29.2	17.0	4.8	33.1
2003	703.3	533.7	212.8	30.1	3.8	102.3	33.4	31.5	17.3	5.2	37.2
2004	854.1	682.7	199.5	28.2	3.5	134.5	37.9	45.0	18.3	134.2	45.7
2005	878.0	694.0	195.0	23.8	2.4	149.4	36.4	49.6	21.7	131.2	57.2
2006	919.7	734.2	189.3	18.8	2.1	165.1	35.5	57.3	23.5	154.8	65.6
2007	942.7	745.4	189.3	17.3	1.9	179.5	38.7	69.3	28.8	133.8	67.2
2008	980.9	813.7	187.8	24.8	2.2	196.4	46.4	72.9	33.5	159.6	65.1
2009	998.3	856.6	185.7	24.3	0.9	215.7	58.4	71.2	36.6	172.2	67.5
2010	1031.6	905.4	189.0	22.7	0.9	228.2	64.7	74.9	42.4	193.5	65.3
2011	1069.7	955.8	188.8	20.1	0.7	243.0	75.9	90.1	50.6	210.6	59.3
2012	1107.3	996.1	188.3	19.8	0.7	261.6	83.2	92.7	54.3	227.9	50.8
2013	1141.0	1073.0	189.5	17.5	0.7	278.0	85.4	96.1	56.1	265.9	64.8
2014	1156.7	1066.2	188.6	18.8	0.5	290.6	86.2	94.5	58.7	254.6	55.7
2015	1186.1	1107.1	182.9	16.9	0.4	300.3	103.5	90.6	59.7	273.3	56.4
2016	1220.1	1141.1	188.1	13.9	0.3	305.1	116.9	81.6	61.2	298.4	51.4
2017	1246.8	1166.2	183.4	14.3	0.3	318.3	124.4	79.7	65.2	307.7	45.6
2018	1237.8	1161.9	177.8	13.1	0.4	330.2	128.2	76.8	67.7	302.4	40.2
2019	1273.0	1198.9	170.8	14.9	0.2	327.0	112.6	74.5	71.1	372.6	35.0

资料来源：表中2002—2013年私营从业人员数据来源于北京市市场监督管理局，2014年及以后数据为市统计局根据劳动工资制度，规模以上单位采用全面调查，规模以下单位采用抽样调查推算得到；个体从业人员数据来源于北京市市场监督管理局。

Source: Figures of employed persons in private enterprises from 2002 to 2013 in this table were from Beijing Municipal Administration of Market Supervision. Date after 2014 were calculated on the basis of comprehensive surveys for entities above designated size and sample surveys for entities below designated size, according to the labor and wage system; and figures on self-employed individuals were from Beijing Municipal Administration of Market Supervision.

3-13 全市法人单位从业人员年末人数和平均工资
YEAR-END EMPLOYED PERSONS IN LEGAL ENTITIES AND AVERAGE WAGES

项目	Item	从业人员年末人数（万人）Year-end Employed Persons (10000 persons)		从业人员平均工资（元）Average Wage (yuan)	
		2019	2018	2019	2018
合计	**Total**	**1163.9**	**1121.7**	**140581**	**127107**
按登记注册类型分	**By Registration Type**				
内资	Domestically-invested Enterprises	1018.3	977.3	132082	119311
国有	State-owned Enterprises	170.9	177.8	189849	162118
集体	Collectively-owned Enterprises	14.9	13.1	68765	66211
股份合作	Joint-equity Cooperative Enterprises	3.8	3.7	63494	57572
联营	Associated Enterprises	0.2	0.4	97267	79695
有限责任公司	Limited Liability Companies	327.0	330.2	138288	123239
股份有限公司	Companies Limited by Shares	112.6	128.2	198220	164780
私营	Private Enterprises	372.6	302.5	85262	76908
其他	Others	16.3	21.4	95684	84465
港、澳、台商投资	Hong Kong, Macao and Taiwan-invested Enterprises	71.1	67.7	193110	171261
外商投资	Foreign-invested Enterprises	74.5	76.7	206698	188538
按国民经济行业分	**By Sector**				
农、林、牧、渔业	Agriculture, Forestry, Animal Production and Hunting, Fishing	0.6	3.5	84856	55138
采矿业	Mining and Quarrying	3.3	3.6	133077	123098
制造业	Manufacturing	86.9	95.0	123448	110484
电力、热力、燃气及水生产和供应业	Production and Distribution of Electricity, Heating Power, Gas and Water	10.3	10.4	169992	154436
建筑业	Construction	72.4	72.9	104619	95651
批发和零售业	Wholesale and Retail Trade	134.6	128.9	107030	98102
交通运输、仓储和邮政业	Transport, Storage and Post	67.9	66.3	115638	102919
住宿和餐饮业	Lodging and Catering Services	43.1	44.2	59700	56100
信息传输、软件和信息技术服务业	Information Transmission, Software and Information Technology Services	112.9	111.5	216842	187334
金融业	Financial Intermediation	69.1	58.2	251432	261214
房地产业	Real Estate	68.8	63.4	102237	98569
租赁和商务服务业	Leasing and Business Services	167.8	157.1	110441	102350
科学研究和技术服务业	Scientific Research and Development, Technical Services	118.1	104.3	154109	143023
水利、环境和公共设施管理业	Management of Water Conservancy, Environment and Public Facilities	16.0	15.0	95529	86796
居民服务、修理和其他服务业	Resident Service, Repair and Other Services	18.6	21.2	63413	51520
教育	Education	64.0	60.4	172823	154924
卫生和社会工作	Health Care and Social Works	35.0	32.7	200164	180343
文化、体育和娱乐业	Culture, Sports and Entertainment	24.3	24.9	178266	149144
公共管理、社会保障和社会组织	Public Management, Social Security and Social Organizations	50.2	48.2	159193	140310
国际组织	International Organizations				

3-14 城镇单位在岗职工年末人数及工资总额(1978-2019年)
YEAR-END NUMBER AND WAGES OF FULLY EMPLOYED STAFF AND WORKERS IN URBAN ENTITIES (1978-2019)

年份 Year	在岗职工年末人数(万人) Year-end Fully Employed Staff and Workers (10000 persons)	国有单位 State-owned	集体单位 Collectively-owned	其他单位 Others	在岗职工工资总额(亿元) Total Wages of Fully Employed Staff and Workers (100 million yuan)	国有单位 State-owned	集体单位 Collectively-owned	其他单位 Others
1978	291.6	240.9	50.7		18.7	16.2	2.5	
1979	311.9	254.2	57.7		22.4	19.4	3.0	
1980	326.5	269.4	57.1		26.9	23.3	3.6	
1981	344.4	283.1	61.3		28.3	24.2	4.1	
1982	360.1	293.0	67.1		30.5	25.9	4.6	
1983	371.9	303.4	68.5		33.8	28.5	5.3	
1984	375.4	302.5	71.6	1.3	40.4	33.7	6.6	0.1
1985	382.3	308.1	72.6	1.6	50.7	41.5	9.0	0.3
1986	397.9	324.4	71.1	2.4	58.0	48.5	9.1	0.4
1987	405.2	331.8	70.7	2.7	66.7	56.0	10.1	0.6
1988	410.4	336.4	69.9	4.1	81.2	68.1	12.1	1.0
1989	418.4	343.8	67.4	7.2	96.3	81.0	13.4	1.9
1990	454.9	357.9	86.8	10.2	118.9	96.1	19.7	3.1
1991	470.0	367.8	89.0	13.2	132.2	106.1	21.5	4.6
1992	476.6	371.5	90.5	14.6	158.5	128.6	23.9	6.0
1993	467.3	362.3	79.6	25.4	218.9	176.6	28.5	13.8
1994	471.8	363.5	73.4	34.9	306.5	243.4	36.2	26.9
1995	470.9	358.2	72.1	40.6	382.0	295.6	46.5	39.9
1996	460.6	349.0	64.8	46.8	442.4	339.4	46.2	56.8
1997	465.3	348.7	65.0	51.6	514.8	383.6	53.8	77.4
1998	450.1	321.7	50.8	77.6	558.2	391.9	45.0	121.3
1999	438.0	303.0	49.6	85.4	614.5	420.0	44.8	149.7
2000	434.2	283.0	46.0	105.2	695.5	453.6	46.7	195.2
2001	400.3	235.9	40.0	124.4	777.3	477.8	44.8	254.7
2002	434.2	212.6	32.7	188.9	950.9	508.8	40.0	402.1
2003	436.3	197.6	26.1	212.6	1098.9	565.5	35.0	498.4
2004	446.4	183.7	24.8	237.9	1315.1	625.7	34.0	655.4
2005	448.4	178.5	20.7	249.2	1520.1	694.9	30.8	794.4
2006	453.1	172.9	16.4	263.8	1805.5	738.0	30.5	1037.0
2007	478.9	172.7	15.4	290.8	2194.3	862.4	31.2	1300.7
2008	526.1	171.0	22.7	332.4	2874.3	1008.8	48.2	1817.3
2009	560.4	170.9	22.4	367.1	3227.2	1074.3	53.3	2099.6
2010	587.7	175.1	21.1	391.5	3789.1	1221.2	56.7	2511.2
2011	640.3	177.1	18.7	444.5	4778.6	1421.1	62.3	3295.2
2012	670.4	177.3	18.6	474.5	5657.9	1582.5	71.6	4003.8
2013	695.5	178.4	16.5	500.6	6502.0	1724.7	70.2	4707.1
2014	708.8	177.7	17.8	513.3	7293.3	1884.5	81.5	5327.3
2015	724.8	172.8	16.0	536.0	8225.2	2059.0	81.5	6084.7
2016	733.5	178.0	13.1	542.4	9005.0	2299.0	80.1	6625.9
2017	756.4	174.3	13.5	568.6	10182.8	2611.0	80.9	7490.9
2018	762.1	168.9	12.4	580.8	11562.8	2812.6	84.2	8666.0
2019	727.8	162.7	14.0	551.1	12627.3	3166.3	97.3	9363.7

注：1．2007年及以前城镇单位是指乡及乡以上独立核算法人单位，不包括乡镇企业、私营单位和个体工商户。2008年及以后城镇单位是指不包括私营单位和个体工商户的独立核算法人单位(下表同)。

2．表中2000年及以前数据为职工口径，职工包括在岗职工和不在岗职工(下表同)。

Note: a) Urban entities in and before 2007 referred to legal entities with independent accounting at and above township level, excluding township enterprises, private entities and self-employed businesses. Urban entities in and after 2008 referred to legal entities with independent accounting excluding private entities and self-employed businesses (the same to the follow tables).

b) Figures before 2000 were counted by the statistical range of employees including on-the-job and off-the-job ones (the same to the follow tables).

3–15 城镇单位在岗职工平均工资(1978–2019年)
AVERAGE WAGES OF FULLY EMPLOYED STAFF AND WORKERS IN URBAN ENTITIES (1978-2019)

单位：元 (yuan)

年 份 Year	在岗职工 平均工资 Average Wage of Fully Employed Staff and Workers	国有单位 State-owned Enterprises	集体单位 Collectively-owned Enterprises	其他单位 Others
1978	673	703	471	
1979	742	778	556	
1980	848	889	635	
1981	837	880	685	
1982	863	896	715	
1983	931	964	785	
1984	1086	1127	946	1170
1985	1343	1367	1231	1768
1986	1488	1530	1287	2080
1987	1670	1712	1449	2267
1988	2000	2048	1738	2661
1989	2312	2366	1992	2761
1990	2653	2713	2334	3243
1991	2877	2937	2504	3713
1992	3402	3500	2828	4289
1993	4780	4920	3834	5469
1994	6540	6695	5009	8179
1995	8144	8237	6516	10278
1996	9579	9645	7133	13851
1997	11019	10917	8259	15370
1998	12285	11971	8800	15989
1999	13778	13483	8928	17748
2000	15726	15483	9844	19165
2001	19155	19776	11063	20594
2002	21852	23754	11997	21432
2003	25312	28464	13580	23769
2004	29674	34009	13422	28026
2005	34191	39067	14695	32324
2006	40117	43298	17781	39513
2007	46507	50524	20379	45508
2008	54913	59361	20990	54983
2009	58140	63239	23553	57911
2010	65683	70320	26607	65755
2011	75834	81215	32469	75584
2012	85307	90456	38596	85234
2013	93997	97356	42482	94513
2014	103400	106097	45772	104473
2015	113073	119046	49969	113066
2016	122749	129542	59507	122096
2017	134994	150622	58900	132062
2018	149843	166977	66776	146730
2019	173205	195783	69344	169239

3-16 城镇单位在岗职工年末人数
YEAR-END NUMBER OF FULLY EMPLOYED STAFF AND WORKERS IN URBAN ENTITIES

单位：人 (person)

项目	Item	2019	2018	2019年为2018年% 2019 as % of 2018
合计	**Total**	**7277700**	**7620907**	**95.5**
按登记注册类型分	**By Registration Type**			
内资	Domestically-invested Enterprises	6013293	6326064	95.1
国有	State-owned Enterprises	1627047	1689344	96.3
集体	Collectively-owned Enterprises	140047	124074	112.9
股份合作	Joint-equity Cooperative Enterprises	34888	33794	103.2
联营	Associated Enterprises	2381	3904	61.0
有限责任公司	Limited Liability Companies	3073977	3139410	97.9
股份有限公司	Companies Limited By Shares	995538	1143401	87.1
其他	Others	139415	192137	72.6
港、澳、台商投资	Hong Kong, Macao and Taiwan-invested Enterprises	617234	613609	100.6
外商投资	Foreign-invested Enterprises	647173	681234	95.0
按国民经济行业分	**By Sector**			
农、林、牧、渔业	Agriculture, Forestry, Animal Production and Hunting, Fishing	3420	25421	13.5
#农业	Agriculture	170	11440	1.5
采矿业	Mining and Quarrying	31636	35851	88.2
制造业	Manufacturing	639940	727480	88.0
电力、热力、燃气及水生产和供应业	Production and Distribution of Electricity, Heating Power, Gas and Water	93909	95682	98.1
建筑业	Construction	432064	452115	95.6
批发和零售业	Wholesale and Retail Trade	560196	688960	81.3
批发业	Wholesale	340945	385206	88.5
零售业	Retail Trade	219251	303754	72.2
交通运输、仓储和邮政业	Transport, Storage and Post	576765	586485	98.3
#铁路运输业	Transport via Railway	102584	103708	98.9
道路运输业	Transport via Road	256607	274401	93.5
邮政业	Post	93053	80441	115.7
住宿和餐饮业	Lodging and Catering Services	217831	231772	94.0
住宿业	Lodging	91172	100914	90.3
餐饮业	Catering Services	126659	130858	96.8
信息传输、软件和信息技术服务业	Information Transmission, Software and Information Technology Services	840588	820976	102.4
金融业	Financial Intermediation	409961	397760	103.1
房地产业	Real Estate	444142	442854	100.3
租赁和商务服务业	Leasing and Business Services	710841	786954	90.3
租赁业	Leasing	15351	34969	43.9
商务服务业	Business Services	695490	751985	92.5
科学研究和技术服务业	Scientific Research and Development, Technical Services	652784	674666	96.8
水利、环境和公共设施管理业	Management of Water Conservancy, Environment and Public Facilities	117639	116518	101.0
居民服务、修理和其他服务业	Resident Services, Repair and Other Services	64478	107363	60.1
#居民服务业	Resident Services	21473	49444	43.4
教育	Education	532070	514470	103.4
卫生和社会工作	Health Care and Social Works	305932	288609	106.0
#卫生	Health Care	284907	270626	105.3
文化、体育和娱乐业	Culture, Sports and Entertainment	176964	179224	98.7
#文化艺术业	Cultures and Arts	35784	35537	100.7
体育	Sports Activities	17777	20601	86.3
公共管理、社会保障和社会组织	Public Management, Social Security and Social Organizations	466540	447747	104.2
国际组织	International Organizations			

3-17 城镇单位在岗职工工资总额
TOTAL WAGES OF FULLY EMPLOYED STAFF AND WORKERS IN URBAN ENTITIES

单位：亿元 (100 million yuan)

项 目	Item	2019	2018	2019年为2018年% 2019 as % of 2018
合 计	**Total**	**12627.3**	**11562.8**	**109.2**
按登记注册类型分	**By Registration Type**			
内 资	Domestically-invested Enterprises	9934.5	9146.8	108.6
国 有	State-owned Enterprises	3166.3	2812.6	112.6
集 体	Collectively-owned Enterprises	97.3	84.2	115.6
股份合作	Joint-equity Cooperative Enterprises	22.6	20.0	112.9
联 营	Associated Enterprises	2.5	3.2	79.3
有限责任公司	Limited Liability Companies	4376.0	4050.3	108.0
股份有限公司	Companies Limited By Shares	2139.3	2015.5	106.1
其 他	Others	130.5	161.0	81.0
港、澳、台商投资	Hong Kong, Macao and Taiwan-invested Enterprises	1278.1	1084.1	117.9
外商投资	Foreign-invested Enterprises	1414.7	1331.9	106.2
按国民经济行业分	**By Sector**			
农、林、牧、渔业	Agriculture, Forestry, Animal Production and Hunting, Fishing	3.3	16.2	20.6
#农 业	Agriculture	0.3	6.4	5.5
采矿业	Mining and Quarrying	43.1	46.9	91.8
制造业	Manufacturing	896.6	907.0	98.9
电力、热力、燃气及水生产和供应业	Production and Distribution of Electricity, Heating Power, Gas and Water	165.2	150.4	109.9
建筑业	Construction	555.7	530.6	104.7
批发和零售业	Wholesale and Retail Trade	881.6	891.8	98.8
批发业	Wholesale	669.6	634.3	105.6
零售业	Retail Trade	212.0	257.5	82.3
交通运输、仓储和邮政业	Transport, Storage and Post	728.2	678.7	107.3
#铁路运输业	Transport via Railway	138.3	129.6	106.7
道路运输业	Transport via Road	234.7	254.6	92.2
邮政业	Post	129.6	78.4	165.4
住宿和餐饮业	Accommodation and Restaurants	165.0	161.2	102.4
住宿业	Accommodation	76.1	78.9	96.4
餐饮业	Restaurants	88.9	82.2	108.2
信息传输、软件和信息技术服务业	Information Transmission, Software and Information Technology Services	1983.9	1695.6	117.0
金融业	Finance	1417.3	1310.5	108.1
房地产业	Real Estate	493.2	459.9	107.2
租赁和商务服务业	Renting and Leasing Activities and Business Services	1030.2	1002.0	102.8
租赁业	Renting and Leasing Activities	21.7	32.6	66.5
商务服务业	Business Services	1008.5	969.4	104.0
科学研究和技术服务业	Scientific Research and Development, Technical Services	1299.2	1173.4	110.7
水利、环境和公共设施管理业	Management of Water Conservancy, Environment and Public Facilities	132.2	112.1	118.0
居民服务、修理和其他服务业	Resident Services, Repair and Other Services	54.7	60.1	91.1
#居民服务业	Resident Services	18.3	25.2	72.6
教 育	Education	977.6	848.5	115.2
卫生和社会工作	Health Care and Social Works	648.3	548.7	118.2
#卫 生	Health Care	630.4	532.9	118.3
文化、体育和娱乐业	Culture, Sports and Entertainment	369.1	314.2	117.5
#文化艺术业	Cultures and Arts	59.5	50.3	118.2
体 育	Sports Activities	29.5	27.7	106.5
公共管理、社会保障和社会组织	Public Management, Social Security and Social Organizations	782.9	655.3	119.5
国际组织	International Organizations			

3-18 城镇单位在岗职工平均工资
AVERAGE WAGES OF FULLY EMPLOYED STAFF AND WORKERS IN URBAN ENTITIES

单位：元 (yuan)

项　　目	Item	2019	2018	2019年为2018年% 2019 as % of 2018
合　计	**Total**	**173205**	**149843**	**115.6**
按登记注册类型分	**By Registration Type**			
内　资	Domestically-invested Enterprises	165438	142659	116.0
国　有	State-owned Enterprises	195783	166977	117.3
集　体	Collectively-owed Enterprises	69344	66776	103.8
股份合作	Joint-equity Cooperative Enterprises	64025	57949	110.5
联　营	Associated Enterprises	97854	79447	123.2
有限责任公司	Limited Liability Companies	143096	125954	113.6
股份有限公司	Companies Limited By Shares	211895	175237	120.9
其　他	Others	91952	81817	112.4
港、澳、台商投资	Hong Kong, Macao and Taiwan-invested Enterprises	204413	177391	115.2
外商投资	Foreign-invested Enterprises	214298	191968	111.6
按国民经济行业分	**By Sector**			
农、林、牧、渔业	Agriculture, Forestry, Animal Production and Hunting, Fishing	95092	60261	157.8
#农　业	Agriculture	191591	50388	380.2
采矿业	Mining and Quarrying	135064	124024	108.9
制造业	Manufacturing	137616	120552	114.2
电力、热力、燃气及水生产和供应业	Production and Distribution of Electricity, Heating Power, Gas and Water	178623	162149	110.2
建筑业	Construction	129804	116589	111.3
批发和零售业	Wholesale and Retail Trade	152524	126147	120.9
批发业	Wholesale	191182	161398	118.5
零售业	Retail Trade	93071	82025	113.5
交通运输、仓储和邮政业	Transport, Storage and Post	123491	108011	114.3
#铁路运输业	Transport via Railway	133299	125137	106.5
道路运输业	Transport via Road	88584	79463	111.5
邮政业	Post	131937	102848	128.3
住宿和餐饮业	Accommodation and Restaurants	74013	67824	109.1
住宿业	Accommodation	81939	75755	108.2
餐饮业	Restaurants	68357	61630	110.9
信息传输、软件和信息技术服务业	Information Transmission, Software and Information Technology Service	236143	207285	113.9
金融业	Finance	347994	329709	105.5
房地产业	Real Estate	112875	103869	108.7
租赁和商务服务业	Renting and Leasing Activities and Business Services	145471	123866	117.4
租赁业	Renting and Leasing Activities	135452	87136	155.4
商务服务业	Business Services	145703	125646	116.0
科学研究和技术服务业	Scientific Research and Development, Technical Services	200622	174532	114.9
水利、环境和公共设施管理业	Management of Water Conservancy, Environment and Public Facilities	110917	97113	114.2
居民服务、修理和其他服务业	Resident Services, Repair and Other Services	82528	57830	142.7
#居民服务业	Resident Services	84907	54625	155.4
教　育	Education	187328	166310	112.6
卫生和社会工作	Health Care and Social Works	214997	192354	111.8
#卫　生	Health Care	224717	199473	112.7
文化、体育和娱乐业	Culture, Sports and Entertainment	207737	174827	118.8
#文化艺术业	Cultures and Arts	166796	141866	117.6
体　育	Sports Activities	166115	134938	123.1
公共管理、社会保障和社会组织	Pulic Management,Social Security and Social Organizations	168150	147277	114.2
国际组织	International Organizations			

3−19 国民经济各行业城镇单位在岗职工平均工资(2019年)
AVERAGE WAGES OF URBAN ENTITIES FULLY EMPLOYED STAFF AND WORKERS IN DIFFERENT SECTORS OF NATIONAL ECONOMY (2019)

单位：元 (yuan)

项　目	Item	平均工资 Average Wages	国有单位 State-owned	集体单位 Collectively-Owned	其他单位 Others
合　计	**Total**	**173205**	**195783**	**69344**	**169239**
农、林、牧、渔业	**Agriculture, Forestry, Animal Production and Hunting, Fishing**	**95092**	**125700**	**55877**	**95974**
#农、林、牧、渔服务业	Service Activities for Agriculture, Forestry, Animal Production and Hunting, Fishing	72495	125700	83739	46653
采矿业	**Mining and Quarrying**	**135064**		**43900**	**135122**
煤炭开采和洗选业	Mining and Washing of Coal	87263		24000	90778
石油和天然气开采业	Extraction of Petroleum and Natural Gas	220438			220438
黑色金属矿采选业	Mining and Processing of Ferrous Metal Ores	121145			121145
有色金属矿采选业	Mining and Processing of Non-Ferrous Metal Ores				
非金属矿采选业	Mining and Processing of Nonmetal Ores	44947		44947	
开采专业及辅助性活动	Mining and Support Service Activities	139331			139331
其他采矿业	Mining of Other Ores	101273			101273
制造业	**Manufacturing**	**137616**	**179018**	**60933**	**137798**
农副食品加工业	Processing of Food from Agricultural Products	88132	85667	41837	88434
食品制造业	Manufacture of Foods	108886		47568	109069
酒、饮料和精制茶制造业	Manufacture of Wine, Beverage and Refined Tea	89646	23609	45611	90092
烟草制品业	Manufacture of Cigarettes and Tobacco	284781	284781		
纺织业	Manufacture of Textile	80068	34000	31113	81713
纺织服装、服饰业	Manufacture of Textile, Wearing Apparel and Ornament	68910	86364	58304	69390
皮革、毛皮、羽毛及其制品和制鞋业	Manufacture of Leather, Fur, Feather and Its Products, and Footwear	50136		60188	48512
木材加工和木、竹、藤、棕、草制品业	Processing of Timbers, Manufacture of Wood, Bamboo, Rattan, Palm and Straw Products	58783		43292	65650
家具制造业	Manufacture of Furniture	80589		36000	80689
造纸和纸制品业	Manufacture of Paper and Paper Products	89057		48420	96155
印刷和记录媒介复制业	Printing, Reproduction of Recording Media	114935	139934	84474	114141
文教、工美、体育和娱乐用品制造业	Manufacture of Articles for Culture, Education, Artwork, Sport and Entertainment Activities	85861	58050	44181	87507
石油、煤炭及其他燃料加工业	Processing of Petroleum, Coal and Other Fuels	163904			163904
化学原料和化学制品制造业	Manufacture of Chemical Raw Materials and Chemical Products	117882	98095	61904	118926
医药制造业	Manufacture of Medicines	175421	207488	64856	175278
化学纤维制造业	Manufacture of Chemical Fibers	77992			77992
橡胶和塑料制品业	Manufacture of Rubber and Plastics Products	83820	137226	48057	84679
非金属矿物制品业	Manufacture of Non-metallic Mineral Products	100185	92667	60869	101718
黑色金属冶炼和压延加工业	Manufacture and Pressing of Ferrous Metals	97024		57200	97810

3-19 续表 1 Continued 1

单位：元 (yuan)

行业	Sector	平均工资 Average Wages	国有单位 State-owned	集体单位 Collectively-Owned	其他单位 Others
有色金属冶炼和压延加工业	Manufacture and Pressing of Nonferrous Metals	116088	160013	51444	115295
金属制品业	Manufacture of Fabricated Metal Products	111519	72122	55827	115073
通用设备制造业	Manufacture of General-Purpose Machinery	131612	48831	55677	134129
专用设备制造业	Manufacture of Special-Purpose Machinery	136968	113443	71619	138021
汽车制造业	Manufacture of Motor Vehicles	140975	61500	46639	141329
铁路、船舶、航空航天和其他运输设备制造业	Manufacture of Railway Locomotives, Building of Ships and Boats, Manufacture of Air and Spacecrafts and Other Transportation Equipment	180016	198202	65934	173166
电气机械和器材制造业	Manufacture of Electrical Machinery and Equipment	150017	76514	59147	151437
计算机、通信和其他电子设备制造业	Manufacture of Computers, Communication Equipment and Other Electronic Equipment	162064	151525	59606	162229
仪器仪表制造业	Manufacture of Measuring Instruments and Meters	150827	110621	86349	151754
其他制造业	Other Manufacturing	166938	123241	40500	168092
废弃资源综合利用业	Waste Rrecycling and Recovery	95531		38797	102572
金属制品、机械和设备修理业	Repair of Fabricated Metal Products, Machinery and Equipment	177481	45000	39318	178226
电力、热力、燃气及水生产和供应业	**Production and Distribution of Electricity, Heating Power, Gas and Water**	**178623**	**223038**	**70804**	**174204**
电力、热力生产和供应业	Production and Distribution of Electricity and Heating Power	191052	224697	71711	186276
燃气生产和供应业	Production and Distribution of Gas	171803	60000	36000	171856
水的生产和供应业	Production and Distribution of Water	125529	82212	69446	126509
建筑业	**Construction**	**129804**	**125192**	**72098**	**130587**
房屋建筑业	Construction of Buildings	141891	110830	81152	143382
土木工程建筑业	Civil Engineering Construction	140766	140472	48184	141205
建筑安装业	Construction Installation	109904	76743	52393	110510
建筑装饰、装修和其他建筑业	Building Decoration, Finishing and Other Construction	85483	120580	50979	85447
批发和零售业	**Wholesale and Retail Trade**	**152524**	**162830**	**69156**	**153181**
批发业	Wholesale	191182	227474	79075	191242
零售业	Retail Trade	93071	112218	63716	92915
交通运输、仓储和邮政业	**Transport, Storage and Post**	**123491**	**122670**	**34972**	**124157**
铁路运输业	Transport via Railway	133299			133299
道路运输业	Transport via Road	88584	72123	30305	89516
水上运输业	Water Transport	198511			198511
航空运输业	Air Transport	213355	219985	97633	213439
管道运输业	Transport via Pipeline	208791			208791
多式联运和运输代理业	Multimodal Transport and Transport Agent Service	136426	111859	37932	136638
装卸搬运和仓储业	Loading, Unloading, Portage and Storage	105195	100420	72360	106251
邮政业	Post	131937	128387		132654
住宿和餐饮业	**Accommodation and Restaurants**	**74013**	**83097**	**68866**	**73110**
住宿业	Accommodation	81939	83933	75195	81764
餐饮业	Restaurants	68357	76740	52577	68383
信息传输、软件和信息技术服务业	**Information Transmission, Software and Information Technology Services**	**236143**	**217125**	**64757**	**236644**
电信、广播电视和卫星传输服务	Telecommunications, Broadcasting, Television and Satellite Transmission Services	272001	240661	80464	273075
互联网和相关服务	Internet and Related Services	255218	192717	58556	256431
软件和信息技术服务业	Software and Information Technology Services	226426	219861	61970	226722

3-19 续表 2 Continued 2

单位：元 (yuan)

行业	Sector	平均工资 Average Wages	国有单位 State-owned	集体单位 Collectively-Owned	其他单位 Others
金融业	**Finance**	**347994**	**306346**	**107357**	**349147**
货币金融服务	Monetary Financial Services	361465	299326		363917
资本市场服务	Capital Market Services	362801	251251		365887
保险业	Insurance	268925	376588	20000	268658
其他金融业	Other Financial Services	427227	555819	110593	425372
房地产业	**Real Estate**	**112875**	**124987**	**70606**	**114545**
租赁和商务服务业	**Renting and Leasing Activities and Business Services**	**145471**	**90980**	**40797**	**169884**
租赁业	Renting and Leasing Activities	135452	92015	59620	139850
商务服务业	Business Services	145703	90978	40507	170778
科学研究和技术服务业	**Scientific Research and Development, Technical Services**	**200622**	**233088**	**147835**	**187788**
研究和试验发展	Research and Experimental Development	231127	239203	218564	210969
专业技术服务业	Professional Technique Services	187463	220912	120520	182991
科技推广和应用服务业	Technique Generalization and Application Services	190145	214321	79236	187998
水利、环境和公共设施管理业	**Management of Water Conservancy, Environment and Public Facilities**	**110917**	**124105**	**57921**	**100319**
水利管理业	Management of Water Conservancy	170287	176962	101292	146081
生态保护和环境治理业	Ecological Protection and Environmental Control	153335	184549	52140	147254
公共设施管理业	Management of Public Facilities	97428	113278	54084	82015
土地管理业	Management of Land	265390	193227	29000	281995
居民服务、修理和其他服务业	**Resident Services, Repair and Other Services**	**82528**	**80741**	**49230**	**86290**
居民服务业	Resident Services	84907	88528	51171	89480
机动车、电子产品和日用产品修理业	Repair of Motor Vehicles, Electronics and Household Appliances	129413	102301	51686	138495
其他服务业	Other Services	55876	54304	44521	56782
教 育	**Education**	**187328**	**223166**	**115390**	**112639**
卫生和社会工作	**Health Care and Social Works**	**214997**	**246519**	**126968**	**112700**
卫 生	Health Care	224717	250328	141119	124455
社会工作	Social Works	84994	126479	65123	63773
文化、体育和娱乐业	**Culture, Sports and Entertainment**	**207737**	**240213**	**77230**	**176445**
新闻和出版业	Journalism and Publishing	213332	212942	112946	215040
广播、电视、电影和录音制作业	Radio Broadcasting, Television, Movies and Sound Recording	268226	387647	73813	165616
文化艺术业	Culture and Arts	166796	176921	91136	144766
体 育	Sports Activities	166115	164816	41099	169737
娱乐业	Entertainment	145112	155964	63591	146627
公共管理、社会保障和社会组织	**Public Management, Social Security and Social Organizations**	**168150**	**177571**	**139298**	**74345**
中国共产党机关	Organs of Communist Party of China	187642	187642		
国家机构	Organs of State	177894	178046	144778	149259
人民政协、民主党派	Peole's Political Consultative Conference and Democratic Parties	201860	201860		
社会保障	Social Security	174699	189154		54500
群众团体、社会团体和其他成员组织	Mass Communities, Social Organizations and Other Membership Organizations	162943	174388	138163	150593
基层群众自治组织	Grass Roots Self-Government Organization	31821	34549		31585
国际组织	**International Organizations**				

3–20 城镇登记失业率和城镇新增就业人数(1979–2019年)
REGISTERED UNEMPLOYED RATE IN URBAN AREA AND NEWLY EMPLOYED PERSONS IN URBAN AREA (1979-2019)

单位：万人 (10000 persons)

年 份 Year	年末实有登记失业人员 Year-end Number of Actual Registed Unemployed Persons	城镇登记失业率(%) Registered Unemployment Rate in Urban Area	城镇新增就业人数 Newly Employed Persons in Urban Area
1979	4.96	1.60	
1980	8.67	1.60	
1981	8.36	1.28	
1982	7.03	1.62	
1983	4.20	1.09	
1984	2.03	0.54	
1985	1.61	0.40	
1986	1.25	0.30	
1987	2.24	0.45	
1988	1.58	0.40	
1989	1.71	0.40	
1990	1.67	0.30	
1991	1.92	0.40	
1992	1.72	0.36	
1993	1.92	0.41	
1994	1.91	0.41	
1995	2.19	0.46	
1996	2.80	0.58	
1997	3.29	0.73	
1998	2.95	0.66	
1999	2.80	0.62	
2000	3.32	0.76	
2001	5.19	1.18	
2002	6.02	1.35	
2003	6.96	1.43	
2004	6.46	1.30	
2005	10.57	2.11	31.50
2006	10.40	1.98	34.39
2007	10.63	1.84	40.71
2008	10.33	1.82	41.97
2009	8.16	1.44	42.44
2010	7.73	1.37	44.64
2011	7.89	1.39	44.69
2012	7.20	1.27	43.89
2013	6.81	1.21	42.87
2014	8.77	1.31	42.65
2015	9.16	1.39	42.62
2016	9.14	1.41	42.80
2017	9.22	1.43	42.20
2018	10.24	1.40	42.30
2019	9.35	1.30	35.10

注：2014年开始年末实有登记失业人员指标统计口径为全市口径，2014年以前为城镇口径。
资料来源：北京市人力资源和社会保障局。
Note: Since 2014, the year-end number of actual registered unemployed persons refers to the statistic of the whole city;while the number before 2014 refers to the statistic in urban and rural areas.
Source: Beijing Municipal Bureau of Human Resource and Social Security.

主要统计指标解释

户籍人口 指公民依照《中华人民共和国户口登记条例》已在其经常居住地的公安户籍管理机关登记了常住户口的人。

常住人口 指在某地区实际居住半年以上的人口。

常住外来人口 指不具有本市户籍户口，来自北京市行政区划以外的省、自治区、直辖市，且在京居住半年以上的人口。

出生率 指在一定时期内（通常为一年）出生人数与同期平均人数(或期中人数)之比，一般用千分比表示。计算公式：

$$出生率=\frac{年出生人数}{年平均人数}\times 1000‰$$

出生人数是指活产，即脱离母体时（不管怀孕月数），有过呼吸或其他生命现象的活婴儿总和。年平均人数是年初、年末人口数的平均数，也可用年中人口数代替。

死亡率 指在一定时期内（通常为一年）死亡人数与同期平均人数（或期中人数）之比，一般用千分比表示。计算公式：

$$死亡率=\frac{年死亡人数}{年平均人数}\times 1000‰$$

自然增长率 指在一定时期内（通常为一年）人口自然增加数（出生人数减死亡人数）与该时期内平均人数（或期中人数）之比，一般用千分比表示。计算公式：

$$自然增长率=\frac{年出生人数-年死亡人数}{年平均人数}\times 1000‰$$

人口自然增长率=人口出生率－人口死亡率

从业人员 指在各级国家机关、党政机关、社会团体及企业、事业单位中工作，取得工资或其他形式的劳动酬的全部人员。包括：在岗职工、聘用的离退休人员以及在单位中工作的港澳台及外籍人员、兼职人员、借用的外单位人员和第二职业者。不包括本单位的不在岗职工。

在岗职工 指在本单位工作并由单位支付工资的人员，以及有工作岗位，但由于学习、病伤产假（六个月以内）等原因暂未工作，仍由单位支付工资的人员。

在岗职工工资总额 与在岗职工指标相对应，根据1990年1月1日的国家统计局令（一号）修订，指单位在报告期内直接支付给本单位在岗职工的劳动报酬总额。包括基础工资、职务工资、级别工资、工龄工资、计件工资、奖金、各种津贴和补贴、交通补贴、洗理费、书报费、旅游费、过节费、伙食补助、住房补贴、住房提租补贴、由单位从个人工资中直接为其代扣或代缴的个人所得税、房水电费以及住房公积金和社会保险基金个人缴纳部分等。

在岗职工平均工资 指企业、事业、机关等单位的在岗职工在一定时期内的人均劳动报酬。它表明一定时期在岗职工工资收入的高低程度，是反映在岗职工工资水平的主要指标。计算公式为：

$$在岗职工平均工资=\frac{报告期实际支付的全部在岗职工工资总额}{报告期全部在岗职工平均人数}$$

从业人员平均工资 指企业、事业、机关等单位的从业人员在一定时期内的人均劳动报酬。计算公式为：

$$从业人员平均工资=\frac{报告期实际支付的全部从业人员劳动报酬总额}{报告期全部从业人员平均人数}$$

期末实有登记失业人员 指报告期末实有的登记失业人员总数，包括城镇登记失业人员和城市化建设地区的登记失业农民（失地农民）。

城镇登记失业率 指城镇登记失业人数与城镇从业人数和城镇登记失业人数二者之和的比。计算公式如下：

$$城镇登记失业率=\frac{年末实有登记失业人数}{城镇从业人数+年末实有登记失业人数}\times 100\%$$

Explanatory Notes on Main Statistical Indicators

Registered Population refers to persons who have registered their permanent residence with the public security register authority of their habitual residence according to the *Households Registration Regulations of PRC*.

Permanent Population refers to persons actually living for more than half a year at a place.

Permanent Migrant Population refers to persons who have no permanent residence registration in Beijing, come from other provinces, autonomous regions and municipalities, and have stayed in Beijing for more than half a year.

Birth Rate refers to the ratio of the number of births to the average population (or mid-period population) during a certain period of time (usually a year), which is often expressed in ‰. The following formula is used:

Birth Rate = Annual Number of Births/Annual Average Number of Population×1,000‰

Number of births refers to live births, i.e. the births when babies has breathed or shown any vital phenomena regardless of the length of pregnancy. Annual average number of population is the average of the number of population at the beginning of the year and that at the end of the year. Sometimes it is substituted with the mid-year population.

Death Rate refers to the ratio of the number of deaths to the average population (or mid-period population) during a certain period of time (usually a year), which is often expressed in ‰. The following formula is used:

Death Rate= Annual Number of Deaths/Annual Average Number of Population×1,000‰

Natural Growth Rate refers to the ratio of the natural growth of population (births minus deaths) to the average population (or mid-period population) during a certain period of time (usually a year), which is often expressed in ‰. The following formula is used:

Natural Growth Rate of Population = (Annual Number of Births - Annual Number of Deaths)/Annual Average Number of Population×1,000‰

Natural Growth Rate of Population = Birth Rate - Death Rate

Employed Persons refer to all persons working in government agencies, Party and political organs, social groups, enterprises and public institutions at all levels, and receiving wages or labor remuneration in other forms. They include: fully employed staff and workers, retired persons employed, persons from Hong Kong, Macao, Taiwan and foreign countries who are employed, part-time employees, employees transferred from other entities, and employees with a second job. They exclude employees that are not on the job in the entity.

Fully Employed Staff and Workers refer to persons working in the entity and paid by the entity, as well as persons having a job in the entity, but not working temporarily due to study, illness, injury or maternity leaves (less than 6 months) and other reasons, and still paid by the entity.

Total Wages of Fully Employed Staff and Workers correspond to the indicator of Fully Employed Staff and Workers. The indicator was revised in accordance with No. 1 Decree of the National Bureau of Statistics dated January 1, 1990, referring to the total wages directly paid by an entity to fully employed staff and workers of the entity during the reporting period. It consists of basic wage, post wage, wage of a rank, seniority wage, piece rate wage, bonus, allowances and subsidies, traffic subsidy, washing and haircutting allowance, books and newspaper allowance, travel benefit, festival bonus, food subsidy, housing subsidy, subsidy for incremental house rent, as well as personal income tax, water and electricity fees and the personally payable portion of housing accumulation fund and social security fund withheld directly by the employer from the employee's wage.

Average Wage of Fully Employed Staff and Workers refers to the per-capita labor remuneration of fully employed staff and workers in enterprises, public institutions and government agencies within a given period of time. It shows the level of wage income of fully employed staff and workers within a given period of time, serving as a main indicator reflecting the level of wage of fully employed staff and workers. The following formula is used:

Average Wage of Fully Employed Staff and Workers = Total Wages of All Fully Employed Staff and Workers Actually Paid in the Reporting Period / Average Number of All Fully Employed Staff and Workers in the Reporting Period

Average Wage of Employed Persons refers to the per-capita labor remuneration of employed persons in enterprises, public institutions and government agencies within a given period of time. The following formula is used:

Average Wage of Employed Persons = Total Labor Remuneration of All Employed Persons Actually Paid in the Reporting Period / Average Number of All Employed Persons in the Reporting Period

Period-end Actual Registered Unemployed Persons refer to the total number of actual unemployed persons registered at the end period, including unemployed persons registered in urban regions and the unemployed peasants registered in urbanization regions (land-lost peasants).

Registered Unemployment Rate in Urban Area refers to the ratio of urban registered unemployed persons to the sum of urban employed persons and urban registered unemployed persons. The following formula is used:

Registered Unemployment Rate in Urban Area
=Number of Actual Registered Unemployed Persons at Year-end / (Urban Employed Persons + Number of Actual Registered Unemployed Persons at Year-end) × 100%

04

价格指数
PRICE INDEX

简要说明

一、主要内容

本章价格指数资料，反映生产、流通、消费与投资的价格变动趋势和变动幅度。主要包括居民消费价格指数；商品零售价格指数；农产品生产者价格指数；工业生产者出厂价格指数；工业生产者购进价格指数；固定资产投资价格指数；住宅销售价格指数。

二、调查方法

（一）居民消费价格指数和商品零售价格指数

编制居民消费价格指数、商品零售价格指数的资料采用抽样调查和重点调查相结合的方法取得，即在全市选择不同的区域，按照布局合理的原则抽选价格调查点，由国家确定调查商品和服务项目，在此基础上按照消费量大、价格变动趋势有较强代表性的原则选择调查样本，对其市场价格进行定期调查，以样本推算总体。

抽选价格调查点。按照布局合理等原则，将不同区域各种类型的商场、农贸市场、服务网点分别按销售额、成交额和经营规模为标志，从高到低排队，依据所需调查点的数量进行等距抽样。

选择代表规格品。代表商品和服务项目由国家确定，代表规格品由各省市按照有关原则选择。选择原则：（1）消费量较大；（2）价格变动趋势和变动程度有较强的代表性，即选中规格品的价格变动特征与未选中规格品之间价格变动的相关性愈高愈好；（3）选中的规格品之间，性质相隔愈远愈好，价格变动特征的相关性愈低愈好；选中的工业消费品必须是合格产品，产品包装上有注册商标、产地、规格等级等标识。

目前，居民消费价格调查按用途划分为 8 个大类，262 个基本分类，国家规定大城市调查规格品数量应在 600 种左右，北京市由于编制分收入层居民消费价格指数，代表规格品数量增加到 1779 种。商品零售价格指数划分为 16 个大类，197 个基本分类，北京市代表规格品数量为 1267 种。

价格资料的采集。采取定人、定点、定时直接调查的方法采集价格资料。

权数资料来源与计算。居民消费价格指数的权数根据城市居民家庭生活消费支出调查资料整理计算。商品零售价格指数的权数根据商业统计中社会消费品零售总额计算。

按照国家统计局统一要求，自 2016 年 1 月起，北京流通消费价格统计专业执行新的《流通和消费价格统计报表制度》，其中居民消费价格和商品零售价格调查项目目录均重新进行了修订调整。

（二）工业生产者出厂价格指数和工业生产者购进价格指数

工业生产者出厂价格是工业品第一次出售时的出厂价格。该项调查采用重点调查与典型调查相结合的调查方法。重点调查对象为选中的全年主营业务收入 2000 万元及以上的工业法人样本单位及部分生产特定产品的全年主营业务收入 2000 万元以下的工业法人样本单位。

工业生产者购进价格是工业企业作为中间投入的价格。调查对象从填报工业生产者出厂价格的企业中选择。

选择代表企业的原则：（1）按工业行业选择调查企业，各中类行业原则上都要有调查企业；（2）大型（或占相当大比重）企业应尽量都选作调查企业；（3）选择生产正常、稳定的企业作为调查对象。

选择代表产品的原则：（1）按工业行业选择代表产品；（2）选择对国计民生影响大的产品；（3）选择生产较为稳定的产品；（4）选择有发展前景的产品；（5）选择具有地方特色的产品。

权数的确定。编制工业生产者出厂价格小类及以上的权数资料来源于工业统计中分行业工业销售产值数据资料；基本分类的权数资料来源于独立的工业企业产品权数调查。购进价格权数资料主要来源于独立的工业企业产品权数调查，中类及以上的权数还要参考分行业的投入产出数据资料和相应行业的出厂权数资料。权数五年更换一次。

根据国家统计制度要求，2016 年开始使用 2015 年作为新一轮的对比基期，同时在按行业分组的工业生产者出厂价格指数中新增加开采辅助活动行业。

（三）固定资产投资价格指数

固定资产投资价格调查采用重点调查、典型调查和非传统数据替代相结合的方法。固定资产投资价格调查所涉及的价格是构成固定资产投资额实体的实际购进价格（或结算价格）。调查的内容包括构成当年建筑工程实体的钢材、木材、水泥、地方建筑材料、电料、化工材料等主要建筑材料价格，投入的劳动力价格（单位工资）和各种施工机械使用费用；设备工器具购置和其他费用投资价格。

选择建筑安装工程调查点的原则：（1）样本单位应具有一定覆盖面；（2）投资经济活动代表性强；（3）兼顾不同经济类型；（4）选择重点工程；（5）兼顾不同工程类别。

选择其他费用调查点的原则：在选择其他费用调查点时，所遵循的原则与建筑安装工程调查点的原则基本相同，特别是要注意选择那些投资额大的工程。但由于其他费用不易取得，所以在实际操作过程中，应同时在建设单位、施工单位开展重点调查，并辅以典型调查（从有关管理部门取得资料）。

权数的确定。固定资产投资价格指数的计算权数是建筑安装工程、设备工器具购置和其他费用三者前三年投资完成额的平均比重。

（四）住宅销售价格指数是反映住宅销售价格总水平变动趋势和程度的相对数。包括新建商品住宅销售价格指数和二手住宅销售价格指数。

新建商品住宅销售价格的调查方法：新建商品住宅销售面积、金额等资料直接采用当地房地产管理部门的网签数据。新建商品住宅的网签数据内容主要包括：住宅项目（楼盘）名称、项目地址、幢号、总层数、所在层数、房屋结构、建筑面积、成交总价（合同金额）、签约时间等。

二手住宅销售价格的调查方法：二手住宅销售价格调查为非全面调查，采用重点调查与典型调查相结合的方法，按照房地产经纪机构上报的方式收集基础数据。

（五）农产品生产者价格指数

农产品生产者价格调查采取抽样调查和重点调查相结合的调查方法。抽取 360 个农产品生产和出售的农业生产经营单位及行政村作为调查对象。对一些区域性比较强的农产品采取在主产区主观选样的方法选择农业生产经营单位及行政村作为调查对象。

由于北京市林业产品（树苗）产值比重较少，不足 1%，根据国家统计局统计制度要求，不需要进行林业产品生产者价格调查。

Brief Introduction

I. Main Content

Price indexes in this chapter reflect the trend and rate of changes in prices of production, circulation, consumption and investment, mainly consisting of consumer price index (CPI), retail price index (RPI), producer price index for farm products, producer price index for industrial products (PPI); purchasing price index for industrial products; price index for investment in fixed assets; and selling price index for residential houses.

II. Survey Methods

1. Consumer Price Index (CPI) and Retail Price Index (RPI)

Data for compilation of the consumer price index and retail price index are collected through a combination of sample surveys and surveys of key units. Different areas are selected across the city, and price survey sites are selected in accordance with the principle of reasonable layout. Commodity and service items for survey are determined by the country. On this basis, survey samples are selected according to the principle of large quantity of consumption, and strong representativeness in price change trend. Regular surveys are conducted to collect data on their market prices. General indexes are inferred on the basis of the sample data.

The selection of price survey sites: By adopting the principle of reasonable layout, an equidistant sampling is conducted for department stores, agricultural product trade markets and service outlets in different types and in different areas by their sales value, transaction value and operational scale, which will be ranked in a descending order based on the number of survey sites required.

The selection of representative specifications: Representative commodities and service items are determined by the country. Representative specifications are selected by provinces and cities according to relevant principles. Principles for selection: (1) large quantity of consumption; (2) strongly representative trend and extent of price changes, which means the characteristics of price changes of selected specifications shall be highly correlated with price changes of those that are not selected; (3) selected specifications shall be different in their nature and least correlated in the characteristics of price changes between each other; the selected industrial consumer goods must be qualified products, with registered trademark, origin, specifications, grade and other marks on the their package.

At present, data are collected under 262 basic headings in 8 categories in the consumer price surveys according to their specific purposes. The quantity of specifications for survey in big cities should be about 600 according to state regulations. In Beijing, due to the development of CPI by income class, the quantity of representative specifications has increased to 1779. Retail price index consists of 197 basic headings in 16 categories. The quantity of representative specifications in Beijing is1267.

Collection of price data: Price data are collected through direct surveys by designated personnel at designated sites on periodic basis.

Source and calculation of the weights: CPI weights are calculated according to survey information on living expenditures of urban residents. RPI weights are calculated according to the total retail sales of consumer goods in business statistics.

According to the uniform requirement of the National Bureau of Statistics, since January 2016, the new *Circulation and Consumption Price Statistical Reporting System* has been implemented for statistics of circulation and consumption price in Beijing, of which the survey catalogues of consumer prices of household and retail prices of commodities have been revised and adjusted.

2. Producer Price Index for Industrial Products (PPI) and Purchasing Price Index for Industrial Products

The producer price for industrial products refers to the producer's price of industrial products when sold for the first time. The survey program is a combination of the key units' survey and typical units' survey methods. Key units refer to the chosen sample units of industrial enterprises with annual main business income at and above RMB 20 million and part of the sample units of industrial enterprises that make specific products and with annual main business income below RMB 20 million.

Purchasing price for industrial products refers to the price of intermediate inputs of industrial enterprise. Enterprises for survey are selected among those that have submitted the producer price for industrial products.

Principles for selecting the representative enterprises: (1) enterprises to be covered in the survey are selected by industrial sectors. In principle, every branch should have enterprises selected; (2) Large-sized enterprises (or enterprises accounting for large proportion) should be selected; (3) Enterprises selected should be those with normal and stable production.

Principles for selecting representative products: (1) representative products shall be selected by industrial sectors; (2) the selected products should have significant impact on the national economy and people's livelihood; (3) the production of the goods selected should be relatively more stable; (4) the prospects of the goods selected should be promising; (5) the products selected should be representative to the localities.

Determination of weights: Materials of weights used for compiling producer price index for industrial products (PPI) of small class and above come from data of industrial sales value collected by sectors in industrial statistics. Materials of weights in basic classification come from independent survey on industrial enterprise product weights. Materials of purchase price weights mainly come from independent survey on industrial enterprise product weights. Weights of medium class and above shall also take reference to input and output data collected by sectors and materials of factory weights in relevant sectors. The weights are changed every five years.

According to the requirements of the national statistical system, since 2016, 2015 shall be taken as a new round of comparison base period; in addition, the new sector of mining support service activities shall be added in the producer price index for industrial products grouped by sectors.

3. Price Index for Investment in Fixed Assets

A combined method of key survey, typical survey and nontraditional data substitution is used for the survey of data on prices of investment in fixed assets. The prices collected in the surveys on prices of investment in fixed assets are the actual purchasing prices (or settlement prices) of entities of investment in fixed assets. The survey covers the prices of main construction materials that constitute the architectural engineering entities in the year, such as steel, timber, cement, local construction materials, electric parts and chemical materials in construction projects; prices of labor input (wages) and costs of use of construction machines; purchasing price of equipment, tools and instruments as well as other expenditures.

Principles for selecting survey sites of construction and installation projects: (1) the sample unit shall have certain coverage; (2) the economic activity of investment should have strong representativeness; (3) different economic types should be considered; (4) key projects shall be selected; (5) attention should be given to various types of projects.

Principles for selecting survey sites of other expenditures: in the selection of survey sites of other expenditures, the same principles shall be followed as in the selection of survey sites of construction and installation projects. Especially projects with larger amount of investment shall be selected. Since it is not easy to obtain data on other expenditures, during the actual data gathering operations, survey on key builders and construction units is to be conducted concurrently with survey on typical units (with information from administration units).

Determination of weights: Weights used for calculating the fixed assets investment price index are determined according to the average proportion of investment amount of construction and installation projects, purchase of equipment, tools and instruments and other expenditures completed in the previous three years.

4. Selling Price Index for Residential Houses is a relative number reflecting the trend and extent of overall level of house selling prices. It includes selling price index for new commercial residential houses and second-hand houses.

Survey method of new commercial residential house selling price: For new commercial residential houses, area, amount and other data are taken directly from the online data recorded by local real estate authorities. Online data of new commercial residential house transaction mainly consist of the name of construction project, project location, building number, total number of floors, floor number, house structure, building area, total price of transaction (contractual amount), and date of contract signing, etc.

Survey method of second-hand house selling price: Survey of second-hand house selling price is incomplete survey conducted with the combined method of key survey and typical survey. Basic data are collected in accordance with the manner of reporting by real estate broker agencies.

5. Producer Price Index for Farm Products

A combined method of sample survey and key survey was used for the survey of producer prices of farm products. 360 entities and administrative villages producing and selling agricultural products are sampled. For some regional agricultural products, data on farm entities and administrative villages are collected with the method of subjective sampling in main production areas.

As the proportion of output value of forestry products (saplings) in Beijing is relatively small, taking no more than 1%, so no survey on producer price for forestry products is conducted according to statistical requirements of National Bureau of Statistics.

4−1 各种价格指数(1978−2019年)
PRICE INDEXES (1978-2019)

(上年=100) (preceding year=100)

年 份 Year	居民消费价格指数 Consumer Price Index	商品零售价格指数 Retail Price Index	农产品生产者价格指数 Producer Price Index for Farm Products	工业生产者出厂价格指数 Producer Price Index for Industrial Products (PPI)	工业生产者购进价格指数 Purchasing Price Index for Industrial Products	固定资产投资价格指数 Price Index for Investment in Fixed Assets
1978	100.6	100.6				
1979	101.8	101.8	109.5			
1980	106.0	106.7	105.5			
1981	101.3	101.4	109.4			
1982	101.8	102.0	101.9			
1983	100.5	100.6	101.8			
1984	102.2	102.1	102.3			
1985	117.6	118.6	117.6			
1986	106.8	106.7	108.1			
1987	108.6	108.7	116.1			
1988	120.4	121.9	123.2			
1989	117.2	118.5	106.8			
1990	105.4	104.1	101.9	107.9	114.8	
1991	111.9	108.5	101.7	105.8	111.7	107.3
1992	109.9	108.3	102.4	100.9	103.3	112.2
1993	119.0	116.9	107.0	121.8	133.2	126.6
1994	124.9	117.9	133.4	112.9	118.7	116.2
1995	117.3	112.6	130.6	107.3	106.7	113.9
1996	111.6	107.3	101.5	100.7	100.3	108.2
1997	105.3	103.8	92.8	101.1	103.4	102.7
1998	102.4	98.3	93.6	95.1	98.1	100.8
1999	100.6	98.8	97.5	97.7	95.8	99.9
2000	103.5	98.9	95.0	102.5	100.0	101.0
2001	103.1	98.8	102.0	99.4	100.5	100.6
2002	98.2	98.4	92.4	96.6	97.1	100.4
2003	100.2	98.2	102.5	101.5	104.7	102.2
2004	101.0	99.2	106.2	103.0	114.2	104.3
2005	101.5	99.7	102.9	101.3	111.4	100.7
2006	100.9	100.2	99.1	99.1	105.5	100.4
2007	102.4	100.8	114.4	99.7	105.0	102.8
2008	105.1	104.4	112.3	103.3	115.8	107.8
2009	98.5	97.8	98.3	94.4	88.6	97.1
2010	102.4	100.4	106.5	102.2	110.5	102.5
2011	105.6	103.2	110.7	102.3	108.4	105.7
2012	103.3	100.6	104.7	98.4	98.7	101.3
2013	103.3	99.8	104.7	97.4	97.8	99.9
2014	101.6	99.1	99.7	99.1	98.8	100.0
2015	101.8	98.5	99.8	96.9	93.7	97.6
2016	101.4	98.1	99.7	98.1	98.5	99.7
2017	101.9	99.2	96.2	100.7	104.4	104.7
2018	102.5	101.1	103.6	100.0	100.8	103.8
2019	102.3	100.5	109.9	99.6	99.6	102.1

注：1．从2011年开始工业品出厂价格指数更名为工业生产者出厂价格指数，原材料、燃料、动力购进价格指数更名为工业生产者购进价格指数，下同。

2．从2013年起，"农产品生产价格指数"更名为"农产品生产者价格指数"。

Note: a) From 2011 ,the Ex-factory Price Index for Manufactured Products has been renamed as Producer Price Index for Industrial Products (PPI), and the Purchasing Price Index for Raw Materials, Fuels and Power has been renamed as Purchasing Price Index for Industrial Products, the same below.

b) From 2013,the Producer Price Index For Agricultural Products has been renamed as Producer Price Index For Farm Products.

4–2 各种价格定基指数(1978–2019年)
FIXED-BASE PRICE INDEXES (1978-2019)

年 份 Year	居民消费价格指数 Consumer Price Index (1978=100)	商品零售价格指数 Retail Price Index (1978=100)	工业生产者出厂价格指数 Producer Price Index for Industrial Products (1990=100)	工业生产者购进价格指数 Purchasing Price Index for Industrial Products (1990=100)	固定资产投资价格指数 Price Index for Investment in Fixed Assets (1990=100)
1978	100.0	100.0			
1979	101.8	101.8			
1980	107.9	108.6			
1981	109.3	110.1			
1982	111.3	112.3			
1983	111.8	113.0			
1984	114.3	115.4			
1985	134.4	136.8			
1986	143.5	145.9			
1987	155.8	158.6			
1988	187.6	193.3			
1989	219.9	229.1			
1990	231.8	238.5	100.0	100.0	100.0
1991	259.4	258.8	105.8	111.7	107.3
1992	285.1	280.3	106.8	115.4	120.4
1993	339.3	327.7	130.0	153.7	152.4
1994	423.8	386.4	146.8	182.4	177.1
1995	497.1	435.1	157.5	194.7	201.7
1996	554.8	466.9	158.6	195.2	218.3
1997	584.2	484.6	160.4	201.9	224.2
1998	598.2	476.4	152.5	198.0	226.0
1999	601.8	470.7	149.0	189.7	225.7
2000	622.9	465.5	152.7	189.7	228.0
2001	642.2	459.9	151.8	190.7	229.4
2002	630.6	452.5	146.6	185.1	230.3
2003	631.9	444.4	148.8	193.8	235.3
2004	638.2	440.8	153.3	221.4	245.5
2005	647.8	439.5	155.3	246.6	247.2
2006	653.6	440.4	153.9	260.2	248.2
2007	669.3	443.9	153.5	273.3	255.1
2008	703.4	463.4	158.6	316.3	275.0
2009	692.8	453.2	149.8	280.3	266.9
2010	709.4	455.0	153.1	309.7	273.6
2011	749.1	469.6	156.6	335.7	289.2
2012	773.8	472.4	154.1	331.3	293.0
2013	799.3	471.5	150.1	324.0	292.7
2014	812.1	467.3	148.7	320.1	292.7
2015	826.7	460.3	144.1	299.9	285.7
2016	838.3	451.6	141.4	295.4	284.8
2017	854.2	448.0	142.4	308.4	298.2
2018	875.6	452.9	142.4	310.8	309.5
2019	895.7	455.2	141.9	309.5	316.0

4-3 居民消费价格分类指数(2019年)
CONSUMER PRICE INDEX BY CATEGORY (2019)

项目	Item	2018=100
居民消费价格指数	**Consumer Price Index**	**102.3**
#非食品价格指数	Non-food Price Index	101.6
#服务项目价格指数	Price Index for Services	102.5
#消费品价格指数	Price Index for Consumer Goods	102.2
食品烟酒	**Food, Tobacco and Liquor**	**105.2**
食品	Food	106.2
粮食	Grain	99.6
薯类	Tubers	101.8
豆类	Beans	102.1
食用油	Edible Oil	99.6
菜	Vegetables	100.6
#鲜菜	Fresh Vegetables	100.7
畜肉类	Livestock Meat	120.9
禽肉类	Poultry Meat	111.2
水产品	Aquatic Products	98.4
蛋类	Eggs	103.8
奶类	Milk	101.0
干鲜瓜果类	Dried and Fresh Melons and Fruits	108.8
#鲜瓜果	Fresh Fruits	111.2
糖果糕点类	Confectionery	100.0
调味品	Condiment	101.3
其他食品类	Other Dood	101.8
茶及饮料	Tea and Drinks	102.2
烟酒	Tobacco and Liquor	100.5
烟草	Tobacco	99.9
酒类	Liquor	101.1
在外餐饮	Outside Food and Drinks	104.3
衣着	**Clothing**	**101.9**
服装	Garments	102.7
服装材料	Clothing Materials	102.8
其他衣着及配件	Other Clothing and Accessories	100.5
衣着加工服务费	Clothing Processing Fee	109.1
鞋类	Shoes	99.4
居住	**Living**	**101.3**
租赁房房租	Rental	101.7
住房保养维修及管理	Housing Maintenance and Management	100.8
水电燃料	Utilities and Fuels	101.1
自有住房	Own Housing	101.5
生活用品及服务	**Daily Necessities and Services**	**99.7**
家具及室内装饰品	Furniture and Interior Decorations	100.4
家具	Furniture	100.8
室内装饰品	Interior Decorations	96.4
家用器具	Domestic Appliances	95.2
大型家用器具	Large Domestic Appliances	94.9
小家电	Sall Domestic Appliances	96.0
家用纺织品	Home Textiles	98.8
家庭日用杂品	Daily Groceries for Households	98.9
个人护理用品	Personal Care Products	101.2
家庭服务	Home Service	105.6
交通和通信	**Traffic and Communication**	**97.2**
交通	Traffic	97.9
交通工具	Vehicles	97.1
交通工具用燃料	Fuels for Vehicles	94.2
交通工具使用和维修	Vehicle Use and Maintenance	103.2
交通费	Transportation Fee	100.5
通信	Communication	95.5
通信工具	Communication Devices	95.9
通信服务	Communication Services	94.8
邮递服务	Mail Service	100.0
教育文化和娱乐	**Education,Culture and Entertainment**	**101.0**
教育	Education	102.9
教育用品	Educational Supplies	100.8
教育服务	Education Services	103.0
文化娱乐	Culture and Entertainment	99.7
文娱耐用消费品	Durable Consumer Goods for Cultural and Recreation Use	95.6
其他文娱用品	Other Recreational Supplies	101.9
文化娱乐服务	Cultural and Recreational Services	101.6
旅游	Tourism	101.6
医疗保健	**Medical Care**	**108.4**
药品及医疗器具	Medicine and Medical Equipment	101.3
中药	Traditional Chinese Medicine	102.2
西药	Western Medicine	102.7
滋补保健品	Nourishing Health Care Products	100.7
医疗卫生器具	Medical and Health Equipment	96.1
保健器具	Health Care Equipment	101.2
医疗服务	Medical Service	121.6
其他用品和服务	**Other Supplies and Services**	**103.2**
其他用品类	Other Supplies	106.5
首饰手表	Jewelry and Watches	107.9
其他杂项用品	Other Miscellaneous	96.7
其他服务类	Other Services	101.1
旅馆住宿	Hotel Accommodation	104.8
美容美发洗浴	Beauty Salon and Bath	102.3
养老服务	Pension Services	102.6
金融保险	Financial Insurance	97.9
其他服务类	Other Services	98.9

4-4 商品零售价格分类指数(2019年)
RETAIL PRICE INDEX BY CATEGORY (2019)

项 目	Item	2018 =100	项 目	Item	2018 =100
商品零售价格指数	**Retail Price Index**	**100.5**	专业音像器材	Professional Audio Equipment	96.5
食 品	**Food**	**105.6**	**文化办公用品**	**Cultural Office Supplies**	**98.3**
粮 食	Grain	99.6	**日用品**	**Daily Necessities**	**98.3**
薯 类	Tubers	101.8	日用百货	Articles of Daily Use	97.0
豆 类	Beans	102.1	厨具餐具茶具	Kitchen Utensils, Tableware and Teaware	99.9
食用油	Edible Oil	99.6	清洗用品	Cleaning Supplies	102.1
菜	Vegetables	100.6	其他日用品	Other Daily Necessities	96.1
畜肉类	Livestock Meat	120.8	**体育娱乐用品**	**Sports and Entertainment Supplies**	**99.6**
禽肉类	Poultry Meat	111.2	体育户外用品	Sports and Outdoor Supplies	99.4
水产品	Aquatic Products	98.4	娱乐用品	Entertainment Supplies	99.7
蛋 类	Eggs	103.8	**交通、通信用品**	**Transportation and**	**97.0**
奶 类	Milk	101.0		**Communication Supplies**	
干鲜瓜果类	Dried and Fresh Melons	108.8	交通运输机械	Transportation Machinery	97.4
	and Fruits		通信器材	Communication Equipment	96.2
糖果糕点类	Confectionery	100.0	**家具**	**Furniture**	**100.8**
调味品	Condiment	101.2	**化妆品**	**Cosmetic**	**101.6**
其他食品类	Other Food	101.8	**金银饰品**	**Gold and Silver Jewelry**	**110.9**
在外餐饮	Outside Food and Drinks	104.3	**中西药品及医疗**	**Chinese Traditional Medicine, Western**	
饮料、烟酒	**Drinks, Tobacco and Liquor**	**101.1**	**保健用品**	**Medicines and Health Care Products**	**101.7**
茶及饮料	Tea and Drinks	102.2	医疗卫生器具	Medical and Health Equipment	96.1
烟 草	Tobacco	99.9	中药	Traditional Chinese Medicine	102.2
酒 类	Liquor	101.1	西药	Western Medicine	102.8
服装、鞋帽	**Clothing, Shoes and Hats**	**101.7**	保健器具及用品	Health Care Equipment and Supplies	100.8
服 装	Garments	102.7	**书报杂志及电子**	**Books, Newspapers, Magazines and**	
鞋帽袜	Footgear and Hats	99.5	**出版物**	**Electronic Publications**	**104.7**
其他衣着配件	Other Clothing Accessories	100.2	教材及参考书	Teaching Materials and Reference Books	100.8
纺织品	**Textile**	**99.5**	书报杂志	Books, Newspapers and Magazines	108.4
服装材料	Clothing Materials	102.8	计算机办公软件	Computer Office Software	99.3
床上用品	Bedding	98.9	**燃 料**	**Fuel**	**96.4**
家用电器及	**Domestic Appliances, Audio**		煤炭及制品	Coal and Coal Products	102.4
音像器材	**& Video Equipment**	**94.8**	石油及制品	Petroleum and Oil Products	96.4
家庭设备	Home Equipment	95.1	**建筑材料及五金电料**	**Building Materials and Hardware**	**100.3**
文娱用耐用	Durable Consumer Goods for		建筑装璜材料	Building Decoration Materials	100.1
消费品	Cultural and Recreation Use	93.4	五金水暖	Hardware and Plumbing	100.5

4–5 农产品生产者价格指数
PRODUCER PRICE INDEX FOR FARM PRODUCTS

(上年=100) (preceding year=100)

项 目	Item	2019	2018
总 指 数	**General Index**	**109.9**	**103.6**
农业产品	Agricultural Products	98.6	109.7
#粮 食	Grain	99.0	107.9
蔬菜及食用菌	Vegetable and Edible Fungus	101.5	102.0
林业产品	Forestry Products		
畜牧业产品	Animal Husbandry Products	123.3	97.0
#肉 牛	Beef Cattle	106.9	105.7
肉 羊	Mutton Sheep	113.2	116.6
奶产品	Milk Products	103.8	101.3
猪	Hogs	149.8	85.2
肉禽(毛重)	Poultry (Gross Weight)	101.4	101.7
禽 蛋	Eggs	102.3	108.0
渔业产品	Fishing	99.6	96.6

4-6 工业生产者出厂价格及购进价格指数(2000-2019年)

(上年=100)

年 份 Year	工业生产者出厂价格指数 Producer Price Index for Industrial Products (PPI)	轻工业 Light Industry	重工业 Heavy Industry	生产资料 Means of Production	生活资料 Comsumer Goods	工业生产者购进价格指数 Purchasing Price Index for Industrial Products	燃料、动力类 Fuels and Power
2000	102.5	98.0	104.2	103.4	98.8	100.0	104.3
2001	99.4	99.6	99.4	99.4	99.6	100.5	101.7
2002	96.6	97.6	96.4	96.4	97.9	97.1	102.3
2003	101.5	98.0	104.5	102.2	99.1	104.7	109.6
2004	103.0	100.2	105.3	103.7	100.6	114.2	120.0
2005	101.3	98.7	103.3	101.9	99.1	111.4	117.1
2006	99.1	97.9	99.6	99.0	99.3	105.5	113.1
2007	99.7	100.7	99.2	99.3	101.3	105.0	105.1
2008	103.3	101.8	104.0	103.8	101.3	115.8	132.3
2009	94.4	96.2	93.6	93.3	99.1	88.6	85.1
2010	102.2	98.7	103.8	102.7	100.3	110.5	121.3
2011	102.3	104.6	102.0	102.5	101.6	108.4	117.8
2012	98.4	101.1	98.0	97.8	101.0	98.7	99.0
2013	97.4	100.7	96.9	96.7	100.5	97.8	96.4
2014	99.1	100.8	98.8	98.7	100.9	98.8	99.4
2015	96.9	100.0	96.4	96.1	99.9	93.7	85.6
2016	98.1	101.8	97.6	98.0	98.3	98.5	98.0
2017	100.7	99.3	100.9	101.5	99.4	104.4	108.4
2018	100.0	99.9	100.0	100.4	99.3	100.8	102.0
2019	99.6	103.6	99.1	99.6	99.6	99.6	99.5

PRODUCER PRICE INDEX AND PURCHASING PRICE INDEX FOR INDUSTRIAL PRODUCTS (2000-2019)

(preceding year=100)

黑色金属材料类 Ferrous Metal Materials	有色金属材料和电线类 Nonferrous Metal Materials and Electric Wires	化工原料类 Chemical Raw Materials	木材及纸浆类 Timber and Paper Pulp	建筑材料及非金属矿类 Construction Materials and Nonmetal Ores	其他工业原材料及半成品类 Other Industrial Materials and Semi-finished Products	农副产品类 Agricultural Products	纺织原料类 Textile Raw Materials
100.5	106.9	103.4	94.8	101.9	98.4	94.5	91.5
100.3	97.9	97.6	98.3	99.5	98.8	103.5	100.6
96.4	96.1	99.3	102.5	97.6	92.3	93.6	97.8
110.9	101.4	107.3	100.6	99.0	95.2	114.3	98.1
124.5	120.9	111.1	100.7	105.8	103.8	122.3	102.8
108.3	123.3	114.9	103.6	101.8	102.8	96.3	106.2
96.7	138.3	104.1	100.3	99.4	98.0	101.3	100.9
115.6	112.2	106.7	101.7	103.5	95.3	138.6	99.2
128.5	97.9	108.3	108.5	115.2	94.9	132.6	101.5
79.8	81.1	82.3	97.0	99.4	95.3	88.2	97.6
115.4	121.6	111.7	104.2	102.7	99.0	106.6	102.8
112.7	115.2	112.7	105.7	103.0	98.9	128.8	108.2
92.2	96.7	102.5	99.0	93.9	98.8	98.5	100.8
94.6	92.1	98.6	98.4	94.2	98.9	102.2	99.6
95.3	95.3	99.2	99.9	96.8	98.9	97.5	100.7
87.2	93.7	94.1	99.0	95.7	98.4	103.1	99.8
99.7	97.2	96.6	99.1	100.6	98.3	112.8	99.8
111.3	123.4	102.9	101.4	106.3	99.9	93.0	101.9
105.7	105.8	101.5	101.1	105.0	98.8	90.7	100.8
100.4	97.2	97.0	98.4	99.3	99.4	111.9	100.2

4-7 工业生产者出厂价格指数
PRODUCER PRICE INDEX FOR INDUSTRIAL PRODUCTS

(上年=100) (preceding year=100)

项目	Item	2019	2018
总指数	**General Index**	**99.6**	**100.0**
按轻、重工业分	**By Light Industry and Heavy Industry**		
轻工业	Light Industry	103.6	99.9
以农产品为原料	Using Farming Products as Raw Materials	104.4	100.4
以非农产品为原料	Using Non-agricultural Products as Raw Materials	102.5	99.2
重工业	Heavy Industry	99.1	100.0
采掘	Excavation	103.6	99.4
原料	Raw Materials	99.5	101.3
加工	Processing	98.5	99.5
按生产、生活资料分	**By Capital Goods and Living Goods**		
生产资料	Means of Production	99.6	100.4
采掘	Excavation	103.6	99.4
原料	Raw Materials	99.5	101.3
加工	Processing	99.1	99.9
生活资料	Living Goods	99.6	99.3
食品	Foods	103.9	100.3
衣着	Clothing	101.1	99.1
一般日用品	Articles for Daily Use	102.9	99.9
耐用消费品	Durable Consumer Goods	97.5	98.9

4-8 工业生产者出厂价格指数(按行业分)
PRODUCER PRICE INDEX FOR INDUSTRIAL PRODUCTS (BY SECTOR)

(上年=100) (preceding year=100)

项目	Item	2019	2018
总指数	**General Index**	**99.6**	**100.0**
煤炭开采和洗选业	Mining and Washing of Coal	100.6	101.1
黑色金属矿采选业	Mining and Processing of Ferrous Metal Ores	119.0	94.6
非金属矿采选业	Mining and Processing of Nonmetal Ores	101.9	104.7
开采专业及辅助性活动	Mining Support Service Activities	102.9	98.2
农副食品加工业	Processing of Food from Agriculture Products	110.9	98.3
食品制造业	Manufacture of Foods	101.4	100.7
酒、饮料及精制茶制造业	Manufacture of Wines, Beverage and Refined Tea	100.5	102.1
烟草制品业	Manufacture of Cigarettes and Tobacco	105.0	101.4
纺织业	Manufacture of Textile	98.3	97.8
纺织服装、服饰业	Manufacture of Textile Wearing Apparel and Ornament	101.2	99.0
皮革、毛皮、羽毛及其制品和制鞋业	Manufacture of Leather, Fur, Feather and Its Products, and Footwear	100.1	100.0
木材加工和木、竹、藤、棕、草制品业	Processing of Timbers, Manufacture of Wood, Bamboo, Rattan, Palm and Straw Products	101.8	101.3
家具制造业	Manufacture of Furniture	102.6	101.7
造纸和纸制品业	Manufacture of Paper and Paper Products	98.7	104.3
印刷和记录媒介复制业	Printing, Reproduction of Recording Media	99.7	101.3
文教、工美、体育和娱乐用品制造业	Manufacture of Articles for Culture, Education, Artwork, Sports and Entertainment Activity	116.5	99.4
石油、煤炭及其他燃料加工业	Processing of Petroleum, Coking, Processing of Nucleus Fuel	99.8	110.8
化学原料和化学制品制造业	Manufacture of Chemical Raw Material and Chemical Products	97.3	101.7
医药制造业	Manufacture of Medicines	99.7	100.1
化学纤维制造业	Manufacture of Chemical Fibres	101.6	100.2
橡胶和塑料制品业	Manufacture of Rubber and Plastics Products	99.8	100.9
非金属矿物制品业	Manufacture of Non-Metallic Mineral Products	101.2	106.9
黑色金属冶炼和压延加工业	Manufacture and Processing of Ferrous Metals	100.3	103.9
有色金属冶炼和压延加工业	Manufacture and processing of Non-Ferrous Metals	97.1	106.2
金属制品业	Manufacture of Fabricated Metal Products	100.0	103.2
通用设备制造业	Manufacture of General-Purpose Machinery	100.0	100.3
专用设备制造业	Manufacture of Special-Purpose Machinery	99.6	99.3
汽车制造业	Manufacture of Motor Vehicles	99.4	98.6
铁路、船舶、航空航天和其他运输设备制造业	Manufacture of Railway Locomotives, Building of Ships and Boats, Manufacture of Air and Spacecrafts and Other Transportation Equipments	99.7	99.9
电气机械和器材制造业	Manufacture of Electrical Machinery and Equipment	99.9	99.2
计算机、通信和其他电子设备制造业	Manufacture of Computer, Communication Equipment and Other Electronic Equipment	95.5	98.3
仪器仪表制造业	Manufacture of Measuring Instrument and Meter	100.0	99.7
其他制造业	Other Manufacturing	127.2	100.6
废弃资源综合利用业	Waste Recycling and Recovery	101.5	101.7
金属制品、机械和设备修理业	Repair of Fabricated Metal Products, Machinery and Equipment	100.0	100.0
电力、热力生产和供应业	Production and Supply of Electricity and Heating Power	99.7	98.9
燃气生产和供应业	Production and Distribution of Gas	99.1	100.0
水的生产和供应业	Production and Distribution of Water	101.4	100.8

4-9 工业生产者购进价格指数
PURCHASING PRICE INDEX FOR INDUSTRIAL PRODUCTS

(上年=100) (preceding year=100)

项目	Item	2019	2018
总指数	**General Index**	**99.6**	**100.8**
燃料、动力类	Fuels and Power	99.5	102.0
黑色金属材料类	Ferrous Metal Materials	100.4	105.7
#钢材	Steel Products	99.5	103.3
其他	Others	106.5	124.8
有色金属材料和电线类	Nonferrous Metal Materials and Electric Wires	97.2	105.8
化工原料类	Chemical Raw Materials	97.0	101.5
木材及纸浆类	Timber and Paper Pulp	98.4	101.1
建筑材料及非金属类	Construction Materials and Non-metallic materials	99.3	105.0
其他工业原材料及半成品类	Other Industrial Materials and Semi-finished Products	99.4	98.8
农副产品类	Agricultural Products	111.9	90.7
纺织原料类	Textile Raw Materials	100.2	100.8

4-10 固定资产投资价格指数(2019年)
PRICE INDEX FOR INVESTMENT IN FIXED ASSETS (2019)

项目	Item	1992=100	1993=100	1994=100	2000=100	2004=100	2005=100	2006=100	2007=100	2008=100
总指数	**General Index**	**262.5**	**207.5**	**178.4**	**138.5**	**128.8**	**127.8**	**127.4**	**123.9**	**114.9**
建筑安装工程	Construction and Installation Projects	331.6	252.8	210.9	154.5	134.0	133.3	133.8	128.4	114.9
人工费	Labor Cost									
材料费	Cost of Materials	1265.0	894.5	618.3	271.3	233.6	224.5	215.8	203.3	186.3
机械费	Cost of Machinery	256.9	190.5	162.0	139.4	119.4	119.6	121.4	116.7	103.3
机械费	Cost of Machinery Use				132.1	128.4	128.4	126.8	124.7	118.6
设备、工器具购置	Purchase of Equipment, Tools and Instruments	102.5	89.1	87.3	69.9	84.4	85.8	86.1	87.1	88.7
其他费用	Others	223.7	183.3	148.4	140.4	136.5	133.9	131.6	128.8	122.9

4-10 续表 continued

项目	Item	2009=100	2010=100	2011=100	2012=100	2013=100	2014=100	2015=100	2016=100	2017=100	2018=100
总指数	**General Index**	**118.3**	**115.5**	**109.2**	**107.8**	**107.9**	**107.9**	**110.6**	**110.9**	**106.0**	**102.1**
建筑安装工程	Construction and Installation Projects	121.8	117.2	106.8	107.9	110.9	112.6	119.2	120.7	109.2	101.0
人工费	Labor Cost										
材料费	Cost of Materials	178.7	168.0	150.6	137.3	129.0	122.5	117.7	113.8	109.1	104.4
机械费	Cost of Machinery	112.6	108.4	98.6	102.2	107.4	110.8	120.5	123.4	109.5	100.1
机械费	Cost of Machinery Use	117.7	115.8	112.0	108.6	107.2	106.3	105.7	104.7	103.6	101.5
设备、工器具购置	Purchase of Equipment, Tools and Instruments	91.7	92.6	93.6	96.1	98.4	99.0	99.5	100.5	100.4	100.0
其他费用	Others	121.9	119.6	115.0	110.6	107.4	105.6	105.1	104.4	104.4	103.8

4-11 住宅销售价格指数(2019年各月)
SELLING PRICE INDEX OF RESIDENTIAL HOUSES (EACH MONTH OF 2019)

(上年同月=100) (same month of previous year=100)

项 目	Item	1月 Jan.	2月 Feb.	3月 Mar.	4月 Apr.	5月 May	6月 Jun.
新建商品住宅	**New Commercial Residential Houses**	**102.8**	**102.9**	**103.2**	**103.5**	**103.9**	**103.9**
90平方米及以下	90sq.m and below	101.9	101.8	101.9	102.2	102.5	102.4
90-144平方米	90-144sq.m	101.7	101.9	101.9	101.9	101.8	102.0
144平方米以上	Above 144sq.m	104.2	104.5	105.1	105.6	106.7	106.4
二手住宅	**Second-hand Residential Houses**	**98.6**	**99.3**	**99.9**	**100.6**	**100.2**	**100.1**
90平方米及以下	90sq.m and below	99.4	100.2	100.9	101.4	101.0	100.3
90-144平方米	90-144sq.m	97.9	98.5	99.0	99.6	99.0	99.5
144平方米以上	Above 144sq.m	97.9	98.4	98.9	100.0	100.3	100.9

4-11 续表 Continued

(上年同月=100) (same month of previous year=100)

项 目	Item	7月 Jul.	8月 Aug.	9月 Sep.	10月 Oct.	11月 Nov.	12月 Dec.
新建商品住宅	**New Commercial Residential Houses**	**104.3**	**104.8**	**104.7**	**104.3**	**105.4**	**104.8**
90平方米及以下	90sq.m and below	102.5	102.8	102.7	102.0	102.4	102.3
90-144平方米	90-144sq.m	102.4	102.3	102.3	101.7	102.7	102.4
144平方米以上	Above 144sq.m	107.0	108.1	108.0	108.0	109.7	108.4
二手住宅	**Second-hand Residential Houses**	**99.5**	**99.1**	**98.8**	**98.5**	**98.7**	**99.5**
90平方米及以下	90sq.m and below	99.7	99.4	98.8	98.3	98.4	99.1
90-144平方米	90-144sq.m	99.1	98.6	98.8	98.9	99.2	100.1
144平方米以上	Above 144sq.m	99.4	99.2	99.1	98.3	98.7	99.8

主要统计指标解释

居民消费价格指数 是度量消费商品及服务项目价格水平随着时间而变动的相对数，反映一定时期内居民家庭购买的消费品及服务价格水平的变动趋势和变动程度。居民消费价格指数变动率通常被用来作为反映通货膨胀（或紧缩）程度的指标。

商品零售价格指数 是度量工业、商业、餐饮业和其他零售企业向城乡居民、机关团体出售生活消费品和办公用品价格水平随着时间而变动的相对数，反映市场商品零售价格的变动趋势和变动程度。

工业生产者出厂价格指数 是反映全部工业产品出厂价格总水平变动程度的相对数。其中包括工业企业售给商业、外贸、物资部门的产品，还包括售给工业和其他部门的生产资料以及直接售给居民的生活消费品。通过工业生产者价格指数能观察工业产品出厂价格变动对工业总产值的影响。

工业生产者购进价格指数 是反映全部工业原材料、燃料、动力购进价格总水平变动程度的相对数。用其可以观察和研究工业企业原材料价格变动对生产的影响，以及企业对原材料涨价的消化能力和承受能力，为制定价格政策提供依据。

固定资产投资价格指数 是反映固定资产投资额价格变动程度的相对数。固定资产投资额由建筑安装装饰工程投资完成额，设备、工器具购置投资完成额和其他费用投资完成额三部分组成。编制固定资产投资价格指数可以准确地反映固定资产投资中涉及的各类商品和取费项目价格变动幅度，消除按现价计算的固定资产投资指标中的价格变动因素，真实地反映固定资产投资的规模、速度、结构和效益，为国家科学地制定、检查固定资产投资计划，提高宏观调控水平，为完善国民经济核算体系提供科学、可靠的依据。

住宅销售价格指数 是反映住宅销售价格总水平变动趋势和程度的相对数。包括新建商品住宅销售价格指数和二手住宅销售价格指数。

农产品生产者价格指数 是指农产品生产者价格总水平变动程度的相对数。农产品生产者价格是指农产品生产者第一次出售其产品时的单位产品价格。

Explanatory Notes on Main Statistical Indicators

Consumer Price Index (CPI) is a relative number measuring the changes in prices of consumer goods and service over time, reflecting the trend and degree of changes in prices of consumer goods and service purchased by households over a period of time. CPI is usually used for reflecting the level of inflation (or deflation).

Retail Price Index is a relative number measuring the changes in prices of consumer goods and office supplies provided by industry, commerce, restaurants and other retail businesses for urban and rural residents and government agencies and organizations over time. It reflects the trend and degree of changes in retail price of commodities in the market.

Producer Price Index for Industrial Products (PPI) is a relative number reflecting the degree of changes in general producer prices of all industrial products, including products sold by industrial enterprises to commercial, foreign trade and materials companies, as well as production materials sold to industrial and other enterprises, and consumer goods directly sold to consumers. It can be used to analyze the impact of producer prices of industrial products on gross industrial output value.

Purchasing Price Index for Industrial Products is a relative number reflecting the degree of changes in the overall level of prices of all industrial materials, fuels and power. It can be used to observe and analyze the effect of changes in prices of raw materials in industrial enterprises on their production, as well as the enterprises' capacity of digesting and bearing the rising prices of raw materials, thus providing basis for formulating price policies.

Price Index for Investment in Fixed Assets is a relative number reflecting the degree of changes in prices of investment in fixed assets. The investment in fixed assets consists of three components, i.e. the investment in construction and installation, the investment in purchasing equipment and instrument, and the investment in other items. Removing the factor of price change in the aggregates of investment at current prices, this indicator shows the changes in the prices of commodities and fees involved in the investment of fixed assets, and can be used to observe the actual size, growth, structure, and efficiency of investment in fixed assets and provides reliable and scientific basis for government planning on and examination of fixed assets investment, thus to improve overall adjustment and controlling skill, and further improve the national accounting system.

Selling Price Index of Residential Houses is a relative number reflecting the trend and degree of changes in the overall level of house selling prices, including newly built residential house selling price index and second-hand house selling price index.

Producer Price Index for Farm Products is a relative number reflecting the degree of changes in the overall production prices of farm products. Producer price of farm products refers to the price of unit product at which the producers of farm products sell their products for the first time.

05

北京统计年鉴2020 BEIJING STATISTICAL YEARBOOK

人民生活
PEOPLE'S LIVING CONDITIONS

简要说明

一、主要内容

本章资料反映北京市居民生活现状及变化情况，分为全市居民生活、城镇居民生活和农村居民生活三部分，主要包括家庭基本情况、家庭收入和消费支出情况、居住状况和耐用消费品拥有量等。

二、调查方法

城乡居民生活状况调查方法和方案由国家统计局统一制定，采用抽样调查的方法，按对全市及分区居民主要收支指标有代表性的原则在全市城乡住户中抽取样本，并按一定的周期对样本进行轮换以保证其代表性。对抽中的住户采用日记账和问卷相结合的方式采集数据。

三、本章资料的调查范围

城镇住户调查的口径范围：2000—2003 年为 1000 户城市居民，覆盖城八区；2004—2006 年为 2000 户城市居民，覆盖城八区；2007 年为 3000 户城镇居民，覆盖所有区县；2008—2012 年为 5000 户城镇居民，覆盖所有区县。

农村住户调查的口径范围：2000—2002 年为 2710 户，覆盖 14 个郊区县；2003 年为 2670 户（石景山区全部农民转居民，40 个样本取消），覆盖 13 个郊区县；2004—2012 年为 3000 户，覆盖 13 个郊区 。

城乡住户调查一体化：2013 年，根据国家统计局实施城乡住户调查一体化改革的要求和《住户收支与生活状况调查方案》的有关规定，国家统计局北京调查总队、北京市统计局对全市城乡住户进行了统一的样本抽取，城乡住户调查样本量共计 10000 户。

按照国家统计局要求，自 2015 年起，北京按照改革后的新口径发布全市和分城乡的居民收支数据。与老口径相比，新口径的差异主要体现在三个方面：一是对居民收支指标口径进行了调整，将反映居民收入的核心指标由原来的城镇居民人均可支配收入和农村居民人均纯收入统一为人均可支配收入；二是按照国家城乡划分标准，将城镇地区的村委会由原来的农村划入城镇进行统计；三是在分城乡的居民收支数据基础上，增加了全体居民的人均可支配收入、人均消费支出数据。

四、按收入水平分组的含义

是指将住户调查样本按人均可支配收入从低到高排队分成五等份，即低收入组、中低收入组、中等收入组、中高收入组和高收入组五部分，各组的户数均占总户数的 20%。

Brief Introduction

I. Main Content

Statistics in this chapter reflect the living conditions of residents in Beijing and their changes, consisting of three parts, including the living conditions of the residents of the whole city, urban residents and rural residents. Figures include the basic family situation, household income and consumption expenditure, housing conditions and number of durable consumer goods in possession.

II. Method of Survey

Methods and plans of survey for living conditions of urban and rural residents are designated by National Bureau of Statistics. The method of sampling survey is adopted to take samples across urban and rural residents of the whole city following the principle of selecting representative residents in terms of major income and expenditure indicators across the city and the districts. Samples are changed in certain periods to ensure their representativeness. For selected residents, statistics are gathered through journals and questionnaires.

III. Scope of Survey

Scope of survey for urban residents: In 2000-2003, the survey covered 1,000 urban households in 8 urban districts; in 2004-2006, covered 2,000 urban households in 8 urban districts; in 2007 covered 3,000 urban households in all districts and counties; in 2008-2012, covered 5,000 households in all districts and counties.

Scope of survey for rural residents: In 2000-2002, the survey covered 2,710 households in 14 suburban districts and counties; in 2003, covered 2,670 households (All rural residents became urban residents in Shijingshan District, so 40 samples were cancelled.) in 13 suburban districts and counties; in 2004-2012 covered 3,000 households in 13 suburban districts.

Integration of survey on urban and rural residents: in 2013, according to the requirements of the National Bureau of Statistics on carrying out integrated reforms of urban and rural resident survey, and *Survey Plan on Income and Expenditure, and Living Conditions of Households*, the NBS Survey Office in Beijing and Beijing Municipal Bureau of Statistics took a total of 10,000 samples of urban and rural residents in an integrated way.

According to requirements of National Bureau of Statistics, since 2015, Beijing has started to issue data on income and expenditure of residents in the city and residents in urban and rural areas according to new standards after the reform. As compared with former standards, the new standards mainly show differences in the following 3 aspects: first, standards on resident income and expenditure indicators are adjusted. Core indicators reflecting resident income are unified from original per capita disposable income of urban residents and per capita net income of rural residents to per capita disposable income; second, according to national standards on division of urban and rural areas, village committees in urban areas that were classified into rural areas are now classified into urban areas; third, based on data on resident income and expenditure in urban and rural areas, data on per capita disposable income and per capita consumption expenditure of residents in Beijing are added.

IV. Meaning of Income level Grouping

Means that households are divided into five groups in a low-to-high order regarding the per capita disposable income. These five groups are the low income, medium-low income, medium income, medium-high income and high income groups. The number of households in each group accounts for 20% of the total.

5-1 全市居民家庭生活基本情况(1978-2019年)
BASIC LIVING CONDITIONS OF HOUSEHOLDS OF THE WHOLE CITY (1978-2019)

年 份 Year	人均可支配收入(元) Per Capita Disposable Income (yuan)	人均可支配收入实际增长(%) Real Growth Rate of Per Capita Disposable Income (%)	人均消费支出(元) Per Capita Consumption Expenditure (yuan)	#食品烟酒 Food, Tobacco and Liquor	全市居民家庭恩格尔系数(%) Engel Coefficient of Households of the Whole City (%)
1978	302		281	169	60.1
1979	344	11.9	321	191	59.5
1980	412	13.0	390	214	55.0
1981	469	12.4	428	240	56.1
1982	507	6.2	463	264	57.1
1983	561	10.0	496	278	56.2
1984	682	18.9	572	315	55.1
1985	854	6.5	757	376	49.6
1986	971	6.4	900	444	49.3
1987	1078	2.2	974	502	51.5
1988	1292	-0.4	1234	614	49.7
1989	1457	-3.8	1312	705	53.7
1990	1741	13.4	1469	787	53.6
1991	1975	1.3	1578	846	53.6
1992	2303	6.1	1882	981	52.1
1993	3126	14.0	2514	1198	47.7
1994	4419	13.2	3502	1636	46.7
1995	5501	6.1	4366	2125	48.7
1996	6429	4.7	4972	2317	46.6
1997	6837	0.9	5629	2466	43.8
1998	7472	6.7	6099	2515	41.2
1999	8155	8.4	6670	2620	39.3
2000	9230	9.4	7644	2750	36.0
2001	10399	9.3	8150	2885	35.4
2002	11300	10.7	9480	3061	32.3
2003	12628	11.5	10451	3131	30.0
2004	14342	12.5	11672	3490	29.9
2005	16853	15.8	13289	3912	29.4
2006	19296	13.5	15123	4228	28.0
2007	21458	8.6	15933	4572	28.7
2008	24371	8.1	17447	5157	29.6
2009	26571	10.7	19381	5561	28.7
2010	29228	7.4	21834	5853	26.8
2011	33176	7.5	24298	6086	25.0
2012	36817	7.5	26562	6574	24.8
2013	40830	7.4	29176	7008	24.0
2014	44489	7.3	31103	7468	24.0
2015	48458	7.0	33803	7584	22.4
2016	52530	6.9	35416	7609	21.5
2017	57230	6.9	37425	7549	20.2
2018	62361	6.3	39843	8065	20.2
2019	67756	6.3	43038	8489	19.7

注：本表数据为城乡住户调查一体化改革后的可比口径数据，下同。
Note: Data in this table are that of comparable standard after the reform to the integration of survey on urban and rural residents, the same below.

5-2 全市居民家庭生活基本情况(2015-2019年)
BASIC LIVING CONDITIONS OF HOUSEHOLDS OF THE WHOLE CITY (2015-2019)

单位：元 (yuan)

项　目	Item	2015	2016	2017	2018	2019	2019年为2018年% 2019 as % of 2018
全市居民家庭生活基本情况	**Basic Living Conditions of Households of the Whole City**						
人均可支配收入	Per Capita Disposable Income	48458	52530	57230	62361	67756	108.7
人均消费支出	Per Capita Consumption Expenditure	33803	35416	37425	39843	43038	108.0
居民家庭恩格尔系数(%)	Engel's Coefficient of Households (%)	22.4	21.5	20.2	20.2	19.7	
人均住房建筑面积(平方米)	Per Capita Floor Space of Houses (sq.m)	33.23	34.02	34.23	34.86	34.52	99.0
城镇居民家庭生活基本情况	**Basic Living Conditions of Urban Households**						
人均可支配收入	Per Capita Disposable Income	52859	57275	62406	67990	73849	108.6
人均消费支出	Per Capita Consumption Expenditure	36642	38256	40346	42926	46358	108.0
居民家庭恩格尔系数(%)	Engel's Coefficient of Households (%)	22.1	21.1	19.8	20.0	19.3	
人均住房建筑面积(平方米)	Per Capita Floor Space of Houses (sq.m)	31.69	32.38	32.56	33.08	32.54	98.4
农村居民家庭生活基本情况	**Basic Living Conditions of Rural Households**						
人均可支配收入	Per Capita Disposable Income	20569	22310	24240	26490	28928	109.2
人均消费支出	Per Capita Consumption Expenditure	15811	17329	18810	20195	21881	108.3
居民家庭恩格尔系数(%)	Engel's Coefficient of Households (%)	27.7	26.9	24.7	23.8	25.3	
人均住房建筑面积(平方米)	Per Capita Floor Space of Houses (sq.m)	43.03	44.50	44.89	46.26	47.19	102.0

5-3 全市居民家庭基本情况(2015-2019年)
BASIC DATA ON HOUSEHOLDS OF THE WHOLE CITY (2015-2019)

项　目	Item	2015	2016	2017	2018	2019
平均每户常住人口 (人)	Average Permanent Population Per Household (person)	2.8	2.7	2.7	2.8	2.8
平均每户就业人口数 (人)	Average Employee Per Household (person)	1.4	1.3	1.3	1.3	1.3
平均每一就业者负担人数 (人)	Average Dependents Per Employee (person)	1.6	1.6	1.6	1.6	1.7
平均每人年可支配收入 (元)	Per Capita Annual Disposable Income (yuan)	48458	52530	57230	62361	67756
平均每人年消费支出 (元)	Per Capita Annual Consumption Expenditure (yuan)	33803	35416	37425	39843	43038

5-4 全市居民家庭人均可支配收入(2015-2019年)
PER CAPITA DISPOSABLE INCOME OF HOUSEHOLDS OF THE WHOLE CITY (2015-2019)

单位：元 (yuan)

项　目	Item	2015	2016	2017	2018	2019	2019年为2018年% 2019 as % of 2018
可支配收入	**Disposable Income**	**48458**	**52530**	**57230**	**62361**	**67756**	**108.7**
工资性收入	Wage Income	30241	33114	35217	37687	41214	109.4
经营净收入	Net Business Income	1421	1396	1408	1201	1201	100.0
财产净收入	Net Property Income	7499	8230	9306	10612	11257	106.1
转移净收入	Net Transfer Income	9297	9790	11299	12861	14084	109.5

注：2019年全市居民人均可支配收入实际增长6.3%。
Note: Real growth rate of the per capita disposable income of residents of the whole city in 2019 is 6.3%.

5-5 全市居民人均可支配收入(按收入水平分)(2015-2019年)
PER CAPITA DISPOSABLE INCOME OF RESIDENTS OF THE WHOLE CITY (BY INCOME LEVEL)(2015-2019)

单位：元 (yuan)

组　别	Group	2015	2016	2017	2018	2019
低收入户　(20%)	Low income 20%	18343	20204	22170	23926	25723
中低收入户　(20%)	Medium-low income 20%	32968	36277	38452	41886	44971
中等收入户　(20%)	Medium income 20%	45239	49342	53023	57864	62596
中高收入户　(20%)	Medium-high income 20%	60627	65555	71451	77910	85170
高收入户　(20%)	High income 20%	99621	105425	116018	126970	139298

5-6 全市居民家庭人均消费支出(2015-2019年)
PER CAPITA CONSUMPTION EXPENDITURE OF HOUSEHOLDS OF THE WHOLE CITY (2015-2019)

单位：元 (yuan)

项　目	Item	2015	2016	2017	2018	2019	2019年为2018年% 2019 as % of 2018
人均消费支出	**Per Capita Consumption Expenditure**	**33803**	**35416**	**37425**	**39843**	**43038**	**108.0**
食品烟酒	Food, Tobacco and Liquor	7584	7609	7549	8065	8489	105.3
衣　着	Clothing	2426	2433	2238	2176	2230	102.5
居　住	Housing	10350	11188	12295	14110	15751	111.6
生活用品及服务	Living Articles and Services	2098	2327	2492	2372	2387	100.6
交通通信	Transportation and Communication	4490	4702	5034	4767	4979	104.4
教育文化娱乐	Educational, Cultural and Recreational	3635	3687	3917	3999	4311	107.8
医疗保健	Healthcare	2229	2456	2900	3275	3740	114.2
其他用品及服务	Other Supplies and Services	991	1015	1000	1079	1151	106.7

注：2019年全市居民人均消费支出实际增长5.6%。
Note: Real growth rate of the per capita consumption expenditure of residents of the whole city in 2019 is 5.6%.

5-7 全市居民家庭每百户主要耐用消费品拥有量(2019年)
NUMBER OF MAIN DURABLE CONSUMER GOODS PER 100 HOUSEHOLDS OF THE WHOLE CITY(2019)

项　　目		Item		全市居民 Residents	城镇居民 Urban Residents	农村居民 Rural Residents
家用汽车	(辆)	Household Cars	(unit)	52	53	45
摩托车	(辆)	Motorcycles	(unit)	4	3	8
助力车	(台)	Powered Bicycles	(unit)	27	19	83
洗衣机	(台)	Washing Machines	(unit)	101	101	102
电冰箱(柜)	(台)	Refrigerators	(unit)	104	103	112
微波炉	(台)	Microwave Ovens	(unit)	77	79	66
彩色电视机	(台)	Color TV Sets	(unit)	127	125	136
空调	(台)	Air Conditioners	(unit)	181	182	180
热水器	(台)	Water Heaters	(unit)	100	99	108
洗碗机	(台)	Dishwashers	(unit)	2	3	1
排油烟机	(台)	Smoke Exhaust Ventilators	(unit)	93	94	85
固定电话	(线)	Fixed-line Telephones	(unit)	54	54	47
移动电话	(部)	Mobile Phones	(unit)	233	230	249
#接入互联网的移动电话	(部)	Mobile Phones Accessed to the Internet	(unit)	187	188	179
计算机	(台)	Computers	(unit)	96	101	65
#接入互联网的计算机	(台)	Computers Accessed to the Internet	(unit)	89	92	59
照相机	(台)	Cameras	(unit)	43	47	12
中高档乐器	(架)	Musical Instruments of Middle and High-grade	(unit)	14	16	4
健身器材	(台)	Fitness Equipment	(unit)	9	9	4
空气净化器(含新风系统)	(台)	Air Purifiers (with Fresh Air System)	(unit)	37	41	8
吸尘器	(台)	Vacuum Cleaners	(unit)	29	31	10

5-8 全市居民家庭居住构成情况(2019年)
COMPOSITION OF HOUSING CONDITIONS FOR HOUSEHOLDS OF THE WHOLE CITY (2019)

单位：% (%)

项目	Item	全市居民 Residents	城镇居民 Urban Residents	农村居民 Rural Residents
居住空间样式	**Style of Living Space**	**100.0**	**100.0**	**100.0**
单栋楼房占比重	Individual Storied Buildings	2.9	2.7	4.5
单栋平房占比重	Individual Single-storey Buildings	17.6	8.1	84.5
四居室及以上单元房占比重	Four-bedroom and above Flat	0.9	1.0	
三居室单元房占比重	Three-bedroom Flat	19.4	22.0	1.2
二居室单元房占比重	Two-bedroom Flat	45.7	51.7	3.2
一居室单元房占比重	One-bedroom Flat	8.8	9.8	1.8
筒子楼或连片平房占比重	Tube-shaped Apartment or Closely Grouped Single-storey Buildings	4.8	4.8	4.7
其他占比重	Others			
房屋来源	**Housing Source**	**100.0**	**100.0**	**100.0**
租赁公房占比重	Public Houses Rented	6.8	7.8	
租赁私房占比重	Private Houses Rented	7.1	7.5	3.9
自建住房占比重	Self-built Houses	19.3	9.5	89.1
购买商品房占比重	Purchased Commercial Houses	28.7	32.7	0.5
购买房改住房占比重	Purchased Houses from Housing Reform	17.7	20.2	
购买保障性住房占比重	Purchased Indemnificatory Housing	5.0	5.7	
拆迁安置房占比重	Resettlement Housing	11.4	12.4	4.4
继承或获赠住房占比重	Housing under Inheritance or Donation	0.8	0.9	0.5
免费借用房占比重	Free Borrowed Houses	2.4	2.5	1.1
雇主提供免费住房占比重	Free Housing Supplied by Employers	0.4	0.4	0.4
其他来源占比重	Others	0.5	0.6	
取水位置	**Water-taking Location**	**100.0**	**100.0**	**100.0**
住宅内管道取水	Water-taking through Pipes in the House	96.5	98.4	82.9
住宅内其他方式取水	Water-taking by Other Means in the House	0.1	0.1	0.4
院内管道取水	Water-taking through Pipes in the Yard	3.0	1.1	16.5
院内其他方式取水	Water-taking by Other Means in the Yard	0.3	0.4	0.3
其他位置取水	Water-taking from Other Locations			
饮用水来源情况	**Source of Drinking Water**	**100.0**	**100.0**	**100.0**
经过净化处理的自来水占比重	Tap Water via Purification Treatment	90.4	93.8	66.2
受保护的井水和泉水占比重	Protected Well Water and Spring Water	8.0	4.4	33.5
不受保护的井水和泉水占比重	Unprotected Well Water and Spring Water			

5-8 续表 continued

单位：% (%)

项目	Item	全市居民 Residents	城镇居民 Urban Residents	农村居民 Rural Residents
江河湖泊水占比重	Water from Rivers and Lakes			
收集雨水占比重	Collecting Rainwater			
桶装水占比重	Barreled Water	1.6	1.8	0.3
其他占比重	Others			
住户厕所类型	**Toilet Type of Households**	**100.0**	**100.0**	**100.0**
水冲式卫生厕所占比重	Water-flushing Sanitary Toilets	98.8	99.5	94.0
水冲式非卫生厕所占比重	Water-flushing Non-sanitary Toilets	0.3		2.1
卫生旱厕占比重	Sanitary Pit Toilet	0.5	0.4	1.5
普通旱厕占比重	Common Pit Toilet	0.4	0.1	2.4
无厕所占比重	Households Without Toilet			
住户厕所使用情况	**Toilet Use Conditions of Households**	**100.0**	**100.0**	**100.0**
本住户独用占比重	Exclusive Use by One Household	95.8	95.5	97.8
几户合用占比重	One Toilet Shared by Several Households	2.1	2.2	1.4
公用厕所占比重	Communal Toilet	2.1	2.3	0.7
主要炊用能源状况	**Main Cooking Energy Conditions**	**100.0**	**100.0**	**100.0**
柴草占比重	Firewood	0.1		0.7
煤炭占比重	Coal			
罐装液化石油气占比重	Bottled LPG	21.1	14.3	69.8
管道液化石油气占比重	Pipeline LPG	0.2	0.3	
管道煤气占比重	Pipeline Gas			
管道天然气占比重	Pipeline Natural Gas	76.3	83.5	25.2
电占比重	Electricity	2.0	1.9	3.0
燃料用油占比重	Oil Used in Fuel			
沼气占比重	Marsh Gas	0.1		0.8
其他占比重	Others			
无炊用行为占比重	Non-cooking Behaviors	0.2	0.1	0.4
住宅外道路路面状况	**Pavement Conditions of Roads Outside Houses**	**100.0**	**100.0**	**100.0**
水泥或柏油路面的户数占比重	Cement or Tar-coated Surface	97.2	97.3	96.3
沙石或石板等硬质路面的户数占比重	Hard Surface Paved with Sand and Stones or Slates	2.7	2.6	3.7
其他路面的户数占比重	Other Pavements	0.1	0.1	

5-9 全市居民家庭主要食品人均消费量(2019年)
PER CAPITA CONSUMPTION OF MAJOR FOODS OF HOUSEHOLDS OF THE WHOLE CITY (2019)

单位：公斤 (kg)

项 目	Item	全市居民 Residents	城镇居民 Urban Residents	农村居民 Rural Residents
粮 食	Grain	97.3	95.7	107.2
豆 类	Beans	8.3	8.2	9.2
蔬菜及菜制品	Vegetables and Vegetable Products	114.9	115.9	108.9
植物油	Vegetable Oil	6.7	6.5	7.9
猪 肉	Pork	14.6	14.2	16.7
牛羊肉	Beef and Mutton	6.2	6.4	5.0
禽 类	Poultry	6.5	6.7	5.8
蛋类及其制品	Eggs and Egg Products	14.5	14.4	15.2
奶及奶制品	Milk and Dairy Products	28.9	31.1	14.6
水产品	Aquatic Products	10.1	10.3	8.7
食 糖	Sugar	1.1	1.1	1.2
酒 类	Liquor	10.5	9.9	14.1
茶 叶	Tea	0.5	0.5	0.4
干鲜瓜果类	Nuts, Fresh Melons and Fruits	85.5	87.1	75.3

5-10 城镇居民家庭生活基本情况(1978-2019年)
BASIC LIVING CONDITIONS OF URBAN HOUSEHOLDS (1978-2019)

年份 Year	人均可支配收入(元) Per Capita Disposable Income (yuan)	人均可支配收入实际增长(%) Real Growth Rate of Per Capita Disposable Income (%)	人均消费支出(元) Per Capita Consumption Expenditure (yuan)	#食品烟酒 Food, Tobacco and Liquor	城镇居民家庭恩格尔系数(%) Engel Coefficient of Urban Households (%)	每一城镇就业者负担人数(人) Dependents Per Urban Employee (person)	城镇居民人均住房建筑面积(平方米) Per Capita Floor Space of Houses in Urban Areas (sq.m)
1978	365		360	211	58.7	1.86	6.70
1979	415	11.6	409	237	57.9	1.83	6.73
1980	501	14.0	490	271	55.3	1.80	7.06
1981	555	9.3	511	295	57.7	1.72	7.48
1982	561	-0.7	535	318	59.3	1.66	7.92
1983	591	4.7	574	338	58.8	1.65	8.37
1984	694	15.0	667	379	56.8	1.63	8.72
1985	908	11.2	923	467	50.6	1.66	9.09
1986	1068	10.1	1067	543	50.9	1.66	9.20
1987	1182	1.9	1148	605	52.7	1.65	9.75
1988	1437	1.0	1456	743	51.1	1.71	10.30
1989	1597	-5.2	1520	841	55.3	1.52	10.74
1990	1902	13.0	1646	892	54.2	1.52	11.17
1991	2170	2.0	1748	955	54.7	1.47	11.64
1992	2556	7.2	2135	1126	52.8	1.43	12.09
1993	3547	16.6	2940	1405	47.8	1.42	12.45
1994	5085	14.8	4134	1919	46.4	1.41	12.85
1995	6235	4.5	5020	2436	48.5	1.41	13.34
1996	7332	5.4	5730	2672	46.6	1.41	13.82
1997	7813	1.2	6532	2854	43.7	1.43	14.36
1998	8536	6.7	7069	2906	41.1	1.40	14.96
1999	9322	8.5	7712	3030	39.3	1.41	15.88
2000	10590	9.8	8866	3174	35.8	1.41	16.75
2001	11939	9.3	9443	3352	35.5	1.39	17.62
2002	12949	10.5	11050	3558	32.2	1.41	19.22
2003	14535	12.0	12122	3627	29.9	1.39	19.71
2004	16502	12.4	13487	4026	29.9	1.44	21.49
2005	18775	12.1	14851	4363	29.4	1.39	22.03
2006	21415	13.1	16869	4692	27.8	1.40	23.65
2007	23752	8.3	17682	5058	28.6	1.40	24.77
2008	26918	7.8	19253	5684	29.5	1.40	26.90
2009	29329	10.7	21230	6125	28.9	1.40	27.69
2010	32132	7.0	23999	6437	26.8	1.40	28.94
2011	36365	7.2	26467	6610	25.0	1.50	29.38
2012	40306	7.3	28949	7123	24.6	1.40	29.26
2013	44564	7.1	31632	7515	23.8	1.50	31.31
2014	48532	7.2	33717	8007	23.7	1.50	31.54
2015	52859	7.0	36642	8091	22.1	1.50	31.69
2016	57275	6.9	38256	8070	21.1	1.56	32.38
2017	62406	7.0	40346	8003	19.8	1.58	32.56
2018	67990	6.2	42926	8577	20.0	1.61	33.08
2019	73849	6.2	46358	8951	19.3	1.63	32.54

5-11 城镇居民家庭基本情况(2015-2019年)
BASIC DATA ON URBAN HOUSEHOLDS (2015-2019)

项目		Item		2015	2016	2017	2018	2019
平均每户常住人口	(人)	Average Permanent Population Per Household	(person)	2.7	2.6	2.6	2.8	2.7
平均每户就业人口数	(人)	Average Employee Per Household	(person)	1.3	1.3	1.2	1.2	1.2
平均每一就业者负担人数	(人)	Average Dependents Per Employee	(person)	1.5	1.6	1.6	1.6	1.6
平均每人年可支配收入	(元)	Per Capita Annual Disposable Income	(yuan)	52859	57275	62406	67990	73849
平均每人年消费支出	(元)	Per Capita Annual Consumption Expenditure	(yuan)	36642	38256	40346	42926	46358

5-12 城镇居民家庭人均可支配收入(2015-2019年)
PER CAPITA DISPOSABLE INCOME OF URBAN HOUSEHOLDS (2015-2019)

单位：元 (yuan)

项目	Item	2015	2016	2017	2018	2019	2019年为2018年% 2019 as % of 2018
可支配收入	**Disposable Income**	**52859**	**57275**	**62406**	**67990**	**73849**	**108.6**
工资性收入	Wage Income	32568	35701	37883	40489	44327	109.5
经营净收入	Net Business Income	1337	1292	1293	1073	1034	96.4
财产净收入	Net Property Income	8492	9310	10520	11983	12690	105.9
转移净收入	Net Transfer Income	10462	10972	12710	14445	15798	109.4

注：2019年城镇居民人均可支配收入实际增长6.2%。
Note: Real growth rate of the per capita disposable income of urban residents in 2019 is 6.2%.

5-13 城镇居民家庭人均消费支出(2015-2019年)
PER CAPITA CONSUMPTION EXPENDITURE OF URBAN HOUSEHOLDS (2015-2019)

单位：元 (yuan)

项目	Item	2015	2016	2017	2018	2019	2019年为2018年% 2019 as % of 2018
人均消费支出	**Per Capita Consumption Expenditure**	**36642**	**38256**	**40346**	**42926**	**46358**	**108.0**
食品烟酒	Food, Tobacco and Liquor	8091	8070	8003	8577	8951	104.4
衣　着	Clothing	2651	2643	2429	2346	2391	101.9
居　住	Housing	11252	12128	13347	15391	17235	112.0
生活用品及服务	Living Articles and Services	2273	2511	2633	2496	2569	102.9
交通通信	Transportation and Communication	4860	5078	5396	5033	5229	103.9
教育文化娱乐	Educational, Cultural and Recreational	4028	4055	4325	4402	4738	107.6
医疗保健	Healthcare	2370	2630	3088	3476	3974	114.3
其他用品及服务	Other Supplies and Services	1117	1141	1125	1205	1271	105.5

注：2019年城镇居民人均消费支出实际增长5.6%。
Note: Real growth rate of the per capita consumption expenditure of urban residents in 2019 is 5.6%.

5-14 城镇居民家庭每百户主要耐用消费品拥有量(1978-2019年)
NUMBER OF MAIN DURABLE CONSUMER GOODS PER 100 URBAN HOUSEHOLDS (1978-2019)

年份 Year	热水器 (台) Water Heaters (unit)	洗衣机 (台) Washing Machines (unit)	彩色电视机 (台) Color TV Sets (unit)	电冰箱 (台) Refrigerators (unit)	照相机 (台) Cameras (unit)	空调 (台) Air Conditioners (unit)	计算机 (台) Computers (unit)	移动电话 (部) Mobile Phones (unit)	家用汽车 (辆) Household Cars (unit)
1978					8				
1979		…			10				
1980		2		…	11				
1981		12	2	2	13				
1982		19	2	3	17				
1983		29	4	7	21				
1984		42	8	15	29				
1985		58	32	42	35				
1986		76	51	62	47				
1987		83	58	72	56				
1988		86	70	81	60				
1989		90	81	89	62				
1990		93	91	96	67				
1991		93	97	102	73	…			
1992	17	96	101	101	77	1			
1993	23	100	107	101	82	2			
1994	39	103	112	104	85	5			
1995	45	100	114	104	87	12			
1996	52	101	119	105	87	14			
1997	58	101	124	104	88	27	12	1	1
1998	65	102	133	105	95	34	15	3	1
1999	67	100	141	103	95	50	24	13	3
2000	74	103	146	107	96	70	32	28	3
2001	78	102	149	107	101	90	45	62	3
2002	84	99	148	102	100	107	56	94	4
2003	85	99	147	100	103	119	68	134	7
2004	94	102	151	103	100	136	79	165	13
2005	97	105	153	104	109	147	89	190	14
2006	98	107	155	105	113	157	96	206	18
2007	99	102	147	108	99	157	92	207	20
2008	95	99	134	103	82	152	86	191	23
2009	98	100	138	104	89	163	97	213	30
2010	98	100	140	103	92	169	104	221	34
2011	97	100	138	103	85	171	104	215	38
2012	99	101	141	103	90	179	112	226	42
2013	99	100	140	103	85	180	110	225	43
2014	99	101	141	104	88	186	114	229	45
2015	93	96	130	98	65	161	107	220	47
2016	93	95	127	97	58	166	103	223	49
2017	92	95	126	97	58	168	105	224	50
2018	99	100	124	103	46	179	100	226	52
2019	99	101	125	103	47	182	101	230	53

5-15 农村居民家庭生活基本情况(1978-2019年)
BASIC LIVING CONDITIONS OF RURAL HOUSEHOLDS (1978-2019)

年 份 Year	人均可支配收入(元) Per Capita Disposable Income (yuan)	人均可支配收入实际增长(%) Real Growth Rate of Per Capita Disposable Income (%)	人均消费支出(元) Per Capita Consumption Expen-diture (yuan)	#食品烟酒 Food, Tobacco and Liquor	农村居民家庭恩格尔系数(%) Engel Coefficient of Rural Households (%)	每一农村劳动力负担人数(人) Dependents Per Rural Labor Force (person)	农村居民人均住房面积(平方米) Per Capita Living Space of Rural Residents (sq.m)
1978	225		185	117	63.2	2.15	9.20
1979	250	9.2	205	131	63.9	2.16	9.67
1980	290	9.6	253	138	54.5	2.13	10.09
1981	351	19.2	313	164	52.4	2.14	12.35
1982	433	21.2	362	190	52.5	1.97	13.01
1983	519	19.5	384	194	50.5	1.82	14.24
1984	664	25.2	435	223	51.3	1.79	14.22
1985	775	-0.8	510	240	47.1	1.64	16.48
1986	823	-0.6	644	292	45.3	1.66	17.41
1987	916	2.5	706	341	48.4	1.64	18.38
1988	1063	-3.7	883	408	46.2	1.63	19.23
1989	1231	-1.2	976	484	49.6	1.62	20.09
1990	1297	-0.04	981	497	50.7	1.61	20.62
1991	1422	-2.0	1100	537	48.8	1.59	21.92
1992	1572	0.6	1149	559	48.7	1.58	22.67
1993	1883	0.7	1255	587	46.8	1.51	23.70
1994	2401	2.1	1584	780	49.2	1.49	24.42
1995	3224	14.5	2336	1158	49.6	1.47	24.74
1996	3562	-1.0	2565	1191	46.4	1.45	25.74
1997	3662	-2.4	2693	1202	44.7	1.48	27.39
1998	3932	4.9	2873	1215	42.3	1.44	27.64
1999	4183	5.8	3123	1226	39.3	1.43	28.65
2000	4533	4.7	3426	1286	37.5	1.51	28.91
2001	4921	5.3	3553	1222	34.4	1.52	31.01
2002	5259	8.9	3733	1239	33.2	1.48	32.58
2003	5429	3.0	4149	1260	30.4	1.45	33.95
2004	5948	8.5	4619	1406	30.4	1.46	34.21
2005	7041	16.7	5318	1611	30.3	1.45	36.94
2006	7888	11.0	5728	1731	30.2	1.42	39.10
2007	8948	10.7	6403	1924	30.0	1.40	39.54
2008	10052	6.9	7289	2189	30.0	1.40	39.40
2009	10942	10.6	8904	2365	26.6	1.39	39.42
2010	12368	10.4	9262	2460	26.6	1.39	40.62
2011	13742	5.2	11086	2895	26.1	1.38	48.63
2012	15365	8.2	11888	3197	26.9	1.40	49.08
2013	17101	7.7	13564	3786	27.9	1.49	51.35
2014	18867	8.6	14535	4048	27.9	1.50	52.42
2015	20569	7.1	15811	4372	27.7	1.60	43.03
2016	22310	7.0	17329	4667	26.9	1.62	44.50
2017	24240	6.7	18810	4653	24.7	1.68	44.89
2018	26490	6.6	20195	4802	23.8	1.70	46.26
2019	28928	6.7	21881	5542	25.3	1.76	47.19

5-16 农村居民家庭基本情况(2015-2019年)
BASIC DATA ON RURAL HOUSEHOLDS (2015-2019)

项　　目	Item	2015	2016	2017	2018	2019
平均每户常住人口 (人)	Average Permanent Population Per Household (person)	2.9	3.0	2.9	3.1	3.0
平均每户整半劳动力 (个)	Average Full/Semi Labor Force Per Household (person)	2.3	2.4	2.4	2.3	2.4
平均每一劳动力负担人口 (人)	Average Dependents Per Labor Force (person)	1.6	1.6	1.7	1.7	1.8
人均住房面积 (平方米)	Per Capita Living Space (sq.m)	43.03	44.50	44.89	46.26	47.19
人均可支配收入 (元)	Per Capita Disposable Income (yuan)	20569	22310	24240	26490	28928
人均消费支出 (元)	Per Capita Consumption Expenditure (yuan)	15811	17329	18810	20195	21881
农村居民家庭恩格尔系数 (%)	Engel Coefficient of Rural Households (%)	27.7	26.9	24.7	23.8	25.3

5-17 农村居民家庭人均可支配收入(2015-2019年)
PER CAPITA DISPOSABLE INCOME OF RURAL HOUSEHOLDS (2015-2019)

单位：元 (yuan)

项　　目	Item	2015	2016	2017	2018	2019	2019年为2018年% 2019 as % of 2018
人均可支配收入	**Per Capita Disposable Income**	**20569**	**22310**	**24240**	**26490**	**28928**	**109.2**
工资性收入	Wage Income	15491	16637	18223	19827	21376	107.8
经营净收入	Net Business Income	1959	2062	2140	2021	2262	111.9
财产净收入	Net Property Income	1204	1350	1570	1877	2127	113.3
转移净收入	Net Transfer Income	1915	2260	2307	2765	3163	114.4

注：2019年农村居民人均可支配收入实际增长6.7%。
Note: Real growth rate of the per capita disposable income of rural residents in 2019 is 6.7%.

5-18 农村居民家庭人均消费支出(2015-2019年)
PER CAPITA CONSUMPTION EXPENDITURE OF RURAL HOUSEHOLDS (2015-2019)

单位：元 (yuan)

项　　目	Item	2015	2016	2017	2018	2019	2019年为2018年% 2019 as % of 2018
人均消费支出	**Per Capita Consumption Expenditure**	**15811**	**17329**	**18810**	**20195**	**21881**	**108.3**
食品烟酒	Food, Tobacco and Liquor	4372	4667	4653	4802	5542	115.4
衣　着	Clothing	996	1095	1025	1088	1200	110.3
居　住	Housing	4636	5199	5588	5951	6298	105.8
生活用品及服务	Living Articles and Services	993	1157	1595	1580	1230	77.8
交通通信	Transportation and Communication	2140	2306	2730	3078	3385	110.0
教育文化娱乐	Educational, Cultural and Recreational	1145	1342	1314	1436	1587	110.5
医疗保健	Healthcare	1336	1347	1699	1992	2247	112.8
其他用品及服务	Other Supplies and Services	193	217	206	268	392	146.3

注：2019年农村居民人均消费支出实际增长5.9%。
Note: Real growth rate of the per capita consumption expenditure of rural residents in 2019 is 5.9%.

5-19 农村居民家庭每百户主要耐用消费品拥有量(1985-2019年)
NUMBER OF MAIN DURABLE CONSUMER GOODS PER 100 RURAL HOUSEHOLDS (1985-2019)

年 份 Year	洗衣机 (台) Washing Machines (unit)	彩 色 电视机 (台) Color TV Sets (unit)	电冰箱 (台) Refrige-rators (unit)	照相机 (台) Cameras (unit)	空 调 (台) Air Conditioners (unit)	计算机 (台) Computers (unit)	移动电话 (部) Mobile Phones (unit)	家用汽车 (辆) Household Cars (unit)
1985	23	7	2	2				
1986	39	12	5	4				
1987	48	15	9	5				
1988	56	20	14	7				
1989	61	25	19	8				
1990	63	29	23	8				
1991	69	42	36	11				
1992	73	46	40	14				
1993	76	56	47	15				
1994	80	65	53	17	1			
1995	81	74	63	21	2			
1996	83	79	67	21	2			
1997	84	85	72	25	3			
1998	85	92	75	26	5			
1999	86	101	81	29	9			
2000	85	107	84	26	20	7	14	3
2001	91	112	86	29	27	12	30	5
2002	94	116	91	32	35	16	52	6
2003	94	116	94	32	39	22	77	6
2004	96	119	96	35	47	27	102	8
2005	97	129	100	37	63	36	139	10
2006	97	131	100	38	72	41	161	10
2007	99	134	104	37	78	46	182	11
2008	101	137	104	39	89	52	201	12
2009	101	138	105	42	98	58	212	12
2010	103	139	107	42	107	64	224	16
2011	99	134	104	37	108	63	231	19
2012	99	136	103	37	113	67	235	21
2013	95	132	102	32	123	74	221	34
2014	97	132	103	32	127	75	222	35
2015	90	131	95	21	118	69	230	32
2016	94	138	101	20	135	74	243	38
2017	94	138	103	21	141	74	244	38
2018	100	136	111	13	168	66	248	45
2019	102	136	112	12	180	65	249	45

5-20 农村居民家庭人均粮食收支情况(2015-2019年)
PER CAPITA GRAIN BALANCE OF RURAL HOUSEHOLDS(2015-2019)

单位：公斤 (kg)

项目	Item	2015	2016	2017	2018	2019
年内粮食收入实物量	**Grain Collected in the Year**	**226.9**	**219.2**	**174.1**	**145.0**	**130.1**
家庭经营生产	Household-based Production	139.6	132.2	91.7	48.8	35.2
购买	Purchased	87.3	87.0	82.4	96.2	94.9
年内粮食消费量	**Grain Consumed in the Year**	**105.6**	**102.1**	**96.7**	**110.2**	**107.2**
#稻谷	Rice	33.4	32.0	29.3	34.0	28.8
小麦	Wheat	57.3	54.7	52.5	58.6	59.4
年内粮食出售量	**Grain Sold in the Year**	**99.6**	**102.8**	**92.3**	**79.2**	**43.0**
出售谷物	Cereal Sold	99.1	102.6	92.3	79.1	42.9
#小麦	Wheat	19.8	20.0	9.6	3.6	2.2

主要统计指标解释

可支配收入 指调查户在调查期内获得的、可用于最终消费支出和储蓄的总和，即调查户可以用来自由支配的收入。可支配收入既包括现金，也包括实物收入。按照收入的来源，可支配收入包含四项，分别为：工资性收入、经营净收入、财产净收入和转移净收入。计算公式为：

可支配收入＝工资性收入+经营净收入+财产净收入+转移净收入

其中：经营净收入=经营收入-经营费用-生产性固定资产折旧-生产税

财产净收入=财产性收入-财产性支出

转移净收入=转移性收入-转移性支出

工资性收入 指就业人员通过各种途径得到的全部劳动报酬和各种福利，包括受雇于单位或个人、从事各种自由职业、兼职和零星劳动得到的全部劳动报酬和福利。

经营净收入 指住户或住户成员从事生产经营活动所获得的净收入，是全部经营收入中扣除经营费用、生产性固定资产折旧和生产税之后得到的净收入。计算公式为：

经营净收入=经营收入-经营费用-生产性固定资产折旧-生产税

财产净收入 指住户或住户成员将其所拥有的金融资产、住房等非金融资产和自然资源交由其他机构单位、住户或个人支配而获得的回报并扣除相关的费用之后得到的净收入。财产净收入不包括转让资产所有权的溢价所得，计入“非收入所得”。

转移净收入 指国家、单位、社会团体对住户的各种经常性转移支付和住户之间的经常性收入转移，在扣减调查户对国家、单位、住户或者个人的经常性或义务性转移支付后的净收入。

计算公式为：转移净收入=转移性收入-转移性支出

转移性收入 指国家、单位、社会团体对住户的各种经常性转移支付和住户之间的经常性收入转移。包括养老金或退休金、社会救济和补助、政策性生产补贴、政策性生活补贴、救灾款、经常性捐赠和赔偿、报销医疗费、住户之间的赡养收入，以及本住户非常住成员寄回带回的收入等。转移性收入不包括住户之间的实物馈赠。

转移性支出 指调查户对国家、单位、住户或个人的经常性或义务性转移支付。包括缴纳的税款、各项社会保障支出、赡养支出、经常性捐赠和赔偿支出以及其他经常转移支出等。

消费支出 指住户用于满足家庭日常生活消费需要的全部支出，包括用于消费品的支出和用于服务性消费的支出。根据用途不同，消费支出可划分为食品烟酒、衣着、居住、生活用品及服务、交通通信、教育文化娱乐、医疗保健、其他用品及服务八大类。根据来源不同，消费支出可划分为现金消费支出、实物消费支出（含自产自用、来自单位或雇主、来自政府和其他社会组织）。

平均每一劳动力负担人口 是由调查户常住人口除以整半劳动力计算得到的。计算公式为：

$$\text{平均每一劳动力负担人口}=\frac{\text{调查户常住人口}}{\text{整半劳动力}}$$

农村居民家庭整半劳动力 指农村常住居民家庭成员中有劳动能力并经常参加实际劳动的人员。是生产的基本要素指标之一，是发展生产增加农民家庭收入的重要源泉。按规定，农村男18周岁至50周岁、女18周岁至45周岁为整劳动力；男16周岁至17周岁、51周岁到60周岁，女16周岁到17周岁、46周岁至55周岁为半劳动力。农民家庭整半劳动力既包括在上述规定劳动年龄内和在劳动年龄以外有劳动能力并经常参加实际劳动的男女整半劳动力，也包括农民家庭常住人员中属于职工的劳动力。但不包括在劳动年龄内已丧失劳动能力的人员。

现住房总建筑面积 指调查户现住房的总建筑面积。现住房计算总建筑面积时以房屋产权证或租赁证为准，建筑面积也可按使用面积×1.333计算得出。应扣除住房中专门用于出租的建筑面积。

恩格尔系数 随着家庭和个人收入增加，收入中用于食品方面的支出比例将逐渐减小，这一定律被称为恩格尔定律，反映这一定律的系数被称为恩格尔系数。计算公式为：

$$\text{恩格尔系数}=\frac{\text{食品支出总额}}{\text{家庭或个人消费支出总额}}\times 100\%$$

Explanatory Notes on Main Statistical Indicators

Disposable Income refers to the total income at the disposal of sampled households gained during the survey, which can be used for final consumption expenditure and savings. Disposable income includes cash and income in kind. By income source, disposable income can be divided into 4 types, namely wage income, net business income, net property income and net transfer income. The following formula is used:

Disposable Income = wage income + net business income + net property income + net transfer income

Of which: Net business income = business income - business expense - depreciation of productive fixed assets - production tax

Net property income = property income - property expenditure

Net transfer income = transfer income - transfer expenditure

Wage Income refers to all payments of labor and various welfares earned by employed persons through all channels, including all payments of labor and welfare gained from institutional or individual employers, various freelance work, part-time job, and scattered work.

Net Business Income refers to the net income of a family or family members from productive and operating activities. It is the net income of all operating income deducting business expense, depreciation of productive fixed assets and production tax. The following formula is used:

Net business income = business income - business expense - depreciation of productive fixed assets - production tax

Net Property Income refers to the net income of a family or family members earned by deducting relevant expenses from returns of their financial assets, non-financial assets (such as house) and natural resource delivered to other institutions, families or individuals for management. Net property income does not include income from premium of property ownership transfer and it shall be regarded as non-revenue proceeds.

Net Transfer Income refers to net income after deducting recurrent or compulsory transfer payment of sampled households to the nation, institutions, households or individuals from various recurrent transfer payments by the nation, institutions, social groups to households and recurrent income transfer among households.

The following formula is used: Net transfer income = transfer income - transfer expenditure

Transfer Income refers to various recurrent transfer payment from the nation, institutions and social groups to households, along with recurrent income transfer among households, including retirement pension, social relief and allowance, policy production subsidiary, policy living subsidiary, disaster relief fund, recurrent donation and compensations, medical expense reimbursement, alimony income among households and income mailed or brought by non-permanent members of such household, etc. Transfer income does not include physical donation among households.

Transfer Expenditure refers to the recurrent or compulsory transfer payment made by the sampled households to the nation, institutions, households or individuals, including tax payment, various social security expenditures, alimony expenditure, recurrent donation and compensation expenditure and other recurrent transfer expenditure, etc.

Consumption Expenditure refers to total expenditures of households for consumption in daily life, including expenditures on consumer goods and services. By usage, it includes 8 categories, i.e. expenditures on food, tobacco and liquor, clothing, housing, living articles and services, transportation and communication, educational, cultural and recreational services, healthcare and medical services, and other goods and services. By source, it includes cash consumption and physical consumption (including self-produced and self-used products and those from institutions or employers, government and other social organizations).

Dependents Per Labor Force refers to the number of permanent population in the sampled household divided by the number of full/semi labor force. The following formula is used:

Dependents Per Labor Force = Number of Permanent Population in the Sampled Households / Number of Full/Semi labor force

Full/Semi Labor Force in Rural Households refers to persons among permanent family members in rural households who are capable of working and work frequently. This is one of the indicators for basic production elements, and an important source for production development and increase of farmer's household income. As stated in regulations, rural males aged 18-50 and females aged 18-45 are full labor force. Males aged 16-17 and 51-60 and females aged 16-17 and 46-55 are semi labor force. Full/Semi Labor Force in Rural Households includes the male and female full/semi labor force within the above-mentioned range age as well as those beyond such range of ages who are capable of working and work frequently; also include labor force among permanent members in rural households who are employees. But it excludes persons who are within the range of labor age but incapable of working.

Total Building Area of Current Houses refers to the total building area of house resided by the surveyed households, which is calculated on the basis of the property ownership certificate or lease certificate. The building area can also be calculated as the usable floor space multiplied by 1.333, which shall deduct the building area of the house specially used for lease.

Engel Coefficient Along with the increase in household and personal income, a gradually smaller proportion of income is used for purchase of food. This law is called Engel's law, and the coefficient reflecting such law is called Engel's Coefficient. The following formula is used:

$$\text{Engel Coefficient} = \frac{\text{expenditure on food}}{\text{total household or individual consumption expenditure}} \times 100\%$$

06

北京统计年鉴2020 BEIJING STATISTICAL YEARBOOK

财政与税收
GOVERNMENT FINANCE AND TAX REVENUES

简要说明

一、主要内容

本章资料包括北京市政府预算收支情况，北京市税收收入情况。

二、有关情况的说明

地方政府预算收支包括一般公共预算收支、政府性基金预算收支、国有资本经营预算收支和社会保险基金预算收支情况，相关数据为决算数。2015 年，财政部门对财政收支统计口径进行了调整，将 11 项政府性基金收入纳入一般公共预算收入。2016 年，根据财政部、国家税务总局《营业税改征增值税试点实施办法》，在全国全面推开营改增试点。因此，自 2017 年起，“营业税”无数据。

2017 年及以前，税收收入情况包括国税收入和地税（费）收入。自 2018 年起，根据机构改革要求，北京市地方税务局与北京市国家税务局合并为国家税务总局北京市税务局，取消“国税收入”和“地税（费）收入”，统一使用税收收入。

Brief Introduction

I. Main Content

Statistics in this chapter include budgetary revenue and expenditure of Beijing Municipal Government and the tax revenues of Beijing.

II. Condition Explanation

Local government budgetary revenue and expenditure includes general public budgetary revenue and expenditure, governmental fund budgetary revenue and expenditure, budgetary revenue and expenditure of state-owned capital operation, and social insurance fund budgetary revenue and expenditure; the relevant data are final accounts. In 2015, the financial department adjusted the statistical caliber of financial revenue and expenditure, and incorporated 11 governmental fund revenues into general public budgetary revenue. In 2016, the pilot program of replacing business tax with value-added tax was implemented in an all-round manner throughout the country in accordance with the *Measures for Implementation of the Pilot Program of Replacing Business Tax with Value-added Tax* issued by the Ministry of Finance and the State Taxation Administration. Therefore, there has been no data on business tax since 2017.

In and before 2017, the statistics for tax revenues included state tax revenues and local tax revenues. Since 2018, according to the institutional reform requirements, Beijing Local Taxation Bureau and Beijing Municipal Bureau of State Taxation have been merged into Beijing Municipal Tax Service of the State Taxation Administration; the state tax revenue and local tax revenue are cancelled and uniformly replaced with tax revenue.

6-1 地方政府预算收入(1978-2019年)

单位：亿元

年 份 Year	一般公共预算收入 General Public Budget Revenue	税收收入 Tax Revenue	#增值税 Value-added Tax	#房产税 Housing Property Tax	#土地增值税 Increment Tax On Land Value	#契税 Deed Tax	#营业税 Operation Tax
1978		18.25					
1979		19.41					
1980		21.22					
1981		24.22					
1982		25.81	0.05				
1983		38.03	1.30				
1984		43.91	2.20				1.23
1985		59.99	4.79				10.23
1986		60.83	7.61				13.19
1987		67.77	9.09				15.42
1988		84.04	15.10				21.11
1989		91.09	16.75				25.33
1990		94.23	16.47				27.95
1991		100.58	19.53				30.78
1992		110.54	22.29				35.86
1993		148.19	42.30				52.07
1994		120.53	25.54				45.63
1995		163.40	27.22				64.46
1996		201.32	29.53				81.61
1997	182.32	235.82	32.67				97.54
1998	229.45	272.23	37.58				113.00
1999	281.37	315.10	39.72				128.86
2000	345.00	372.79	45.96				149.05
2001	454.17	475.00	59.00				181.35
2002	533.99	539.87	66.69				227.79
2003	592.54	588.96	75.26	30.79	3.07	20.40	263.69
2004	744.49	726.50	68.88	31.97	1.85	43.68	333.16
2005	919.21	886.13	97.60	35.21	2.38	60.68	383.76
2006	1117.15	1076.82	117.80	43.29	5.67	64.87	460.99
2007	1492.64	1435.67	134.84	51.75	24.34	80.30	601.06
2008	1837.32	1775.58	158.34	63.84	34.67	82.97	651.78
2009	2026.81	1913.97	179.73	73.98	54.16	103.16	752.60
2010	2353.93	2251.59	210.01	83.83	85.86	134.27	855.40
2011	3006.28	2854.63	237.76	99.40	121.29	136.17	1071.51
2012	3314.93	3124.75	314.00	110.72	132.07	126.58	1152.74
2013	3661.11	3514.52	574.89	122.54	187.24	177.49	1034.79
2014	4027.16	3861.29	646.69	140.22	214.33	192.52	1068.64
2015	4723.86	4263.91	716.12	152.06	174.86	210.23	1186.13
2016	5081.26	4452.97	1214.34	198.22	177.35	254.29	584.41
2017	5430.79	4676.68	1671.90	273.11	288.99	197.46	
2018	5785.92	4988.83	1801.43	299.52	209.13	245.30	
2019	5817.10	4822.98	1820.90	354.43	225.37	225.19	

资料来源：北京市财政局。

LOCAL GOVERNMENT BUDGETARY REVENUE(1978-2019)

(100 million yuan)

#个人所得税 Individual Income Tax	#企业所得税 Company Income Tax	#城市维护建设税 Urban Maintenance and Construction Tax	非税收入 Non-tax Revenue	政府性基金预算收入 Governmental Fund Budgetary Revenue	国有资本经营预算收入 Budgetary Revenue of State-owned Capital Operation	社会保险基金预算收入 Social Insurance Fund Budgetary Revenue
0.02	1.76					
0.05	1.43					
0.07	11.70					
0.13	12.70					
0.34	16.18	2.16				
0.97	20.46	2.51				
1.54	21.87	2.70				
1.23	27.70	3.37				
1.53	24.31	3.74				
2.02	22.55	4.35				
2.56	20.59	4.77				
3.15	19.08	5.13				
4.30	14.20	6.57				
9.24	21.70	7.18				
16.21	29.67	10.42				
22.67	37.22	11.36				
28.76	41.05	12.74	-53.50	27.59		
36.49	41.42	14.12	-42.78	32.56		
45.88	45.99	15.27	-33.74	39.07		
56.38	58.03	17.35	27.79	53.39		
79.52	86.07	20.53	-20.83	53.51		
61.29	100.00	24.91	-5.88	66.97		
57.21	93.70	28.85	3.58	73.40		
73.34	121.70	34.72	17.99	85.55		
84.52	164.76	38.83	33.08	88.14		
102.28	213.86	45.17	40.33	118.63		
135.20	309.34	56.63	56.97	389.40		
171.33	497.52	63.95	61.75	444.71		
177.84	430.42	71.28	112.84	651.96		
215.33	513.09	80.00	102.34	1456.98		
272.90	683.71	145.65	151.65	1352.82		
281.49	752.47	160.34	190.18	1197.92		
333.84	802.12	177.41	146.59	1841.76	63.21	
383.52	915.84	187.24	165.87	3122.91	64.46	
478.12	1024.73	204.36	459.95	2028.37	61.60	
571.26	1095.23	221.64	628.29	1316.47	64.75	3446.83
643.20	1229.80	225.41	754.11	3132.76	61.63	3587.41
728.46	1287.74	245.58	797.09	2009.26	65.41	4186.00
544.16	1228.53	234.98	994.12	2216.30	74.99	4734.44

Source: Beijing Municipal Finance Bureau.

6-2 地方政府预算支出(1997-2019年)

单位：亿元

年 份 Year	一般公共预算支出 General Public Budget Expenditures	#一般公共服务 General Public Service	#教育 Education	#科学技术 Science and Technology	#文化旅游体育与传媒 Culture, Tourism, Sports and Media	#社会保障和就业 Social Security and Employment	#卫生健康 Health
1997	236.39						
1998	280.68						
1999	355.19						
2000	443.00						
2001	559.11						
2002	628.35						
2003	734.80						
2004	898.28						
2005	1058.31						
2006	1296.84	159.95	209.21	70.14	40.51	149.22	100.95
2007	1649.50	179.56	263.00	90.74	53.62	179.28	118.95
2008	1959.29	196.27	316.30	112.19	61.11	209.33	145.05
2009	2319.37	212.21	365.67	126.31	74.75	234.29	166.63
2010	2717.32	239.57	450.22	178.92	79.36	275.90	186.82
2011	3245.23	261.38	520.08	183.07	87.01	354.88	225.49
2012	3685.31	286.57	628.65	199.94	141.37	424.31	256.06
2013	4173.66	297.12	681.18	234.67	154.71	469.13	276.13
2014	4524.67	272.23	742.05	282.71	163.90	509.01	322.29
2015	5737.70	300.12	855.67	287.80	188.50	700.48	370.52
2016	6406.77	367.20	887.38	285.78	198.35	716.21	397.95
2017	6824.53	493.24	964.62	361.76	208.96	795.38	427.87
2018	7471.43	512.40	1025.51	425.87	245.43	835.65	490.09
2019	7408.19	499.43	1137.18	433.42	279.32	972.98	534.41

注：自2019年起，原“文化体育与传媒”更名为“文化旅游体育与传媒”，原“医疗卫生与计划生育”更名为“卫生健康”，下同。
资料来源：北京市财政局。

LOCAL GOVERNMENT BUDGETARY EXPENDITURE(1997-2019)

(100 million yuan)

#节能环保 Energy Conservation and Environmental Protection	#交通运输 Transportation	#城乡社区 Urban and Rural Community	#农林水 Agriculture Forestry and Water Conservancy	政府性基金预算支出 Governmental Fund Budget Expenditure	国有资本经营预算支出 Budget Expenditure of State-owned Capital Operation	社会保障基金预算支出 Social Security Fund Budget Expenditure
20.14	7.05	153.26	88.62	114.74		
29.27	33.09	187.43	102.51	418.15		
35.47	80.35	199.84	121.77	441.64		
54.04	147.07	347.82	142.01	501.50		
60.85	154.99	294.30	158.64	1347.65		
94.51	199.12	339.27	187.34	1329.71		
113.54	243.76	430.76	222.69	1118.45		
138.17	231.79	510.67	297.62	1798.81	66.95	
213.36	214.55	567.40	343.67	2559.09	63.99	
303.26	295.63	995.39	424.78	2281.30	61.72	
363.38	353.48	1120.37	443.55	1432.09	45.63	2497.23
458.44	446.48	1034.14	518.35	2461.60	58.86	2594.95
399.45	462.99	1246.22	576.04	2560.27	52.80	3011.72
308.81	401.59	1074.61	584.62	2960.23	52.24	3755.05

Note: Since 2019, the original Culture, Sports and Media has been changed to Culture, Tourism, Sports and Media; and the original Health Care and Family Planning has been changed to Health.
Source: Beijing Municipal Finance Bureau.

6-3 地方政府预算收入
LOCAL GOVERNMENT BUDGETARY REVENUE

单位：亿元 (100 million yuan)

项　　目	Item	2019	2018	2019年为2018年% 2019 as % of 2018
一般公共预算收入	**General Public Budget Revenue**	**5817.10**	**5785.92**	**100.5**
#增值税	Value-added Tax	1820.90	1801.43	101.1
房产税	House Property Tax	354.43	299.52	118.3
土地增值税	Increment Tax on Land Value	225.37	209.13	107.8
契税	Deed Tax	225.19	245.30	91.8
个人所得税	Personal Income Tax	544.16	728.46	74.7
企业所得税	Company Income Tax	1228.53	1287.74	95.4
城市维护建设税	Urban Maintenance and Construction Tax	234.98	245.58	95.7
耕地占用税	Arable Land Occupation Tax	3.23	2.82	114.7
罚没收入	Income of Fines and Confiscations	76.00	53.64	141.7
行政事业性收费收入	Administrative Fees	64.86	57.41	113.0
政府性基金预算收入	**Government Fund Budget Revenue**	**2216.30**	**2009.26**	**110.3**
国有资本经营预算收入	**Budget Revenue of State-owned Capital Operation**	**74.99**	**65.41**	**114.6**
社会保险基金预算收入	**Social Insurance Fund Budget Revenue**	**4734.44**	**4186.00**	**113.1**

资料来源：北京市财政局。
Source: Beijing Municipal Finance Bureau.

6-4 地方政府预算支出
LOCAL GOVERNMENT BUDGETARY EXPENDITURE

单位：亿元 (100 million yuan)

项　　目	Item	2019	2018	2019年为2018年% 2019 as % of 2018
一般公共预算支出	**General Public Budget Expenditures**	**7408.19**	**7471.43**	**99.2**
#一般公共服务	General Public Service	499.43	512.40	97.5
教　育	Education	1137.18	1025.51	110.9
科学技术	Science and Technology	433.42	425.87	101.8
文化旅游体育与传媒	Culture, Tourism, Sports and Media	279.32	245.43	113.8
社会保障和就业	Social Security and Employment	972.98	835.65	116.4
卫生健康	Health	534.41	490.09	109.0
节能环保	Energy Conservation and Environmental Protection	308.81	399.45	77.3
交通运输	Transportation	401.59	462.99	86.7
城乡社区	Urban and Rural Community	1074.61	1246.22	86.2
农林水	Agriculture, Forestry and Water Conservancy	584.62	576.04	101.5
政府性基金预算支出	**Governmental Fund Budget Expenditure**	**2960.23**	**2560.27**	**115.6**
国有资本经营预算支出	**Budget Expenditure of State-owned Capital Operation**	**52.24**	**52.80**	**98.9**
社会保险基金预算支出	**Social Insurance Fund Budget Expenditure**	**3755.05**	**3011.72**	**124.7**

资料来源：北京市财政局。
Source: Beijing Municipal Finance Bureau.

6–5 地税税费收入分税种、分行业完成情况(2010–2017年)
LOCAL TAX REVENUE BY CATEGORY AND INDUSTRY (2010-2017)

单位：亿元 (100 million yuan)

项　　目	Item	2010	2011	2012	2013	2014	2015	2016	2017
地税税费收入	**Local Tax Revenue**	**2104.9**	**2666.6**	**2865.3**	**3061.6**	**3387.8**	**3868.2**	**3261.8**	**3683.1**
按税种分	**By Category**								
#增值税	Business Tax							44.6	41.5
营业税	Operation Tax	855.4	1071.5	1152.7	1032.4	1067.9	1186.1		
企业所得税	Coporate Income Tax	173.2	210.5	221.0	258.1	333.9	374.1	479.8	555.9
个人所得税	Personal Income Tax	536.3	681.3	703.5	834.5	958.8	1195.3	1428.1	1608.0
按行业分	**By Sector**								
第一产业	Primary Industry	3.7	4.0	4.9	5.0	7.7	7.9	7.4	7.8
第二产业	Secondary Industry	235.2	303.1	326.2	348.5	388.5	408.7	345.5	386.4
#制造业	Manufacturing	101.8	138.4	150.4	160.7	179.4	206.3	219.5	235.8
电力、燃气及水的生产和供应业	Production and Distribution of Electricity, Gas and Water	15.7	19.4	21.2	25.2	28.9	29.2	35.1	37.5
建筑业	Construction	109.9	134.4	144.6	154.0	171.7	166.5	85.1	106.6
第三产业	Tertiary Industry	1866.0	2359.5	2534.1	2708.1	2991.6	3451.6	2908.9	3288.9
#交通、运输、仓储及邮政业	Transport, Storage and Post	51.4	64.0	60.6	38.1	40.5	46.4	47.1	52.5
信息传输、计算机服务和软件业	Information Transmission, Computer Servicesand Software	98.0	125.5	132.8	123.7	141.8	147.1	171.1	192.0
批发和零售业	Wholesale and Retail Trade	111.4	159.4	169.3	188.8	206.2	230.1	244.2	283.9
金融业	Finance	276.4	366.4	446.7	478.0	599.5	763.0	411.2	429.4
房地产业	Real Estate	437.4	520.4	525.4	659.3	734.2	745.7	841.7	938.0

资料来源：国家税务总局北京市税务局。
Source: Beijing Municipal Tax Service of State Taxation Administration.

6-6 国税税收收入分税种、分行业完成情况(2010—2017年)
STATE TAX REVENUE BY CATEGORY AND INDUSTRY (2010-2017)

单位：亿元 (100 million yuan)

项 目	Item	2010	2011	2012	2013	2014	2015	2016	2017
国税税收收入	**State Tax Revenue**	**4346.8**	**5332.5**	**6339.4**	**7470.9**	**8325.2**	**8655.2**	**9378.5**	**9605.7**
按税种分	**By Category**								
#增值税	Value-added Tax	868.3	961.7	1096.0	1456.3	1659.8	1710.5	2486.2	3286.1
营业税	Operation Tax	145.4	161.3	191.3	203.7	80.7	150.7		
企业所得税	Corporate Income Tax	2642.0	3506.5	3609.4	5024.4	5757.3	5937.2	5976.0	5373.9
按行业分	**By Sector**								
第一产业	Primary Industry	5.8	0.7	0.3	2.6	0.9	2.5	4.3	4.5
第二产业	Secondary Industry	779.1	881.1	843.8	1069.3	1159.4	1182.2	1198.0	1339.7
#制造业	Manufacturing	623.2	709.2	764.6	832.0	889.5	963.2	960.7	985.3
电力、燃气及水的生产和供应业	Production and Distribution of Electricity, Gas and Water	105.2	103.5	131.0	261.4	194.1	171.1	169.2	203.2
建筑业	Construction	30.1	45.3	54.8	57.0	50.9	63.9	170.2	260.3
第三产业	Tertiary Industry	3561.9	4450.8	5495.3	6399.0	7164.8	7470.5	8176.1	8261.5
#交通、运输、仓储及邮政业	Transport, Storage and Post	157.9	209.2	212.1	245.1	242.6	242.6	189.4	239.3
信息传输、计算机服务和软件业	Information Transmission, Computer Services and Software	30.8	105.9	245.9	373.2	296.2	285.0	306.3	371.4
批发和零售业	Wholesale and Retail Trade	1081.6	1410.8	1314.6	1451.0	1474.0	1420.6	1468.5	1645.7
金融业	Finance	1831.2	2158.0	3034.0	3500.2	4153.2	4401.4	4828.6	4115.7
房地产业	Real Estate	107.6	122.3	111.6	157.0	156.9	104.3	274.9	380.9

资料来源：国家税务总局北京市税务局。
Source: Beijing Municipal Tax Service of State Taxation Administration.

6-7 税收收入情况(2017-2019年)
STATISTICS FOR TAX REVENUE(2017-2019)

单位：亿元 (100 million yuan)

项　目	Item	2017	2018	2019
税收收入	**Tax Revenue**	**12403.9**	**12655.5**	**13098.1**
按税种分	**By Category**			
#增值税	Business Tax	3327.6	3595.3	3629.9
企业所得税	Corporate Income Tax	5929.8	5727.5	6501.1
个人所得税	Personal Income Tax	1610.3	1824.2	1363.1
按行业分	**By Sector**			
第一产业	Primary Industry	11.7	11.2	12.6
第二产业	Secondary Industry	1665.8	1808.3	1746.4
#制造业	Manufacturing	1179.0	1202.5	1222.7
电力、燃气及水的生产和供应业	Production and Distribution of Electricity, Gas and Water	235.9	213.6	186.0
建筑业	Construction	354.0	367.3	351.2
第三产业	Tertiary Industry	10726.4	10836.0	11339.1
#交通、运输、仓储及邮政业	Transport, Storage and Post	286.0	344.7	354.7
信息传输、计算机服务和软件业	Information Transmission, Computer Services and Software	550.4	630.7	664.6
批发和零售业	Wholesale and Retail Trade	1324.5	1529.1	1243.9
金融业	Finance	4515.4	4252.7	5217.0
房地产业	Real Estate	1302.1	1175.8	1203.1

注：本表税收收入不含各项非税收入，2017年为同口径数据。
资料来源：国家税务总局北京市税务局。
Note: Tax revenue in this table doesn't include the non-tax revenues. That of 2017 was the data of the same caliber.
Source: Beijing Municipal Tax Service of State Taxation Administration.

主要统计指标解释

财政部分

一般公共预算收入 是通过一定的形式和程序，由各级财政部门组织并纳入预算管理的各项收入。

政府性基金预算收入 是按规定收取，转入或通过当年财政安排，由财政管理并具有指定用途的政府性基金预算收入等。

国有资本经营预算收入 指国家以所有者身份依法取得国有资本收益，并对所得收益进行分配而发生的各项收支预算，是政府预算的重要组成部分。

社会保险基金预算收入 社会保险基金预算是指社会保险经办机构根据国家预算管理和社会保险相关法律法规编制的、经规定程序审批的具有法律效力的年度基金财务收支计划。

税收收入 包括增值税、营业税、企业所得税、个人所得税、资源税、城市维护建设税、房产税、印花税、城镇土地使用税、土地增值税、车船税、耕地占用税、契税等。

非税收收入 包括专项收入、行政事业性收费、罚没收入和其他收入。

一般公共预算支出 是各级财政部门对集中的一般预算收入有计划地分配和使用而安排的支出。

政府性基金预算支出 是各级财政部门用基金预算收入安排的支出。

一般公共服务支出 指政府提供基本公共管理与服务的支出，包括人大事务、政协事务、政府办公厅（室)及相关机构事务、发展与改革事务、统计信息事务、财政事务、税收事务、审计事务、海关事务、人力资源事务、纪检监察事务、人口与计划生育事务、 商贸事务、知识产权事务、工商行政管理事务、国土资源事务、 海洋管理事务、 测绘事务、地震事务、气象事务、民族事务、宗教事务、港澳台侨事务、档案事务、共产党事务、民主党派事务及工商联事务、群众团体事务、彩票事务等。

教育支出 指政府教育事务支出，包括教育行政管理、学前教育、小学教育、初中教育、普通高中教育、普通高等教育、初等职业教育、中专教育、技校教育、职业高中教育、高等职业教育、广播电视教育、留学生教育、特殊教育、干部继续教育、教育机关服务等。

科学技术支出 指用于科学技术方面的支出，包括科学技术管理事务、基础研究、应用研究、技术研究与开发、科技条件与服务、社会科学、科学技术普及、科技交流与合作等。

文化旅游体育与传媒支出 指政府在文化、文物、体育、广播影视、新闻出版等方面的支出。

社会保障和就业支出 指政府在社会保障与就业方面的支出，包括社会保障和就业管理事务、民政管理事务、财政对社会保险基金的补助、补充全国社会保障基金、行政事业单位离退休、企业改革补助、就业补助、抚恤、退役安置、社会福利、残疾人事业、城市居民最低生活保障、其他城镇社会救济、农村社会救济、自然灾害生活救助、红十字事务等。

卫生健康 指政府医疗卫生与计划生育管理方面的支出。

节能环保支出 指政府环境保护支出，包括环境保护管理事务支出、环境监测与监察支出、污染治理支出、自然生态保护支出、天然林保护工程支出、退耕还林支出、风沙荒漠治理支出、退牧还草支出、已垦草原退耕还草、能源节约利用、污染减排、可再生能源和资源综合利用等支出。

交通运输支出 指政府交通运输和邮政业方面的支出，包括公路运输支出、水路运输支出、铁路运输支出、民用航空运输支出、邮政业支出等。

城乡社区支出 指政府城乡社区事务支出，包括城乡社区管理事务支出、城乡社区规划与管理支出、城乡社区公共设施支出、城乡社区住宅支出、城乡社区环境卫生支出、建设市场管理与监督支出等。

农林水支出 指政府农林水事务支出，包括农业支出、林业支出、水利支出、扶贫支出、农业综合开发支出等。

税收部分

税费收入 指由各级地方税务局征缴的各项税收收入和罚没收入。包括企业所得税、个人所得税、资源税、房产税、契税、城市维护建设税等。

税收收入 指由税务局征缴的各项税收收入。包括增值税、消费税、企业所得税、个人所得税、城市维护建设税等。

企业所得税 是对中国境内全部企业的生产经营所得和其他所得征收的一种税。

增值税 指以商品或劳务销售额为计税依据并实行扣除已征税款制度的一种流转税。

个人所得税 是对个人（自然人）取得的各项应税所得征收的一种税。

Explanatory Notes on Main Statistical Indicators

Finance

General Public Budgetary Revenue refers to the revenue organized by finance authorities at all levels in certain form and through certain procedures and involved in budgetary management.

Governmental Fund Budgetary Revenue refers to governmental fund budgetary revenues collected, transferred or allocated by government finance in the current year in accordance with regulations, and regulated by government finance and used for specific purpose.

Budgetary Revenue of State-owned Capital Operation refers to the state-owned capital income of the country as the owner and all kinds of income and expenditure budgets resulted from the allocation of the income. It is an important part of governmental budget.

Social Insurance Fund Budgetary Revenue refers to a legally effective annual financial revenue and expenditure plan of fund formulated by social insurance agencies in accordance with relevant laws and regulations of state budget management and social insurance as well as specified approval procedures.

Tax Revenue includes value-added tax, business tax, corporate income tax, individual income tax, resource tax, urban maintenance and construction tax, house property tax, stamp tax, urban land use tax, land appreciation tax, tax on vehicles and boat operation, farm land occupation tax, deed tax, etc.

Non-tax Revenue includes special program receipts, charge of administrative and institutional units, income of fines and confiscation, and other non-tax revenues.

General Public Budgetary Expenditure refers to the expenditure arranged by finance authorities at all levels from the general budgetary revenue according to the planned distribution.

Governmental Fund Budgetary Expenditure refers to the expenditure arranged by finance authorities at all levels according to the fund budget revenue.

Expenditure for General Public Services refers to the spending on the basic public management and services provided by the government, including the expenses on affairs of Beijing Municipal People's Congress, CPC Beijing Municipal Committee, General Office of Beijing Municipal Government and relative institutions, development and reform, statistical information, finance, taxation, audit, customs, human resources, discipline inspection and supervision, population and family planning, commerce and trade, intellectual property, administration for industry and commerce, land and resources, oceanic administration, surveying and mapping, earthquake, weather, ethnics, religions, Hong Kong, Macao, Taiwan, and Overseas Chinese, archive administration, Chinese Communist Party, democratic parties, federation of industry and commerce, mass organizations, and lottery, etc.

Expenditure for Education refers to the spending of government on education, including the expenses on the administration of education, pre-school education, primary education, junior high school education, senior high school education, general higher education, primary vocational education, secondary vocational education, technical school education, vocational senior high school education and higher vocational education, radio and television education, overseas student education, special education, continuing education for management personnel, and services for education authorities, etc.

Expenditure for Science and Technology refers to the spending on science and technology (S&T), including the expense on the administration of S&T, basic research, applied research, technology research and development, conditions and services of S&T, popularization of social science and S&T, exchanges and cooperation of S&T, etc.

Expenditure for Cultural, Tourism Sport and Media refers to the spending on culture, cultural relics, sports, radio, films, television, press and publication, etc.

Expenditure for Social Security and Employment refers to the spending on social security and employment, including the expenses on social security and employment administration affairs, civil affairs, budgetary subsidy on the social insurance funds, subsidy on National Social Security Fund, subsidy on retirees of administrative and institutional units, subsidy on enterprise reform, subsidy on employment, pension, reemployment of ex-serviceman, social welfare, the handicapped undertakings, subsistence allowances for urban residents, other urban social relief, rural social relief, relief for natural disasters, affairs of Red Cross, etc.

Expenditure for Health refers to the spending of government on health care and family planning.

Expenditure for Energy Conservation and Environmental Protection refers to the spending of government on environmental protection, including the expenses on administration of environmental protection, environment monitoring and supervision, pollution control, natural and ecological protection, projects of natural forest protection, reforestation, control of sand storms, returning pasture and grazing land to grassland, energy conservation and utilization, emission reduction, comprehensive utilization of renewable energy and resources, etc.

Expenditure for Transportation refers to the spending of government on transportation and postal services, including the expenses on highway transportation, waterway transportation, railway transportation, civil aviation transportation and postal services, etc.

Expenditure for Urban and Rural Community refers to the spending of government on urban and rural community affairs, including the expenses on administration of urban and rural communities, planning and management of urban and rural communities, public facilities in urban and rural communities, residential houses in urban and rural communities, sanitation in urban and rural communities, management and supervision of construction markets, etc.

Expenditure for Agriculture, Forestry and Water Conservancy refers to the spending of government on agriculture affairs, forestry affairs, water conservancy affairs, poverty alleviation and comprehensive agricultural development, etc.

Taxes

Local Tax Revenue refers to the revenue of taxes, fines and confiscations levied and collected by local tax bureaus at all levels, including, corporate income tax, personal income tax, resource tax, house property tax, deed tax, urban maintenance and construction tax, etc.

State Tax Revenue refers to the revenue of taxes levied and collected by tax authorities at all levels, including value-added tax, excise tax, corporate income tax, individual income tax, urban maintenance and construction tax, etc.

Corporate Income Tax is a sort of tax levied against income of China domestic enterprises from their production and operation and other income.

Value-Added Tax is a sort of commodity turnover tax based on commodity and service sales, with a system of deduction of tax levied.

Personal Income Tax is a sort of tax levied against taxable income earned by individuals (natural persons).

07

能源、资源和环境
ENERGY, RESOURCES AND ENVIRONMENT

简要说明

一、主要内容

本章资料包括北京市能源生产与消费情况、万元地区生产总值能耗、能源平衡表、能源消费弹性系数和北京地区用电量情况、土地利用情况、气象情况、水资源情况、排水及节水情况、园林绿化及森林情况、大气环境、固体废物处置情况等。

二、能源统计范围及测算方法

（一）关于统计范围。能源部分统计范围为全社会口径，调查方法包括：第二、三产业限额以上法人单位能源消费情况全面调查、限额以下法人单位能源消费情况抽样调查、农业生产能源消费统计、居民生活能源消费情况抽样调查及能源供应部门的能源供应情况等。

（二）关于测算方法。从全市范围看，各能源品种的生产量、供应量和消费量存在平衡关系。因此，在进行生产和居民生活的能源消费量测算时，根据全市各能源品种的生产量、供应量和供应结构进行平衡修正。

三、关于历史数据调整的问题

2004年能源消费数据为北京市第一次全国经济普查数据，1995-2003年的能源消费数据根据第一次经济普查的数据结果进行了修订。

2008年能源消费数据为北京市第二次全国经济普查数据，1995-2007年的能源消费数据根据第二次经济普查的数据结果进行了修订。

2010年，根据北京市第六次全国人口普查的数据结果对2006-2010年的人均指标数据进行了修订。

2013年能源消费数据为北京市第三次全国经济普查数据。2005-2012年的能源生产量、能源消费总量、万元地区生产总值能耗及下降率，以及2010-2012年的能源消费构成、能源消费弹性系数、平均每万元地区生产总值能源消费量、人均生活用能源、主要能源日均消费量数据已根据第三次全国经济普查的数据结果进行了修订。

2018年能源消费数据为北京市第四次全国经济普查数据。2015-2017年的能源消费数据根据第四次全国经济普查的数据结果进行了修订。1992-2017年的万元地区生产总值能耗及下降率、万元地区生产总值水耗及下降率、能源消费弹性系数、平均每万元地区生产总值能源消费量中使用的地区生产总值数据，根据北京市第四次全国经济普查的数据结果进行了修订。

四、有关统计标准的变化说明

（一）关于行业划分。2012年以前，执行《国民经济行业分类》（GB/T 4754-2002）标准。2012-2017年执行《国民经济行业分类》（GB/T 4754-2011）标准。自2018年起，执行《国民经济行业分类》（GB/T 4754-2017）标准。.

（二）关于三次产业划分。2003年，根据《国民经济行业分类》（GB/T 4754—2002），国家统计局印发了《国家统计局关于印发〈三次产业划分规定〉的通知》（国统字〔2003〕14号）。2012年，根据国家质检总局和国家标准委颁布的《国民经济行业分类》（GB/T 4754—2011），国家统计局对2003年《三次产业划分规定》进行了修订。主要在以下方面作出调整：一是将门类“农、林、牧、渔业”中的“农、林、牧、渔服务业”，“采矿业”中的“开采辅助活动”，“制造业”中的“金属制品、机械和设备修理业”等三个大类一并调整到第三产业。调整后，第一产业为4个大类；第二产业为2个门类和36个大类；第三产业为15个门类和3个大类。二是明确第三产业即为服务业。

Brief Introduction

I. Main Content

Statistics in this chapter include the energy production and energy consumption in Beijing, energy consumption in regions with RMB 10,000 of GDP, energy balance sheet, energy consumption elasticity coefficient, electricity consumption in Beijing, land utilization, meteorology, water resources, water drainage and water saving, landscaping and forest, atmospheric environment, solid waste disposal and other environmental protection data.

II. Scope of Statistics and Calculation Method for Energy

(I) Scope of Statistics. Statistics on energy cover the entire society. The survey methods include: comprehensive survey on energy consumption of legal entities above designated size in the secondary and tertiary industries, sample survey on energy consumption of legal entities below designated size, statistics on energy consumption in agricultural production, sample survey on household energy consumption, and energy supply by energy supply departments, etc.

(II) Calculation Method. From the perspective of the whole city, there is a relationship of balance among the production, supply and consumption of various energy varieties. Therefore, balance correction shall be conducted according to the production, supply and supply structure of various energy varieties of the whole city when calculating the energy consumption for production and the household energy consumption.

III. Adjustment to Historical Data

Data on energy consumption for 2004 were collected from the first national economic census in Beijing; data on energy consumption for the period between 1995 and 2003 had been revised according to the data of the first economic census.

Data on energy consumption for 2008 were collected from the second national economic census in Beijing; data on energy consumption for the period between 1995 and 2007 had been revised in accordance with the data of the second economic census.

The per-capita energy consumption for living and per-capita water resources are calculated by annual average permanent population; in 2010, the per-capita index data from 2006 to 2010 were revised in accordance with the results of the sixth national population census in Beijing.

Data on energy consumption for 2013 were collected from the third national economic census in Beijing. Data on energy production, total energy consumption, energy consumption per RMB 10,000 of GDP and the decrease rate for the period between 2005 and 2012, and the data on composition of energy consumption from 2010 to 2012, the data on energy consumption elasticity coefficient, average energy consumption per RMB 10,000 of GDP, per-capita energy consumption for living, daily average consumption of main energy, have been revised in accordance with the results of the third national economic census.

Data on energy consumption for 2018 were collected from the fourth national economic census in Beijing. Data on energy consumption for the period between 2015 and 2017 had been revised according to the results of the fourth national economic census. Data on energy consumption per RMB 10,000 of GDP and the decrease rate, water consumption per RMB 10,000 of GDP and the decrease rate, energy consumption elasticity coefficient, and the GDP data for energy consumption per RMB 10,000 of GDP, for the period between 1992 and 2017 have been revised in accordance with the results of the fourth national economic census in Beijing.

IV. Changes in Relevant Statistical Standards

(I) Classification of Sectors. The standards in the *Classification of National Economic Sectors* (GB/T 4754-2002) were implemented before 2012. The standards in the *Classification of National Economic Sectors (GB/T 4754-2011)* were implemented from 2012 to 2017. The standards in the *Classification of National Economic Sectors* (GB/T 4754-2017) are implemented since 2018.

(II) Classification of Three Industries. According to the *Classification of National Economic Sectors* (GB/T 4754-2002), the National Bureau of Statistics issued the *Notice of the National Bureau of Statistics on the Issuance of the 'Regulations on Three Industries Classification'* (G.T.Z. [2003] No. 14) in 2003. According to the *Classification of National Economic Sectors* (GB/T 4754-2011) promulgated by the General Administration of Quality Supervision, Inspection and Quarantine of the People's Republic of China and the Standardization Administration of the People's Republic of China, the National Bureau of Statistics revised the *Regulations on Three Industries Classification* of 2003 version in 2012. Adjustments were mainly made in the following aspects: Firstly, the "service activities for agriculture, forestry, animal husbandry and fishing" in the category of "agriculture, forestry, animal production and hunting, fishing", the "mining support service activities" in the category of "mining and quarrying", and the "repair of fabricated metal products, machinery and equipment" in the category of "manufacturing" were adjusted to the tertiary industry. After adjustment, the primary industry fell into 4 categories; the secondary industry fell into 2 classes and 36 categories; and the tertiary industry fell into 15 classes and 3 categories. Secondly, the tertiary industry was defined as the service industry.

7-1 能源生产量(2005-2019年)
ENERGY PRODUCTION (2005-2019)

年 份 Year	一次能源 合计 (万吨标准煤) Primary Energy Total (10000 tons of SCE)	#原 煤 (万吨) Raw Coal (10000 tons)	#水 电 (亿千瓦时) Hydropower (100 million kWh)	#风 电 (亿千瓦时) Wind Power (100 million kWh)	#光伏发电 (亿千瓦时) Photovoltaic Power (100 million kWh)
2005	679.5	945.2	4.0		
2006	460.6	642.1	4.1		
2007	466.1	648.8	4.2		
2008	414.2	578.5	4.5	0.9	
2009	475.7	641.3	4.4	1.4	
2010	499.9	500.1	4.3	3.1	
2011	500.3	500.1	4.5	3.1	
2012	507.2	493.1	4.2	3.1	
2013	541.7	500.1	4.7	3.3	0.1
2014	514.0	457.5	6.8	2.8	0.1
2015	545.6	450.1	6.6	2.6	0.5
2016	445.8	317.6	12.2	3.3	1.1
2017	416.9	255.0	11.2	3.5	2.0
2018	611.5	176.2	9.9	3.5	3.1
2019	691.1	36.1	10.2	3.4	4.8

7-1 续表 Continued

年 份 Year	二次能源 合计 (万吨标准煤) Secondary Energy (10000 tons of SCE)	#汽 油 (万吨) Gasoline (10000 tons)	#煤 油 (万吨) Kerosene (10000 tons)	#柴 油 (万吨) Diesel Oil (10000 tons)	#燃料油 (万吨) Fuel Oil (10000 tons)	#液化石油气 (万吨) Liquefied Petroleum Gas (10000 tons)	#热 力 (万百万千焦) Heat Petroleum Gas (10000 million kilo-joule)	#电 力 (亿千瓦时) Electricity (100 million kWh)
2005	2772.6	142.2	12.4	154.7	64.5	47.3	11335.7	209.8
2006	2632.9	145.6	11.6	167.1	57.9	23.0	12181.6	209.7
2007	2767.9	160.4	36.4	244.7	36.7	41.0	12686.9	224.2
2008	3104.9	202.3	85.2	354.8	28.6	42.9	13650.5	244.7
2009	3146.9	242.1	111.6	314.8	28.0	28.8	14226.1	241.9
2010	3397.8	247.7	116.1	314.5	33.7	29.0	15345.0	262.0
2011	3080.9	245.3	126.4	309.3	21.3	27.2	14795.5	256.1
2012	3135.6	255.2	132.9	274.5	18.4	31.9	15400.5	283.3
2013	3000.2	223.9	99.4	194.7	16.9	28.1	14893.6	326.7
2014	3314.3	287.4	152.3	219.8	4.7	32.1	15055.4	351.6
2015	3460.4	296.3	160.0	180.4	1.4	34.0	15819.7	412.5
2016	3267.7	260.5	149.8	152.5	0.7	41.3	16091.9	419.0
2017	3316.6	271.0	190.8	156.6	3.6	41.6	16473.3	376.2
2018	3523.4	276.2	187.6	159.8	4.2	42.4	18380.0	432.1
2019	3601.5	285.5	191.3	173.1	0.7	46.1	18195.2	443.0

7-2 能源消费总量及构成情况(2010-2019年)
PRIMARY ENERGY CONSUMPTION AND ITS COMPOSITION(2010-2019)

年 份 Year	能源消费总量 (万吨标准煤) Total Energy Consumption (10000 tons of SCE)	占能源消费总量的比重 (%) As Percentage of Primary Energy Production (%) 煤 炭 Coal	石 油 Petroleum	天然气 Natural Gas	一次电力 Primary Electricity	电力净调入(+)、调出(-)量 Net Amount of Electricity Transferred in/out	其他能源 Other Energy
2010	6359.49	29.59	30.94	14.58	0.45	24.35	0.09
2011	6397.30	26.66	32.92	14.02	0.45	25.62	0.33
2012	6564.10	25.22	31.61	17.11	0.42	25.38	0.26
2013	6723.90	23.31	32.19	18.20	0.35	24.99	0.96
2014	6831.23	20.37	32.56	21.09	0.41	24.03	1.54
2015	6802.79	13.05	33.79	29.18	0.40	21.71	1.88
2016	6916.72	9.22	33.14	31.88	0.66	23.37	1.73
2017	7088.33	5.06	34.00	32.00	0.65	26.15	2.14
2018	7269.76	2.77	34.14	34.17	0.61	25.68	2.63
2019	7360.32	1.81	34.55	34.01	0.67	25.79	3.17

7–3 能源消费总量及万元地区生产总值能耗(1980–2019年)
TOTAL ENERGY CONSUMPTION AND ENERGY CONSUMPTION PER 10000 YUAN OF GDP (1980-2019)

单位：万吨标准煤 (10000 tons of SCE)

年 份 Year	能源消费总量 Total Energy Consumption	第一产业 Primary Industry	第二产业 Secondary Industry	第三产业 Tertiary Industry	生活消费 Residential Consumption	万元地区生产总值能耗（吨标准煤）Energy Consumption per 10000 Yuan of GDP (ton of SCE)	万元地区生产总值能耗下降率(%) Decrease Rate of Energy Consumption per 10000 Yuan GDP(%)
1980	1907.7	66.8	1400.3	297.6	143.0	13.715	
1981	1902.6	53.3	1339.4	334.9	175.0	13.668	-0.23
1982	1920.4	55.7	1346.2	338.0	180.5	12.398	6.02
1983	1984.7	73.4	1379.4	313.6	218.3	10.839	11.22
1984	2144.1	85.8	1470.9	347.3	240.1	9.899	7.98
1985	2211.4	90.7	1488.3	351.6	280.8	8.601	5.12
1986	2400.0	95.7	1612.0	380.4	311.9	8.424	-0.49
1987	2475.8	89.0	1647.8	424.7	314.3	7.576	5.88
1988	2612.6	111.7	1748.1	412.2	340.6	6.369	6.45
1989	2653.2	114.4	1735.9	427.0	375.9	5.818	2.73
1990	2709.7	105.7	1720.1	515.3	368.6	5.411	2.92
1991	2872.0	126.7	1807.6	542.0	395.7	4.795	3.56
1992	2987.5	143.6	1888.1	552.4	403.4	4.877	6.54
1993	3264.6	133.6	2150.9	561.0	419.1	4.745	2.69
1994	3385.9	143.6	2234.1	574.8	433.4	4.329	8.78
1995	3533.3	120.4	2328.4	632.7	451.8	4.033	6.83
1996	3734.5	110.8	2477.0	698.1	448.6	3.882	3.76
1997	3719.2	95.7	2369.6	799.8	454.1	3.508	9.64
1998	3808.1	96.2	2400.5	856.4	455.0	3.277	6.58
1999	3906.6	86.9	2370.7	971.8	477.2	3.029	7.57
2000	4144.0	104.8	2424.8	1080.9	533.5	2.868	5.29
						(1.264)	
2001	4229.2	105.4	2366.6	1196.2	561.0	1.154	8.71
2002	4436.1	103.0	2414.6	1334.5	584.0	1.083	6.18
2003	4648.2	99.9	2476.7	1391.0	680.6	1.021	5.69
2004	5139.6	85.6	2664.2	1638.0	751.8	0.997	2.41
2005	5049.8	85.4	2363.7	1771.7	829.0	0.872	4.33
						(0.706)	
2006	5399.3	91.1	2421.2	1962.8	924.2	0.669	5.21
2007	5747.7	95.1	2434.6	2198.4	1019.6	0.623	6.96
2008	5786.2	95.2	2215.6	2394.3	1081.1	0.575	7.63
2009	6008.6	97.1	2206.5	2527.3	1177.7	0.543	5.63
2010	6359.5	98.5	2364.1	2654.4	1242.5	0.521	4.12
						(0.425)	
2011	6397.3	98.3	2160.1	2818.9	1320.0	0.396	6.94
2012	6564.1	98.1	2082.1	2967.0	1416.9	0.377	4.74
2013	6723.9	97.3	2079.2	3109.1	1438.3	0.358	4.93
2014	6831.2	91.7	1998.4	3236.5	1504.6	0.339	5.40
2015	6802.8	84.6	1902.7	3312.6	1502.9	0.316	6.18
						(0.275)	
2016	6916.7	80.4	1870.8	3414.4	1551.1	0.261	4.91
2017	7088.3	72.0	1844.2	3519.3	1652.8	0.251	4.04
2018	7269.8	60.7	1835.2	3681.4	1692.4	0.241	3.88
2019	7360.3	55.8	1850.7	3762.5	1691.4	0.230	4.53

注：1. 本表能源消费量指标按等价值计算，万元地区生产总值能耗下降率按可比价格计算。
2. 1992年以前万元地区生产总值能耗按当年价格计算；1992年及以后按可比价格计算。更换基期年份计算两个可比价数据，括号内数据按新基期价格计算。
3. 第一产业中包含农林牧渔服务业能源消费；2017年及以前，第二产业中包含开采专业及辅助性活动、金属制品、机械和设备修理业的能源消费，下同。
4. 2019年，万元地区生产总值能耗及其下降率为初步统计数据，下同。

Note: a) Energy consumption in this table is calculated at equivalent prices. Decrease rate of energy consumption per 10000 yuan of GDP is calculated at comparable prices

b) Energy consumption per 10000 yuan of GDP before 1992 was calculated at the price of that year; figures in and after 1992 were calculated at comparable prices. Two figures at comparable prices were calculated for the year in which the base period was changed. Figures in brackets were calculated at the price of new base period.

c) In the primary industry, the energy consumption of the service activities for agriculture, forestry, animal husbandry and fishing were included; the energy consumption in the mining and support activities, repair of fabricated metal products, machinery and equipment were included in the secondary industry in and before 2017, the same below.

d) The data for 2019 on the energy consumption per 10000 yuan of GDP and its decrease rate were the preliminary statistical data, the same below.

7-4 按行业分能源消费总量
TOTAL ENERGY CONSUMPTION BY SECTOR

单位：万吨标准煤 (10000 tons of SCE)

项 目	Item	2019	2018
能源消费总量	**Total Energy Consumption**	**7360.3**	**7269.8**
按产业分	**By Three Industies**		
第一产业	Primary Industry	55.8	60.7
第二产业	Secondary Industry	1850.7	1835.2
第三产业	Tertiary Industry	3762.5	3681.4
生活消费	Residential Consumption	1691.4	1692.4
按行业分	**By Sector**		
#采矿业	Mining and Quarrying	6.4	9.2
制造业	Manufacturing	1162.9	1148.9
电力、热力、燃气及水生产和供应业	Production and Distribution of Electricity, Heating Power, Gas and Water	559.6	554.2
建筑业	Construction	126.9	127.3
批发和零售业	Wholesale and Retail Trade	207.8	210.8
交通运输、仓储和邮政业	Transport, Storage and Post	1533.8	1491.9
住宿和餐饮业	Accommodation and Restaurants	229.3	248.7
信息传输、软件和信息技术服务业	Information Transmission,Software and Information Technology Services	240.3	219.0
金融业	Finance	66.3	66.4
房地产业	Real Estate	441.6	427.6
租赁和商务服务业	Renting and Leasing Activities and Business Services	189.6	192.0
科学研究和技术服务业	Scientific Research and Development, Technical Services	183.3	182.1
水利、环境和公共设施管理业	Management of Water Conservancy, Environment and Public Facilities	80.2	73.9
居民服务、修理和其他服务业	Resident Services, Repair and Other Services	33.4	30.7
教 育	Education	235.3	236.9
卫生和社会工作	Healthcare and Social Works	96.2	94.9
文化、体育和娱乐业	Culture, Sports and Entertainment	70.4	70.3
公共管理、社会保障和社会组织	Public Administration, Social Security and Social Organizations	149.87	131.9

7-5 按三次产业分万元地区生产总值能耗(2000-2019年)
ENERGY CONSUMPTION PER 10000 YUAN OF GDP BY THREE INDUSTRIES (2000-2019)

单位：吨标准煤 (ton of SCE)

年 份 Year	万元地区生产总值能耗 Energy Consumption per 10000 yuan of GDP	按产业分 By Three Industies			按行业分 By Sector	
		第一产业 Primary Industry	第二产业 Secondary Industry	第三产业 Tertiary Industry	#工 业 Industry	#交通运输、仓储和邮政业 Transport, Storage and Post
	地区生产总值按2000年可比价计算 GDP calculated at the comparable prices of 2000					
2000	1.264	1.322	2.369	0.497	2.836	1.420
2001	1.154	1.284	2.121	0.485	2.525	1.653
2002	1.083	1.218	2.007	0.475	2.397	1.732
2003	1.021	1.199	1.868	0.443	2.202	1.798
2004	0.997	1.032	1.742	0.462	2.003	2.162
2005	0.872	1.046	1.409	0.439	1.619	2.091
	地区生产总值按2005年可比价计算 GDP calculated at the comparable prices of 2005					
2005	0.706	0.983	1.239	0.344	1.422	1.502
2006	0.669	1.041	1.155	0.334	1.341	1.806
2007	0.623	1.065	1.037	0.324	1.201	1.968
2008	0.575	1.048	0.941	0.315	1.089	2.262
2009	0.543	1.022	0.852	0.302	0.989	2.294
2010	0.521	1.054	0.805	0.289	0.923	2.228
	地区生产总值按2010年可比价计算 GDP calculated at the comparable prices of 2010					
2010	0.425	0.802	0.731	0.229	0.852	1.711
2011	0.396	0.793	0.627	0.224	0.724	1.723
2012	0.377	0.767	0.566	0.218	0.658	1.717
2013	0.358	0.738	0.525	0.212	0.611	1.725
2014	0.339	0.696	0.472	0.205	0.554	1.716
2015	0.316	0.720	0.437	0.194	0.527	1.733
	地区生产总值按2015年可比价计算 GDP calculated at the comparable prices of 2015					
2015	0.275	0.603	0.430	0.164	0.516	1.689
2016	0.261	0.627	0.402	0.157	0.484	1.684
2017	0.251	0.590	0.380	0.151	0.454	1.605
2018	0.241	0.507	0.364	0.147	0.434	1.631
2019	0.230	0.478	0.351	0.141	0.425	1.641

7-6 按三次产业分万元地区生产总值能耗下降率(2001-2019年)
ENERGY CONSUMPTION PER 10000 YUAN OF GDP DECREASE RATE BY THREE INDUSTRIES (2001-2019)

单位：% (%)

年份 Year	万元地区生产总值能耗下降率 Decrease Rate of Energy Consumption per 10000 yuan GDP	按产业分 By Three Industies			按行业分 By Sector	
		第一产业 Primary Industry	第二产业 Secondary Industry	第三产业 Tertiary Industry	#工业 Industry	#交通运输、仓储和邮政业 Transport, Storage and Post
2001	8.71	2.92	10.45	2.43	10.94	-16.41
2002	6.18	5.12	5.39	2.04	5.07	-4.76
2003	5.69	1.53	6.91	6.83	8.15	-3.79
2004	2.41	13.97	6.77	-4.40	9.03	-20.27
2005	4.33	-2.46	7.52	-2.98	7.64	-4.09
2006	5.21	-5.87	6.83	2.87	5.66	-20.22
2007	6.96	-2.31	10.16	3.00	10.49	-8.99
2008	7.63	1.52	9.27	2.83	9.34	-14.92
2009	5.63	2.50	9.50	4.12	9.15	-1.43
2010	4.12	-3.10	5.51	4.16	6.63	2.89
2011	6.94	1.09	14.29	2.19	15.07	-0.73
2012	4.74	3.34	9.73	2.56	9.10	0.37
2013	4.93	3.69	7.29	2.78	7.13	-0.46
2014	5.40	5.73	10.01	3.28	9.32	0.50
2015	6.18	-3.44	7.37	5.38	4.96	-0.98
2016	4.91	-4.07	6.67	4.00	6.13	0.27
2017	4.04	5.94	5.38	4.06	6.32	4.70
2018	3.88	15.90	4.22	2.50	4.38	-1.61
2019	4.53	5.72	3.48	3.95	1.98	-0.60

注：表内万元地区生产总值能耗下降率按可比价格计算。
Note: Decrease rate of energy consumption per 10000 yuan of GDP in the table is calculated at comparable prices.

7-7 电力平衡表
ELECTRICITY BALANCE

单位：亿千瓦时 (100 million kWh)

项目	Item	2019	2018
可供本地区消费的能源量	**Total Energy Available for Local Consumption**	**723.38**	**709.90**
加工转换投入(-)产出(+)量	**Input(-) or Output(+) in Processing and Conversion**	**443.02**	**432.13**
火力发电	Thermal Power	443.02	432.13
供热	Heating		
煤炭洗选	Washing of Coal		
炼焦	Coking		
炼油及煤制油	Oil Refining and Coal to Liquid		
#油品再投入量(-)	Oil Product Re-input(-)		
制气	Gas Production		
#焦炭再投入量(-)	Coke Re-input(-)		
煤制品加工	Coal Product Processing		
回收能	Energy Recycled		
损失量	**Losses**	**66.28**	**69.41**
#运输和输配损失	In Transportation and Transmission	66.28	69.41
终端消费量	**End-use Energy Consumption**	**1100.12**	**1072.97**
农、林、牧、渔业	Agriculture, Forestry, Animal Production and Hunting, Fishing	17.68	18.84
工业	Industry	232.79	226.01
#用作原料、材料	Use as Materials		
建筑业	Construction	26.39	25.30
交通运输、仓储和邮政业	Transport, Storage and Post	57.98	55.87
批发和零售业、住宿和餐饮业	Wholesale and Retail Trade, Accommodation and Restaurants	96.51	102.90
其他	Others	417.17	387.68
居民生活	Residential Consumption	251.60	256.36
城镇	Urban	204.95	210.62
乡村	Rural	46.65	45.74
平衡差额	**Balance**		**-0.34**
消费量合计	**Total Energy Consumption**	**1166.40**	**1142.38**

7-8 综合能源平衡表(标准量)
COMPREHENSIVE ENERGY BALANCE (STANDARD VOLUME)

单位：万吨标准煤 (10000 tons of SCE)

项　　目	Item	2019	2018
可供本地区消费的能源量	**Total Energy Available for Local Consumption**	**7360.35**	**7268.80**
加工转换投入(-)产出(+)量	**Input(-) or Output(+) in Procesing and Conversion**	**-61.57**	**-64.52**
火力发电	Thermal Power		
供　热	Heating	-70.00	-73.36
煤炭洗选	Washing of Coal		
炼　焦	Coking		
炼油及煤制油	Oil Refining and Coal to Liquid	450.37	431.74
#油品再投入量(-)	Oil Product Re-input(-)	-455.97	-436.78
制　气	Gas Production		
#焦炭再投入量(-)	Coke Re-input(-)		
煤制品加工	Coal Product Processing		
回收能	Energy Recycled	13.98	13.88
损失量	**Losses**	**244.09**	**265.72**
#运输和输配损失	In Transportation and Transmission	178.44	186.80
终端消费量	**End-use Energy Consumption**	**7054.66**	**6939.52**
农、林、牧、渔业	Agriculture, Forestry, Animal Production and Hunting, Fishing	55.75	60.73
工　业	Industry	1423.26	1382.14
#用作原料、材料	Use as Materials	267.84	242.28
建筑业	Construction	126.92	127.31
交通运输、仓储和邮政业	Transport, Storage and Post	1533.82	1491.90
批发和零售业、住宿和餐饮业	Wholesale and Retail Trade, Accommodation and Restaurants	437.09	459.52
其　他	Others	1786.41	1725.57
居民生活	Residential Consumption	1691.41	1692.36
城　镇	Urban	1445.88	1446.45
乡　村	Rural	245.53	245.91
平衡差额	**Balance**	**0.03**	**-0.96**
消费量合计	**Total Energy Consumption**	**7360.32**	**7269.76**

7-9 能源平衡表(实物量简表)(2018年)
ENERGY BALANCE (PHYSICAL VOLUME) (SIMPLE EDITION) (2018)

单位：万吨 (10000 tons)

项目	Item	原煤 Coal	洗精煤 Washed Coal	其他洗煤 Other Washed Coal	煤制品 Coal Products	焦炭 Coke	原油 Crude Oil	汽油 Gaso-line	煤油 Kero-sene
可供本地区消费的能源量	**Total Energy Available for Local Consumption**	**221.57**			**54.61**	**0.01**	**911.77**	**217.38**	**503.46**
加工转换投入(-)产出(+)量	**Input(-) or Output(+) in Procesing and Conversion**	**-146.37**					**-911.34**	**276.21**	**187.57**
火力发电	Thermal Power	-49.67							
供热	Heating	-96.70							
煤炭洗选	Washing of Coal								
炼焦	Coking								
炼油及煤制油	Oil Refining and Coal to Liquid						-911.34	276.21	187.57
#油品再投入量(-)	Oil Product Re-input(-)								
制气	Gas Production								
#焦炭再投入量(-)	Coke Re-input(-)								
煤制品加工	Coal Product Processing								
回收能	Energy Recycled								
损失量	**Losses**						**0.44**		
#运输和输配损失	In Transportation and Transmission								
终端消费量	**End-use Energy Consumption**	**75.20**			**54.61**	**0.01**		**493.60**	**691.03**
农、林、牧、渔业	Agriculture, Forestry, Animal Production and Hunting, Fishing	4.02						2.50	
工业	Industry	43.34				…		10.83	0.05
#用作原料、材料	Use as Materials							0.01	0.01
建筑业	Construction	0.20						9.02	
交通运输、仓储和邮政业	Transport, Storage and Post	0.94				…		42.57	690.47
批发和零售业、住宿和餐饮业	Wholesale and Retail Trade, Accommodation and Restaurants	1.85				…		21.90	
其他	Others	3.29				…		49.55	0.51
居民生活	Residential Consumption	21.57			54.61			357.23	
城镇	Urban	21.57						357.23	
乡村	Rural				54.61				
平衡差额	**Balance**	**-0.01**				**…**			
消费量合计	**Total Energy Consumption**	**221.58**			**54.61**	**0.01**	**911.78**	**493.60**	**691.03**

7-9 续表 1 Continued 1

单位：万吨　　(10000 tons)

项　目	Item	柴　油 Diesel Oil	燃料油 Fuel Oil	石脑油 Naphtha	润滑油 Grease Oil	石　蜡 Oilfin	溶剂油 Solvent Oil	石油沥青 Oil Asphalt	石油焦 Petroleum Coal
可供本地区消费的能源量	**Total Energy Available for Local Consumption**	**19.01**	**-2.62**	**79.92**	**1.15**		**0.04**	**-9.78**	**-22.78**
加工转换投入(-)产出(+)量	**Input(-) or Output(+) in Procesing and Conversion**	**159.27**	**3.17**	**-2.73**				**20.92**	**22.79**
火力发电	Thermal Power	-0.19							-5.10
供　热	Heating	-0.32	-0.99						-19.56
煤炭洗选	Washing of Coal								
炼　焦	Coking								
炼油及煤制油	Oil Refining and Coal to Liquid	159.77	4.16	178.45				20.92	47.45
#油品再投入量(-)	Oil Product Re-input(-)			-181.18					
制　气	Gas Production								
#焦炭再投入量(-)	Coke Re-input(-)								
煤制品加工	Coal Product Processing								
回收能	Energy Recycled								
损失量	**Losses**								
#运输和输配损失	In Transportation and Transmission								
终端消费量	**End-use Energy Consumption**	**178.28**	**0.55**	**77.19**	**1.15**		**0.04**	**11.14**	**0.01**
农、林、牧、渔业	Agriculture, Forestry, Animal Production and Hunting, Fishing	1.95							
工　业	Industry	11.25	0.45	77.19	1.15		0.04	11.14	0.01
#用作原料、材料	Use as Materials			77.19	1.15		0.04	11.14	
建筑业	Construction	24.83							
交通运输、仓储和邮政业	Transport, Storage and Post	110.11	0.08						
批发和零售业、住宿和餐饮业	Wholesale and Retail Trade, Accommodation and Restaurants	4.28	0.01						
其　他	Others	25.85	0.01						
居民生活	Residential Consumption								
城　镇	Urban								
乡　村	Rural								
平衡差额	**Balance**								
消费量合计	**Total Energy Consumption**	**178.78**	**1.54**	**258.37**	**1.15**		**0.04**	**11.14**	**24.66**

7-9 续表 2 Continued 2

单位：万吨 (10000 tons)

项　　目	Item	液化石油气 Liquefied Petroleum Gas	炼厂干气 Refinery Gas	其它石油制品 Other Petroleum Products	天然气（亿立方米） Natural Gas (100 million cu.m)	液化天然气 Liquefied Natural Gas	热力（万百万千焦） Heat (10000 million kilo-joule)	电力（亿千瓦时） Electricity (100 million kWh)	其他能源（万吨标准煤） Others (10000 tons of SCE)
可供本地区消费的能源量	**Total Energy Available for Local Consumption**	**-6.27**		**15.94**	**184.85**	**21.95**	**541.32**	**709.90**	**172.54**
加工转换投入(−)产出(+)量	**Input(-) or Output(+) in Procesing and Conversion**	**40.01**	**65.02**	**87.59**	**-113.46**	**-1.40**	**18380.00**	**432.13**	**-72.96**
火力发电	Thermal Power	-0.20	-0.22	-0.12	-67.11			432.13	-86.85
供　热	Heating	-2.15	-5.34	-8.26	-46.35	-1.40	18380.00		
煤炭洗选	Washing of Coal								
炼　焦	Coking								
炼油及煤制油	Oil Refining and Coal to Liquid	42.36	70.58	233.48					
#油品再投入量(−)	Oil Product Re-input(-)			-137.51					
制　气	Gas Production								
#焦炭再投入量(−)	Coke Re-input(-)								
煤制品加工	Coal Product Processing								
回收能	Energy Recycled								13.88
损失量	**Losses**				**6.67**			**69.41**	
#运输和输配损失	In Transportation and Transmission							69.41	
终端消费量	**Final Consumption Industry**	**33.74**	**65.02**	**103.53**	**64.72**	**20.56**	**18921.33**	**1072.97**	**99.58**
农、林、牧、渔业	Agriculture, Forestry, Animal Production and Hunting, Fishing	0.05			0.04		0.45	18.84	
工　业	Industry	1.02	65.02	103.53	15.61	2.02	4437.59	226.01	8.13
#用作原料、材料	Use as Materials	0.05	9.48	77.41	0.03	0.02			
建筑业	Construction	0.46			0.36		124.19	25.30	0.30
交通运输、仓储和邮政业	Transport, Storage and Post	1.55			3.72	18.54	582.03	55.87	2.87
批发和零售业、住宿和餐饮业	Wholesale and Retail Trade, Accommodation and Restaurants	4.01			7.48		1274.02	102.90	4.64
其　他	Others	2.75			23.40		7675.05	387.68	27.26
居民生活	Residential Consumption	23.89			14.11		4828.00	256.36	56.38
城　镇	Urban	15.99			11.67		4828.00	210.62	4.61
乡　村	Rural	7.89			2.44			45.74	51.77
平衡差额	**Balance**							**-0.34**	
消费量合计	**Total Energy Consumption**	**36.09**	**70.58**	**249.42**	**184.85**	**21.97**	**18921.33**	**1142.38**	**186.42**

7-10 能源平衡表(实物量简表)(2019年)
ENERGY BALANCE (PHYSICAL VOLUME) (SIMPLE EDITION) (2019)

单位：万吨 (10000 tons)

项　目	Item	原煤 Coal	洗精煤 Washed Coal	其他洗煤 Other Washed Coal	煤制品 Coal Products	焦炭 Coke	原油 Crude Oil	汽油 Gaso-line	煤油 Kero-sene
可供本地区消费的能源量	**Total Energy Available for Local Consumption**	**147.03**			**35.76**		**936.99**	**215.45**	**506.51**
加工转换投入(-)产出(+)量	**Input(-) or Output(+) in Processing and Transformation**	**-86.42**					**-936.51**	**285.45**	**191.30**
火力发电	Thermal Power	-35.89							
供　热	Heating	-50.54							
煤炭洗选	Washing of Coal								
炼　焦	Coking								
炼油及煤制油	Oil Refining and Coal to Liquid						-936.51	285.45	191.30
#油品再投入量(-)	Oil Product Re-input(-)								
制　气	Gas Production								
#焦炭再投入量(-)	Coke Re-input(-)								
煤制品加工	Coal Product Processing								
回收能	Energy Recycled								
损失量	**Losses**						**0.48**		
#运输和输配损失	In Transportation and Transmission								
终端消费量	**Final Consumption Industry**	**60.61**			**35.76**			**500.90**	**697.80**
农、林、牧、渔业	Agriculture, Forestry, Animal Production and Hunting, Fishing	2.69						2.31	
工　业	Industry	40.98						9.59	0.06
#用作原料、材料	Use as Materials								0.01
建筑业	Construction	0.12						8.89	
交通运输、仓储和邮政业	Transport, Storage and Post	0.41						49.74	697.17
批发和零售业、住宿和餐饮业	Wholesale and Retail Trade, Accommodation and Restaurants	2.21						19.53	
其　他	Others	1.32						40.63	0.57
居民生活	Residential Consumption	12.89			35.76			370.20	
城　镇	Urban	12.89						370.20	
乡　村	Rural				35.76				
平衡差额	**Balance**								
消费量合计	**Total Energy Consumption**	**147.03**			**35.76**		**936.99**	**500.90**	**697.80**

7-10 续表 1 Continued 1

单位：万吨 (10000 tons)

项目	Item	柴油 Diesel Oil	燃料油 Fuel Oil	石脑油 Naphtha	润滑油 Grease Oil	石蜡 Oilfin	溶剂油 Solvent Oil	石油沥青 Oil Asphalt	石油焦 Petroleum Coal
可供本地区消费的能源量	**Total Energy Available for Local Consumption**	**-11.24**	**-0.23**	**85.84**	**0.83**		**0.01**	**-2.19**	**-16.01**
加工转换投入(-)产出(+)量	**Input(-) or Output(+) in Procesing and Conversion**	**172.65**	**0.66**	**-9.24**				**27.19**	**16.03**
火力发电	Thermal Power	-0.20							-6.45
供 热	Heating	-0.27	-0.06						-26.25
煤炭洗选	Washing of Coal								
炼 焦	Coking								
炼油及煤制油	Oil Refining and Coal to Liquid	173.11	0.72	181.29				27.19	48.74
#油品再投入量(-)	Oil Product Re-input(-)			-190.53					
制 气	Gas Production								
#焦炭再投入量(-)	Coke Re-input(-)								
煤制品加工	Coal Product Processing								
回收能	Energy Recycled								
损失量	**Losses**								
#运输和输配损失	In Transportation and Transmission								
终端消费量	**End-use Energy Consumption**	**161.41**	**0.42**	**76.60**	**0.82**		**0.01**	**25.00**	**0.02**
农、林、牧、渔业	Agriculture, Forestry, Animal Production and Hunting, Fishing	1.81							
工 业	Industry	11.03	0.14	76.60	0.82		0.01	25.00	0.02
#用作原料、材料	Use as Materials			76.60	0.82		0.01	25.00	
建筑业	Construction	22.28							
交通运输、仓储和邮政业	Transport, Storage and Post	99.81	0.27						
批发和零售业、住宿和餐饮业	Wholesale and Retail Trade, Accommodation and Restaurants	4.54							
其 他	Others	21.95	0.01						
居民生活	Residential Consumption								
城 镇	Urban								
乡 村	Rural								
平衡差额	**Balance**				…				
消费量合计	**Total Energy Consumption**	**161.87**	**0.48**	**267.13**	**0.82**		**0.01**	**25.00**	**32.72**

7-10 续表 2 Continued 2

单位：万吨 (10000 tons)

项　目	Item	液化石油气 Liquefied Petroleum Gas	炼厂干气 Refinery Gas	其它石油制品 Other Petroleum Products	天然气(亿立方米) Natural Gas (100 million cu.m)	液化天然气 Liquefied Natural Gas	热力(万百万千焦) Heat (10000 million kilo-joule)	电力(亿千瓦时) Electricity (100 million kWh)	其他能源(万吨标准煤) Others (10000 tons of SCE)
可供本地区消费的能源量	**Total Energy Available for Local Consumption**	**3.38**		**33.05**	**186.37**	**21.98**	**560.46**	**723.38**	**214.45**
加工转换投入(-)产出(+)量	**Input(-) or Output(+) in Procesing and Conversion**	**39.91**	**73.75**	**72.66**	**-116.87**	**-0.90**	**18195.17**	**443.02**	**-105.45**
火力发电	Thermal Power	-0.08	-0.12	-0.59	-69.36			443.02	-119.43
供　热	Heating	-1.41	-5.60	-13.94	-47.51	-0.90	18195.17		
煤炭洗选	Washing of Coal								
炼　焦	Coking								
炼油及煤制油	Oil Refining and Coal to Liquid	46.05	79.47	222.37					
#油品再投入量(-)	Oil Product Re-input(-)	-4.65		-135.17					
制　气	Gas Production								
#焦炭再投入量(-)	Coke Re-input(-)								
煤制品加工	Coal Product Processing								
回收能	Energy Recycled								13.98
损失量	**Losses**				**5.39**			**66.28**	
#运输和输配损失	In Transportation and Transmission							66.28	
终端消费量	**Final Consumption Industry**	**43.29**	**73.75**	**105.72**	**64.10**	**21.09**	**18755.63**	**1100.12**	**109.00**
农、林、牧、渔业	Agriculture, Forestry, Animal Production and Hunting, Fishing	0.05						17.68	
工　业	Industry	0.77	73.75	105.72	14.99	1.56	4370.82	232.79	7.17
#用作原料、材料	Use as Materials	0.09	13.74	78.79	0.03				
建筑业	Construction	0.48			0.41		121.36	26.39	0.30
交通运输、仓储和邮政业	Transport, Storage and Post	17.41			3.42	19.52	617.55	57.98	6.26
批发和零售业、住宿和餐饮业	Wholesale and Retail Trade, Accommodation and Restaurants	3.47			7.35		1206.89	96.51	4.65
其　他	Others	2.32			23.35		7504.01	417.17	28.57
居民生活	Residential Consumption	18.80			14.59		4935.00	251.60	62.06
城　镇	Urban	10.70			12.04		4935.00	204.95	5.67
乡　村	Rural	8.10			2.55			46.65	56.39
平衡差额	**Balance**								
消费量合计	**Total Energy Consumption**	**49.43**	**79.47**	**255.42**	**186.37**	**21.98**	**18755.63**	**1166.40**	**228.43**

7−11 能源平衡表(标准量简表)(2018年)
ENERGY BALANCE (STANDARD VOLUME) (SIMPLE EDITION) (2018)

单位：万吨标准煤 (10000 tons of SCE)

项　目	Item	合　计 Total	原　煤 Coal	洗精煤 Washed Coal	其　他 洗　煤 Other Washed Coal	煤制品 Coal Products	焦　炭 Coke	原 油 Crude Oil	汽　油 Gaso-line	煤　油 Kero-sene
可供本地区消费的能源量	**Total Energy Available for Local Consumption**	**7268.80**	**172.35**			**28.87**	**0.01**	**1302.56**	**319.85**	**740.79**
加工转换投入(−)产出(+)量	**Input(-) or Output(+) in Processing and Transformation**	**-64.52**	**-112.72**					**-1301.94**	**406.42**	**275.99**
火力发电	Thermal Power		-38.12							
供　热	Heating	-73.36	-74.60							
煤炭洗选	Washing of Coal									
炼　焦	Coking									
炼油及煤制油	Oil Refining and Coal to Liquid	431.74						-1301.94	406.42	275.99
#油品再投入量(−)	Oil Product Re-input(-)	-436.78								
制　气	Gas Production									
#焦炭再投入量(−)	Coke Re-input(-)									
煤制品加工	Coal Product Processing									
回收能	Energy Recycled	13.88								
损失量	**Losses**	**265.72**						**0.63**		
#运输和输配损失	In Transportation and Transmission	186.80								
终端消费量	**Final Consumption Industry**	**6939.52**	**59.64**			**28.87**	**0.01**		**726.28**	**1016.78**
农、林、牧、渔业	Agriculture, Forestry, Animal Production and Hunting, Fishing	60.72	2.94						3.68	
工　业	Industry	1382.14	31.75				…		15.93	0.08
#用作原料、材料	Use as Materials	242.28							0.01	0.01
建筑业	Construction	127.30	0.15						13.27	
交通运输、仓储和邮政业	Transport, Storage and Post	1491.90	0.69				…		62.63	1015.96
批发和零售业、住宿和餐饮业	Wholesale and Retail Trade, Accommodation and Restaurants	459.52	1.36				…		32.22	
其　他	Others	1725.57	2.42				…		72.91	0.75
居民生活	Residential Consumption	1692.36	20.33			28.87			525.63	
城　镇	Urban	1446.45	20.33						525.63	
乡　村	Rural	245.91				28.87				
平衡差额	**Balance**	**-0.96**					**…**	**-0.01**	**-0.01**	
消费量合计	**Total Energy Consumption**	**7269.76**								

7-11 续表 1 Continued 1

单位：万吨标准煤 (10000 tons of SCE)

项　目	Item	柴　油 Diesel Oil	燃料油 Fuel Oil	石脑油 Naphtha	润滑油 Grease Oil	石　蜡 Oilfin	溶剂油 Solvent Oil	石油沥青 Oil Asphalt	石油焦 Petroleum Coal
可供本地区消费的能源量	**Total Energy Available for Local Consumption**	**27.70**	**-3.74**	**119.88**	**1.63**		**0.06**	**-13.02**	**-25.59**
加工转换投入(-)产出(+)量	**Input(-) or Output(+) in Processing and Transformation**	**232.07**	**4.52**	**-4.09**				**27.84**	**25.60**
火力发电	Thermal Power	-0.27							-5.73
供　热	Heating	-0.47	-1.42						-21.97
煤炭洗选	Washing of Coal								
炼　焦	Coking								
炼油及煤制油	Oil Refining and Coal to Liquid	232.81	5.94	267.68				27.84	53.30
#油品再投入量(-)	Oil Product Re-input(-)			-271.77					
制　气	Gas Production								
#焦炭再投入量(-)	Coke Re-input(-)								
煤制品加工	Coal Product Processing								
回收能	Energy Recycled								
损失量	**Losses**								
#运输和输配损失	In Transportation and Transmission								
终端消费量	**Final Consumption Industry**	**259.77**	**0.78**	**115.79**	**1.63**		**0.05**	**14.82**	**0.01**
农、林、牧、渔业	Agriculture, Forestry, Animal Production and Hunting, Fishing	2.84							
工　业	Industry	16.39	0.64	115.79	1.63		0.05	14.82	0.01
#用作原料、材料	Use as Materials			115.79	1.63		0.05	14.82	
建筑业	Construction	36.19							
交通运输、仓储和邮政业	Transport, Storage and Post	160.44	0.12						
批发和零售业、住宿和餐饮业	Wholesale and Retail Trade, Accommodation and Restaurants	6.24	0.01						
其　他	Others	37.67	0.02						
居民生活	Residential Consumption								
城　镇	Urban								
乡　村	Rural								
平衡差额	**Balance**						**0.01**		
消费量合计	**Total Energy Consumption**								

7-11 续表 2 Continued 2

单位：万吨标准煤 (10000 tons of SCE)

项目	Item	液化石油气 Liquefied Petroleum Gas	炼厂干气 Refinery Gas	其它石油制品 Other Petroleum Products	天然气 Natural Gas (100 million cu.m)	液化天然气 Liquefied Natural Gas	热力 Heat	电力 Electricity	其它能源 Others
可供本地区消费的能源量	**Total Energy Available for Local Consumption**	**-10.75**		**22.58**	**2445.54**	**38.58**	**18.46**	**1910.51**	**172.54**
加工转换投入(-)产出(+)量	**Input(-) or Output(+) in Proce-ssing and Transformation**	**68.58**	**102.17**	**104.00**	**-1607.27**	**-2.46**	**626.76**	**1162.97**	**-72.96**
火力发电	Thermal Power	-0.34	-0.35	-0.16	-1031.15			1162.97	-86.85
供　热	Heating	-3.69	-8.39	-11.00	-576.12	-2.46	626.76		
煤炭洗选	Washing of Coal								
炼　焦	Coking								
炼油及煤制油	Oil Refining and Coal to Liquid	72.62	110.91	280.17					
#油品再投入量(-)	Oil Product Re-input(-)			-165.01					
制　气	Gas Production								
#焦炭再投入量(-)	Coke Re-input(-)								
煤制品加工	Coal Product Processing								
回收能	Energy Recycled								13.88
损失量	**Losses**				**78.30**			**186.80**	
#运输和输配损失	In Transportation and Transmission							186.80	
终端消费量	**Final Consumption Industry**	**57.84**	**102.17**	**126.58**	**759.97**	**36.14**	**645.22**	**2887.61**	**99.58**
农、林、牧、渔业	Agriculture, Forestry, Animal Production and Hunting, Fishing	0.09			0.45		0.02	50.71	
工　业	Industry	1.75	102.17	126.58	183.30	3.55	151.32	608.25	8.13
#用作原料、材料	Use as Materials	0.08	14.89	94.64	0.33	0.03			
建筑业	Construction	0.80			4.28		4.23	68.09	0.30
交通运输、仓储和邮政业	Transport, Storage and Post	2.66			43.73	32.58	19.85	150.37	2.87
批发和零售业、住宿和餐饮业	Wholesale and Retail Trade, Accommodation and Restaurants	6.87			87.79		43.44	276.94	4.64
其　他	Others	4.72			274.77		261.72	1043.34	27.26
居民生活	Residential Consumption	40.95			165.65		164.63	689.91	56.38
城　镇	Urban	27.42			137.00		164.63	566.82	4.61
乡　村	Rural	13.53			28.65			123.09	51.77
平衡差额	**Balance**					**-0.02**		**-0.93**	
消费量合计	**Total Energy Consumption**								

7-12 能源平衡表(标准量简表)(2019年)
ENERGY BALANCE (STANDARD VOLUME) (SIMPLE EDITION) (2019)

单位：万吨标准煤 (10000 tons of SCE)

项目	Item	合计 Total	原煤 Coal	洗精煤 Washed Coal	其他洗煤 Other Washed Coal	煤制品 Coal Products	焦炭 Coke	原油 Crude Oil	汽油 Gasoline	煤油 Kerosene
可供本地区消费的能源量	**Total Energy Available for Local Consumption**	**7360.35**	**114.15**			**18.90**		**1338.59**	**317.01**	**745.28**
加工转换投入(-)产出(+)量	**Input(-) or Output(+) in Processing and Transformation**	**-61.57**	**-66.11**					**-1337.90**	**420.01**	**281.48**
火力发电	Thermal Power		-27.45							
供热	Heating	-69.95	-38.66							
煤炭洗选	Washing of Coal									
炼焦	Coking									
炼油及煤制油	Oil Refining and Coal to Liquid	450.37						-1337.90	420.01	281.48
#油品再投入量(-)	Oil Product Re-input(-)	-455.97								
制气	Gas Production									
#焦炭再投入量(-)	Coke Re-input(-)									
煤制品加工	Coal Product Processing									
回收能	Energy Recycled	13.98								
损失量	**Losses**	**244.09**						**0.69**		
#运输和输配损失	In Transportation and Transmission	178.43								
终端消费量	**Final Consumption Industry**	**7054.66**	**48.04**			**18.90**			**737.02**	**1026.75**
农、林、牧、渔业	Agriculture, Forestry, Animal Production and Hunting, Fishing	55.75	2.02						3.40	
工业	Industry	1423.26	30.78						14.11	0.09
#用作原料、材料	Use as Materials	267.84							0.01	0.01
建筑业	Construction	126.92	0.09						13.08	0.01
交通运输、仓储和邮政业	Transport, Storage and Post	1533.82	0.31						73.19	1025.81
批发和零售业、住宿和餐饮业	Wholesale and Retail Trade, Accommodation and Restaurants	437.09	1.66						28.74	
其他	Others	1786.41	1.03						59.78	0.85
居民生活	Residential Consumption	1691.41	12.15			18.90			544.72	
城镇	Urban	1445.88	12.15						544.72	
乡村	Rural	245.53				18.90				
平衡差额	**Balance**	**0.03**								**0.01**
消费量合计	**Total Energy Consumption**	**7360.32**								

7-12 续表 1 Continued 1

单位：万吨标准煤 (10000 tons of SCE)

项目	Item	柴油 Diesel Oil	燃料油 Fuel Oil	石脑油 Naphtha	润滑油 Grease Oil	石蜡 Oilfin	溶剂油 Solvent Oil	石油沥青 Oil Asphalt	石油焦 Petroleum Coal
可供本地区消费的能源量	**Total Energy Available for Local Consumption**	**-16.37**	**-0.33**	**128.76**	**1.17**		**0.01**	**-2.91**	**-17.99**
加工转换投入(-)产出(+)量	**Input(-) or Output(+) in Proce -ssing and Transformation**	**251.56**	**0.94**	**-13.86**				**36.18**	**18.01**
火力发电	Thermal Power	-0.29							-7.25
供热	Heating	-0.39	-0.09						-29.49
煤炭洗选	Washing of Coal								
炼焦	Coking								
炼油及煤制油	Oil Refining and Coal to Liquid	252.24	1.03	271.93				36.18	54.75
#油品再投入量(-)	Oil Product Re-input(-)			-285.80					
制气	Gas Production								
#焦炭再投入量(-)	Coke Re-input(-)								
煤制品加工	Coal Product Processing								
回收能	Energy Recycled								
损失量	**Losses**								
#运输和输配损失	In Transportation and Transmission								
终端消费量	**Final Consumption Industry**	**235.19**	**0.60**	**114.90**	**1.17**		**0.01**	**33.26**	**0.02**
农、林、牧、渔业	Agriculture, Forestry, Animal Production and Hunting, Fishing	2.64							
工业	Industry	16.07	0.20	114.90	1.17		0.01	33.26	0.02
#用作原料、材料	Use as Materials			114.90	1.17		0.01	33.26	
建筑业	Construction	32.46							
交通运输、仓储和邮政业	Transport, Storage and Post	145.43	0.38						
批发和零售业、住宿和餐饮业	Wholesale and Retail Trade, Accommodation and Restaurants	6.61							
其他	Others	31.98	0.02						
居民生活	Residential Consumption								
城镇	Urban								
乡村	Rural								
平衡差额	**Balance**		**0.01**				**0.01**		
消费量合计	**Total Energy Consumption**								

7-12 续表 2

单位：万吨标准煤

项　　目	Item	液　化 石油气 Liquefied Petroleum Gas	炼　厂 干　气 Refinery Gas
可供本地区消费的能源量	**Total Energy Available for Local Consumption**	**5.80**	
加工转换投入(-)产出(+)量	**Input(-) or Output(+) in Processing and Transformation**	**68.42**	**115.89**
火力发电	Thermal Power	-0.14	-0.19
供　热	Heating	-2.42	-8.79
煤炭洗选	Washing of Coal		
炼　焦	Coking		
炼油及煤制油	Oil Refining and Coal to Liquid	78.94	124.87
#油品再投入量(-)	Oil Product Re-input(-)	-7.97	
制　气	Gas Production		
#焦炭再投入量(-)	Coke Re-input(-)		
煤制品加工	Coal Product Processing		
回收能	Energy Recycled		
损失量	**Losses**		
#运输和输配损失	In Transportation and Transmission		
终端消费量	**Final Consumption Industry**	**74.21**	**115.89**
农、林、牧、渔业	Agriculture, Forestry, Animal Production and Hunting, Fishing	0.08	
工　业	Industry	1.32	115.89
#用作原料、材料	Use as Materials	0.16	21.59
建筑业	Construction	0.82	
交通运输、仓储和邮政业	Transport, Storage and Post	29.84	
批发和零售业、住宿和餐饮业	Wholesale and Retail Trade, Accommodation and Restaurants	5.95	
其　他	Others	3.98	
居民生活	Residential Consumption	32.23	
城　镇	Urban	18.35	
乡　村	Rural	13.88	
平衡差额	**Balance**	**0.01**	
消费量合计	**Total Energy Consumption**		

7-12 Continued 2

(10000 tons of SCE)

其它石油制品 Other Petroleum Products	天然气 Natural Gas (100 million cu.m)	液化天然气 Liquefied Natural Gas	热力 Heat	电力 Electricity	其它能源 Others
43.98	**2464.56**	**38.63**	**19.11**	**1947.54**	**214.45**
85.28	**-1627.62**	**-1.58**	**620.46**	**1192.73**	**-105.45**
-0.79	-1037.20			1192.73	-119.43
-18.57	-590.42	-1.58	620.46		
266.84					
-162.20					
					13.98
	64.96			**178.43**	
				178.43	
129.27	**771.98**	**37.05**	**639.57**	**2961.82**	**109.00**
	0.01			47.60	
129.27	180.49	2.75	149.04	626.73	7.17
96.34	0.40				
	4.97		4.14	71.06	0.30
	41.14	34.30	21.06	156.09	6.26
	88.48		41.15	259.84	4.65
	281.19		255.89	1123.13	28.57
	175.69		168.28	677.37	62.06
	144.94		168.28	551.77	5.67
	30.76			125.60	56.39
				0.01	

7-13 分行业能源消费总量和主要能源品种消费量(2018年)

单位：万吨

项　　目	Item	能源消费总量(万吨标准煤) Total Energy Consumption (10000 tons of SCE)	煤　炭 Coal
合　计	**Total**	**7269.76**	**276.19**
农、林、牧、渔业	Agriculture, Forestry, Animal Production and Hunting, Fishing	60.72	4.02
采矿业	Mining and Quarrying	9.24	
煤炭开采和洗选业	Mining and Washing of Coal	2.38	
石油和天然气开采业	Extraction of Petroleum and Natural Gas		
黑色金属矿采选业	Mining of Ferrous Metal Ores	6.68	
有色金属矿采选业	Mining of Non-ferrous Metal Ores	0.02	
非金属矿采选业	Mining and Processing of Nonmetal Ores	0.04	
开采专业及辅助性活动	Professional and Support Activities for Mining	0.10	
其他采矿业	Mining of Other Ores n.e.c	0.01	
制造业	Manufacturing	1148.91	41.27
农副食品加工业	Processing of Food from Agricultural Products	18.75	
食品制造业	Manufacture of Foods	27.56	
酒、饮料和精制茶制造业	Manufacture of Wine, Beverage and Refined Tea	23.30	
烟草制品业	Manufacture of Cigarettes and Tobacco	1.94	
纺织业	Manufacture of Textile	1.42	
纺织服装、服饰业	Manufacture of Textile Wearing Apparel and Ornament	6.14	
皮革、毛皮、羽毛及其制品和制鞋业	Manufacture of Leather, Fur, Feather and Its Products, and Footwear	0.61	
木材加工和木、竹、藤、棕、草制品业	Processing of Timbers, Manufacture of Wood, Bamboo, Rattan, Palm, and Straw Products	1.04	0.02
家具制造业	Manufacture of Furniture	4.62	
造纸和纸制品业	Manufacture of Paper and Paper Products	7.69	
印刷和记录媒介复制业	Printing, Reproduction of Recording Media	18.56	
文教、工美、体育和娱乐用品制造业	Manufacture of Articles for Culture, Education, Artwork, Sport and Entertainment Activities	2.83	
石油、煤炭及其他燃料加工业	Processing of Petroleum, Coal and Other Fuels	468.84	
化学原料和化学制品制造业	Manufacture of Chemical Raw Materials and Chemical Products	99.42	0.01
医药制造业	Manufacture of Medicines	43.00	
化学纤维制造业	Manufacture of Chemical Fibers	1.86	
橡胶和塑料制品业	Manufacture of Rubber and Plastics Products	11.67	
非金属矿物制品业	Manufacture of Non-Metallic Mineral Products	95.39	41.14

注：各行业能源消费总量不等于各品种能源消费量(标准煤)的简单加总，应扣除能量重复计算部分。

CONSUMPTION OF TOTAL ENERGY AND MAIN ENERGY VARIETIES BY SECTOR (2018)

(10000 tons)

汽 油 Gasoline	煤 油 Kerosene	柴 油 Diesel Oil	燃料油 Fuel Oil	液 化 石油气 Liquefied Petroleum Gas	液化 天然气 Liquefied Natural Gas	天然气 (亿立方米) Natural Gas (100 million cu.m)	热 力 (万百万千焦) Heat (10 billion kilo-joule)	电 力 (亿千瓦时) Electricity (100 million kwh)
493.60	**691.03**	**178.78**	**1.54**	**36.09**	**21.97**	**184.85**	**18921.33**	**1142.38**
2.50		1.95		0.05		0.04	0.45	18.84
0.07		0.51		0.01		0.04	18.82	2.72
0.01		0.01		0.01			9.45	0.75
0.04		0.50				0.04	9.37	1.92
								0.01
0.01								0.01
0.02								0.03
9.92	0.05	10.24	0.45	0.76	2.01	12.65	4276.94	160.93
0.27		0.29		0.03	0.21	0.39	75.91	3.82
0.36		0.31		0.08	0.20	0.76	91.10	5.20
0.19		0.20		0.02	0.06	0.84	77.34	3.76
						0.09	0.07	0.31
0.05		0.01		0.01		0.02	2.52	0.37
0.24		0.05		0.01	0.07	0.12	23.34	1.20
0.03						0.01	1.20	0.16
0.07		0.02				0.01	1.24	0.27
0.24		0.04		0.02		0.05	5.60	1.23
0.17		0.08		0.01	0.24	0.18	3.49	1.72
0.40		0.15		0.01		0.18	34.80	5.35
0.09		0.01		0.03	0.02	0.02	18.45	0.64
0.04		0.11		0.04		3.15	1648.39	17.60
0.39		0.32		0.06	0.35	0.31	1223.33	13.94
0.45		0.11		0.03	0.05	0.95	201.18	8.96
0.01						0.05	1.70	0.44
0.22		0.10		0.02		0.13	12.06	3.44
0.58		6.37	0.44	0.04	0.48	1.26	21.71	10.31

Note: The data on total energy consumption of all sectors is not equal to the simplesum of consumption (SCE equivalent) of all sorts of energy,which should exclude the double-counted part of energy.

7-13 续表

单位：万吨

项　　目	Item	能源消费总量（万吨标准煤）Total Energy Consumption (10000 tons of SCE)	煤　炭 Coal
黑色金属冶炼及压延加工业	Manufacture and Pressing of Ferrous Metals	17.08	
有色金属冶炼及压延加工业	Manufacture and Pressing of Non-Ferrous Metals	4.48	
金属制品业	Manufacture of Fabricated Metal Products	17.85	
通用设备制造业	Manufacture of General-purpose Machinery	21.75	0.09
专用设备制造业	Manufacture of Special-purpose Machinery	19.98	
汽车制造业	Manufacture of Motor Vehicles	98.66	
铁路、船舶、航空航天和其他运输设备制造业	Manufacture of Railway Locomotives, Building of Ships and Boats, Manufacture of Air and Spacecrafts and Other Transportation Equipment	15.14	
电气机械和器材制造业	Manufacture of Electrical Machinery and Equipment	16.29	
计算机、通讯和其他电子设备制造业	Manufacture of Computer, Communication Equipment and Other Electronic Equipment	87.58	
仪器仪表制造业	Manufacture of Measuring Instruments and Meters	6.63	
其他制造业	Other Manufacturing	3.23	
废弃资源综合利用业	Waste recycling and recovery	1.23	
金属制品、机械和设备修理业	Repair of Fabricated Metal Products, Machinery and Equipment	4.35	
电力、燃气及水的生产和供应业	Production and Distribution of Electricity, Gas and Water	554.23	148.44
电力、热力生产和供应业	Production and Supply of Electric Power and Heat Power	406.19	148.44
燃气生产和供应业	Production and Distribution of Gas	83.10	
水的生产和供应业	Production and Distribution of Water	64.94	
建筑业	Construction	127.30	0.20
批发和零售业	Wholesale and Retail Trade	210.81	1.60
交通运输、仓储和邮政业	Transport, Storage and Post	1491.90	0.94
住宿和餐饮业	Accommodation and Restaurants	248.71	0.25
信息传输、软件和信息技术服务业	Information transmission,software and information technology services	218.95	0.19
金融业	Finance	66.38	
房地产业	Real Estate Trade	427.60	0.23
租赁和商务服务业	Renting and Leasing Activities and Business Services	191.95	0.69
科学研究和技术服务业	Scientific Research and Development, Technical Services	182.10	0.56
水利、环境和公共设施管理业	Water, Environment and Municipal Engineering Conservancy	73.88	0.04
居民服务、修理和其他服务业	Resident services, repair and other services	30.69	0.07
教　育	Education	236.94	0.16
卫生和社会工作	Healthcare and Social Works	94.85	0.04
文化、体育和娱乐业	Culture, Sports and Entertainment	70.28	0.14
公共管理、社会保障和社会组织	Public Administration, Social Security and Social Organizations	131.93	1.19
生活消费	Residential Consumption	1692.36	76.18
城　镇	Urban	1446.45	21.57
乡　村	Rural	245.91	54.61

7-13 Continued

(10000 tons)

汽 油 Gasoline	煤 油 Kerosene	柴 油 Diesel Oil	燃料油 Fuel Oil	液 化 石油气 Liquefied Petroleum Gas	液化 天然气 Liquefied Natural Gas	天然气 (亿立方米) Natural Gas (100 million cu.m)	热 力 (万百万千焦) Heat (10 billion kilo-joule)	电 力 (亿千瓦时) Electricity (100 million kwh)
0.02						0.76	0.84	3.03
0.05		0.03			0.01	0.03	5.52	1.41
0.73		0.18		0.04	0.03	0.28	29.43	4.48
0.78		0.10		0.09	0.02	0.22	88.29	5.31
0.90		0.18		0.02	0.03	0.08	122.44	4.90
1.63		0.97		0.12	0.01	2.11	119.66	23.96
0.21		0.07		0.01		0.18	102.60	3.37
0.65		0.05		0.04	0.04	0.11	72.18	3.91
0.45		0.06		0.01		0.20	207.98	28.71
0.41		0.01		0.01		0.05	47.18	1.37
0.05		0.22				0.01	26.42	0.65
0.02		0.01			0.16	0.01	0.26	0.28
0.20	0.05	0.18		0.01		0.10	10.72	0.83
0.83		1.01	0.99	2.61	1.42	123.05	141.82	131.77
0.47		0.75	0.99	2.57	1.40	115.89	105.45	107.69
0.20		0.19			0.02	7.12	6.10	0.94
0.16		0.08		0.03		0.04	30.27	23.14
9.02		24.83		0.46		0.36	124.19	25.30
20.55		3.98		0.77		0.89	655.27	51.66
42.57	690.47	110.11	0.08	1.55	18.54	3.72	582.03	55.87
1.35		0.30		3.24		6.58	618.75	51.24
4.34		0.98		0.08		0.40	363.27	71.53
1.71		0.11		0.03		0.16	356.37	18.43
3.95		0.46		0.22		9.52	1630.93	92.29
16.61		14.02		0.62		1.84	677.87	36.70
10.13	0.51	1.73	0.01	0.31		2.01	998.63	38.87
2.09		5.22		0.16		0.92	63.44	18.25
2.43		1.51		0.14		0.89	49.32	4.61
1.99		0.96		0.43		4.74	1654.99	41.82
0.98		0.13		0.28		1.32	538.74	20.99
1.76		0.24		0.15		0.55	405.21	16.92
3.56		0.50		0.33		1.05	936.28	27.27
357.23				23.89		14.11	4828.00	256.36
357.23				15.99		11.67	4828.00	210.62
				7.89		2.44		45.74

7-14 分行业能源消费总量和主要能源品种消费量(2019年)

单位：万吨

项目	Item	能源消费总量（万吨标准煤）Total Energy Consumption (10000 tons of SCE)	煤炭 Coal
合计	**Total**	**7360.32**	**182.80**
农、林、牧、渔业	Agriculture, Forestry, Animal Production and Hunting, Fishing	55.75	2.69
采矿业	Mining and Quarrying	6.35	
煤炭开采和洗选业	Mining and Washing of Coal		
石油和天然气开采业	Extraction of Petroleum and Natural Gas		
黑色金属矿采选业	Mining of Ferrous Metal Ores	6.23	
有色金属矿采选业	Mining of Non-ferrous Metal Ores		
非金属矿采选业	Mining and Processing of Nonmetal Ores	0.03	
开采专业及辅助性活动	Professional and Support Activities for Mining	0.09	
其他采矿业	Mining of Other Ores n.e.c		
制造业	Manufacturing	1162.92	39.73
农副食品加工业	Processing of Food from Agricultural Products	17.05	
食品制造业	Manufacture of Foods	26.63	
酒、饮料和精制茶制造业	Manufacture of Wine, Beverage and Refined Tea	21.57	
烟草制品业	Manufacture of Cigarettes and Tobacco	1.69	
纺织业	Manufacture of Textile	1.29	
纺织服装、服饰业	Manufacture of Textile Wearing Apparel and Ornament	5.84	
皮革、毛皮、羽毛及其制品和制鞋业	Manufacture of Leather, Fur, Feather and Its Products, and Footwear	0.57	
木材加工和木、竹、藤、棕、草制品业	Processing of Timbers, Manufacture of Wood, Bamboo, Rattan, Palm, and Straw Products	0.38	
家具制造业	Manufacture of Furniture	4.78	
造纸和纸制品业	Manufacture of Paper and Paper Products	6.87	
印刷和记录媒介复制业	Printing, Reproduction of Recording Media	19.18	
文教、工美、体育和娱乐用品制造业	Manufacture of Articles for Culture, Education, Artwork, Sport and Entertainment Activities	2.49	
石油、煤炭及其他燃料加工业	Processing of Petroleum, Coal and Other Fuels of Nucleus Fuel	483.47	
化学原料和化学制品制造业	Manufacture of Chemical Raw Materials and Chemical Products	101.91	0.01
医药制造业	Manufacture of Medicines	45.83	
化学纤维制造业	Manufacture of Chemical Fibers	1.65	
橡胶和塑料制品业	Manufacture of Rubber and Plastics Products	10.11	
非金属矿物制品业	Manufacture of Non-Metallic Mineral Products	112.24	39.72

注：各行业能源消费总量不等于各品种能源消费量(标准煤)的简单加总，应扣除能量重复计算部分。

CONSUMPTION OF TOTAL ENERGY AND MAIN ENERGY VARIETIES BY SECTOR (2019)

(10000 tons)

汽 油 Gasoline	煤 油 Kerosene	柴 油 Diesel Oil	燃料油 Fuel Oil	液 化 石油气 Liquefied Petroleum Gas	液化 天然气 Liquefied Natural Gas	天然气 (亿立方米) Natural Gas (100 million cu.m)	热 力 (万百万千焦) Heat (10 billion kilo-joule)	电 力 (亿千瓦时) Electricity (100 million kwh)
500.90	**697.80**	**161.87**	**0.48**	**49.43**	**21.98**	**186.37**	**18755.63**	**1166.40**
2.31		1.81		0.05				17.68
0.04		0.48				0.03	8.24	1.84
0.03		0.48				0.03	8.24	1.80
								0.01
0.01								0.03
8.80	0.06	10.08	0.14	5.32	1.56	10.99	4162.67	162.47
0.23		0.24		0.02	0.18	0.30	73.89	3.67
0.31		0.28		0.04	0.20	0.68	83.05	5.29
0.17		0.16		0.01	0.02	0.72	74.41	3.63
						0.07		0.31
0.05		0.01				0.01	2.41	0.37
0.22		0.04		0.01	0.05	0.11	21.14	1.15
0.02		0.01				0.01		0.16
0.06		0.01						0.09
0.24		0.03				0.06	5.19	1.29
0.14		0.07		0.01	0.10	0.15	3.26	1.65
0.38		0.15		0.01		0.17	31.88	5.65
0.07				0.02		0.02	16.10	0.59
0.03		0.02		0.05		2.93	1746.40	18.86
0.33		0.33		4.78	0.24	0.22	1110.34	14.15
0.40		0.08		0.04	0.02	0.89	202.18	10.23
						0.05		0.40
0.19		0.07		0.01		0.09	7.76	3.11
0.46		6.32	0.14	0.04	0.62	1.19	20.64	10.59

Note: The data on total energy consumption of all sectors is not equal to the simplesum of consumption (SCE equivalent) of all sorts of energy,which should exclude the double-counted part of energy.

7-14 续表

单位：万吨

项目	Item	能源消费总量(万吨标准煤) Total Energy Consumption (10000 tons of SCE)	煤炭 Coal
黑色金属冶炼及压延加工业	Manufacture and Pressing of Ferrous Metals	16.85	
有色金属冶炼及压延加工业	Manufacture and Pressing of Non-Ferrous Metals	4.38	
金属制品业	Manufacture of Fabricated Metal Products	17.28	
通用设备制造业	Manufacture of General-purpose Machinery	20.47	
专用设备制造业	Manufacture of Special-purpose Machinery	21.44	
汽车制造业	Manufacture of Motor Vehicles	86.96	
铁路、船舶、航空航天和其他运输设备制造业	Manufacture of Railway Locomotives, Building of Ships and Boats, Manufacture of Air and Spacecrafts and Other Transportation Equipment	12.94	
电气机械和器材制造业	Manufacture of Electrical Machinery and Equipment	13.40	
计算机、通讯和其他电子设备制造业	Manufacture of Computer, Communication Equipment and Other Electronic Equipment	89.62	
仪器仪表制造业	Manufacture of Measuring Instruments and Meters	6.13	
其他制造业	Other Manufacturing	3.42	
废弃资源综合利用业	Waste recycling and recovery	1.42	
金属制品、机械和设备修理业	Repair of Fabricated Metal Products, Machinery and Equipment	5.07	
电力、燃气及水的生产和供应业	Production and Distribution of Electricity, Gas and Water	559.64	87.67
电力、热力生产和供应业	Production and Supply of Electric Power and Heat Power	420.70	87.67
燃气生产和供应业	Production and Distribution of Gas	69.37	
水的生产和供应业	Production and Distribution of Water	69.57	
建筑业	Construction	126.92	0.12
批发和零售业	Wholesale and Retail Trade	207.84	2.20
交通运输、仓储和邮政业	Transport, Storage and Post	1533.82	0.41
住宿和餐饮业	Accommodation and Restaurants	229.26	
信息传输、软件和信息技术服务业	Information transmission,software and information technology services	240.26	
金融业	Finance	66.31	
房地产业	Real Estate Trade	441.58	
租赁和商务服务业	Renting and Leasing Activities and Business Services	189.59	
科学研究和技术服务业	Scientific Research and Development, Technical Services	183.34	0.25
水利、环境和公共设施管理业	Water, Environment and Municipal Engineering Conservancy	80.20	0.09
居民服务、修理和其他服务业	Resident services, repair and other services	33.35	0.01
教育	Education	235.33	
卫生和社会工作	Healthcare and Social Works	96.16	0.03
文化、体育和娱乐业	Culture, Sports and Entertainment	70.41	0.14
公共管理、社会保障和社会组织	Public Administration, Social Security and Social Organizations	149.87	0.81
生活消费	Residential Consumption	1691.41	48.65
城镇	Urban	1445.88	12.89
乡村	Rural	245.53	35.76

7-14 Continued

(10000 tons)

汽 油 Gasoline	煤 油 Kerosene	柴 油 Diesel Oil	燃料油 Fuel Oil	液 化 石油气 Liquefied Petroleum Gas	液化 天然气 Liquefied Natural Gas	天然气 (亿立方米) Natural Gas (100 million cu.m)	热 力 (万百万千焦) Heat (10 billion kilo-joule)	电 力 (亿千瓦时) Electricity (100 million kwh)
0.02						0.71	0.54	3.06
0.04		0.01				0.03	8.40	1.37
0.62		0.15		0.04	0.02	0.24	27.47	4.55
0.64		0.09		0.09	0.02	0.18	81.85	5.15
0.77		0.17		0.02	0.02	0.09	139.79	5.23
1.53		0.86		0.04	0.02	1.60	105.70	22.03
0.20		0.06		0.01		0.06	94.32	3.21
0.53		0.05		0.05	0.03	0.09	54.54	3.33
0.40		0.06		0.01		0.19	174.84	29.94
0.35		0.01		0.01		0.02	38.93	1.50
0.06		0.35				0.01	24.57	0.67
0.02		0.01			0.02	0.03	2.56	0.33
0.33	0.05	0.45		0.01		0.08	10.50	0.92
0.75		0.93	0.06	1.59	0.90	126.24	199.91	134.76
0.48		0.79	0.06	1.53	0.90	120.34	166.34	108.98
0.13		0.01				5.84	7.57	0.96
0.14		0.13		0.05		0.06	26.00	24.82
8.89		22.28		0.48		0.41	121.36	26.39
18.31		4.29		0.66		1.01	625.66	51.27
49.74	697.17	99.81	0.27	17.41	19.52	3.42	617.55	57.98
1.22		0.25		2.81		6.34	581.23	45.24
4.09		0.22		0.06		0.35	343.45	80.38
1.62		0.08		0.03		0.16	335.82	18.66
3.41		0.41		0.21		10.03	1521.73	95.78
9.32		11.49		0.28		2.04	663.56	40.68
9.40	0.57	1.57		0.37		1.87	980.32	40.35
1.98		5.63		0.16		0.80	60.63	20.89
2.84		0.92		0.12		0.94	49.24	5.28
1.98		0.89		0.40		4.32	1596.99	43.34
0.90		0.10		0.26		1.24	533.61	21.81
1.71		0.21		0.13		0.51	392.83	17.31
3.39		0.43	0.01	0.32		1.10	1025.83	32.69
370.20				18.80		14.59	4935.00	251.60
370.20				10.70		12.04	4935.00	204.95
				8.10		2.55		46.65

7-15 能源消费弹性系数(2000-2019年)
ELASTICITY COEFFICIENT OF ENERGY CONSUMPTION (2000-2019)

项 目 Item	能源消费比上年增长 (%) Growth of Energy Consumption over the Previous Year	电力消费比上年增长 (%) Growth of Electricity Consumption over the Previous Year	能源消费弹性系数 Elasticity Coefficient of Energy Consumption	电力消费弹性系数 Elasticity Coefficient of Electricity Consumption
2000	6.08	9.53	0.51	0.79
2001	2.06	5.68	0.17	0.48
2002	4.89	9.54	0.41	0.81
2003	4.78	5.71	0.43	0.51
2004	10.57	10.60	0.79	0.80
2005	7.44	11.16	0.60	0.91
2006	6.92	9.16	0.54	0.72
2007	6.45	9.06	0.45	0.63
2008	0.67	4.90	0.07	0.55
2009	3.84	7.15	0.38	0.71
2010	5.84	9.49	0.56	0.91
2011	0.59	2.21	0.07	0.27
2012	2.61	5.91	0.34	0.77
2013	2.44	4.42	0.32	0.57
2014	1.60	2.72	0.22	0.37
2015	0.31	1.91	0.04	0.28
2016	1.67	7.25	0.24	1.05
2017	2.48	4.57	0.36	0.67
2018	2.56	7.08	0.38	1.06
2019	1.25	2.10	0.21	0.35

7-16 平均每万元地区生产总值能源消费量(2010-2019年)
ENERGY CONSUMPTION PER 10000 YUAN OF GROSS DOMESTIC PRODUCT (2010-2019)

项目 Item	能源总消费量 (吨标准煤) Total (ton of SCE)	煤炭 (千克) Coal (kg)	电力 (千瓦时) Electricity (kwh)	石油 (千克) Petroleum (kg)	天然气 (立方米) Natural Gas (cu.m)
	地区生产总值按2010年可比价计算 GDP calculated at the comparable prices of 2010				
2010	0.42	169.07	537.23	90.59	49.98
2011	0.40	140.04	508.04	89.50	45.45
2012	0.38	125.10	499.50	82.02	52.85
2013	0.36	107.57	484.10	78.89	52.64
2014	0.34	86.14	463.00	76.30	56.40
2015	0.32	54.06	441.32	73.48	68.14
	地区生产总值按2015年可比价计算 GDP calculated at the comparable prices of 2015				
2015	0.27	47.02	383.89	63.92	59.28
2016	0.26	31.99	385.10	59.58	61.26
2017	0.25	17.33	377.06	58.52	58.16
2018	0.24	9.15	378.40	56.55	62.23
2019	0.23	5.71	364.31	54.73	59.16

7-17 人均生活用能源(2010-2019年)
PER CAPITA ENERGY CONSUMPTION FOR NON-PRODUCTIVE PURPOSE (2010-2019)

年 份 Year	合 计 (千克标准煤) Total (kg of SCE)	煤 炭 (千克) Coal (kg)	电 力 (千瓦时) Electricity (kWh)	液化石油气 (千克) Liquefied Petroleum Gas(kg)	天然气 (立方米) Natural Gas (cu.m)	汽 油 (升) Gasoline (liter)
2010	650.2	173.6	729.1	11.3	53.1	164.9
2011	663.2	167.1	727.2	10.7	52.7	167.6
2012	693.2	159.0	791.8	9.3	56.5	174.4
2013	687.5	147.7	750.6	9.9	57.1	180.7
2014	705.3	137.6	793.5	11.0	59.6	182.5
2015	695.5	126.3	808.7	11.6	63.7	194.3
2016	714.2	110.8	899.9	12.1	59.0	198.3
2017	761.0	83.3	1004.0	12.0	75.5	207.3
2018	782.6	35.2	1185.5	11.0	65.2	226.3
2019	785.3	22.6	1168.1	8.7	67.7	235.4

注：本表人均生活用能源按常住人口年平均数计算。
Note: Per-capita energy consumption for non-productive prupose is calculated by average permanent population.

7-18 主要能源日均消费量(2010-2019年)
DAILY CONSUMPTION OF MAIN ENERGY VARIETIES(2010-2019)

年 份 Year	合 计 (万吨标准煤) Total (10000 tons of SCE)	煤 炭 (吨) Coal (ton)	原 油 (吨) Crude Oil (ton)	汽 油 (吨) Gasoline (ton)	煤 油 (吨) Kerosene (ton)	柴 油 (吨) Diesel Oil (ton)	燃料油 (吨) Fuel Oil (ton)	电 力 (万千瓦时) Electricity (10000 kWh)	天然气 (万立方米) Natural Gas (10000 cu.m)
2010	17.4	69315.4	30175.6	9935.4	10757.0	5333.0	442.3	22024.9	2048.9
2011	17.5	62056.8	29778.2	10418.6	11503.7	5366.2	340.3	22512.5	2014.0
2012	18.0	59714.8	29072.1	11116.6	12146.1	5166.4	302.4	23842.3	2522.4
2013	18.4	55321.3	23860.7	11605.7	13070.1	5312.2	227.3	24896.0	2707.2
2014	18.7	47576.5	28345.6	12071.7	13906.3	5382.5	154.3	25572.9	3115.0
2015	18.6	31922.7	27165.5	12678.2	14914.6	4995.9	134.5	26061.7	4024.1
2016	18.9	23222.5	22493.2	12886.8	16281.2	4731.2	127.1	27952.1	4446.9
2017	19.4	13437.3	24453.0	13420.6	17643.7	4797.5	77.1	29229.7	4508.5
2018	19.9	7566.8	24980.2	13523.2	18932.4	4898.2	42.3	31298.1	5147.4
2019	20.2	5008.1	25671.1	13723.3	19117.9	4434.9	13.3	31956.1	5189.1

7-19 全社会用电量情况(1978-2019年)
TOTAL ELECTRICITY CONSUMPTION IN BEIJING (1978-2019)

单位：万千瓦时 (10000 kWh)

年 份 Year	全社会用电量 Electricity Consumption	第一产业 Primary Industry	第二产业 Secondary Industry	工 业 Industry	建筑业 Construction	第三产业 Tertiary Industry	城乡居民生活用电 Residential Electricity Consumption	城 市 Urban	乡 村 Rural
1978	735000	48993	570621	570621		94555	20831	11022	9809
1979	802317	52134	620262	620262		107437	22484	11495	10989
1980	854638	65283	648496	648496		116947	23912	12441	11471
1981	867153	80027	643976	643976		121883	21267	9452	11815
1982	925700	104842	657060	657060		139403	24395	10820	13575
1983	956293	92601	687937	687937		151290	24465	12320	12145
1984	1029420	105234	716653	716653		177455	30078	16025	14053
1985	1106255	111110	746324	746324		210622	38199	22479	15720
1986	1181155	105688	851519	835725	15794	175090	48858	31008	17850
1987	1285023	77909	923797	899760	24037	224747	58570	35063	23507
1988	1378574	83809	970885	943383	27502	248446	75434	48624	26810
1989	1421817	100151	979216	949629	29587	258067	84383	56120	28263
1990	1504785	93049	1014037	986356	27681	302775	94924	65262	29662
1991	1613977	93256	1061207	1032064	29143	348769	110745	77575	33170
1992	1759611	101985	1155514	1123835	31679	375874	126238	88621	37617
1993	1924978	107010	1243115	1206001	37114	429835	145018	103579	41439
1994	2054504	101134	1307898	1262961	44937	479679	165791	119025	46766
1995	2225922	102099	1403864	1341398	62466	538936	181022	130897	50125
1996	2443709	111904	1496968	1422590	74378	617286	217551	158474	59077
1997	2636078	120444	1529201	1449129	80072	721774	264659	196641	68018
1998	2762080	108267	1548485	1457149	91336	811283	294045	220543	73502
1999	2972629	121242	1581977	1478523	103454	912834	356576	276642	79934
2000	3844266	130865	2172604	2066892	105712	1064322	476475	385396	91079
2001	3999415	131811	2105819	1978673	127146	1222471	539314	439058	100256
2002	4399637	137370	2293735	2145292	148443	1342490	626042	517386	108656
2003	4676056	107372	2418419	2250525	167894	1447344	702921	574623	128298
2004	5131804	104234	2593504	2391414	202090	1628731	805335	647474	157861
2005	5705364	114308	2795753	2605832	189921	1906093	889210	706405	182805
2006	6115719	122550	2943550	2744127	199423	2090888	958731	768884	189847
2007	6670089	133557	3091374	2881807	209567	2378399	1066759	862604	204155
2008	6897189	136065	2943893	2763399	180494	2654140	1163091	949878	213213
2009	7391465	157310	3027974	2853018	174956	2918229	1287952	982720	305232
2010	8099029	168992	3278682	3081364	197319	3258009	1393346	951811	441535
2011	8217055	170368	3109174	2894464	214708	3490143	1447370	945588	501782
2012	8742835	181391	3209078	2980645	228430	3734022	1618344	1370932	247412
2013	9131113	185749	3345854	3110626	235229	4029145	1570365	1347401	222964
2014	9370485	185633	3352904	3129060	223846	4139319	1692629	1457398	235231
2015	9527169	185031	3238220	3030638	207583	4356332	1747586	1496078	251508
2016	10202704	196243	3343189	3129675	213514	4708959	1954313	1664539	289774
2017	10668904	112930	3323724	3105551	218276	5063019	2169231	1842219	327012
2018	11423809	106382	3316045	3073165	253012	5437818	2563564	2106181	457383
2019	11663964	98872	3254317	2990649	263949	5794810	2515964	2049447	466517

注：1. 1985年以前农、林、牧、渔和水利业用电量中，只包含农业排灌、农副业和社队企业的用电量。
2. 1980年以前的城市居民用电量以全市市政用电量的 1/10计算。
3. 2000年以前工业用电量不包含输配损失和发电企业自产自用电量。
4. 自2018年起，行业划分执行《国民经济行业分类》(GB/T 4754-2017)标准，为保证数据可比，对2017年数据进行了修订。

资料来源：北京市电力公司。

Note: a) Before 1985, electricity consumption by agriculture, forestry, animal production and hunting, fishing and water conservancy only included the electricity consumption by farming irrigation, agricultural and sideline products, and village enterprises.
b) Before 1980, electricity consumption by urban residents was one-tenth of the total electricity consumption by municipal administration in Beijing.
c) Before 2000, electricity consumption by industry excluded transmission and distribution losses and electricity generated and consumed by power generating enterprises.
d) Sectors are classified in accordance with the standard in the Classification of National Economic Sectors (GB/T 4754-2017) since 2018. In order to keep the data comparable, the data of 2017 have been revised.

Source: Beijing Electric Power Corporation.

7-20 主要土地利用状况(2009-2018年)
LAND UTILIZATION (2009-2018)

单位：公顷 (hectare)

年 份 Year	耕地面积 Arable Land	园地面积 Garden Plot	林地面积 Forest Land	草地面积 Grass Land	城镇村及工矿用地面积 Land for Urban, Rural,Industrial and Mining Use	交通运输用地面积 Land for Transportation	水域及水利设施用地面积 Water Areas and Land for Water Conservancy Facilities
2009	227170.43	141617.22	743696.19	84843.14	284791.79	44446.42	80235.85
2010	223779.38	139298.50	742018.50	85827.05	290782.01	45335.78	79774.99
2011	221956.16	138072.99	740730.87	85651.69	295116.72	45452.68	79380.05
2012	220856.16	137117.72	739633.48	85491.29	297758.79	46327.98	79088.32
2013	221157.28	135573.37	738036.45	85348.82	300847.83	46626.41	78739.52
2014	219948.76	135103.71	737542.89	85139.49	302939.17	47006.28	78378.65
2015	219326.49	134857.89	737078.88	85066.77	304393.05	47062.78	78304.28
2016	216345.43	133453.18	739705.54	84721.53	306615.41	47480.86	77968.73
2017	213730.65	132799.79	744473.56	84479.43	306825.68	47704.86	76373.77
2018	212840.60	132531.10	746634.08	84323.67	303247.34	48526.72	76291.41

注：表中2009年数据为第二次全国土地调查数据，2010年及以后为各年土地变更调查数据。
资料来源：北京市规划和自然资源委员会。
Note: Statistics for 2009 were from the 2nd National Land Survey, and statistics for 2010-2016 were survey data of land changed.
Source:Beijing Municipal Commission of Planning and Natural Resources.

7-21 水资源情况(2001-2019年)

单位：亿立方米

项　目	Item	2001	2002	2003	2004	2005
全年水资源总量	**Total Volume of Water Resource in the Year**	**19.2**	**16.1**	**18.4**	**21.4**	**23.2**
地表水资源量	Volume of Surface Water Resource	7.8	5.3	6.1	8.2	7.6
地下水资源量	Volume of Underground Water Resource	15.7	14.7	14.8	16.5	15.6
人均水资源(立方米)	**Per-capita Water Resource(cu.m)**	**139.7**	**114.7**	**127.8**	**145.1**	**153.1**
全年供水总量	**Total Volume of Water Supplied in the Year**	**38.9**	**34.6**	**35.8**	**34.6**	**34.5**
按来源分	By Source					
地表水	Surface Water	11.7	10.4	8.3	5.7	7.0
地下水	Underground Water	27.2	24.2	25.4	26.8	24.9
再生水	Recycled Water			2.1	2.0	2.6
南水北调水	Water Transit from South to North					
全年用水总量	**Total Volume of Water Consumed in the Year**	**38.9**	**34.6**	**35.8**	**34.6**	**34.5**
按用途分	By Purpose					
农业用水	Water Used by Agriculture	17.4	15.5	13.8	13.5	13.2
工业用水	Water Used by Industry	9.2	7.6	8.4	7.7	6.8
生活用水	Domestic Water	12.0	10.8	13.0	12.8	13.4
生态环境用水	Water for the Environment	0.3	0.8	0.6	0.6	1.1
万元地区生产总值水耗(立方米)	**Water Consumption per 10000 yuan GDP (cu.m)**	**100.81**	**76.50**	**67.97**	**55.26**	**48.25**
万元地区生产总值水耗下降率(%)	**Decrease Rate of Water Consumption per 10000 yuan GDP (%)**	**13.81**	**20.46**	**6.92**	**14.82**	**11.08**

注：1. 本表人均水资源按常住人口年平均数计算。2006—2010年数据根据全国第六次人口普查进行了修订。
2. 万元地区生产总值水耗按现价计算，下降率按可比价计算，如按可比价计算，2018年、2019万元地区生产总值水耗均为13.02立方米。
3. 2018年及以前的万元地区生产总值水耗及下降率数据中使用的地区生产总值数据，根据北京市第四次全国经济普查结果进行了修订；2019年万元地区生产总值水耗及下降率为初步统计数。

资料来源：除人均数据和万元地区生产总值水耗以外其它数据来自北京市水务局。

STATISTICS FOR WATER RESOURCES(2001-2019)

(100 million cu.m)

2006	2007	2008	2009	2010	2011	2012	2013	2014	2015	2016	2017	2018	2019
22.1	**23.8**	**34.2**	**21.8**	**23.1**	**26.8**	**39.5**	**24.8**	**20.3**	**26.8**	**35.1**	**29.8**	**35.5**	**24.6**
6.7	7.6	12.8	6.8	7.2	9.2	18.0	9.4	6.5	9.3	14.0	12.0	14.3	8.6
15.4	16.2	21.4	15.1	15.9	17.6	21.6	15.4	13.8	17.4	21.1	17.7	21.1	16.0
140.6	**145.3**	**198.5**	**120.3**	**120.8**	**134.7**	**193.3**	**118.6**	**94.9**	**123.8**	**161.4**	**137.1**	**164.0**	**114.0**
34.3	**34.8**	**35.1**	**35.5**	**35.2**	**36.0**	**35.9**	**36.4**	**37.5**	**38.2**	**38.8**	**39.5**	**39.3**	**41.7**
6.4	5.7	5.5	4.6	4.6	5.5	5.2	4.8	8.5	2.9	2.9	3.6	3.0	6.6
24.3	24.2	22.9	21.8	21.2	20.9	20.4	20.1	19.6	18.2	17.5	16.6	16.3	15.5
3.6	5.0	6.0	6.5	6.8	7.0	7.5	8.0	8.6	9.5	10.0	10.5	10.8	11.5
		0.7	2.6	2.6	2.6	2.8	3.5	0.8	7.6	8.4	8.8	9.3	8.1
34.3	**34.8**	**35.1**	**35.5**	**35.2**	**36.0**	**35.9**	**36.4**	**37.5**	**38.2**	**38.8**	**39.5**	**39.3**	**41.7**
12.8	12.4	12.0	12.0	11.4	10.9	9.3	9.1	8.2	6.5	6.1	5.1	4.2	3.7
6.2	5.8	5.2	5.2	5.1	5.0	4.9	5.1	5.1	3.8	3.8	3.5	3.3	3.3
13.7	13.9	14.7	14.7	14.7	15.6	16.0	16.3	17.0	17.5	17.8	18.3	18.4	18.7
1.6	2.7	3.2	3.6	4.0	4.5	5.7	5.9	7.2	10.4	11.1	12.6	13.4	16.0
40.90	**33.38**	**29.71**	**27.52**	**23.50**	**20.92**	**18.86**	**17.21**	**16.35**	**15.42**	**14.35**	**13.22**	**11.87**	**11.78**
11.86	**11.32**	**7.45**	**8.08**	**10.28**	**5.38**	**7.37**	**5.89**	**4.05**	**4.70**	**4.98**	**4.70**	**6.75**	**0.02**

Note: a) Data on per-capita water resource in the table are calculated by the annual average permanent population. Data for 2006-2010 have been revised in accordance with the sixth national population census.

b) Water consumption per 10000 yuan of GDP is at calculated current prices, and decrease rate is calculated at comparable prices. If calculated at comparable prices, the water consumption per 10000 yuan of GDP in 2018 and 2019 was both 13.02 cubic metres.

c) the GDP data used in the data of water consumption per 10000 yuan of GDP and its decrease rate in and before 2018 were revised according to the results of the fourth national economic census in Beijing; the data for 2019 on water consumption per 10000 yuan of GDP and its decrease rate were the preliminary statistical data.

Source: Except for per-capita figures and water consumption per 10000 yuan GDP,other figures are from Beijing Water Authority.

7-22 分行业规模以上工业用水量情况
WATER CONSUMPTION OF INDUSTRIAL ENTERPRISESDESIGNATED SIZE ABOVE SIZE BY SECTOR

项目	Item	用水量（万立方米）Water Consumption (10000 cu.m)		重复用水率（%）Reuse Rate of Water (%)	
		2019	2018	2019	2018
合计	**Total**	**23485**	**24700**	**95.7**	**95.8**
采矿业	**Mining and Quarrying**	**1287**	**1401**	**91.6**	**90.8**
煤炭开采和洗选业	Mining and Washing of Coal	138	245	11.2	29.2
石油和天然气开采业	Extraction of Petroleum and Natural Gas	8	8		
黑色金属矿采选业	Mining of Ferrous Metal Ores	1005	1076	93.3	92.7
有色金属矿采选业	Mining of Non-Ferrous Metal Ores				
非金属矿采选业	Mining and Processing of Nonmetal Ores				
开采专业及辅助性活动	Mining Support Service Activities	136	72		
其他采矿业	Mining of Other Ores				
制造业	**Manufacturing**	**12048**	**13060**	**95.4**	**95.2**
农副食品加工业	Processing of Food from Agricultural Products	398	451	70.5	65.3
食品制造业	Manufacture of Foods	692	733	89.4	89.0
酒、饮料和精制茶制造业	Manufacture of Wine, Beverage and Refined Tea	1653	1719	64.0	70.4
烟草制品业	Manufacture of Cigarettes and Tobacco	26	27	98.1	89.2
纺织业	Manufacture of Textile	8	11		
纺织服装、服饰业	Manufacture of Textile, Wearing Apparel and Ornament	66	81		
皮革、毛皮、羽毛及其制品和制鞋业	Manufacture of Leather, Fur, Feather and Its Products, and Footwear	2	3	86.2	83.1
木材加工和木、竹、藤、棕、草制品业	Processing of Timbers, Manufacture of Wood, Bamboo, Rattan, Palm and Straw Products	1	5	33.3	
家具制造业	Manufacture of Furniture	40	40	0.2	0.5
造纸和纸制品业	Manufacture of Paper and Paper Products	59	65	69.7	67.5
印刷和记录媒介复制业	Printing, Reproduction of Recording Media	190	201	64.0	64.6
文教、工美、体育和娱乐用品制造业	Manufacture of Articles for Culture, Education, Artwork, Sport and Entertainment Activities	30	34		
石油、煤炭及其他燃料加工业	Processing of Petroleum, Coal and Other Fuels	1198	1101	98.9	99.0
化学原料和化学制品制造业	Manufacture of Chemical Raw Materials and Chemical Products	690	693	98.6	98.6
医药制造业	Manufacture of Medicines	1193	1144	84.0	84.2
化学纤维制造业	Manufacture of Chemical Fibres	9	10	96.7	96.1
橡胶和塑料制品业	Manufacture of Rubber and Plastics Products	95	93	94.3	94.1
非金属矿物制品业	Manufacture of Non-metallic Mineral Products	868	845	85.9	86.4
黑色金属冶炼和压延加工业	Manufacture and Pressing of Ferrous Metals	191	194	97.8	97.8
有色金属冶炼和压延加工业	Manufacture and Processing of Non-ferrous Metals	53	80	97.3	97.0
金属制品业	Manufacture of Fabricated Metal Products	142	157	93.8	95.3
通用设备制造业	Manufacture of General-Purpose Machinery	218	237	88.5	87.9
专用设备制造业	Manufacture of Special-Purpose Machinery	259	274	47.2	48.5
汽车制造业	Manufacture of Motor Vehicles	1240	1920	90.5	87.6
铁路、船舶、航空航天和其他运输设备制造业	Manufacture of Railway Locomotives, Building of Ships and Boats, Manufacture of Air and Spacecrafts and Other Transportation Equipments	79	104	94.2	76.4
电气机械和器材制造业	Manufacture of Electrical Machinery and Equipment	137	167	11.2	15.0
计算机、通信和其他电子设备制造业	Manufacture of Computers, Communication Equipment and Other Electronic Equipment	2243	2271	94.7	95.3
仪器仪表制造业	Manufacture of Measuring Instrument and Meter	71	71	71.2	69.7
其他制造业	Other Manufacturing	3	5		
废弃资源综合利用业	Waste Rrecycling and Recovery	8	8	93.7	93.7
金属制品、机械和设备修理业	Repair of Fabricated Metal Products, Machinery and Equipment	191	318		
电力、热力、燃气及水生产和供应业	**Production and Distribution of Electricity, Heating Power, Gas and Water**	**10150**	**10239**	**96.1**	**96.5**
电力、热力生产和供应业	Production and Supply of Electric Power and Heat Power	6590	6815	97.3	97.5
燃气生产和供应业	Production and Distribution of Gas	92	94	0.6	1.2
水的生产和供应业	Production and Distribution of Water	3467	3331	80.6	81.3

注：重复用水率=重复用水量/(用新水量+重复用水量)*100%。

Note: Reuse Rate of Water = Volume of Water Used Repeatedly / (Volume of New Water Used + Volume of Water Used Repeatedly) * 100%.

7-23 气象情况(1978-2019年)
METEOROLOGY (1978-2019)

年份 Year	降水量(毫米) Precipitation (mm)	平均气温(℃) Average Temperature (℃)	最高 Highest	最低 Lowest	日照时数(时) Hours of Sunshine (hours)	平均风速(米/秒) Average Wind Speed (meter/second)	平均气压(百帕) Average Air Pressure (100 pa)	大风日数(日) Days of Strong Wind (day)	雨日数(日) Days of Rain (day)
1978	664.8	11.6	37.5	-14.4	2865.4	2.6	1012.8	35	64
1979	718.4	11.1	35.9	-15.4	2667.4	2.5	1012.2	33	63
1980	380.7	11.0	35.1	-15.4	2920.8	2.5	1012.7	29	83
1981	393.2	12.3	38.1	-14.0	2803.9	2.5	1010.8	15	92
1982	544.4	12.8	37.3	-14.3	2825.1	2.6	1010.5	26	92
1983	489.9	13.0	37.2	-15.0	2844.3	2.4	1010.3	29	100
1984	488.8	11.9	36.1	-14.9	2767.6	2.4	1010.6	18	90
1985	721.0	11.5	35.1	-15.2	2511.9	2.2	1010.4	12	104
1986	665.3	12.1	38.5	-15.4	2804.1	2.3	1010.7	21	96
1987	683.9	12.3	36.1	-15.5	2631.9	2.4	1010.3	23	102
1988	673.3	12.7	38.1	-13.2	2558.1	2.4	1010.8	17	96
1989	442.2	13.2	35.8	-11.0	2626.2	1.9	1011.1	3	78
1990	697.3	12.7	37.5	-14.8	2325.0	1.9	1010.6	12	113
1991	747.9	12.5	35.7	-12.6	2536.6	2.1	1010.8	8	98
1992	541.5	12.8	37.5	-8.7	2712.5	2.2	1011.0	6	100
1993	506.7	13.0	35.8	-13.0	2669.8	2.6	1010.8	12	91
1994	813.2	13.7	37.2	-11.5	2470.5	2.5	1010.1	9	92
1995	572.5	13.3	35.0	-9.2	2519.1	2.6	1010.3	16	89
1996	700.9	12.7	36.0	-10.0	2418.7	2.6	1011.0	16	103
1997	430.9	13.1	38.2	-14.0	2596.5	2.5	1012.9	11	76
1998	731.7	13.1	37.2	-14.2	2420.7	2.3	1012.5	10	93
1999	266.9	13.1	41.9	-12.2	2594.0	2.4	1012.5	7	86
2000	371.1	12.8	39.4	-15.0	2667.2	2.5	1012.7	10	83
2001	338.9	12.9	39.6	-17.0	2611.7	2.4	1012.9	10	78
2002	370.4	13.2	41.1	-12.8	2588.4	2.3	1012.7	15	84
2003	444.9	12.9	37.6	-15.0	2260.2	2.5	1013.3	6	93
2004	483.5	13.5	38.9	-12.9	2515.4	2.4	1012.6	12	94
2005	410.7	13.2	38.9	11.5	2576.1	2.4	1012.8	5	79
2006	318.0	13.4	37.3	-14.7	2192.7	2.2	1012.5	5	86
2007	483.9	14.0	37.3	-11.7	2351.1	2.2	1012.6	5	78
2008	626.3	13.4	36.3	-13.5	2391.4	2.2	1012.6	8	100
2009	480.6	13.3	39.6	-12.2	2511.8	2.2	1011.9	15	86
2010	522.5	12.6	40.6	-16.7	2382.9	2.3	1012.2	14	88
2011	720.6	13.4	35.9	-11.6	2485.7	2.2	1013.2	3	82
2012	733.2	12.9	38.0	-13.7	2450.2	2.2	1012.2	3	85
2013	578.9	12.8	38.2	-14.1	2371.1	2.1	1012.2	3	71
2014	461.5	14.1	41.1	-11.2	2344.1	2.1	1013.0	8	77
2015	458.6	13.7	38.9	-9.2	2420.2	2.1	1013.2	7	99
2016	669.1	13.8	37.8	-15.2	2502.1	2.1	1013.1	2	86
2017	576.2	14.2	38.5	-10.1	2600.1	2.1	1013.1	4	78
2018	546.5	13.6	39.9	-13.9	2483.7	2.0	1013.2	3	73
2019	406.3	13.8	38.0	-14.4	2542.3	2.1	1013.1	8	65

资料来源：北京市气象局。
Source: Beijing Municipal Bureau of Meteorology.

7-24 气　象(2019年)
METEOROLOGY (2019)

月份 Month	降水量(毫米) Precipitation (mm)	平均气温(℃) Average Temperature (℃)	日照时数(时) Hours of Sunshine (hours)	平均风速(米/秒) Average Wind Speed (meter/second)	平均气压(百帕) Average Air Pressure (100 pa)	大风日数(日) Days of Strong Wind (day)	雨日数(日) Days of Rain (day)
全　年 Total	**406.3**	**13.8**	**2542.3**	**2.1**	**1013.1**	**8**	**65**
1		-1.7	200.3	2.0	1025.9		
2	2.0	-0.8	150.5	2.0	1023.3		
3	2.5	9.7	271.3	2.6	1013.9	1	2
4	39.4	14.7	246.4	2.5	1010.9		6
5	58.5	22.3	270.5	2.5	1005.3	2	5
6	9.4	26.3	217.8	2.2	1000.9		8
7	90.0	28.0	194.9	1.9	999.5	1	17
8	63.9	25.9	205.9	2.0	1002.7		12
9	90.8	23.1	239.8	1.6	1011.8		5
10	22.8	13.3	196.4	1.7	1017.3		5
11	21.3	5.8	151.5	1.8	1021.5	3	4
12	5.7	-1.2	197.0	2.1	1024.0	1	1

注：1．无霜期203天。
　　2．年极端最高气温38.0℃，出现日期7月4日。
　　3．年极端最低气温-14.4℃，出现日期12月31日。
资料来源：北京市气象局。
Note: a) Annual frost-free period is 203 days.
　　b) Annual utmost highest air temperature is 38.0℃, seen on the 4th of July.
　　c) Annual utmost lowest air temperature is -14.4℃, seen on the 31th of December.
Source: Beijing Municipal Bureau of Meteorology.

7-25 污水处理及环境卫生(1978-2019年)
SEWAGE DISPOSAL AND ENVIRONMENTAL SANITATION (1978-2019)

年份 Year	污水管道长度(公里) Length of Sewage Pipes (km)	污水处理能力(万立方米/日) Sewage Treatment Capacity (10000 cu.m/day)	污水处理率(%) Sewage Treatment Rate (%)	再生水利用量(万立方米) Volume of Recycled Water Used (10000 cu.m)	生活垃圾无害化处理能力(吨/日) Harmless Disposal Capacity of Domestic Waste (ton/day)	生活垃圾产生量(万吨) Output of Domestic Garbage (10000 tons)	生活垃圾清运量(万吨) Domestic Waste Removed and Transported (10000 tons)	生活垃圾无害化处理率(%) Rate of Harmless Disposal of Domestic Waste (%)	粪便清运量(万吨) Excrement Removed and Transported (10000 tons)
1978	290	23.2	7.6				107.2		88.9
1979	309	23.2	10.2				128.0		89.4
1980	334	23.2	9.4				147.0		95.1
1981	347	25.2	10.8				174.0		97.6
1982	365	25.2	10.9				204.7		99.3
1983	411	25.2	10.2				221.4		99.5
1984	568	25.2	10.0				235.4		98.8
1985	706	25.2	10.0				248.1		142.2
1986	747	26.4	8.9				274.4		167.5
1987	805	26.4	7.7				298.3		181.0
1988	770	26.4	7.4				319.9		190.0
1989	860	26.4	6.6				337.0		196.0
1990	904	30.4	7.3				384.1		210.0
1991	968	30.4	6.6				397.1		210.3
1992	1036	4.5	1.2				430.9		216.0
1993	1064	4.5	3.1				446.3		220.6
1994	1122	24.5	9.6				467.2		238.1
1995	1065	58.5	19.4				483.9		258.4
1996	1597	58.5	21.2				483.0		268.0
1997	1635	58.5	22.0				490.0		279.0
1998	1712	58.5	22.5				495.1		295.6
1999	1754	58.5	25.0				505.0		298.0
2000	1852	128.5	39.4		6550		295.6	56.40	274.0
2001	2163	143.5	42.0		6750		309.3	82.15	301.0
2002	2658	180.6	45.0		8750		321.4	86.36	311.7
2003	2903	215.0	50.1		9400		361.4	91.31	268.0
2004	2909	255.0	53.9		10050	495.5	405.9	93.78	175.0
2005	2521	324.0	62.4	23816	10350	536.9	454.6	95.96	171.7
2006	3398	331.0	73.2	36088	10350	585.1	538.3	92.45	175.7
2007	4357	348.0	76.2	49501	10350	619.5	600.9	95.70	189.1
2008	4458	329.4	78.9	60000	12148	672.8	656.6	97.71	206.8
2009	4495	356.0	80.3	64999	13680	669.1	656.1	98.22	211.2
2010	4479	365.0	81.0	68014	16680	634.9	633.0	96.95	194.4
2011	4765	369.4	82.0	71012	16930	634.4	634.4	98.24	207.5
2012	5735	388.5	83.0	75003	17530	648.3	648.3	99.12	207.2
2013	6363	393.0	84.6	80108	21971	671.7	671.7	99.30	220.7
2014	6536	425.0	86.1	86620	21971	733.8	733.8	99.59	216.1
2015	7157	439.5	87.9	94826	27321	790.3	790.3	99.80	204.7
2016	7889	612.0	90.0	100398	24341	872.6	872.6	99.84	204.0
2017	10207	665.6	92.4	105085	24341	924.8	924.8	99.88	214.3
2018	12147	670.6	93.4	107633	28591	975.7	975.7	99.94	201.1
2019	13188	679.2	94.5	115152	32711	1011.2	1011.2	99.98	198.0

注：1．污水处理能力等指标1992年及以后为污水无害化处理情况，1992年以前为污水简易处理情况。
2．生活垃圾无害化处理率按清运量计算。

资料来源：北京市水务局、北京市城市管理委员会。

Note: a) Disposal capacity and other indicators in and after 1992 were about harmless disposal, and those before 1992 were about simple disposal.
b) The harmless disposal rate of domestic waste is calculated with the volume of waste cleared and transported.

Source: Beijing Water Authority，Beijing Municipal Commission of City Administration.

7–26 排水及节水
WATER DRAINAGE AND SAVING

项　目	Item	2019	2018
排　水	**Water Drainage**		
污水处理能力（万立方米/日）	Sewage Treatment Capacity (10000cu.m/day)	679.2	670.6
污水年处理量（万立方米）	Annual Treatment Volume of Sewage (10000 cu.m)	199678	190358
#污水厂	Treated by Sewage Treatment Plants	193356	185948
污水处理率 (%)	Sewage Treatment Rate (%)	94.5	93.4
污水排放总量（万立方米）	Total Volume of Sewage Drainage (10000 cu.m)	211209	203703
排水管道长度（公里）	Length of Drainage Pipelines (km)	22585	21878
污水管	Sewage Pipes	13188	12147
雨水管	Rain Pipes	7868	8241
雨污合流管	Rain-sewage Sewer	1528	1489
再生水利用量（万立方米）	Volume of Recycled Water Used (10000 cu.m)	115152	107633
节　水	**Water Saving**		
节水量（万立方米）	Volume Saved (10000 cu.m)	11176	8315
节水措施（项）	Water Saving Measures Implemented (unit)	122	163

资料来源：北京市水务局。
Source: Beijing Water Authority.

7-27 环境卫生
MUNICIPAL ENVIRONMENT AND SANITATION

项　　目		Item		2019	2018
工作量		**Work Load**			
清扫街道面积	（万平方米／日）	Area of Cleaned Streets	(10000 sq.m/day)	15602	14443
生活垃圾无害化处理能力	（吨/日）	Harmless Disposal Capacity of Domestic Waste	(ton/day)	32711	28591
生活垃圾清运量	（万吨）	Domestic Waste Removed and Transported	(10000 tons)	1011.2	975.7
生活垃圾无害化处理量	（万吨）	Volume of Harmless Disposal of Domestic Waste	(10000 tons)	1010.9	975.1
生活垃圾无害化处理率		Rate of Harmless Disposal of Domestic Waste			
（按清运量计算）	（%）	(Calculated by Volume of Waste Cleared and Transported)	(%)	99.98	99.94
餐厨垃圾处理量	（万吨）	Kitchen Waste Removed and Transported	(10000 tons)	67.9	46.3
粪便清运量	（万吨）	Excrement Removed and Transported	(10000 tons)	198.0	201.1
环卫机械数量	**（辆）**	**Number of Environmental Sanitation Machinery**	**(unit)**	**12526**	**12638**
环卫设施		**Environmental Sanitation Facilities**			
公共厕所	（座）	Public Lavatories	(unit)	6034	5270

资料来源：北京市城市管理委员会。
Source: Beijing Municipal Commission of City Administration.

7–28 环境保护(2000–2019年)
ENVIRONMENTAL PROTECTION (2000-2019)

年 份 Year	可吸入颗粒物 (PM_{10}) 年平均浓度值 (微克/立方米) Annual Average Concentration of Inspiratory Particulate Matter (μg/cu.m)	细颗粒物 ($PM_{2.5}$) 年平均浓度值 (微克/立方米) Annual Average Concentration of $PM_{2.5}$ (μg/cu.m)	二氧化硫 (SO_2) 年平均浓度值 (微克/立方米) Annual Average Concentration of Dioxide (μg/cu.m)	二氧化氮 (NO_2) 年平均浓度值 (微克/立方米) Annual Average Concentration of Nitrogen Dioxide (μg/cu.m)	化学需氧量 (COD) 排放量 (万吨) COD Emission Volume (10000 tons)	二氧化硫 (SO_2) 排放量 (万吨) SO_2 Emission Volume (10000 tons)	区域环境 噪 声 平 均 值 (分贝) Average Value of Noises in Regional Environment (db)	道路交通 干线噪声 平 均 值 (分贝) Average Value of Noises in Road Transportation (db)
2000	162		71	71	17.9	22.4	53.9	71.0
2001	165		64	71	17.0	20.1	53.9	69.6
2002	166		67	76	15.3	19.2	53.5	69.5
2003	141		61	72	13.4	18.3	53.6	69.7
2004	149		55	71	13.0	19.1	53.8	69.6
2005	142		50	66	11.6	19.1	53.2	69.5
2006	161		53	66	11.0	17.6	53.9	69.7
2007	148		47	66	10.7	15.2	54.0	69.9
2008	122		36	49	10.1	12.3	53.6	69.6
2009	121		34	53	9.9	11.9	54.1	69.7
2010	121		32	57	9.2	11.5	54.1	70.0
2011	114		28	55	19.3	9.8	53.7	69.6
2012	109		28	52	18.7	9.4	54.0	69.2
2013	108	89.5	27	56	17.8	8.7	53.9	69.1
2014	116	85.9	22	57	16.9	7.9	53.6	69.1
2015	102	80.6	14	50	16.2	7.1	53.3	69.2
2016	92	73.0	10	48	8.7	3.3	54.3	69.3
2017	84	58.0	8	46	8.2	2.0	53.2	69.3
2018	78	51.0	6	42	5.6	1.1	53.7	69.6
2019	68	42.0	4	37	5.1	0.6	53.7	69.6

注：化学需氧量(COD)排放量和二氧化硫排放量(SO_2)指标自2011年起对统计口径和核算方法进行调整，自2016年起为环境统计年报初步数据。

资料来源：北京市生态环境局。

Note: In 2011, the statistical standard and calculation method were adjusted for COD emission volume and SO_2 emission volume; since 2016, the data on COD emission volume and SO_2 emission volume refer to the preliminary data in the annual statistical report on environment.

Source: Beijing Municipal Ecology and Environment Bureau.

7—29 环境保护
ENVIRONMENTAL PROTECTION

项目		Item		2019	2018
水环境		**Water Environment**			
废水排放总量	(万吨)	Total Discharge of Sewage	(10000 tons)	116266.12	126413.03
#工业废水排放量		Industrial Waste Water Discharge Volume		7716.14	8422.15
化学需氧量(COD)排放量	(吨)	COD Emission Volume	(ton)	51121	55956
#工业废水中COD排放量		Emission of COD in Industrial Waster Water		1619	1951
氨氮排放量	(吨)	Ammonia Nitrogen Discharge	(ton)	3467	3680
#工业废水中氨氮排放量		Ammonia Nitrogen Discharge in Industrial Waster Water		58	53
大气环境		**Atmosphere Environment**			
二氧化硫(SO_2)排放量	(吨)	SO_2 Emission Volume	(ton)	6248	11428
#工业二氧化硫排放量		Emission of Industrial SO_2		1132	1554
氮氧化物排放量	(吨)	Emission of Nitrogen Oxides	(ton)	104577	122132
#工业氮氧化物排放量		Emission of Industrial Nitrogen Oxides		12961	14988
烟(粉)尘排放量	(吨)	Smoke and Dust Emission	(ton)	6169	15343
#工业烟(粉)尘排放量		Emission of Industrial Smoke and Dust		3349	4404
固体废物		**Solid Waste**			
一般工业固体废物产生量	(万吨)	General Industrial Solid Waste Generated	(10000 tons)	598.36	628.23
一般工业固体废物综合利用量	(万吨)	General Industrial Solid Waste Recycled	(10000 tons)	382.52	433.40
一般工业固体废物处置量	(万吨)	General Industrial Solid Waste Disposed	(10000 tons)	216.05	195.32
危险废物产生量	(吨)	Hazardous Wastes Generated	(ton)	245855	179418
危险废物综合利用量	(吨)	Hazardous Wastes Recycled	(ton)	77212	75289
危险废物处置量	(吨)	Hazardous Wastes Disposed	(ton)	164186	102414
生态环境		**Ecological Environment**			
自然保护区个数	(个)	Number of Nature Reserves	(unit)	21	21
#国家级自然保护区		State-level Nature Reserves		2	2
自然保护区面积	(万公顷)	Area of Nature Reserves	(10000 hectares)	13.8	13.8

注：本表水环境、大气环境和固体废物数据为环境统计年报初步数据。
资料来源：北京市生态环境局、北京市园林绿化局。
Note: Data on water environment, atmosphere environment and solid waste in this table refer to the preliminary data in the annual statistical report on environment.
Source: Beijing Municipal Ecology and Environment Bureau, Beijing Gardening and Green Bureau.

7-30 园林绿化及森林情况(1978-2019年)

年 份 Year	年末公园绿地面积 (公顷) Green Land and Park (year-end) (hectare)	人均公园绿地面积 (平方米) Per Capita Park Green Area (sq.m)	城市绿化覆盖率 (%) Urban Green Coverage (%)	林木绿化率 (%) Forest Coverage (%)	年末园林绿地面积 (公顷) Garden Green Area (year-end) (hectare)
1978	2693	5.1	22.3		
1979	2693	5.1	22.3		
1980	2746	5.1	20.1	16.6	
1981	2751	5.1	20.1	16.6	
1982	2779	5.1	20.1	16.6	
1983	2823	5.1	20.1	16.6	
1984	2878	5.1	20.1	16.6	
1985	3263	4.9	22.1	16.6	
1986	3606	5.1	22.9	16.6	
1987	3570	5.1	22.9	16.6	
1988	4074	5.8	25.0	16.6	
1989	6910	6.0	26.0	16.6	
1990	7110	6.1	28.0	28.3	
1991	4279	6.4	28.4	28.3	
1992	4213	6.7	30.3	28.3	
1993	4452	7.8	31.3	28.3	
1994	5221	7.9	32.4	28.3	
1995	5017	7.5	32.7	36.3	
1996	5147	7.5	33.2	36.3	
1997	5408	7.8	34.2	36.3	
1998	6351	9.0	35.6	36.3	
1999	6457	9.1	36.3	36.3	
2000	7140	9.7	36.5	42.0	26680
2001	7554	10.1	38.8	44.0	30224
2002	7907	10.7	40.6	45.5	32572
2003	9115	11.4	40.9	47.5	38475
2004	10446	11.5	41.9	49.5	36755
2005	11365	12.0	42.0	50.5	38877
2006	11788	12.0	42.5	51.0	45495
2007	12101	12.6	43.0	51.6	46320
2008	12316	13.6	43.5	52.1	46993
2009	18070	14.5	44.4	52.6	61695
2010	19020	15.0	45.0	53.0	62672
2011	19728	15.3	45.6	54.0	63541
2012	21178	15.5	46.2	55.5	65540
2013	22215	15.7	46.8	57.4	67048
2014	28798	15.9	47.4	58.4	80223
2015	29503	16.0	48.4	59.0	81305
2016	30069	16.1	48.4	59.3	82113
2017	31019	16.2	48.4	61.0	83501
2018	32619	16.3	48.4	61.5	85286
2019	35157	16.4	48.5	62.0	88704

资料来源：自2019年起，森林火灾数据来源于北京市应急管理局，其余年份及其他指标数据均来源于北京市园林绿化局。

STATISTICS FOR LANDSCAPING AND FORESTS (1978-2019)

森林面积 (公顷) Forest Area (hectare)	森林覆盖率 (%) Forest Coverage Rate (%)	活立木蓄积量 (万立方米) Total Stock of Standing Trees (10000 cu.m)	森林蓄积量 (万立方米) Forest Stock (10000 cu.m)	森林火灾次数 (次) Number of Forest Fires (unit)	森林火灾经济损失 (万元) Economic Loss of Forest Fires (10000 yuan)
619243.2		1521.4	1295.3	9	11.4
626006.3	35.9	1521.4	1295.3	13	96.7
636565.7	36.5	1559.5	1368.9	8	28.1
641368.3	36.5	1574.0	1394.4		
658914.1	36.7	1810.3	1406.2	2	
666050.7	37.0	1854.7	1435.4	4	1.4
673411.8	37.6	1899.4	1468.7	3	1.7
691341.1	38.6	1943.3	1499.0	1	
716456.1	40.1	1993.4	1536.8		
734530.6	41.0	2109.1	1669.9	1	
744956.1	41.6	2149.3	1701.1	3	29.7
756000.7	42.3	2180.0	1724.6	4	
767665.1	43.0	2211.1	1749.8	3	206.2
777603.5	43.5	2246.8	1798.0	1	
791972.0	44.0	2306.2	1850.0	8	

Source: Since 2019, the data on forest fires have been provided by Beijing Emergency Management Bureau; the data for other years and other indicator data were provided by Beijing Gardening and Greening Bureau.

主要统计指标解释

能源生产量 能源生产量是反映能源生产规模、构成、生产成果的重要指标。按能源的成因分为一次能源（亦称天然能源）生产量和二次能源（亦称人工能源）生产量。

一次能源生产量 指报告期内生产一次能源的企业将自然界现存的能源资源经过开采而产出的合格产品，主要包括原煤、原油、天然气、水电等。

二次能源生产量 指报告期内将一次能源经过各种加工转换设备生产出的另一种形式的各种合格的能源产品。如火电、热力、洗煤、焦炭、各种石油制品、焦炉煤气、其他煤气等。

能源消费总量 指一定地域（行政或地理区域）内，国民经济各行业和居民家庭在一定时期所消费的各种能源的总和。能源消费总量包括终端能源消费量、能源加工转换损失量、能源运输和管理过程的损失量三部分。

能源消费总量（等价值） 是电力按等价热值计算的能源消费总量。等价热值是能源统计中经常使用的一个热值概念，是指加工转换产出的某种二次能源所投入的一次能源的量，即获得一个度量单位的某种二次能源所消耗的以热值表示的一次能源。

能源加工转换投入产出量 能源具有由一种能量形式转换为另一种能量形式及耗用过程中可用一种能源替代另一种能源的特征。为提高能源的利用价值和效率，对能源进行加工、转换，产出适合生产和生活需要的更高级的能源产品。在加工转换投入(-)产出(+)量中，“-”表示能源加工转换的投入量，“+”表示二次能源的产出量。

投入量 是指为生产二次能源产品，所投入到能源加工转换设备的各种能源数量。在表中以负数表示。

产出量 是指各种能源（一次能源或少量再投入的二次能源）经过加工转换后，产出的各种二次能源产品（包括不作为能源使用的副产品，联产品）数量。

加工转换损失量 是指在能源加工、转换过程中损失的能量（能源），即能源加工、转换过程中投入的能源和产出的二次能源之间的差额。

损失量 指能源在经营管理和生产、输送、分配、储存等过程中发生的损失以及由于自然因素等原因造成的损失数量。不包括加工转换损失量。

终端消费量 是指能源消费环节的最后一个环节的能源消费，包括直接用作燃料、原材料和动力的各种能源的消费。它们的消费过程体现了能源消费的终止，不会再重新作为能源投入使用。终端消费量不包括用于能源加工转换投入量、加工转换损失量和损失量。

能源消费弹性系数 指能源消费总量增长率与地区生产总值增长率的比值。

电力消费弹性系数 指电力消费量增长率与地区生产总值增长率的比值。

平均每万元地区生产总值能源消费量 能源总消费量或分品种能源消费量与地区生产总值之比。

人均生活用能量 指用于生活消费的各种能源数量与人口总数之比。

日均能源消费量 指各品种能源消费量与当年实际天数之比。

垃圾无害化处理能力 指垃圾无害化处理场（厂）按工艺设计每天所能处理生活垃圾的数量。垃圾无害化处理场（厂）必须是按照有关技术、环境、卫生标准和规范进行设计、建设、运行、维护和管理的各种生活垃圾处理设施，主要包括卫生填埋场、堆肥厂和焚烧厂等。

大风日数 指出现瞬时风速达到或超过 17.0m/s（或目测估计风力达到或超过 8 级）大风的天数。

水资源总量 指降水形成的地表和地下水总量，不包括过境水量。

排水管道长度 指所有排水总管、干管、支管、检查井及连接井进出口等长度之和。计算时应按单管计算，即在同一条街道上如有两条或两条以上并排的排水管道时，应按每条排水管道的长度相加计算。

污水处理能力 指污水处理厂（或处理装置）每昼夜处理污水量的设计能力。

污水处理量 指污水处理厂和处理装置实际处理的污水量。包括物理处理量、生物处理量和化学处理量。

污水处理率 指污水处理量与污水排放总量的比率。计算公式：

$$\text{污水处理率} = \frac{\text{污水处理量}}{\text{污水排放总量}} \times 100\%$$

生活垃圾清运量 指报告期内收集和运送到各垃圾处理场（厂）的垃圾的数量。

粪便清运量 指报告期内收集和运送到各粪便处理场（厂）的粪便的数量。

生活垃圾无害化处理量 指报告期内简易处理场和各种垃圾无害化处理场（厂）处理垃圾的总量。垃圾简易处理量指垃圾简易填埋场所处理的垃圾总量。垃圾无害化处理量指垃圾无害化处理场（厂）所处理的垃圾总量。

生活垃圾无害化处理率 指报告期垃圾无害化处理量与垃圾产生量的比率。计算公式：

$$垃圾无害化处理率 = \frac{垃圾无害化处理量}{垃圾产生量} \times 100\%$$

在统计时，如果生活垃圾产生量不易取得，可用清运量代替。

化学需氧量（COD）排放量 指工业废水中 COD 排放量与生活污水中 COD 排放量之和。指用化学氧化剂氧化水中有机污染物时所需的氧量。COD 值越高，表示水中有机污染物污染越重。

二氧化硫（SO_2）排放量 指报告期内工业 SO_2 排放量与生活 SO_2 排放量之和。

工业固体废物综合利用量 指报告期内企业通过回收、加工、循环、交换等方式，从固体废物中提取或者使其转化为可以利用的资源、能源和其他原材料的固体废物量（包括当年利用的往年工业固体废物贮存量）。如用做农业肥料、生产建筑材料、筑路等。

公园绿地 指向公众开放，以游憩为主要功能，兼具生态、美化、防灾等作用，其绿地率达到 65%以上，配有多种乔灌木及地被植物，有一定设施和艺术布局的绿地。人均公园绿地面积计算口径为常住人口。

绿化覆盖率 指报告期末区域内绿化覆盖面积与区域面积的比率。

计算公式：

$$绿化覆盖率 = \frac{区域内绿化覆盖面积}{区域面积} \times 100\%$$

森林面积 指由乔木树种构成，郁闭度 0.20 以上(含 0.20)的林地或冠幅宽度 10 米以上的林带的面积，即有林地面积。它是反映森林资源总面积的重要指标。森林面积包括天然起源和人工起源的针叶林面积、阔叶林面积、针阔混交林面积和竹林面积。

活立木蓄积量 指一定范围土地上全部树木蓄积的总量，包括森林蓄积、疏林蓄积、散生木蓄积和四旁树蓄积。

森林蓄积量 指一定森林面积上存在着的林木树干部分的总材积，以立方米为计量单位。

森林火灾次数 指发生在城市市区外的一切森林、林木和林地的火灾次数，包括森林火警、一般灾害、重大灾害和特大灾害。

Explanatory Notes on Main Statistical Indicators

Energy Production is an important indicator reflecting the size, composition and results of energy production. By the cause of formation, it consists of the production of primary energy (also known as natural energy) and that of secondary energy (also known as artificial energy).

Production of Primary Energy means up-to-grade products produced by primary energy producers in the reporting period through extraction of existing energy in the nature, mainly including raw coal, crude oil, natural gas, hydroelectricity, etc.

Production of Secondary Energy means various up-to-grade energy products in another form that are made from primary energy with various processing and converting equipment in the reporting period, including thermal power, heating power, washed coal, coke, various petroleum products, coke oven gas and other gases, etc.

Total Energy Consumption means the total consumption of various energies by national economic sectors and resident households in a specific region (administrative or geographic). Total energy consumption can be divided into three parts: end-use energy consumption, loss during energy processing and conversion and loss during energy transport and management.

Total Energy Consumption (in Equivalent Caloricity) means the total consumption of electric power calculated in equivalent caloricity. Equivalent caloricity is a caloricity concept frequently used in statistics of energy. It means the quantity of primary energy input for a secondary energy produced through processing and conversion, i.e. the primary energy in terms of caloricity which is consumed to produce one measuring unit of a secondary energy.

Input and Output of Energy Processing and Conversion One form of energy can be converted into another form of energy. And in consumption, one sort of energy can be replaced with another. In order to improve the energy use value and efficiency, energy is processed and converted to produce energy products at higher levels which are suitable for productive and living needs. In the processing and conversion input (-) and output (+), "-" means the input for energy processing and conversion. And "+" means the output from energy processing and conversion.

Input means the volume of energy put into the energy processing and converting equipment in order to produce secondary energy products. It is shown as a negative number in the table.

Output means the volume of secondary energy products (including byproducts and multi-products that cannot be used as energy) from processing and conversion of energy sources (primary energy or a small amount of secondary energy re-input).

Loss during Processing and Conversion means the energy lost in the processing and conversion of energy, namely the difference between the energy input and the secondary energy output during energy processing and conversion.

Energy Loss means the loss of energy during operation, management, production, transportation, distribution and storage, as well as the loss due to natural factors and other reasons. It excludes the loss during processing and conversion.

End-use Energy Consumption means the energy consumption in the last section of energy consumption, including the consumption of various energy sources used as fuel, raw materials and power. Such consumption represents the end of energy consumption, and the energy will not be put into use again as energy. End-use energy consumption does not include the input for energy processing and conversion, loss during the processing and conversion of energy, and energy loss.

Elasticity Coefficient of Energy Consumption means the ratio of growth rate of total energy consumption to the growth rate of GDP.

Elasticity Coefficient of Electric Power Consumption means the ratio of growth rate of electric power consumption to the growth rate of GDP.

Average Energy Consumption per RMB 10000 of GDP means the ratio of total energy consumption or energy consumption by variety to GDP.

Per-capital Energy Consumption by Households means the ratio of quantity of energy consumed by households to the total population.

Daily Energy Consumption means the ratio of energy consumption to the actual days in the same year.

Harmless Disposal Capacity of Waste means the daily quantity of domestic waste that can be disposed at harmless disposal facilities (sites) according to the process designed. Harmless disposal facilities (sites) must be domestic waste disposal facilities, including landfills, manure yards, incineration facilities and so on, which are designed, built, operated and managed in accordance with relevant technological, environmental, and sanitary standards and criterion.

Total Water Resources means the total volume of surface water and underground water caused by rainfall, excluding passing-by water.

Number of windy days means the number of days with an instantaneous wind speed of 17.0 m/s or more (or with visually estimated force 8 or above wind).

Length of Sewage Pipes means the total length of all main drainage pipes, trunk pipes, branch pipes, access manholes, and connector well entrances and exits, and so on. The length of single pipes shall be included, i.e. if there are two or more drainage pipes parallel on a street, the length of every pipe shall be included.

Sewage Treatment Capacity means the designed capacity of sewage disposal day and night for a sewage disposal plant (or facility).

Volume of Sewage Treated means the volume of sewage actually disposed by sewage disposal plants and facilities, consisting of physical volume, biological volume and chemical volume of waste water disposed.

Sewage Treatment Rate means the ratio of sewage disposed to the total discharge of sewage. The formula is:

Sewage Disposal Rate = Volume of Sewage Disposed / Total Discharge of Sewage × 100%

Domestic Waste Removed and Transported means the quantity of waste collected and transported to waste treatment sites (plants) in the reporting period.

Excrement Removed and Transported means the quantity of excrement collected and transported to waste treatment sites (plants) in the reporting period.

Volume of Harmless Disposal of Domestic Waste means the total volume of waste disposed by simple disposal sites and harmless waste disposal sits (plants) in the reporting period. Simple disposal of waste means the total volume of waste by simple landfills. Harmless waste disposal means the total volume of waste disposed by harmless waste disposal sites (plants).

Rate of Harmless Disposal of Domestic Waste means the ratio of harmless waste disposal to the waste produced in the reporting period. The formula is:

Rate of Harmless Disposal of Domestic Waste = Harmless Waste Disposal / Waste Produced × 100%

In practical statistics, if it is hard to get figures on the volume of domestic waste produced, the volume removed and transported may be used.

COD Emission Volume means the sum of COD emission in industrial sewage and in domestic waste water. It means the amount of oxygen required when chemical oxidants are used to oxidize organic pollutants in water. A higher value of COD corresponds to more serious pollution by organic pollutants.

SO_2 Emission Volume means the sum of industrial SO_2 emission and domestic SO_2 emission in the reporting period.

Industrial Solid Waste Utilized means the volume of solid wastes from which useful materials can be extracted or which can be converted into usable resources, energy or other materials by means of reclamation, processing, recycling and exchange (including utilizing in the year the stocks of industrial solid wastes of the previous year). Examples of such utilizations include fertilizers, building materials and road materials.

Green Land and Parks means the green land open to the public, with main function of recreation, together with ecological, landscaping and disaster preventing functions, and with more than 65% green coverage, provided with multiple arbors, shrubs and ground-cover plants, along with certain facilities and artistic layouts. Per capita area of green land is calculated on the basis of Permanent population.

Green Land Coverage means the ratio of area of green land in a region to the total area of the region in the reporting period. The formula is:

Green Land Coverage = Area of Green Land in a Region / Total Area of the Region × 100%

Forest Area means the area of forest where arbor trees grow with canopy density above 0.2 (and at 0.2) or forest area with crown width more than 10m, i.e. the area of land with forest. It is an important indicator reflecting the total area of forest resources. Forest Area includes the area of coniferous forest, broad leaf forest, mixed coniferous-broad-leaf forest and bamboo forest from both natural and artificial origins.

Total Stock of Standing Trees mean the total stock of all trees on specific area of land, including trees in forest, trees in sparse forest, scattered trees and trees planted by the side of villages, farm houses and along roads and rivers.

Forest Stock means the total volume of timber of forest tree trunks growing on specific area of forest, which are measured in cubic meters.

Number of Forest Fires means the number of all fires occurring in forests, woods, woodlands outside the urban districts, including forest fires, general fires, severe fires and fire disasters.

08

北京统计年鉴2020　　BEIJING STATISTICAL YEARBOOK

城市公用事业
PUBLIC UTILITIES

简 要 说 明

主要内容

本章资料反映北京市城市公用事业的综合水平，主要包括四部分：历年城市公用事业基本情况，水、气、热等供应及消费情况，城市公交、出租车情况，市政主要设施情况。

Brief Introduction

Main Content

Statistics in this chapter show the overall level of urban public utilities in Beijing, which consist of four parts: Basic statistics for urban public utilities in previous years，Water, gas and heating supply and consumption，Urban public transport and taxi services，Main public facilities.

8-1 公路、城市道路及桥梁(1978–2019年)
HIGHWAYS, URBAN ROADS AND BRIDGES (1978-2019)

年份 Year	境内道路总里程(公里) Total Length of Highways and Roads (km)	公路里程(公里) Total Length of Highways (km)	#高速公路 Express-ways	城市道路里程(公里) Length of Urban Roads (km)	#快速路 Rapid Roads	#主干路 Trunk Roads	城市道路面积(万平方米) Area of Urban Roads (10000 sq.m)	城市道路桥梁(座) Number of Bridges (unit)	#立交桥 Overpasses
1978		6562		2078			1611	351	2
1979		7278		2131			1618	348	2
1980		7487		2185			1664	351	6
1981		7566		2234			1742	342	8
1982		7683		2671			2098	408	9
1983		8058		2820			2265	431	10
1984		8271		2928			2393	440	11
1985		8482		2979			2485	460	16
1986		8995		3038			2559	479	16
1987		9103		3087			2631	510	22
1988		9124		3151			2701	522	23
1989		9371		3235			2815	552	27
1990		9648	35	3276			2905	562	33
1991		10259	63	3308			3134	569	40
1992		10827	71	3189			3212	595	55
1993		11260	99	3285			3398	596	64
1994		11532	112	3316			3470	616	75
1995		11811	113	3194			3494	582	84
1996		12084	114	3665			3807	646	133
1997		12306	144	3637			4061	693	140
1998		12498	190	3721			4214	715	138
1999		12825	230	3753			4353	787	141
2000		13600	268	4126			4921	834	149
2001		13891	335	4312			6062	891	160
2002		14359	463	5444			7645	1051	180
2003	18239	14453	499	3055			5345	848	119
2004	19010	14630	525	4067	219	834	6417	949	271
2005	19015	14696	548	4073	239	922	7437	964	304
2006	25377	20503	625	4380	232	955	7286	1079	376
2007	25765	20754	628	4421	236	960	7632	1230	377
2008	26921	20340	777	6143	242	755	8940	1738	381
2009	27436	20755	884	6204	242	805	9179	1765	393
2010	27907	21114	903	6312	263	855	9395	1855	411
2011	28446	21347	912	6258	263	861	9164	1885	418
2012	28585	21492	923	6271	263	865	9236	1950	413
2013	28808	21673	923	6295	269	953	9611	1998	414
2014	29209	21849	982	6426	383	965	10002	2042	422
2015	29069	21885	982	6423	383	969	10029	2069	427
2016	29282	22026	1013	6374	390	970	10275	2088	431
2017	29463	22226	1013	6359	390	984	10347	2094	435
2018	29429	22256	1115	6203	390	998	10328	2156	435
2019	29531	22366	1168	6156	390	1006	10459	2165	437

注：1. 境内道路总里程为全市道路和公路里程之和(剔除道路、公路交叉重复部分)。
2. 道路及桥梁1978年—1981年统计范围为城八区及通县；1982年—2002年统计范围为城八区及14个县城；2003年—2009年统计范围为城八区和北京经济技术开发区。2010年起城市道路及其附属设施统计范围为城六区。
3. 2008年道路数据为北京市城市道路普查数据。

资料来源：北京市交通委员会。

Note: a) Total length of highways and roads means the sum of roads and highways across the city (excluding intersections of roads and highways).
b) Statistics for roads and bridges covered 8 urban districts and Tongzhou County in 1978-1981; the coverage was extended to 8 urban districts and 14 counties in 1982-2002; in 2003-2009, the coverage included 8 central urban districts and Beijing Economic-Technological Development Zone; since 2010, statistics for urban roads and the auxiliary facilities have been confined to 6 urban districts.
c) Statistics for roads and highways in 2008 were from Beijing Urban Road Census.

Source: Beijing Municipal Commission of Transport.

8-2 城市公共交通(1978-2019年)

年 份 Year	公共交通运营线路条数(条) Number of Operating Public Transport Routes (line)	公共电汽车 Buses and Trolley Buses	轨道交通 Rail Transit	公共交通运营线路长度(公里) Length of Operating Public Transport Lines (km)	公共电汽车 Buses and Trolley Buses	轨道交通 Rail Transit	公共交通运营车辆(辆) Number of Operating Public Transport Vehicles in Operation (vehicle)
1978	119	118	1	1427	1403	24	2743
1979	121	120	1	1469	1446	24	2997
1980	123	122	1	1479	1455	24	3113
1981	127	126	1	1525	1501	24	3375
1982	139	138	1	1678	1654	24	3620
1983	151	150	1	1820	1797	24	3907
1984	164	162	2	1939	1899	40	4221
1985	191	189	2	2312	2272	40	4583
1986	200	198	2	2574	2534	40	4576
1987	194	192	2	2382	2342	40	4776
1988	199	197	2	2445	2405	40	4787
1989	207	205	2	2525	2485	40	4890
1990	216	214	2	2654	2614	40	5160
1991	223	221	2	2755	2715	40	5182
1992	262	260	2	3379	3338	42	5223
1993	268	266	2	3532	3491	42	5213
1994	284	282	2	4117	4075	42	5319
1995	300	298	2	4538	4497	42	5367
1996	399	397	2	7317	7276	42	6828
1997	667	665	2	14011	13969	42	10479
1998	690	688	2	14929	14888	42	10819
1999	750	748	2	16566	16513	54	12509
2000	682	680	2	15639	15585	54	14191
2001	555	553	2	13180	13126	54	15420
2002	592	589	3	15835	15760	75	17580
2003	620	616	4	16131	16017	114	17445
2004	621	617	4	15247	15133	114	19343
2005	626	622	4	18328	18214	114	19471
2006	624	620	4	18582	18468	114	20489
2007	649	644	5	17495	17353	142	20525
2008	679	671	8	18057	17857	200	23221
2009	701	692	9	18498	18270	228	23730
2010	727	713	14	19079	18743	336	24011
2011	764	749	15	19832	19460	372	24478
2012	795	779	16	19989	19547	442	25831
2013	830	813	17	20153	19688	465	27590
2014	895	877	18	20776	20249	527	28331
2015	894	876	18	20740	20186	554	28311
2016	895	876	19	20392	19818	574	27892
2017	908	886	22	19898	19290	608	30966
2018	910	888	22	19881	19245	637	29732
2019	1181	1158	23	28331	27632	699	29459

注：自2006年5月1日起，公共电汽车、轨道交通售票采取刷卡方式，并陆续进行了票制票价改革，客运量统计口径方法相应调整，因此与历史数据不可比。

资料来源：本表2005年及以后数据来源于北京市交通委员会。

URBAN PUBLIC TRANSPORT (1978-2019)

		公共交通			出租小汽车 Taxis Service	
公共电汽车 Buses and Trolley Buses	轨道交通 Rail Transit	客运量（万人次） Passengers Traffic of Public Transport (10000 person-times)	公共电汽车 Buses and Trolley Buses	轨道交通 Rail Transit	运营车辆（辆） Operating Vehicles (vehicle)	客运量（万人次） Passenger Traffic (10000 persons)
2627	116	172559	169465	3094		
2889	108	205703	200918	4785		
3001	112	236998	231477	5521		
3259	116	263944	257478	6466		
3500	120	284175	276922	7253		
3753	154	302501	294301	8200		
4037	184	324437	314132	10305		
4398	185	335227	321264	13963		
4371	205	328770	312990	15780		
4524	252	330417	311190	19227		
4535	252	337094	306396	30698		
4587	303	306435	275383	31052		
4857	303	334673	296495	38178		
4877	305	344525	307438	37087		
4900	323	348770	305959	42811		
4890	323	335378	286268	49110		
4984	335	353289	299993	53296		
4984	383	371579	315777	55802		
6427	401	349847	305433	44414		
10044	435	391182	346676	44507		
10382	437	418825	372494	46331		
12018	491	426706	378483	48223		
13604	587	406691	363213	43478		
14803	617	449720	402850	46870		
16939	641	492122	443880	48242		
16753	692	426628	379380	47248		
18451	892	499830	439130	60700		
18503	968	517769	449793	67976	66000	65000
19522	967	468225	397919	70306	66646	64121
19395	1130	488138	422645	65493	66646	64111
21507	1714	592523	470863	121660	66646	69000
21716	2014	658785	516517	142268	66646	68000
21548	2463	689788	505144	184645	66646	69000
21628	2850	722552	503272	219280	66646	69600
22146	3685	761578	515416	246162	66646	69862
23592	3998	804775	484306	320469	67046	69946
23667	4664	815849	477180	338668	67546	66828
23287	5024	738384	406003	332381	68284	58750
22688	5204	734953	369019	365934	68484	47665
25624	5342	713396	335595	377801	68484	39378
24076	5656	703818	318975	384843	70035	34021
23010	6449	709604	313366	396238	71517	33110

Note: Since May 1, 2006, buses, trolley buses and rail transit tickets were sold by card swiping. Ticket system and prices were also reformed successively. The statistical coverage and methods for passenger traffic were adjusted accordingly, so these figures were incomparable with historical data.

Source: Since 2005, data in this table were provided by Beijing Municipal Commission of Transport.

8-3 城市供水、供气及供热(1978-2019年)
URBAN WATER SUPPLY, GAS SUPPLY AND HEAT SUPPLY (1978-2019)

年份 Year	全市集中供热管道长度(公里) Total Length of Pipelines for Centralized Heating (km)	全市集中供热面积(万平方米) Centralized Heating Area in Beijing (10000 sq.m)	#住宅 Residence	煤气销售量(万立方米) Sales Volume of Coal Gas (10000 cu.m)	液化石油气销售量(吨) Sales Volume of Liquefied Petroleum Gas (ton)	天然气销售量(万立方米) Sales Volume of Natural Gas (10000 cu.m)
1978				32687	97255	
1979				32113	114350	
1980				34935	128990	
1981				36309	134771	
1982				36748	149805	
1983				37319	150058	
1984				38710	156421	
1985				41678	169720	
1986				44542	182239	
1987				47594	178205	
1988				49595	177112	287
1989				56056	175814	1805
1990		3702		59508	172688	3544
1991		4560		66111	174326	5062
1992		5281		73615	174694	6040
1993		5730		80163	177065	6702
1994		7056		80409	173105	7623
1995		7537		85201	177637	11003
1996		7838		88356	185304	13504
1997		8399		76429	172879	16565
1998		9102		68998	174464	32619
1999		9992		61846	188450	64833
2000		10860		46719	190571	95919
2001		14729		33960	182188	150585
2002		18172		21077	234680	176504
2003		25108		23991	311657	208837
2004		28150	18962	17714	431660	250326
2005	6272	31736	22218	16776	356551	294279
2006	7013	34977	23158	9763	415268	389202
2007	10424	37203	23697		319631	441327
2008	11948	42501	26738		289576	578626
2009	12156	44240	27694		332693	645356
2010	12224	46715	32305		299392	677009
2011	11734	50794	34563		394437	726229
2012	11031	52555	35104		379371	883385
2013	11192	54591	36806		453546	956852
2014	12038	56786	38085		531556	1088999
2015	12207	58465	39031		523391	1427808
2016	13545	61136	41084		489473	1538425
2017	60169	60751	42215		457024	1577065
2018	60549	62932	43460		448107	1807388
2019	60166	63928	44419		395029	1823476

注：1.2006年6月开始全市煤气家庭用户已全部置换为天然气用户，因此2007年以后煤气销售量无数据。
2.自2012年起，自来水数据口径调整为城镇公共供水。
3.自2017年起，全市集中供热管道长度数据包含一级、二级管网数据，2016年及以前只包含一级管网数据。
4.自2011年起，液化石油气销售量数据包含市内销售量数据和市外销售量数据。自2019年起，天然气销售量数据包含市内销售量数据和市外销售量数据，下同。

资料来源：北京市城市管理委员会、北京市水务局。

Note: a) Since June 2006, all households using coal gas have started to use natural gas. Therefore, there are no data on sales volume of coal gas since 2007.
b) Since 2012, relevant figures of tap water were changed to cover urban public water supply.
c) Since 2017, the figures of total length of pipelines for centralized heating included that of the primary and secondary heating network; in and before 2016, the said figures included the primary network data only.
d) Since 2011, the figures of sales volume of liquefied petroleum gas included data on volume of sales in Beijing and that outside Beijing. Since 2019, the figures of sales volume of natural gas included data on volume of sales in Beijing and that outside Beijing, the same below.

Source: Beijing Municipal Commission of Urban Administration、Beijing Water Authority.

8-3 续表 Continued

年 份 Year	居 民 燃气用户 (万户) Gas Using Households (10000 households)	自来水综合 生产能力 (万立方米/日) Gereral Production Capacity of Tap Water (10000 cu.m/day)	自来水供水 管道长度 (公里) Length of Water Supply Pipelines (km)	自 来 水 销售总量 (万立方米) Total Sales Volume of Tap Water (10000 cu.m)
1978	65.2	134	2926	32664
1979	76.7	151	3083	36232
1980	80.3	163	3272	38933
1981	85.1	167	3435	41634
1982	88.0	164	4216	41136
1983	90.9	166	4452	42778
1984	96.9	167	4622	43716
1985	102.3	176	4927	45601
1986	153.6	188	5079	46695
1987	160.9	185	5257	47680
1988	165.4	189	5550	50059
1989	172.6	206	5647	50145
1990	176.1	215	5770	52718
1991	184.7	221	5947	56107
1992	192.4	226	6130	58704
1993	197.5	234	6367	60794
1994	210.3	242	6727	67977
1995	219.8	264	6907	67877
1996	188.1	266	6907	69684
1997	243.0	302	6339	79046
1998	254.4	330	6989	75969
1999	259.8	357	7179	78098
2000	291.9	367	7610	75364
2001	310.0	371	8146	69807
2002	336.4	428	8555	79322
2003	406.0	429	9278	71583
2004	438.6	399	9981	82986
2005	462.6	348	9831	71600
2006	540.2	373	11899	74970
2007	556.4	391	13133	77778
2008	591.0	404	14118	80792
2009	600.0	424	14791	86881
2010	634.2	445	16144	89185
2011	644.1	473	16963	94622
2012	713.5	411	14029	93826
2013	737.4	444	14495	98178
2014	846.0	503	14994	103402
2015	885.7	506	15421	103929
2016	886.5	504	15742	108386
2017	929.0	522	16105	110587
2018	926.4	527	16448	115852
2019	873.2	599	16735	120059

8-4 液化石油气及天然气
LIQUEFIED PETROLEUM GAS AND NATURAL GAS

项　　目		Item		2019	2018	2019年为2018年% 2019 as % of 2018
液化石油气		**Liquefied Petroleum Gas**				
供气总量	（吨）	Gas Supply	(ton)	434286	481775	90.1
销售气量	（吨）	Gas Sales	(ton)	395029	448107	88.2
#家庭用量		Househlod Consumption		114224	140480	81.3
家庭用户	（万户）	Househlod Consumers	(10000 households)	173.3	254.0	68.2
天然气		**Natural Gas**				
供气总量	（万立方米）	Gas Supply	(10000 cu.m)	1877422	1874070	100.2
销售气量	（万立方米）	Gas Sales	(10000 cu.m)	1823476	1807388	100.9
#家庭用量		Househlod Consumption		145888	141076	103.4
家庭用户	（万户）	Househlod Consumers	(10000 households)	699.9	672.5	104.1
居民燃气用户	（万户）	**Household Gas Users**	**(10000 households)**	**873.2**	**926.4**	**94.3**

注：本表液化石油气、天然气供气总量和销售气量数据均包含燕山石化数据。
资料来源：北京市城市管理委员会、中国石化集团北京燕山石化有限公司。
Note: Data on liquefied petroleum gas and natural gas consumption consumption in this table include the consumption of Yanshan Petrochemical.
Source: Beijing Municipal Commission of City Administration, and SINOPEC Beijing Yanshan Petrochemical Co., Ltd.

8-5 自来水及自备水源
TAP WATER AND SELF-PROVIDED SOURCES OF WATER

项　　目		Item		2019	2018
自来水		**Tap Water**			
综合生产能力	（万立方米/日）	General Production Capacity	(10000cu.m/day)	598.9	526.8
供水管道长度	（公里）	Length of Water Supply Pipelines	(km)	16735	16448
销售总量	（万立方米）	Total Sales Volume	(10000 cu.m)	120059	115852
生产用水		For Production Use		12764	13072
生活用水		For Public Service Use		104439	100271
生态环境用水		For Domestic Use		2855	2508
自备井水		**Self-provided Well Water**			
用水量	（万立方米）	Consumption	(10000 cu.m)	45811	54324
生产用水		For Production Use		10724	11623
生活用水		For Public Service Use		29524	34715
生态环境用水		For Domestic Use		5563	7986

注：自来水数据口径为城镇公共供水。自备井水数据口径为城镇范围，2019年，自备井用水量中不包含乡镇集中供水数据。
资料来源：北京市水务局。
Note: Statistical basis for tap water is urban public water supply. Since 2013, statistical scope for the data on self-provided well water were changed to cover urban area, satellite city, central town, town with general organizational structure, except agriculture.
Source: Beijing Water Authority.

8-6 市政设施情况
BASIC STATISTICS FOR MUNICIPAL FACILITIES

项 目		Item		2019	2018
境内道路总里程	（公里）	Total Length of Highways and Roads	(km)	29531	29429
高速公路里程	（公里）	Length of Expressways	(km)	1168	1115
城市道路里程	（公里）	Length of Urban Roads	(km)	6156	6203
#快速路		Rapid Roads		390	390
#主干路		Trunk Roads		1006	998
城市道路面积	（万平方米）	Coverage of Urban Roads	(10000 sq.m)	10459	10328
#铺装步道		Paved Roads		1776	1730
城市道路立交桥数	（座）	Number of Overpasses in City	(unit)	437	435
城市过街天桥数	（座）	Number of Pedestrain Overpasses in City	(unit)	545	545
城市地下通道数	（座）	Number of Underpasses in City	(unit)	215	214
备案停车场个数	（个）	Number of Parking Lots Recorded	(unit)	5402	6324
备案停车场车位总数	（个）	Total Capacity of Parking Lots Recorded	(unit)	1703607	1890573
路口电视监视点位	（台）	TV Monitors at Crossings	(unit)	1256	1250
城六区照明线路长度	（公里）	Length of Lighting Lines in 6 Urban Districts	(km)	8402	8402

注：本表统计范围为城六区。
资料来源：北京市交通委员会、北京市公安局公安交通管理局、北京市路灯管理中心。
Note: Data in this table covers 6 urban districts .
Source: Beijing Municipal Communission of Transport, Beijing Traffic Management Bureau., Beijing Street Lamp Administration Center.

主要统计指标解释

自来水综合生产能力 指按供水设施取水、净化、送水、出厂输水干管等环节实际测定计算的综合生产能力。不包括供水高峰阶段，超负荷增加的生产能力。计算时，以四个环节中最薄弱的环节为主确定能力。

自来水供水管道长度 指从送水泵至用户水表之间所有管道的长度。不包括新安装尚未使用的管道。

生产用水 指在生产活动中取用的水量，包含工业用水量和农业用水量两个部分。

生活用水 指城乡居民家庭日常生活及除工业企业外的建筑业、商业、饮食业、宾馆业、服务业、机关团体、医院、学校部队等范围的用水。

生态环境用水 指通过人为措施补充给河湖、湿地的水量及园林绿化、环境卫生（公厕冲洗、道路喷洒等）等用水。

公共交通年末运营车辆 指公交企业（单位）用于运营业务的全部车辆数。

运营线路总长度 指全部运营线路长度之和。计算公式：

$$运营线路长度=\sum 各条运营线路长度$$

$$=\sum\left[\begin{pmatrix}上行起点至终点里程+下行起点至终点里程\\+上下行终点掉头里程\end{pmatrix}\right]$$

公路里程 指公路的长度，凡达到《公路工程技术标准（JTGB01-2003)》规定的技术等级的公路，均统计公路里程，包括大、中城市的郊区公路里程，公路通过城镇（指县城、集镇）街道的里程和公路桥梁长度、隧道长度、渡口的宽度以及分期修建的公路已验收交付使用的里程。国道、省道、县道、乡道和专用公路中新增的人工修建的、路基宽度在 4.5 米以上的等外路里程也纳入公路里程统计。按技术等级公路可分为高速公路、一级公路、二级公路、三级公路、四级公路和等外公路。

道路里程 指道路长度和与道路相通的桥梁、隧道的长度，按车行道中心线计算。城市道路由车行道和人行道两部分组成。在统计时只统计路面宽度在 3.5 米（含 3.5 米）以上的各种铺装道路，包括开放型工业区和住宅区道路在内。

道路面积 指道路面积和与道路相通的广场、桥梁、隧道的面积（统计时，将人行道面积单独统计）。人行道面积按道路两侧面积相加计算。包括步行街和广场，不含人车混行的道路。

Explanatory Notes on Main Statistical Indicators

General Production Capacity of Tap Water means the comprehensive production capacity of water facilities calculated by on-site measurement, including capacity of the water in-taking, treatment, transmission and delivery; while overloaded capacity during water supply peak hours are not included. Calculation of the capacity was mainly dependent upon the weakest link of the whole production process.

Length of Tap Water Supply Pipelines means the length of all pipes linking between the water outlet pumps and users' water meters, excluding the ones newly installed and not yet put into use.

Water for Production Use means the water used for production and operation of business entities within the city, covering sectors including agriculture, forestry, animal production and hunting, fishing, industry, construction, transportation, etc.

Water for Public Service Use means the water used for urban public services, including water supply for administrative and public institutions, military units, public facilities, social services, wholesale and retail trades, hotels and catering, and social service organizations.

Water for ecological and environmental protection refers to the replenishment of water into rivers, lakes and wetlands through artificial measures, and refers to the water used for landscaping and environmental sanitation (toilet flushing and road spraying, etc.).

Year-end Public Transport Vehicles in Operation means the number of all vehicles used for operational businesses in public transit enterprises (institutions).

Total Length of Public Transport Routes means the sum of all lines in operation. It is calculated with the formula:

Length of Public Transit Lines = ∑ Length of all lines in operation = ∑ [(mileage from the upward starting point to the end point + mileage from the downward starting point to the end point + mileage of double back from upward and downward end points)]

Total Length of Highways means the length of highways. Such statistics apply for any highway reaching the technical grade stated in *Highway Engineering Technical Standards (JTGB01-2003)*, including the mileage of highways in suburbs of middle and large cities, mileage of highways passing through streets in towns (counties and townships), length of highway bridges, length of tunnels, width of ferries, and mileage of highways constructed in several phases and put into use. The mileage of non-graded new highways built manually onto national highways, provincial highways, county highways, township highways and special highways, with roadbed width of 4.5m and above, are also incorporated. In terms of technical grade, highways fall into expressways, first-grade highways, second-grade highways, third-grade highways, fourth-grade highways, and non-graded highways.

Length of Highways and Roads means the length of roads and bridges and tunnels connecting with roads, calculated by the central lines of carriage ways. Urban roads consist of carriageways and sidewalks. Statistics only cover paved roads with width of pavement above 3.5m (including 3.5m), roads in open industrial zones and residential zones included.

Area of Roads means the area of roads and the area of squares, bridges and tunnels connecting to the roads (the area of sidewalks is calculated separately). The area of sidewalks is the sum of area on both sides of roads, including pedestrian streets and squares, excluding roads passable for both pedestrians and vehicles.

09

固定资产投资和房地产开发

INVESTMENT IN FIXED ASSETS AND REAL ESTATE DEVELOPMENT

简要说明

一、主要内容

本章资料包括北京市固定资产投资、房屋建筑施工及竣工情况、房地产开发情况、保障性安居工程建设情况等。

二、统计范围和调查方法

（一）统计范围。1996 年及以前固定资产投资统计起点为 5 万元及以上，1996 年以后调整为 50 万元及以上，从 2011 年开始调整为 500 万元及以上。

（二）调查方法。除农户固定资产投资统计采用抽样调查方法外，其他均为全面调查。

三、有关统计标准的变化说明

（一）关于行业划分。自 2018 年开始执行《国民经济行业分类》（GB/T 4754-2017）标准。

（二）关于三次产业划分。2003 年，根据《国民经济行业分类》（GB/T 4754—2002），国家统计局印发了《国家统计局关于印发〈三次产业划分规定〉的通知》（国统字〔2003〕14 号）。2012 年，根据国家质检总局和国家标准委颁布的《国民经济行业分类》（GB/T 4754—2011），国家统计局对 2003 年《三次产业划分规定》进行了修订。主要在以下方面作出调整：一是将门类“农、林、牧、渔业”中的“农、林、牧、渔服务业”，“采矿业”中的“开采辅助活动”，“制造业”中的“金属制品、机械和设备修理业”等三个大类一并调整到第三产业。调整后，第一产业为 4 个大类；第二产业为 2 个门类和 36 个大类；第三产业为 15 个门类和 3 个大类。二是明确第三产业即为服务业。

本章2012年及以后三次产业的分类执行调整后的划分规定。

Brief Introduction

I. Main Content

Statistics in this chapter include figures on investment in fixed assets, buildings under construction and buildings completed, real estate development as well as figures on government-subsidized housing projects, in Beijing over the years.

II. Scope of Statistics and Method for Survey

(I) Scope of Statistics. Before and in 1996, the threshold of fixed assets investment statistics was RMB 50,000 and above; after 1996, it was adjusted to RMB 500,000 and above; since 2011, the figure has been set at RMB 5 million and above.

(II) Method for Survey. Except for the statistics for investment in fixed assets of rural households in which the sampling survey method is adopted, the statistics for all other items are made with the comprehensive survey method.

III. Changes in Relevant Statistical Standards

(I) Classification of Sectors. The standards in the *Classification of National Economic Sectors (GB/T 4754-2017) are implemented since 2018.*

(II) Classification of Three Industries. According to the *Classification of National Economic Sectors* (GB/T 4754-2002), the National Bureau of Statistics issued the *Notice of the National Bureau of Statistics on the Issuance of the 'Regulations on Three Industries Classification'* (G.T.Z. [2003] No. 14) in 2003. According to the *Classification of National Economic Sectors* (GB/T 4754-2011) promulgated by the General Administration of Quality Supervision, Inspection and Quarantine of the People's Republic of China and the Standardization Administration of the People's Republic of China, the National Bureau of Statistics revised the *Regulations on Three Industries Classification* of 2003 version in 2012. Adjustments were mainly made in the following aspects: Firstly, the "service activities for agriculture, forestry, animal husbandry and fishing" in the category of "agriculture, forestry, animal production and hunting, fishing", the "mining support service activities" in the category of "mining and quarrying", and the "repair of fabricated metal products, machinery and equipment" in the category of "manufacturing" were adjusted to the tertiary industry. After adjustment, the primary industry fell into 4 categories; the secondary industry fell into 2 classes and 36 categories; and the tertiary industry fell into 15 classes and 3 categories. Secondly, the tertiary industry was defined as the service industry.

The classification of thee industries since 2012 as mentioned in this chapter has all been subject to the classification provisions after adjustment.

9-1 全社会固定资产投资和增长速度情况(1978-2018年)
TOTAL INVESTMENT IN FIXED ASSETS AND GROWTH RATE(1978-2018)

单位：亿元 (100 million yuan)

年 份 Year	全社会固定资产投资 Total Investment in Fixed Assets		#房地产开发投资 Investment in Real Estate Development		#基础设施投资 Infrastructure Investment		#建筑安装投资 Construction and Installation Investment	
	绝对量 Absolute Volume	比上年增长(%) Growth Rate (%)	绝对量 Absolute Volume	比上年增长(%) Growth Rate (%)	绝对量 Absolute Volume	比上年增长(%) Growth Rate (%)	绝对量 Absolute Volume	比上年增长(%) Growth Rate (%)
1978	22.6				5.4			
1979	26.5	17.3			5.8	7.4		
1980	33.2	25.3			6.0	3.4		
1981	36.6	10.2			5.8	-3.3		
1982	38.6	5.5			6.1	5.2		
1983	51.3	32.9			6.7	9.8		
1984	66.3	29.2			8.8	31.3		
1985	94.0	41.8			13.2	50.0		
1986	106.2	13.0			14.5	9.8		
1987	136.2	28.2			22.1	52.4		
1988	163.0	19.7			23.2	5.0		
1989	139.5	-14.4			26.5	14.2		
1990	179.2	28.5	22.5		31.6	19.2		
1991	192.0	7.1	24.0	6.7	35.2	11.4	107.3	
1992	266.0	38.5	33.7	40.4	58.8	67.0	136.2	26.9
1993	410.4	54.3	58.4	73.3	91.4	55.4	232.0	70.3
1994	648.8	58.1	99.5	70.4	153.4	67.8	362.6	56.3
1995	841.5	29.7	352.8	254.6	156.1	1.8	459.0	26.6
1996	876.9	4.2	328.2	-7.0	188.8	20.9	515.8	12.4
1997	961.2	9.6	330.3	0.6	218.3	15.6	546.2	5.9
1998	1155.6	20.2	377.4	14.3	320.4	46.8	626.9	14.8
1999	1170.6	1.3	421.5	11.7	302.7	-5.5	679.1	8.3
2000	1297.4	10.8	522.1	23.9	351.9	16.3	701.5	3.3
2001	1530.5	18.0	783.8	50.1	356.4	1.3	801.6	14.3
2002	1814.3	18.5	989.4	26.2	411.9	15.6	964.9	20.4
2003	2157.1	18.9	1202.5	21.5	417.8	1.4	1151.3	19.3
2004	2528.3	17.2	1473.3	22.5	463.2	10.9	1438.9	25.0
2005	2827.2	11.8	1525.0	3.5	610.7	31.8	1569.5	9.1
2006	3371.5	19.3	1719.9	12.8	935.3	53.2	1836.0	17.0
2007	3966.6	17.6	1995.8	16.0	1175.8	25.7	2117.9	15.4
2008	3848.5	-3.0	1908.7	-4.4	1160.7	-1.3	1798.8	-15.1
2009	4858.4	26.2	2337.7	22.5	1462.0	26.0	1983.0	10.2
2010	5493.5	13.1	2901.1	24.1	1403.5	-4.0	2124.9	7.2
	(5218.3)							
2011	5910.6	13.3	3036.3	10.1	1400.2	0.3	2585.3	22.4
2012	6462.8	9.3	3153.4	3.9	1789.2	27.8	3076.6	19.0
2013	7032.2	8.8	3483.4	10.5	1785.7	-0.2	3482.2	13.2
2014	7562.3	7.5	3911.3	12.3	2018.1	13.0	3468.1	-0.4
2015	7990.9	5.7	4226.3	8.1	2174.5	7.7	2996.5	-13.6
2016	8461.7	5.9	4045.4	-4.3	2399.5	10.3	3132.8	4.5
2017	8948.1	5.7	3745.9	-7.4	2984.2	24.4	3279.1	4.7
2018		-9.9		3.4		-10.7		3.6

注：1.根据国家统计局有关规定，从2004年起，全社会固定资产投资中不包括零星购置投资，下同。
2.从2011年起，根据国家统计局有关规定，固定资产投资统计起点由50万元调整至500万元。2010年未加括号的为原口径数，括号内为调整后的数据，固定资产投资增长速度按可比口径计算。

Note: a) According to related regulations of National Bureau of Statistics, since 2004, total investment in fixed assets has not included investment in acquiring minor items, the same below.
b) Since 2011, the statistical threshold of investment in fixed assets has been adjusted from RMB 500,000 to RMB 5 million according to the related regulations of National Bureau of Statistics. Figures in 2010 with no brackets are based on the former standard.Figures in brackets are data after adjustment. The growth rates of fixed assets investment are calculated in comparable terms.

9-2 按产业分全社会固定资产投资和增长速度情况(1978-2018年)
INVESTMENT IN FIXED ASSETS AND GROWTH RATE BY INDUSTRY (1978-2018)

单位：亿元 (100 million yuan)

年 份 Year	全社会固定资产投资 Total Investment in Fixed Assets		第一产业 Primary Industry		第二产业 Secondary Industry		第三产业 Tertiary Industry	
	绝对量 Absolute Volume	比上年增长(%) Growth Rate (%)	绝对量 Absolute Volume	比上年增长(%) Growth Rate (%)	绝对量 Absolute Volume	比上年增长(%) Growth Rate (%)	绝对量 Absolute Volume	比上年增长(%) Growth Rate (%)
1978	22.6		1.4		10.8		10.4	
1979	26.5	17.3	1.0		12.0		13.5	
1980	33.2	25.3	0.7		15.7		16.8	
1981	36.6	10.2	0.6		13.6		17.2	
1982	38.6	5.5	1.2		15.4		17.9	
1983	51.3	32.9	1.2		16.4		20.9	
1984	66.3	29.2	1.3		20.3		30.6	
1985	94.0	41.8	1.6		32.4		43.8	
1986	106.2	13.0	1.5		41.4		51.6	
1987	136.2	28.2	1.6		46.9		72.9	
1988	163.0	19.7	2.0		48.8		87.9	
1989	139.5	-14.4	1.9		38.4		81.9	
1990	179.2	28.5	2.4		43.3		89.9	
1991	192.0	7.1	2.7		51.3		90.4	
1992	266.0	38.5	3.9		82.9		114.2	
1993	410.4	54.3	2.1		150.4		165.7	
1994	648.8	58.1	3.7		185.8		318.4	
1995	841.5	29.7	3.1		153.7		284.8	
1996	876.9	4.2	2.8		174.9		319.7	
1997	961.2	9.6	0.9		201.1		380.1	
1998	1155.6	20.2	1.5		201.7		479.7	
1999	1170.6	1.3	1.7		179.4		470.4	
2000	1297.4	10.8	3.0		157.2		510.3	
2001	1530.5	18.0	8.4		154.2		1367.9	
2002	1814.3	18.5	7.5		185.0		1621.8	
2003	2157.1	18.9	21.0		260.7		1875.4	
2004	2528.3	17.2	14.6		401.0		2112.7	
2005	2827.2	11.8	11.9		409.7		2405.6	
2006	3371.5	19.3	14.5	21.8	363.2	-11.4	2993.8	24.5
2007	3966.6	17.6	16.7	15.5	484.1	33.3	3465.8	15.8
2008	3848.5	-3.0	28.1	68.2	386.0	-20.3	3434.4	-0.9
2009	4858.4	26.2	57.4	104.6	411.4	6.6	4389.5	27.8
2010	5493.5	13.1	43.2	-24.8	528.1	28.4	4922.3	12.1
2011	5910.6	13.3	47.2	13.8	762.2	47.2	5101.3	9.5
2012	6462.8	9.3	145.4	208.4	719.8	-5.6	5597.5	9.7
2013	7032.2	8.8	175.5	20.6	755.0	4.9	6101.7	9.0
2014	7562.3	7.5	163.9	-6.6	716.8	-5.1	6681.6	9.5
2015	7990.9	5.7	111.0	-32.2	677.1	-5.5	7202.8	7.8
2016	8461.7	5.9	99.8	-10.1	722.9	6.8	7639.0	6.1
2017	8948.1	5.7	95.9	-3.9	893.8	23.6	7958.4	4.2
2018		-9.9		8.9		-43.2		-6.3

注：2000年及以前按产业划分中，不含房地产开发投资及农村投资。2001年以后含房地产开发投资及农村固定资产投资。

Note: Data of investment in fixed assets grouped by industry excluded investment in real estate development and rural investment in 2000 and before. After 2001, data of investment in fixed assets included investment in real estate development and rural fixed assets.

9-3 固定资产投资资金来源情况(1978-2019年)
INVESTMENT IN FIXED ASSETS BY SOURCE OF FUNDS (1978-2019)

单位：亿元 (100 million yuan)

年 份 Year	上年末结余资金 Surplus Funds by the End of the Previous Year	本年资金来源小计 Subtotal of Funds at Current Year	中央预算资金 Central Budgetary Fund	国内贷款 Domestic Loans	债券 Bonds	利用外资 Foreign Investment	自筹资金 Self-raised Funds	其他资金 Others
1978		22.5	16.9					
1979		26.5	19.2					
1980		33.2	18.5					
1981		31.4	15.4					
1982		34.5	14.1					
1983		38.5	16.0					
1984		52.2	22.5					
1985		77.8	30.4					
1986		94.5	33.0					
1987		126.2	43.1					
1988		149.4	37.4					
1989		123.1	35.0	12.8		18.2	44.5	12.6
1990		136.2	34.4	22.8		15.2	52.3	11.5
1991		151.1	35.5	28.2		13.9	65.5	8.0
1992		216.7	42.2	40.1		14.9	109.9	9.6
1993	54.3	425.2	47.1	79.2	1.6	28.0	205.2	64.1
1994	71.1	695.7	64.1	91.5	0.8	96.9	331.2	111.2
1995	200.8	915.8	70.3	122.7	1.1	187.3	339.8	194.6
1996	204.9	926.1	76.7	152.8	1.0	161.2	330.5	203.9
1997	183.1	1016.7	86.3	194.3		139.2	383.4	213.5
1998	207.1	1140.1	98.4	223.8	17.0	132.1	450.2	218.6
1999	212.1	1183.8	136.2	262.2	1.4	82.7	461.3	240.0
2000	293.1	1439.1	107.0	373.8	0.6	51.5	505.6	400.6
2001	325.5	1796.8	136.7	429.4	2.5	35.6	595.6	597.0
2002	433.2	2075.3	108.5	543.8	1.9	41.5	672.8	706.8
2003	542.7	2674.0	78.4	755.2		52.6	887.9	899.9
2004	654.6	3712.8	118.6	804.7		120.5	1245.7	1423.3
2005	924.4	4553.7	128.8	1055.8		70.9	1452.8	1845.4
2006	1043.8	4927.3	126.4	1347.5	32.7	76.2	1532.2	1812.3
2007	1202.2	6193.0	102.2	1513.3	22.4	82.8	2195.6	2276.7
2008	1469.5	5184.7	104.2	1394.2	35.5	80.0	2016.4	1554.5
2009	1321.7	8702.2	118.1	3038.5	17.5	39.3	2441.3	3047.4
2010	2109.1	8327.8	99.5	2218.7	4.3	43.8	3209.1	2752.4
2011	2341.4	8235.4	71.7	1853.6	85.4	29.8	3588.6	2606.3
2012	2830.7	9156.0	156.1	2186.3	12.7	24.9	3478.4	3297.6
2013	3133.1	10580.3	159.6	2554.1	0.8	23.5	4295.2	3547.2
2014	3586.5	10208.7	161.7	2841.0	8.0	33.3	4347.9	2816.8
2015	4238.6	10773.9	184.9	2390.1	10.6	13.2	4853.6	3321.5
2016	4585.2	12065.0	107.9	2677.3	9.2	13.1	5047.8	4209.6
2017	4780.5	11396.2	123.0	2729.7	29.6	21.6	4884.2	3608.1
2018	5229.3	9154.7	289.4	2116.1	27.3	24.6	3877.7	2819.6
2019	4571.7	8767.3	148.2	2021.2	12.5	3.5	2564.8	4017.1

注：1.1978—1992年不含房地产开发和农村投资；1993—2003年不含农村投资。
2.2017年起，原“国家预算内资金”调整为“中央预算资金”。
3.2018年及以前，固定资产投资资金来源数据为全社会口径，2019年为不含农户口径。

Note: a) Figures from 1978 to 1992 did not include investment in real estate development and rural investment; figures from 1993 to 2003 did not include rural investment.
b) Since 2017, the original State Budgets was renamed Central Budgetary Fund.
c) In and before 2018, the data on investment in fixed asset by source of funds were those of full coverage. The data for 2019 were those that excluding rural households.

9-4 基础设施投资和增长速度情况(1978—2019年)
INVESTMENT IN INFRASTRUCTURE AND GROWTH RATE (1978-2019)

单位：亿元 (100 million yuan)

年 份 Year	基础设施投资 Infrastructure Investment		#能 源 Energy		#公共服务业 Public Services		#交通运输 Transportation		#邮政电信 Post & Telecommunications		基础设施投资占固定资产投资比重(%) Infrastructure Investment as Percentage of Investment in Fixed Assets (%)
	绝对量 Absolute Volume	比上年增长(%) Growth Rate (%)	绝对量 Absolute Volume	比上年增长(%) Growth Rate (%)	绝对量 Absolute Volume	比上年增长(%) Growth Rate (%)	绝对量 Absolute Volume	比上年增长(%) Growth Rate (%)	绝对量 Absolute Volume	比上年增长(%) Growth Rate (%)	
1978	5.4		1.4		0.6		1.7		0.4		23.9
1979	5.8		1.1		1.3		1.7		0.4		21.9
1980	6.0		0.9		2.3		2.3		0.5		17.9
1981	5.8		1.3		2.0		1.8		0.4		15.8
1982	6.1		1.4		1.9		1.9		0.4		15.8
1983	6.7		1.5		1.9		2.6		0.6		13.1
1984	8.8		1.4		3.0		2.3		1.1		13.3
1985	13.2		3.8		2.5		2.6		2.7		14.0
1986	14.5		4.8		2.1		3.1		3.5		13.7
1987	22.1		8.0		3.1		6.6		3.2		16.2
1988	23.2		8.8		5.3		4.7		3.0		14.2
1989	26.5		9.2		6.6		5.2		5.2		19.0
1990	31.6		9.0		8.3		8.7		5.4		17.6
1991	35.2		12.4		7.5		9.3		5.8		18.3
1992	58.8		17.7		8.2		20.1		12.3		22.1
1993	91.4		19.3		4.1		29.4		24.2		22.3
1994	153.4		38.0		27.2		30.0		48.6		23.6
1995	156.1		46.7		15.9		34.2		46.4		18.6
1996	188.8		59.2		29.1		54.0		44.1		21.5
1997	218.3		75.6		24.3		51.2		60.3		22.7
1998	320.4		85.1		38.0		104.6		77.5		27.7
1999	302.7		90.3		75.0		63.0		54.0		25.9
2000	351.9		53.2		154.6		64.6		63.7		27.1
2001	356.4		40.8		114.6		104.4		84.8		23.3
2002	411.9		49.5		101.6		159.7		78.7		22.7
2003	417.8		36.1		152.8		129.2		82.2		19.4
2004	463.2		73.0		139.3		148.8		68.5		18.3
2005	610.7		102.3		160.3		224.1		69.9		21.6
2006	935.3	53.2	113.4	10.9	265.3	65.4	439.6	96.2	72.3	3.5	27.7
2007	1175.8	25.7	200.2	76.5	289.5	9.2	548.0	24.7	84.8	17.2	29.6
2008	1160.7	-1.3	144.1	-28.0	291.6	0.7	604.2	10.3	86.7	2.3	30.2
2009	1462.0	26.0	165.4	14.8	434.5	49.0	698.6	15.6	124.9	44.1	30.1
2010	1403.5	-4.0	157.2	-5.0	359.1	-17.3	720.5	3.1	94.2	-24.5	25.5
2011	1400.2	0.3	171.1	10.7	379.4	6.4	680.7	-5.4	82.3	-12.6	23.7
2012	1789.2	27.8	231.9	35.5	508.1	33.9	712.0	4.6	122.0	48.2	27.7
2013	1785.7	-0.2	270.2	16.5	451.3	-11.2	664.5	-6.7	132.9	8.9	25.4
2014	2018.1	13.0	352.7	30.5	502.5	11.3	756.5	13.9	127.3	-4.2	26.7
2015	2174.5	7.7	297.3	-15.7	494.4	-1.6	827.0	9.3	172.3	35.3	27.2
2016	2399.5	10.3	332.0	11.7	643.8	30.2	973.0	17.7	147.5	-14.3	28.4
2017	2984.2	24.4	502.5	51.4	694.5	7.9	1327.0	36.4	194.4	31.8	33.4
2018		-10.7		-45.4		-6.8		1.1		2.3	32.7
2019		-3.8		-15.4		2.4		-9.2		17.8	33.1

注：1.2004年及以后基础设施投资包括农村基础设施投资。

2.2018年及以前的基础设施投资占比为基础设施投资占全社会固定资产投资比重，从2019年起为基础设施投资占固定资产投资(不含农户)的比重。

Note: a) Investment in infrastructure in and after 2004 includes that in rural infrastructure investment.

b) The proportion of infrastructure investment in and before 2018 referred to the percentage for infrastructure investment of the total investment in fixed assets; since 2019, it refers to the percentage for infrastructure investment of the fixed assets investment(excluding peasant households).

9–5 固定资产投资增长速度情况(2019年)
GROWTH TRATE OF INVESTMENT IN FIXED ASSETS (2019)

单位：% (%)

项 目	Item	2019
固定资产投资(不含农户)		**-2.4**
#建筑安装	Construction and Installation Investment	5.9
#房地产开发	Investment in Real Estate Development	-0.9
按产业分	**By Three Industies**	
第一产业	Primary Industry	20.6
第二产业	Secondary Industry	-9.0
第三产业	Tertiary Industry	-2.3
按行业分	**By Sector**	
农、林、牧、渔业	Agriculture, Forestry, Animal Production and Hunting, Fishing	20.9
采矿业	Mining and Quarrying	-9.5
制造业	Manufacturing	0.8
电力、热力、燃气及水生产和供应业	Production and Distribution of Electricity, Heating Power, Gas and Water	-15.4
工业	Industry	-8.2
建筑业	Construction	-52.8
批发和零售业	Wholesale and Retail Trade	-46.1
交通运输、仓储和邮政业	Transport, Storage and Post	-15.4
住宿和餐饮业	Accommodation and Restaurants	116.2
信息传输、软件和信息技术服务业	Information Transmission, Software and Information Technology Services	-13.3
金融业	Finance	6.9
房地产业	Real Estate	-3.9
租赁和商务服务业	Renting and Leasing Activities and Business Services	157.7
科学研究和技术服务业	Scientific Research and Development, Technical Services	27.0
水利、环境和公共设施管理业	Management of Water Conservancy, Environment and Public Facilities	1.8
居民服务、修理和其他服务业	Resident Services, Repair and Other Services	
教 育	Education	-13.0
卫生和社会工作	Health Care and Social Works	49.0
文化、体育和娱乐业	Culture, Sports and Entertainment	77.0
公共管理、社会保障和社会组织	Pulic Administration,Social Security and Social Organizations	-27.9
国际组织	International Organizations	

9-6 房屋建筑施工及竣工面积(1978-2019年)
FLOOR SPACE OF BUILDINGS UNDER CONSTRUCTION AND COMPLETED (1978-2019)

单位：万平方米 (10000 sq.m)

年 份 Year	施工面积 Floor Space of Buildings under Construction	#住 宅 Residential Buildings	竣工面积 Floor Space of Buildings Completed	#住 宅 Residential Buildings	中 央 Central	地 方 Local
1978	956.3	456.8	407.0	190.4	158.7	248.3
1979	1340.6	780.2	537.6	304.9	235.2	302.4
1980	1704.1	1037.0	648.4	396.9	315.8	332.6
1981	1875.8	1189.9	726.9	462.6	327.2	399.7
1982	1938.6	1210.1	728.3	463.8	303.7	424.6
1983	1952.1	1163.6	775.5	514.0	312.3	463.2
1984	2351.9	1327.1	818.7	437.6	352.7	466.0
1985	2802.7	1599.2	892.2	505.4	427.3	464.9
1986	2760.7	1557.4	906.5	532.7	424.5	482.0
1987	2578.0	1273.2	1042.2	608.9	507.8	534.4
1988	2642.2	1226.2	1065.6	623.5	499.6	566.0
1989	2450.8	1167.8	1046.9	601.8	565.8	481.1
1990	2864.9	1561.9	1081.2	573.0	637.4	443.8
1991	2818.0	1612.0	1036.4	601.8	396.2	640.2
1992	3126.8	1784.7	1111.4	681.2	399.3	712.1
1993	3607.5	1866.4	1158.0	654.8	320.5	837.5
1994	4460.9	2315.1	1370.7	832.1	366.8	1003.9
1995	5524.3	2897.6	1530.2	937.3	386.4	1143.8
1996	5633.2	2696.9	1517.5	870.4	452.0	1065.5
1997	5819.4	2881.3	1625.7	996.8	492.2	1133.5
1998	6496.1	3473.7	1821.5	1093.1	508.4	1313.1
1999	6556.5	3754.8	2321.4	1519.9	655.3	1666.1
2000	6995.9	4083.3	2358.2	1499.7	618.8	1739.4
2001	8203.3	5226.4	2554.6	1804.9	490.6	2064.0
2002	9697.7	6193.3	3121.8	2191.4	441.8	2680.0
2003	11262.2	7011.3	3222.8	2322.3	242.1	2980.7
2004	13121.9	7513.1	4203.2	2649.5	301.9	3901.3
2005	14096.2	8043.2	4679.2	3024.1	256.6	4422.6
2006	14069.2	7113.0	4191.0	2391.6	388.6	3802.4
2007	14146.7	6788.8	3866.4	2098.0	399.6	3466.8
2008	14145.3	6656.3	3840.7	1871.1	496.8	3343.9
2009	14380.6	7058.4	4252.6	2369.6	388.4	3864.2
2010	15572.1	7932.9	3908.4	2263.5	329.2	3579.1
2011	18065.2	8817.1	4032.9	2121.8	425.5	3607.4
2012	20045.4	9217.8	3723.5	1992.5	216.9	3506.6
2013	21526.0	9469.0	3989.7	2154.8	255.2	3734.4
2014	21677.7	8978.3	4967.5	2547.6	541.4	4426.1
2015	20009.1	7962.3	4170.2	1900.7	480.2	3690.0
2016	22721.4	7744.2	3594.0	1763.3	299.8	3294.2
2017	21512.7	7298.9	2671.1	1137.4	196.5	2474.5
2018	17956.3	6950.5	2384.9	899.2	189.9	2195.0
2019	16893.5	6472.2	1990.4	747.1	323.3	1667.1

注：2007年及以前，表中数据不包含农村农户房屋施工和竣工面积。
Note: Figures in and before 2007 excluded floor space of buildings under construction and completed in rural areas.

9–7 房屋建筑施工及竣工面积
FLOOR SPACE OF BUILDINGS UNDER CONSTRUCTION AND COMPLETED

单位：万平方米 (10000 sq.m)

项　目	Item	2019	2018	占竣工面积比重(%) Proportion in Completed Floor Space (%)	
				2019	2018
施工总面积	**Floor Space of Buildings under Construction**	**16893.5**	**17956.3**		
竣工总面积	**Floor Space of Buildings Completed**	**1990.4**	**2384.9**	**100.0**	**100.0**
按隶属关系分	**By Affiliation**				
中　央	Central	323.3	189.9	16.2	8.0
地　方	Local	1667.1	2195.0	83.8	92.0
#国　有	State-owned	395.2	474.6	19.9	19.9
集　体	Collectively-owned	8.7	24.5	0.4	1.0
按地区分	**By District**				
东 城 区	Dongcheng District	10.1	18.7	0.5	0.8
西 城 区	Xicheng District	29.2	23.3	1.5	1.0
朝 阳 区	Chaoyang District	340.1	244.9	17.1	10.3
丰 台 区	Fengtai District	192.1	213.4	9.7	8.9
石景山区	Shijingshan District	24.3	22.0	1.2	0.9
海 淀 区	Haidian District	310.4	215.7	15.6	9.0
门头沟区	Mentougou District	162.2	226.8	8.1	9.5
房 山 区	Fangshan District	126.2	181.9	6.3	7.6
通 州 区	Tongzhou District	116.7	250.4	5.9	10.5
顺 义 区	Shunyi District	183.1	291.1	9.2	12.2
昌 平 区	Changping District	196.7	216.7	9.9	9.1
大 兴 区	Daxing District	143.0	252.5	7.2	10.6
怀 柔 区	Huairou District	41.3	43.9	2.1	1.8
平 谷 区	Pinggu District	22.2	84.7	1.1	3.6
密 云 区	Miyun District	48.8	65.5	2.5	2.7
延 庆 区	Yanqing District	44.0	33.2	2.2	1.4

9-8 房地产开发面积(1990-2019年)

单位：万平方米

年 份 Year	房 屋 施工面积 Floor Space of Buildings under Construction	#本 年 新开工 面 积 Floor Space of Buildings Newly Started Construction in Current Year	住 宅 Residential Houses	办公楼 Office Buildings	商业、营业用房及其他 Buildings for Commercial, Business Operation Use and Others	房 屋 竣工面积 Floor Space of Buildings Completed	住 宅 Residential Houses
1990	774.0	249.1	643.4	17.4	41.2	271.6	226.5
1991	815.1	317.6	692.1	2.1	57.6	275.2	240.4
1992	1021.1	508.6	865.4	7.6	54.8	331.4	300.8
1993	1262.0	524.8	887.6			356.4	280.6
1994	1593.2	659.4	1107.6			445.7	385.6
1995	2810.2	1012.2	1728.7	462.7	252.6	653.0	506.3
1996	2824.6	578.7	1520.7	638.7	283.9	663.4	470.8
1997	2869.6	848.4	1541.1	637.7	260.8	682.3	478.3
1998	3499.1	1193.4	2107.2	590.7	297.7	842.8	588.7
1999	3784.0	1061.8	2447.9	484.4	281.3	1208.5	908.3
2000	4455.0	1676.9	2971.6	449.1	281.3	1365.6	1013.7
2001	5966.7	2789.8	4349.6	495.5	330.6	1707.4	1393.4
2002	7510.7	3206.0	5397.5	672.5	400.3	2384.4	1926.2
2003	9070.7	3433.8	6352.9	901.3	557.7	2593.7	2080.8
2004	9931.3	3054.3	6759.4	1122.4	641.8	3067.0	2343.9
2005	10748.5	2965.9	7283.4	1209.8	809.2	3770.9	2841.4
2006	10483.5	3179.4	6311.3	1245.8	1403.0	3193.9	2193.3
2007	10438.6	2557.4	5914.5	1364.6	1482.1	2891.7	1854.0
2008	10014.3	2337.2	5538.2	1287.2	1429.8	2558.0	1399.3
2009	9719.1	2246.6	5551.9	1132.2	1323.4	2678.6	1613.2
2010	10300.9	2974.2	6176.0	1054.8	1229.3	2386.7	1498.5
2011	12065.4	4246.1	7168.1	1422.7	1187.5	2245.2	1316.1
2012	13122.5	3224.2	7510.4	1711.9	1236.9	2390.9	1522.7
2013	13886.9	3577.5	7406.9	2114.1	4365.9	2666.4	1692.0
2014	13641.5	2502.8	6999.7	2277.1	4364.7	3054.1	1804.3
2015	13095.0	2790.2	6314.6	2426.8	4353.6	2631.5	1378.2
2016	13089.8	2813.7	5927.6	2447.3	4714.9	2383.1	1275.2
2017	12608.6	2475.7	5506.6	2428.4	4673.6	1466.7	604.0
2018	12962.6	2321.1	5877.1	2220.5	4865.0	1557.9	731.2
2019	12515.0	2073.2	5640.1	1951.0	4923.9	1343.3	583.2

注：1．2005年以前的商品房销售面积为竣工后的全部商品房销售面积，2005年及以后为期房与现房销售面积之和。
2．2010年起，商品房销售面积中包含定向安置房数据。
3．2012年及以前商业、营业用房及其他只包括商业及服务性等营业性用房，自2013年起包括：厂房、仓库、商业营业用房、服务业用房、教育用房、文化体育用房、医疗用房、科研用房及其他用房(下同)。2017年起，原“商业、非公益用房及其他”更名为“商业、营业用房及其他”。

STATISTICS FOR FLOOR SPACE OF REAL ESTATE DEVELOPENT (1990–2019)

(10000 sq.m)

办公楼 Office Buildings	商业、营业用房及其他 Buildings for Commercial, Business Operation Use and Others	商品房销售面积 Floor Space of Commercial Buildings Sold	住宅 Residential Houses	办公楼 Office Buildings	商业、营业用房及其他 Buildings for Commercial, Business Operation Use and Others	年末商品房待售面积 Floor Space of Vacant Commercial Buildings at the Year End	住宅 Residential Houses	办公楼 Office Buildings	商业、营业用房及其他 Buildings for Commercial, Business Operation Use and Others
9.7	13.3	142.2							
0.9	10.9	154.0	152.5						
2.7	8.3	159.1	153.0						
		182.0	182.0						
		168.6	149.0	17.2	1.1				
27.9	43.5	191.9	180.0	4.0	4.5	81.5			
79.0	38.3	215.3	183.1	13.7	14.4	214.8	179.6		
80.9	42.4	290.9	256.2	18.8	8.0	298.3	258.9		
92.3	69.8	409.2	377.0	23.2	7.0	334.8	262.9		
108.8	43.1	544.4	484.7	48.0	6.8	624.3	529.1		
97.2	48.7	956.9	898.2	41.2	6.1	627.4	515.1		
98.0	48.2	1205.0	1127.5	49.8	17.4	774.0	634.1		
97.4	82.9	1708.3	1604.4	44.0	32.9	919.0	763.2		
94.0	117.5	1895.8	1771.1	38.1	50.8	1123.4	896.9		
153.9	225.3	2472.0	2285.8	92.5	60.2	1044.1	723.8		
287.8	180.9	2803.2	2566.0	131.2	66.9	1374.2	799.7		
304.4	289.2	2607.6	2205.0	260.3	108.6	1039.7	494.1		
314.8	315.1	2176.6	1731.5	265.7	134.8	1136.2	411.8		
364.6	313.1	1335.4	1031.4	139.4	112.4	1438.3	522.7		
316.6	322.4	2362.3	1880.5	255.8	157.1	1351.4	426.8		
198.4	271.9	1639.5	1201.4	208.1	142.1	1482.7	511.9		
245.2	232.4	1440.0	1035.0	211.4	108.7	1792.6	699.8		
226.8	240.1	1943.7	1483.4	253.5	114.0	1911.8	789.5		
273.1	701.3	1903.1	1363.7	317.9	221.5	1861.4	829.3	180.1	852.0
387.5	862.3	1459.0	1141.3	136.8	180.9	2065.7	864.8	307.2	893.7
385.4	867.8	1554.7	1127.3	243.0	184.4	2168.1	867.7	332.5	968.0
343.7	764.2	1675.1	993.5	415.4	266.2	2160.8	845.8	320.7	994.3
321.2	541.5	875.0	612.8	108.3	153.9	2092.1	811.2	336.1	944.8
249.9	576.8	696.2	526.8	75.8	93.6	2153.3	833.7	390.6	929.0
290.3	469.8	938.9	789.0	53.4	96.5	2489.5	893.1	569.0	1027.4

Note: a) Before 2005, the floor space of commercial buildings sold referred to the total floor space of completed commercial buildings sold, since 2005, the figure is the sum of floor space of completed commercial buildings sold and those under construction sold.

b) Since 2010, the floor space of commercial buildings sold has included figures of targeted resettlement buildings.

c) In and before 2012, buildings for commercial, business operation use and others only included business and commercial buildings. Since 2013, it has included: factory buildings, warehouses, commercial buildings,buildings for service industy, education buildings, cultural and sports buildings, medical buildings, scientific research buildings and others(the same below).Since 2017,the original "Buildings for Commercial Use, Non-public Buildings and Others"was renamed"Buildings for Commercial, Business Operation Use and Others".

9-9 房地产开发情况(1990-2019年)
STATISTICS FOR REAL ESTATE DEVELOPMENT (1990-2019)

单位：亿元 (100 million yuan)

年 份	房地产开发投资 Investment in Real Estate Development		#住 宅 Residential Buildings		#办公楼 Office Buildings	
	绝对量 Absolute Volume	比上年增长(%) Growth Rate (%)	绝对量 Absolute Volume	比上年增长(%) Growth Rate (%)	绝对量 Absolute Volume	比上年增长(%) Growth Rate (%)
1990	22.5		12.3			
1991	24.0		14.0			
1992	33.7		20.0			
1993	58.4		38.1			
1994	99.5		50.3			
1995	352.8		142.4		71.5	
1996	328.2	-7.0	124.9	-12.3	84.2	17.8
1997	330.3	0.6	132.9	6.4	91.1	8.2
1998	377.4	14.3	168.0	26.4	78.5	-13.8
1999	421.5	11.7	236.6	40.8	52.5	-33.1
2000	522.1	23.9	288.3	21.9	45.2	-13.9
2001	783.8	50.1	464.2	61.0	72.0	59.3
2002	989.4	26.2	586.7	26.4	97.3	35.1
2003	1202.5	21.5	633.0	7.9	142.7	46.7
2004	1473.3	22.5	776.0	22.6	187.9	31.7
2005	1525.0	3.5	779.5	0.5	196.2	4.4
2006	1719.9	12.8	863.6	10.8	216.7	10.4
2007	1995.8	16.0	991.7	14.8	242.2	11.8
2008	1908.7	-4.4	940.6	-5.2	170.5	-29.6
2009	2337.7	22.5	906.6	-3.6	166.7	-2.2
2010	2901.1	24.1	1509.0	66.4	259.1	55.4
2011	3036.3	4.7	1778.3	17.8	363.8	40.4
2012	3153.4	3.9	1628.0	-8.5	384.8	5.8
2013	3483.4	10.5	1724.6	5.9	611.7	59.0
2014	3911.3	12.3	1962.0	13.8	750.2	22.6
2015	4226.3	8.1	1962.7	…	906.6	20.8
2016	4045.4	-4.3	1950.9	-0.6	699.1	-22.9
2017	3745.9	-7.4	1725.5	-11.6	742.9	6.3
2018		3.4		17.4		-29.7
2019		-0.9		0.7		-27.3

9-10 房地产开发企业经营情况(2018年)
REAL ESTATE DEVELOPMENT ENTERPRISES (2018)

项　　目	Item	企业单位个数(个) Number of Enterprises (unit)	实收资本合计(万元) Paid-in Capital (10000 yuan)	资产总计(万元) Total Assets (10000 yuan)	主营业务收入(万元) Main Business Income (10000 yuan)	利润总额(万元) Total Profits (10000 yuan)
合　　计	**Total**	**1544**	**57150476**	**571725818**	**35155039**	**5920470**
按企业登记注册类型分	**By Registration Type**					
内资企业	Domestically-Funded Enterprises	1439	49385846	521967016	32617979	5397290
国有企业	State-owned Enterprises	19	932581	6791549	297406	63085
集体企业	Collectively-owned Enterprises	6	24268	2062260	32867	23424
私营企业	Private Enterprises	290	3187530	39202532	1129787	-168759
股份合作企业	Joint-equity Cooperative Enterprises					
股份有限公司	Companies Limited by Shares	23	2063600	40789794	952308	1165596
有限责任公司	Limited Liability Companies	1101	43177867	433120880	30205612	4313945
港澳台商投资企业	Hong Kong, Macao and Taiwan-invested Enterprises	59	5160857	34240723	1471985	177477
港澳台合资经营	Joint Ventures	20	2257567	19530430	887261	292230
港澳台合作经营	Cooperative	18	913014	4465395	236111	-85254
港澳台商独资企业	Solely-funded Enterprises	20	1566841	9651647	335720	-27582
其他港澳台商投资企业	Others	1	***	***	***	***
外商投资企业	Foreign-invested Enterprises	46	2603773	15518079	1065076	345703
中外合资经营	Joint Ventures	22	1458726	5104601	648276	195667
中外合作经营	Cooperative	11	197418	3365713	276032	669
外资(独资)企业	Solely-funded Enterprises	11	904847	4655863	82993	37250
外商投资股份有限公司	Companies Limited by Shares	1	***	***	***	***
其他外商投资企业	Others	1	***	***	***	***
按隶属关系分	**By Affiliation**					
中　央	Central	59	4972111	43205498	3218271	1023256
地　方	Local	1485	52178365	528520320	31936769	4897214
按资质等级分	**By Qualification Grade**					
一　级	First-grade	68	11076774	128605465	3941258	2835019
二　级	Second-grade	105	6153197	71126190	5572917	608909
三　级	Third-grade	108	5373344	43426084	2766318	141233
四　级	Fourth-grade	753	21096727	196013708	12927412	1137253
暂　定	Provisional	369	11638779	114443111	8694799	911855
其　他	Others	141	1811655	18111260	1252335	286201
按营业状况分	**By Operating Condition**					
营　业	Operating	1527	57090692	571412457	35154654	5919439
停　业	Closed	13	57784	312250	167	-1284
其　他	Others	4	2000	1111	218	2315

9-11 房地产开发企业经营情况(2019年)
REAL ESTATE DEVELOPMENT ENTERPRISES (2019)

项目	Item	企业单位个数(个) Number of Enterprises (unit)	实收资本合计(万元) Paid-in Capital (10000 yuan)	资产总计(万元) Total Assets (10000 yuan)	主营业务收入(万元) Main Business Income (10000 yuan)	利润总额(万元) Total Profits (10000 yuan)
合计	**Total**	**1340**	**56510460**	**552274674**	**34258353**	**4183944**
按企业登记注册类型分	**By Registration Type**					
内资企业	Domestically-Funded Enterprises	1247	49520122	508395656	32134603	3733637
国有企业	State-owned Enterprises	13	875581	5887173	185165	40720
集体企业	Collectively-owned Enterprises	4	22060	1778435	28194	20077
私营企业	Private Enterprises	209	3101591	33110076	1369218	-198371
股份合作企业	Joint-equity Cooperative Enterprises	2	22675	349940	11735	6702
联营企业	Associated Enterprise	1	***	***		***
股份有限公司	Companies Limited by Shares	21	1818362	43243036	794163	917622
有限责任公司	Limited Liability Companies	995	43664852	423872883	29517903	2924416
其他企业	Others	2	10000	149179	228225	23160
港澳台商投资企业	Hong Kong, Macao and Taiwan-invested Enterprises	51	4409080	29317323	1055675	226071
港澳台合资经营	Joint Ventures	16	1106449	4149897	440955	173348
港澳台合作经营	Cooperative	15	618567	3713934	130316	-14266
港澳台商独资企业	Solely-funded Enterprises	20	2684064	21453492	484404	66989
外商投资企业	Foreign-invested Enterprises	42	2581258	14561695	1068075	224236
中外合资经营	Joint Ventures	20	1453948	7286616	643784	176376
中外合作经营	Cooperative	10	163748	3146579	280618	40750
外资(独资)企业	Solely-funded Enterprises	11	955781	4121588	138152	7901
外商投资股份有限公司	Companies Limited by Shares	1	***	***	***	***
按隶属关系分	**By Affiliation**					
中央	Central	52	4276308	38975718	1828249	517263
地方	Local	1288	52234153	513298956	32430104	3666682
按资质等级分	**By Qualification Grade**					
一级	First-grade	59	9777959	117047220	4376980	2370217
二级	Second-grade	85	7692337	69547312	3599684	59594
三级	Third-grade	83	4292479	39932335	1792376	-106935
四级	Fourth-grade	673	20657744	187968745	12854316	1112970
暂定	Provisional	344	11897132	120865831	10671011	582311
其他	Others	96	2192809	16913231	963987	165788
按营业状况分	**By Operating Condition**					
营业	Operating	1333	56495200	551713586	34258193	4189333
停业	Closed	6	14260	167382	160	-3711
其他	Others	1	***	***		***

9-12 房地产开发企业开发建设情况(2019年)
DEVELOPMENT OF REAL ESTATE DEVELOPMENT ENTERPRISES (2019)

单位：亿元、万平方米 (100 million yuan,10000 sq.m)

项　　目	Item	2019	2019年为2018年% 2019 as % of 2018
本年实际到位资金	**Total Actual Funds in Place This Year**	**5672.5**	**99.1**
#国内贷款	Incl.: Domestic Loans	1346.2	81.2
自筹资金	Self-raised Funds	1205.0	78.5
定金及预收款	Down Payment and Advance Payment	2516.7	122.8
个人按揭贷款	Personal Mortgage Loans	362.2	118.9
本年购置土地面积	**Land Space Purchased in Current Year**	**144.0**	**66.0**

9-13 保障性安居工程建设情况
CONSTRUCTION OF GOVERNMENT-SUBSIDIZED HOUSING PROJECTS

单位：万平方米 (10000 sq.m)

项　　目	Item	2019	2018	2019年为2018年% 2019 as % of 2018
施工面积	**Floor Space Under Construction**	**5168.8**	**5484.9**	**94.2**
经济适用房	Affordable Housing	232.6	246.7	94.3
限价房	Price-capped Housing	196.0	484.4	40.5
公租(廉租)房	Public Rental (Low-rent) Housing	338.5	341.5	99.1
定向安置房	Resettlement Housing	3689.1	3630.8	101.6
共有产权房	Shared Ownership Housing	712.5	781.5	91.2
竣工面积	**Floor Space Completed**	**494.5**	**664.7**	**74.4**
经济适用房	Affordable Houses	33.3	14.7	226.5
限价房	Price-capped Houses	87.4	177.4	49.3
公租(廉租)房	Public Rental (Low-rent) Houses	80.0	33.9	236.0
定向安置房	Targeted Resettlement Houses	255.0	260.9	97.7
共有产权房	Shared Ownership Housing	38.8	177.8	21.8
本年新开工面积	**Floor Space Newly Started in the Year**	**757.3**	**1049.2**	**72.2**
经济适用房	Affordable Houses	2.2	70.2	3.1
限价房	Price-capped Houses	0.1	19.2	0.5
公租(廉租)房	Public Rental (Low-rent) Houses	36.8	70.1	52.5
定向安置房	Targeted Resettlement Houses	564.9	530.3	106.5
共有产权房	Shared Ownership Housing	153.3	359.4	42.7

主要统计指标解释

全社会固定资产投资 包括城镇固定资产投资（含房地产开发投资）和农村固定资产投资。

固定资产投资（不含农户） 是以货币形式表现的在一定时期内完成的建造和购置固定资产的工作量以及与此有关的费用的总称。

新增固定资产投资 是指报告期内交付使用的固定资产价值。包括本年内建成投入生产或交付使用的工程投资和达到固定资产标准的设备、工具、器具的投资及有关应摊入的费用。属于增加固定资产价值的其他建设费用，应随同交付使用的工程一并计入新增固定资产。

基础设施投资 是指能够为企业提供作为中间投入用于生产的基本需求；能够为消费者提供所需的基本消费服务；能够为社区提供用于改善不利的外部环境的服务等建设的投资，包括固定资产投资中用于市政工程、电信工程、公共设施和水利环保等建设的投资。

上年末结余资金 是指上年资金来源中没有形成固定资产投资额而结余的资金。包括尚未用到工程上去的材料价值、未开始安装的需要安装设备价值及结存的现金和银行存款等。

本年资金来源小计 是指固定资产投资单位在报告期收到的，用于固定资产投资的各种货币资金。包括中央预算内资金、国内贷款、债券、利用外资、自筹资金和其他资金。

中央预算资金 指来源于中央公共预算安排的用于项目建设的资金数额。

国内贷款 是指报告期固定资产投资项目单位向银行及非银行金融机构借入的用于固定资产投资的各种国内借款，包括银行利用自有资金及吸收存款发放的贷款、上级主管部门拨入的国内贷款、国家专项贷款(包括煤代油贷款、劳改煤矿专项贷款等)，地方财政专项资金安排的贷款、国内储备贷款、周转贷款等。

利用外资 是指报告期收到的用于固定资产建造和购置投资的境外资金(包括设备、材料、技术在内)。包括外商直接投资、对外借款(外国政府贷款、国际金融组织贷款、出口信贷、外国银行商业贷款、对外发行债券和股票)及外商其他投资(包括利用外商投资收益在国内进行固定资产再投资活动的资金)。不包括我国自有外汇资金(包括国家外汇、地方外汇、留成外汇、调剂外汇和国内银行自有资金发行的外汇贷款等)。

自筹资金 指固定资产投资单位报告期收到的，由各地区、各部门及企业、事业单位筹集用于固定资产投资的预算外资金，包括中央各部门、各级地方和企业、事业单位的自有资金。

其他资金来源 是指在报告期收到的除以上各种资金之外其他用于固定资产投资的资金。包括社会集资、个人资金、无偿捐赠的资金、其他单位拨入的资金、市级预算资金和区级预算资金等。

建筑安装投资（建筑安装工作量） 是指各种房屋、建筑物的建造工程，各种设备、装置的安装工程，又称建筑安装工作量。建筑工程投资必须经过兴工动料，通过施工活动才能实现。在安装工程中，不包括被安装设备本身价值。

房地产开发投资 指从本年1月1日起至本年最后一天止完成的全部用于房屋建设工程和土地开发工程的投资额，以及公益性建筑和土地购置费等投资。

经济适用房 指政府提供政策优惠，限定套型面积和销售价格，按照合理标准建设，面向城镇低收入住房困难家庭供应的具有保障性质的政策性住房。

限价商品住房（限价房） 指政府控制土地出让价格，限定销售价格和套型面积，向城镇中等收入家庭供应的普通商品住房。

公共租赁住房（公租房） 指政府提供财政投入和政策支持，限定套型建筑面积标准，按照合理标准组织建设，或通过长期租赁等方式筹集，按照当地政府规定的供应标准，面向城镇中等偏下收入住房困难家庭、新就业职工和有稳定职业并在城镇居住一定年限的外来务工人员供应的保障性住房。

廉租住房（廉租房） 指政府提供财政投入和政策支持，限定套型建筑面积标准，按照合理标准组织建设，或通过购买、改建和租赁等方式筹集，按照当地政府规定的供应标准，面向城镇低收入住房困难家庭供应的具有保障性质的住房。

房屋施工面积 是指报告期内施工的全部房屋建筑面积。包括本期新开工的面积和上年开工跨入本期继续施工房屋面积，以及上期已停建在本期恢复施工的房屋面积。本期竣工和本期施工后又停建、缓建的房屋面积仍包括在施工面积中，多层建筑应填各层建筑面积之和。

房屋竣工面积 是指报告期内房屋建筑按照设计要求已全部完工，达到住人和使用条件，经验收鉴定合格(或达到竣工验收标准)，可正式移交使用的各栋房屋建筑面积的总和。

待售面积 指报告期末已竣工的可供销售或出租的商品房屋建筑面积中，尚未销售或出租的商品房屋建筑面积，包括以前年度竣工和本期竣工的房屋面积，但不包括报告期已竣工的拆迁还建，统建代建，公共配套建筑、房地产公司自用及周转房等不可销售或出租的房屋面积。

Explanatory Notes on Main Statistical Indicators

Total Investment in Fixed Assets includes urban investment in fixed assets (including the investment in real estate development) and rural investment in fixed assets.

Investment in Fixed Assets (Excluding Rural Households) refers to the completed volume of activities in construction and purchase of fixed assets and the related fees, expressed in monetary terms during the reference period.

Incremental Fixed Assets Investment means the value of fixed assets put into use in the reporting period, including investment in projects completed and put into use within the year, and investment in equipment, tools and appliances that reach the standard of fixed assets, together with expenses incurred in these activities. Other construction costs adding value to fixed assets shall be calculated in the incremental fixed assets together with the projects put into use.

Infrastructure Investment refers to investment that provides intermediate inputs for enterprise to meet their basic production needs, provides consumers with basic consumer services needed, or provides communities with services for improving external environment, which includes the investment in municipal projects, telecom projects, public facilities, water conservancy and environmental protection.

Surplus Funds by the Year End of the Previous Year refers to the fund in the previous year that was not included in the investment in fixed assets, including the value of materials not yet used for projects, value of equipment to be installed, and balance of cash and bank deposits.

Subtotal of Funds at Current Year refers to monetary capital received by investors that was used for investment in fixed assets, including funds from central budentary funds, domestic loans, bonds, foreign investment, self-raised funds and other funds.

Central Budgetary Fund refers to the amount of fund that comes from the central public budget arrangement is used for project construction.

Domestic Loans refer to loans of various forms borrowed by fixed assets investment project entities from banks and non-bank financial institutions for the purpose of investment in fixed assets during the reporting period, including loans issued by banks from their equity funds and deposits, loans appropriated by higher authorities, special loans allocated by the central government (including loans for replacing oil with coal, and special loans for labor camp coal mines), loans arranged by local government from special funds, domestic reserve loans and revolving loans.

Foreign Investment refers to foreign funds received during the reporting period for the investment in construction and purchase of fixed assets (including equipment, materials and technologies), including foreign direct investment, foreign loans (loans from foreign governments and international financial institutions, export credit, commercial loans from foreign banks, issued bonds and stocks overseas), and other foreign investments (including funds for domestic re-investment in fixed assets by earnings from foreign investment). It does not include foreign exchanges owned by China (foreign exchanges owned by the central and local governments, foreign exchanges retained, foreign exchange swap, loans in foreign exchanges issued by the domestic banks with their own funds, etc.).

Self-raised Funds refer to non-budgetary funds for investment in fixed assets received during the reporting period by different regions, departments, enterprises and public institutions, including self-owned funds of central departments, local authorities, enterprises and public institutions.

Other Funds refer to funds for investment in fixed assets received from sources other than those listed above, including social funds, personal funds, donated funds and funds transferred from other institutions, actual budget fund and district-level budget fund, etc.

Construction and Installation Investment (Workload of Construction and Installation) refers to the investment in construction projects of various houses and buildings, and installation projects of various equipment and devices, also known as the workload of construction and installation. It can only be realized through construction work and consumption of materials. For installation projects, the value of equipment installed is not included.

Real Estate Development Investment refers to all investment used for housing projects and land development projects, together with public welfare buildings and land purchase costs spent from January 1st to the last day of the year.

Affordable Houses refer to government-subsidized houses that are supplied to urban low-income households and built in line with reasonable standards, limited size and fixed pricing.

Price-capped Houses refer to ordinary commercial houses with limited size and fixed pricing that are supplied to middle-income urban households, and their land transfer price is controlled by the government.

Public Rental Houses refer to government-subsidized houses that are built in line with reasonable standards and limited size, and can be rented by lower middle-income urban households with housing difficulties, new employees and migrant workers with stable jobs and have lived in the urban area for a certain period.

Low-rent Houses refer to government-subsidized houses that are built in line with reasonable standards and limited size, with funds raised by purchasing, reconstruction or leasing, and can be rented by low-income urban households with housing difficulties.

Floor Space of Buildings under Construction refers to the total floor space of all houses and buildings under construction during the reference period, including floor space of newly started buildings in current period, floor space of construction extended from the previous period to the current period, and floor space of construction suspended during the previous period and resumed in the current period. Floor space of construction completed in the current period, and floor space of construction started and then suspended in the current period are also included in the floor space under construction. For multi-storey buildings, the sum of floor space of all floors shall be calculated.

Floor Space of Buildings Completed refers to the total floor space of all houses and buildings fully completed as required in the design plan during the reference period, which have been examined as qualified for living and use, and can be handed over and put into use.

Floor Space of Vacant Commercial Buildings refers to total floor space of commercial buildings for sale or for renting by the end of the reference period. It consists of the floor space of completed buildings in previous years and in the current year, but does not include relocated houses or buildings of unified construction or agent contract, as well as houses not for sale or renting such as public facilities, houses used by real estate companies and temporary houses.

10

对外经济贸易
FOREIGN ECONOMIC RELATIONS AND TRADE

简要说明

一、主要内容

本章资料主要反映北京市对外经济贸易的发展状况，包括对外贸易、利用外资、对外经济合作的历年概况。

二、统计范围

1.货物进出口情况

货物进出口统计的范围是凡能引起北京市海关境内物质资源存量增加或减少的进出口货物，除制度另有规定者外，均列入该项统计，调查方法采用全面调查。主要内容包括北京地区进出口总值；主要产品进出口数量等。

2.口岸运营情况

口岸运营的统计范围是北京首都国际机场空港口岸、北京丰台货运口岸、北京朝阳口岸、北京西站铁路口岸、北京平谷国际陆港、北京天竺综合保税区。主要内容包括旅客吞吐量、货邮吞吐量、监管货物的数量、征收关税等。

3.服务贸易情况

服务贸易情况的统计范围是北京地区涉及服务贸易进出口业务的企业，包括跨境提供、境外消费、商业存在和自然人移动等内容。

4.利用外资情况

利用外资情况的统计范围是凡经工商行政管理机关核准登记，在中华人民共和国北京地域内所有使用外资（包括港澳台地区投资）的单位和部门，经批准设立的中外合资经营企业、合作经营企业、外资企业、外商投资股份制企业、合作开发项目等具有法人资格的独立核算企业(包括港澳台地区投资企业)，在华从事经营活动的外国及港澳台地区企业及外国公司在中国境内设立的分支机构。主要内容包括实际利用外商直接投资，外商投资企业经营情况，调查方法采用全面调查。

5.对外经济合作

对外经济合作的统计范围是经各级商务部门批准的从事对外承包、劳务合作和设计咨询业务并具有法人资格的对外承包劳务企业；调查方法采用全面调查。主要内容包括对外承包工程、劳务合作和设计咨询。

Brief Introduction

I. Main Content

Data in this chapter show the development of foreign economic relations and trade in Beijing, including foreign trade, foreign capital utilization, and foreign economic cooperation in Beijing over the years, as well as friendly exchanges.

II. Scope of Statistical

1. Foreign Trade

Foreign trade statistics apply for: any imports and exports that lead to increase or decrease in the stock of physical resources at Beijing customs, except for those otherwise stated in regulations, and were obtained through comprehensive survey. Foreign trade data include: total volume of import and export in Beijing, and quantity of main import and export products, and so on..

2. Statistics for Port Operation

The statistical scope of port operation covers the Port of Beijing Capital International Airport, Beijing Fengtai Cargo Transport Port, Beijing Chaoyang Transport Port, Railway Port at Beijing West Railway Station, Beijing Pinggu International Land Port, and Beijing Tianzhu Comprehensive Bonded Zone. Statistics in this chapter, which is sourced from Port Administration Office of the People's Government of Beijing Municipality, mainly include passenger throughput, cargo throughput, cargos under customs regulation and duties levied.

3. Service Trade

The statistical scope of service trade covers the enterprises involved in import export of service trade in Beijing.

4.Scope of Statistics

The statistical slope of scope of statistics covers all entities and organizations registered with administration for industry and commerce upon approval, and using foreign capital (including investment from Hong Kong, Macao and Taiwan region) within the jurisdiction of Beijing, P.R.C, enterprises with legal person statues and independent accounting system (including enterprises invested by companies from Hong Kong, Macao and Taiwan region), including joint ventures, cooperative enterprises and foreign-invested enterprises, foreign-invested joint-stock enterprises, and cooperative development projects, and enterprises of foreign countries and Hong Kong, Macao and Taiwan region conducting operations in China as well as branch offices opened by foreign companies in China. Foreign capital utilization data include foreign direct investment, operation of foreign-invested enterprises, and were obtained through comprehensive survey.

5. Foreign Economic Cooperation

Statistics cover foreign labor service enterprises with legal person statues that are engaged in foreign contracting, labor service cooperation and design consulting with approval from departments of commerce at different levels. Comprehensive survey was used. Foreign economic cooperation statistics apply for: foreign contracting projects, labor service cooperation and design consulting.

10-1 北京地区对外经济贸易(1980-2019年)
FOREIGN ECONOMIC RELATIONS AND TRADE IN BEIJING (1980-2019)

年 份 Year	货物进出口总值(亿美元) Total Value of Imports and Exports of Goods (USD 100 million)	出 口 Exports	#高新技术产品 High-tech Products	#机电产品 Mechanical and Electrical Products	进 口 Imports	#高新技术产品 High-tech Products	#机电产品 Mechanical and Electrical Products
1980							
1981							
1982							
1983	306.0	146.9			159.1		
1984	355.9	175.2			180.8		
1985	325.4	43.7			281.7		
1986	306.0	37.1			268.9		
1987	267.0	35.4			231.6		
1988	298.9	39.6			259.3		
1989	286.1	30.2			255.9		
1990	236.4	44.1			192.3		
1991	242.4	45.7			196.7		
1992	249.8	56.1		15.8	193.7	27.1	73.1
1993	279.2	67.0		15.1	212.2	30.3	88.5
1994	288.8	83.4		19.5	205.4	42.1	112.1
1995	370.4	102.5		28.2	267.9	40.7	122.5
1996	293.2	81.2		25.4	212.0	24.1	73.4
1997	303.9	96.1		27.1	207.8	34.6	76.6
1998	305.1	105.1		32.5	199.9	34.8	90.9
1999	343.6	99.0		32.1	244.6	56.8	121.4
2000	494.0	119.7	22.7	43.7	374.3	74.0	142.6
2001	515.0	117.7	26.3	47.8	397.3	99.3	188.3
2002	525.1	126.1	31.4	57.1	398.9	91.6	170.2
2003	685.0	168.9	39.6	71.5	516.1	99.0	194.9
2004	945.8	205.7	58.1	97.0	740.1	105.3	227.2
2005	1255.1	308.7	97.1	155.7	946.4	136.6	269.6
2006	1580.4	379.5	138.9	217.1	1200.8	170.5	378.7
2007	1930.0	489.3	179.8	286.2	1440.7	236.0	447.8
2008	2716.9	575.0	190.6	335.4	2141.9	241.8	498.8
2009	2147.9	483.6	175.2	308.0	1664.3	235.7	519.4
2010	3016.6	554.4	193.7	339.4	2462.2	274.9	666.1
2011	3895.8	590.0	181.2	352.3	3305.9	314.5	766.8
2012	4081.1	596.3	190.2	373.8	3484.8	298.8	721.8
2013	4299.4	631.0	203.6	389.5	3668.4	292.4	716.8
2014	4155.4	623.4	187.5	379.0	3532.0	293.7	778.5
2015	3194.2	546.7	140.3	314.4	2647.5	261.3	659.2
2016	2823.8	520.2	113.2	272.8	2303.6	255.0	655.3
2017	3237.2	585.0	112.8	284.1	2652.2	264.9	659.4
2018	4124.3	741.7	152.2	322.1	3382.6	278.3	691.1
2019	4162.8	750.5	157.5	312.5	3412.3	270.3	659.4

注：货物进出口总值为海关统计的北京地区进出口数据(包括中央单位)。
资料来源：中华人民共和国北京海关、北京市商务局。
Note: Figures of total value of imports and exports of goods are imports and exports data of Beijing counted by Beijing Customs (including central government entities).
Source: Beijing Customs of the People's Republic of China and Beijing Municipal Commerce Bureau.

10-1 续表 Continued

年 份 Year	货物进出口总值(亿元) Total Value of Imports and Exports of Goods (100 million yuan)	出 口 Exports	进 口 Imports	服务贸易进出口总额(亿美元) Total Export-Import Volume of Service Trade (USD 100 million)	出 口 Exports	进 口 Imports	外商直接投资项目(合同)个数(个) Number of Foreign Direct Investment Projects (Contracts) (unit)	实际利用外商直接投资额(万美元) Actal Use of Foreign Direct Investment (USD10000)
1980							4	
1981							3	
1982							4	
1983							5	
1984							29	
1985							83	
1986							63	
1987							72	9534
1988							148	50278
1989							185	31846
1990							241	27696
1991							724	24482
1992	1377.1	309.2	1067.9				2208	34984
1993	1607.9	385.8	1222.1				3753	66693
1994	2492.4	719.2	1773.1				2675	144460
1995	3108.2	863.2	2244.9				1552	140277
1996	2450.3	680.9	1769.4				868	155290
1997	2522.5	798.4	1724.0				790	159286
1998	2530.6	872.2	1658.4				651	206415
1999	2356.9	665.6	1691.3				644	223004
2000	4090.1	991.4	3098.7				1147	245799
2001	4262.2	974.3	3287.8				1147	177000
2002	4345.7	1043.9	3301.8				1370	178964
2003	5674.5	1398.6	4275.9	162.24		66.12	1362	214675
2004	7824.5	1702.1	6122.4	235.70		93.08	1806	308354
2005	10331.9	2540.4	7791.4	300.74		109.62	2136	352638
2006	12670.7	3039.9	9630.8	393.23		154.08	2106	455191
2007	14831.0	3764.7	11066.3	503.06	252.81	250.25	2177	506572
2008	19113.6	4044.2	15069.4	691.92	341.69	350.23	1897	608172
2009	14648.2	3301.9	11346.3	644.10	311.60	332.50	1423	612094
2010	20478.2	3766.1	16712.1	798.29	388.22	410.07	1629	636358
2011	25303.9	3835.4	21468.5	895.40	415.00	480.40	1345	705447
2012	25765.2	3766.8	21998.4	1000.20	445.11	555.09	1360	804160
2013	26691.0	3920.1	22770.9	1023.30	426.90	596.40	1190	852418
2014	25517.9	3829.4	21688.6	1106.10	435.00	671.10	1318	904085
2015	19827.7	3395.0	16432.6	1302.78	490.67	812.11	1386	1299635
2016	18652.2	3433.5	15218.6	1508.60	532.13	976.47	1073	1302858
2017	21923.9	3962.5	17961.4	1434.26	437.21	997.06	1309	2432909
2018	27182.5	4878.5	22303.9	1606.19	562.75	1043.43	1639	1731089
2019	28677.2	5172.4	23504.8				1636	1421299

注：2019年服务贸易进出口额为10646.9亿元，其中：出口3720.1亿元，进口6926.8亿元。

Note: The total export-import volume of service trade in 2019 was RMB 1.06469 trillion, including the export volume of RMB 372.01 billion and the import volume of RMB 692.68 billion.

10-2 北京地区货物进出口贸易总值(按企业性质、贸易方式分)
TOTAL VALUE OF IMPORTS AND EXPORTS OF GOODS IN BEIJING (BY ENTERPRISE TYPE AND COMPOSITION)

项 目	Item	金额(万美元) Value (USD 10000) 2019	2018	金额(万元) Value (10000 yuan) 2019	2018
进出口总值	**Total Value of Imports and Exports**	**41627600**	**41242626**	**286771763**	**271824754**
出 口	**Local Exports**	**7504956**	**7417025**	**51723764**	**48785416**
按企业性质分	**By Enterprise Type**				
#国有企业	State-owned Enterprises	4798054	4951914	33049401	32518192
外商投资企业	Foreign-invested Enterprises	1617321	1506238	11155593	9942456
中外合资	Joint Ventures	256322	284893	1765959	1877142
中外合作	Cooperatives	4708	4336	32189	28684
外商独资	Solely-funded Enterprises	1356291	1217010	9357445	8036629
民营企业	Private Enterprises	959093	926600	6612042	6103402
集体企业	Collectively-owned Enterprises	1428	2284	9812	15191
私营企业	Privately-owned Enterprises	957554	924049	6601466	6086476
个体工商户	Privately or Individually-owned Business	110	266	764	1734
按贸易方式分	**By Composition**				
#一般贸易	General Trade	5729742	5571101	39471207	36632298
来料加工贸易	Trade of Processing & Supplied Materials	81229	101847	558556	670496
进料加工贸易	Trade of Processing Imported Materials	390700	507726	2695667	3347101
对外承包工程货物	Contracted Foreign Goods and Projects	681903	704058	4711777	4619114
出料加工贸易	Trade of Processing Exported Materials	1191	1728	8176	11326
进 口	**Imports**	**34122644**	**33825601**	**235047999**	**223039338**
按企业性质分	**By Enterprise Type**				
#国有企业	State-owned Enterprises	26011032	26003223	179118547	171431601
外商投资企业	Foreign-invested Enterprises	5800867	5750966	39978309	37908099
中外合资	Joint Ventures	1078650	1022743	7427235	6728661
中外合作	Cooperatives	4393	5146	30195	33472
外商独资	Solely-funded Enterprises	4717824	4723076	32520880	31145967
民营企业	Private Enterprises	2147576	2002456	14805417	13227038
集体企业	Collectively-owned Enterprises	128416	87789	882816	581486
私营企业	Privately-owned Enterprises	2018897	1914374	13920793	12643620
个体工商户	Privately or Individually-owned Business	263	293	1807	1932
按贸易方式分	**By Composition**				
#一般贸易	General Trade	29666787	29823086	204342212	196572478
来料加工装配贸易	Trade of Processing and Assembling Supplied Materials	1639646	1476924	11290431	9744912
进料加工贸易	Trade of Processing Imported Materials	199320	231788	1372986	1529221
外商投资企业进口设备、物品	Equipment and Goods Imported by Foreign-invested Enterprises	5328	10348	37306	66541
租赁贸易	Leasing Trade	19829	22443	136417	154716

资料来源：中华人民共和国北京海关。
Source: Beijing Customs of the People's Republic of China.

10-3 北京地区货物进出口贸易总值(按国别、地区分)
TOTAL VALUE OF IMPORTS AND EXPORTS OF GOODS IN BEIJING (BY COUNTRY AND REGION)

项目	Item	金额(万美元) Value (USD 10000)		金额(万元) Value (10000 yuan)	
		2019	2018	2019	2018
进出口总值	**Total Value of Imports and Exports**	**41627600**	**41242626**	**286771763**	**271824754**
出口	**Exports**	**7504956**	**7417025**	**51723764**	**48785416**
按国别(地区)分	**By Country (Region)**				
#中国香港	Hong Kong, China	1015690	763466	6996817	5035919
中国澳门	Macao, China	35805	42366	246336	278365
中国台湾	Taiwan, China	107581	106124	741874	699121
日本	Japan	282347	305911	1944789	2013936
新加坡	Singapore	879245	914521	6054329	5989165
韩国	Korea	281678	308298	1939553	2036492
越南	Vietnam	299590	242322	2065560	1597858
伊朗	Iran	56995	145465	390252	953231
印度	India	154420	139098	1065224	917720
印度尼西亚	Indonesia	154594	136991	1066473	900827
英国	United Kingdom	67368	73430	464233	484339
德国	Germany	96464	103097	666426	677865
法国	France	74815	71850	516742	473306
意大利	Italy	77736	56503	536525	369913
匈牙利	Hungary	7520	7760	51781	51100
俄罗斯联邦	Russian Federation	179275	160847	1236963	1058867
美国	United States	425190	525938	2931468	3467484
澳大利亚	Australia	246342	214677	1698403	1402910
进口	**Imports**	**34122644**	**33825601**	**235047999**	**223039338**
按国别(地区)分	**By Country (Region)**				
#中国香港	Hong Kong, China	58588	24254	407370	159693
日本	Japan	1328383	1316441	9157814	8674235
新加坡	Singapore	344278	335518	2372097	2218710
韩国	Korea	464876	590702	3204293	3885145
沙特阿拉伯	Saudi Arabia	2687133	1927283	18512071	12760887
英国	United Kingdom	743510	563290	5118962	3729067
德国	Germany	2463092	2350473	16962994	15517712
法国	France	294056	281910	2029966	1871501
意大利	Italy	260290	228369	1795349	1509502
瑞士	Switzerland	842848	1095205	5813302	7158984
比利时	Belgium	92306	74773	634581	493655
俄罗斯联邦	Russian Federation	1618487	1605378	11170036	10623063
加拿大	Canada	738226	729442	5062912	4785576
美国	United States	2432816	2897633	16769629	18926889
澳大利亚	Australia	2768964	2061860	19058210	13581895
阿曼	Oman	1049052	1097681	7240005	7242615
安哥拉	Angola	1445511	1709624	9944741	11302362

资料来源：中华人民共和国北京海关。
Source: Beijing Customs of the People's Republic of China.

10–4 北京地区海关主要商品进口量及金额(2019年)
VOLUME & VALUE OF MAJOR COMMODITIES IMPORTED AT BEIJING CUSTOMS (2019)

项　目		Item		进口数量 Import Volume	进口金额 (万美元) Import Value (USD 10000)
粮　食	(吨)	Grain	(ton)	26912171	1016653
食用植物油	(吨)	Edible Vegetable Oil	(ton)	1860307	136170
食　糖	(吨)	Sugar	(ton)	1063898	37808
酒类及饮料		Alcohol and Beverage			38449
天然及合成橡胶(包括胶乳)	(吨)	Natural and Synthetic Rubber(Including Latex)	(ton)	148194	21523
纸　浆	(吨)	Paper Pulp	(ton)	1660395	101877
羊毛及毛条	(吨)	Wool and Wool Top	(ton)	42126	32522
棉　花	(吨)	Cotton	(ton)	354389	67907
合成纤维纱线	(吨)	Synthetic Fiber Yarn	(ton)	2738	2133
铁矿砂及其精矿	(吨)	Iron Sand and Iron Ore Concentrates	(ton)	166936444	1595387
原　油	(吨)	Crude Oil	(ton)	299220415	14240964
成品油	(吨)	Product Oil	(ton)	7376422	380642
医药材及药品	(吨)	Medicinal and Pharmaceutical Materials and Medicines	(ton)	29543	907814
肥　料	(吨)	Fertilizers	(ton)	8026481	264602
塑料制品		Plastic Products			79964
纸浆、纸及其制品	(吨)	Paper Pulp, Paper and Paper Products	(ton)	1942900	134467
纺织纱线、织物及制品		Textile Yarn, Fabric and Products			62291
服装及衣着附件		Clothes and Clothing Accessories			45092
钢　材	(吨)	Steel Products	(ton)	168704	40608
印刷、装订机械及其零件		Printing and Binding Machinery and Parts Thereof			111934
自动数据处理设备及其部件		Automatic Data Processing Equipment and Their Components			112806
变压器	(个)	Voltage Transformers	(unit)	1743451	2907
电视摄像机、数字照相机及视频摄录一体机	(台)	Television Cameras, Digital Cameras and Integrated Video Cameras and Recorders	(set)	1754137	73029
印刷电路	(万块)	Printed Circuits	(10000 pieces)	231100	7112
集成电路	(万个)	Integrated Circuits	(10000 units)	1427738	241579
电线和电缆	(吨)	Wires and Cables	(ton)	4939	15737
汽车		Automobiles			2472389
汽车零配件		Auto Spare Parts			529324
飞机及其他航空器	(架)	Aircrafts and Others	(unit)	117	42278
船　舶		Ships and Boats			24746
医疗仪器及器械		Medical Instruments and Devices			244396
计量检测分析自控仪器及器具		Automatically-controlled Measuring, Testing and Analyzing Instruments			536801

资料来源：中华人民共和国北京海关。
Source: Beijing Customs of the People's Republic of China.

10-5 北京地区海关主要商品出口量及金额(2019年)

VOLUME & VALUE OF MAIN COMMODITIES EXPORTED AT BEIJING CUSTOMS (2019)

项目		Item		出口数量 Export Volume	出口金额 Export Value (万美元) (USD 10000)
粮食	(吨)	Grain	(ton)	2534089	91019
果蔬汁	(吨)	Fruit and Vegetable Juice	(ton)	91993	9598
肥料	(吨)	Fertilizers	(ton)	1975167	53135
煤及褐煤	(吨)	Coal and Lignite	(ton)	2927921	38826
焦炭、半焦炭	(吨)	Coke and Semi-coke	(ton)	910517	23785
成品油	(吨)	Product Oil	(ton)	51061478	2922967
医药材及药品	(吨)	Medicinal and Pharmaceutical Materials and Medicines	(ton)	37413	59739
纺织纱线、织物及制品		Textile Yarn, Fabric and Products			70855
铁合金	(吨)	Ferroalloy	(ton)	2959	4449
钢材	(吨)	Steel Products	(ton)	2528494	233915
未锻轧铝及铝材	(吨)	Non-forged Aluminum and Aluminum Products	(ton)	76307	20421
纺织机械及零件		Textile Machinery and Parts			14463
机床	(台)	Machine Tools	(set)	44539	9965
自动数据处理设备及其部件		Automatic Data Processing Equipment and Their Components			76007
液晶显示板	(个)	LCD Plates	(unit)	17779051	85933
变压器	(个)	Voltage Transformers	(unit)	2922632	53807
蓄电池	(个)	Storage Cells	(unit)	1129694	5953
手机	(台)	Cell phones	(set)	48992261	632513
二极管及类似半导体器件	(万个)	Diode and Similar Semiconductor Devices	(10000 units)	97731	25603
集成电路	(万个)	Integrated Circuits	(10000 units)	815865	177150
电线和电缆	(吨)	Wires and Cables	(ton)	38234	35402
汽车		Automobiles			88630
汽车零配件		Auto Spare Parts			133049
船舶		Boats and Ships			113209
医疗仪器及器械		Medical Instruments and Devices			68865
家具及其零件		Furniture and Their Parts			16999
服装及衣着附件		Clothes and Clothing Accessories			97768
鞋靴		Shoes and Boots			14931
塑料制品		Plastic Products			53707

资料来源：中华人民共和国北京海关。
Source: Beijing Customs of the People's Republic of China.

10-6 北京口岸运营情况
STATISTICS FOR PORT OPERATION IN BEIJING

项　　目		Item		2019	2018	2019年为2018年% 2019 as % of 2018
北京首都国际机场空港口岸		**Port of Beijing Capital International Airport**				
旅客吞吐量	(万人次)	Passenger Throughput	(10000 person-times)	10001	10081	99.2
进出境人员	(万人次)	Inbound/Outbound Visitors	(10000 person-times)	2655	2685	98.9
#外籍人员进出境		Inbound/Outbound Foreign Visitors		696	715	97.4
货邮吞吐量	(万吨)	Cargos Carried	(10000 tons)	195	205	95.0
飞机起降	(架次)	Takeoff and Landing of Airplanes	(unit)	594286	613118	96.9
#进出境飞机起降		Takeoff and Landing of Airplanes Inbound/Outbound		149475	150539	99.3
海关监管货物	(万吨)	Cargos under Customs Regulation	(10000 tons)	10305	8719	118.2
北京丰台货运口岸		**Beijing Fengtai Cargo Transport Port**				
海关监管货物	(吨)	Cargos under Customs Regulation	(ton)	8782	18273	48.1
北京朝阳口岸		**Beijing Chaoyang Transport Port**				
海关监管货物	(吨)	Cargos under Customs Regulation	(ton)	823743	1249014	66.0
北京西站铁路口岸		**Railway Port at Beijing West Railway Station**				
进出境人员	(人次)	Inbound/Outbound Visitors	(person-times)	30618	44864	68.2
#外籍人员进出境		Inbound/Outbound Foreign Visitors		1348	2817	47.9
北京平谷国际陆港		**Beijing Pinggu International Land Port**				
海关监管货物	(吨)	Cargos under Customs Regulation	(ton)	70833	101140	70.0
北京天竺综合保税区		**Beijing Tianzhu Comprehensive Bonded Zone**				
实际进出货物	(吨)	Cargos under Customs Regulation	(ton)	71737	77264	92.8
海关征收税款净入库税额	**(亿元)**	**Net Paid-in Duties Levied and Collected by Customs**	**(100 million yuan)**	**677.86**	**678.47**	**99.9**

资料来源：北京市人民政府口岸办公室。
Source: Port Administration Office of the People's Government of Beijing Municipality.

10-7 外商投资企业实际利用外资情况(2006-2019年)

单位：万美元

项　　目	Item	2006	2007
实际利用外商直接投资额	**Actual Use of Foreign Direct Investment**	**455191**	**506572**
按登记注册类型分	**By Registration Type**		
合资经营	Joint Ventures	80570	77887
合作经营	Cooperatives	33039	18037
独资经营	Solely-funded Enterprises	341367	408754
外商投资股份制	Companies Limited by Shares	215	1894
按产业分	**By Industry**		
第一产业	Primary Industry	544	4774
第二产业	Secondary Industry	109380	93391
第三产业	Tertiary Industry	345267	408407
按行业分	**By Sector**		
农、林、牧、渔业	Agriculture, Forestry, Animal Production and Hunting, Fishing	544	4774
制造业	Manufacturing	105590	89618
建筑业	Construction	1254	878
信息传输、计算机服务和软件业	Information Transmission, Computer Services and Software	44341	78470
批发与零售业	Wholesale and Retail Trade	24378	33318
住宿和餐饮业	Accommodation and Restaurants	1882	5824
房地产业	Real Estate	72242	119476
租赁和商务服务业	Renting and Leasing Activities, Business Services	174342	92896
其他行业	Other Sectors	30618	81318
按外商国别(地区)分	**By Country (Region) of Foreign Investors**		
#中国香港	Hong Kong,China	86600	149291
英属维尔京群岛	Virgin Islands	78445	104154
开曼群岛	Cayman Islands	27596	68646
日　本	Japan	67580	30386
韩　国	Korea	35357	24420
美　国	United States	20043	18280
新加坡	Singapore	17616	15328
巴巴多斯	Barbados	7278	13789
德　国	Germany	47797	11476
毛里求斯	Mauritius	10166	8068
百慕大	Bermuda	1658	7540
萨摩亚	Samoan	1483	6189
荷　兰	Netherlands	4610	4876
法　国	France	3578	3824
英　国	United Kingdom	2977	3304

资料来源：北京市商务局。

ACTUAL USE OF FOREIGN CAPITAL BY FOREIGN INVESTED ENTERPRISES (2006-2019)

(USD 10000)

2008	2009	2010	2011	2012	2013	2014	2015	2016	2017	2018	2019
608172	**612094**	**636358**	**705447**	**804160**	**852418**	**904085**	**1299635**	**1302858**	**2432909**	**1731089**	**1421299**
90916	91049	91335	78983	191944	190667	154808	268500	792030	200974	312084	172711
21372	32249	22890	15068	14184	22887	5166	202	4021	8441	11375	79
490252	448912	516766	594890	592310	593258	704367	995202	487714	2195168	1136891	968413
5632	39884	5367	16506	5722	45606	39744	35731	19093	28326	270739	280096
2032	3833	1246	214	733	1717	13947	7620	2303	838	6725	63
162515	88536	71899	80798	112326	149687	97254	59528	68266	111886	238435	71615
443625	519725	563213	624435	691101	701014	792884	1232487	1232289	2320185	1485929	1349621
2032	3833	1246	214	733	1717	13947	7620	2303	838	6725	63
150056	75364	68496	63303	86378	106848	84226	59397	63806	39318	102868	33682
1715	2493	411	2343	383	193	703	131	113	2651	15	813
105396	94752	95453	109246	135121	119547	115292	48611	113490	1317877	452240	534844
34677	55411	66032	115437	74311	92739	54792	242167	584292	182005	77612	52899
3357	8427	3525	1705	2877	1822	2047	549	3010	3161	30180	1873
78787	79682	141728	112539	87739	148057	136822	27541	66160	206915	194690	70022
132541	225888	175580	190363	161595	171079	339759	71199	120407	229595	271400	110025
99611	66244	83887	110297	255023	210416	156497	842420	349277	450549	595359	617078
173292	270295	312863	323041	440357	360481	541495	993199	561687	2145130	1249888	1063358
125045	123201	76255	112981	28882	51111	37592	189644	210649	30907	29389	12837
75463	41389	45209	35982	59320	43982	36835	5774	269682	36757	59455	54177
47174	23905	40692	77196	59022	44781	31125	12193	12449	29609	20291	14352
27841	17601	14725	22372	70959	21029	18584	8143	37807	31878	57825	70562
17888	18628	21370	30221	21097	38882	15634	3677	10182	14036	34892	25146
10520	12600	24888	12898	31656	19383	35631	16468	54266	11389	10744	20046
15803	2384	941	821	200	2839	3000	3				
26654	14308	22344	17939	25763	107467	99968	35761	95500	11784	28587	20887
7780	5615	7179	1311	1392	3297	3586	275	774	3612	1509	2168
1699	4441	4860	813	1483	265	2005		150	73939	131362	40214
2468	1310	1705	893	1163	589	311	1463	95	100	50	443
28520	4906	10639	3677	8542	14619	12119	508	845	16181	3092	16605
2583	6349	3700	6642	2286	1409	6284	16054	13446	7050	7437	2424
4897	4242	1120	6245	3828	2387	1738	2010	1741	759	916	1431

Source: Beijing Municipal Commission of Commerce.

10-8 限额以上港澳台及外商投资法人企业基本情况(2018)
STATISTICS FOR HONGKONG，MACAO，TAIWAN AND FOREIGN-INVESTED CORPORATE ENTERPRISES ABOVE DESIGNATED SIZE(2018)

项　目	Item	企业单位数(个) Number of Enterprises (unit)	从业人员平均人数(人) Average Number of Persons Employed (person)	营业收入(万元) Business Income (10000 yuan)	利润总额(万元) Total Profits (10000 yuan)
合　计	**Total**	**3578**	**1367810**	**352320182**	**49406806**
按登记注册类型分	**By Registration Type**				
港澳台商投资企业	Hong Kong, Macao and Taiwan -invested Enterprises	1443	647189	152831263	10147693
与港澳台商合资	Joint Ventures	423	153447	15787417	1864138
与港澳台商合作	Cooperatives	74	17700	1564543	225150
港澳台商独资	Solely-funded Enterprises	899	406178	121282436	6144179
港澳台商投资股份有限公司	Companies Limited by Shares	33	52781	12725485	1599412
其他港澳台投资企业	Others	14	17083	1471382	314813
外商投资企业	Foreign-invested Enterprises	2135	720621	199488919	39259113
中外合资	Joint Ventures	630	273043	75170091	9065477
中外合作	Cooperatives	52	11197	888318	61538
外商独资	Solely-funded Enterprises	1392	401783	120857953	30119676
外商投资股份有限公司	Companies Limited by Shares	44	24653	1944776	-89266
其他外商投资企业	Others	17	9945	627781	101688
按国民经济行业分	**By Sector**				
农、林、牧、渔业	Agriculture, Forestry, Animal Production and Hunting, Fishing				
制造业	Manufacturing	650	276018	83388251	6763249
建筑业	Construction	70	9027	1752170	58783
批发和零售业	Wholesale and Retail Trade	566	192131	152724787	7328190
住宿和餐饮业	Accommodation and Restaurants	160	134483	3828723	363214
交通运输、仓储和邮政业	Transport,Storage and Post	97	126502	18844387	2191789
信息传输、软件和信息技术服务业	Information Transmission, Software and Information Technology Services	513	283878	39511685	20231169
房地产业	Real Estate	284	78053	6164741	1010412
租赁和商务服务业	Renting and Leasing Activities, Business Services	528	97415	17742220	3998481
其他行业	Other Sectors	710	170303	28363219	7461517
按三次产业分	**By Industry**				
第一产业	Primary Industry				
第二产业	Secondary Industry	725	283463	88917957	7415159
第三产业	Tertiary Industry	2853	1084347	263402224	41991647

注：1.行业划分执行《国民经济行业分类》(GB/T 4754-2017)标准。
2.从业人员平均人数中，金融业为从业人员期末人数；利润总额中，金融业为营业利润数据。

Note: a) Sectors in this table are classified in accordance with the Standard for Industrial Classification for National Economic Activities (GB/T 4754-2017).
b) In the Average Number of Persons Employed, the data of finance referred to the period-end number of employed persons; and in the Total Profits, the data of finance referred to the operating profit data.

10-9 限额以上港澳台及外商投资法人企业基本情况(2019)
STATISTICS FOR HONGKONG，MACAO，TAIWAN AND FOREIGN-INVESTED CORPORATE ENTERPRISES ABOVE DESIGNATED SIZE(2019)

项目	Item	企业单位数(个) Number of Enterprises (unit)	从业人员平均人数(人) Average Number of Persons Employed (person)	营业收入(万元) Business Income (10000 yuan)	利润总额(万元) Total Profits (10000 yuan)	应交税金合计(万元) Total Taxes Payable (10000 yuan)
合计	**Total**	**3877**	**1374575**	**383439193**	**40711028**	**14932298**
按登记注册类型分	**By Registration Type**					
港澳台商投资企业	Hong Kong, Macao and Taiwan-invested Enterprises	1596	668555	175691186	11294909	4697469
与港澳台商合资	Joint Ventures	440	153270	14978628	2024102	968593
与港澳台商合作	Cooperatives	72	16799	1458290	329708	225176
港澳台商独资	Solely-funded Enterprises	1046	433275	147773507	7864566	3140160
港澳台商投资股份有限公司	Companies Limited by Shares	22	52441	10820603	1044512	338512
其他港澳台投资企业	Others	16	12770	660158	32020	25028
外商投资企业	Foreign-invested Enterprises	2281	706020	207748007	29416119	10234829
中外合资	Joint Ventures	669	262059	77755584	8482337	5221547
中外合作	Cooperatives	55	11163	1126904	116058	140582
外商独资	Solely-funded Enterprises	1499	406030	124314621	20443904	4805068
外商投资股份有限公司	Companies Limited by Shares	42	22061	3686132	321351	16304
其他外商投资企业	Others	16	4707	864766	52469	51328
按国民经济行业分	**By Sector**					
农、林、牧、渔业	Agriculture, Forestry, Animal Production and Hunting, Fishing					
制造业	Manufacturing	639	249889	84613702	7699087	4818003
建筑业	Construction	64	7912	1705813	38189	38325
批发和零售业	Wholesale and Retail Trade	671	190650	172072435	7652907	3285975
住宿和餐饮业	Accommodation and Restaurants	190	148167	4141861	325456	165487
交通运输、仓储和邮政业	Transport,Storage and Post	99	123945	19881914	2279289	764736
信息传输、软件和信息技术服务业	Information Transmission, Software and Information Technology Services	586	309881	46032455	11300298	2073057
房地产业	Real Estate	302	71185	6060018	1065257	1145874
租赁和商务服务业	Renting and Leasing Activities, Business Services	592	105118	20846569	4132702	636738
其他行业	Other Sectors	734	167828	28084426	6217844	2004104
按三次产业分	**By Industry**					
第一产业	Primary Industry					
第二产业	Secondary Industry	711	256125	89989078	8166429	4941629
第三产业	Tertiary Industry	3166	1118450	293450115	32544599	9990668

注：1.行业划分执行《国民经济行业分类》(GB/T 4754—2017)标准。
2.应交税金合计包括应交增值税、所得税费用和税金及附加。

Note: a) Sectors in this table are classified in accordance with the Standard for Industrial Classification for National Economic Activities (GB/T 4754-2017).
b) Total tax payable includes VAT payable, income tax expense, tax and surtax.

10–10 境外投资情况(2003–2019年)
STATISTICS FOR OVERSEAS INVESTMENT (2003-2019)

单位：万美元 (USD 10000)

年 份 Year	中方投资额 Amount of Investment by China	截至各年期末直接投资存量 Diret Investment Stock by the Year End
2003	30054	44844
2004	15739	70086
2005	11306	92940
2006	5612	91873
2007	15295	159195
2008	47299	251019
2009	45185	375865
2010	76614	480882
2011	117503	603380
2012	168900	757800
2013	413010	1276456
2014	727353	2848870
2015	1228033	3879895
2016	1557362	5438141
2017	665126	6484394
2018	647042	6995279
2019	826601	7368891

资料来源：北京市商务局。
Source: Beijing Municipal Commerce Bureau.

10–11 对外经济合作(1984–2019年)
STATISTICS FOR FOREIGN ECONOMIC COOPERATION (1984-2019)

年 份 Year	合同数 (份) Number of Contracts (unit)	#对外承包工程 Foreign Contracted Works	合同额 (万美元) Contract Value (USD 10000)	#对外承包工程 Foreign Contracted Works	完成营业额 (万美元) Turnover (USD 10000)	#对外承包工程 Foreign Contracted Works	年末在外人数 (人) Year-end Workers Staying Abroad (person)	对外承包工程 Foreign Contracted Works	对外劳务合作 Foreign Labor Service Cooperation
1984	9	2	2801	2768	502	331	541	163	378
1985	12	2	852	736	2083	355	2401	18	2383
1986	30	7	446	319	1535	90	837	71	766
1987	37	5	547	354	696	186	690	20	670
1988	46	5	885	344	802	281	819	104	715
1989	111	7	1685	235	1018	459	600	83	517
1990	105	16	3756	2253	1056	625	336	25	311
1991	114	9	3202	1671	1897	1469	980	306	674
1992	130	16	8889	7762	3140	2543	952	264	688
1993	143	48	29397	27625	9748	8871	1555	532	1023
1994	114	34	15715	15089	18783	17822	2720	1694	1026
1995	116	35	15613	14014	12789	12156	2604	1297	1307
1996	116	49	67689	62945	43057	38124	2516	1559	957
1997	107	37	35640	23374	29629	17945	3122	1993	1129
1998	180	48	25526	19292	31009	24930	3647	2239	1408
1999	90	28	25232	18715	26167	19690	3476	2199	1277
2000	104	54	16285	9936	19799	13543	3205	1660	1545
2001	105	54	21439	14758	18628	11680	3494	2141	1353
2002	73	42	27949	19376	23160	14453	2134	1112	1022
2003	117	99	48271	30761	34926	17334	2097	1270	827
2004	128	116	81185	51136	59630	29241	2552	1629	923
2005	272	238	93732	56709	71281	35554	4424	2528	1896
2006	232	166	176752	160328	83518	70062	8962	6760	2202
2007	317	143	236881	211560	94077	71727	11299	7060	4239
2008	486	197	558714	520973	168416	131686	11422	6366	5056
2009	190	182	336223	296851	226893	185017	17121	11805	5316
2010	199	170	286179	251114	259794	222514	22499	17145	5354
2011	229	229	264019	262078	252951	249146	17821	12393	5428
2012	340	340	405885	403475	295639	289902	16747	12143	4604
2013	349	349	564383	562440	341046	335854	21036	16549	4487
2014	283	283	437463	429369	365358	357432	29457	21683	7774
2015	208	208	471988	464808	370880	354868	34183	19287	14896
2016	229	229	515670	514151	260173	249642	20436	13176	7260
2017	272	272	908136	905968	419082	402944	24588	11806	12782
2018	230	230	740714	730314	419200	399820	31127	12383	18744
2019	186	186	1203947	1173673	487960	421872	64942	11043	53899

注：1984–2008年，对外承包工程统计中含对外设计咨询统计数据。
资料来源：北京市商务局。
Note: In 1984-2008, statistics for foreign contracted projects included statistics for consultation on foreign design.
Source: Beijing Municipal Commerce Bureau.

主要统计指标解释

货物进出口总值 指实际进、出我国海关并能引起我国境内物质资源增加或减少的进出口货物总金额。包括我国境内法人和其他组织以一般贸易、易货贸易、加工贸易、补偿贸易、寄售代销贸易等方式进出口的货物、租赁期一年及以上的租赁进出口货物、边境小额贸易货物、国际援助物资或捐赠品、保税区和保税仓库进出口货物等的金额合计。进出口总值用以观察一个国家在对外贸易方面的总规模。我国规定出口货物按离岸价格统计，进口货物按到岸价格统计。

一般贸易 指我国境内有进出口经营权的企业单边进口或单边出口的货物。

来料加工装配贸易 指由外商提供全部或部分原材料、辅料、零部件、元器件、配套件和包装物料，必要时提供设备，由我方按对方的要求进行加工装配，成品交对方销售，我方收取工缴费；或对方提供的作价设备价款，我方用工缴费偿还的交易形式。

进料加工贸易 指我方用外汇购买进口的原料、材料、辅料、元器件、零部件、配套件和包装物料，加工成品或半成品后再外销出口的交易形式。

旅客吞吐量 指经乘航班进出北京民用运输机场的中国公民、港澳台同胞、华侨及外国人等旅客数量的总和。

货邮吞吐量 指通过民用运输机场的航班运输的货物、邮寄物品和随身携带的行李物品重量总和。

飞机起降架次 指进出民用运输机场的正常航班架次，不包括包机和其他非正常航班。

海关征收税款净入库税额 指北京海关征收的税款合计，包含进出口关税和进口环节税。

服务贸易 服务贸易包括跨境提供、境外消费、商业存在和自然人移动等内容。

批准外商直接投资企业项目个数 指外商直接投资中批准设立的外商投资企业个数、批准的合作开发项目个数。

实际利用外商直接投资额 指批准的合同外资金额的实际执行数，外国投资者根据批准外商投资企业的合同（章程）的规定实际缴付的出资额和企业投资总额内外国投资者以自己的境外自有资金实际直接向企业提供的贷款。

对外承包工程 指企业按照国际通行做法，在国（境）外承揽和实施各类工程项目的经济活动。企业承揽的我国对外经济援助项目、我国驻外使（领）馆等建设项目视同对外承包工程项目。

对外劳务合作 指企业按照与国（境）外政府有关机构、团体、企业、私人雇主所签合同规定，向国（境）外派遣各类劳务人员的经济活动。企业自带设备以提供技术服务的形式在国（境）外承揽的项目视同对外劳务合作项目。

Explanatory Notes on Main Statistical Indicators

Total Value of Imports and Exports refer to the total value of goods actually imported and exported at China's customs, which lead to increase or decrease in the physical resources in China, including goods imported/exported by China domestic legal persons and other organizations in such manners as general trade, barter trade, processing trade, compensation trade, commission-based sales trade, leasing imports/exports with a lease period of one year and more, small-sum border trade goods, international aid goods and donations, imports/exports in bonded zones and bonded warehouses. The indicator of the Total Value of Imports and Exports can be used to observe the total size of foreign trade in a country. In accordance with the stipulation of the Chinese government, imports are calculated at CIF, while exports are calculated at FOB.

General Trade means goods imported and exported unilaterally by domestic enterprises with import/export rights.

Trade of Processing and Assembling Supplied Materials is a form of transaction in which all or part of raw materials, auxiliary materials, parts and components, elements, fittings, and packaging materials, and equipment if necessary are provided by the foreign party, processed or assemble by Chinese party according to requirements of the foreign party, and the finished products are sold by the foreign party. The Chinese party charges processing fees and pays back the money of priced equipment provided by the foreign party with processing charges.

Trade of Processing Imported Materials is a form of transaction in which the Chinese party purchases raw materials, auxiliary materials, parts and components, elements, fittings, and packaging materials with foreign exchange, processing them into finished or semi-finished products and export them.

Passenger Throughput means the total number of Chinese citizens, compatriots form Hong Kong, Macao and Taiwan, oversea Chinese and foreigners that take off and land at civil airports in Beijing by flights.

Cargos Throughput means the sum of goods, mailed articles and luggage transported by flights taking off from and landing at civil airports in Beijing.

Takeoff and Landing of Airplanes means the number of regular flights taking off from and landing at civil airports in Beijing, excluding chartered flights and other non-regular flights.

Net Paid-in Duties Levied and Collected by Customs mean the sum of duties actually levied by customs in Beijing, including import and export duties and import linkage taxs.

Service Trade includes overseas provision, overseas consumption, commercial existence, movement of natural persons, and so on.

Number of Direct Foreign-invested Enterprises Approved means the number of foreign-invested enterprises and joint development projects approved in foreign direct investment (FDI).

Actual Use of Foreign Direct Investment means the value of approved contractual foreign investment actually used, the amount of actual capital contribution by foreign investors according to the contract (articles of incorporation) of the foreign-invested enterprise approved and, in the total investment of an enterprise, the amount of loans provided directly by foreign investor with its own overseas money for the enterprise.

Foreign Contracted Projects refer to economic activities in which enterprises undertake and implement various projects in foreign (overseas) countries in line with international practices. Foreign economic aid projects and construction projects of Chinese Embassies (Consulates) undertaken by enterprises are deemed as foreign contracted projects.

Foreign Labor Service Cooperation means any economic activity in which enterprises dispatch labors to foreign (overseas) countries as stated in contracts signed with foreign (overseas) government agencies, groups, enterprises, and private employers. Projects undertaken by enterprises in foreign (overseas) countries in a manner of providing technical service with their own equipment are deemed as foreign labor service cooperation projects.

11

北京统计年鉴2020　BEIJING STATISTICAL YEARBOOK

农业及农村经济
AGRICULTURE AND RURAL ECONOMY

简要说明

一、主要内容

本章资料反映北京市农业生产和农村经济基本情况，主要包括农村基本情况、农业生产条件、农林牧渔业产值及主要农产品生产情况、农作物播种面积、设施农业、农业观光园、乡村旅游、乡镇企业情况等。

二、统计范围和调查方法

（一）统计范围

农林牧渔业统计范围包括辖区内全部农林牧渔业生产单位、非农行业单位附属的农林牧渔业生产活动单位以及农户的农业生产活动。军委系统的农林牧渔业生产（除军马外）也应包括在内，但不包括农业科学试验机构进行的农业生产。

1．农业：指各种农作物的种植活动。包括谷物、豆类、薯类、棉花、油料、糖料、麻类、烟叶、蔬菜、食用菌及花卉盆景园艺产品、水果、坚果、饲料和香料作物、药材及其它作物的种植。

2．林业：包括林木的栽培(不包括茶园、桑园和果园的栽培、管理和收获等活动)、木材和竹材的采运、林产品的采集。

3．畜牧业：包括牲畜饲养和放牧、家禽饲养以及野生动物的捕猎和饲养。

4．渔业：分为淡水养殖和海水养殖，包括水生动物和海藻类植物的养殖和捕捞。

农村社会经济统计范围包括所有乡镇辖区内的社会经济活动。

（二）调查方法

农林牧渔业生产统计采取全面调查方法，村级起报。主要粮食播种面积数据通过卫星遥感测量方法取得,粮食产量数据通过抽样调查方法取得。

三、农林牧渔总产值的核算方法

根据农业生产特点，农林牧渔业总产值的核算采用“产品法”计算，即用产品产量乘以价格求出各种产品的产值，按产品产值类别分别汇总，计算出农林牧渔各业的产值，各业相加为农林牧渔业总产值。

1．农业：包括谷物和其他作物；蔬菜、食用菌及花卉盆景园艺产品；水果、坚果、饲料、香料；中药材。

2．林业：包括林木的培育和种植；木材、竹材采运；林产品的采集。

3．牧业：包括除渔业养殖以外的一切动物饲养和放牧以及野生动物的捕猎和饲养。

4．渔业：包括水生动物和海藻类植物的养殖和捕捞。

5．农林牧渔专业及辅助性活动：产值等于农林牧渔专业及辅助性活动营业收入。

（一）核算内容的变化情况。1958 年及以后的林业产值中增加了村及村以下竹木采伐产值；牧业中取消了厩肥产值；副业中取消了农民自给性手工业产值；渔业中增加了海洋捕捞水产品产值。1980 年及以后的农业总产值，在副业中增加了农民家庭兼营工业商品部分的产值。从 1984 年起村及村以下办工业产值划归工业。从 1993 年起，取消副业，将野生动物的捕猎划入牧业，野生植物采集和农民家庭兼营商品性工业划归农业。从 2003 年起按照新的《国民经济行业分类》标准取消了“其他农业”；将农林牧渔服务业产值纳入农林牧渔业总产值中；从农林牧渔业总产值中取消了“家庭兼营商品性工业”；将村以上木材和竹材的采运划入了林业。

（二）核算方法变化情况。2003 年以后，计算农林牧渔业总产值使用的价格从农产品综合平均价调整为农产品生产价格。2004 年，国家统计局报表制度规定农林牧渔业总产值增加按可比价计算的产值及发展速度（计算方法：用现价产值的中类数据除以中类缩减指数求得各中类的可比价产值，各中类相加得大类的可比价产值，最后用大类数据相加得农业可比价总产值，可比价产值除以上年现价产值得发展速度）。从 2005 年起，取消了按 1990 年价格计算的农业产值。由于 2006 年农业普查后对农业生产历史数据进行了修订，新修订的农业产值数据只到大类，如果按大类缩减计算农业可比价总产值不符合国家报表制度要求，故 2005 年及以前年度没有按可比价计算的发展速度。

四、有关统计标准的变化说明

关于行业划分标准。2003 年至 2011 年执行《国民经济行业分类》(GB/T 4754—2002) 标准；2012-2017 年执行《国民经济行业分类》(GB/T 4754-2011)标准；自 2018 年起，执行《国民经济行业分类》(GB/T 4754—2017) 标准。

五、关于历史数据调整

根据 2006 年北京市第二次全国农业普查结果，北京市统计局、国家统计局北京调查总队按照国务院农普办要求，依照国际通用做法，对 1997—2005 年的相关指标历史数据进行了修订。

2010 年起，根据新的《统计用产品分类目录》，将原林业产值中的核桃、栗子、白果、松子等干果产值调整至农业产值中，为同口径对比，将 2009 年数据也作了相应调整。

Brief Introduction

I. Main Content

Statistics in this chapter show basic situation of agricultural production and rural economy in Beijing, mainly consisting of basic statistics on rural areas, agricultural production conditions, output of agriculture, forestry, animal production and hunting, fishing, and statistics on production of main agricultural products, sown area, facility agriculture, agricultural sightseeing gardens, rural tourism, and township enterprises, and so on.

II. Scope of Statistics and Method for Survey

Statistics on agriculture, forestry, animal production and hunting, fishing cover all related producing entities, producers affiliated to non-agricultural departments, as well as farmers' agricultural production activities. Production by the military commission system shall also be included (except for army horse breeding), but the production by scientific testing agencies is not included.

1. Agriculture: It refers to the growing of various agricultural crops, including grains, beans, potatoes, cotton, oil plants, sugar plants, fiber plants, tobacco leaves, vegetables, edible fungus, flower bonsai and gardening products, fruits, nuts, feedstuff, and spice crops, herbs, and other crops.

2. Forestry: It includes tree planting (except for the cultivation, management and harvest of tea gardens, mulberry fields, and orchards), the logging of timber and bamboo, and the collection of forestry products.

3. Animal production and hunting: It includes the breeding and grazing of livestock, poultry agriculture, as well as hunting and breeding of wildlife.

4. Fishing: It falls into two parts: freshwater agriculture and mariculture, including the cultivation and fishing for aquatic animals and algae.

Statistics for social and economic development in rural areas cover social and economic activities of all villages and towns within the jurisdiction.

III. Method for Survey and Counting

Based on agricultural production characteristics, the gross output value of agriculture, forestry, animal production and hunting, fishing was calculated by the "product approach"--that is to multiply production volume by the unit price, so as to get output value of each product, then sum it up by category, namely agriculture, forestry, animal production and hunting, fishing; and the sum total of these categories will be gross output value of the whole sector.

1. Agriculture: including cereal and other crops; vegetables, edible mushrooms, flower bonsai and gardening products; fruits, nuts, beverage, spices, and herbs.

2. Forestry: including the cultivation and planting of forest trees; logging of timber and bamboo; and collection of forestry products.

3. Animal production and hunting: including the breeding and grazing of animals other than fish breeding, as well as hunting and breeding of wildlife.

4. Fishing: including cultivation and catching of aquatic animals and seaweed plants.

5. Professional and Supporting Activities of Agricultare, Forestry,Animal Production and Hunting,Fishing: the output value equals the operating income of professional and supporting activities of agriculture, forestry, animal production and hunting, fishing.

(I) Changes in Accounting Content. Since 1958, output value of bamboo and timber logging by villages and units subordinated to villages has been included in the statistics of forestry; output value of barnyard manure has been excluded from animal production and hunting statistics; output value of subsistence handicrafts has been excluded from sideline products output value; and the output value of aquatic products by marine fishing has been added to fishing. Since 1980, the output value of industrial commodities operated by rural households has been included in the output value of sideline products. Since 1984, industrial output value produced by villages and units subordinated to villages has been added in the sector of industry. In 1993, the group "sideline products" was cancelled; the hunting of wild animals has been classified as animal production and hunting, and the gathering of wild plants and commercial industrial businesses run by rural households have been included in agriculture. A new standard for *Classification of National Economic Sectors* was introduced in 2003. According to the new classification, the group "other agricultural activities" was cancelled; the output value of service activities for agriculture, forestry, animal husbandry and fishing is included in the gross output value of agriculture, forestry, animal production and hunting, fishing; the value of industrial output by households is excluded from the gross output value of agriculture, forestry, animal production and hunting, fishing; output value of wood and bamboo logging of units above village level is included in forestry statistics.

(II) Changes in Accounting Method. Since 2003, the price used for calculating the gross output value of agricultures, forestry, animal production and hunting, fishing has been adjusted from the overall average price of farm products into the producer price for farm products. In 2004, the Reporting System of the National Bureau of Statistics stated that, for incremental gross output value of agriculture, forestry, animal production and hunting, fishing, the output value and growth rate shall be calculated at comparable prices (calculation method: use the output value of groups at present prices to divide the groups' deflator, so as to get the output value at comparable prices; then add up the groups' output value to get the whole division's output value at comparable prices; in the end, add up all divisions' output value to get the gross output value at comparable prices for agriculture sector and divide the output value at comparable prices by the output value at current prices in the previous year to get the growth rate). Since 2005, the practice of using prices of 1990 as reference numbers to calculate agricultural output value has been cancelled. As historical data of agricultural production were revised after the agricultural census in 2006, revised agricultural production output value figures were presented only in divisions; and it does not meet the requirements of national reporting system to calculate the gross agricultural output value at comparable prices by divisions' deflator. Therefore, there were no figures of growth rate at comparable prices in and prior to 2005.

IV. Changes in Relevant Statistical Standards

Standard for Classification of Sectors. The standards in the *Classification of National Economic Sectors* (GB/T 4754-2002) were implemented from 2003 to 2011. The standards in the *Standard for Classification of National Economic Sectors* (GB/T 4754-2002) were implemented from 2012 to 2017. The standards in the *Classification of National Economic Sectors (GB/T 4754-2017) are implemented since 2018.*

V. Adjustments to Historical Statistics

Based on the results of the second national agricultural census in 2006 in Beijing, Beijing Municipal Bureau of Statistics and Survey Office of the National Bureau of Statistics in Beijing revised related historical statistics during 1997-2005 as required by the Agricultural Census Office of the State Council and in accordance with the international practice.

Since 2010, the output value of nuts such as walnuts, chestnuts, gingkoes and pine nuts formerly included in forestry has been added in the output value of agriculture according to the new *Catalog on Statistical Product Classification*. In order to conduct same-caliber comparison, data in 2009 annual report have also been adjusted accordingly.

11-1 农村基本情况(1978-2019年)
BASIC STATISTICS FOR RURAL AREAS (1978-2019)

年 份 Year	乡政府 (个) Township Governments (unit)	镇政府 (个) Town Governments (unit)	村民委员会 (个) Villagers' Committees (unit)	乡镇及行政村常住户数 (万户) Number of Permanent Households in Towns and Administrative Villages (10000 households)	乡镇及行政村常住人口 (万人) Permanent Population in Towns and Administrative Villages (10000 persons)	乡镇及行政村从业人员 (万人) Employed Persons in Towns and Administrative Villages (10000 persons)
1978				91.9	382.1	165.3
1979				92.9	374.7	165.1
1980				95.0	374.3	167.4
1981				98.9	377.6	172.9
1982				103.2	381.8	179.4
1983				106.6	384.0	184.6
1984				108.9	385.6	188.9
1985	350	15	4394	111.8	387.2	190.0
1986	327	15	4400	113.1	386.9	189.5
1987	324	14	4326	115.7	388.9	189.8
1988	321	13	4111	118.6	389.6	189.2
1989	322	14	4483	121.5	390.0	186.1
1990	252	77	4481	124.5	392.0	184.3
1991	209	77	4480	125.5	390.7	182.1
1992	209	77	4229	126.2	387.6	178.7
1993	192	81	4476	126.5	382.4	176.0
1994	174	92	4464	124.9	376.0	171.6
1995	166	100	4355	125.0	371.5	163.6
1996	166	100	4357	124.6	368.9	164.2
1997	132	108	4348	124.6	365.3	161.2
1998	126	105	4032	125.9	364.4	161.0
1999	125	103	4040	125.9	363.9	165.3
2000	70	142	4039	126.8	363.7	165.8
2001	52	139	4010	127.6	361.6	165.3
2002	51	141	4005	128.0	357.6	165.6
2003	45	142	3985	131.1	360.6	169.6
2004	42	142	3985	132.8	359.9	171.4
2005	43	142	3953	142.2	381.8	184.0
2006	41	142	3957	143.6	501.6	316.9
2007	41	142	3955	176.9	510.0	313.4
2008	40	142	3951	189.8	547.4	321.3
2009	40	142	3950	203.8	572.5	338.7
2010	40	142	3943	216.0	589.4	347.8
2011	38	144	3941	212.4	574.8	338.3
2012	38	144	3940	215.2	582.5	341.7
2013	38	144	3938	221.9	599.5	353.5
2014	38	144	3937	225.2	606.9	357.0
2015	38	144	3936	221.4	593.5	348.0
2016	38	143	3941	232.6	612.6	385.9
2017	38	143	3920	216.7	566.6	352.2
2018	38	143	3915	211.9	558.0	337.5
2019	38	143	3891	211.7	555.7	333.7

资料来源：乡政府、镇政府和村民委员会个数由中共北京市委社会工作委员会北京市民政局提供。

Source: Numbers of township governments, town governments, villagers' committees are provided by Social Work Committee of Beijing Municipal Committee of the Communist Party of China Beijing Municipal Civil Affairs Bureau.

11-2 农业生产条件(1978-2019年)
CONDITIONS FOR AGRICULTURAL PRODUCTION (1978-2019)

年 份 Year	年末实有耕地面积(万公顷) Actual Area of Arable Land (year-end) (10000 hectares)	农业机械总动力(万千瓦) Total Power of Agricultural Machinery (10000 kW)	农村用电量(万千瓦时) Rural Electricity Consumption (10000 kWh)	化肥施用量(万吨) Consumption of Chemical Fertilizers (10000 tons)
1978	42.9	189.4	58802	11.6
1979	42.7	212.2	63124	11.3
1980	42.6	234.6	76753	12.3
1981	42.5	244.8	91844	11.2
1982	42.4	242.2	96961	12.0
1983	42.3	261.8	104608	12.0
1984	42.2	290.8	119289	10.7
1985	42.1	320.4	126830	8.2
1986	41.9	345.5	180640	9.1
1987	41.8	388.4	159450	10.0
1988	41.6	399.7	163986	10.6
1989	41.4	423.9	128414	11.8
1990	41.3	416.2	122711	14.4
1991	41.1	384.8	111347	14.4
1992	40.9	399.8	143963	14.4
1993	40.6	450.5	169911	14.9
1994	40.2	459.2	172042	19.8
1995	39.4	468.1	201731	18.8
1996	34.4	468.4	275871	18.9
1997	34.2	433.2	301655	19.7
1998	34.1	415.5	290859	19.3
1999	33.8	410.4	330069	19.0
2000	32.9	399.2	572257	17.9
2001	29.2	394.9	619806	15.7
2002	27.5	381.8	414248	14.9
2003	26.0	366.9	427266	14.3
2004	23.6	340.3	383954	14.5
2005	23.3	337.7	421680	14.8
2006	23.3	325.5	416459	14.8
2007	23.2	300.5	411238	14.0
2008	23.2	267.0	427377	13.6
2009	22.7	271.5	439099	13.8
2010	22.4	276.0	443774	13.7
2011	22.2	265.2	454009	13.8
2012	22.1	241.1	473121	13.7
2013	22.1	207.7	485320	12.8
2014	22.0	195.8	505559	11.6
2015	21.9	185.9	516705	10.5
2016	21.6	144.4	547099	9.7
2017	21.4	133.5	615078	8.5
2018	21.3	125.6	651370	7.3
2019		122.8	677672	6.2

注：1．化肥施用量为折纯量。
2．2003年以前农村用电量由原北京市供电局提供。
3．农业机械总动力数据由北京市农业农村局提供。

Note: a) Data on consumption of chemical fertilizers were net amount.
b) Figures of rural electricity consumption before 2003 were provided by the former Beijing Electric Power Supply Bureau.
c) Figures of total power of agricultural machinery were provided by Beijing Municipal Bureau of Agriculture and Rural Affairs.

11-3 农作物播种面积和造林面积(1978-2019年)
SOWN AND AFFORESTATION AREA (1978-2019)

单位：万公顷 (10000 hectares)

年份 Year	农作物播种面积 Sown Area	#粮食作物 Grain Crops	#玉米 Corn	#小麦 Wheat	#油料 Oil-bearing Crops	#蔬菜及食用菌 Vegetables and Edible Mushrooms	#瓜类及草莓 Melons & Strawberries	#饲料 Forage	造林面积 Afforestation Area
1978	69.1	56.1	16.9	19.2	3.3	5.6	0.2	2.0	1.4
1979	67.7	56.0	18.2	19.7	3.0	5.4	0.3	2.0	1.6
1980	65.7	54.9	19.7	18.8	2.8	5.1	0.4	1.8	2.4
1981	64.4	53.0	19.8	18.4	2.7	5.5	0.6	1.7	2.7
1982	64.2	52.7	19.7	18.1	2.4	5.9	0.8	1.6	2.8
1983	63.8	53.0	20.1	18.7	1.9	5.7	0.5	1.5	3.3
1984	63.3	52.3	20.6	19.5	1.8	5.8	0.7	1.5	3.2
1985	61.8	51.1	21.7	19.1	2.0	5.4	0.9	1.3	3.0
1986	60.5	49.9	21.6	18.5	2.0	5.8	1.1	1.0	1.5
1987	59.8	49.5	22.3	18.3	1.6	6.0	0.9	1.1	2.0
1988	59.5	48.8	22.2	18.6	1.5	6.3	1.0	1.2	1.6
1989	58.9	48.3	21.9	18.5	1.3	6.8	0.8	1.1	0.8
1990	59.0	48.4	22.4	18.8	1.2	7.0	0.6	1.1	1.3
1991	59.0	48.3	22.3	19.2	1.2	7.3	0.5	1.0	1.5
1992	58.5	47.7	22.4	19.2	1.2	7.5	0.5	0.8	1.5
1993	56.5	45.6	21.8	17.8	1.3	7.8	0.5	0.7	4.8
1994	55.1	43.0	20.6	16.4	1.2	9.1	0.6	0.6	5.5
1995	55.3	43.4	20.8	17.2	1.2	9.1	0.5		4.7
1996	53.8	42.7	20.8	17.1	1.1	8.8	0.5	0.5	4.0
1997	53.6	42.5	20.6	17.1	1.0	8.9	0.5	0.5	3.8
1998	53.5	42.3	20.8	17.1	1.0	9.0	0.5	0.5	3.7
1999	52.6	41.0	19.8	16.8	1.0	9.2	0.5	0.5	3.0
2000	45.4	30.8	13.6	12.2	1.5	10.4	0.8	1.2	2.6
2001	38.0	21.4	10.0	7.3	1.4	11.3	0.9	1.9	3.2
2002	33.5	16.9	8.7	4.7	1.6	11.5	0.9	1.8	4.8
2003	30.1	14.1	7.5	3.6	1.4	10.8	0.9	1.9	4.7
2004	30.4	15.4	9.4	3.9	1.1	9.1	0.8	2.8	3.2
2005	30.8	19.2	12.0	5.3	0.9	7.9	0.8	1.5	1.2
2006	32.0	22.0	13.6	6.3	0.7	7.1	0.9	0.6	1.3
2007	29.5	19.7	13.9	4.1	0.7	7.0	0.9	0.4	1.1
2008	32.2	22.6	14.6	6.4	0.7	6.8	0.8	0.4	0.9
2009	32.0	22.6	15.1	6.1	0.6	6.8	0.8	0.4	1.8
2010	31.7	22.3	15.0	6.2	0.5	6.8	0.8	0.5	1.4
2011	30.3	20.9	14.1	5.8	0.5	6.7	0.8	0.5	2.1
2012	28.3	19.4	13.2	5.2	0.5	6.4	0.8	0.3	3.6
2013	24.2	15.9	11.4	3.6	0.3	6.2	0.7	0.2	4.4
2014	20.0	12.0	8.9	2.4	0.3	5.7	0.6	0.3	2.3
2015	17.7	10.4	7.6	2.1	0.2	5.4	0.5	0.2	0.8
2016	15.1	8.7	6.5	1.6	0.2	4.7	0.4	0.3	1.0
2017	12.6	6.7	5.0	1.1	0.2	4.2	0.4	0.3	0.9
2018	10.6	5.6	4.0	1.0	0.2	3.6	0.4	0.2	2.0
2019	9.2	4.7	3.4	0.8	0.1	3.1	0.3	0.3	2.2

注：造林面积2009年以前为人工造林面积，2009年起调整为人工造林、无林地和疏林地新封面积之和。

Note: Afforestation area before 2009 was artificial afforestation area, and after 2009 it became the sum of the area of artificial forests, non-forest land and newly enclosed forest land.

11-4 农林牧渔业总产值(1978-2019年)
GROSS OUTPUT VALUE OF AGRICULTURE, FORESTRY, ANIMAL PRODUCTION AND HUNTING, FISHING (1978-2019)

年份 Year	农林牧渔业总产值(亿元) Gross Output Value of Agriculture, Forestry, Animal Production and Hunting, Fishing (100 million yuan)	农业 Agriculture	林业 Forestry	牧业 Animal Production and Hunting	渔业 Fishing	农林牧渔专业及辅助性活动 Professional and Supporting Activities of Agricultare,Forestry, Animal Production and Hunting,Fishing	农林牧渔业总产值比上年增长(%) Growth Rate (%): 按现价计算 Calculated at Current Price	按可比价计算 Calculate at Comparable Price
1978	11.5	8.9	0.2	2.4	0.01			
1979	12.3	8.8	0.2	3.3	0.02		7.0	
1980	14.3	9.8	0.5	3.9	0.05		16.3	
1981	14.9	10.1	0.7	4.1	0.05		4.2	
1982	16.8	11.3	0.7	4.7	0.05		12.8	
1983	19.6	12.7	0.8	6.0	0.1		16.7	
1984	22.2	14.4	0.9	6.7	0.2		13.3	
1985	25.9	16.1	0.8	8.6	0.4		16.7	
1986	28.1	17.2	0.8	9.4	0.7		8.5	
1987	34.4	20.3	0.8	12.3	1.0		22.4	
1988	52.6	31.4	0.9	18.6	1.7		52.9	
1989	60.4	34.2	0.7	23.3	2.2		14.8	
1990	70.2	39.0	0.9	28.0	2.3		16.2	
1991	76.5	39.6	1.5	32.8	2.6		9.0	
1992	84.5	43.2	1.6	36.3	3.4		10.5	
1993	100.4	51.1	2.3	42.7	4.3		18.8	
1994	144.3	72.5	3.1	64.0	4.7		43.7	
1995	164.4	86.8	2.7	68.8	6.1		13.9	
1996	168.9	89.2	2.8	71.1	5.8		2.7	
1997	170.5	86.8	2.9	74.6	6.2		0.9	
1998	174.8	88.3	3.2	75.8	7.5		2.5	
1999	180.6	89.4	4.1	79.5	7.6		3.3	
2000	188.6	88.1	5.2	87.5	7.8		4.4	
2001	202.2	84.7	9.0	99.3	9.2		7.2	
2002	213.5	83.5	11.9	108.6	9.5		5.6	
2003	224.7	80.9	12.3	114.3	9.3	7.9	5.2	
2004	234.9	83.1	11.4	124.3	8.9	7.2	4.5	
2005	239.3	91.0	12.4	120.8	8.7	6.4	1.9	
2006	240.2	104.5	14.8	105.1	9.8	6.0	0.4	0.9
2007	272.3	115.5	17.8	122.4	10.1	6.5	13.4	0.8
2008	303.9	128.1	20.5	140.5	9.8	5.0	11.6	0.8
2009	315.0	146.1	17.2	136.1	10.3	5.3	3.6	5.5
2010	328.0	154.2	16.8	139.6	11.5	5.9	4.1	-1.7
2011	363.1	163.4	18.9	162.7	11.5	6.6	10.7	0.9
2012	395.7	166.3	54.8	154.2	13.0	7.5	9.0	2.9
2013	421.8	170.4	75.9	154.8	12.8	8.0	6.6	2.1
2014	420.1	155.1	90.7	152.7	13.2	8.4	-0.4	…
2015	368.2	154.5	57.3	135.9	11.9	8.7	-12.3	-11.7
2016	338.1	145.2	52.2	122.7	9.2	8.7	-8.2	-9.9
2017	308.3	129.8	58.8	101.4	9.6	8.7	-8.8	-6.9
2018	296.8	114.7	95.1	72.0	6.1	8.8	-3.7	-6.0
2019	281.7	102.3	115.6	49.3	5.3	9.1	-5.1	-6.3

11-5 主要农业产品产量(1978-2019年)
OUTPUT OF MAJOR AGRICULTURAL PRODUCTS (1978-2019)

单位：万吨 (10000 tons)

年份 Year	粮食 Grain	油料 Oil-bearing Crops	蔬菜及食用菌 Vegetables and Edible Mushroom	干鲜果品 Nuts and Fresh Fruits	牛奶 Milk	肉类 Meat	#猪牛羊肉 Pork, Beef and Mutton	禽蛋产量 Poultry and Eggs	水产品 Aquatic Products
1978	186.0	2.6	164.5	17.5	5.4	11.9	11.9	2.1	0.2
1979	172.8	2.6	181.3	15.8	6.0	13.1	13.1	3.1	0.3
1980	186.0	3.1	175.9	15.9	6.8	15.1	15.1	3.4	0.4
1981	180.7	2.2	172.8	15.6	7.6	13.2	13.2	3.7	0.4
1982	185.5	2.3	208.3	13.8	8.9	13.9	13.9	5.4	0.4
1983	201.5	2.1	199.1	18.2	10.6	14.9	14.9	8.9	0.6
1984	217.4	2.6	218.0	20.2	12.6	13.4	13.4	12.2	1.0
1985	219.7	3.9	204.0	18.9	13.5	13.6	13.6	14.1	1.6
1986	216.5	3.0	222.7	18.7	14.6	13.3	13.3	14.7	2.2
1987	227.0	3.3	241.1	22.5	15.5	12.9	12.9	16.8	3.0
1988	234.6	3.0	271.3	23.8	18.0	14.5	14.5	21.8	3.9
1989	239.2	2.8	331.0	26.7	19.9	23.3	17.2	24.7	4.6
1990	264.6	3.1	356.1	27.6	21.7	26.8	20.4	25.8	5.1
1991	279.7	3.3	368.4	29.3	23.9	33.9	24.8	27.9	5.6
1992	281.9	3.4	381.4	34.0	24.5	35.9	27.3	30.0	6.4
1993	284.1	3.8	418.8	39.6	22.5	36.7	28.2	31.4	7.0
1994	249.2	3.8	350.0	48.8	22.2	34.4	24.8	31.2	7.6
1995	259.8	3.3	397.3	46.8	20.6	39.8	28.9	28.5	8.1
1996	237.4	2.9	403.2	51.3	21.0	38.2	27.3	24.7	7.8
1997	237.5	2.7	408.8	54.8	22.2	39.9	27.8	23.8	7.7
1998	239.3	2.8	403.8	59.5	22.7	43.4	30.3	17.9	7.6
1999	201.0	2.8	419.8	60.2	24.0	46.1	30.2	15.8	7.6
2000	144.2	3.8	466.3	66.0	30.3	50.5	30.9	16.0	7.5
2001	104.9	4.3	491.0	71.9	42.9	55.9	33.0	15.6	7.4
2002	82.3	4.6	507.4	78.7	55.1	60.9	35.2	15.2	7.4
2003	58.0	3.3	486.7	84.1	63.3	60.6	35.2	16.2	7.1
2004	70.2	2.9	444.1	90.9	70.0	57.4	34.0	15.9	6.7
2005	94.9	2.5	373.1	93.9	64.2	53.3	31.7	16.0	6.4
2006	109.2	2.2	341.2	88.7	61.9	45.3	26.9	15.2	5.4
2007	102.1	2.2	340.1	91.1	62.2	47.9	27.1	15.6	6.0
2008	125.5	2.2	321.3	89.8	66.4	45.1	25.9	15.2	6.1
2009	124.8	1.8	317.1	90.3	67.4	47.2	27.6	15.4	5.8
2010	115.7	1.6	303.0	85.4	64.1	46.3	27.5	15.1	6.3
2011	121.8	1.4	296.9	87.8	64.0	44.4	27.6	15.1	6.1
2012	113.8	1.3	279.9	84.3	65.1	43.2	27.3	15.2	6.4
2013	96.1	1.0	266.9	79.5	61.5	41.8	27.9	17.5	6.4
2014	63.9	0.7	236.2	74.5	59.5	39.3	26.9	19.7	6.8
2015	62.6	0.6	205.1	71.4	57.2	36.4	25.2	19.6	6.6
2016	52.8	0.6	183.6	66.1	45.7	30.4	24.4	18.3	5.4
2017	41.1	0.5	156.8	61.1	37.4	26.4	21.7	15.7	4.5
2018	34.1	0.4	130.6	49.9	31.1	17.5	15.1	11.2	3.0
2019	28.8	0.3	111.5	48.9	26.4	5.1	3.4	9.6	3.0

注：1. 肉类产量1988年及以前为猪牛羊肉产量。
2. 2006年及以前水产品产量为淡水鱼产量，2007年以后含远洋捕捞量。水产品数据由北京市农业农村局提供。

Note: a) Output of meat in and before 1988 was the output of pork, beef and mutton.
b) Output of aquatic products was output of fresh water fish in and before 2006, and long-range fishing has been included since 2007. Figures of aquatic products were provided by Beijing Municipal Bureau of Agriculture and Rural Affairs.

11-6 平均每一从业人员创造农、林、牧、渔业产值(1990-2019年) AVERAGE OUTPUT VALUE OF AGRICULTURE, FORESTRY, ANIMAL PRODUCTION AND HUNTING, FISHING CREATED BY EACH PERSON (1990-2019)

单位：元 (yuan)

年 份 Year	农林牧渔业总产值 Total Output Value of Agriculture, Forestry, Animal Production and Hunting, Fishing	#农 业 Agriculture	#林 业 Forestry	#畜牧业 Animal Production and Hunting	#渔 业 Fishing
1990	8507	5537	1540	54837	22729
1991	9523	5722	2807	68268	26442
1992	11329	6678	3826	78905	33689
1993	13859	8271	4558	92901	39518
1994	21002	12461	6507	139136	39182
1995	25110	15760	5750	156332	47266
1996	25250	15504	6741	173404	53133
1997	26101	15605	6886	169541	56211
1998	25817	15653	7724	124279	68379
1999	25396	15621	8398	101869	63684
2000	27061	16454	8416	99481	65223
2001	29772	16838	12287	109151	76321
2002	33313	18193	15209	116799	86784
2003	37770	19579	14634	129862	92879
2004	40569	20934	12376	153518	98619
2005	40834	22700	12496	156911	96184
2006	36559	21147	17398	166889	195867
2007	44276	25892	19324	177359	126998
2008	49175	28405	22031	212910	122318
2009	51750	33061	18507	215008	128750
2010	54579	35130	17886	228814	164441
2011	62556	38613	20344	285988	155637
2012	70258	40585	59852	282916	175234
2013	77516	43643	81323	294659	179937
2014	81816	42790	98094	313314	199704
2015	74570	45000	60007	292513	183929
2016	66069	38680	69071	308089	168466
2017	63838	36110	75790	328636	173260
2018	65896	34106	116210	330368	123936
2019	66477	32357	136943	352263	122272

11-7 耕地面积
ARABLE LAND AREA

单位：公顷 (hectare)

项　目	Item	2018	2017
年初耕地总资源	**Total Arable Land Resources at the Beginning of the Year**	**213730.65**	**216345.43**
年内增加	**Increase in the Year**	**398.45**	**392.94**
#土地综合整治	Comprehensive Land Improvement	189.12	373.01
农业结构调整	Agricultural Structure Adjustment	209.33	0.02
年内减少	**Decrease in the Year**	**1288.50**	**3007.72**
#建设占用	Occupied by Construction	1206.39	860.49
灾害损毁	Disaster Damage		2147.23
生态退耕	Farmland Converted for EcologicalPreservation		
农业结构调整	Agricultural Structure Adjustment	82.11	
年末耕地面积	**Total Arable Land Resources at the End of the Year**	**212840.60**	**213730.65**
水　田	Paddy Field	1861.38	1872.46
水浇地	Irrigable Land	161040.63	161737.93
其　他	Others	49938.59	50120.26

资料来源：北京市规划和自然资源委员会。
Source: Beijing Municipal Commission of Planning and Natural Resources.

11－8 农业观光园、乡村旅游、种业和设施农业(2005－2019年)

项 目	Item	2005	2006
农业观光园	**Agricultural Sightseeing Gardens**		
农业观光园个数 (个)	Number of Agricultural Sightseeing Gardens (unit)	1012	1230
高峰期从业人员 (人)	Employed Persons in Peak Production Period (person)	40729	52828
接待人次 (万人次)	Visits Received (10000 person-times)	892.5	1210.6
经营总收入 (亿元)	Total Operating Income (100 million yuan)	7.9	10.5
乡村旅游	**Rural Tourism**		
从事乡村旅游实际经营接待户 (户)	Number of Actual Operating Households in Rural Tourism Reception (household)	7268	8726
高峰期从业人员 (人)	Employed Persons in Peak Production Period of the Term (person)	14070	18253
乡村旅游接待人次 (万人次)	Number of Visits Received by Rural Tourism (10000 person-times)	758.9	982.5
乡村旅游总收入 (亿元)	Total Income of Rural Tourism (100 million yuan)	3.1	3.7
种 业	**Seed Industry**		
种业收入 (亿元)	Income (100 million yuan)	5.9	7.7
#销往外埠收入	Sales to Other Areas		
#牧业收入	Income from Animal Production and Hunting		
设施农业	**Facility Agriculture**		
设施农业实际利用占地面积 (公顷)	Actual Area Utilized by Facility Agriculture (hectare)	15645	17832
设施农业播种面积 (公顷)	Sown Area of Facility Agriculture (hectare)		
设施农业产值 (亿元)	Output Value of Facility Agriculture (100 million yuan)	18.6	21.1

注：2018年及以前乡村旅游为民俗旅游口径；2019年起，乡村旅游统计范围除包括民俗旅游农户外，还包括乡镇及乡镇以下范围内为乡村旅游服务的宾馆、饭店、旅游商品专卖店等。

AGRICULTURAL SIGHTSEEING GARDENS, RURAL TOURISM, BREEDING OF SEEDS AND FACILITY AGRICULTURE (2005-2019)

2007	2008	2009	2010	2011	2012	2013	2014	2015	2016	2017	2018	2019
1302	1332	1294	1303	1300	1283	1299	1301	1328	1258	1216	1172	948
51392	49366	49504	42561	46038	48906	50406	47088	42617	40349	39624	39726	33815
1446.8	1498.2	1597.4	1774.9	1842.9	1939.9	1944.4	1911.2	1903.3	2250.5	2105.3	1897.6	1538.0
13.1	13.6	15.2	17.8	21.7	26.9	27.4	24.9	26.3	28.0	29.9	27.3	23.2
10323	9151	8705	7979	8396	8367	8530	8863	8941	9026	8363	7783	7354
20750	19421	19790	16856	18232	18705	19578	21493	22313	22215	22455	21203	23720
1167.6	1205.6	1393.1	1553.6	1668.9	1695.8	1806.5	1914.2	2139.7	2297.4	2232.1	2042.3	1920.1
5.0	5.3	6.1	7.3	8.7	9.1	10.2	11.3	12.9	14.4	14.2	13.0	14.4
9.9	10.9	12.8	14.6	18.1	16.1	14.0	14.0	12.7	14.0	12.7	12.4	15.1
4.0	5.8	7.3	8.1	11.7	9.7	8.2	8.0	6.6	7.7	6.7	7.4	10.6
8.3	9.3	10.6	12.1	15.1	13.6	12.6	12.5	11.2	12.9	11.1	10.8	13.3
18022	17051	18762	18323	18616	19059	18852	18232	17397	15404	14941	13880	12900
30331	33889	36203	36811	38006	37797	38763	38115	41088	37666	35740	32324	27068
28.1	28.2	33.9	40.7	45.6	52.0	57.3	51.3	55.5	54.4	54.5	51.7	47.1

Note: In and before 2018, rural tourism was uniformly called folk-custom tourism; since 2019, the scope of statistics of rural tourism covered not only the peasant households engaging in folk-custom tourism, but also the hotels, restaurants and tourists commodities stores, etc. at or below township level that served the rural tourism.

11-9 农业生产条件
PRODUCTIVE CONDITIONS OF AGRICULTURE

项目		Item		2019	2018	2019年为2018年% 2019 as % of 2018
主要农业机械拥有量		**Possession of Major Agricultural Machinery**				
农业机械总动力	(万千瓦)	Total Power of Agricultural Machinery	(10000 kW)	122.8	125.6	97.8
大中型拖拉机	(混合台)	Large and Medium-sized Tractors	(unit)	4314	4699	91.8
小型拖拉机	(台)	Mini Tractors	(unit)	2124	2232	95.2
机引农具	(台)	Tractor-propelled Farm Tools	(unit)	12223	12251	99.8
机动喷雾器	(部)	Motorized Sprayers	(unit)	11523	11363	101.4
联合收割机	(台)	Combine Harvesters	(unit)	975	1341	72.7
机动脱粒机	(台)	Motorized Shellers	(unit)	3742	3798	98.5
米面加工机	(台)	Processing Machines of Rice and Flour	(unit)	3196	3220	99.3
机动挤奶器	(台)	Motorized Milkers	(unit)	1570	1599	98.2
饲料粉碎机	(台)	Fodder Grinders	(unit)	2219	2496	88.9
农业机械作业面积		**Operation Area of Agricultural Machinery**				
机耕面积	(公顷)	Cultivated Area by Machinery	(hectare)	18052	20083	89.9
占全部耕地面积比重	(%)	Share in the Total Arable Land	(%)	95.8	97.4	
机播面积	(公顷)	Sown Area by Machinery	(hectare)	46820	51819	90.4
占播种面积比重	(%)	Share in the Total Sown Area	(%)	95.1	96.5	
机收面积	(公顷)	Harvest Area by Machinery	(hectare)	38554	42084	91.6
占收获面积比重	(%)	Share in the Total Harvest Area	(%)	78.3	77.7	
农村用电量及小水电		**Rural Electricity Consumption and Small Hydropower Stations**				
农村用电量	(万千瓦时)	Rural Electricity Consumption	(10000 kWh)	677672	651370	104.0
农田水利		**Irrigation and Water Conservancy**				
排灌用动力机械	(台)	Irrigation Machinery	(unit)	31336	32788	95.6
排灌用动力机械动力	(万千瓦)	Power of Irrigation Machinery	(10000 kW)	38.8	39.9	97.1
机(电)井	(万眼)	Motor-pumped Wells	(10000 unit)	33136	32396	102.3
有效灌溉面积	(公顷)	Effective Irrigation Area	(hectare)	109237	109672	99.6
化肥施用量(折纯)		**Consumption of Chemical Fertilizers (converted into net amount)**				
化肥施用量	(吨)	Consumption of Chemical Fertilizers	(ton)	61727.0	72934.1	84.6
#氮肥	(吨)	Nitrogenous Fertilizers	(ton)	22481.3	30163.0	74.5
磷肥	(吨)	Phosphate Fertilizers	(ton)	3351.2	4008.1	83.6
钾肥	(吨)	Potash Fertilizers	(ton)	3372.0	3857.1	87.4

注：1．农村小水电站是指乡村两级小水电站实有数。
2．主要农业机械拥有量、农业机械作业面积及排灌动力机械数据由北京市农业农村局提供。
3．机(电)井、固定机电排灌站及有效灌溉面积数据由北京市水务局提供。

Note: a) Figures of rural small hydropower stations refer to actual number of small hydropower stations at township and village level.
b) Figures of possession of major agricultural machinery, operation area of agricultural machinery, and irrigation machiner, are provided by Beijing Municipal Bureau of Agriculture and Rural Affairs.
c) Figures of motor-pumped wells,drainage and irrigation stations with fixed machinery and effective irrigation area are provided by Beijing Water Authority.

11-10 农林牧渔业总产值
GROSS OUTPUT VALUE OF AGRICULTURE, FORESTRY, ANIMAL PRODUCTION AND HUNTING, FISHING

单位：万元 (10000 yuan)

项　目	Item	总产值 Gross Output Value 2019	2018	2019年为2018年% 2019 as % of 2018
合　计	**Total**	**2817044.6**	**2967694.8**	**94.9**
农　业	**Agriclture**	**1023274.8**	**1147488.9**	**89.2**
谷　物	Cereal	55772.3	64367.8	86.6
豆　类	Beans	2458.5	3316.6	74.1
经济作物	Cash Crops	2481.2	3335.3	74.4
蔬菜、食用菌	Vegetables and Edible Mushromms	424161.4	523757.2	81.0
水果（含瓜果类）	Fruits (including melons)	515878.8	423667.5	121.8
其　他	Others	22522.6	129044.5	17.5
林　业	**Forestry**	**1156294.1**	**951268.5**	**121.6**
牧　业	**Animal Production and Hunting**	**493203.1**	**719739.0**	**68.5**
牲畜饲养	Animal Breeding	196601.9	227874.4	86.3
养　猪	Hogs	59379.5	279587.0	21.2
家禽饲养	Poultry	231685.1	187359.9	123.7
#禽　蛋	Poultry Eggs	128415.6	134408.8	95.5
其　他	Others	5536.6	24917.6	22.2
渔　业	**Fishing**	**52821.4**	**61497.2**	**85.9**
农林牧渔专业及辅助性活动	**Professional and Supporting Activities of Agricultare, Forestry,Animal Production and Hunting,Fishing**	**91451.2**	**87701.2**	**104.3**

11-11 主要农作物播种面积及产量
SOWN AREA AND OUTPUT OF MAJOR CROPS

项 目	Item	2019 播种面积(公顷) Sown Areas (hectare)	2019 单产(公斤/公顷) Output Per Unit (kg/hectare)	2019 总产量(吨) Total Output (ton)	2018 播种面积(公顷) Sown Areas (hectare)	2018 单产(公斤/公顷) Output Per Unit (kg/hectare)	2018 总产量(吨) Total Output (ton)
粮 食	**Grain**	**46515.3**	**6183.1**	**287609.2**	**55638.9**	**6136.7**	**341437.4**
按季节分	By Season						
夏 粮	Summer Grain	8212.7	5427.6	44575.2	10140.4	5274.9	53490.0
秋 粮	Autumn Grain	38302.6	6345.1	243034.0	45498.5	6328.7	287947.4
按品种分	Grouped by Variety						
稻 谷	Rice	148.2	6651.6	985.8	168.3	6752.7	1136.7
冬小麦	Winter Wheat	7998.2	5493.6	43938.9	9745.4	5370.8	52340.3
玉 米	Corn	33663.1	6781.7	228291.3	40089.6	6770.3	271416.4
薯 类	Tubers	1164.6	5533.1	6444.0	1181.1	5555.3	6561.5
大 豆	Soybeans	1402.8	2019.1	2832.5	1851.0	1986.7	3677.4
棉 花	**Cotton**	**6.8**	**1073.5**	**7.3**	**7.5**	**1066.7**	**8.0**
油 料	**Oil-bearing Crops**	**1232.2**	**2483.8**	**3060.4**	**1580.7**	**2636.4**	**4167.3**
#花 生	Peanuts	869.5	2830.1	2460.9	1148.6	2774.9	3187.2
中草药材	**Chinese medicine herbs**	**2032.1**	**861.2**	**1750.0**	**2067.7**	**383.4**	**792.8**
蔬菜及食用菌	**Vegetables and Edible Mushrooms**	**31175.7**	**35750.1**	**1114534.1**	**36010.2**	**36254.0**	**1305512.4**
瓜类及草莓	**Melons & Strawberries**	**3252.9**	**44001.6**	**143132.9**	**3603.8**	**41829.9**	**150746.8**
#西 瓜	Watermelons	2383.1	52442.7	124976.9	2757.0	48034.6	132431.3
饲 料	**Forage**	**3128.8**	**31444.2**	**98382.7**	**2441.4**		
#牧 草	Forage Grass	14.5	19700.5	285.0	20.6		
花 卉	**Flowers**	**2531.9**			**2444.8**		

11-12 林业及干鲜果品生产
FORESTRY, NUTS AND FRESH FRUIT PRODUCTION

项目	Item	2019	2018	2019年为2018年% 2019 as % of 2018
林业生产	**Forestry**			
营造林面积 (公顷)	Sulviculture and Afforestation Area (hectare)	138975	126240	110.1
#人工造林面积	Artificial Afforestation Area	18698	18427	101.5
育苗面积 (公顷)	Seedling Growing Area (hectare)	14792	14921	99.1
果类生产	**Fruits**			
干鲜果总产量 (吨)	Output of Nuts and Fresh Fruit (ton)	488802	498910	98.0
干　果	Nuts	32904	35078	93.8
#核　桃	Walnuts	9574	9946	96.3
板　栗	Chinese Chestnuts	21689	23442	92.5
鲜　果	Fresh Fruits	455898	463832	98.3
#苹　果	Apples	47126	42626	110.6
梨	Pears	75358	78522	96.0
葡　萄	Grapes	20556	21577	95.3
柿　子	Persimmons	18642	23415	79.6
桃	Peaches	250736	250626	100.0
年末实有果园面积 (公顷)	**Actual Orchard Area (year-end) (hectare)**	**43821**	**46407**	**94.4**

注：本表中营造林面积为人工造林、飞播造林、封山育林、退化林修复、人工更新、森林抚育面积之和。
资料来源：林业生产数据由北京市园林绿化局提供。
Note: The Silviculture and Afforestation Area in this table refers to the sum of the area of the artificial afforestation, air seeding and afforestation, closing hillsides for afforestation, restoration of degraded forest, artificial regeneration and forest tending.
Source: Figures of forestry are from Beijing Municipal Bureau of Landscape and Forestry.

11-13 牲畜饲养及畜产品产量
LIVESTOCK BREEDING AND OUTPUT

项 目		Item		2019	2018	2019年为2018年% 2019 as % of 2018
畜禽存栏		**Amount of Livestock and Poultry on Hand**				
大牲畜	(万头)	Large Animals	(10000 heads)	8.5	10.9	77.4
#牛		Cattle and Buffaloes		8.1	10.6	76.7
猪	(万头)	Hogs	(10000 heads)	13.2	45.4	29.0
羊	(万只)	Sheep	(10000 units)	16.9	24.2	69.6
山 羊		Goats		4.8	5.7	84.6
绵 羊		Sheep		12.1	18.6	65.0
家 禽	(万只)	Poultry	(10000 units)	974.8	990.7	98.4
#产蛋鸡		Hens		877.5	887.9	98.8
肉 鸡		Chickens		65.2	58.6	111.2
鸭		Ducks		31.2	43.0	72.5
兔	(万只)	Rabbits	(10000 units)	0.3	0.7	49.2
畜禽出栏		**Amount of Livestock and Poultry Marketed**				
牛	(万头)	Cattle	(10000 heads)	4.2	5.3	78.9
猪	(万头)	Hogs	(10000 heads)	28.4	169.4	16.7
羊	(万只)	Sheep	(10000 units)	22.6	35.6	63.5
畜禽产品产量		**Output of Livestock and Poultry Products**				
肉类产量	(万吨)	Output of Meat	(10000 tons)	5.1	17.5	29.4
#猪 肉		Pork		2.3	13.5	16.9
牛 肉		Beef		0.7	0.9	79.2
羊 肉		Mutton		0.4	0.6	64.1
牛奶产量	(万吨)	Output of Milk	(10000 tons)	26.4	31.1	85.1
禽 蛋	(万吨)	Poultry Eggs	(10000 tons)	9.6	11.2	85.5
#鸡 蛋		Eggs		9.4	11.1	85.4
蜂 蜜	(吨)	Honey	(ton)	1229.4	1032.0	119.1

11－14 水产品生产
AQUATIC PRODUCTS

项　目	Item	2019	2018	2019年为2018年% 2019 as % of 2018
渔业水域面积　(公顷)	**Area of Fishery Waters (hectare)**	**33821**	**31290**	**108.1**
#淡水养殖面积	Freshwater Agriculture	2178	2606	83.6
#池　塘	Puddles and Ponds	2177	2568	84.8
水产品产量　(吨)	**Output of Aquatic Products (ton)**	**30190**	**30028**	**100.5**
#淡水鱼产量	Output of Freshwater Fish	23529	28322	83.1
#大水库	Large Reservoirs	2450	2289	107.0
池　塘	Puddles and Ponds	21079	23267	90.6

资料来源：北京市农业农村局。
Source: Beijing Municipal Bureau of Agriculture and Rural Affairs.

11－15 种业生产
STATISTICS FOR PRODUCTION OF SEED INDUSTRY

项　目	Item	产　量 Output			收　入(万元) Income (10000 yuan)		
		2019	2018	2019年为2018年% 2019 as % of 2018	2019	2018	2019年为2018年% 2019 as % of 2018
合　计	**Total**				**150813.6**	**124351.6**	**121.3**
农　业	**Agriculture**				**9495.8**	**8673.1**	**109.5**
#小麦种　(公斤)	Wheat Seeds (kg)	693600	622000	111.5	144	141	102.5
玉米种　(公斤)	Corn Seeds (kg)	70466	68219	103.3	47	47	99.4
蔬菜种　(公斤)	Vegetable Seeds (kg)	102989	157045	65.6	1192	3227	37.0
林　业	**Forestry**				**6609.1**	**5046.2**	**131.0**
#树　苗　(百株)	Saplings (100 units)	5517.1	4484.1	123.0	6609.1	5046.2	131.0
牧　业	**Animal Production and Hunting**				**132526.1**	**108381.4**	**122.3**
#种　猪　(头)	Boars (head)	4393	71718	6.1	2057	16710	12.3
种雏禽　(万只)	Breeding Birds (10000 units)	2115.3	2734.4	77.4	74732.4	42324.4	176.6
种　蛋　(万枚)	Breeding Eggs (10000 units)	31499.6	29456.0	106.9	45785.6	39356.2	116.3
渔　业	**Fishing**				**2182.6**	**2250.9**	**97.0**
#种鱼苗　(万尾)	Breeding Fish Fry (10000 units)	4372.0	9836.9	44.4	2182.6	2246.4	97.2

11—16 设施农业(2019年)
FACILITY AGRICULTURE (2019)

项　　目	Item	设施农业播种面积(公顷) Sown Area of Facility Agriculture (hectare)	设施农业产量(吨) Output of Facility Agriculture (ton)	设施农业产值(万元) Output Value of Facility Agriculture (10000 yuan)
合　计	**Total**	**27068.5**		**471035.8**
温　室	**Greenhousse**	**13565.0**		**317321.5**
蔬菜及食用菌	Vegetables and Edible Mushrooms	11608.1	430732.0	205231.3
花卉苗木	Flowers and Saplings	706.7		35143.2
#切　花	Cut Flowers	66.3	85367.4	2324.0
盆　花	Potted Flowers	617.2	1154428.4	32365.1
瓜果类	Melons	851.2	18203.8	61223.5
园林水果	Fruits	350.1	2157.8	8400.5
其　他	Others	48.9		7323.0
大　棚	**Greenhouse Garden**	**12256.6**		**141896.0**
蔬菜及食用菌	Vegetables and Edible Mushrooms	9789.8	334045.4	87165.2
花卉苗木	Flowers and Sapling	240.1		8050.8
#切　花	Cut Flowers	64.3	189402.2	1471.5
盆　花	Potted Flowers	166.8	397675.5	6577.3
瓜果类	Melons	1959.3	104757.2	40561.6
园林水果	Fruits	214.0	1473.1	3901.1
其　他	Other	53.3		2217.3
中小棚	**Medium and Small Shed**	**1246.9**		**11818.3**
蔬菜及食用菌	Vegetables and Edible Mushrooms	1024.3	26061.7	8092.2
花卉苗木	Flowers and Sapling	33.6		1178.7
#切　花	Cut Flowers	5.9	5680.0	32.8
盆　花	Potted Flowers	27.7	32246.4	1145.9
瓜果类	Melons	185.6	7106.5	2534.4
园林水果	Fruits	3.5	4.5	13.0
其　他	Other			

注：切花产量的计量单位是百枝，盆花产量的计量单位是百盆。
Note: Cut flowers output are measured in 100 ones; and potted flowers, 100 pots.

11-17 乡镇企业各行业基本情况(2019年)
BASIC STATISTICS FOR TOWN AND TOWNSHIP ENTERPRISES IN DIFFERENT SECTORS (2019)

项 目	Item	企业个数(个) Number of Enterprises (unit)	从业人员(人) Employed Persons (person)	总收入(万元) Total Income (10000 yuan)	利润总额(万元) Total Profits (10000 yuan)
合 计	**Total**	**66724**	**500160**	**39672372**	**2045547**
农 业	Agriculture	2002	13504	332840	12273
工 业	Industry	19791	25221	30919118	1356695
建筑业	Construction	2828	4038	3693871	47453
交通运输、仓储和邮政业	Transportation, Storage and Post	3074	71354	1526083	167979
批发零售业	Wholesale and Retail Trade	14147	77300	1372293	44454
住宿及餐饮业	Lodging and Catering Services	5179	47112	96665	28640
居民服务、其他服务和娱乐业	Household Services, Other Services and Entertainment	17725	172896	437586	124566
其 他	Others	1978	88735	1293916	263487

资料来源：北京市经济和信息化局。
Source: Beijing Municipal Bureau of Economy and Information Technology.

11-18 乡镇企业出口供货情况
GOODS SUPPLIES FOR EXPORT OF TOWN AND TOWNSHIP ENTERPRISES

单位：万元 (10000 yuan)

项 目	Item	2019	2018
合 计	**Total**	**569262**	**709987**
化 工	Chemical Products	12077	15062
机 械	Machinery	280814	350233
矿 产	Mineral Products	4026	5021
轻 工	Light Industry	59584	74313
食 品	Food	28594	35662
土产畜产	Local and Livestock Products	14256	17780
纺织服装	Textile and Garments	39275	48984
工 艺 品	Artworks	5431	6773
其 他	Others	125207	156159

资料来源：北京市经济和信息化局。
Source: Beijing Municipal Bureau of Economy and Information Technology.

11-19 农村双层经营主要指标情况(2019年)
MAIN INDICATORS OF RURAL DOUBLE-LAYER MANAGEMENT SYSTEM (2019)

项目		Item		2019
集体经济组织情况		**Organizations of Collective Economy**		
乡镇级集体经济组织数	(个)	Number of Township-level Collective Economic Organizations	(unit)	184
村级集体经济组织数	(个)	Number of Village-level Collective Economic Organizations	(unit)	3944
汇总农户数	(户)	Total Number of Peasant Households	(household)	1336110
汇总人口数	(人)	Total Number of Population	(person)	3130272
劳动力总人数	(人)	Total Number of Labor Force	(person)	1824027
就业率	(%)	Employment Rate	(%)	93.2
集体经济经营情况		**Operation of Collective Economy**		
集体经济总收入	(亿元)	Gross Income of Collective Economy	(100 million yuan)	673.8
#主营业务收入		Of which: Main Business Income		418.3
利润总额	(亿元)	Total Profit	(100 million yuan)	31.0
净利润	(亿元)	Net Profit	(100 million yuan)	17.8
可供分配的利润	(亿元)	Profit Available for Distribution	(100 million yuan)	-85.9
未分配利润	(亿元)	Undistributed Profit	(100 million yuan)	-115.1
资产总计	(亿元)	Total Assets	(100 million yuan)	8349.3
乡镇级		Township Level		3198.6
村级		Village Level		5150.8
所有者权益合计	(亿元)	Total Owner's Equity	(100 million yuan)	2648.5
乡镇级		Township Level		533.7
村级		Village Level		2114.8
人均所有者权益	(元)	Per-capita Owner's Equity	(yuan)	84610
农户收入情况		**Income of Peasant Households**		
农户总收入	(亿元)	Total Income	(100 million yuan)	1459.8
农户所得总额	(亿元)	Total Earnings	(100 million yuan)	836.2
人均所得	(元)	Per-capita Earnings	(yuan)	26715
农户从集体经济获取的所得总额	(亿元)	Total Earnings of Peasant Household from Collective Economy	(100 million yuan)	189.5
农户经营休闲农业及乡村旅游收入	(亿元)	Income of Peasant Household from Operating Leisure Agriculture and Rural Tourism	(100 million yuan)	8.5

注：双层经营指农民家庭分散经营和集体统一经营相结合。
资料来源：北京市农业农村局。
Note: Double-layer management system refers to a system with integration of decentralized management of peasant households and collective unified management.
Source: Beijing Municipal Bureau of Agriculture and Rural Affairs.

主要统计指标解释

农林牧渔业总产值 是以货币表现的农林牧渔业的全部产品总量和对农林牧渔业生产活动进行的各种支持性服务活动的价值。

耕地 指种植农作物的土地，包括熟地，新开发、复垦、整理地，休闲地（含轮歇地、轮作地）；以种植农作物（含蔬菜）为主，间有零星果树、桑树或其他树木的土地；平均每年能保证收获一季的已垦滩地和海涂。耕地中包括南方宽度<1.0米、北方宽度<小于2.0米固定的沟、渠、路和地坎(埂)；临时种植药材、草皮、花卉、苗木等的耕地，以及其他临时改变用途的耕地。

农作物播种面积 指实际播种或移植有农作物的面积。凡是实际种植有农作物的面积，不论种植在耕地上还是种植在非耕地上，均包括在农作物播种面积中。在播种季节基本结束后，因遭灾而重新改种和补种的农作物面积，也包括在内。

设施农业 指以工厂化生产方式，建造人工设施，改变气候条件，提高农作物抵御自然灾害的能力，改良生物特性，使作物实现错季或反季节生产，达到农作物均衡生产的目的。

农业机械总动力 指主要用于农、林、牧、渔业的各种动力机械的动力总和。包括耕作机械、排灌机械、收获机械、农用运输机械、植物保护机械、牧业机械、渔业机械和其他农用机械[内燃机按引擎马力折成瓦（特）计算，电动机按功率折成瓦（特）计算]。不包括专门用于乡、镇、村、组办工业、基本建设、非农业运输、科学实验和教学等非农业生产方面用的动力机械与作业机械。

农村用电量 指本年度内，扣除在农村中的国有经济工业交通、基建等单位的用电量以后的农村生产和生活的全年用电总量（计量单位千瓦小时，按全年累计数统计），即包括国家电网供电，也包括农村自办电站供电量。

农用化肥施用量 指本年度内实际用于农业生产的化学肥料数量，包括氮肥、磷肥、钾肥和复合肥。施用量要求按折纯量计算数量，即各类化学肥料的实际施用数量按其含氮、含五氧化二磷、含氧化钾的比例折成百分之百计算。

折纯量＝实物量×某种化肥有效成份含量的百分比

乡镇及行政村单位常住户数 指长期（一年以上）居住在乡镇（不包括城关镇）行政管理区域内的住户，还包括居住在城关镇所辖行政村范围内的农村住户。户口不在本地而在本地居住一年及以上的住户也包括在本地农村住户内；有本地户口，但举家外出谋生一年以上的住户，无论是否保留承包耕地都不包括在本地农村住户范围内。不包括乡村地区内的国有经济的机关、团体、学校、企业、事业单位的集体户。

乡镇及行政村常住人口 指乡村地区常住居民户数中的常住人口数，即经常在家或在家居住6个月以上，而且经济和生活与本户连成一体的人口。外出从业人员在外居住时间虽然在6个月以上，但收入主要带回家中，经济与本户连为一体，仍视为家庭常住人口；在家居住，生活和本户连成一体的国家职工、退休人员也为家庭常住人口。但是现役军人、中专及以上（走读生除外）的在校学生、以及常年在外（不包括探亲、看病等）且已有稳定的职业与居住场所的外出从业人员，不应当作家庭常住人口。

乡镇及行政村从业人员 指全部乡镇及行政村人口中16岁以上实际参加生产经营活动并取得实物或货币收入的人员，既包括劳动年龄内经常参加劳动的人员，也包括超过劳动年龄但经常参加劳动的人员。但不包括户口在家的在外学生、现役军人和丧失劳动能力的人，也不包括待业人员和家务劳动者。从业人员按从事主业时间最长（时间相同按收入）分为农业从业人员，工业从业人员，建筑业从业人员，交通运输仓储及邮政业从业人员，信息传输、计算机服务和软件业，批发与零售业从业人员，住宿和餐饮业从业人员，其它从业人员。

Explanatory Notes on Main Statistical Indicators

Gross Output Value of Agriculture, Forestry, Animal Production and Hunting, Fishing refers to the monetary value of all products of agriculture, forestry, animal production and hunting, fishing, as well as the monetary value of services provided in support of all the above-mentioned sectors.

Arable Land refers to the land suitable for growing crops, including cultivated land; any land newly opened up, reclaimed and cultivated; fallow land (including swidden and rotated land); land mostly for growing crops (including vegetables), supplemented by mulberry trees, fruit trees, and other trees; cultivated bottomland and shallows that can secure an average of one harvest annually. Arable land includes furrows, ditches, paths and field ridges less than 1m wide in the southern part of China, or less than 2m wide in the northern part. It also covers arable land that is temporarily for growing medicinal materials, turf, flowers, nursery stock and other uses.

Sown Area refers to the area of all lands actually sown or transplanted with crops, including both the cultivated and non-cultivated land. Area of lands re-planted after seedtime has passed due to natural disasters is also included.

Facility Agriculture means to produce in an industrialized manner, put in place facilities of manual intervention, change climate conditions, increase the crops' capability to resist natural disasters, and improve the crops' biological property, so as to stagger harvest seasons, create anti-season production, and achieve balanced production of crops.

Total Power of Agricultural Machinery refers to the total power of motive power machines used in agriculture, forestry, animal production and hunting, fishing sectors, including machinery for ploughing, irrigation and drainage, harvesting, agricultural transport, plant protection, animal production and hunting, fishing and other farm machinery (The horsepower of internal combustion engines is converted into watts, and the output of electric motors is also converted into watts). Motive power machines and operating machines exclusively used for non-agricultural production activities, such as industrial operations run by counties, towns, villages and teams, capital construction, non-agricultural transport, scientific experiments and teaching, are not included.

Rural Electricity Consumption refers to the total rural production and rural residents' electricity consumption in the whole year (unit of measurement: kilowatt-hour; the data representing accumulative usage of the year), deducting the consumption by entities like state-owned industry, transport, and infrastructure construction. The data cover both power supplies by the State Grid and by the rural self-run power stations.

Consumption of Chemical Fertilizers refers to the total quantity of chemical fertilizers applied in agricultural production within the year, including nitrogenous fertilizer, phosphate fertilizer, potash fertilizer, and compound fertilizer. The amount of chemical fertilizers applied is calculated in terms of net amount, that is, to use the gross weight of the respective fertilizers in calculating the quantity of effective ingredients (e.g. nitrogen content in nitrogenous fertilizer, phosphorous pent oxide content in phosphate fertilizer, and potassium oxide content in potash fertilizer).

Net Amount = Physical Quantity× Content (%) of Effective Ingredients in Certain Chemical Fertilizer

Number of Resident Households in Towns and Administrative Villages refers to households living in the administrative areas of towns and villages (excluding township government premises) on a long-term basis (more than one year), including those living in administrative villages within township government premises. Households with non-local household registration but having been living locally for more than one year are also counted as local rural households; while households with local household registration but left to make a living elsewhere for more than one year, with or without contract lands, are not counted as local rural households. Collective households of state-owned organs, groups, schools, enterprises, and public institutions, as well as households living in grouped commercial residential quarters in rural areas are not included.

Permanent Population in Towns and Administrative Villages refers to the population of permanent households in rural areas, namely those who stay home regularly or live at home for more than 6 months with their economic life and livelihood incorporated into the household. Migrant workers who live away from home for more than 6 months but taking most of their earnings back home, with their economic life still incorporated into the household, are also counted as permanent population of the household; state employees and retirees who live locally with their life incorporated into the household are also considered permanent population. But soldiers in active service, enrolled students (externs excluded) in technical secondary schools or above, as well as migrant workers who lived away from home for years (excluding those who travel to visit their families or to seek medical care) with a stable job and residence elsewhere, are not regarded as permanent population.

Employ Persons in Towns and Administrative Villages refer to persons aged above 16 in all towns and administrative villages, who actually participate in productive and operating activities and earn incomes in kind or cash, including persons within the range of labor age and regularly participating in labor, and persons beyond the range of labor age but regularly participating in labor; while local registered students who left home for education, soldiers in active service, and people who lost the ability to work are not included, neither are the people waiting for employment or domestic workers. In terms of the length of employment period (or in terms of income if the employment periods are identical), employment falls into the following categories: agriculture, industry, construction, transportation, storage and post, information transmission, software and information technology services, wholesale and retail trade, accommodation and restaurants, and other sectors.

12

工　业
INDUSTRY

简要说明

一、主要内容

本章资料反映北京市工业基本情况，主要包括按登记注册类型、轻重工业、企业规模、行业大类等分组的主要经济指标数据。

具体指标包括单位数、工业总产值、资产总计、负债合计、营业收入、营业成本、税金及附加、利润总额、应交增值税、总资产贡献率、资产负债率、主要工业产品产量等。

二、统计范围

1984年以前农村的村及村以下办工业归属农业，1984年及以后划归工业。

1999年及以前，工业的统计范围按隶属关系划分为乡及乡以上独立核算工业企业和非独立核算生产单位、村办工业、城镇合作工业、农村合作工业、城镇个体工业、农村个体工业六大部分（1984年以前村办工业不在工业统计范围内）。

2000年及以后，工业统计调查范围由按隶属关系划分，改变为按企业规模划分。其中，2000-2006年规模以上工业统计范围为全部国有及年主营业务收入在500万元及以上非国有工业企业；2007-2010年为年主营业务收入在500万元及以上法人工业企业；2011年及以后为年主营业务收入在2000万元及以上法人工业企业。

三、有关统计标准的变化说明

（一）关于行业划分。2002年及以前，工业行业分类执行《国民经济行业分类及代码》(GB/T 4754- 94)标准，2003-2011年执行《国民经济行业分类标准》(GB/T 4754-2002)标准，2012-2017年执行《国民经济行业分类》(GB/T 4754-2011)标准，自2018年起执行《国民经济行业分类》(GB/T 4754-2017)标准。

与2002版相比，2011版《国民经济行业分类》标准中，将原“交通运输设备制造业”调整为“汽车制造业”，将原“通信设备、计算机及其他电子设备制造业”调整为“计算机、通信和其它电子设备制造业”，将原“石油加工业”与“炼焦、煤气及煤制品业”合并为“石油加工、炼焦和核燃料加工业”。

（二）关于企业标准划分。2010年以前企业大中小型划分执行2003年《统计上大中小型企业划分办法（暂行）》。2011年至2017年大中小微型企业划分标准执行国家统计局《关于统计上大中小微型企业划分办法》（国统字[2011]75号）；自2018年起，执行《统计上大中小微型企业划分办法（2017）》（国统字[2017]213号）。

四、关于历史数据调整

1993-2003年规模以上工业总产值历史资料根据北京市第一次全国经济普查的结果采用“趋势离差法”进行了修订，2004年为第一次全国经济普查数据，2008年为第二次全国经济普查数据，2013年为第三次全国经济普查数据，2018年为第四次全国经济普查数据。

Brief Introduction

I. Main Content

Data in this chapter show the basic situation of industry in Beijing, mainly including: major economic indicators grouped by type of registration, light or heavy industry, enterprise scale, and industries.

Specific indicators include: unit number, gross industrial output value, total assets, total liabilities, business income, business cost, business tax and surtax, total profits, payable VAT, contribution rate to total assets, asset-liability ratio, and output of main industrial products, etc.

II. Scope of Statistics

Prior to 1984, the rural industrial production run by villages and units subordinated to villages was classified as agriculture. Since 1984, it has been grouped into industry.

Before 1999, industrial statistics coverage was divided into six parts by administrative relationship, i.e. independent accounting industrial enterprises and non-independent accounting production units at the township-level and above, village-run industry, urban cooperative industry, rural cooperative industry, urban individual operated industry, and rural individual operated industry (village-run industry was not included in the industrial statistics before 1984).

In and after 2000, the scope of industrial statistics was grouped by enterprise scale instead of administrative relationship. Specifically, from 2000 to 2006, the scope of statistics of industry above designated size covers all state-owned enterprises and non-state-owned industrial enterprises with annual main business income of RMB 5 million and above; from 2007 to 2010, the scope of statistics covers the corporate industrial enterprises with annual main business income of RMB 5 million and above; since 2011, the scope of statistics covers the corporate industrial enterprises with annual main business income of RMB 20 million and above.

III. Changes in Relevant Statistical Standards

(I) Classification of Sectors: The standards in the *Classification and Codes of National Economic Sectors (GB/T 4754-94)* were implemented in the classification of industrial sectors before 2002. The standards in the *Standard for Classification of National Economic Sectors* (GB/T 4754-2002) were implemented from 2003 to 2011. The standards in the *Classification of National Economic Sectors* (GB/T 4754-2011) were implemented from 2012 to 2017. The standards in the *Classification of National Economic Sectors* (GB/T 4754-2017) are implemented since 2018.

Contrary to the 2002 version, in the standards in the *Classification of National Economic Sectors* 2011, the original manufacture of transport equipment was adjusted to "manufacture of motor vehicles, the original manufacture of communication equipment, computer and electronic equipment was adjusted to "manufacture of computer, communication equipment and other electronic equipment, and the original petroleum processing and coking, gas and coal products were combined into processing of petroleum ,coking, processing of nucleus fuel.

(II) Before 2010, the classification of small, medium and large-sized enterprises should comply with the standards in the *Measures for Statistical Classification of Small, Medium and Large-sized Enterprises (Temporary)* 2003. The classification of micro, small, medium and large-sized enterprises should comply with the standards in the *Measures for Statistical Classification of Micro, Small, Medium and Large-sized Enterprises* (G.T.Z. [2011] No. 75) of the National Bureau of Statistics from 2011 to 2017. Since 2018, the classification has been in line with the standards in the *Measures for Statistical Classification of Micro, Small, Medium and Large-sized Enterprises (2017)* (G.T.Z. [2017] No. 213).

IV. Adjustment to Historical Data

The historical data on gross output value of industry above designated size for the period between 1993 and 2003 had been revised based on results from the first national economic census in Beijing by the trend deviation method. The data for 2004 were collected from the first national economic census, the data for 2008 were collected from the second national economic census, the data for 2013 were collected from the third national economic census, and the data for 2018 were collected from the fourth national economic census.

12-1 规模以上工业总产值(1984—2019年)

单位：亿元

年 份 Year	合 计 Total	轻工业 Light Industry	重工业 Heavy Industry	#大中型工业 Medium and Large-sized Industry	#计算机、通信和其他电子设备制造业 Manufacture of Computers, Communication Equipment and Other Electronic Equipment	#汽 车制造业 Manufacture of Motor Vehicles	#电力、热力生产和供应业 Production and Supply of Electricity and Heating Power	#铁路、船舶、航空航天和其他运输设备制造业 Manufacture of Railway Locomotives, Building of Ships Manufacture Air and Spacecrafts and Other Transportation Equipment
1984	276.2	118.0	158.2	178.7				
1985	324.2	135.8	188.4	213.7				
1986	336.5	140.8	195.7	231.6	14.5	23.1	9.2	
1987	387.6	160.1	227.5	272.1	19.5	28.6	9.4	
1988	495.6	212.5	283.1	345.4	28.9	39.2	11.0	
1989	602.7	264.1	338.6	408.3	33.6	44.0	13.7	
1990	625.9	262.2	363.7	433.8	37.3	48.7	16.1	
1991	730.2	298.1	432.1	507.4	45.7	69.6	18.7	
1992	860.0	306.5	553.5	587.4	47.8	100.9	22.5	
1993	1166.6	361.9	804.7	747.6	71.4	126.6	28.9	
1994	1576.6	497.9	1078.7	990.7	120.3	162.1	39.9	
1995	1493.3	472.2	1021.1	937.7	154.8	173.8	41.1	
1996	1590.6	509.1	1081.5	962.3	199.2	166.6	17.5	
1997	1819.7	577.8	1241.9	999.6	300.9	158.5	75.5	
1998	1947.0	598.2	1348.8	1059.8	467.1	112.9	71.1	
1999	2183.5	621.8	1561.7	1090.9	611.8	121.6	74.8	
2000	2842.0	719.3	2122.7	1653.1	934.1	109.7	83.2	
2001	3270.1	842.4	2427.7	2298.4	1066.0	180.9	83.8	
2002	3620.2	882.4	2737.8	2434.7	1018.9	269.4	99.9	
2003	4410.8	936.7	3474.1	3183.9	1091.1	528.0	118.3	
2004	5733.3	1084.7	4648.6	3699.3	1235.6	748.9	492.8	
2005	6946.2	1164.9	5781.3	5242.1	1775.5	817.7	600.0	
2006	8210.0	1258.2	6951.8	6237.9	2234.2	1003.6	847.6	
2007	9648.4	1505.5	8142.9	7365.9	2663.1	1057.4	1068.0	
2008	10413.1	1674.3	8738.8	7898.9	2385.9	1153.3	1242.4	
2009	11039.1	1766.7	9272.4	8349.3	2095.5	1663.8	1435.6	
2010	13699.8	2000.0	11699.8	10505.3	2229.1	2177.7	2120.2	
2011	14513.6	2227.2	12286.4	11289.3	2026.2	2495.6	2283.4	
2012	15596.2	2402.1	13194.1	12239.6	2054.9	2521.5	3018.1	200.2
2013	17370.9	2541.5	14829.4	13941.3	2217.0	3269.2	3739.1	262.0
2014	18452.9	2568.0	15884.9	15039.5	2424.5	3647.6	4087.0	381.5
2015	17449.6	2610.8	14838.8	14250.3	2110.2	3882.9	4085.6	384.5
2016	18087.3	2731.6	15355.7	15053.2	2019.9	4771.6	4105.5	391.5
2017	18901.1	2924.1	15977.0	15747.2	2199.5	4492.5	4496.7	423.7
2018	19669.0	2975.7	16693.3	16224.5	2492.0	3945.3	5032.2	434.8
2019	20386.1	2964.1	17422.0	16541.0	2600.5	3964.5	5474.9	457.3

注：工业总产值按现价计算。

GROSS OUTPUT VALUE OF INDUSTRY ABOVE DESIGNATED SIZE (1984–2019)

(100 million yuan)

#化学原料和化学制品制造业 Manufacture of Chemical Raw Materials and Chemical Products	#通用设备制造业 Manufacture of General-Purpose Machinery	#专用设备制造业 Manufacture of Special-Purpose Machinery	#电气机械和器材制造业 Manufacture of Electrical Machinery and Equipment	#仪器仪表制造业 Manufacture of Measuring Instruments and Meters	#医药制造业 Manufacture of Medicines	#非金属矿物制品业 Manufacture of Non-Metallic Mineral Products	#石油加工、炼焦和核燃料加工业 Processing of Petroleum, Coking, Processing of Nuclear Fuel
48.1			15.7	3.7	5.4	15.9	4.8
57.2			17.0	4.0	7.1	17.6	5.6
69.4			22.2	5.3	9.8	20.1	7.0
83.4			27.0	5.5	10.8	24.7	8.2
87.1			22.1	4.9	11.4	24.1	9.7
42.8			25.7	5.7	14.0	27.1	65.6
62.0			30.5	7.4	15.8	31.8	67.4
70.1	64.8	33.8	40.9	12.2	18.2	50.3	92.4
90.6	76.1	62.1	53.4	15.4	21.8	81.1	117.3
101.4	55.3	40.4	37.0	24.3	21.9	54.5	133.9
104.3	54.3	41.4	44.8	32.1	26.4	71.4	133.3
100.1	49.9	53.1	52.2	30.6	32.3	73.7	148.4
100.1	53.5	81.0	69.2	33.2	38.9	92.6	111.8
116.6	43.4	100.0	87.5	37.0	47.1	95.0	156.7
144.2	49.1	123.4	97.7	42.4	58.5	102.8	289.2
145.6	71.9	98.0	111.5	49.7	71.5	102.8	269.8
168.0	81.4	130.2	119.1	74.8	98.6	132.9	318.0
312.7	128.1	151.0	169.2	97.8	123.0	143.4	241.9
399.0	186.7	189.8	197.5	124.4	119.7	184.5	274.6
236.9	237.1	232.0	222.3	158.2	131.1	193.8	592.5
257.5	292.5	300.9	260.7	183.9	150.1	234.6	540.4
318.0	347.8	331.9	333.7	215.7	202.3	258.5	601.7
306.7	409.2	434.4	387.2	211.4	263.9	296.5	753.2
255.9	377.9	423.1	596.4	205.4	313.1	344.4	682.1
358.3	547.7	502.4	699.1	227.9	372.8	392.5	825.2
371.2	597.9	565.6	775.1	242.3	452.9	445.2	902.5
345.9	524.7	510.3	669.7	224.3	543.3	461.1	886.3
349.6	516.9	614.7	714.1	245.8	599.1	491.1	767.2
352.1	550.6	590.3	737.6	257.3	669.0	488.0	845.4
319.3	488.0	543.7	786.2	257.7	733.0	392.2	591.1
302.3	490.0	512.1	678.6	254.9	814.4	432.1	494.4
333.9	537.3	557.2	665.8	269.1	981.6	432.1	580.0
303.4	532.0	694.8	665.1	241.9	1142.7	464.5	638.5
270.1	507.7	789.0	686.0	294.0	1221.6	482.1	579.8

Note: Gross output value is calculated at current prices.

12-2 规模以上工业企业主要指标(1978-2019年)
MAIN INDICATORS FOR INDUSTRIAL ENTERPRISES ABOVE DESIGNATED SIZE (1978-2019)

单位：亿元 (100 million yuan)

年份 Year	企业单位个数(个) Number of Enterprises (unit)	平均用工人数(万人) Average Number of Employed Persons (10000 persons)	资产总计 Total Assets	负债合计 Total Liabilities	固定资产原价 Original Value of Fixed Assets	营业收入 Business Income	营业成本 Business Cost	利润总额 Total Profits	利税总额 Total Taxes & Profits
1978	4225	114.8			130.5	109.8		37.1	50.2
1979	3746	116.8	141.7		137.1	118.6		41.4	55.5
1980	3733	140.9	154.7		149.5	198.8		45.3	60.4
1981	3778	152.9	165.1		162.2	205.5		44.1	59.9
1982	3867	158.7	174.9		175.1	218.3		44.0	60.4
1983	4011	162.0	184.7		188.7	240.9		46.9	64.2
1984	4291	165.5	200.4		204.5	272.9		50.5	70.7
1985	4458	165.6	233.8		233.7	317.6		54.9	82.9
1986	5461	169.9	272.0		262.7	338.5		52.4	81.4
1987	5746	170.5	314.7		300.9	393.5		57.1	88.5
1988	5932	170.5	360.7		341.3	503.2		70.2	108.1
1989	6175		434.3		389.0	559.8		63.8	108.7
1990	6272	173.5	498.3		438.2	610.5		48.9	95.7
1991	6344	172.4	567.3		505.2	727.2		58.3	110.6
1992	6205	175.5	640.9		575.4	852.7		74.8	134.7
1993	10320	167.9	1521.0		998.7	1282.2		109.5	181.2
1994	10889	179.5	1969.2		964.8	1320.7		96.2	185.7
1995	10712	176.2	2582.6	1528.8	1390.0	1590.4		85.3	193.0
1996	16905	166.6	2875.6	1722.1	1632.0	1580.1		33.1	122.5
1997	19387	157.5	3408.3	2049.7	1850.3	1707.1	1409.1	40.5	140.5
1998	18089	167.1	4012.9	2483.9	2221.3	2034.5	1669.7	48.4	161.7
1999	19682	161.1	4254.1	2586.3	2312.1	2218.6	1824.7	69.8	184.6
2000	16027	145.6	4612.7	2676.4	2531.6	2821.4	2338.0	127.1	256.1
2001	4356	108.0	4448.2	2459.6	2503.7	3006.9	2533.4	137.0	279.5
2002	4551	107.6	4742.9	2527.8	2655.4	3182.8	2612.9	165.5	322.0
2003	4019	100.8	5178.0	2751.2	2756.0	3885.7	3203.2	235.3	419.0
2004	6872	113.6	12049.5	4143.1	3922.2	5992.7	4288.5	397.4	641.8
2005	6301	117.1	12829.8	4706.7	4434.0	7279.1	6309.6	413.5	683.1
2006	6400	117.4	14244.4	5542.3	5030.6	8914.2	7779.9	531.1	847.9
2007	6398	119.3	16215.5	6508.3	5814.8	10440.2	9034.1	695.6	1055.2
2008	7206	123.4	16802.4	8085.0	6574.6	11275.8	9866.7	557.0	937.9
2009	6891	120.4	19540.7	9874.6	7083.6	12173.1	10406.4	742.9	1269.9
2010	6885	124.2	22750.6	11548.1	7936.1	14807.1	12611.2	1028.3	1649.0
2011	3740	117.9	25321.7	12648.6	8620.8	16105.8	13681.9	1129.5	1806.2
2012	3692	120.2	28613.2	14837.2	10277.2	17277.1	14595.8	1267.9	2010.4
2013	3641	116.1	30800.7	16208.0	10788.6	19058.7	16124.8	1282.9	2125.2
2014	3686	116.6	33557.0	17137.6	11532.9	20179.4	17012.1	1515.8	2407.9
2015	3548	110.4	38609.8	18102.4	12265.5	19256.1	15998.5	1597.7	2528.0
2016	3340	104.4	43093.7	19798.1	12978.0	20213.8	16750.7	1608.3	2521.6
2017	3231	99.5	45985.8	20671.0	13964.0	21181.0	17481.1	2023.7	2937.0
2018	3108	92.7	49321.5	22270.2	14651.0	22348.1	18482.2	1647.0	2594.9
2019	3121	86.8	52222.0	21974.5	15448.8	23419.1	19364.2	1710.3	2544.7

注：2010年及以前，营业收入为主营业务收入数据，营业成本为主营业务成本数据。

Note: In and before 2010, the data of business income referred to the data of main business income, and the data of business cost referred to the data of main business cost.

12–3 规模以上工业产品产量(1978–2019年)
OUTPUT OF INDUSTRIAL PRODUCTS ABOVE DESIGNATED SIZE (1978-2019)

年 份 Year	布 (万米) Cloth (10000 m)	机制纸及纸板 (万吨) Machine-made Paper and Paperboard (10000 tons)	饮料酒 (万千升) Alcoholic Beverage (10000 kL)	乳制品 (万吨) Dairy Products (10000 tons)	家用电冰箱 (万台) Household Refrigerators (10000 units)	照相机 (万台) Camera (10000 units)	家 具 (万件) Furniture (10000 pieces)	原 煤 (万吨) Raw Coal (10000 tons)
1978	25436	12.1	8.4			0.5	137.8	818.7
1979	27297	13.9	9.9		2.0	0.7	171.3	711.1
1980	28940	14.0	11.6		2.6	1.0	200.2	791.0
1981	28635	14.5	13.4		3.1	4.2	217.7	788.7
1982	29758	15.8	14.9	0.2	4.5	0.9	243.5	811.3
1983	30068	17.1	17.4	0.3	6.4	2.8	254.2	840.5
1984	27621	18.9	20.3	0.6	10.3	5.3	297.9	884.3
1985	25998	20.6	21.3	0.9	17.3	12.5	335.1	944.3
1986	27503	21.9	21.5	0.7	18.1	15.9	303.8	917.2
1987	29738	24.1	22.7	0.8	19.4	16.5	283.0	899.8
1988	32262	23.3	23.9	1.0	23.6	15.8	347.1	906.0
1989	32271	25.8	28.7	1.0	24.7	13.5	572.1	1016.8
1990	31258	25.4	34.6	1.2	10.7	12.9	590.6	1005.5
1991	31497	27.2	43.8	1.3	7.1	5.4	602.0	996.5
1992	29717	22.6	56.6	1.2	9.1	4.2	570.0	1015.2
1993	26816	19.1	72.6	1.6	4.2	39.3	729.0	835.4
1994	21440	21.0	83.1	0.3	6.6	158.8	605.0	1008.5
1995	24524	26.6	91.2	1.5		243.1	755.0	995.4
1996	22585	15.3	102.2	1.2	6.3	234.3	510.6	1013.7
1997	25185	18.1	...	1.7	...	157.7	469.4	1011.7
1998	21299	13.1		0.9	0.3	177.7	348.5	989.5
1999	14753	13.0	148.8	1.4	5.8	81.6	386.2	792.1
2000	12183	10.6	185.6	2.1	3.6	55.2	272.1	553.0
2001	11353	8.8	135.8	3.7	5.9	61.3	370.6	690.2
2002	10314	6.2	138.7	1.4	16.2	220.7	368.3	880.9
2003	8393	7.9	132.8	1.3	22.8	238.3	323.8	822.6
2004	4081	19.6	148.0	56.4	63.1	116.8	567.7	1067.9
2005	4270	17.0	145.6	56.9	81.7	47.9	406.5	897.9
2006	930	14.0	170.8	63.5	74.1	49.2	893.4	629.2
2007	536	10.4	189.1	57.9	73.1	34.7	638.8	633.3
2008	1583	14.9	180.0	44.9	79.0	49.0	690.9	567.7
2009	965	14.1	181.1	52.2	128.7	27.1	719.4	641.3
2010	495	10.6	185.8	52.3	92.1	29.2	822.8	500.0
2011	339	10.0	187.0	58.6	73.5	26.6	750.2	500.1
2012	351	11.3	191.7	56.6	80.4	18.2	720.1	493.1
2013	361	10.0	198.0	58.5	83.7	17.9	995.9	500.1
2014	361	6.6	187.4	60.6		6.6	674.7	457.5
2015	174	5.0	167.1	62.1		1.6	700.5	450.1
2016		6.1	167.5	62.2		0.1	776.2	317.6
2017		5.9	164.9	59.7		0.1	686.3	255.0
2018		4.4	148.5	53.2			626.1	176.2
2019		4.2	128.2	55.4			463.1	36.1

12-3 续表 1 continued

年 份 Year	原 油 加工量 (万吨) Crude Oil Processed (10000 tons)	乙 烯 (万吨) Ethylene (10000 tons)	发电量 (万千瓦时) Electricity Generated (10000 kWh)	粗 钢 (万吨) Crude Steel (10000 tons)	钢 材 (万吨) Rolled Steel (10000 tons)	水 泥 (万吨) Cement (10000 tons)	交 流 电动机 (万千瓦) Alternator (10000 kW)
1978			990750	191.0	116.8	191.5	152.5
1979			1042870	196.5	137.5	196.9	179.7
1980	591.1		1065060	200.9	152.1	217.4	142.7
1981	533.5	24.7	993071	190.3	149.5	225.7	104.0
1982	533.5	25.6	1003446	200.4	159.4	249.1	123.3
1983	563.8	27.3	1028826	214.1	177.9	270.8	148.3
1984	589.4	26.9	1038842	241.7	200.1	291.6	165.4
1985	591.1	27.8	1037171	267.7	221.0	318.5	172.0
1986	619.0	25.3	1043208	303.6	255.5	310.5	178.4
1987	640.2	27.0	1057493	335.5	283.4	319.6	196.4
1988	645.0	30.3	1110758	369.0	314.9	334.3	199.5
1989	651.9	29.1	1191269	386.0	327.9	345.9	163.8
1990	654.4	30.1	1253554	443.7	375.0	339.0	151.6
1991	653.4	31.1	1318000	499.7	402.9	377.6	156.7
1992	662.5	32.8	1423000	575.0	438.3	403.0	174.9
1993	664.0	27.2	1410900	702.7	525.3	477.9	162.3
1994	642.0	28.1	1298718	828.7	617.6	531.7	165.0
1995	648.0	53.0	1322114	804.9	629.8	574.2	165.4
1996	633.6	57.5	1415555	794.7	654.3	666.0	151.9
1997	657.0	58.0	1464302	801.7	652.4	700.9	148.7
1998	602.3	57.0	1566621	803.2	676.1	762.0	149.7
1999	701.9	68.0	1431772	734.5	663.8	803.0	142.0
2000	741.7	65.5	1452564	803.4	696.7	827.0	161.0
2001	647.9	54.3	1326588	824.9	727.3	809.0	175.1
2002	695.2	90.4	1419754	816.9	750.0	884.0	199.3
2003	701.1	88.8	1451197	816.4	785.0	882.0	253.1
2004	783.4	98.2	2038933	827.5	868.3	1204.5	279.4
2005	796.9	99.0	2133451	827.6	966.3	1183.8	262.9
2006	828.9	99.1	2136918	818.1	1016.3	1269.4	269.0
2007	915.0	90.9	2278658	810.8	1030.4	1167.3	281.9
2008	1114.6	85.4	2431255	466.8	656.8	880.8	259.7
2009	1161.3	84.1	2424839	464.9	769.6	1077.4	159.0
2010	1123.4	96.2	2688350	427.5	794.0	1049.0	191.1
2011	1103.1	89.6	2628331	2.9	287.0	911.5	146.0
2012	1075.0	84.0	2908214	2.6	253.8	874.5	117.1
2013	881.6	72.3	3312116	2.3	221.8	868.4	145.4
2014	1051.1	77.6	3385699	2.1	195.0	703.1	115.0
2015	1000.1	78.6	4173847	1.5	175.0	553.5	40.3
2016	844.8	69.6	4336690		162.8	510.3	46.1
2017	898.9	79.3	3878163		179.0	374.4	48.2
2018	911.3	79.4	4372998		179.1	397.0	35.4
2019	936.5	81.5	4311921		170.7	318.7	20.7

12-3 续表 2 continued

年 份 Year	汽 车 (万辆) Motor Vehicles (10000 units)	#轿 车 Sedan Cars	移动通信手持机 (万台) Mobile Phones (10000 units)	微型计算机设备 (万台) Micro-Computers (10000 units)	数控金属切削机床 (台) CNC Metal Cutting Lathe (unit)	显示器 (万台) Display Devices (10000 units)	集成电路 (亿块) IC (100 million units)
1978	1.8						
1979	2.4						
1980	2.8						
1981	2.7						
1982	2.8						
1983	3.1			0.3			
1984	3.6			1.2			
1985	5.0			0.5			
1986	5.8			0.5			
1987	7.4			0.9			
1988	9.0			3.0			
1989	8.5			1.3			
1990	8.8			1.2			
1991	11.0			1.7			
1992	13.8			3.0			
1993	13.4			4.1			
1994	14.7			4.3			
1995	17.9			19.2			
1996	13.4			28.1	326		0.5
1997	11.0			59.8	433		0.6
1998	8.5			160.9	430		0.6
1999	12.3	1.0		180.0	481		1.3
2000	12.5	0.5	1549.6	257.8	568		2.4
2001	14.3	0.5	2163.4	339.7	1004		2.1
2002	18.1	0.7	2280.1	415.7	912		2.5
2003	34.7	7.3	3334.5	469.3	1188		4.7
2004	53.9	15.0	4172.1	532.7	1024		11.1
2005	58.6	22.2	9131.1	649.6	1655		12.6
2006	68.3	27.0	14068.0	736.1	1875	680.7	11.8
2007	70.7	20.3	22719.9	843.3	2382	513.6	15.7
2008	76.6	28.3	20725.5	691.7	3108	478.1	19.1
2009	127.1	53.8	21355.3	842.7	6125	655.6	18.3
2010	150.3	62.2	27388.0	938.6	9766	877.8	25.3
2011	150.5	67.1	25962.3	1083.7	12537	851.4	32.0
2012	167.0	78.5	19949.3	1074.5	13332	796.9	31.9
2013	203.8	94.5	18783.4	1106.9	6983	305.3	38.4
2014	216.7	118.6	17983.6	1015.6	13890	548.1	54.3
2015	221.9	118.9	9540.8	885.6	12471	519.0	62.7
2016	260.4	120.7	6923.9	684.1	12420	503.5	80.5
2017	225.0	107.6	7483.1	742.4	14877	360.8	93.1
2018	163.2	78.8	8448.0	555.5	11862	406.3	149.5
2019	164.0	77.8	8373.3	513.2	7611	470.1	154.5

12-4 规模以上工业企业主要经济指标(2018年)

单位：万元

项目	Item	企业单位个数(个) Number of Enterprises (unit)	#亏损企业 LossSuffering Enterprises	工业总产值(当年价格) Gross Output Value of Industry (at current year's prices)	工业销售产值(当年价格) Sales Value of Industry (at current)	#出口交货值 Delivery Value of Exports
合　计	**Total**	**3108**	**677**	**196690179**	**193509320**	**12393626**
按行业分	**By Sector**					
采矿业	Mining and Quarrying	16	10	2767392	2785054	217542
制造业	Manufacturing	2958	640	137691765	134501236	12176084
电力、热力、燃气及水生产和供应业	Production and Distribution of Electricity, Heating Power, Gas and Water	134	27	56231022	56223030	
按轻重工业分	**By Light and Heavy Industries**					
轻工业	Light Industry	1053	224	29757205	28778676	1349219
重工业	Heavy Industry	2055	453	166932974	164730644	11044407
按规模分	**By Size**					
#大　型	Large-sized	126	27	126912520	125081340	8573552
中　型	Medium-sized	469	83	35332372	34276515	1950514
小　型	Small-sized	2321	510	33420851	33110677	1832325
按隶属关系分	**By Affiliation**					
中　央	Central	213	33	68972922	68402074	480007
地　方	Local	2895	644	127717257	125107246	11913619
按登记注册类型分	**By Registration Type**					
内资企业	Domestially-Invested Enterprises	2447	504	122684503	120735112	4293586
国有企业	State-owned Enterprises	36	12	8363716	8365394	9201
集体企业	Collectively-owned Enterprises	27	8	211258	208650	193
股份合作企业	Joint-equity Cooperative Enterprises	32	6	751864	753153	8584
有限责任公司	Limited Liability Companies	1082	249	78975529	77859070	2572616
股份有限公司	Companies Limited by Shares	255	59	23118036	22539162	1182651
私营企业	Private Enterprises	1014	170	11253382	10998965	520342
其他企业	Others	1		***	***	***
港澳台商投资企业	Hong Kong, Macao and Taiwan-invested Enterprises	153	38	21859754	20627460	3946875
港澳台合资经营	Joint Ventures	74	18	3445573	3334433	486470
港澳台合作经营	Cooperatives	3		***	***	***
港澳台商独资企业	Solely-funded Enterprises	67	20	18088606	16985591	3398027
港澳台商投资股份有限公司	Companies Limited by Shares	9		299593	283090	62373
外商投资企业	Foreign-invested Enterprises	508	135	52145922	52146748	4153165
#中外合资经营	Joint Ventures	187	34	34264734	34325840	1377674
中外合作经营	Cooperatives	8	3	203293	193696	16253
外资(独资)企业	Solely-funded Enterprises	299	93	16718944	16608627	2438387
外商投资股份有限公司	Companies Limited by Shares	12	5	802168	858530	316301
按控股类型分	**By Holding Types**					
#国有控股	State-holding Enterprises	643	142	115618998	114774749	3447914
集体控股	Collectively-holding Enterprises	80	24	2985912	2954381	166593
私人控股	Private-holding Enterprises	1787	349	29185313	28388171	1281380
港澳台控股	Hong Kong, Macao, and Taiwan-holding Enterprises	114	29	19781239	18527021	3688274
外商控股	Foreign-Investor-holding Enterprises	436	123	27242011	27078735	3792083

注：应交税金合计包括应交增值税、所得税费用、税金及附加，下同。

MAIN ECONOMIC INDICATORS OF INDUSTRIAL ENTERPRISES ABOVE DESIGNATED SIZE (2018)

(10000 yuan)

平均用工人数（人） Average Number of Employed Persons (person)	资产负债					
	资产总计 Total Assets	流动资产合计 Total Current Assets	#存货 Inventories	#产成品 Finished Products	#应收账款 Accounts Receivable (Net)	固定资产原价 Total Original Value of Fixed Assets
927430	**493214891**	**187213730**	**27599999**	**10310680**	**45256007**	**146509574**
36884	39564621	8774566	334369	66575	1861150	9693642
799903	238796898	147664093	27050968	10227566	37918810	53848127
90643	214853372	30775072	214662	16540	5476047	82967805
282226	45735936	28846789	6691752	3111654	6161628	11730799
645204	447478955	158366941	20908247	7199026	39094379	134778776
392758	348277067	101011174	12401022	4925317	20632662	114263205
252465	73052505	42336814	6418851	2168969	10835346	17786221
272786	66376847	41954081	8426534	3104994	12981708	14299945
171233	223935740	46354662	4826103	1101740	8585757	76815267
756197	269279151	140859068	22773896	9208940	36670250	69694307
638849	397706057	126064685	17189920	5687523	31217935	117527382
24167	14610082	2139807	742507	60323	264594	19711123
4197	329625	237820	36946	16981	43897	140444
2900	339762	282708	84874	16222	96080	66842
334799	291698112	75864762	8731807	2926691	18203724	82833496
141461	72084840	34027971	4507195	1450932	7948563	11069662
131147	18623407	13498923	3085247	1215030	4654250	3693620
***	***	***	***	***	***	***
67942	32103467	19464831	3517710	1773668	4875437	7392390
25909	6992923	4193573	723602	347509	1051304	3265986
***	***	***	***	***	***	***
38543	20169953	13240530	2723044	1392616	3632025	3841784
3159	4902202	1995858	65736	30130	181673	277325
220639	63405367	41684214	6892369	2849488	9162635	21589803
107327	38419816	23634783	3571235	1594067	5202018	12465853
6260	330963	253158	3472	4740	25181	135322
97070	22205845	17049776	3170258	1222924	3641265	8683081
9005	2165851	660895	122628	22410	276838	266735
390996	354394284	98521265	11462090	4034901	20613007	118455666
20764	4464290	3263646	652564	219004	1202654	714264
281227	71251519	42170545	7708460	2693214	12665400	9070772
52228	23130665	14988019	3042966	1602313	4150508	4426423
160412	35241552	25386804	4370624	1660970	5786173	12876717

Note: Total tax payable includes VAT payable, income tax expense, tax and surtax, the same below.

12-4 续表

单位：万元

项目	Item	资产负债 Assets and Liabilities				
		负债合计 Total Liabilities	#流动负债合计 Total Current Liabilities	#应付账款 Accounts Receivable	所有者权益合计 Total Owner's Equity	#实收资本 Paid-up Capital
合计	**Total**	**222701900**	**162735914**	**46281788**	**270512977**	**156704127**
按行业分	**By Sector**					
采矿业	Mining and Quarrying	23320905	12796162	1342935	16243716	6327697
制造业	Manufacturing	127278902	108086053	37227394	111517983	47951141
电力、热力、燃气及水生产和供应业	Production and Distribution of Electricity, Heating Power, Gas and Water	72102093	41853699	7711460	142751277	102425289
按轻重工业分	**By Light and Heavy Industries**					
轻工业	Light Industry	21253699	18187952	5555048	24482232	9231333
重工业	Heavy Industry	201448201	144547962	40726741	246030745	147472794
按规模分	**By Size**					
#大型	Large-sized	148700360	101515058	25858362	199576706	126145411
中型	Medium-sized	36949832	29303026	8404144	36102672	15087028
小型	Small-sized	33584232	29736949	11704182	32792605	14954642
按隶属关系分	**By Affiliation**					
中央	Central	78793428	51035856	10279477	145142312	104207311
地方	Local	143908472	111700058	36002311	125370665	52496816
按登记注册类型分	**By Registration Type**					
内资企业	Domestically-Invested Enterprises	170277893	116688318	28967648	227428153	138821067
国有企业	State-owned Enterprises	9239988	5504675	1172918	5370095	3084828
集体企业	Collectively-owned Enterprises	159307	126518	34601	170318	30610
股份合作企业	Joint-equity Cooperative Enterprises	246028	216658	130560	93735	54099
有限责任公司	Limited Liability Companies	121353569	79440959	18175763	170344540	119175068
股份有限公司	Companies Limited by Shares	29060807	22011490	5912506	43024032	13017693
私营企业	Private Enterprises	10215144	9384968	3540434	8408257	3452129
其他企业	Others	***	***	***	***	***
港澳台商投资企业	Hong Kong, Macao and Taiwan-invested Enterprises	18896757	16671240	6108788	13206708	4042558
港澳台合资经营	Joint Ventures	3451138	2663939	711173	3541784	1622103
港澳台合作经营	Cooperatives	***	***	***	***	***
港澳台商独资企业	Solely-funded Enterprises	13047526	12416498	5315817	7122426	1374211
港澳台商投资股份有限公司	Companies Limited by Shares	2393385	1586094	80689	2508817	1039575
外商投资企业	Foreign-invested Enterprises	33527250	29376356	11205353	29878116	13840503
#中外合资经营	Joint Ventures	19208807	16477185	7111808	19211009	8929746
中外合作经营	Cooperatives	130397	117834	44618	200566	186101
外资(独资)企业	Solely-funded Enterprises	13356355	12120118	3762450	8849488	4260527
外商投资股份有限公司	Companies Limited by Shares	685458	607859	263808	1480394	453731
按控股类型分	**By Holding Types**					
#国有控股	State-holding Enterprises	149427439	98126444	23914950	204966843	131483474
集体控股	Collectively-holding Enterprises	2366286	1916349	772612	2098003	524333
私人控股	Private-holding Enterprises	35227228	30212702	9300145	36024283	13111739
港澳台控股	Hong Kong, Macao, and Taiwan-holding Enterprises	14819239	13737610	5688236	8311424	1830714
外商控股	Foreign-Investor-holding Enterprises	18820931	16829803	6042954	16420619	8911686

12-4 Continued

(10000 yuan)

损益 Profits and Losses						应交税金合计		
营业收入 Business Income	营业成本 Business Cost	销售费用 Sales Expenses	管理费用 Management Expenses	财务费用 Financial Expenses	利润总额 Total Profits	Total Tax Payable	#税金及附加 Tax and Surtax	#应交增值税 Value Added Tax Payable
223480751	**184821926**	**11943498**	**11506975**	**2324175**	**16470016**	**12294858**	**3797641**	**5681458**
5495925	5369652	21638	404597	666730	-871917	185760	57265	90184
161012762	125404467	11814060	10491253	1162925	11951019	9969886	3319006	4539929
56972063	54047807	107801	611125	494521	5390914	2139212	421371	1051346
35512836	22199242	6361455	2869530	252302	3739709	3119091	726681	1727834
187967915	162622684	5582044	8637444	2071872	12730307	9175767	3070960	3953624
142449217	122069061	6424183	4840175	1262982	10076854	7893322	3007748	3108546
39827705	29775466	3179148	3028145	578431	4034239	2475719	533551	1341503
39861927	31774951	2300115	3434647	436282	2580700	1880948	248413	1201327
71318822	64438128	520044	1928140	540037	5323764	3785467	1408914	1583636
152161928	120383798	11423455	9578835	1784138	11146253	8509391	2388727	4097822
135382057	115233867	5087947	7564062	1961231	9062726	7042911	2278251	3370013
8656872	8045279	77667	231793	119924	5762	570922	296752	255998
218845	192042	7137	21571	-624	8531	13113	1557	9170
806439	772629	10588	19303	544	-226	12437	4081	7853
86731949	77086579	2193603	3789455	1378962	5787674	3490572	678601	1856151
26200571	19661634	1658308	2163586	367080	2490433	2347956	1230485	814524
12756662	9469136	1139481	1336111	95268	770306	607525	66707	425976
***	***	***	***	***	***	***	***	***
29566063	25756720	1497132	1195432	158629	1246756	540400	77699	327958
3747194	2733291	322088	340023	77705	325264	274808	31341	166207
***	***	***	***	***	***	***	***	***
25282806	22578100	1156617	812784	-7239	714629	244739	40541	148925
511331	431745	16291	38053	88299	202670	17866	5558	10760
58532630	43831339	5358419	2747481	204314	6160535	4711547	1441692	1983487
36853687	27534999	2804207	1513889	94812	4551849	3588922	1318183	1334298
371393	274519	52988	25875	-1418	19218	20458	2418	10981
19839495	14794653	2336026	1103448	80738	1479207	1017498	111409	589515
1223437	1028798	144232	91731	23875	106503	75336	7039	42776
125600476	108257131	3405336	4913810	1693873	10058564	8324032	3310375	3219812
3320225	2573471	244357	266648	13589	247070	145827	16126	89062
32796811	24070789	3146461	3233773	464565	2645352	1623904	201327	1087454
27235075	24004582	1356077	980447	25579	875437	360285	54622	213339
32443919	24598794	3409622	1886157	120644	2486969	1692752	180305	985695

12-5 规模以上工业企业主要经济指标(2019年)

单位：万元

项目	Item	企业单位个数(个) Number of Enterprises (unit)	#亏损企业 LossSuffering Enterprises	工业总产值(当年价格) Gross Output Value of Industry (at current year's prices)	平均用工人数(人) Average Number of Employed Persons (person)	资产总计 Total Assets
合计	**Total**	**3121**	**702**	**203861154**	**868087**	**522220073**
按行业分	**By Sector**					
采矿业	Mining and Quarrying	15	5	3248509	32241	40232503
制造业	Manufacturing	2951	666	139973569	742495	238853202
电力、热力、燃气及水生产和供应业	Production and Distribution of Electricity, Heating Power, Gas and Water	155	31	60639076	93351	243134368
按轻重工业分	**By Light and Heavy Industries**					
轻工业	Light Industry	1056	244	29641197	271174	48000386
重工业	Heavy Industry	2065	458	174219957	596913	474219688
按规模分	**By Size**					
#大型	Large-sized	115	24	132613840	358599	375925999
中型	Medium-sized	437	62	32796277	233307	71343466
小型	Small-sized	2370	558	37106359	267349	69338344
按隶属关系分	**By Affiliation**					
中央	Central	202	25	74388109	162987	249996414
地方	Local	2919	677	129473045	705100	272223659
按登记注册类型分	**By Registration Type**					
内资企业	Domestially-Invested Enterprises	2471	515	130066743	606750	425188580
#国有企业	State-owned Enterprises	32	8	8041387	19927	14928340
集体企业	Collectively-owned Enterprises	29	6	179874	3590	341230
股份合作企业	Joint-equity Cooperative Enterprises	28	6	262044	2231	244486
有限责任公司	Limited Liability Companies	1079	253	85980342	323400	314877202
股份有限公司	Companies Limited by Shares	255	57	23194555	135917	75918296
私营企业	Private Enterprises	1047	184	12405134	121485	18853581
其他企业	Others					
港澳台商投资企业	Hong Kong, Macao and Taiwan-invested Enterprises	155	33	21702456	61950	27575209
港澳台合资经营	Joint Ventures	83	17	3142887	24430	5287267
港澳台合作经营	Cooperatives	2	1	***	***	***
港澳台商独资企业	Solely-funded Enterprises	64	13	18347546	34971	21445754
港澳台商投资股份有限公司	Companies Limited by Shares	6	2	197510	2277	809109
外商投资企业	Foreign-invested Enterprises	495	154	52091955	199387	69456285
#中外合资经营	Joint Ventures	189	48	35095960	100047	43217899
中外合作经营	Cooperatives	10	3	223319	4877	439978
外资(独资)企业	Solely-funded Enterprises	288	102	16274715	89864	24661314
外商投资股份有限公司	Companies Limited by Shares	6	1	367667	3552	885608
按控股类型分	**By Holding Types**					
#国有控股	State-holding Enterprises	656	135	123104607	369730	379311251
集体控股	Collectively-holding Enterprises	75	22	2867615	18171	4203605
私人控股	Private-holding Enterprises	1809	381	30220486	270491	72461504
港澳台控股	Hong Kong, Macao, and Taiwan-holding Enterprises	112	23	19847931	47374	23841613
外商控股	Foreign-Investor-holding Enterprises	420	133	25618014	141425	37470744

注：应交税金合计包括应交增值税、所得税费用、税金及附加，下同。

MAIN ECONOMIC INDICATORS OF INDUSTRIAL ENTERPRISES ABOVE DESIGNATED SIZE (2019)

(10000 yuan)

资产负债							
流动资产合计 Total Current Assets	#存货 Inventories	#产成品 Finished Products	#应收账款 Accounts Receivable (Net)	固定资产原价 Total Original Value of Fixed Assets	负债合计 Total Liabilities	#流动负债合计 Total Current Liabilities	
190542547	**28604003**	**10147190**	**46015467**	**154487867**	**219744824**	**166804339**	
8959615	316653	39217	1764907	10120946	24856305	13949078	
151783969	28056484	10094637	38729667	55797484	123090766	107641709	
29798963	230865	13336	5520893	88569438	71797753	45213552	
29872316	7037473	3166462	6408623	12543117	20919818	17764749	
160670231	21566530	6980728	39606844	141944750	198825006	149039590	
104228628	13040833	4628124	20502410	121017559	150897745	109032192	
41188099	6141333	2026501	11971663	17008389	31632448	25910824	
43312011	9102259	3395858	13167472	16159952	35102634	30745793	
43218433	5020544	1124304	8371262	80725248	73553781	51709379	
147324114	23583459	9022886	37644204	73762618	146191043	115094960	
125809192	17625489	5804615	32089604	124529337	166211436	118916529	
1943433	626710	50230	160870	20519555	9556440	5400982	
244208	37688	14980	41485	128590	175105	153672	
195340	111380	11431	38473	56973	176931	176606	
73839220	9004818	3132700	17654822	88056969	115041708	78907503	
36012521	4624372	1364331	9446724	11987410	31293384	25319237	
13562756	3218878	1229464	4745739	3776027	9944945	8937276	
17829832	3747588	1517581	4668745	7231693	15723741	14323355	
3262745	542406	285015	839790	3243667	2154983	1817670	
***	***	***	***	***	***	***	
14053946	3047454	1178820	3619923	3889771	13197519	12306591	
482678	154612	50952	196236	91363	367404	195259	
46903522	7230926	2824995	9257118	22726837	37809647	33564456	
26938826	3730730	1462788	5359370	13563933	22261120	19445867	
366790	47173	6223	65310	146541	192084	183744	
19299346	3398182	1333412	3720840	8822093	14987074	13648319	
231812	40111	17821	101493	161308	243373	236765	
98892978	11750540	3895677	21770646	125276275	148185822	103212471	
2895320	689931	198872	899566	736152	2095754	1703826	
42032814	7792539	2766552	12737585	9655954	32797045	28603305	
15740552	3365310	1391068	4102186	4457080	14421067	13304953	
27874430	4599165	1806178	5724321	13268283	20177506	18033743	

Note: Total tax payable includes VAT payable, income tax expense, tax and surtax, the same below.

12-5 续表

单位：万元

项 目	Item	资产负债 Assets and Liabilities #应付账款 Accounts Receivable	所有者权益合计 Total Owner's Equity	#实收资本 Paid-up Capital
合 计	**Total**	**50305266**	**302475233**	**206000416**
按行业分	**By Sector**			
采矿业	Mining and Quarrying	1521340	15376198	6323012
制造业	Manufacturing	40131065	115762420	46066697
电力、热力、燃气及水生产和供应业	Production and Distribution of Electricity, Heating Power, Gas and Water	8652862	171336615	153610708
按轻重工业分	**By Light and Heavy Industries**			
轻工业	Light Industry	5534878	27080561	9506702
重工业	Heavy Industry	44770388	275394672	196493714
按规模分	**By Size**			
#大 型	Large-sized	28672951	225028253	175544105
中 型	Medium-sized	8841299	39711017	13884855
小 型	Small-sized	12462557	34235697	15840274
按隶属关系分	**By Affiliation**			
中 央	Central	11666201	176442632	154883975
地 方	Local	38639065	126032601	51116441
按登记注册类型分	**By Registration Type**			
内资企业	Domestically-Invested Enterprises	30574882	258977129	188591070
#国有企业	State-owned Enterprises	1363790	5371900	3298853
集体企业	Collectively-owned Enterprises	29682	166125	26153
股份合作企业	Joint-equity Cooperative Enterprises	114010	67555	51783
有限责任公司	Limited Liability Companies	19212313	199835487	168964266
股份有限公司	Companies Limited by Shares	6201326	44624911	12534773
私营企业	Private Enterprises	3652618	8908630	3709242
其他企业	Others			
港澳台商投资企业	Hong Kong, Macao and Taiwan-invested Enterprises	7370544	11851466	3039737
港澳台合资经营	Joint Ventures	613091	3132283	1609520
港澳台合作经营	Cooperatives	***	***	***
港澳台商独资企业	Solely-funded Enterprises	6713396	8248234	1307819
港澳台商投资股份有限公司	Companies Limited by Shares	42949	441705	116309
外商投资企业	Foreign-invested Enterprises	12359840	31646637	14369609
#中外合资经营	Joint Ventures	8132082	20956779	9694566
中外合作经营	Cooperatives	74555	247895	133089
外资(独资)企业	Solely-funded Enterprises	3981292	9674240	4357960
外商投资股份有限公司	Companies Limited by Shares	151840	642235	174485
按控股类型分	**By Holding Types**			
#国有控股	State-holding Enterprises	26784007	231125427	180093702
集体控股	Collectively-holding Enterprises	553171	2107850	508145
私人控股	Private-holding Enterprises	9217218	39664447	13335679
港澳台控股	Hong Kong, Macao, and Taiwan-holding Enterprises	7040700	9420545	1700946
外商控股	Foreign-Investor-holding Enterprises	6163025	17293237	9422801

12-5 Continued

(10000 yuan)

损益 Profits and Losses							应交税金合计 Total Tax Payable	#税金及附加 Tax and Surtax	#应交增值税 Value Added Tax Payable
营业收入 Business Income	营业成本 Business Cost	销售费用 Sales Expenses	管理费用 Management Expenses	研发费用 R&D Expenses	财务费用 Financial Expenses	利润总额 Total Profits			
234190962	**193641682**	**12375475**	**8567129**	**4108849**	**2142005**	**17102542**	**11313670**	**3723458**	**4620751**
5519783	5127923	22481	289174	35267	747166	-346812	145579	50360	53277
167136416	130446102	12240796	7359613	3864238	853367	12515772	9415225	3269876	3949250
61534763	58067657	112197	918342	209345	541472	4933582	1752866	403222	618224
36527298	22934907	6317023	2241202	884292	260568	3828850	2764025	713184	1383137
197663664	170706775	6058452	6325927	3224558	1881437	13273692	8549645	3010274	3237614
151261361	129956508	6629049	3652710	1649798	1392348	9695495	7226426	2945023	2383450
37250720	27143401	3266032	2164159	1171033	332667	4807108	2296308	517040	1192994
43987613	35044185	2437560	2578211	1257909	375599	2678153	1714522	250986	999496
76493034	68988208	518073	1724508	690070	405650	5501258	3359121	1458458	1061657
157697928	124653475	11857401	6842621	3418780	1736355	11601285	7954549	2265000	3559094
144832654	123042259	5269420	5517660	3031460	1945295	8901380	6363981	2322583	2643763
8375223	7817285	67223	265384	57362	97464	-112186	438651	298030	150945
201754	166120	7972	19730	2440	208	14459	11308	1212	7362
268640	242092	6504	11706	3811	490	866	3752	4363	-1081
94025984	83395115	2177122	2884507	1306873	1291181	6439016	3061450	653312	1339532
28565019	21646448	1859066	1439143	1139908	452658	1501658	2242857	1301021	747763
13390425	9772013	1149505	896487	520954	103309	1058041	605814	64591	399149
31263426	27172694	1824298	707806	404728	-32761	1991297	572158	86143	237398
3514464	2544811	312357	180690	119725	4764	345147	210801	30160	109057
***	***	***	***	***	***	***	***	***	***
27470520	24446400	1469383	491961	278976	-47103	1614795	350900	53532	120436
262077	173024	41023	32165	5187	9679	29161	8634	2257	6510
58094882	43426729	5281757	2341664	672662	229470	6209866	4377531	1314733	1739590
36912255	27662768	2867811	1337368	449760	107228	4572652	3420286	1210155	1233157
408630	288069	38819	29129	7646	-4384	59454	23676	2997	13338
19996208	14902829	2211070	944894	206599	119504	1561667	915741	98459	480369
569951	412550	143785	18028	6179	848	13271	8902	1547	5785
134968118	117251723	3385284	4074211	1473760	1560071	9518419	7518147	3241535	2515033
3032511	2283179	233823	162073	95517	13477	272593	120543	14588	65195
33455720	23748110	3359196	2100590	1654112	448280	2687925	1591534	208128	992885
29240354	25594254	1701924	598647	328334	-36472	1843858	450361	64345	171698
31026713	23132261	3296845	1516863	455245	149523	2484059	1480980	158563	791454

12-6 分行业规模以上工业企业主要经济指标(2018年)

单位：万元

项 目	Item	企业单位个数(个) Number of Enterprises (unit)	#亏损企业 Loss-Suffering Enterprises	工业总产值(当年价格) Gross Output Value of Industry (at current year's prices)
合 计	**Total**	**3108**	**677**	**196690179**
采矿业	**Mining and Quarrying**	**16**	**10**	**2767392**
煤炭开采和洗选业	Mining and Washing of Coal	2		***
石油和天然气开采业	Extraction of Petroleum and Natural Gas	2	2	***
黑色金属矿采选业	Mining and Processing of Ferrous Metal Ores	6	5	896196
非金属矿采选业	Mining and Processing of Nonmetal Ores	1		***
开采专业及辅助性活动	Mining and Support Service Activities	5	3	1340608
制造业	**Manufacturing**	**2958**	**640**	**137691765**
农副食品加工业	Processing of Food from Agricultural Products	114	31	2748633
食品制造业	Manufacture of Foods	122	26	3259577
酒、饮料和精制茶制造业	Manufacture of Wines, Beverage and Refined Tea	39	11	2686442
烟草制品业	Manufacture of Cigarettes and Tobacco	1		***
纺织业	Manufacture of Textile	12	2	85458
纺织服装、服饰业	Manufacture of Textile Wearing Apparel and Ornament	95	31	1102917
皮革、毛皮、羽毛及其制品和制鞋业	Manufacture of Leather, Fur, Feather and Its Products, and Footwear	6	1	55296
木材加工和木、竹、藤、棕、草制品业	Processing of Timbers, Manufacture of Wood, Bamboo, Rattan, Palm, and Straw Products	7		65018
家具制造业	Manufacture of Furniture	41	5	877061
造纸和纸制品业	Manufacture of Paper and Paper Products	37	9	588659
印刷和记录媒介复制业	Printing, Reproduction of Recording Media	90	21	1294079
文教、工美、体育和娱乐用品制造业	Manufacture of Articles for Culture, Education, Artwork, Sport and Entertainment Activities	31	7	1383318
石油、煤炭及其他燃料加工业	Processing of Petroleum, Coal and Other Fuels	16	2	6385008
化学原料和化学制品制造业	Manufacture of Chemical Raw Materials and Chemical Products	160	32	3034230
医药制造业	Manufacture of Medicines	217	33	11427107
化学纤维制造业	Manufacture of Chemical Fibres	2		***
橡胶和塑料制品业	Manufacture of Rubber and Plastics Products	80	21	773934
非金属矿物制品业	Manufacture of Non-metallic Mineral Products	197	50	4644768
黑色金属冶炼和压延加工业	Manufacture and Pressing of Ferrous Metals	9	1	1034890
有色金属冶炼和压延加工业	Manufacture and Pressing of Non-ferrous Metals	23	5	701995
金属制品业	Manufacture of Fabricated Metal Products	167	34	2830002
通用设备制造业	Manufacture of General-purpose Machinery	209	54	5319813
专用设备制造业	Manufacture of Special-purpose Machinery	299	48	6947722
汽车制造业	Manufacture of Motor Vehicles	225	86	39453045
铁路、船舶、航空航天和其他运输设备制造业	Manufacture of Railway Locomotives, Building of Ships and Boats, Manufacture of Air and Spacecrafts and Other Transportation Equipment	77	7	4347822
电气机械和器材制造业	Manufacture of Electrical Machinery and Equipment	225	40	6650892
计算机、通信和其他电子设备制造业	Manufacture of Computers, Communication Equipment and Other Electronic Equipment	269	62	24920434
仪器仪表制造业	Manufacture of Measuring Instruments and Meters	156	18	2419072
其他制造业	Other Manufacturing	12	2	1142177
废弃资源综合利用业	Waste Recycling and Recovery	7		47825
金属制品、机械和设备修理业	Repair of Fabricated Metal Products, Machinery and Equipment	13	1	926190
电力、热力、燃气及水生产和供应业	**Production and Distribution of Electricity, Heating Power, Gas and Water**	**134**	**27**	**56231022**
电力、热力生产和供应业	Production and Distribution of Electricity and Heating Power	83	15	50321630
燃气生产和供应业	Production and Distribution of Gas	25	7	4654418
水的生产和供应业	Production and Distribution of Water	26	5	1254975

MAIN ECONOMIC INDICATORS OF INDUSTRIAL ENTERPRISES ABOVE DESIGNATED SIZE (BY SECTOR) (2018)

(10000 yuan)

工业销售产值(当年价格) Sales Value of Industry (at current year's prices)	#出口交货值 Delivery Value of Exports	平均用工人数(人) Average Number of Employed Persons (person)	资产负债 资产总计 Total Assets	流动资产合计 Total Current Assets	#存货 Inventories	#产成品 Finished Products	#应收账款 Accounts Receivable	固定资产原价 Total Original Value of Fixed Assets
193509320	**12393626**	**927430**	**493214891**	**187213730**	**27599999**	**10310680**	**45256007**	**146509574**
2785054	**217542**	**36884**	**39564621**	**8774566**	**334369**	**66575**	**1861150**	**9693642**
***	***	***	***	***	***	***	***	***
***	***	***	***	***	***	***	***	***
893043		15265	32213024	5367883	114666	34729	1169887	6921390
***	***	***	***	***	***	***	***	***
1341295	38762	16754	4287180	2120361	193289	6279	673582	2638996
134501236	**12176084**	**799903**	**238796898**	**147664093**	**27050968**	**10227566**	**37918810**	**53848127**
2750494	51962	22241	3696680	2045092	402187	196425	318312	596233
3309249	123931	41392	4377097	2533990	404996	203408	592519	1439630
2667103	23316	24560	5623771	3511047	392826	198713	260294	1562426
***	***	***	***	***	***	***	***	***
85654	25681	2083	359779	242861	30825	14247	40891	81179
981952	207552	29845	1408803	1076246	451207	268000	196626	320411
49804	9643	1201	100143	66162	45554	29214	12693	14322
65518		1063	155600	96180	19530	10400	31578	14244
873097	25028	8226	1259286	777106	322185	246843	154240	263282
591063	57237	3918	553715	373782	90291	33895	105230	323408
1299916	5242	19610	2183065	1359539	267927	101089	191587	1543101
1391052	43783	5472	1112477	825943	452591	191587	49559	190299
6379227	2164	8443	2861712	1124817	568125	124628	173667	3461221
2968914	73304	21187	4533861	2991528	545839	283576	733371	1655779
10661882	134935	78386	16582656	10469250	2847580	1239074	2804372	3711688
***	***	***	***	***	***	***	***	***
766387	88689	10904	1021253	727803	146546	66126	241678	413721
4615921	156767	35959	14411165	9506337	855016	285301	2789978	1944425
1035700	85404	1807	804359	297100	132564	50192	76671	732682
684556	63524	3809	828565	535058	190355	77836	96287	208594
2887951	212206	25356	6938454	3747774	578040	187249	829445	1253217
5225685	791366	46306	11870715	8057185	2024022	612792	1691037	2044559
6504988	959564	63200	21698718	13381255	2321070	667429	3649267	1878255
39578915	627756	122054	56911553	31111792	4284862	1992270	7624892	13951969
4149114	37772	33657	8262747	6028268	1834316	366632	1780550	1723307
6618969	303604	44220	12575713	9656507	1549067	436384	3883850	1471697
23498631	7752755	98831	46754441	30568055	4961814	2134374	7635554	10874633
2386196	171945	27128	5545170	3866447	808965	182129	1247046	673181
975254	44440	3684	1453795	1115449	248768	6640	383103	289140
46183		701	126098	63347	3756	1583	18194	76573
917072	67219	13245	4318297	1175390	197840	6302	282654	837918
56223030		**90643**	**214853372**	**30775072**	**214662**	**16540**	**5476047**	**82967805**
50313470		64868	195579844	26426049	179959	6279	4071981	71533929
4654514		12569	7352604	1508777	12135	6518	334353	3365620
1255047		13206	11920923	2840245	22568	3743	1069713	8068255

12-6 续表

单位：万元

项目	Item	资产负债 Assets and Liabilities 负债合计 Total Liabilities	#流动负债合计 Total Current Liabilities	#应付账款 Accounts Payable	所有者权益合计 Total Owner's Equity
合计	**Total**	**222701900**	**162735914**	**46281788**	**270512977**
采矿业	**Mining and Quarrying**	**23320905**	**12796162**	**1342935**	**16243716**
煤炭开采和洗选业	Mining and Washing of Coal	***	***	***	***
石油和天然气开采业	Extraction of Petroleum and Natural Gas	***	***	***	***
黑色金属矿采选业	Mining and Processing of Ferrous Metal Ores	20454506	10834321	650617	11758517
非金属矿采选业	Mining and Processing of Nonmetal Ores	***	***	***	***
开采专业及辅助性活动	Mining and Support Service Activities	1566039	1471044	581994	2721141
制造业	**Manufacturing**	**127278902**	**108086053**	**37227394**	**111517983**
农副食品加工业	Processing of Food from Agricultural Products	2098667	1869180	317373	1598013
食品制造业	Manufacture of Foods	2026082	1933761	810765	2351014
酒、饮料和精制茶制造业	Manufacture of Wines, Beverage and Refined Tea	2594249	2157454	429868	3029523
烟草制品业	Manufacture of Cigarettes and Tobacco	***	***	***	***
纺织业	Manufacture of Textile	155533	99980	22235	204246
纺织服装、服饰业	Manufacture of Textile Wearing Apparel and Ornament	802272	735556	206553	606530
皮革、毛皮、羽毛及其制品和制鞋业	Manufacture of Leather, Fur, Feather and Its Products, and Footwear	58084	58084	9074	42060
木材加工和木、竹、藤、棕、草制品业	Processing of Timbers, Manufacture of Wood, Bamboo, Rattan, Palm, and Straw Products	129746	129496	23293	25853
家具制造业	Manufacture of Furniture	900915	608152	176511	358371
造纸和纸制品业	Manufacture of Paper and Paper Products	269591	246702	99639	284124
印刷和记录媒介复制业	Printing, Reproduction of Recording Media	785830	678707	266631	1397235
文教、工美、体育和娱乐用品制造业	Manufacture of Articles for Culture, Education, Artwork, Sport and Entertainment Activities	893388	858544	365910	219089
石油、煤炭及其他燃料加工业	Processing of Petroleum, Coal and Other Fuels	1395368	1278431	437906	1466344
化学原料和化学制品制造业	Manufacture of Chemical Raw Materials and Chemical Products	2219153	1790376	685513	2314707
医药制造业	Manufacture of Medicines	6602294	5465599	1753767	9980361
化学纤维制造业	Manufacture of Chemical Fibres	16199	15383	312	23835
橡胶和塑料制品业	Manufacture of Rubber and Plastics Products	508481	443772	204898	512771
非金属矿物制品业	Manufacture of Non-metallic Mineral Products	9933569	8726462	2422576	4477597
黑色金属冶炼和压延加工业	Manufacture and Pressing of Ferrous Metals	857024	281643	194901	-52665
有色金属冶炼和压延加工业	Manufacture and Pressing of Non-ferrous Metals	281347	254201	63843	547218
金属制品业	Manufacture of Fabricated Metal Products	3398737	2920054	665821	3539715
通用设备制造业	Manufacture of General-purpose Machinery	5627741	4816641	1318264	6242975
专用设备制造业	Manufacture of Special-purpose Machinery	11426437	9184948	2768622	10272279
汽车制造业	Manufacture of Motor Vehicles	31978239	25387160	10211473	24933315
铁路、船舶、航空航天和其他运输设备制造业	Manufacture of Railway Locomotives, Building of Ships and Boats, Manufacture of Air and Spacecrafts and Other Transportation Equipment	4607572	3935255	1369956	3655176
电气机械和器材制造业	Manufacture of Electrical Machinery and Equipment	7447543	6969921	2984392	5128169
计算机、通信和其他电子设备制造业	Manufacture of Computers, Communication Equipment and Other Electronic Equipment	25189219	23238604	8226088	21565220
仪器仪表制造业	Manufacture of Measuring Instruments and Meters	2445262	2187066	890977	3099907
其他制造业	Other Manufacturing	923169	861994	148784	530626
废弃资源综合利用业	Waste Recycling and Recovery	66377	43929	6527	59721
金属制品、机械和设备修理业	Repair of Fabricated Metal Products, Machinery and Equipment	1533118	801399	135239	2785179
电力、热力、燃气及水生产和供应业	**Production and Distribution of Electricity, Heating Power, Gas and Water**	**72102093**	**41853699**	**7711460**	**142751277**
电力、热力生产和供应业	Production and Distribution of Electricity and Heating Power	63642199	37391134	6359653	131937644
燃气生产和供应业	Production and Distribution of Gas	2804525	2015053	309240	4548079
水的生产和供应业	Production and Distribution of Water	5655369	2447512	1042567	6265554

12-6 Continued

(10000 yuan)

	损益 Profits and Losses						应交税金合计		
#实收资本 Paid-up Capital	营业收入 Business Income	营业成本 Business Cost	销售费用 Sales Expenses	管理费用 Management Expenses	财务费用 Financial Expenses	利润总额 Total Profits	应交税金合计 Total Tax Payable	#税金及附加 Tax and Surtax	#应交增值税 Value Added Tax Payable
156704127	**223480751**	**184821926**	**11943498**	**11506975**	**2324175**	**16470016**	**12294858**	**3797641**	**5681458**
6327697	**5495925**	**5369652**	**21638**	**404597**	**666730**	**-871917**	**185760**	**57265**	**90184**
***	***	***	***	***	***	***	***	***	***
***	***	***	***	***	***	***	***	***	***
2948109	3670583	3707873	8285	244234	656171	-583195	59029	27563	31908
***	***	***	***	***	***	***	***	***	***
3001702	1387309	1386757	3471	60181	-10065	-279407	50814	8092	9005
47951141	**161012762**	**125404467**	**11814060**	**10491253**	**1162925**	**11951019**	**9969886**	**3319006**	**4539929**
937507	3717314	3298691	190801	165705	34783	102924	47075	6654	24340
1068269	6006982	3803537	1440032	317639	4695	430136	448199	41912	301032
1207898	2890074	1881312	341429	197230	6789	310521	442412	227582	155153
***	***	***	***	***	***	***	***	***	***
121579	171365	134136	5571	21562	2872	9348	5976	2088	1730
273945	1278053	876917	231723	118935	5900	44520	75510	9003	56343
9453	76436	65674	4840	5143	101	493	2869	302	2233
15051	94141	77835	5067	9854	857	677	3120	461	2513
213851	898797	711620	60980	75741	22415	26303	43471	4841	28942
147658	719758	568823	27876	41087	-1091	78266	47597	3873	24911
724404	1565473	1196854	43133	182653	-1602	139980	120349	16366	75767
238829	1655896	1524308	57304	56500	10256	12471	22289	4414	15986
78748	7035849	5599534	56816	206475	12402	261379	1197228	881598	245813
1604361	3681294	2853448	310083	305116	25977	198350	103287	19787	121662
2664253	11530924	5025435	3384431	1091295	129866	2048978	1237473	116006	800294
9200	32142	21704	1384	3308	-38	5223	2160	454	940
266271	1017509	850851	41893	93349	5163	22329	38481	5480	27853
2104233	5053543	4245826	183604	370226	234417	112199	227782	29561	161634
283665	1086133	1035685	18786	14915	13002	1486	10653	4352	7113
140561	748316	661015	10019	45705	4491	28728	16474	2624	10247
1476943	3540517	3012666	86106	289824	44287	116237	107381	17741	66217
2313479	5993629	4534113	362303	526345	66244	479594	333614	39443	197135
3346093	8037025	5756963	556151	891821	125159	1051638	410332	54399	247455
11481131	43458398	35407083	2234870	1892954	346331	3904358	3362828	1378340	1167822
1392607	4348722	3263733	74975	499955	42816	497932	236233	23692	128233
2725535	7669833	6001440	488668	661675	38615	548445	358461	40417	210763
10612905	33223838	29043925	1343513	1780004	-83321	1033276	488518	97098	240537
1125601	2835921	1937445	225874	383233	13138	256279	180746	22350	114421
280724	1108030	1005753	7461	71648	112	26965	9760	1292	3496
28716	57616	45791	492	8420	760	9365	5778	652	3729
964696	968436	792494	5687	122314	60495	160000	58311	7648	38648
102425289	**56972063**	**54047807**	**107801**	**611125**	**494521**	**5390914**	**2139212**	**421371**	**1051346**
96552204	50767857	48750352	14601	288683	365448	4835228	1731478	189920	938377
1048344	4718483	4302485	38634	229276	33452	319634	95164	7153	37931
4824741	1485723	994970	54565	93166	95620	236052	312571	224298	75037

12-7 分行业规模以上工业企业主要经济指标(2019年)

单位：万元

项目	Item	企业单位个数(个) Number of Enterprises (unit)	#亏损企业 Loss-Suffering Enterprises	工业总产值(当年价格) Gross Output Value of Industry (at current year's prices)
合 计	**Total**	**3121**	**702**	**203861154**
采矿业	**Mining and Quarrying**	**15**	**5**	**3248509**
煤炭开采和洗选业	Mining and Washing of Coal	1		***
石油和天然气开采业	Extraction of Petroleum and Natural Gas	3	1	***
黑色金属矿采选业	Mining and Processing of Ferrous Metal Ores	5	2	1142228
非金属矿采选业	Mining and Processing of Nonmetal Ores	1		***
开采专业及辅助性活动	Mining and Support Service Activities	5	2	1569925
制造业	**Manufacturing**	**2951**	**666**	**139973569**
农副食品加工业	Processing of Food from Agricultural Products	107	29	2455712
食品制造业	Manufacture of Foods	118	28	3181976
酒、饮料和精制茶制造业	Manufacture of Wines, Beverage and Refined Tea	39	13	2236953
烟草制品业	Manufacture of Cigarettes and Tobacco	1		***
纺织业	Manufacture of Textile	12	2	103019
纺织服装、服饰业	Manufacture of Textile Wearing Apparel and Ornament	84	31	1006990
皮革、毛皮、羽毛及其制品和制鞋业	Manufacture of Leather, Fur, Feather and Its Products, and Footwear	8	3	48236
木材加工和木、竹、藤、棕、草制品业	Processing of Timbers, Manufacture of Wood, Bamboo, Rattan, Palm, and Straw Products	8	2	61269
家具制造业	Manufacture of Furniture	40	6	818738
造纸和纸制品业	Manufacture of Paper and Paper Products	36	7	549473
印刷和记录媒介复制业	Printing, Reproduction of Recording Media	95	15	1340012
文教、工美、体育和娱乐用品制造业	Manufacture of Articles for Culture, Education, Artwork, Sport and Entertainment Activities	29	6	1386307
石油、煤炭及其他燃料加工业	Processing of Petroleum, Coal and Other Fuels	16	7	5797609
化学原料和化学制品制造业	Manufacture of Chemical Raw Materials and Chemical Products	149	35	2700629
医药制造业	Manufacture of Medicines	235	48	12216089
化学纤维制造业	Manufacture of Chemical Fibres	2		***
橡胶和塑料制品业	Manufacture of Rubber and Plastics Products	73	15	637991
非金属矿物制品业	Manufacture of Non-metallic Mineral Products	188	42	4820971
黑色金属冶炼和压延加工业	Manufacture and Pressing of Ferrous Metals	7	1	881908
有色金属冶炼和压延加工业	Manufacture and Pressing of Non-ferrous Metals	23	3	632807
金属制品业	Manufacture of Fabricated Metal Products	160	33	3022115
通用设备制造业	Manufacture of General-purpose Machinery	213	52	5076938
专用设备制造业	Manufacture of Special-purpose Machinery	314	60	7889649
汽车制造业	Manufacture of Motor Vehicles	210	85	39645173
铁路、船舶、航空航天和其他运输设备制造业	Manufacture of Railway Locomotives, Building of Ships and Boats, Manufacture of Air and Spacecrafts and Other Transportation Equipment	77	6	4573250
电气机械和器材制造业	Manufacture of Electrical Machinery and Equipment	220	41	6860380
计算机、通信和其他电子设备制造业	Manufacture of Computers, Communication Equipment and Other Electronic Equipment	276	66	26005205
仪器仪表制造业	Manufacture of Measuring Instruments and Meters	175	23	2940354
其他制造业	Other Manufacturing	13	5	1367102
废弃资源综合利用业	Waste Recycling and Recovery	7		62932
金属制品、机械和设备修理业	Repair of Fabricated Metal Products, Machinery and Equipment	16	2	1115044
电力、热力、燃气及水生产和供应业	**Production and Distribution of Electricity, Heating Power, Gas and Water**	**155**	**31**	**60639076**
电力、热力生产和供应业	Production and Distribution of Electricity and Heating Power	98	16	54749363
燃气生产和供应业	Production and Distribution of Gas	26	7	4690254
水的生产和供应业	Production and Distribution of Water	31	8	1199459

MAIN ECONOMIC INDICATORS OF INDUSTRIAL ENTERPRISES ABOVE DESIGNATED SIZE (BY SECTOR) (2019)

(10000 yuan)

平均用工人数(人) Average Number of Employed Persons (person)	资产负债							
	资产总计 Total Assets	流动资产合计 Total Current Assets	#存货 Inventories	#产成品 Finished Products	#应收账款 Accounts Receivable	固定资产原价 Total Original Value of Fixed Assets	负债合计 Total Liabilities	#流动负债合计 Total Current Liabilities
868087	**522220073**	**190542547**	**28604003**	**10147190**	**46015467**	**154487867**	**219744824**	**166804339**
32241	**40232503**	**8959615**	**316653**	**39217**	**1764907**	**10120946**	**24856305**	**13949078**
***	***	***	***	***	***	***	***	***
***	***	***	***	***	***	***	***	***
14524	33745152	6107680	96328	30839	1052890	7255321	22334402	11737283
***	***	***	***	***	***	***	***	***
16029	4388094	2114598	215905	5835	642454	2719959	1665288	1575153
742495	**238853202**	**151783969**	**28056484**	**10094637**	**38729667**	**55797484**	**123090766**	**107641709**
19241	3678725	2032105	382941	204094	259734	625546	1994219	1795829
37752	4510029	2671650	372283	190209	658219	1467565	1947512	1866669
24463	5669628	3495379	397654	170550	304596	1630476	2365726	2031554
***	***	***	***	***	***	***	***	***
1715	347626	224281	30619	16375	41181	78364	139327	85814
26590	1369904	1039015	430333	274094	212043	304830	784012	700816
1076	106612	72641	46176	29062	11835	11273	63984	56159
360	49928	43414	11173	1248	10065	8042	36836	36801
7253	1294140	823039	301851	195753	168639	246667	954713	650107
3759	530685	370281	96085	39843	88908	297317	298249	282319
18919	2232437	1429702	301911	110983	232903	1577817	758180	603685
4792	1102688	806299	510900	178351	49767	210758	847235	807954
8072	2693759	797202	539755	106857	126914	3607891	1248978	948085
19442	3828737	2550764	533797	304312	564411	1376962	1946349	1395389
81104	18641468	11611013	3212141	1384636	3166994	4383955	7276820	6197265
***	***	***	***	***	***	***	***	***
9662	955847	702158	140354	65642	239191	397538	501843	452318
31371	9519721	6403889	710536	302642	2990521	1754892	5958680	5528204
1710	749128	269080	123838	32208	52466	736347	812075	212233
2748	688636	431549	141974	44939	97498	176437	218634	193804
23115	7708666	4345712	780478	193470	865258	1250532	4092752	3631929
43484	10582522	7364807	1924918	673562	1576456	2011214	4295345	4059794
63636	22066578	13478197	2527358	728989	3707367	2058125	10768041	9543681
103498	54562271	33419981	4129592	1799905	8637434	14561587	32829919	27821307
30106	8646871	6495874	1961627	363622	1851238	1695843	4554626	4241669
40629	11550649	8614869	1468504	397853	3328685	1450396	6534045	5722323
90440	52971426	35229730	5419171	2033197	7560032	11589198	26622293	24503624
27564	5980449	4250859	922727	225468	1327417	711468	2649645	2460426
3721	1720119	1387881	349815	11179	239754	358637	938736	885355
748	134900	76685	1997	975	25713	77441	54874	35803
14088	4439141	962045	221869	7131	323207	841068	1485429	779625
93351	**243134368**	**29798963**	**230865**	**13336**	**5520893**	**88569438**	**71797753**	**45213552**
68730	222432147	24759890	200495	7276	3912136	76526365	62295030	40614234
10968	7848140	1792521	6812	1222	316598	3417468	3048406	2098768
13653	12854081	3246553	23558	4839	1292159	8625604	6454318	2500550

12-7 续表

单位：万元

项目	Item	资产负债 Assets and Liabilities #应付账款 Accounts Payable	所有者权益合计 Total Owner's Equity	#实收资本 Paid-up Capital
合 计	**Total**	**50305266**	**302475233**	**206000416**
采矿业	**Mining and Quarrying**			
煤炭开采和洗选业	Mining and Washing of Coal	***	***	***
石油和天然气开采业	Extraction of Petroleum and Natural Gas	***	***	***
黑色金属矿采选业	Mining and Processing of Ferrous Metal Ores	753628	11410750	2959864
非金属矿采选业	Mining and Processing of Nonmetal Ores	***	***	***
开采专业及辅助性活动	Mining and Support Service Activities	668956	2722806	2998124
制造业	**Manufacturing**			
农副食品加工业	Processing of Food from Agricultural Products	245391	1684506	985678
食品制造业	Manufacture of Foods	759394	2562516	1024404
酒、饮料和精制茶制造业	Manufacture of Wines, Beverage and Refined Tea	450215	3303902	1172508
烟草制品业	Manufacture of Cigarettes and Tobacco	***	***	***
纺织业	Manufacture of Textile	21198	208299	115404
纺织服装、服饰业	Manufacture of Textile Wearing Apparel and Ornament	190708	585891	256028
皮革、毛皮、羽毛及其制品和制鞋业	Manufacture of Leather, Fur, Feather and Its Products, and Footwear	8559	42629	10003
木材加工和木、竹、藤、棕、草制品业	Processing of Timbers, Manufacture of Wood, Bamboo, Rattan, Palm, and Straw Products	12071	13092	10436
家具制造业	Manufacture of Furniture	173847	339426	206250
造纸和纸制品业	Manufacture of Paper and Paper Products	73235	232437	134600
印刷和记录媒介复制业	Printing, Reproduction of Recording Media	278721	1474256	761995
文教、工美、体育和娱乐用品制造业	Manufacture of Articles for Culture, Education, Artwork, Sport and Entertainment Activities	336330	255453	287175
石油、煤炭及其他燃料加工业	Processing of Petroleum, Coal and Other Fuels	419507	1444781	106105
化学原料和化学制品制造业	Manufacture of Chemical Raw Materials and Chemical Products	602916	1882387	1446763
医药制造业	Manufacture of Medicines	2039790	11364647	2930458
化学纤维制造业	Manufacture of Chemical Fibres	***	***	***
橡胶和塑料制品业	Manufacture of Rubber and Plastics Products	226765	454003	259195
非金属矿物制品业	Manufacture of Non-metallic Mineral Products	2629691	3561041	1615255
黑色金属冶炼和压延加工业	Manufacture and Pressing of Ferrous Metals	146360	-62947	279051
有色金属冶炼和压延加工业	Manufacture and Pressing of Non-ferrous Metals	66421	470002	113170
金属制品业	Manufacture of Fabricated Metal Products	819979	3615913	1475016
通用设备制造业	Manufacture of General-purpose Machinery	1329273	6287174	2315393
专用设备制造业	Manufacture of Special-purpose Machinery	2861994	11298536	3695253
汽车制造业	Manufacture of Motor Vehicles	11004714	21732351	8517360
铁路、船舶、航空航天和其他运输设备制造业	Manufacture of Railway Locomotives, Building of Ships and Boats, Manufacture of Air and Spacecrafts and Other Transportation Equipment	1724475	4092245	1369954
电气机械和器材制造业	Manufacture of Electrical Machinery and Equipment	2423921	5016602	2771616
计算机、通信和其他电子设备制造业	Manufacture of Computers, Communication Equipment and Other Electronic Equipment	9999131	26349131	11628853
仪器仪表制造业	Manufacture of Measuring Instruments and Meters	923545	3330803	1166827
其他制造业	Other Manufacturing	186552	781383	281195
废弃资源综合利用业	Waste Recycling and Recovery	9073	80026	32723
金属制品、机械和设备修理业	Repair of Fabricated Metal Products, Machinery and Equipment	156454	2953712	987003
电力、热力、燃气及水生产和供应业	**Production and Distribution of Electricity, Heating Power, Gas and Water**	**8652862**	**171336615**	**153610708**
电力、热力生产和供应业	Production and Distribution of Electricity and Heating Power	7127993	160137117	147910646
燃气生产和供应业	Production and Distribution of Gas	425566	4799734	824445
水的生产和供应业	Production and Distribution of Water	1099303	6399763	4875616

12-7 Continued

(10000 yuan)

损益 Profits and Losses							应交税金合计		
营业收入 Business Income	营业成本 Business Cost	销售费用 Sales Expenses	管理费用 Manage-ment Expenses	研发费用 R&D Expenses	财务费用 Financial Expenses	利润总额 Total Profits	Total Tax Payable	#税金及附加 Tax and Surtax	#应交增值税 Value Added Tax Payable
234190962	**193641682**	**12375475**	**8567129**	**4108849**	**2142005**	**17102542**	**11313670**	**3723458**	**4620751**
***	***	***	***		***	***	***	***	***
***	***	***	***	***	***	***	***	***	***
3507830	3399883	7586	184787	3921	732275	-465841	59011	28145	29795
***	***	***	***		***	***	***	***	***
1668176	1520985	7283	54709	13541	1761	38313	36564	8036	9415
3943779	3537802	175673	112078	26584	27172	112592	43086	6510	25085
5755106	3744830	1199461	283394	32645	-4683	533372	372933	33714	220190
2572526	1766823	270886	200975	17493	12323	179681	354338	233074	99687
***	***	***	***	***	***	***	***	***	***
201492	162675	5583	15895	3679	2135	10334	6133	2029	1829
1226391	829215	231898	102625	17063	6437	38538	58515	7775	43312
71507	63068	4960	3060	67	333	-328	1103	264	723
65959	60276	1846	2714	543	229	526	1448	162	1150
840524	655564	55204	57143	13309	22666	34460	34036	4307	22250
652559	507843	27255	32666	5615	1211	73515	47934	4034	19616
1549706	1162117	41642	166182	37562	-1066	138867	98244	14304	59932
1685873	1569091	43277	51350	5891	7968	19065	23146	4479	14723
6365150	5038566	57195	181107	12162	15920	-46190	1126821	956407	163982
3224322	2449612	269812	231385	66735	15790	203423	159500	18017	97307
12984162	5948324	3677080	798006	463217	154781	2142809	1123706	105806	671559
***	***	***	***	***	***	***	***	***	***
812671	674984	36994	67649	20144	6039	-1551	26651	4002	18850
5130604	4365436	194892	276741	123516	56390	165586	219188	25528	164303
914753	870039	15455	13336	2154	12773	-5294	13771	5290	10645
651592	570389	7518	24804	19954	1878	31080	14951	2332	9012
3589648	3033484	79219	233490	67064	58230	167038	97632	18810	55151
5777413	4384732	333332	345845	199521	14010	572840	260151	33107	143557
8863712	6177050	666303	605692	431864	116303	1048810	438526	53809	241579
44881170	36923150	2269006	1368920	683279	217225	3325290	3186257	1256805	1105014
4582801	3495569	83148	287855	166861	33501	519442	196442	20786	108457
7959748	6276167	479559	403911	274415	26022	552517	300173	36797	169740
36249925	31481306	1696243	977663	924817	-20938	1992338	603559	122363	265852
3299657	2224677	285579	266663	188141	20356	380498	188752	24151	118106
1411941	1245706	8429	62917	22457	492	80613	25292	2066	10259
75805	60197	762	6022	2519	69	10795	6569	781	4208
1234802	975211	10428	140451	29067	55205	191556	59407	7914	32550
61534763	**58067657**	**112197**	**918342**	**209345**	**541472**	**4933582**	**1752865**	**403222**	**618224**
55345651	52743113	18103	674737	79826	385811	4538835	1398207	167213	530350
4761205	4279313	18662	147858	120703	42196	345379	63305	6806	29105
1427907	1045231	75432	95748	8816	113466	49368	291354	229203	58769

12−8 分行业规模以上国有控股工业企业主要经济指标(2018年)

单位：万元

项 目	Item	企业单位个数(个) Number of Enterprises (unit)	#亏损企业 Loss-Suffering Enterprises	工业总产值(当年价格) Gross Output Value of Industry (at current year's prices)
合 计	**Total**	**643**	**142**	**115618998**
采矿业	**Mining and Quarrying**	**9**	**7**	**2699016**
煤炭开采和洗选业	Mining and Washing of Coal	1		***
石油和天然气开采业	Extraction of Petroleum and Natural Gas	2	2	***
黑色金属矿采选业	Mining and Processing of Ferrous Metal Ores	3	2	***
非金属矿采选业	Mining and Processing of Nonmetal Ores			
开采专业及辅助性活动	Mining and Support Service Activities	3	3	***
制造业	**Manufacturing**	**541**	**115**	**60906684**
农副食品加工业	Processing of Food from Agricultural Products	16	5	983146
食品制造业	Manufacture of Foods	13	2	642427
酒、饮料和精制茶制造业	Manufacture of Wines, Beverage and Refined Tea	9	2	1329613
烟草制品业	Manufacture of Cigarettes and Tobacco	1		***
纺织业	Manufacture of Textile	4	1	14914
纺织服装、服饰业	Manufacture of Textile Wearing Apparel and Ornament	5		85925
皮革、毛皮、羽毛及其制品和制鞋业	Manufacture of Leather, Fur, Feather and Its Products, and Footwear	1	1	***
木材加工和木、竹、藤、棕、草制品业	Processing of Timbers, Manufacture of Wood, Bamboo, Rattan, Palm, and Straw Products			
家具制造业	Manufacture of Furniture	2		***
造纸和纸制品业	Manufacture of Paper and Paper Products	2		***
印刷和记录媒介复制业	Printing, Reproduction of Recording Media	31	10	731436
文教、工美、体育和娱乐用品制造业	Manufacture of Articles for Culture, Education, Artwork, Sport and Entertainment Activities	7	2	181023
石油、煤炭及其他燃料加工业	Processing of Petroleum, Coal and Other Fuels	7	2	5640738
化学原料和化学制品制造业	Manufacture of Chemical Raw Materials and Chemical Products	23	2	1250159
医药制造业	Manufacture of Medicines	31	1	1983241
化学纤维制造业	Manufacture of Chemical Fibres	2		***
橡胶和塑料制品业	Manufacture of Rubber and Plastics Products	6	1	50723
非金属矿物制品业	Manufacture of Non-metallic Mineral Products	50	16	1756136
黑色金属冶炼和压延加工业	Manufacture and Pressing of Ferrous Metals	2		***
有色金属冶炼和压延加工业	Manufacture and Pressing of Non-ferrous Metals	7		517742
金属制品业	Manufacture of Fabricated Metal Products	25	8	1344309
通用设备制造业	Manufacture of General-purpose Machinery	39	10	938077
专用设备制造业	Manufacture of Special-purpose Machinery	47	12	1476287
汽车制造业	Manufacture of Motor Vehicles	42	11	28580110
铁路、船舶、航空航天和其他运输设备制造业	Manufacture of Railway Locomotives, Building of Ships and Boats, Manufacture of Air and Spacecrafts and Other Transportation Equipment	34	2	3712085
电气机械和器材制造业	Manufacture of Electrical Machinery and Equipment	23	7	818572
计算机、通信和其他电子设备制造业	Manufacture of Computers, Communication Equipment and Other Electronic Equipment	64	15	4766486
仪器仪表制造业	Manufacture of Measuring Instruments and Meters	38	4	726548
其他制造业	Other Manufacturing	5	1	1103826
废弃资源综合利用业	Waste Recycling and Recovery	1		***
金属制品、机械和设备修理业	Repair of Fabricated Metal Products, Machinery and Equipment	4		849117
电力、热力、燃气及水生产和供应业	**Production and Distribution of Electricity, Heating Power, Gas and Water**	**93**	**20**	**52013297**
电力、热力生产和供应业	Production and Distribution of Electricity and Heating Power	57	11	50025114
燃气生产和供应业	Production and Distribution of Gas	15	5	783826
水的生产和供应业	Production and Distribution of Water	21	4	1204357

MAIN ECONOMIC INDICATORS OF INDUSTRIAL ENTERPRISES ABOVE DESIGNATED SIZE (BY SECTOR) (2018)

(10000 yuan)

工业销售产值(当年价格)	#出口交货值	平均用工人数(人)	资产负债					
Sales Value of Industry (at current year's prices)	Delivery Value of Exports	Average Number of Employed Persons (person)	资产总计 Total Assets	流动资产合计 Total Current Assets	#存货 Inventories	#产成品 Finished Products	#应收账款 Accounts Receivable	固定资产原价 Total Original Value of Fixed Assets
114774749	**3447914**	**390996**	**354394284**	**98521265**	**11462090**	**4034901**	**20613007**	**118455666**
2715737	**217542**	**35356**	**38953991**	**8387272**	**314325**	**59213**	**1746499**	**9570455**
***	***	***	***	***	***	***	***	***
***		***	***	***	***	***	***	***
***		***	***	***	***	***	***	***
***	***	***	***	***	***	***	***	***
60048580	**3230372**	**278320**	**107676108**	**60890854**	**10968102**	**3964039**	**13730012**	**29052371**
994370		6420	1042315	776502	152141	104720	101937	167315
682674	871	6509	1157658	468337	53577	30009	148414	226835
1340076	3061	7982	2194812	1714022	219474	146896	20212	451631
***	***	***	***	***	***	***	***	***
14190	1383	953	214807	120886	7561	5558	7365	52678
94910	63241	843	90840	70587	37797	11028	11964	25256
***	***	***	***	***	***	***	***	***
***		***	***	***	***	***	***	***
***		***	***	***	***	***	***	***
732512	94	10238	1225889	794791	160626	67625	67628	959697
176319	3075	1578	279398	182225	118932	54508	11259	60818
5630778	2164	7223	2494792	962659	505188	117873	125863	3413171
1214698	20627	4193	1492343	998320	209916	148449	157027	848786
1860158	6099	17480	5014900	2697920	837734	301112	514029	1178509
***	***	***	***	***	***	***	***	***
54021	16320	1320	133076	100271	15598	7694	29186	38725
1730700	88304	13462	8650483	5392834	290757	127029	1030455	1075537
***	***	***	***	***	***	***	***	***
502809	41748	2066	618908	387015	140569	44386	59475	122528
1343558	79717	9139	2776197	1398472	226708	44018	231281	680103
944094	14543	10004	2179249	1574177	600286	106640	318706	407405
1362680	87130	16545	3851906	2813452	791274	270677	797845	692886
28500554	410685	73723	45838184	24470355	3032442	1558721	5441705	10087547
3513788	28967	27758	6550648	4793673	1594338	277014	1304581	1553534
847815	2977	5159	1864552	1388549	212373	37003	570931	300948
4598641	2136279	29261	11995234	6094136	935801	370703	1762587	4387463
704533	3766	7721	1381941	1101023	261086	69432	360683	190253
937428	35684	3020	1385090	1073597	243221	3869	372555	281353
***		***	***	***	***	***	***	***
839521	64913	12462	4052060	987397	176036	85	224986	807445
52010432		**77320**	**207764185**	**29243138**	**179662**	**11650**	**5136495**	**79832840**
50023404		60158	194857104	26050804	161572	2977	4002420	71182811
783826		4331	1351178	474047	8036	5338	81218	624111
1203202		12831	11555903	2718287	10054	3335	1052858	8025918

12-8 续表

单位：万元

项 目	Item	资产负债 Assets and Liabilities 负债合计 Total Liabilities	#流动负债合计 Total Current Liabilities	#应付账款 Accounts Payable	所有者权益合计 Total Owner's Equity
合 计	**Total**	**149427439**	**98126444**	**23914950**	**204966843**
采矿业	**Mining and Quarrying**	**22884780**	**12385702**	**1267490**	**16069211**
煤炭开采和洗选业	Mining and Washing of Coal	***	***	***	***
石油和天然气开采业	Extraction of Petroleum and Natural Gas	***	***	***	***
黑色金属矿采选业	Mining and Processing of Ferrous Metal Ores	***	***	***	***
非金属矿采选业	Mining and Processing of Nonmetal Ores				
开采专业及辅助性活动	Mining and Support Service Activities	***	***	***	***
制造业	**Manufacturing**	**57136123**	**45790976**	**15164145**	**50539984**
农副食品加工业	Processing of Food from Agricultural Products	719452	703435	100015	322863
食品制造业	Manufacture of Foods	336849	314346	165977	820809
酒、饮料和精制茶制造业	Manufacture of Wines, Beverage and Refined Tea	1248144	954799	40440	946668
烟草制品业	Manufacture of Cigarettes and Tobacco	***	***	***	***
纺织业	Manufacture of Textile	91011	38758	1637	123795
纺织服装、服饰业	Manufacture of Textile Wearing Apparel and Ornament	67102	53191	18514	23738
皮革、毛皮、羽毛及其制品和制鞋业	Manufacture of Leather, Fur, Feather and Its Products, and Footwear	***	***	***	***
木材加工和木、竹、藤、棕、草制品业	Processing of Timbers, Manufacture of Wood, Bamboo, Rattan, Palm, and Straw Products				
家具制造业	Manufacture of Furniture	***	***	***	***
造纸和纸制品业	Manufacture of Paper and Paper Products	***	***	***	***
印刷和记录媒介复制业	Printing, Reproduction of Recording Media	380554	342338	135632	845335
文教、工美、体育和娱乐用品制造业	Manufacture of Articles for Culture, Education, Artwork, Sport and Entertainment Activities	231116	202393	121400	48282
石油、煤炭及其他燃料加工业	Processing of Petroleum, Coal and Other Fuels	1182702	1158742	366879	1312091
化学原料和化学制品制造业	Manufacture of Chemical Raw Materials and Chemical Products	964734	630947	245976	527609
医药制造业	Manufacture of Medicines	1568283	1071353	286779	3446617
化学纤维制造业	Manufacture of Chemical Fibres	***	***	***	***
橡胶和塑料制品业	Manufacture of Rubber and Plastics Products	35965	32681	11896	97111
非金属矿物制品业	Manufacture of Non-metallic Mineral Products	6178953	5464634	844306	2471530
黑色金属冶炼和压延加工业	Manufacture and Pressing of Ferrous Metals	***	***	***	***
有色金属冶炼和压延加工业	Manufacture and Pressing of Non-ferrous Metals	138992	119162	21073	479916
金属制品业	Manufacture of Fabricated Metal Products	1420568	1209451	264042	1355628
通用设备制造业	Manufacture of General-purpose Machinery	1332149	1234409	319761	847100
专用设备制造业	Manufacture of Special-purpose Machinery	2527099	2135106	797193	1324808
汽车制造业	Manufacture of Motor Vehicles	25770663	19686934	7235565	20067521
铁路、船舶、航空航天和其他运输设备制造业	Manufacture of Railway Locomotives, Building of Ships and Boats, Manufacture of Air and Spacecrafts and Other Transportation Equipment	3924164	3334029	1114672	2626485
电气机械和器材制造业	Manufacture of Electrical Machinery and Equipment	1234672	1154447	645687	629880
计算机、通信和其他电子设备制造业	Manufacture of Computers, Communication Equipment and Other Electronic Equipment	3686200	3300139	1730814	8309033
仪器仪表制造业	Manufacture of Measuring Instruments and Meters	790927	720579	250555	591014
其他制造业	Other Manufacturing	894152	832978	144666	490938
废弃资源综合利用业	Waste Recycling and Recovery	***	***	***	***
金属制品、机械和设备修理业	Repair of Fabricated Metal Products, Machinery and Equipment	1466250	741171	119340	2585810
电力、热力、燃气及水生产和供应业	**Production and Distribution of Electricity, Heating Power, Gas and Water**	**69406536**	**39949766**	**7483315**	**138357648**
电力、热力生产和供应业	Production and Distribution of Electricity and Heating Power	63135139	37021551	6285330	131721965
燃气生产和供应业	Production and Distribution of Gas	892997	551839	179520	458180
水的生产和供应业	Production and Distribution of Water	5378401	2376376	1018465	6177503

12-8 Continued

(10000 yuan)

#实收资本 Paid-up Capital	损益 Profits and Losses: 营业收入 Business Income	营业成本 Business Cost	销售费用 Sales Expenses	管理费用 Management Expenses	财务费用 Financial Expenses	利润总额 Total Profits	应交税金合计 Total Tax Payable	#税金及附加 Tax and Surtax	#应交增值税 Value Added Tax Payable
131483474	**125600476**	**108257131**	**3405336**	**4913810**	**1693873**	**10058564**	**8324032**	**3310375**	**3219812**
6209901	**5340338**	**5253059**	**17792**	**388342**	**659416**	**-882517**	**180872**	**55878**	**86972**
***	***	***	***	***	***	***	***	***	***
***	***	***	***	***	***	***	***	***	***
***	***	***	***	***	***	***	***	***	***
***	***	***	***	***	***	***	***	***	***
23634263	**67574019**	**52847583**	**3314779**	**4127048**	**557711**	**5904466**	**6091325**	**2839341**	**2117993**
233195	1658540	1550794	64260	30139	4190	15944	13077	2297	8531
253944	870764	620273	183923	37774	-1862	45489	40552	4182	27986
235084	1354041	797146	127359	69081	-3140	198264	312254	187982	83359
***	***	***	***	***	***	***	***	***	***
77317	45501	30991	1488	11062	1024	2685	3220	1515	744
53420	160733	151583	2511	4448	1227	583	1611	413	1074
***	***	***	***	***	***	***	***	***	***
***	***	***	***	***	***	***	***	***	***
***	***	***	***	***	***	***	***	***	***
468678	917471	659356	16932	120991	-3119	119441	87451	12300	51302
139539	203776	160060	25695	16468	3732	2173	11385	1829	9348
59336	6156642	4774649	35263	190879	5892	256504	1182534	875456	238065
971109	1385675	1171058	24755	118625	7990	60000	36929	5618	29358
986138	1997081	1015347	368350	220458	20674	478774	248249	28387	159365
***	***	***	***	***	***	***	***	***	***
36993	126227	101584	5117	14729	-376	732	4782	1026	3208
1223313	2015562	1657525	66445	174438	190540	15850	105207	15462	71834
***	***	***	***	***	***	***	***	***	***
104721	530614	472728	5233	28136	1999	24237	11311	1855	6403
638122	1712106	1500611	16631	136229	9242	11502	32996	8999	11568
517645	1024797	819079	36557	111772	5264	31846	84946	10636	61967
742604	1802388	1441454	82542	199128	19930	50057	73898	15093	50598
9102469	31030034	23986315	1923005	1302059	253975	3776292	3020603	1326885	955711
1134521	3645943	2865531	42345	386450	36443	339412	160402	17382	84719
487207	968943	858819	23519	76467	9901	-9166	27876	5375	18800
4377878	5741067	4836497	172449	521425	-77576	289536	187956	38162	110929
261087	792933	575269	51065	126649	2899	-11210	49047	7240	33275
259632	1069154	981526	4103	64998	-308	23035	6803	989	1513
***	***	***	***	***	***	***	***	***	***
896625	879060	741900	1882	103434	60468	137264	46368	6841	31778
101639309	**52686119**	**50156489**	**72765**	**398421**	**476746**	**5036615**	**2051835**	**415156**	**1014848**
96455807	50423808	48432220	10108	258126	359782	4799420	1721017	188621	937132
431028	827485	765570	9812	51789	25604	5286	21456	2508	4641
4752475	1434826	958700	52845	88505	91360	231909	309363	224027	73074

12-9 分行业规模以上国有控股工业企业主要经济指标(2019年)

单位：万元

项 目	Item	企业单位个数(个) Number of Enterprises (unit)	#亏损企业 Loss-Suffering Enterprises	工业总产值(当年价格) Gross Output Value of Industry (at current year's prices)
合 计	**Total**	**656**	**135**	**123104607**
采矿业	**Mining and Quarrying**	**8**	**4**	**3066108**
煤炭开采和洗选业	Mining and Washing of Coal			
石油和天然气开采业	Extraction of Petroleum and Natural Gas	2	1	***
黑色金属矿采选业	Mining and Processing of Ferrous Metal Ores	3	1	***
非金属矿采选业	Mining and Processing of Nonmetal Ores			
开采专业及辅助性活动	Mining and Support Service Activities	3	2	***
制造业	**Manufacturing**	**545**	**114**	**63733678**
农副食品加工业	Processing of Food from Agricultural Products	16	4	847222
食品制造业	Manufacture of Foods	13	2	675199
酒、饮料和精制茶制造业	Manufacture of Wines, Beverage and Refined Tea	9	3	928270
烟草制品业	Manufacture of Cigarettes and Tobacco	1		***
纺织业	Manufacture of Textile	4	1	18466
纺织服装、服饰业	Manufacture of Textile Wearing Apparel and Ornament	6	2	76456
皮革、毛皮、羽毛及其制品和制鞋业	Manufacture of Leather, Fur, Feather and Its Products, and Footwear	1		***
木材加工和木、竹、藤、棕、草制品业	Processing of Timbers, Manufacture of Wood, Bamboo, Rattan, Palm, and Straw Products			
家具制造业	Manufacture of Furniture	2	1	***
造纸和纸制品业	Manufacture of Paper and Paper Products	3		***
印刷和记录媒介复制业	Printing, Reproduction of Recording Media	31	8	745319
文教、工美、体育和娱乐用品制造业	Manufacture of Articles for Culture, Education, Artwork, Sport and Entertainment Activities	6	1	135425
石油、煤炭及其他燃料加工业	Processing of Petroleum, Coal and Other Fuels	8	4	5536092
化学原料和化学制品制造业	Manufacture of Chemical Raw Materials and Chemical Products	25	5	1161324
医药制造业	Manufacture of Medicines	34	7	1804160
化学纤维制造业	Manufacture of Chemical Fibres	2		***
橡胶和塑料制品业	Manufacture of Rubber and Plastics Products	6	1	36992
非金属矿物制品业	Manufacture of Non-metallic Mineral Products	46	12	1724557
黑色金属冶炼和压延加工业	Manufacture and Pressing of Ferrous Metals	2		***
有色金属冶炼和压延加工业	Manufacture and Pressing of Non-ferrous Metals	6		427755
金属制品业	Manufacture of Fabricated Metal Products	25	6	1558441
通用设备制造业	Manufacture of General-purpose Machinery	38	6	1032730
专用设备制造业	Manufacture of Special-purpose Machinery	47	10	1604596
汽车制造业	Manufacture of Motor Vehicles	45	14	29976795
铁路、船舶、航空航天和其他运输设备制造业	Manufacture of Railway Locomotives, Building of Ships and Boats, Manufacture of Air and Spacecrafts and Other Transportation Equipment	32	1	3841798
电气机械和器材制造业	Manufacture of Electrical Machinery and Equipment	21	3	980569
计算机、通信和其他电子设备制造业	Manufacture of Computers, Communication Equipment and Other Electronic Equipment	68	17	6171768
仪器仪表制造业	Manufacture of Measuring Instruments and Meters	37	5	811471
其他制造业	Other Manufacturing	5	1	1268382
废弃资源综合利用业	Waste Recycling and Recovery	2		***
金属制品、机械和设备修理业	Repair of Fabricated Metal Products, Machinery and Equipment	4		996419
电力、热力、燃气及水生产和供应业	**Production and Distribution of Electricity, Heating Power, Gas and Water**	**103**	**17**	**56304821**
电力、热力生产和供应业	Production and Distribution of Electricity and Heating Power	65	9	54375894
燃气生产和供应业	Production and Distribution of Gas	15	3	794508
水的生产和供应业	Production and Distribution of Water	23	5	1134419

MAIN ECONOMIC INDICATORS OF INDUSTRIAL ENTERPRISES ABOVE DESIGNATED SIZE (BY SECTOR) (2019)

(10000 yuan)

平均用工人数(人) Average Number of Employed Persons (person)	资产负债							
	资产总计 Total Assets	流动资产合计 Total Current Assets	#存货 Inventories	#产成品 Finished Products	#应收账款 Accounts Receivable	固定资产原价 Total Original Value of Fixed Assets	负债合计 Total Liabilities	#流动负债合计 Total Current Liabilities
369730	**379311251**	**98892978**	**11750540**	**3895677**	**21770646**	**125276275**	**148185822**	**103212471**
30816	**39212031**	**8422811**	**298772**	**30839**	**1585245**	**9976830**	**24204302**	**13381773**
***	***	***	***		***	***	***	***
***	***	***	***	***	***	***	***	***
***	***	***	***		***	***	***	***
259256	**105156553**	**62747236**	**11266280**	**3857525**	**15028630**	**30102176**	**55405324**	**46773075**
6525	1068465	783881	154587	121624	68842	184393	738642	691493
6365	1160654	443883	52647	25211	143818	231798	338686	316324
7828	1993624	1491306	201786	110132	21254	504007	989819	731861
***	***	***	***	***	***	***	***	***
828	210448	115046	6434	5166	11739	51278	83878	30365
777	87585	68136	34073	10536	14208	24367	65160	47952
***	***	***	***	***	***	***	***	***
***	***	***	***	***	***	***	***	***
***	***	***	***	***	***	***	***	***
9549	1260403	845731	193505	77720	104086	980146	367556	279423
1338	265428	173833	100788	84921	11337	58439	200560	177311
6824	2349329	642697	429126	100720	125024	3568507	1051458	826905
4245	1512433	1027313	238155	170052	168044	680054	942465	483253
18272	5537563	2800087	859951	299044	583956	1552504	1753602	1309860
***	***	***	***	***	***	***	***	***
1140	130856	101808	15059	9303	24379	38594	31525	27920
11880	4239126	2654955	288766	136066	1096600	873632	2445490	2319596
***	***	***	***	***	***	***	***	***
1251	501935	301543	92073	22921	49677	95152	101734	83689
9072	2936024	1757800	321929	61658	190654	694391	1544863	1429983
9296	2269963	1599080	572420	104101	354744	393315	1268632	1152395
16165	4021795	2934464	750984	256591	821027	706331	2589961	2244872
64345	44614120	26891514	2945775	1310513	6520334	10827703	26839287	22953001
24007	6777917	5085784	1724803	294403	1349597	1500444	3829201	3577720
3806	1974359	1533520	193034	30903	532267	232463	1364871	1129383
28741	13936772	7831850	1078554	476221	1904757	4520623	4802251	4297982
7570	1538061	1231845	321994	102491	417007	211995	812845	766572
3012	1428098	1113591	340733	5746	210237	318439	905910	855980
***	***	***	***	***	***	***	***	***
13089	4100972	712670	196833		257678	801698	1409244	710552
79658	**234942667**	**27722931**	**185488**	**7314**	**5156772**	**85197270**	**68576196**	**43057624**
63663	221319527	24237859	172309	2882	3820648	76084236	61545133	40061909
2740	1290536	449603	2786	161	74912	532727	911814	593963
13255	12332603	3035469	10393	4271	1261212	8580307	6119249	2401752

12-9 续表

单位：万元

项　目	Item	资产负债 Assets and Liabilities		
		#应付账款 Accounts Payable	所有者权益合计 Total Owner's Equity	#实收资本 Paid-up Capital
合 计	**Total**	**26784007**	**231125427**	**180093702**
采矿业	**Mining and Quarrying**	**1442636**	**15007730**	**6151466**
煤炭开采和洗选业	Mining and Washing of Coal			
石油和天然气开采业	Extraction of Petroleum and Natural Gas	***	***	***
黑色金属矿采选业	Mining and Processing of Ferrous Metal Ores	***	***	***
非金属矿采选业	Mining and Processing of Nonmetal Ores			
开采专业及辅助性活动	Mining and Support Service Activities	***	***	***
制造业	**Manufacturing**	**17057891**	**49751228**	**21269679**
农副食品加工业	Processing of Food from Agricultural Products	49662	329823	253752
食品制造业	Manufacture of Foods	159569	821968	253944
酒、饮料和精制茶制造业	Manufacture of Wines, Beverage and Refined Tea	***	***	***
烟草制品业	Manufacture of Cigarettes and Tobacco	9284	334414	92976
纺织业	Manufacture of Textile	1652	126570	76141
纺织服装、服饰业	Manufacture of Textile Wearing Apparel and Ornament	19505	22425	53920
皮革、毛皮、羽毛及其制品和制鞋业	Manufacture of Leather, Fur, Feather and Its Products, and Footwear	***	***	***
木材加工和木、竹、藤、棕、草制品业	Processing of Timbers, Manufacture of Wood, Bamboo, Rattan, Palm, and Straw Products			
家具制造业	Manufacture of Furniture	***	***	***
造纸和纸制品业	Manufacture of Paper and Paper Products	***	***	***
印刷和记录媒介复制业	Printing, Reproduction of Recording Media	134936	892847	482979
文教、工美、体育和娱乐用品制造业	Manufacture of Articles for Culture, Education, Artwork, Sport and Entertainment Activities	122029	64868	158239
石油、煤炭及其他燃料加工业	Processing of Petroleum, Coal and Other Fuels	341823	1297871	87736
化学原料和化学制品制造业	Manufacture of Chemical Raw Materials and Chemical Products	221009	569968	881104
医药制造业	Manufacture of Medicines	285077	3783961	1076157
化学纤维制造业	Manufacture of Chemical Fibres	***	***	***
橡胶和塑料制品业	Manufacture of Rubber and Plastics Products	7166	99332	36993
非金属矿物制品业	Manufacture of Non-metallic Mineral Products	993355	1793636	811991
黑色金属冶炼和压延加工业	Manufacture and Pressing of Ferrous Metals	***	***	***
有色金属冶炼和压延加工业	Manufacture and Pressing of Non-ferrous Metals	26113	400200	78110
金属制品业	Manufacture of Fabricated Metal Products	315781	1391160	621478
通用设备制造业	Manufacture of General-purpose Machinery	372891	1001331	529455
专用设备制造业	Manufacture of Special-purpose Machinery	799495	1431834	779980
汽车制造业	Manufacture of Motor Vehicles	8312877	17774833	6909638
铁路、船舶、航空航天和其他运输设备制造业	Manufacture of Railway Locomotives, Building of Ships and Boats, Manufacture of Air and Spacecrafts and Other Transportation Equipment	1449419	2948715	1065488
电气机械和器材制造业	Manufacture of Electrical Machinery and Equipment	450486	609488	447796
计算机、通信和其他电子设备制造业	Manufacture of Computers, Communication Equipment and Other Electronic Equipment	2215680	9134520	4612289
仪器仪表制造业	Manufacture of Measuring Instruments and Meters	267805	725215	258886
其他制造业	Other Manufacturing	182345	522189	259632
废弃资源综合利用业	Waste Recycling and Recovery	***	***	***
金属制品、机械和设备修理业	Repair of Fabricated Metal Products, Machinery and Equipment	128675	2691727	882284
电力、热力、燃气及水生产和供应业	**Production and Distribution of Electricity, Heating Power, Gas and Water**	**8283479**	**166366470**	**152672557**
电力、热力生产和供应业	Production and Distribution of Electricity and Heating Power	7037182	159774394	147718695
燃气生产和供应业	Production and Distribution of Gas	177250	378722	206129
水的生产和供应业	Production and Distribution of Water	1069047	6213354	4747733

12-9 Continued

(10000 yuan)

损益 Profits and Losses							应交税金合计 Total Tax Payable		
营业收入 Business Income	营业成本 Business Cost	销售费用 Sales Expenses	管理费用 Manage-ment Expenses	研发费用 R&D Expenses	财务费用 Financial Expenses	利润总额 Total Profits	应交税金合计 Total Tax Payable	#税金及附加 Tax and Surtax	#应交增值税 Value Added Tax Payable
134968118	**117251723**	**3385284**	**4074211**	**1473760**	**1560071**	**9518419**	**7518147**	**3241535**	**2515033**
5227103	**4962799**	**8958**	**268979**	**32193**	**738115**	**-424908**	**125533**	**43011**	**50957**
***	***	***	***	***	***	***	***	***	***
***	***	***	***	***	***	***	***	***	***
***	***		***	***	***	***	***	***	***
72630628	**58136079**	**3283542**	**3043104**	**1358731**	**317678**	**5407677**	**5710838**	**2804586**	**1878750**
1942767	1828175	66741	33274	1318	5808	24376	12951	2194	8502
945209	680013	208805	34945	4601	-1567	43662	32052	3631	18357
***	***	***	***	***	***	***	***	***	***
528583	170231	10740	36891	4441	-5387	38047	325281	264032	50132
47169	32691	949	8605	926	807	2133	2743	1498	369
173466	165076	3159	3729	74	1275	-641	2988	435	2483
***	***	***	***	***	***	***	***	***	***
***	***	***	***	***	***	***	***	***	***
***	***	***	***		***	***	***	***	***
883284	632924	15632	112347	19528	-3512	102301	64554	10440	36157
200034	169931	16034	11527	1803	3199	4830	10045	1734	7569
6017590	4746715	35192	166698	8702	9578	-48746	1118224	950843	161531
1279833	1066341	24168	102659	23592	10553	50406	44614	5503	24470
1840699	941761	342009	184739	76774	19889	415310	188765	24707	120350
***	***	***	***	***	***	***	***	***	***
118751	90648	4840	10018	4447	-158	6932	4987	1065	3063
1924681	1636327	74253	107850	60684	17359	79718	84092	12532	60887
***	***	***	***	***	***	***	***	***	***
427718	377771	3078	12960	12130	458	25659	10649	1678	6266
1769774	1512054	16535	103917	32181	7370	114661	37671	10883	14713
1115353	895246	36415	73462	56309	4231	83405	53635	8372	32114
2000438	1628641	88319	146725	68083	16839	61338	77334	15980	52484
34209617	27242868	1965615	1006626	320283	153723	3507423	2974986	1207648	1001545
3817397	3040810	50551	211254	120861	25572	348062	134677	15592	76494
1077525	941036	27196	51772	30778	11835	16815	25609	5329	14136
7034705	6026561	185234	262493	394102	-31021	225853	151553	41937	78527
894713	628195	54167	78708	63981	2400	74806	50865	7605	36316
1315569	1209832	5303	58554	19448	-633	28643	4778	1224	2226
***	***	***	***	***	***	***	***	***	***
1103279	902216	6822	123139	25154	54789	150118	44517	7133	26206
57110387	**54152845**	**92784**	**762128**	**82836**	**504278**	**4535650**	**1681776**	**393939**	**585325**
54905565	52370871	13224	639178	73754	376472	4483954	1387503	165680	529402
845454	785468	5644	32800	1706	24946	-108	11067	1280	2047
1359368	996506	73917	90150	7376	102860	51804	283207	226979	53876

12-10 分行业规模以上港澳台及外商投资工业企业主要经济指标(2018年)

单位：万元

项目	Item	企业单位个数(个) Number of Enterprises (unit)	#亏损企业 Loss-Suffering Enterprises	工业总产值(当年价格) Gross Output Value of Industry (at current year's prices)
合计	**Total**	**661**	**173**	**74005676**
采矿业	**Mining and Quarrying**	**1**		***
煤炭开采和洗选业	Mining and Washing of Coal			
石油和天然气开采业	Extraction of Petroleum and Natural Gas			
黑色金属矿采选业	Mining and Processing of Ferrous Metal Ores			
非金属矿采选业	Mining and Processing of Nonmetal Ores			
开采专业及辅助性活动	Mining and Support Service Activities	1		***
制造业	**Manufacturing**	**650**	**173**	**69418908**
农副食品加工业	Processing of Food from Agricultural Products	16	4	503428
食品制造业	Manufacture of Foods	39	10	2052794
酒、饮料和精制茶制造业	Manufacture of Wines, Beverage and Refined Tea	19	7	822111
烟草制品业	Manufacture of Cigarettes and Tobacco			
纺织业	Manufacture of Textile	2	1	***
纺织服装、服饰业	Manufacture of Textile Wearing Apparel and Ornament	17	7	182530
皮革、毛皮、羽毛及其制品和制鞋业	Manufacture of Leather, Fur, Feather and Its Products, and Footwear	2	1	***
木材加工和木、竹、藤、棕、草制品业	Processing of Timbers, Manufacture of Wood, Bamboo, Rattan, Palm, and Straw Products			
家具制造业	Manufacture of Furniture	8	2	429204
造纸和纸制品业	Manufacture of Paper and Paper Products	11	3	425903
印刷和记录媒介复制业	Printing, Reproduction of Recording Media	11	3	147766
文教、工美、体育和娱乐用品制造业	Manufacture of Articles for Culture, Education, Artwork, Sport and Entertainment Activities	8	2	42464
石油、煤炭及其他燃料加工业	Processing of Petroleum, Coal and Other Fuels	2		***
化学原料和化学制品制造业	Manufacture of Chemical Raw Materials and Chemical Products	30	6	981277
医药制造业	Manufacture of Medicines	43	7	5405031
化学纤维制造业	Manufacture of Chemical Fibres			
橡胶和塑料制品业	Manufacture of Rubber and Plastics Products	18	4	373510
非金属矿物制品业	Manufacture of Non-metallic Mineral Products	17	5	212654
黑色金属冶炼和压延加工业	Manufacture and Pressing of Ferrous Metals	1	1	***
有色金属冶炼和压延加工业	Manufacture and Pressing of Non-ferrous Metals	2	1	***
金属制品业	Manufacture of Fabricated Metal Products	28	6	301936
通用设备制造业	Manufacture of General-purpose Machinery	63	15	3235034
专用设备制造业	Manufacture of Special-purpose Machinery	69	14	1560765
汽车制造业	Manufacture of Motor Vehicles	108	47	31749963
铁路、船舶、航空航天和其他运输设备制造业	Manufacture of Railway Locomotives, Building of Ships and Boats, Manufacture of Air and Spacecrafts and Other Transportation Equipment	2		***
电气机械和器材制造业	Manufacture of Electrical Machinery and Equipment	32	9	2006611
计算机、通信和其他电子设备制造业	Manufacture of Computers, Communication Equipment and Other Electronic Equipment	58	14	16875932
仪器仪表制造业	Manufacture of Measuring Instruments and Meters	35	3	812184
其他制造业	Other Manufacturing	3	1	***
废弃资源综合利用业	Waste Recycling and Recovery	1		***
金属制品、机械和设备修理业	Repair of Fabricated Metal Products, Machinery and Equipment	5		826278
电力、热力、燃气及水生产和供应业	**Production and Distribution of Electricity, Heating Power, Gas and Water**	**10**		**4567624**
电力、热力生产和供应业	Production and Distribution of Electricity and Heating Power	4		657327
燃气生产和供应业	Production and Distribution of Gas	4		3815613
水的生产和供应业	Production and Distribution of Water	2		***

MAIN ECONOMIC INDICATORS OF INDUSTRIAL ENTERPRISES ABOVE DESIGNATED SIZE (BY SECTOR) (2018)

(10000 yuan)

工业销售产值(当年价格) Sales Value of Industry (at current year's prices)	#出口交货值 Delivery Value of Exports	平均用工人数(人) Average Number of Employed Persons (person)	资产负债 资产总计 Total Assets	流动资产合计 Total Current Assets	#存货 Inventories	#产成品 Finished Products	#应收账款 Accounts Receivable	固定资产原价 Total Original Value of Fixed Assets
72774208	**8100041**	**288581**	**95508834**	**61149045**	**10410079**	**4623157**	**14038072**	**28982193**
***		***	***	***	***	***	***	***
***		***	***	***	***	***	***	***
68186762	**8100041**	**278430**	**84396306**	**58113965**	**10386807**	**4618955**	**13545501**	**24408881**
502361	27041	5121	352873	208585	57943	15230	65659	145860
2090356	82791	23484	2941661	1606915	176770	89325	368008	1049111
799804	16878	8173	1085680	765140	73905	33645	214427	505227
***		***	***	***	***	***	***	***
177707	114723	6694	172637	147933	67851	24068	29302	45268
***	***	***	***	***	***	***	***	***
426378	10196	2377	556728	463470	250740	224959	52688	103997
421832	55158	2093	385586	275030	61955	14507	79198	259838
148489	4932	2494	207133	135621	27367	12459	30864	180228
43432	31632	1124	55502	49448	21412	7939	11905	6906
***		***	***	***	***	***	***	***
961928	18226	7144	1229986	793506	98149	31161	154574	619131
5011232	99646	29644	5873896	4215349	1435428	669934	1177454	1170014
357872	48615	4320	411098	290718	55005	25373	94632	198815
215898	25105	3620	324846	226372	29433	10547	81746	179308
***		***	***	***	***	***	***	***
***	***	***	***	***	***	***	***	***
336594	73303	3936	584626	419962	94951	32395	105909	163609
3228486	661354	19948	5293606	3937411	852511	286951	732420	1080030
1510172	493540	14161	3390107	2364405	362235	101693	691571	436445
32053279	398114	66712	32606053	19029040	2869069	1421333	4415363	10573861
***	***	***	***	***	***	***	***	***
2056083	255312	10314	2006661	1765716	296026	105474	592907	366713
15709740	5473982	46739	24440806	19672918	3073618	1446051	4026893	6667523
829947	124686	5951	1270127	1012782	217722	37040	339554	159072
***	***	***	***	***	***	***	***	***
***		***	***	***	***	***	***	***
826278	67109	11308	632844	409217	147882	4427	189307	381965
4567616		**9706**	**10602588**	**2705632**	**11619**	**706**	**400837**	**4528856**
657327		959	4540753	1673125	8443		142410	1756307
3815605		7976	5940537	1001545	2913	706	245344	2718217
***		***	***	***	***		***	***

12-10 续表

单位：万元

项目	Item	资产负债 Assets and Liabilities 负债合计 Total Liabilities	#流动负债合计 Total Current Liabilities	#应付账款 Accounts Payable	所有者权益合计 Total Owner's Equity
合 计	**Total**	**52424007**	**46047596**	**17314140**	**43084824**
采矿业	**Mining and Quarrying**	***	***	***	***
煤炭开采和洗选业	Mining and Washing of Coal				
石油和天然气开采业	Extraction of Petroleum and Natural Gas				
黑色金属矿采选业	Mining and Processing of Ferrous Metal Ores				
非金属矿采选业	Mining and Processing of Nonmetal Ores				
开采专业及辅助性活动	Mining and Support Service Activities	***	***	***	***
制造业	**Manufacturing**	**48243132**	**43009676**	**17104806**	**36153171**
农副食品加工业	Processing of Food from Agricultural Products	218301	148702	64703	134572
食品制造业	Manufacture of Foods	1381335	1338296	589993	1560327
酒、饮料和精制茶制造业	Manufacture of Wines, Beverage and Refined Tea	968548	873428	316009	117132
烟草制品业	Manufacture of Cigarettes and Tobacco				
纺织业	Manufacture of Textile	***	***	***	***
纺织服装、服饰业	Manufacture of Textile Wearing Apparel and Ornament	125419	124396	26448	47219
皮革、毛皮、羽毛及其制品和制鞋业	Manufacture of Leather, Fur, Feather and Its Products, and Footwear	***	***	***	***
木材加工和木、竹、藤、棕、草制品业	Processing of Timbers, Manufacture of Wood, Bamboo, Rattan, Palm, and Straw Products				
家具制造业	Manufacture of Furniture	555183	415023	113583	1545
造纸和纸制品业	Manufacture of Paper and Paper Products	158501	155342	65425	227085
印刷和记录媒介复制业	Printing, Reproduction of Recording Media	69762	67085	27710	137371
文教、工美、体育和娱乐用品制造业	Manufacture of Articles for Culture, Education, Artwork, Sport and Entertainment Activities	38832	38832	20396	16670
石油、煤炭及其他燃料加工业	Processing of Petroleum, Coal and Other Fuels	***	***	***	***
化学原料和化学制品制造业	Manufacture of Chemical Raw Materials and Chemical Products	360355	329668	136260	869631
医药制造业	Manufacture of Medicines	2919853	2324122	944778	2954043
化学纤维制造业	Manufacture of Chemical Fibres				
橡胶和塑料制品业	Manufacture of Rubber and Plastics Products	149201	126273	81488	261897
非金属矿物制品业	Manufacture of Non-metallic Mineral Products	113963	112408	53275	210883
黑色金属冶炼和压延加工业	Manufacture and Pressing of Ferrous Metals	***	***	***	***
有色金属冶炼和压延加工业	Manufacture and Pressing of Non-ferrous Metals	***	***	***	***
金属制品业	Manufacture of Fabricated Metal Products	272988	238124	76437	311638
通用设备制造业	Manufacture of General-purpose Machinery	2473693	2103893	672070	2819913
专用设备制造业	Manufacture of Special-purpose Machinery	1923402	1710898	523277	1466705
汽车制造业	Manufacture of Motor Vehicles	17634854	15179378	6896963	14971200
铁路、船舶、航空航天和其他运输设备制造业	Manufacture of Railway Locomotives, Building of Ships and Boats, Manufacture of Air and Spacecrafts and Other Transportation Equipment	***	***	***	***
电气机械和器材制造业	Manufacture of Electrical Machinery and Equipment	1118380	1046565	495936	888280
计算机、通信和其他电子设备制造业	Manufacture of Computers, Communication Equipment and Other Electronic Equipment	16438194	15517361	5552526	8002612
仪器仪表制造业	Manufacture of Measuring Instruments and Meters	674251	637596	286763	595875
其他制造业	Other Manufacturing	***	***	***	***
废弃资源综合利用业	Waste Recycling and Recovery	***	***	***	***
金属制品、机械和设备修理业	Repair of Fabricated Metal Products, Machinery and Equipment	360704	330487	75492	272140
电力、热力、燃气及水生产和供应业	**Production and Distribution of Electricity, Heating Power, Gas and Water**	**3799153**	**2679078**	**149251**	**6803435**
电力、热力生产和供应业	Production and Distribution of Electricity and Heating Power	1862641	1228396	27904	2678112
燃气生产和供应业	Production and Distribution of Gas	1878866	1430975	110073	4061671
水的生产和供应业	Production and Distribution of Water	***	***	***	***

12-10 Continued

(10000 yuan)

#实收资本 Paid-up Capital	损益 Profits and Losses						应交税金合计 Total Tax Payable	#税金及附加 Tax and Surtax	#应交增值税 Value Added Tax Payable
	营业收入 Business Income	营业成本 Business Cost	销售费用 Sales Expenses	管理费用 Management Expenses	财务费用 Financial Expenses	利润总额 Total Profits			
17883061	**88098693**	**69588059**	**6855551**	**3942913**	**362944**	**7407290**	**5251947**	**1519390**	**2311445**
***	***	***	***	***	***	***	***	***	***
***	***	***	***	***	***	***	***	***	***
15889368	**83388251**	**65427616**	**6827140**	**3732747**	**273273**	**6763249**	**5102477**	**1506061**	**2241850**
100141	669756	583335	45329	33821	3781	-114	13152	2136	8434
772030	4568230	2794541	1239925	218570	-9267	328651	346963	32255	234892
563545	903069	612668	144971	75934	6751	26261	74563	16212	43961
***	***	***	***	***	***	***	***	***	***
34144	256652	216463	21609	17874	2468	-1659	7500	1150	6262
***	***	***	***	***	***	***	***	***	***
33696	341336	265468	22601	29710	14286	7604	18324	1812	10532
111962	530864	400785	24627	27796	-2922	76077	41992	3219	20707
89491	160069	133880	6914	15468	-471	3732	8487	1017	6603
11121	51169	42600	3427	4729	507	-258	1469	345	778
***	***	***	***	***	***	***	***	***	***
406628	1043821	638754	175388	71250	2289	150911	35205	10082	70431
796444	5715654	2645391	1745131	440166	107861	717519	574351	50791	364545
74378	429214	343250	19704	46066	364	19406	19374	2385	13369
105447	237706	191330	8148	20779	-271	17108	17687	2445	11153
***	***	***	***	***	***	***	***	***	***
***	***	***	***	***	***	***	***	***	***
196352	449827	378503	22692	36506	3877	2232	16810	2622	10786
858743	3651753	2748503	199203	240760	42173	418717	180081	20154	82190
497991	2057516	1488426	132291	252288	16502	261850	93162	12767	43948
5517871	33724751	26848097	1896636	1020564	148005	3635222	3169416	1275571	1097092
***	***	***	***	***	***	***	***	***	***
258958	2339928	1707928	127897	153029	1401	344713	177118	15245	89685
4991569	23811353	21448541	903233	821641	-82007	564348	180512	40987	55992
220602	1018670	751845	68001	87062	4945	108629	52370	5094	26855
***	***	***	***	***	***	***	***	***	***
***	***	***	***	***	***	***	***	***	***
197602	833096	692255	1491	89192	6751	39997	45688	5539	28880
1887202	**4610632**	**4086531**	**26102**	**204082**	**82428**	**633123**	**148976**	**13212**	**69219**
1246733	680001	526404	17	16129	76031	310960	67684	7284	30410
598906	3833806	3484485	26085	175494	7524	314468	73069	4576	32935
***	***	***	***	***	***	***	***	***	***

12-11 分行业规模以上港澳台及外商投资工业企业主要经济指标(2019年)

单位：万元

项目	Item	企业单位个数(个) Number of Enterprises (unit)	#亏损企业 Loss-Suffering Enterprises	工业总产值(当年价格) Gross Output Value of Industry (at current year's prices)
合 计	**Total**	**650**	**187**	**73794411**
采矿业	**Mining and Quarrying**	**1**		***
煤炭开采和洗选业	Mining and Washing of Coal			
石油和天然气开采业	Extraction of Petroleum and Natural Gas			
黑色金属矿采选业	Mining and Processing of Ferrous Metal Ores			
非金属矿采选业	Mining and Processing of Nonmetal Ores			
开采专业及辅助性活动	Mining and Support Service Activities	1		***
制造业	**Manufacturing**	**637**	**185**	**69198373**
农副食品加工业	Processing of Food from Agricultural Products	14	2	454818
食品制造业	Manufacture of Foods	42	10	2086472
酒、饮料和精制茶制造业	Manufacture of Wines, Beverage and Refined Tea	19	6	694850
烟草制品业	Manufacture of Cigarettes and Tobacco			
纺织业	Manufacture of Textile	2	1	***
纺织服装、服饰业	Manufacture of Textile Wearing Apparel and Ornament	15	6	174377
皮革、毛皮、羽毛及其制品和制鞋业	Manufacture of Leather, Fur, Feather and Its Products, and Footwear	2	1	***
木材加工和木、竹、藤、棕、草制品业	Processing of Timbers, Manufacture of Wood, Bamboo, Rattan, Palm, and Straw Products			
家具制造业	Manufacture of Furniture	7	2	412934
造纸和纸制品业	Manufacture of Paper and Paper Products	10	2	418470
印刷和记录媒介复制业	Printing, Reproduction of Recording Media	11	3	143017
文教、工美、体育和娱乐用品制造业	Manufacture of Articles for Culture, Education, Artwork, Sport and Entertainment Activities	6	1	41320
石油、煤炭及其他燃料加工业	Processing of Petroleum, Coal and Other Fuels	2		***
化学原料和化学制品制造业	Manufacture of Chemical Raw Materials and Chemical Products	29	9	908912
医药制造业	Manufacture of Medicines	43	10	6020966
化学纤维制造业	Manufacture of Chemical Fibres			
橡胶和塑料制品业	Manufacture of Rubber and Plastics Products	17	6	323772
非金属矿物制品业	Manufacture of Non-metallic Mineral Products	14	4	181804
黑色金属冶炼和压延加工业	Manufacture and Pressing of Ferrous Metals	1	1	***
有色金属冶炼和压延加工业	Manufacture and Pressing of Non-ferrous Metals	2	1	***
金属制品业	Manufacture of Fabricated Metal Products	26	6	245209
通用设备制造业	Manufacture of General-purpose Machinery	63	11	2939053
专用设备制造业	Manufacture of Special-purpose Machinery	75	15	1659637
汽车制造业	Manufacture of Motor Vehicles	103	54	31744535
铁路、船舶、航空航天和其他运输设备制造业	Manufacture of Railway Locomotives, Building of Ships and Boats, Manufacture of Air and Spacecrafts and Other Transportation Equipment	2	1	***
电气机械和器材制造业	Manufacture of Electrical Machinery and Equipment	31	7	2063999
计算机、通信和其他电子设备制造业	Manufacture of Computers, Communication Equipment and Other Electronic Equipment	56	16	16459446
仪器仪表制造业	Manufacture of Measuring Instruments and Meters	35	6	804304
其他制造业	Other Manufacturing	4	3	74624
废弃资源综合利用业	Waste Recycling and Recovery	1		***
金属制品、机械和设备修理业	Repair of Fabricated Metal Products, Machinery and Equipment	5	1	965057
电力、热力、燃气及水生产和供应业	**Production and Distribution of Electricity, Heating Power, Gas and Water**	**12**	**2**	**4591994**
电力、热力生产和供应业	Production and Distribution of Electricity and Heating Power	4		641250
燃气生产和供应业	Production and Distribution of Gas	4	1	3846069
水的生产和供应业	Production and Distribution of Water	4	1	104676

MAIN ECONOMIC INDICATORS OF INDUSTRIAL ENTERPRISES ABOVE DESIGNATED SIZE (BY SECTOR) (2019)

(10000 yuan)

平均用工人数(人) Average Number of Employed Persons (person)	资产负债 资产总计 Total Assets	流动资产合计 Total Current Assets	#存货 Inventories	#产成品 Finished Products	#应收账款 Accounts Receivable	固定资产原价 Total Original Value of Fixed Assets	负债合计 Total Liabilities	#流动负债合计 Total Current Liabilities
261337	**97031494**	**64733355**	**10978514**	**4342575**	**13925863**	**29958530**	**53533388**	**47887810**
***	***	***	***	***	***	***	***	***
***	***	***	***	***	***	***	***	***
251058	**88840701**	**62800077**	**10955601**	**4338025**	**13437466**	**25445912**	**50673263**	**45728919**
4096	307674	189455	59097	11315	56636	151012	144438	128152
21285	3098029	1758779	168676	89109	453049	1064681	1341581	1299891
6440	1109415	799780	71486	36352	210271	479069	907049	878875
***	***	***	***	***	***	***	***	***
6633	176141	145249	63779	22897	26332	45370	130506	126115
***	***	***	***	***	***	***	***	***
2267	547602	465836	239491	172295	61337	98409	562361	441976
1846	355089	260267	63708	17069	71557	238866	173789	170524
2220	219600	151925	28601	11742	30678	166226	77487	55469
1043	49568	45361	21848	8580	12352	5169	33762	33762
***	***	***	***	***	***	***	***	***
6687	1040243	638032	130645	67981	119635	555108	373811	345537
30518	6652162	4820212	1729042	742795	1314515	1289873	3323438	2675042
4100	399984	288391	54156	24413	118795	199800	192553	174663
3186	250521	197827	29807	10589	46561	118584	95214	90007
***	***	***	***	***	***	***	***	***
***	***	***	***	***	***	***	***	***
3144	649491	435296	95274	32215	92289	116675	381796	251550
18863	3986329	3305151	773386	309231	618295	1099085	1260766	1205740
13478	2624945	2029676	383704	121172	538450	477950	1215937	1157472
56390	34856689	21220891	2920061	1261007	4386953	11149617	20039049	17730954
***	***	***	***	***	***	***	***	***
9826	1936650	1661910	307399	99511	581785	414367	1070273	994745
38847	27807242	22397190	3363496	1225294	4065470	7069245	18041487	16875751
5767	1251194	999336	190949	43200	323443	165658	622476	583455
411	251643	239728	7460	4332	12992	36861	11901	8449
***	***	***	***	***	***	***	***	***
11498	771865	486672	168842	4946	223775	397834	439195	358742
9840	**7641231**	**1550433**	**12676**	**419**	**341130**	**4485118**	**2446882**	**1760332**
977	910183	164266	9835		79025	1566668	237685	235006
7968	6507083	1319749	2615	419	239406	2856984	2116124	1488511
895	223965	66419	226		22699	61466	93073	36814

12-11 续表

单位：万元

项目	Item	资产负债 Assets and Liabilities #应付账款 Accounts Payable	所有者权益合计 Total Owner's Equity	#实收资本 Paid-up Capital
合计	**Total**	**19730384**	**43498103**	**17409346**
采矿业	**Mining and Quarrying**	***	***	***
煤炭开采和洗选业	Mining and Washing of Coal			
石油和天然气开采业	Extraction of Petroleum and Natural Gas			
黑色金属矿采选业	Mining and Processing of Ferrous Metal Ores			
非金属矿采选业	Mining and Processing of Nonmetal Ores			
开采专业及辅助性活动	Mining and Support Service Activities	***	***	***
制造业	**Manufacturing**	**19382924**	**38167436**	**16155490**
农副食品加工业	Processing of Food from Agricultural Products	55845	163237	99641
食品制造业	Manufacture of Foods	569928	1756448	763717
酒、饮料和精制茶制造业	Manufacture of Wines, Beverage and Refined Tea	296393	202366	478133
烟草制品业	Manufacture of Cigarettes and Tobacco			
纺织业	Manufacture of Textile	***	***	***
纺织服装、服饰业	Manufacture of Textile Wearing Apparel and Ornament	25896	45635	30714
皮革、毛皮、羽毛及其制品和制鞋业	Manufacture of Leather, Fur, Feather and Its Products, and Footwear	***	***	***
木材加工和木、竹、藤、棕、草制品业	Processing of Timbers, Manufacture of Wood, Bamboo, Rattan, Palm, and Straw Products			
家具制造业	Manufacture of Furniture	91257	-14759	33696
造纸和纸制品业	Manufacture of Paper and Paper Products	44803	181301	100964
印刷和记录媒介复制业	Printing, Reproduction of Recording Media	22366	142113	74491
文教、工美、体育和娱乐用品制造业	Manufacture of Articles for Culture, Education, Artwork, Sport and Entertainment Activities	19869	15806	10457
石油、煤炭及其他燃料加工业	Processing of Petroleum, Coal and Other Fuels	***	***	***
化学原料和化学制品制造业	Manufacture of Chemical Raw Materials and Chemical Products	128180	666433	382109
医药制造业	Manufacture of Medicines	1128304	3328724	767593
化学纤维制造业	Manufacture of Chemical Fibres			
橡胶和塑料制品业	Manufacture of Rubber and Plastics Products	110356	207431	62759
非金属矿物制品业	Manufacture of Non-metallic Mineral Products	36837	155308	86493
黑色金属冶炼和压延加工业	Manufacture and Pressing of Ferrous Metals	***	***	***
有色金属冶炼和压延加工业	Manufacture and Pressing of Non-ferrous Metals	***	5128	5437
金属制品业	Manufacture of Fabricated Metal Products	61771	267695	125607
通用设备制造业	Manufacture of General-purpose Machinery	589859	2725563	802365
专用设备制造业	Manufacture of Special-purpose Machinery	506534	1409009	650741
汽车制造业	Manufacture of Motor Vehicles	7988793	14817640	5325318
铁路、船舶、航空航天和其他运输设备制造业	Manufacture of Railway Locomotives, Building of Ships and Boats, Manufacture of Air and Spacecrafts and Other Transportation Equipment	***	***	***
电气机械和器材制造业	Manufacture of Electrical Machinery and Equipment	471587	866377	274212
计算机、通信和其他电子设备制造业	Manufacture of Computers, Communication Equipment and Other Electronic Equipment	6850717	9765755	5565784
仪器仪表制造业	Manufacture of Measuring Instruments and Meters	229336	628719	225783
其他制造业	Other Manufacturing	1530	239742	16724
废弃资源综合利用业	Waste Recycling and Recovery	***	***	***
金属制品、机械和设备修理业	Repair of Fabricated Metal Products, Machinery and Equipment	86429	332670	230790
电力、热力、燃气及水生产和供应业	**Production and Distribution of Electricity, Heating Power, Gas and Water**	**282628**	**5194350**	**1147365**
电力、热力生产和供应业	Production and Distribution of Electricity and Heating Power	27275	672499	453128
燃气生产和供应业	Production and Distribution of Gas	232999	4390960	598906
水的生产和供应业	Production and Distribution of Water	22354	130892	95331

12-11 Continued

(10000 yuan)

损 益 Profits and Losses							应交税金合计 Total Tax Payable		
营业收入 Business Income	营业成本 Business Cost	销售费用 Sales Expenses	管理费用 Manage-ment Expenses	研发费用 R&D Expenses	财务费用 Financial Expenses	利润总额 Total Profits	应交税金合计 Total Tax Payable	#税金及附加 Tax and Surtax	#应交增值税 Value Added Tax Payable
89358308	**70599423**	**7106055**	**3049469**	**1077389**	**196710**	**8201163**	**4949689**	**1400875**	**1976988**
***	***	***	***	***	***	***	***	***	***
***	***	***	***	***	***	***	***	***	***
84613702	**66467615**	**7089729**	**2904389**	**956831**	**172471**	**7699087**	**4818003**	**1385005**	**1911622**
638937	544959	47001	22144	401	1596	20853	11347	1890	5797
4469902	2844554	1010874	204018	14013	-10531	422735	296706	25769	173878
788996	516180	138063	68045	5694	4846	49576	62865	11945	36999
***	***	***	***		***	***	***	***	***
237791	196228	21016	16939	3118	2529	-2601	4483	1060	3887
***	***	***	***	***	***	***	***	***	***
295939	216082	22037	25242	3666	7589	19576	12258	1453	6534
489029	363573	23873	19898	3080	-691	74398	43557	3302	16639
154505	123299	6979	13206	3607	-318	7683	8153	862	5802
40825	31531	3305	3834	44	301	1761	811	226	420
***	***	***	***	***	***	***	***	***	***
1048024	707871	171555	61937	7656	1448	91595	78458	8488	47756
6966906	3502128	1887736	373005	121517	137447	939168	553373	45492	301942
378875	306331	16963	35038	9640	1166	6440	13172	1778	9436
200973	158055	8856	28906	4659	-12	1849	12330	1891	8001
***	***	***	***		***	***	***	***	***
***	***	***	***		***	***	***	***	***
371247	311898	21395	29713	5846	8523	-2468	12186	1811	7000
3422254	2588465	197652	154736	69819	-23495	432363	148139	16338	72468
2029885	1395873	152247	151795	115740	2608	234089	99444	11669	45657
32554531	25952427	1889814	909757	213418	98838	3457228	2910105	1164014	968143
***	***	***	***		***	***	***	***	***
2497037	1822295	141526	134096	52427	-2245	346684	143629	14009	61925
25455872	22912111	1230470	458244	273181	-79108	1358452	271458	58432	69892
1043983	777140	70146	74034	24149	4398	96303	49344	5399	26836
70975	21465	1891	1880	561	350	48689	18545	675	6757
***	***		***		***	***	***	***	***
972748	778531	6705	93960	21732	10172	63029	43241	5907	20372
4642311	**4054867**	**10398**	**136455**	**119111**	**18040**	**492183**	**128542**	**15524**	**62582**
665480	524290	14	10168		998	132636	66833	8544	30174
3866380	3446587	10373	112992	118997	16986	348221	52436	5484	26753
110452	83990	11	13295	115	56	11325	9273	1496	5655

12-12 分行业规模以上大中型工业企业主要经济指标(2018年)

单位：万元

项 目	Item	企业单位个数(个) Number of Enterprises (unit)	#亏损企业 Loss-Suffering Enterprises	工业总产值(当年价格) Gross Output Value of Industry (at current year's prices)
合 计	**Total**	**595**	**110**	**162244892**
采矿业	**Mining and Quarrying**	**10**	**7**	**2718160**
煤炭开采和洗选业	Mining and Washing of Coal	1		***
石油和天然气开采业	Extraction of Petroleum and Natural Gas	2	2	***
黑色金属矿采选业	Mining and Processing of Ferrous Metal Ores	3	2	***
非金属矿采选业	Mining and Processing of Nonmetal Ores			
开采专业及辅助性活动	Mining and Support Service Activities	4	3	1329890
制造业	**Manufacturing**	**549**	**96**	**106086632**
农副食品加工业	Processing of Food from Agricultural Products	20	3	1307139
食品制造业	Manufacture of Foods	37	5	2384828
酒、饮料和精制茶制造业	Manufacture of Wines, Beverage and Refined Tea	12	2	2326053
烟草制品业	Manufacture of Cigarettes and Tobacco	1		***
纺织业	Manufacture of Textile	1		***
纺织服装、服饰业	Manufacture of Textile Wearing Apparel and Ornament	23	8	662491
皮革、毛皮、羽毛及其制品和制鞋业	Manufacture of Leather, Fur, Feather and Its Products, and Footwear	2	1	***
木材加工和木、竹、藤、棕、草制品业	Processing of Timbers, Manufacture of Wood, Bamboo, Rattan, Palm, and Straw Products	1		***
家具制造业	Manufacture of Furniture	8		666048
造纸和纸制品业	Manufacture of Paper and Paper Products	4		343780
印刷和记录媒介复制业	Printing, Reproduction of Recording Media	16	3	794067
文教、工美、体育和娱乐用品制造业	Manufacture of Articles for Culture, Education, Artwork, Sport and Entertainment Activities	3		***
石油、煤炭及其他燃料加工业	Processing of Petroleum, Coal and Other Fuels	5	2	5641866
化学原料和化学制品制造业	Manufacture of Chemical Raw Materials and Chemical Products	12	3	1250306
医药制造业	Manufacture of Medicines	57	3	9103335
化学纤维制造业	Manufacture of Chemical Fibres	1		***
橡胶和塑料制品业	Manufacture of Rubber and Plastics Products	6	1	317358
非金属矿物制品业	Manufacture of Non-metallic Mineral Products	25	6	2259181
黑色金属冶炼和压延加工业	Manufacture and Pressing of Ferrous Metals	2		***
有色金属冶炼和压延加工业	Manufacture and Pressing of Non-ferrous Metals	4		366037
金属制品业	Manufacture of Fabricated Metal Products	13	4	1446443
通用设备制造业	Manufacture of General-purpose Machinery	32	9	3529271
专用设备制造业	Manufacture of Special-purpose Machinery	50	3	4234894
汽车制造业	Manufacture of Motor Vehicles	58	20	36134631
铁路、船舶、航空航天和其他运输设备制造业	Manufacture of Railway Locomotives, Building of Ships and Boats, Manufacture of Air and Spacecrafts and Other Transportation Equipment	21		3380400
电气机械和器材制造业	Manufacture of Electrical Machinery and Equipment	39	5	4432898
计算机、通信和其他电子设备制造业	Manufacture of Computers, Communication Equipment and Other Electronic Equipment	71	16	20186174
仪器仪表制造业	Manufacture of Measuring Instruments and Meters	19	1	978136
其他制造业	Other Manufacturing	3	1	***
废弃资源综合利用业	Waste Recycling and Recovery			
金属制品、机械和设备修理业	Repair of Fabricated Metal Products, Machinery and Equipment	3		***
电力、热力、燃气及水生产和供应业	**Production and Distribution of Electricity, Heating Power, Gas and Water**	**36**	**7**	**53440100**
电力、热力生产和供应业	Production and Distribution of Electricity and Heating Power	25	5	48348209
燃气生产和供应业	Production and Distribution of Gas	3	1	***
水的生产和供应业	Production and Distribution of Water	8	1	1115183

MAIN ECONOMIC INDICATORS OF INDUSTRIAL ENTERPRISES ABOVE DESIGNATED SIZE (BY SECTOR) (2018)

(10000 yuan)

工 业 销售产值 (当年价格) Sales Value of Industry (at current year's prices)	#出 口 交货值 Delivery Value of Exports	平 均 用工人数 (人) Average Number of Employed Persons (person)	资产负债 资 产 总 计 Total Assets	流动资产 合 计 Total Current Assets	#存 货 Inventories	#产成品 Finished Products	#应收账款 Accounts Receivable	固定资产 原 价 Total Original Value of Fixed Assets
159357855	**10524066**	**645223**	**421329572**	**143347988**	**18819873**	**7094286**	**31468008**	**132049425**
2735567	**217542**	**35801**	**39463931**	**8716721**	**325978**	**62709**	**1838233**	**9614911**
***	***	***	***	***	***	***	***	***
***		***	***	***	***		***	***
***		***	***	***	***	***	***	***
1330577	38762	16576	4266952	2107666	191945	4935	666755	2626800
103190721	**10306524**	**529629**	**175837864**	**107042621**	**18336739**	**7021057**	**24532860**	**43438108**
1294350	17764	11436	2448933	1241250	172932	102553	118856	296491
2449203	76183	31611	3342249	1836869	224749	125564	410740	1115019
2323899	5064	20914	4932123	3094285	310939	175741	229507	1212121
***	***	***	***	***	***	***	***	***
***	***	***	***	***	***	***	***	***
533607	89269	19951	821001	606730	249137	182973	105561	180771
***	***	***	***	***	***	***	***	***
***	***	***	***	***	***	***	***	***
665658	10514	5194	766113	380659	129334	86369	83343	169302
340451	26212	1618	220981	151814	51905	14542	36773	176898
797921	1183	11063	1291425	822439	150950	60159	95740	931171
***	***	***	***	***	***	***	***	***
5639191	2164	7814	2679398	995366	492556	106863	133548	3416328
1197537	1686	9746	1502942	1066664	220489	154906	172080	740952
8420759	96974	56714	13083676	8131014	2319361	1020449	2153197	2769770
***	***	***	***	***	***	***	***	***
314021	30078	4053	325004	243725	34328	14403	83107	148352
2244576	110478	18399	10546560	6562496	451118	95863	1157147	1088476
***	***	***	***	***	***	***	***	***
355691	42655	2345	600000	369854	140097	44891	56648	156099
1467569	108227	9726	3424555	1813546	180156	38349	203985	657250
3469373	605046	27445	6973291	4759104	1187604	335396	919967	1477107
3927708	636742	35058	15825700	8762425	1366934	399680	2114977	1155547
36120359	569474	98676	52433042	28393555	3699356	1790630	6468771	12686465
3181340	18766	24160	5950343	4404618	1488133	249413	1182391	1495079
4309907	240688	26858	6523787	5089228	814066	236041	2246031	988513
19006781	7309674	74649	33362887	24183531	3770545	1613173	5458574	10175182
974806	77778	10310	1757293	1303079	261244	61128	442233	207689
***	***	***	***	***	***	***	***	***
***	***	***	***	***	***	***	***	***
53431567		**79793**	**206027777**	**27588647**	**157156**	**10520**	**5096916**	**78996407**
48340931		57981	188762161	23919766	139967	1449	3757533	68355981
***	***	***	***	***	***	***	***	***
1113928		11146	11143483	2522278	9278	3335	1035472	7818356

12-12 续表

单位：万元

项目	Item	资产负债 Assets and Liabilities 负债合计 Total Liabilities	#流动负债合计 Total Current Liabilities	#应付账款 Accounts Payable	所有者权益合计 Total Owner's Equity
合计	**Total**	**185650192**	**130818084**	**34262506**	**235679378**
采矿业	**Mining and Quarrying**	**23266503**	**12744545**	**1327573**	**16197428**
煤炭开采和洗选业	Mining and Washing of Coal	***	***	***	***
石油和天然气开采业	Extraction of Petroleum and Natural Gas	***	***	***	***
黑色金属矿采选业	Mining and Processing of Ferrous Metal Ores	***	***	***	***
非金属矿采选业	Mining and Processing of Nonmetal Ores				
开采专业及辅助性活动	Mining and Support Service Activities	1562989	1467993	581127	2703963
制造业	**Manufacturing**	**95003075**	**79196565**	**25833468**	**80834787**
农副食品加工业	Processing of Food from Agricultural Products	1252236	1123465	124672	1196697
食品制造业	Manufacture of Foods	1486591	1428072	616035	1855657
酒、饮料和精制茶制造业	Manufacture of Wines, Beverage and Refined Tea	2185662	1850926	350941	2746461
烟草制品业	Manufacture of Cigarettes and Tobacco	***	***	***	***
纺织业	Manufacture of Textile	***	***		***
纺织服装、服饰业	Manufacture of Textile Wearing Apparel and Ornament	382479	348258	99506	438522
皮革、毛皮、羽毛及其制品和制鞋业	Manufacture of Leather, Fur, Feather and Its Products, and Footwear	***	***	***	***
木材加工和木、竹、藤、棕、草制品业	Processing of Timbers, Manufacture of Wood, Bamboo, Rattan, Palm, and Straw Products	***	***	***	***
家具制造业	Manufacture of Furniture	462191	312216	138279	303923
造纸和纸制品业	Manufacture of Paper and Paper Products	125772	125508	37638	95209
印刷和记录媒介复制业	Printing, Reproduction of Recording Media	354895	315648	141824	936530
文教、工美、体育和娱乐用品制造业	Manufacture of Articles for Culture, Education, Artwork, Sport and Entertainment Activities	***	***	***	***
石油、煤炭及其他燃料加工业	Processing of Petroleum, Coal and Other Fuels	1285105	1168272	379832	1394293
化学原料和化学制品制造业	Manufacture of Chemical Raw Materials and Chemical Products	979785	620836	205326	523157
医药制造业	Manufacture of Medicines	5136526	4161774	1247517	7947150
化学纤维制造业	Manufacture of Chemical Fibres	***	***	***	***
橡胶和塑料制品业	Manufacture of Rubber and Plastics Products	132773	112559	57184	192230
非金属矿物制品业	Manufacture of Non-metallic Mineral Products	7068952	6143586	976958	3477608
黑色金属冶炼和压延加工业	Manufacture and Pressing of Ferrous Metals	***	***	***	***
有色金属冶炼和压延加工业	Manufacture and Pressing of Non-ferrous Metals	161116	140972	28125	438884
金属制品业	Manufacture of Fabricated Metal Products	2036307	1677741	259432	1388248
通用设备制造业	Manufacture of General-purpose Machinery	2611637	2298101	702996	4361654
专用设备制造业	Manufacture of Special-purpose Machinery	8339976	6226308	1713253	7485724
汽车制造业	Manufacture of Motor Vehicles	29573255	23147885	8847437	22859788
铁路、船舶、航空航天和其他运输设备制造业	Manufacture of Railway Locomotives, Building of Ships and Boats, Manufacture of Air and Spacecrafts and Other Transportation Equipment	3447088	3150269	984884	2503255
电气机械和器材制造业	Manufacture of Electrical Machinery and Equipment	3928704	3668243	1574759	2595083
计算机、通信和其他电子设备制造业	Manufacture of Computers, Communication Equipment and Other Electronic Equipment	19867312	18478615	6609216	13495575
仪器仪表制造业	Manufacture of Measuring Instruments and Meters	642256	570758	274360	1115037
其他制造业	Other Manufacturing	***	***	***	***
废弃资源综合利用业	Waste Recycling and Recovery				
金属制品、机械和设备修理业	Repair of Fabricated Metal Products, Machinery and Equipment	***	***	***	***
电力、热力、燃气及水生产和供应业	**Production and Distribution of Electricity, Heating Power, Gas and Water**	**67380614**	**38876974**	**7101465**	**138647163**
电力、热力生产和供应业	Production and Distribution of Electricity and Heating Power	60166518	35111400	5998336	128595642
燃气生产和供应业	Production and Distribution of Gas	***	***	***	***
水的生产和供应业	Production and Distribution of Water	5216346	2238742	988838	5927137

12-12 Continued

(10000 yuan)

#实收资本 Paid-up Capital	损益 Profits and Losses: 营业收入 Business Income	营业成本 Business Cost	销售费用 Sales Expenses	管理费用 Management Expenses	财务费用 Financial Expenses	利润总额 Total Profits	应交税金合计 Total Tax Payable	#税金及附加 Tax and Surtax	#应交增值税 Value Added Tax Payable
141232439	**182276921**	**151844527**	**9603331**	**7868320**	**1841413**	**14111094**	**10369041**	**3541299**	**4450049**
6316392	**5440148**	**5326972**	**20101**	**394426**	**666660**	**-871599**	**181367**	**55995**	**87348**
***	***	***	***	***	***	***	***	***	***
***	***	***	***	***	***	***	***	***	***
***	***	***	***	***	***	***	***	***	***
2995062	1376591	1380190	2309	57939	-10142	-279654	50428	8024	8662
34690079	**122829711**	**94994167**	**9497014**	**7003454**	**800668**	**10118892**	**8307133**	**3107915**	**3435964**
723981	1915529	1690831	101808	75370	21533	96199	27541	3579	12599
783279	4973957	3040833	1345151	234655	-8903	361546	374104	35089	255522
779965	2509696	1602737	316383	149728	2525	291219	409271	217307	138831
***	***	***	***	***	***	***	***	***	***
***	***	***	***	***	***	***	***	***	***
146163	727043	415617	179672	72193	3040	55285	57190	6158	42149
***	***	***	***	***	***	***	***	***	***
***	***	***	***	***	***	***	***	***	***
91999	589983	453940	45924	50819	7408	29814	32828	3499	21864
37014	379967	275701	21958	19067	30	60969	34773	2752	16982
442868	964510	721916	18058	111965	-3442	109806	84612	10170	52477
***	***	***	***	***	***	***	***	***	***
42398	6230142	4822305	53107	195354	11139	255049	1184408	876233	239988
835071	1350169	986915	163952	142966	8976	41600	63131	8519	50179
1907292	9184328	3845851	2811916	806955	122670	1749665	1020682	95400	648907
***	***	***	***	***	***	***	***	***	***
87706	368279	298854	13631	40664	1786	10828	14289	1946	11073
1489294	2490259	2036531	62100	201689	214172	80145	103835	16217	73881
***	***	***	***	***	***	***	***	***	***
93197	382839	326818	4821	30093	2810	19497	10897	1607	7067
596133	1783036	1498441	31062	148130	27815	96052	45122	9949	23363
1431094	3799677	2858784	217854	255205	-3358	425992	225851	27596	126449
2269715	4913100	3532540	330890	498505	101894	724439	245236	35154	147656
10737216	39365583	31744814	2135674	1630203	296352	3746117	3210438	1361531	1081979
967818	3281337	2554854	33891	274659	29252	490378	146672	15637	77120
979516	4822914	3654169	346461	391102	16211	409912	253632	26830	136990
8220461	27209620	24068581	1139995	1282582	-125181	692025	285388	70837	123955
379732	1089136	740244	75820	128888	1585	165631	76846	8038	44914
***	***	***	***	***	***	***	***	***	***
***	***	***	***	***	***	***	***	***	***
100225968	**54007062**	**51523388**	**86216**	**470440**	**374084**	**4863801**	**1880541**	**377389**	**926737**
94952248	48693100	46998757	9462	195608	276106	4323497	1517348	167249	822895
***	***	***	***	***	***	***	***	***	***
4601244	1323828	886193	47085	74682	91424	221122	282961	204352	68449

12—13 分行业规模以上大中型工业企业主要经济指标(2019年)

单位：万元

项目	Item	企业单位个数(个) Number of Enterprises (unit)	#亏损企业 Loss-Suffering Enterprises	工业总产值(当年价格) Gross Output Value of Industry (at current year's prices)
合计	**Total**	**552**	**86**	**165410117**
采矿业	**Mining and Quarrying**	**10**	**5**	**3088013**
煤炭开采和洗选业	Mining and Washing of Coal			
石油和天然气开采业	Extraction of Petroleum and Natural Gas	2	1	***
黑色金属矿采选业	Mining and Processing of Ferrous Metal Ores	4	2	1125790
非金属矿采选业	Mining and Processing of Nonmetal Ores			
开采专业及辅助性活动	Mining and Support Service Activities	4	2	1554594
制造业	**Manufacturing**	**505**	**75**	**104790336**
农副食品加工业	Processing of Food from Agricultural Products	18	2	985085
食品制造业	Manufacture of Foods	33	3	2315124
酒、饮料和精制茶制造业	Manufacture of Wines, Beverage and Refined Tea	9	2	1824548
烟草制品业	Manufacture of Cigarettes and Tobacco	1		***
纺织业	Manufacture of Textile	2		***
纺织服装、服饰业	Manufacture of Textile Wearing Apparel and Ornament			
皮革、毛皮、羽毛及其制品和制鞋业	Manufacture of Leather, Fur, Feather and Its Products, and Footwear	20	7	612492
木材加工和木、竹、藤、棕、草制品业	Processing of Timbers, Manufacture of Wood, Bamboo, Rattan, Palm, and Straw Products			
家具制造业	Manufacture of Furniture	7		616171
造纸和纸制品业	Manufacture of Paper and Paper Products	4		362797
印刷和记录媒介复制业	Printing, Reproduction of Recording Media	17	1	816871
文教、工美、体育和娱乐用品制造业	Manufacture of Articles for Culture, Education, Artwork, Sport and Entertainment Activities	3		***
石油、煤炭及其他燃料加工业	Processing of Petroleum, Coal and Other Fuels	3	1	***
化学原料和化学制品制造业	Manufacture of Chemical Raw Materials and Chemical Products	15	3	998623
医药制造业	Manufacture of Medicines	64	7	9804334
化学纤维制造业	Manufacture of Chemical Fibres	1		29187
橡胶和塑料制品业	Manufacture of Rubber and Plastics Products	4	2	195634
非金属矿物制品业	Manufacture of Non-metallic Mineral Products	20	3	1926892
黑色金属冶炼和压延加工业	Manufacture and Pressing of Ferrous Metals	2		***
有色金属冶炼和压延加工业	Manufacture and Pressing of Non-ferrous Metals	3		***
金属制品业	Manufacture of Fabricated Metal Products	13	4	1661420
通用设备制造业	Manufacture of General-purpose Machinery	31	2	3270879
专用设备制造业	Manufacture of Special-purpose Machinery	51	6	4667197
汽车制造业	Manufacture of Motor Vehicles	43	14	35364912
铁路、船舶、航空航天和其他运输设备制造业	Manufacture of Railway Locomotives, Building of Ships and Boats, Manufacture of Air and Spacecrafts and Other Transportation Equipment	19		3501691
电气机械和器材制造业	Manufacture of Electrical Machinery and Equipment	32	5	4121000
计算机、通信和其他电子设备制造业	Manufacture of Computers, Communication Equipment and Other Electronic Equipment	61	12	20093475
仪器仪表制造业	Manufacture of Measuring Instruments and Meters	22	1	1269196
其他制造业	Other Manufacturing	3		***
废弃资源综合利用业	Waste Recycling and Recovery			
金属制品、机械和设备修理业	Repair of Fabricated Metal Products, Machinery and Equipment	4		996419
电力、热力、燃气及水生产和供应业	**Production and Distribution of Electricity, Heating Power, Gas and Water**	**37**	**6**	**57531768**
电力、热力生产和供应业	Production and Distribution of Electricity and Heating Power	27	5	52562894
燃气生产和供应业	Production and Distribution of Gas	2		***
水的生产和供应业	Production and Distribution of Water	8	1	1040257

MAIN ECONOMIC INDICATORS OF INDUSTRIAL ENTERPRISES ABOVE DESIGNATED SIZE (BY SECTOR) (2019)

(10000 yuan)

平均用工人数(人) Average Number of Employed Persons (person)	资产负债							
	资产总计 Total Assets	流动资产合计 Total Current Assets	#存货 Inventories	#产成品 Finished Products	#应收账款 Accounts Receivable	固定资产原价 Total Original Value of Fixed Assets	负债合计 Total Liabilities	#流动负债合计 Total Current Liabilities
591906	**447269465**	**145416726**	**19182166**	**6654625**	**32474073**	**138025948**	**182530193**	**134943017**
31526	**39786883**	**8819108**	**310840**	**34971**	**1733840**	**10033645**	**24643118**	**13805905**
***	***	***	***		***	***	***	***
14317	33724161	6096133	96053	30839	1052890	7255321	22328748	11737283
15839	4363301	2096357	214202	4132	632920	2708467	1660181	1570046
478556	**171498115**	**108809141**	**18704239**	**6613023**	**25510679**	**44260859**	**90391802**	**78396627**
9998	2407250	1230407	168626	106298	77096	265128	1202267	1054892
27776	3342387	1887112	169004	85040	472061	1105539	1434805	1375958
19946	4711123	2889691	302811	137081	258284	1169160	1548661	1257269
***	***	***	***	***	***	***	***	***
***	***	***	***	***	***	***	***	***
18444	846599	638264	264992	189931	132007	174695	422388	366859
4533	712633	337477	110549	33253	89433	158620	422990	275165
1602	258550	205334	58859	17880	38573	182460	162124	161795
10896	1336102	868383	185693	66574	134697	974810	355583	321527
***	***	***	***	***	***	***	***	***
***	***	***	***	***	***	***	***	***
9776	1514798	1080948	241582	169838	162338	608509	867683	516961
59714	14724839	9039705	2666145	1166585	2452145	3308387	5558098	4664718
533	81485	51094	9254	5366	637	19463	9740	9319
2984	199271	132149	29696	13603	51556	117041	104598	83353
13477	4808917	3014328	265902	101685	1114928	823318	2543027	2335564
***	***	***	***	***	***	***	***	***
***	***	***	***	***	***	***	***	***
9544	3601588	2058797	272965	32244	199449	650527	2209629	2018706
25340	7000914	4782405	1215213	452817	853446	1489312	2311947	2211127
34490	15386191	8399004	1435855	411992	2215543	1228698	7296668	6488638
81263	49872218	30028752	3467475	1553928	7255166	12945656	29869477	25061393
22013	6079189	4545991	1592469	241854	1195590	1406375	3545481	3308752
22140	5370615	4077535	700602	169186	1758501	975223	3182418	2958935
64102	37101702	28378624	3980806	1412622	5873876	10564532	21909714	20314983
10811	2250035	1701645	375030	79153	504078	227323	882936	783925
***	***	***	***	***	***	***	***	***
13089	4100972	712670	196833		257678	801698	1409244	710552
81824	**235984467**	**27788478**	**167087**	**6631**	**5229554**	**83731444**	**67495273**	**42740485**
61278	217646828	23566179	154818	2001	3710737	72562026	59455177	38948917
***	***	***	***	***	***	***	***	***
11530	11741878	2816681	9856	4271	1224126	8315811	5818073	2197158

12-13 续表

单位：万元

项 目	Item	资产负债 Assets and Liabilities #应付账款 Accounts Payable	所有者权益合计 Total Owner's Equity	#实收资本 Paid-up Capital
合 计	**Total**	**37514250**	**264739270**	**189428960**
采矿业	**Mining and Quarrying**	**1514379**	**15143765**	**6258217**
煤炭开采和洗选业	Mining and Washing of Coal			
石油和天然气开采业	Extraction of Petroleum and Natural Gas	***	***	***
黑色金属矿采选业	Mining and Processing of Ferrous Metal Ores	753628	11395413	2959864
非金属矿采选业	Mining and Processing of Nonmetal Ores			
开采专业及辅助性活动	Mining and Support Service Activities	667181	2703120	2991485
制造业	**Manufacturing**	**28115221**	**81106311**	**31435891**
农副食品加工业	Processing of Food from Agricultural Products	70068	1204983	661764
食品制造业	Manufacture of Foods	567268	1907582	692903
酒、饮料和精制茶制造业	Manufacture of Wines, Beverage and Refined Tea	180076	3162462	607028
烟草制品业	Manufacture of Cigarettes and Tobacco	***	***	***
纺织业	Manufacture of Textile	***	***	***
纺织服装、服饰业	Manufacture of Textile Wearing Apparel and Ornament	99644	424211	135541
皮革、毛皮、羽毛及其制品和制鞋业	Manufacture of Leather, Fur, Feather and Its Products, and Footwear			
木材加工和木、竹、藤、棕、草制品业	Processing of Timbers, Manufacture of Wood, Bamboo, Rattan, Palm, and Straw Products			
家具制造业	Manufacture of Furniture	111224	289644	89731
造纸和纸制品业	Manufacture of Paper and Paper Products	34456	96426	37014
印刷和记录媒介复制业	Printing, Reproduction of Recording Media	170313	980519	470248
文教、工美、体育和娱乐用品制造业	Manufacture of Articles for Culture, Education, Artwork, Sport and Entertainment Activities	***	***	***
石油、煤炭及其他燃料加工业	Processing of Petroleum, Coal and Other Fuels	***	***	***
化学原料和化学制品制造业	Manufacture of Chemical Raw Materials and Chemical Products	224383	647115	758791
医药制造业	Manufacture of Medicines	1476267	9166741	2152595
化学纤维制造业	Manufacture of Chemical Fibres	1552	71745	16850
橡胶和塑料制品业	Manufacture of Rubber and Plastics Products	47451	94673	27789
非金属矿物制品业	Manufacture of Non-metallic Mineral Products	966395	2265890	904160
黑色金属冶炼和压延加工业	Manufacture and Pressing of Ferrous Metals	***	***	***
有色金属冶炼和压延加工业	Manufacture and Pressing of Non-ferrous Metals	***	***	***
金属制品业	Manufacture of Fabricated Metal Products	340841	1391959	589999
通用设备制造业	Manufacture of General-purpose Machinery	683364	4688966	1472209
专用设备制造业	Manufacture of Special-purpose Machinery	1721413	8089523	2228070
汽车制造业	Manufacture of Motor Vehicles	9392406	20002741	7775258
铁路、船舶、航空航天和其他运输设备制造业	Manufacture of Railway Locomotives, Building of Ships and Boats, Manufacture of Air and Spacecrafts and Other Transportation Equipment	1259642	2533708	799329
电气机械和器材制造业	Manufacture of Electrical Machinery and Equipment	1226593	2188196	990436
计算机、通信和其他电子设备制造业	Manufacture of Computers, Communication Equipment and Other Electronic Equipment	8423463	15191988	8809956
仪器仪表制造业	Manufacture of Measuring Instruments and Meters	296741	1367099	429329
其他制造业	Other Manufacturing	***	***	***
废弃资源综合利用业	Waste Recycling and Recovery			
金属制品、机械和设备修理业	Repair of Fabricated Metal Products, Machinery and Equipment	128675	2691727	882284
电力、热力、燃气及水生产和供应业	**Production and Distribution of Electricity, Heating Power, Gas and Water**	**7884650**	**168489194**	**151734853**
电力、热力生产和供应业	Production and Distribution of Electricity and Heating Power	6659131	158191651	146560697
燃气生产和供应业	Production and Distribution of Gas	***	***	***
水的生产和供应业	Production and Distribution of Water	987039	5923804	4575779

12-13 Continued

(10000 yuan)

损益 Profits and Losses							应交税金合计		
营业收入 Business Income	营业成本 Business Cost	销售费用 Sales Expenses	管理费用 Manage-ment Expenses	研发费用 R&D Expenses	财务费用 Financial Expenses	利润总额 Total Profits	应交税金合计 Total Tax Payable	#税金及附加 Tax and Surtax	#应交增值税 Value Added Tax Payable
188512082	**157099909**	**9895080**	**5816869**	**2820830**	**1725015**	**14502603**	**9522733**	**3462062**	**3576444**
5347339	**5056341**	**14886**	**278980**	**33640**	**744314**	**-415019**	**129160**	**43400**	**54180**
***	***	***	***	***	***	***	***	***	***
3478521	3377203	7584	181179	3921	732313	-468193	57113	27444	28598
1652845	1511907	5928	53451	12911	1675	35470	35630	8007	8930
124848288	**96783422**	**9790876**	**4769168**	**2585963**	**511328**	**10310529**	**7831979**	**3056855**	**2985773**
1949800	1739285	95824	52632	9045	13588	78362	21079	2954	12624
4732036	2996412	1096337	203482	19626	-9258	446379	311521	27314	183359
2096277	1448040	213964	144168	13320	7885	150769	316955	221193	80963
***	***	***	***	***	***	***	***	***	***
***	***	***	***	***	***	***	***	***	***
714379	409478	172540	59597	14471	5043	49830	44650	5251	32315
521770	393405	39877	36568	9821	12798	27292	23000	2829	14703
427926	308265	22926	15427	3824	625	73668	41426	2676	14890
940548	697795	18737	104390	21453	-1378	95540	63574	8709	38379
***	***	***	***	***	***	***	***	***	***
***	***	***	***	***	***	***	***	***	***
1083875	710461	168449	98487	27346	2315	75436	65782	9285	43783
10547149	4788302	3049335	598492	346451	145313	1828830	926684	86025	544553
30078	20077	1313	1966	1302	11	5418	1516	404	340
223722	183406	7162	22577	6445	1817	2484	6994	1228	5260
2084974	1732914	65078	137102	69110	17612	97611	82483	11191	61907
***	***	***	***	***	***	***	***	***	***
***	***	***	***	***	***	***	***	***	***
1891820	1596853	21062	119604	37520	24546	124465	41511	11046	20099
3616724	2762188	204739	164880	103856	-5977	456651	163355	21014	81572
5176303	3590905	407977	315409	250137	88732	659838	261763	31484	142812
39661333	32170973	2163704	1146706	621069	185890	3296948	3085653	1242697	1047351
3406366	2712555	36741	175377	108441	25309	344766	114497	13879	61975
4631361	3572825	319603	203223	139849	8252	381825	208776	23572	115200
28949023	25326120	1484229	639072	629630	-90794	1692472	452480	97259	180902
1254119	786762	125439	95503	76935	3638	214776	78811	8836	45269
***	***	***	***	***	***	***	***	***	***
1103279	902216	6822	123139	25154	54789	150118	44517	7133	26206
58316455	**55260147**	**89319**	**768721**	**201228**	**469373**	**4607093**	**1561594**	**361807**	**536492**
53091972	50792868	10390	575302	75888	351889	4212000	1245324	146828	456649
***	***	***	***	***	***	***	***	***	***
1243921	908559	68610	75823	6342	101653	48190	263247	209344	52763

12−14 规模以上工业企业主要效益指标(2018年)

单位：%

项　　目	Item	总资产贡献率 Contribution Rate of Total Assets	资产保值增值率 Rate of Assets Preservation and Appreciation
合　　计	**Total**	**5.69**	**107.30**
按行业分	**By Sector**		
采矿业	Mining and Quarrying	-0.27	94.86
制造业	Manufacturing	8.72	109.27
电力、热力、燃气及水生产和供应业	Production and Distribution of Electricity, Heating Power, Gas and Water	3.41	107.38
按轻重工业分	**By light and heavy industries**		
轻工业	Light Industry	13.87	99.29
重工业	Heavy Industry	4.85	108.16
按规模分	**By Size**		
#大　型	Large-sized	4.99	105.03
中　型	Medium-sized	8.79	117.43
小　型	Small-sized	6.62	111.04
按隶属关系分	**By Affiliation**		
中　央	Central	3.94	108.35
地　方	Local	7.14	106.11
按登记注册类型分	**By Registration Type**		
内资企业	Domestially-Invested Enterprises	4.17	107.09
国有企业	State-owned Enterprises	4.60	4.63
集体企业	Collectively-owned Enterprises	5.58	105.76
股份合作企业	Joint-equity Cooperative Enterprises	3.58	94.46
有限责任公司	Limited Liability Companies	3.31	363.60
股份有限公司	Companies Limited by Shares	6.75	102.88
私营企业	Private Enterprises	7.20	111.27
其他企业	Others	3.63	
港澳台商投资企业	Hong Kong, Macao and Taiwan-invested Enterprises	5.51	117.94
港澳台合资经营	Joint Ventures	8.32	121.65
港澳台合作经营	Cooperatives	16.90	106.49
港澳台商独资企业	Solely-funded Enterprises	4.36	105.63
港澳台商投资股份有限公司	Companies Limited by Shares	6.17	165.93
外商投资企业	Foreign-invested Enterprises	15.32	104.67
中外合资经营	Joint Ventures	18.95	113.96
中外合作经营	Cooperatives	9.67	123.70
外资(独资)企业	Solely-funded Enterprises	9.94	107.18
外商投资股份有限公司	Companies Limited by Shares	8.14	47.50
按控股类型分组	**By holding types**		
#国有控股	State-holding Enterprises	5.14	107.50

MAIN INDICATORS OF ECONOMIC BENEFITS OF INDUSTRIAL ENTERPRISES ABOVE DESIGNATED SIZE (2018)

(%)

资产负债率 Assets-Liabilities Ratio	流动资产周转率(次) Turnover of Current Assets (times)	收入利润率 Income-Profit Margin	产品销售率 Sales Rate of Products	每百元营业收入成本费用(元) Cost Expense of Per 100 Yuan of Business Income (yuan)	人均营业收入(元) Sales Revenue Per Capita (yuan)
45.15	**1.19**	**7.37**	**98.38**	**94.23**	**2409678**
58.94	0.63	-15.86	100.64	117.59	1490057
53.30	1.09	7.42	97.68	92.46	2012904
33.56	1.85	9.46	99.99	97.00	6285324
46.47	1.23	10.53	96.71	89.21	1258312
45.02	1.19	6.77	98.68	95.18	2913310
42.70	1.41	7.07	97.75	94.49	3626895
50.58	0.94	10.13	97.01	91.80	1577554
50.60	0.95	6.47	99.07	95.19	1461289
35.19	1.54	7.46	99.17	94.54	4165016
53.44	1.08	7.33	97.96	94.09	2012200
42.82	1.07	6.69	98.41	95.91	2119156
63.24	4.05	0.07	100.02	97.90	3582105
48.33	0.92	3.90	98.77	100.59	521432
72.41	2.85	0.03	100.17	99.58	2780826
41.60	1.14	6.67	98.59	97.37	2590568
40.31	0.77	9.51	97.50	91.03	1852141
54.85	0.95	6.04	97.74	94.38	972700
15.08	0.84	2.30	100.00	93.75	602163
58.86	1.52	4.22	94.36	96.76	4351662
49.35	0.89	8.68	96.77	92.69	1446291
12.27	0.71	16.96	93.70	81.50	747175
64.69	1.91	2.83	93.90	97.06	6559636
48.82	0.26	39.64	94.49	112.33	1618649
52.88	1.40	10.52	100.00	89.08	2652869
50.00	1.56	12.35	100.18	86.69	3433776
39.40	1.47	5.17	95.28	94.77	593280
60.15	1.16	7.46	99.34	92.32	2043834
31.65	1.85	8.71	107.03	105.33	1358620
42.16	1.27	8.01	99.27	94.16	3212321

12-15 规模以上工业企业主要效益指标(2019年)

单位：%

项　　目	Item	总资产贡献率 Contribution Rate of Total Assets	资产保值增值率 Rate of Assets Preservation and Appreciation
合　计	**Total**	**5.24**	**111.82**
按行业分	**By Sector**		
采矿业	Mining and Quarrying	1.20	94.66
制造业	Manufacturing	8.56	103.81
电力、热力、燃气及水生产和供应业	Production and Distribution of Electricity, Heating Power, Gas and Water	2.66	120.02
按轻重工业分	**By light and heavy industries**		
轻工业	Light Industry	12.70	110.61
重工业	Heavy Industry	4.49	111.94
按规模分	**By Size**		
#大　型	Large-sized	4.34	112.75
中　型	Medium-sized	9.58	109.99
小　型	Small-sized	6.08	104.40
按隶属关系分	**By Affiliation**		
中　央	Central	3.37	121.57
地　方	Local	6.97	100.53
按登记注册类型分	**By Registration Type**		
内资企业	Domestially-Invested Enterprises	3.70	113.87
国有企业	State-owned Enterprises	2.90	100.03
集体企业	Collectively-owned Enterprises	6.71	97.54
股份合作企业	Joint-equity Cooperative Enterprises	1.86	72.07
有限责任公司	Limited Liability Companies	3.08	117.31
股份有限公司	Companies Limited by Shares	5.21	103.72
私营企业	Private Enterprises	8.54	105.95
其他企业	Others		
港澳台商投资企业	Hong Kong, Macao and Taiwan-invested Enterprises	8.34	89.74
港澳台合资经营	Joint Ventures	9.24	88.44
港澳台合作经营	Cooperatives	11.19	86.83
港澳台商独资企业	Solely-funded Enterprises	8.20	115.81
港澳台商投资股份有限公司	Companies Limited by Shares	5.85	17.61
外商投资企业	Foreign-invested Enterprises		
中外合资经营	Joint Ventures	16.37	109.09
中外合作经营	Cooperatives	17.03	123.60
外资(独资)企业	Solely-funded Enterprises	8.88	109.32
外商投资股份有限公司	Companies Limited by Shares	2.38	43.38
按控股类型分	**By holding types**		
#国有控股	State-holding Enterprises	4.42	112.76

MAIN INDICATORS OF ECONOMIC BENEFITS OF INDUSTRIAL ENTERPRISES ABOVE DESIGNATED SIZE (2019)

(%)

资　产 负债率 Assets-Liabilities Ratio	流动资产 周 转 率 (次) Turnover of Current Assets (times)	收　入 利润率 Income-Profit Margin	每百元营业 收入成本费用 (元) Cost Expense of Per 100 Yuan of Main Business Income (yuan)	人均营业 收　入 (元) Sales Revenue Per Capita (yuan)
42.08	**1.23**	**7.30**	**94.30**	**269778**
61.78	0.62	-6.28	112.72	171204
51.53	1.10	7.49	92.60	225101
29.53	2.07	8.02	97.26	659176
43.58	1.22	10.48	89.35	134701
41.93	1.23	6.72	95.21	331143
40.14	1.45	6.41	94.72	421812
44.34	0.90	12.90	91.48	159664
50.63	1.02	6.09	94.78	164533
29.42	1.77	7.19	94.55	469320
53.70	1.07	7.36	94.17	223653
39.09	1.15	6.15	95.84	238702
64.02	4.31	-1.34	99.16	420295
51.32	0.83	7.17	97.38	56199
72.37	1.38	0.32	98.50	120412
36.54	1.27	6.85	96.84	290742
41.22	0.79	5.26	92.90	210165
52.75	0.99	7.90	92.92	110223
57.02	1.75	6.37	96.20	504656
40.76	1.08	9.82	89.98	143859
11.59	0.54	13.40	83.86	60165
61.54	1.95	5.88	96.98	785523
45.41	0.54	11.13	99.62	115097
51.51	1.37	12.39	87.84	368949
43.66	1.11	14.55	87.92	83787
60.77	1.04	7.81	91.94	222516
27.48	2.46	2.33	102.01	160459
39.07	1.36	7.05	94.65	365045

12-16 规模以上工业企业主要工业产品生产能力
PRODUCTION CAPACITY OF MAIN INDUSTRIAL PRODUCTS IN INDUSTRIAL ENTERPRISES ABOVE DESIGNATED SIZE

主要工业产品名称		Name of Main Industrial Products		2019	2018
原油加工能力	(万吨)	Crude Oil Processing Capacity	(10000 tons)	1100	1150
硅酸盐水泥熟料	(万吨)	Portland Cement Chamotte	(10000 tons)	305	305
发电设备容量总计	(万千瓦)	Total Capacity of Power Generation Equipment	(10000 kW)	1237.2	1206.5
#火电设备容量		Capacity of Thermal Power Equipment		1120.1	1070.4
水电设备容量		Capacity of Hydropower Equipment		93.1	98.1
风电设备容量		Capacity of Wind Power Equipment		0.1	18.7
原　煤	(万吨)	Raw Coal	(10000 tons)		220.0
卷　烟	(亿支)	Cigarette	(10000 units)	288.0	275.4
水　泥	(万吨)	Cement	(10000 tons)	400.0	400.0
钢　材	(万吨)	Rolled Steel	(10000 tons)	171.8	171.8
金属切削机床	(台)	Metal-Cutting Machine Tools	(10000 units)	19693	19983
汽　车	(万辆)	Motor Vehicles	(10000 units)	247.4	282.3
#基本型乘用车(轿车)		Basic-type Passenger Vehicles (Sedans)		187.7	179.2
移动通信手持机(手机)	(万台)	Mobile Communication Handsets (Mobile Phones)	(10000 units)	1174.7	1547.7
微型计算机设备	(万台)	Micro-computers	(10000 units)	1320.0	1040.0

12-17 主要工业产品产量
OUTPUT OF MAIN INDUSTRIAL PRODUCTS

工业产品名称		Name of Main Industrial Product		2019	2018
单晶硅	(千克)	Monocrystalline Silicon	(kg)	190303.3	201301.4
中成药	(万吨)	Finished Traditional Chinese Herbal Medicines	(10000 tons)	3.5	4.4
沥青和改性沥青防水卷材	(万平方米)	Asphalt and Modified Asphalt Waterproof Roll Materials	(10000 sq.m)	71.5	145.1
纤维增强塑料制品	(万吨)	Fiber-reinforced Plastic Products	(10000 tons)	1.4	1.5
耐火材料制品	(万吨)	Products Made from Fire-resistant Materials	(10000 tons)	40.5	45.3
冷轧薄宽钢带	(万吨)	Cold-rolled Thin Broad Steel Bands	(10000 tons)	87.6	90.4
单一稀土金属	(千克)	Single Rare Earth Metals	(kg)	1343806	1443214
发动机	(万千瓦)	Engines	(10000 kW)	19857.5	19064.7
气动元件	(万件)	Pneumatic Components	(10000 units)	31250.4	31008.4
数控金属切削机床	(台)	Digital Metal Cutting Tools	(unit)	7611	11862
机床数控装置	(套)	CNC Units of Lathe	(unit)	8864	61530
工业电炉	(台)	Industrial Electric Cookers	(unit)	729	230
环境污染防治专用设备	(台套)	Special Equipment for Prevention and Control of Environmental Pollution	(set)	58080	96223
汽　车	(万辆)	Automobiles	(10000 units)	164.0	163.2
#基本型成用车(轿车)		Including: Basic-type Passenger Vehicles (Sedans)		77.8	78.8
运动型多用途乘用车(SUV)		Sport Utility Vehicles (SUV)		35.8	41.4
载货汽车		Freight Trucks		48.3	42.4
改装汽车	(万辆)	Refitted Automobiles	(10000 units)	1.1	1.6
风力发电机组	(万千瓦)	Wind Power Generator Units	(10000 kW)	167.3	126.8
锂离子电池	(万只)	Lithiums Ion Batteries	(10000 units)		1058.0
移动通信手持机(手机)	(万台)	Mobile Communication Handsets (Mobile Phones)	(10000 units)	8373.3	8448.0
微型计算机设备	(万台)	Micro-computer Equipment	(10000 units)	513.2	555.5
服务器	(台)	Servers	(unit)	55540	91552
液晶显示模组	(万套)	Liquid Crystal Display Modules	(10000 sets)	17832.3	14046.5
显示器	(万台)	Display Devices	(10000 units)	470.1	406.3
集成电路	(亿块)	Integrated Circuits	(100 million pieces)	154.5	149.5
彩色电视机	(万台)	Color TV Sets	(10000 units)	417.9	456.4

12－18　规模以上高技术制造业主要经济指标(2018年)
MAIN ECONOMIC INDICATORS OF HIGH-TECH MANUFACTURING ENTERPRISES ABOVE DESIGNATED SIZE (2018)

单位：亿元　(100 million yuan)

项　目	Item	工业总产值 Gross Output Value of Industry	营业收入 Business Income	利润总额 Total Profits	应交税金 Tax Payable
合　计	**Total**	**4425.8**	**5313.6**	**400.5**	**216.5**
按登记注册类型分	**By Registration Type**				
内　资	Domestially-Invested Enterprises	1945.7	2076.8	240.0	127.3
国　有	State-owned Enterprises	85.6	86.8	7.7	3.2
集　体	Collectively-owned Enterprises	1.3	1.6	…	…
股份合作企业	Joint-equity Cooperative Enterprises	4.4	4.0	-0.2	0.1
有限责任公司	Limited Liability Companies	1036.2	1113.8	96.3	57.4
股份有限公司	Companies Limited by Shares	498.7	517.8	100.2	44.8
私营企业	Private Enterprises	319.7	352.8	35.9	21.8
其　他	Others				
港澳台商投资	Hong Kong, Macao and Taiwan-invested Enterprises	1485.7	2137.7	47.8	25.0
外商投资	Foreign-invested Enterprises	994.4	1099.2	112.8	64.3
按高技术领域分	**By Field of High Technology**				
医药制造业	Manufacture of Medicines	1142.7	1153.1	204.9	123.7
航空、航天器及设备制造业	Manufacture of Aircrafts and Spacecrafts	314.7	311.1	22.5	9.6
电子及通信设备制造业	Manufacture of Electronic Equipment and Communication Equipment	2294.1	2960.2	95.1	41.8
计算机及办公设备制造业	Manufacture of Computers and Office Equipments	261.8	424.6	11.1	8.9
医疗仪器设备及仪器仪表制造业	Manufacture of Medical Equipments and Meters	407.2	457.6	65.0	32.0
信息化学品制造	Information Chemical Manufacturing	5.3	7.1	1.9	0.5

12−19 规模以上高技术制造业主要经济指标(2019年)
MAIN ECONOMIC INDICATORS OF HIGH-TECH MANUFACTURING ENTERPRISES ABOVE DESIGNATED SIZE (2019)

单位：亿元 (100 million yuan)

项 目	Item	工业总产值 Gross Output Value of Industry	营业收入 Business Income	利润总额 Total Profits	应交税金 Tax Payable
合 计	**Total**	**4703.9**	**5850.1**	**521.9**	**217.5**
按登记注册类型分	**By Registration Type**				
内 资	Domestially-Invested Enterprises	2170.5	2287.8	259.5	120.5
国 有	State-owned Enterprises	73.0	79.9	10.0	3.0
集 体	Collectively-owned Enterprises	1.8	2.0	-0.1	0.1
股份合作企业	Joint-equity Cooperative Enterprises	2.0	1.8	…	0.1
有限责任公司	Limited Liability Companies	1199.0	1279.8	93.6	48.8
股份有限公司	Companies Limited by Shares	525.5	547.9	96.5	43.9
私营企业	Private Enterprises	369.3	376.3	59.5	24.7
其 他	Others				
港澳台商投资	Hong Kong, Macao and Taiwan-invested Enterprises	1487.8	2343.5	127.7	29.0
外商投资	Foreign-invested Enterprises	1045.6	1218.9	134.7	68.0
按高技术领域分	**By Field of High Technology**				
医药制造业	Manufacture of Medicines	1221.6	1298.4	214.3	112.4
航空、航天器及设备制造业	Manufacture of Aircrafts and Spacecrafts	333.7	328.4	24.5	9.0
电子及通信设备制造业	Manufacture of Electronic Equipment and Communication Equipment	2372.6	3214.6	185.6	52.6
计算机及办公设备制造业	Manufacture of Computers and Office Equipments	277.0	465.1	16.9	9.4
医疗仪器设备及仪器仪表制造业	Manufacture of Medical Equipments and Meters	498.8	543.0	80.6	34.2
信息化学品制造	Information Chemical Manufacturing	0.2	0.7	0.1	…

12−20 规模以上工业战略性新兴产业总产值
TOTAL OUTPUT VALUE OF STRATEGIC EMERGING INDUSTRIES AMONG INDUSTRIAL ENTERPRISES ABOVE DESIGNATED SIZE

单位：亿元 (100 million yuan)

项 目	Item	2019	2018
合 计	**Total**	**5127.7**	**4971.1**
节能环保产业	Energy Conservation and Environmental Protection Industry	351.3	347.4
新一代信息技术产业	New Generation IT Industry	1989.0	1930.0
生物产业	Bioindustry	1393.6	1278.5
高端装备制造业	High-end Equipment Manufacturing	722.9	748.9
新能源产业	New Energy Industry	195.2	171.6
新材料产业	New Material Industry	325.3	317.7
新能源汽车产业	New Energy Automobiles	123.0	137.7
数字创意产业	Digital Creative Industry	27.4	39.4
相关服务业	Related Service Industry		

主要统计指标解释

工业 指从事自然资源的开采，对采掘品和农产品进行加工和再加工的物质生产部门。具体包括：(1) 对自然资源的开采，如采矿、晒盐、森林采伐等（但不包括禽兽捕猎和水产捕捞）；(2) 对农副产品的加工、再加工，如粮油加工、食品加工、扎花、纺织、制革等；(3) 对采掘品的加工、再加工，如炼铁、炼钢、化工生产、石油加工、机器制造、木材加工等，以及电力、自来水、煤气的生产和供应等；(4) 对工业品的修理、翻新，如机器设备的修理。

轻工业 指主要提供生活消费品和制作手工工具的工业。按其所使用的原料不同，可分为两大类：(1) 以农业为原料的轻工业，是指直接或间接以农产品为基本原料的轻工业。主要包括食品制造、饮料制造、烟草加工、纺织、缝纫、皮革和毛皮制作、造纸以及印刷等工业；(2) 以非农产品为原料的轻工业，是指以工业品为原料的轻工业。主要包括文教体育用品、化学药品制造、合成纤维制造、日用化学制品、日用玻璃制品、日用金属制品、手工工具制造、医疗器械制造、文化和办公用机械制造等工业。

重工业 是指为国民经济各部门提供物质技术基础的主要生产资料的工业。按其生产性质和产品用途，可以分为下列三类：(1) 采掘（伐）工业，是指对自然资源的开采，包括石油开采、煤炭开采、金属矿开采、非金属矿开采和木材采伐等工业；(2) 原材料工业，指向国民经济各部门提供基本材料、动力和燃料的工业。包括金属冶炼及加工、炼焦及焦炭化学、化工原料、水泥、人造板以及电力、石油和煤炭加工等工业；(3) 加工工业，是指对工业原材料进行再加工制造的工业。包括装备国民经济各部门的机械设备制造工业、金属结构、水泥制品等工业，以及为农业提供的生产资料如化肥、农药等工业。

根据上述划分原则，修理业中以重工业产品为修理作业对象的划为重工业，反之划为轻工业。

工业总产值 指工业企业在报告期内生产的以货币形式表现的工业最终产品和提供工业劳务活动的总价值量。它包括：在本企业内不再进行加工，经检验、包装入库已经销售和准备销售的全部工业成品（包括半成本）价值，对外加工费收入，自制半成品、在制品期末期初差额价值。工业总产值采用“工厂法”计算，即以工业企业作为一个整体，按企业生产活动的最终成果来计算。

工业销售产值 是以货币形式表现的，工业企业在报告期内销售的本企业生产的工业产品或提供工业性劳务价值的总价值量。包括企业在报告期内实际销售（包括本期生产和非本期生产）的全部成品、半成品的总价值，报告期内完成的对外承接的工业品加工的加工费收入，对外工业品修理作业可获取的加工费收入和对内非工业部门提供的加工修理、设备安装等收入。已销售的成品、半成品不论是本期生产的、还是非本期生产的，只要是本期销售出去的均包括在内。企业为本单位基本建设部门、生活福利部门等提供的产品和工业性作业及自制设备也应视同销售，这部分也应作为销售统计。

资产总计 指企业过去的交易或者事项形成的、由企业拥有或者控制的、预期会给企业带来经济利益的资源。资产一般按流动性分为流动资产和非流动资产。其中流动资产可分为货币资金、交易性金融资产、应收票据、应收账款、预付款项、其他应收款、存货等；非流动资产可分为长期股权投资、固定资产、无形资产及其他非流动资产等。

(1) 流动资产合计 资产满足以下条件之一应归为流动资产：①预计在一个正常营业周期中变现、出售或耗用，主要包括存货、应收账款等；②主要为交易目的而持有；③预计在资产负债表日起一年内（含一年）变现；④自资产负债表日起一年内，交换其他资产或清偿负债的能力不受限制的现金或现金等价物。包括货币资金、应收票据、应收账款、存货等项目。

(2) 固定资产原价 指固定资产的成本，包括企业在购置，自行建造、安装、改建、扩建、技术改造某项固定资产时所发生的全部支出总额。

负债合计 指企业过去的交易或者事项形成的，预期会导致经济利益流出企业的现时义务。负债一般按偿还期长短分为流动负债和非流动负债。

(1) 流动负债合计 负债满足下列条件之一的应归为流动负债：①预计在一个正常营业周期中清偿；②主要为交易目的而持有；③自资产负债表日起一年内到期应予清偿；④企业无权自主地将清偿推迟至资产负债表日后一年以上。包括短期借款、应付票据、应付账款、应付职工薪酬、应交税费等项目。

(2) 非流动负债合计 指流动负债之外的负债。包括长期借款、应付债券等。

所有者权益合计 指企业资产扣除负债后由所有者享有的剩余权益。公司的所有者权益又称股东权益。包括实收资本、资本公积、盈余公积、未分配利润等。

实收资本 指企业各投资者实际投入的资本（或股本）总额，包括货币、实物、无形资产等各种形式的投入。实收资本按投资主体可分为国家资本、集体资本、法人资本、个人资本、港澳台资本和外商资本。

营业收入 指企业从事销售商品、提供劳务和让渡资产使用权等生产经营活动形成的经济利益流入。

营业成本 指企业从事销售商品、提供劳务和让渡资产使用权等生产经营活动发生的实际成本。

税金及附加 指企业因从事生产经营活动按税法规定应缴纳的消费税、城市维护建设税、资源税、环境保护税、教育费附加及房产税、土地使用税、车船使用税、印花税等相关税费。

营业利润 指企业从事生产经营活动所取得的利润。

利润总额 指企业在一定会计期间的经营成果，是生产经营过程中各种收入扣除各种耗费后的盈余，反映企业在报告期内实现的亏盈总额。

应交增值税 指企业按税法规定，以销售货物、服务、无形资产或提供加工、修理修配劳务等增加货物价值的活动本期应交纳的税金。

应交增值税=销项税额－（进项税额－进项税额转出）－出口抵减内销产品应纳税额－减免税款+出口退税

应交增值税不含期初末抵扣税额。

工业产品销售率 指报告期工业销售产值与工业总产值之比。计算公式：

$$\text{工业产品销售率(\%)}=\frac{\text{报告期现价工业销售产值}}{\text{报告期现价工业总产值}}\times 100\%$$

平均用工人数 指报告期企业平均实际拥有的、参与本企业生产经营活动的人员数。

流动资产周转率 指在一定时期内流动资产完成的周转次数，反映流动资产的周转速度。计算公式：

$$\text{流动资产周转率(次)}=\frac{\text{营业收入}}{\text{流动资产平均余额}}$$

资产负债率 反映在企业资产总额中有多少资产是通过借债而得的，也可以用于衡量企业利用债权人提供资金进行经营活动的能力以及企业在清算时保护债权人利益的程度。计算公式：

$$\text{资产负债率}=\frac{\text{负债总额}}{\text{资产总额}}\times 100\%$$

总资产贡献率 反映企业全部资产的获利能力，是企业经营业绩和管理水平的集中体现，是评价和考核企业盈利能力的核心指标。计算公式为：

$$\text{总资产贡献率}=(\text{利润总额}+\text{税金总额}+\text{利息支出})\div\text{平均资产总额}\times 100\%$$

其中：税金总额为税金及附加与应交增值税之和；平均资产总额为期初期末资产总计的算术平均值。

资产保值增值率 反映企业净资产的变动状况，是企业发展能力的集中体现。计算公式为：

$$\text{资产保值增值率}=\frac{\text{报告期期末所有者权益}}{\text{上年同期期末所有者权益}}\times 100\%$$

高技术制造业 是指国民经济行业中 R&D 投入强度相对较高的制造业行业，根据国家统计局《高技术产业（制造业）分类（2017)》标准界定。

Explanatory Notes on Main Statistical Indicators

Industry refers to the material production sector which is engaged in extraction of natural resources and processing and reprocessing of minerals and agricultural products, including (1) extraction of natural resources, such as mining, salt production, logging (but not including animal hunting and fishing); (2) processing and reprocessing of agricultural products, such as grain and oil processing, food processing, embroidery, textile manufacturing and leather making; (3) processing and reprocessing of mining products, such as iron making, steel making, chemical production, petroleum processing, machine building, timber processing; and production and supply of electric power, tap water and gas; (4) repair and refurbishment of industrial products, such as the repair of machinery equipment.

Light Industry refers to the industries that produce consumer goods and hand tools. It falls into two categories, based on different raw materials:

(1) Industries basing the raw materials on agriculture, which directly or indirectly use farm products as basic raw materials, mainly include the manufacture of foods and beverages, tobacco processing, textile manufacturing, tailoring, fur and leather manufacturing, paper making, printing, etc.

(2) Industries using non-agricultural products as raw materials, which means the manufactured goods are used as raw materials, mainly include the manufacture of cultural, educational articles and sports goods, chemical medicines, synthetic fiber, daily chemical products, glass products for daily use, metal products for daily use, hand tools, medical appliances and instruments, as well as stationery and office machinery.

Heavy Industry refers to the industries that provide material and technical foundation as key means of production for various sectors of the national economy. It falls into the following three categories according to the purpose of production or the use of products:

(1) Mining, quarrying and logging industry refers to the industry that extracts natural resources, including the extraction of petroleum, coal, metal and non-metal ores and logging.

(2) Raw material industry refers to the industry that provides various sectors of the national economy with basic materials, fuels and power. It includes smelting and processing of metals, coking and coke chemistry, chemical materials, cement, artificial boards, as well as power generation, petroleum refining and coal processing.

(3) Processing industry refers to the industry that reprocesses raw materials. It includes machine manufacturing, which equips various sectors of the national economy, metal structure, cement products, and chemical fertilizer and pesticide industry that provide means of production for agriculture.

According to the above principle of classification, the repair services for products of heavy industry are classified as heavy industry, while the repair services for products of light industry are classified as light industry.

Gross Output Value of Industry is the total value in monetary terms for final industrial products and industrial labor service provided by industrial enterprises during the reporting period. It includes the value of the finished industrial products, which will not be further processed in the enterprises and have been sold or have been prepared for sales upon being inspected, packed and put in storage, the revenue from processing products for others, the difference value of self-made semi-finished products and the articles in process at the end and beginning of the period. The gross industrial output value is calculated with factory method; that is, to take an industrial enterprise as a whole. It calculates the final products created by the enterprise.

Sales Value of Industry refers to the total value of industrial products sold or labor service provided by an industrial enterprise during the reporting period in monetary terms. It includes the total value of all finished and semi-finished products actually sold by the enterprise (including products produced in current period and noncurrent period), revenue from processing products for others, repairing industrial products for others, as well as processing, repairing, and installing equipment for internal non-industrial departments in the reporting period. All finished and semi-finished products sold in the current period will be counted, regardless of whether they were produced in the current period or not. The value of products, industrial work and home-built equipment provided by the enterprise for its capital construction department and welfare department will also be included in the industrial sales value.

Total Assets refer to resources formed by previous transactions or matters of an enterprise, owned or controlled by the enterprise, and expected to bring economic benefits to the enterprise. Classified by the liquidity, assets fall into current assets and non-current assets. Current assets include monetary capital, tradable financial assets, notes receivable, accounts receivable, prepayment, other receivables, and inventory, etc.; while non-current assets include long-term equity investment, fixed assets, intangible assets, and other non-current assets, etc.

(1) Total Current Assets Assets that meet any of the following requirements are considered current assets: a. assets expected to be cashed in, sold or consumed in a normal operating cycle, which mainly includes inventory and accounts receivable, etc.; b. assets held mainly for transaction; c. assets expected to be cashed in within one year (including one year) from the balance sheet date; d. cash or cash equivalents with unrestricted capacity of exchanging for other assets or paying off debts within one year from the balance sheet date, which include monetary capital, notes receivable, accounts receivable, inventory, etc.

(2) Original Value Fixed Assets refers to the cost of fixed assets, including the total amount of expenditure incurred to an enterprise in its acquisition, self-construction, installation, reconstruction, expansion or technological transformation of a certain fixed asset.

Total Liabilities refer to the present obligations formed by previous transactions or matters of an enterprise, expected to lead the flow of economic benefits out of the enterprise. By the term of payment, liabilities generally include current liabilities and non-current liabilities.

(1) Total Current liabilities Liabilities that meet any of the following requirements are considered current liabilities: a. assets expected to be paid off within one normal operating cycle; b. assets held mostly for the purpose of transaction; c. assets expected to be due and paid off within one year from the balance sheet date; d. assets that the enterprise has no right to delay the payment to more than one year after the balance sheet date on its own. They include short-term loans, notes payable, accounts payable, wages payable, taxes and fees payable, etc.

(2) Total Non-current Liabilities refer to liabilities other than current liabilities, including long-term borrowings and bonds payable, etc.

Total Owner's Equity refers to the remaining equity of assets in an enterprise held by owners after deducting the liabilities. Owner's equity of a company is also called shareholders' equity, including paid-up capital, capital reserves, operating surplus reserves and non-distributed profits, etc.

Paid-up Capital refers to the total capital (or equity) actually contributed by investors to an enterprise, including input in various forms, such as monetary investment, physical investment and intangible assets. Categorized by investors, paid-up capital includes state capital, collective capital, legal person's capital, personal capital, capital from Hong Kong, Macao and Taiwan, and foreign capital.

Business Income refers to the inflow of economic benefits formed in an enterprise's production and operating activities such as sales of commodities, rendering of labor services and assignment of the right to use assets, etc.

Business Cost refers to the actual cost incurred by an enterprise in its production and operating activities such as sales of commodities, rendering of labor services and assignment of the right to use assets, etc.

Tax and Surtax refers to the consumption tax, urban maintenance and construction tax, resource tax, environmental protection tax, educational surcharge as well as the house property tax, land use tax, vehicle and vessel use tax, stamp tax and other relevant taxes and fees that are payable by an enterprise for engaging in production and operating activities in accordance with the tax law.

Operating Profits refer to the profits reaped by an enterprise from its productive and operating activities.

Total Profits refer to the operating results of an enterprise during certain accounting period, representing the surplus of various incomes from production and operation deducting various expenses, reflecting the total gains and losses realized by the enterprise during the reporting period.

VAT Payable refer to the tax payable by an enterprise in current period according to provisions in Law of Tax for its activities of adding value to goods, such as selling goods, services and intangible assets or providing labor service for processing, repair and replacement.

VAT Payable = Output Tax – (Input Tax – Transfer-out of Input Tax) – Tax Payable Deducted by Export from Output Tax of Domestically Sold Products – Tax Concession + Export Rebate

VAT Payable excludes the taxes not deducted at the beginning of the period.

Sales Rate of Industrial Products refers to the ratio of the sales value of industry to the gross output value of industry during the reporting period. The following formula is used:

Sales Rate of Industrial Products (%) = Sales Value of Industry at Present Value During the Reporting Period / Gross Output Value of Industry at Present Value During the Reporting Period × 100%

Average Number of Employees refers to the average number of employees actually in the enterprise and engaged in its production and operation activities during the reporting period.

Turnover of Current Assets refers to the number of times for current assets turnover within a period of time. It reflects the turnover velocity of current assets. Calculation formula is listed below:

Turnover of Current Assets (No. of times) = Busiress Income / Average Balance of Current Assets

Assets-liabilities Ratio reflects how many assets—out of the total assets of the enterprise, are obtained by borrowing. It can be used to evaluate the enterprise's capability of operating by using the funds provided by creditors, and to what extent the enterprise will be able to protect the creditors' interests in the case of liquidation. The following formula is used:

Assets-liabilities Ratio = Total Liabilities / Total Assets × 100%

Contribution Rate of Total Assets indicates the profitability of all assets in an enterprise, reflecting the operating performance and management of the enterprise. It serves as a core indicator evaluating the enterprise's profitability. The following formula is used:

Total Assets Contribution rate = (Total Profit + Total Tax + Total Interest Expenses) / Average Total Assets × 100%

Note: the total tax is the sum of tax and surtax, and VAT payable; average total assets are represented by the arithmetic average of total assets at the beginning and the end of the period.

Assets Maintenance and Appreciation Rate reflects the changes in the net assets of an enterprise. It embodies the development ability of the enterprise. Calculation formula is listed below:

Assets Maintenance and Appreciation Rate = Owner's Equity at the End of the Reporting Period / Owner's Equity at the End of the Same Period in the Previous Year × 100%

High-tech Manufacturing Sector refers to the manufacturing industry with relatively high R&D input intensity in national economic sectors, and is defined in accordance with the standards in the High Technology Industry (Manufacturing Industry) Classification 2017 of the National Bureau of Statistics.

13

建筑业
CONSTRUCTION

简要说明

一、主要内容

本章资料主要反映北京市建筑业企业基本情况和生产经营情况。主要指标包括企业个数、从业人员、建筑业总产值、建筑业企业房屋建筑面积、利润、税金等。

二、统计范围

建筑业统计范围从 2004 年起，由原具有建筑业资质等级四级及四级以上的独立核算的建筑业企业调整为具有施工总承包、专业承包资质的所有法人建筑业企业。

三、调查方法

本章建筑业企业统计数据根据国家统计局制定的《建筑业统计报表制度》整理汇总。建筑业统计数据采取全面调查的方法。

四、有关统计标准的变化说明

2002-2011 年建筑业行业分类执行《国民经济行业分类》(GB/T 4754-2002)标准，2012-2017 年执行《国民经济行业分类》(GB/T 4754-2011)标准。自 2018 年起，执行《国民经济行业分类》(GB/T 4754−2017) 标准。

五、关于历史数据调整

2004 年开展了“北京市第一次全国经济普查”，按照国家统计局统一要求和统一方法，1993-2003 年建筑业总产值根据普查结果采用“趋势离差法”进行了修订，2004 年为第一次经济普查数据，2008 年为第二次经济普查数据，2013 年为第三次经济普查数据。

Brief Introduction

I. Main Content

Statistics in this chapter mainly show the basic situation and operation of construction enterprises in Beijing. Main indicators include number of enterprises, employees, gross output value of the construction sector, as well as floor space, profits, and tax of construction enterprises.

II. Scope of Statistics

Since 2004, data on construction sector, which previously covered construction enterprises with independent accounting at or above Level-4 in construction qualifications, have been adjusted to cover all construction enterprises with qualifications of general and specialized contracting.

III. Methods of Survey

Data on construction enterprises in this chapter were gathered based on *Statistical Statement System for Construction Sector* developed by the National Bureau of Statistics. The figures were gained through complete survey.

IV. Changes in Relevant Statistical Standards

Classification of construction sectors during 2002-2011 was based on the standards in the *Classification of National Economic Sectors* (GB/T 4754-2002). The standards in the *Classification of National Economic Sectors* (GB/T 4754-2011) were implemented from 2012 to 2017. The standards in the *Classification of National Economic Sectors (GB/T 4754-2017) are implemented since 2018.*

V. Adjustment to Historical Data

As “the first national economic census in Beijing” was conducted in 2004, in accordance with the unified requirements and methods of the National Bureau of Statistics, the data on gross output value of construction sector during 1993-2003 were adjusted by “trend deviation method” based on the census results. The data for 2004 were collected from the first economic census, the data for 2008 were collected from the second economic census, and the data for 2013 were collected from the third economic census.

13-1 建筑业企业基本情况(1978-2019年) BASIC STATISTICS FOR ENTERPRISES IN THE CONSTRUCTION INDUSTRY (1978-2019)

年份 Year	企业单位数(个) Construction Enterprises (unit)	年末从业人员(万人) Employed Persons (year-end) (10000 persons)	建筑业总产值(亿元) Gross Output Value (100 million yuan)	企业利润总额(亿元) Total Profits (100 million yuan)	房屋建筑面积(万平方米) Floor Space of Buildings (10000 sq.m) 施工面积 Floor Space under Construction	竣工面积 Floor Space Completed
1978	64	25.4	10.5	0.7		
1979	70	26.4	12.7	0.9		
1980	71	27.8	14.7	1.5		
1981	71	27.0	14.5	1.6		
1982	91	30.7	17.3	1.7		
1983	116	37.2	22.6	2.5		
1984	2765	53.0	33.4	3.2		
1985	2549	63.9	43.9	3.9		
1986	2361	61.3	51.3	3.3		
1987	2292	64.4	67.0	4.1		
1988	1659	64.2	81.6	3.9		
1989	1545	60.0	89.0	3.8		
1990	994	60.2	94.7	3.4		
1991	922	60.3	99.6	2.8	2495	1172
1992	976	62.7	122.6	3.1	2774	1227
1993	1098	75.9	215.5	6.1	3499	1428
1994	1259	73.4	336.0	9.4	4035	1437
1995	1332	82.6	426.6	7.8	4602	1593
1996	1292	82.5	494.7	8.9	5328	1967
1997	1297	80.3	556.4	10.4	5801	2117
1998	1482	75.6	678.6	12.4	6525	2225
1999	1588	62.0	750.6	13.6	6824	2632
2000	1697	56.6	812.5	16.4	7247	2809
2001	1811	57.8	1055.4	18.7	8919	3198
2002	2122	57.0	1211.3	24.7	10241	3827
2003	2419	59.1	1521.2	31.5	12160	4486
2004	2623	51.2	1659.8	40.0	14424	5258
2005	2752	67.2	1894.0	67.3	15418	4862
2006	2800	66.9	2167.9	112.8	16202	4786
2007	2845	51.7	2576.8	115.7	18225	4946
2008	3527	47.0	3066.2	84.5	19537	4803
2009	3556	56.2	4059.7	217.4	22721	5225
2010	3594	59.9	5196.0	265.2	29440	5933
2011	3667	49.6	6046.3	219.6	36507	6456
2012	3572	49.2	6588.3	293.0	41660	8414
2013	3522	49.3	7459.6	385.8	49259	8950
2014	3426	51.0	8209.8	473.2	56477	9275
2015	3369	59.0	8436.7	520.1	59777	9886
2016	3218	59.2	8841.2	725.7	61098	10703
2017	2888	60.8	9736.7	773.5	65290	9844
2018	2854	53.4	10939.8	498.5	71969	9771
2019	2877	55.5	11999.4	822.7	80557	10937

注：建筑业企业房屋建筑面积包括在本市和外省完成的施工、竣工面积。
Note: Data on floor space covers buildings under construction and completed in Beijing and other provinces.and outside the city.

13-2 建筑业施工企业基本情况(2019年)
BASIC STATISTICS FOR CONSTRUCTION ENTERPRISES (2019)

项 目	Item	建筑业总产值(亿元) Gross Output Value (10000 yuan)	年末从业人员(人) Employed Persons (year-end) (person)	签订合同额(亿元) Value of Contract Signed (10000 yuan)	竣工产值(亿元) Output Value of Completion (10000 yuan)
合 计	**Total**	**11999.4**	**554590**	**39953.4**	**5221.0**
按企业登记注册类型分	**By Registration Type**				
内资企业	Domestically-funded Enterprises	11890.7	545279	39699.8	5131.4
#国有企业	State-owned Enterprises	150.5	9522	534.6	62.7
集体企业	Collectively-owned Enterprises	57.6	5648	183.2	39.0
股份合作企业	Joint-equity Cooperative Enterprises	33.7	5396	40.7	20.7
有限责任公司	Limited Liability Companies	9789.2	393555	32858.3	4334.7
股份有限公司	Companies Limited by Shares	814.4	16332	4101.0	97.3
私营企业	Private Enterprises	1043.8	114800	1980.2	575.5
港澳台商投资企业	Hong Kong, Macao and Taiwan-invested Enterprises	58.3	5661	110.5	53.9
外商投资企业	Foreign-invested Enterprises	50.4	3650	143.1	35.7
按隶属关系分	**By Affiliation**				
中 央	Central	9732.0	340728	34887.2	3948.3
地 方	Local	2267.4	213862	5066.2	1272.7
按行业分	**By Sector**				
房屋建筑业	Construction of Buildings	6203.2	230977	22799.7	3278.5
土木工程建筑业	Civil Engineering Construction	4100.1	168946	14186.0	873.5
建筑安装业	Construction Installation	835.9	73965	1651.3	565.7
建筑装饰、装修和其他建筑业	Building Decoration, Finishing and Other Construction	860.1	80702	1316.4	503.4

注：统计范围为施工总承包、专业承包的法人建筑业企业（下表同）。
Note: Statistics covers general contracting and specialized contracting corporate construction enterprises(same as the following table).

13-3 建筑业施工企业主要财务指标(2018年)

单位：亿元

项目	Item	企业单位数(个) Number of Enterprises (unit)	资产负债 Assets and Liabilities							
			资产总计 Total Assets	流动资产合计 Total Current Assets	固定资产原价 Total Original Value of Fixed Assets	负债合计 Total Liabilities	#流动负债合计 Total Current Liabilities	#应付账款 Accounts Payable	所有者权益合计 Total Owner's Equity	#实收资本 Paid-up Capital
合　计	**Total**	**2854**	**27814.1**	**17776.7**	**941.7**	**19051.8**	**17070.8**	**6171.7**	**8762.3**	**3494.9**
按企业登记注册类型分	**By Registration Type**									
内资企业	Domestically-funded Enterprises	2783	27598.0	17577.8	930.4	18885.3	16907.5	6103.0	8712.7	3460.7
#国有企业	State-owned Enterprises	38	81.6	76.4	5.6	65.5	62.5	12.2	16.0	9.2
集体企业	Collectively-owned Enterprises	53	128.0	109.4	5.8	103.5	103.2	24.3	24.5	11.3
股份合作企业	Joint-Equity Cooperative Enterprises	43	38.8	35.1	5.3	21.3	20.8	4.6	17.6	9.8
有限责任公司	Limited Liability Companies	1085	16784.9	12824.9	747.5	13164.7	12042.5	5265.0	3620.2	2029.0
股份有限公司	Companies Limited by Shares	49	9125.6	3266.7	61.6	4528.7	3712.8	484.1	4596.9	1067.0
私营企业	Private Enterprises	1514	1438.9	1265.2	104.5	1001.5	965.6	312.8	437.5	334.5
港澳台商投资企业	Hong Kong, Macao and Taiwan- invested Enterprises	38	105.8	97.7	4.1	87.3	84.8	31.4	18.6	17.5
外商投资企业	Foreign-invested Enterprises	33	110.3	101.2	7.2	79.3	78.5	37.3	31.0	16.7
按隶属关系分	**By Affiliation**									
中　央	Central	172	20231.1	11470.9	511.0	13226.0	11788.6	4141.8	7005.1	2423.7
地　方	Local	2682	7583.0	6305.8	430.7	5825.8	5282.1	2029.9	1757.2	1071.2
按国民经济行业分	**By Sector**									
房屋建筑业	Construction of Buildings	535	10467.1	7179.4	340.2	7737.1	6870.5	2854.6	2730.0	1360.7
土木工程建筑业	Civil Engineering Construction	599	14442.4	8236.3	443.6	9323.0	8318.5	2474.0	5119.3	1641.9
建筑安装业	Construction Installation	687	1652.2	1288.5	81.0	1081.6	1012.0	474.2	570.6	253.9
建筑装饰、装修和其他建筑业	Building Decoration and Other Construction	1033	1252.5	1072.4	76.9	910.1	869.8	368.9	342.4	238.4

注：应交税金合计包括应交增值税、所得税费用、税金及附加。

MAIN FINANCIAL INDICATORS OF CONSTRUCTION ENTERPRISES (2018)

(100 million yuan)

损 益 Profits and Loss					应交税金合计 Total Taxes Payable	#税金及附加 Tax and Surtax	#所得税费用 Income Tax Expense	#应交增值税 Value Added Tax Payable	流动比率(倍) Current Ratio (times)	速动比率(倍) Quick Ratio (times)	资产负债率(%) Assets-Liabilities Ratio (%)	资本金利润率(%) Capital-Profit Ratio (%)
营业收入 Business Income	营业成本 Business Cost	管理费用 Management Expenses	财务费用 Financial Expenses	利润总额 Total Profits								
13481.3	**12513.8**	**567.1**	**131.5**	**498.5**	**263.5**	**37.4**	**62.1**	**164.0**	**1.04**	**0.93**	**68.5**	**14.3**
13306.1	12359.0	556.4	130.3	492.6	259.2	36.9	60.7	161.6	1.04	0.93	68.4	14.2
45.2	41.6	2.5	-0.1	1.1	1.6	0.2	0.4	1.0	1.22	0.82	80.3	12.3
104.6	99.5	3.9	0.0	1.1	3.2	0.3	0.4	2.5	1.06	0.82	80.9	9.6
23.6	21.1	1.6	0.0	0.7	0.8	0.1	0.2	0.5	1.69	1.19	54.7	7.2
10931.4	10191.5	436.2	52.3	266.2	197.0	30.3	53.0	113.8	1.06	0.93	78.4	13.1
1191.9	1112.6	39.6	73.8	209.6	20.0	2.3	1.6	16.1	0.88	0.86	49.6	19.6
1009.4	892.7	72.6	4.2	13.9	36.6	3.8	5.0	27.8	1.31	1.13	69.6	4.2
83.8	74.0	5.4	0.5	2.8	2.3	0.3	0.7	1.3	1.15	1.00	82.5	16.0
91.4	80.8	5.3	0.7	3.1	2.0	0.1	0.7	1.1	1.29	0.99	71.9	18.5
8575.9	8039.1	309.7	93.5	413.8	124.3	18.0	37.5	68.8	0.97	0.90	65.4	17.1
4905.4	4474.7	257.4	38.0	84.7	139.2	19.4	24.6	95.2	1.19	0.99	76.8	7.9
5986.5	5640.2	182.0	66.9	148.4	105.1	17.2	28.3	59.6	1.04	0.88	73.9	10.9
5453.4	5058.6	250.1	58.7	285.4	104.9	13.4	21.4	70.2	0.99	0.92	64.6	17.4
1070.0	957.4	67.9	0.3	49.0	25.0	3.3	8.0	13.7	1.27	1.16	65.5	19.3
971.5	857.6	67.2	5.6	15.8	28.4	3.5	4.5	20.5	1.23	1.06	72.7	6.6

Note:Total taxes payable include VAT payable, income tax expense, tax and surtax.

13-4 建筑业施工企业主要财务指标(2019年)

单位：亿元

项目	Item	企业单位数(个) Number of Enterprises (unit)	资产负债 Assets and Liabilities					
			资产总计 Total Assets	流动资产合计 Total Current Assets	固定资产原价 Total Original Value of Fixed Assets	负债合计 Total Liabilities	#流动负债合计 Total Current Liabilities	#应付账款 Accounts Payable
合　计	**Total**	**2877**	**29966.9**	**18531.7**	**947.7**	**20019.0**	**17942.0**	**6495.2**
按企业登记注册类型分	**By Registration Type**							
内资企业	Domestically-funded Enterprises	2813	29761.4	18342.5	937.4	19858.2	17784.0	6425.4
#国有企业	State-owned Enterprises	31	88.3	82.0	4.9	72.0	70.8	17.1
集体企业	Collectively-owned Enterprises	43	120.8	102.1	5.9	94.8	94.2	22.7
股份合作企业	Joint-Equity Cooperative Enterprises	39	38.2	33.8	5.5	20.8	20.4	4.9
有限责任公司	Limited Liability Companies	1022	18249.0	13585.1	739.1	14216.5	13067.9	5455.9
股份有限公司	Companies Limited by Shares	43	9559.5	3036.9	64.2	4199.4	3310.9	532.0
私营企业	Private Enterprises	1634	1702.0	1499.8	117.0	1252.5	1217.7	392.2
港、澳、台商投资企业	Hong Kong, Macao and Taiwan- invested Enterprises	37	105.7	98.0	3.5	86.8	84.9	32.3
外商投资企业	Foreign-invested Enterprises	27	99.8	91.2	6.7	74.0	73.1	37.4
按隶属关系分	**By Affiliation**							
中　央	Central	164	21565.4	11628.6	499.3	13481.0	12026.9	4169.9
地　方	Local	2713	8401.4	6903.1	448.4	6538.1	5915.2	2325.2
按国民经济行业分	**By Sector**							
房屋建筑业	Construction of Buildings	543	11128.4	7447.9	336.8	8132.4	7220.9	2908.5
土木工程建筑业	Civil Engineering Construction	615	15687.7	8523.8	451.3	9697.5	8622.7	2679.3
建筑安装业	Construction Installation	682	1856.0	1449.6	80.0	1193.3	1140.2	519.5
建筑装饰、装修和其他建筑业	Building Decoration and Other Construction	1037	1294.7	1110.5	79.7	995.8	958.2	387.9

注：应交税金合计包括应交增值税、所得税费用、税金及附加。

MAIN FINANCIAL INDICATORS OF CONSTRUCTION ENTERPRISES (2019)

（100 million yuan）

		损益 Profits and Loss						应交			
所有者权益合计 Total Owner's Equity	#实收资本 Paid-up Capital	营业收入 Business Income	营业成本 Business Cost	管理费用 Management Expenses	研发费用 R&D Expenses	财务费用 Financial Expenses	利润总额 Total Profits	税金合计 Total Taxes Payable	#税金及附加 Tax and Surtax	#所得税费用 Income Tax Expense	#应交增值税 Value Added Tax Payable
9947.8	**3656.8**	**15291.4**	**14192.1**	**455.9**	**219.5**	**124.5**	**822.7**	**316.8**	**40.1**	**67.1**	**209.6**
9903.2	3625.9	15120.8	14038.7	447.1	218.8	123.7	818.8	312.9	39.7	65.8	207.4
16.3	10.0	44.7	40.4	2.7	0.3	-0.1	1.0	1.2	0.2	0.3	0.7
26.1	10.9	101.6	95.9	4.0			1.5	2.4	0.3	0.5	1.6
17.3	9.6	25.4	22.9	1.7			0.7	0.7	0.1	0.2	0.4
4032.4	2159.0	12323.0	11489.4	312.3	206.2	52.1	321.9	252.7	32.1	52.5	168.2
5360.2	1085.4	1329.0	1245.9	39.6	4.2	67.0	483.9	21.2	2.4	7.1	11.7
449.5	350.7	1295.3	1142.8	86.2	8.1	4.7	9.8	34.8	4.7	5.2	24.9
18.9	16.2	82.1	72.7	4.8	0.5	0.4	2.5	2.2	0.2	0.8	1.2
25.7	14.7	88.5	80.7	4.0	0.2	0.4	1.3	1.6	0.1	0.5	1.0
8084.5	2498.0	9758.4	9144.8	202.4	169.8	84.4	735.6	168.6	19.1	42.5	107.0
1863.4	1158.8	5532.9	5047.3	253.5	49.7	40.1	87.1	148.1	21.0	24.6	102.6
2996.0	1443.8	6814.9	6421.6	165.5	70.9	51.5	301.0	160.4	18.9	30.8	110.7
5990.2	1689.1	6142.2	5691.5	160.1	124.1	60.0	446.6	100.0	13.1	25.6	61.3
662.7	287.3	1265.0	1128.3	63.6	17.3	6.8	73.2	29.3	4.3	8.0	17.0
298.9	236.6	1069.3	950.7	66.6	7.3	6.2	1.9	27.0	3.7	2.8	20.6

Note:Total taxes payable include VAT payable, income tax expense, tax and surtax.

13-4 续表 Continued

单位：亿元 (100 million yuan)

项　目	Item	流动比率(倍) Current Ratio (times)	速动比率(倍) Quick Ratio (times)	资产负债率(%) Assets-Liabilities Ratio (%)	资本金利润率(%) Capital-Profit Ratio (%)
合　计	**Total**	**1.03**	**0.94**	**66.8**	**22.5**
按企业登记注册类型分	**By Registration Type**				
内资企业	Domestically-funded Enterprises	1.03	0.94	66.7	22.6
#国有企业	State-owned Enterprises	1.16	0.90	81.5	10.3
集体企业	Collectively-owned Enterprises	1.08	0.86	78.4	13.9
股份合作企业	Joint-Equity Cooperative Enterprises	1.66	1.12	54.6	7.4
有限责任公司	Limited Liability Companies	1.04	0.94	77.9	14.9
股份有限公司	Companies Limited by Shares	0.92	0.89	43.9	44.6
私营企业	Private Enterprises	1.23	1.09	73.6	2.8
港澳台商投资企业	Hong Kong, Macao and Taiwan-invested Enterprises	1.15	1.03	82.1	15.6
外商投资企业	Foreign-invested Enterprises	1.25	0.97	74.2	8.9
按隶属关系分	**By Affiliation**				
中　央	Central	0.97	0.93	62.5	29.4
地　方	Local	1.17	0.97	77.8	7.5
按国民经济行业分	**Grouped by Sector**				
房屋建筑业	Construction of Buildings	1.03	0.90	73.1	20.9
土木工程建筑业	Civil Engineering Construction	0.99	0.93	61.8	26.4
建筑安装业	Construction Installation	1.27	1.15	64.3	25.5
建筑装饰、装修和其他建筑业	Building Decoration, Finishing and Other Construction	1.16	1.06	76.9	0.8

13-5 建筑业施工企业竣工率
PROJECT COMPLETION RATE OF CONSTRUCTION ENTERPRISES

单位：% (%)

项 目	Item	产值竣工率 Completion Rate by Output Value		面积竣工率 Completion Rate by Floor Space	
		2019	2018	2019	2018
合 计	**Total**	**43.5**	**40.9**	**11.9**	**13.6**
按企业登记注册类型分	**By Registration Type**				
内资企业	Domestically-funded Enterprises	43.2	40.7	13.5	13.5
国有企业	State-owned Enterprises	41.7	89.0	8.3	55.6
集体企业	Collectively-owned Enterprises	67.7	128.7	14.6	36.5
股份合作企业	Joint-equity Cooperative Enterprises	61.3	73.8	5.7	37.7
有限责任公司	Limited Liability Companies	44.3	41.1	13.5	13.5
股份有限公司	Companies Limited by Shares	11.9	16.9	9.6	23.3
私营企业	Private Enterprises	55.1	43.5	25.4	11.6
港澳台商投资企业	Hong Kong, Macao and Taiwan-invested Enterprises	92.5	63.1	39.2	
外商投资企业	Foreign-invested Enterprises	70.9	71.2	26.2	27.7
按隶属关系分	**By Affiliation Relationship**				
中 央	Central	40.6	32.2	9.7	12.2
地 方	Local	56.1	54.4	61.8	17.4
按国民经济行业分	**By Sector**				
房屋建筑业	Construction of Buildings	52.9	49.5	14.2	13.8
土木工程建筑业	Civil Engineering Construction	21.3	22.1	5.9	9.7
建筑安装业	Construction Installation	67.7	53.7	7.4	17.4
建筑装饰、装修和其他建筑业	Building Decoration, Finishing and Other Construction	58.5	62.8	16.2	25.4

主要统计指标解释

建筑业总产值 指以货币表现的建筑业企业在一定时期内生产的建筑产品和服务的总和。它包括建筑工程产值、安装工程产值、其他产值三部分内容。

(1)**建筑工程产值** 指列入建筑工程预(概)算内的各种工程价值。

(2)**安装工程产值** 指为设备安装而发生的安装工程费用，在设备安装产值中，不得包括被安装设备本身价值。

(3)**其他产值** 建筑业总产值中除建筑工程、安装工程以外的产值，包括房屋构筑物修理产值、非标准设备制造产值、总包企业向分包企业收取的管理费，以及不能明确划分的施工活动所完成的产值。

年末从业人员 指年末最后一日24小时在本单位工作并取得劳动报酬或收入的期末实有人员数。该指标为时点指标，不包括最后一日当天及以前与单位解除劳动合同关系的人员和建筑业整建制使用的人员。

房屋施工面积 指报告期内施工的全部房屋建筑面积，包括：本期新开工的房屋面积、上期施工跨入本期继续施工的房屋面积、上期停缓建本期复工的房屋面积、本期施工又停缓建和本期竣工的房屋面积。

房屋竣工面积 指在报告期内房屋建筑按照设计要求已全部完工，达到了住人和使用条件，经验收鉴定合格或达到竣工验收标准，可正式移交使用的各栋房屋建筑面积的总和。

签订合同额 指建筑业企业在报告期直接同建设单位签订的各种国内工程合同的总价款和以前年度同建设单位签订的各种国内工程合同的未完工程跨入本年度继续施工工程合同的总价款余额。

主营业务收入 指企业确认的销售商品、提供劳务等主营业务的收入。

主营业务成本 指企业经营主要业务所发生的成本总额。

应交增值税 指按照税法规定，以销售货物、服务、无形资产、不动产或提供加工、修理修配劳务的增值额和货物进口金额为计税依据而课征的一种流转税。

利润总额 指企业在一定会计期间的经营成果，是生产经营过程中各种收入扣除各种耗费后的盈余，反映企业在报告期内实现的亏盈总额。

Explanatory Notes on Main Statistical Indicators

Gross Output Value of Construction refers to total of construction products and services, expressed in money terms, completed by construction enterprises during a given period of time. It includes: output value of construction works, output value of installation works and other output value.

(1) Output Value of Construction Works means the value of works involved in project budgets.

(2) Output Value of Installation Works means the costs of installation works incurred for equipment installation. Output value of equipment installation does not include the value of installed equipment itself.

(3) Other Output Value means, of the total output value of construction, the output value other than that of construction and installations works. It includes the repair output value of houses and structures, manufacturing output value of non-standard equipment, management charges collected by general contracting enterprises from subcontracting enterprises, as well as the output value of construction activities falling in no specific categories.

Year-end Employed Persons refers to the year-end actual number of employed persons who still work during the 24 hours of the last day of a year and acquire labor compensation or income. This time-spot index does not include persons who terminate their labor contracts at or before the last day of the year or the persons used in the construction industry as a whole.

House Construction Area means the building area of all houses in the reporting period, including: the area of houses newly started in current period, area of houses built in the previous period and continued in current period, area of houses suspended in the previous period and restarted in current period, area of houses built and suspended in current period, and area of houses completed in current period.

Area of Houses Completed means the total area of all houses and buildings entirely completed in line with requirements of design, meeting conditions of living and use, being checked and accepted as qualified or reaching the acceptance standards of completed projects and officially delivered for use in the reporting period.

Value of Signed Contracts means total price of all kinds of domestic engineering contracts signed directly between construction enterprises and builders in the reporting period and the balance of total price of domestic engineering contracts signed with builders in previous year and continued for implementation in the current year.

Main Business Income means the income recognized by an enterprise from main business such as sale of commodities and rendering of service.

Main Business Cost means the total cost incurred in an enterprise for the operation of main business.

VAT Payable means a kind of turnover tax levied on the basis of the appreciation amount and amount of goods imported for sale of goods, services, intangible assets, real estate or for rendering of processing, repair and replacement services in accordance with the tax laws.

Total Profits mean the operating result of an enterprise in certain accounting period. It is the surplus of all revenues deducting all costs in its production and operation, reflecting its total profit and loss realized in the reporting period.

14

第三产业
TERTIARY INDUSTRY

简要说明

一、主要内容

本章资料包括第三产业主要指标及占全市比重、规模以上第三产业主要指标、规模以上第三产业企业财务状况以及物流业、会展活动情况等。

二、统计范围

1.规模以上第三产业包括除国际组织以外的各行业限额以上的法人单位。具体为：批发业为年主营业务收入 2000 万元及以上的企业；零售业为年主营业务收入 500 万元及以上的企业；住宿业为星级饭店和星级以外年主营业务收入 200 万元及以上企业；餐饮业为年主营业务收入 200 万元及以上的企业；金融业为全部金融监管法人单位及下属产业活动单位、年营业收入 500 万元及以上的非金融监管的金融业法人单位以及从事互联网金融业务的其他法人单位；房地产开发业的全部法人单位。

2018 年居民服务、修理和其他服务业，文化、体育和娱乐业，为年营业收入 500 万元及以上或从业人员期末人数 50 人及以上的企业；其余行业为年营业收入 1000 万元及以上或从业人员期末人数 50 人及以上的企业；执行行政事业、民间非营利组织会计制度年收入合计 1000 万元及以上的法人单位。

2019 年居民服务、修理和其他服务业，文化、体育和娱乐业，社会工作，为年营业收入 500 万元及以上的企业；其余行业为年营业收入 1000 万元及以上的企业；执行事业、民间非营利组织会计制度年收入合计 2000 万元及以上的卫生法人单位，其余行业为年收入合计 1000 万元以及上的法人单位。

2.物流业资料根据物流业法人单位财务状况统计报表以及其他有关统计资料测算取得。

3.会展业统计对象涉及会展活动的举办服务单位和接待单位。具体包括限额以上住宿业法人单位和产业活动单位、从事各种会展活动的场馆、大型会展活动的举办单位（名单主要由北京市公安局提供）以及为会展活动提供各类专业服务的规模以上单位和旅行社。由于每年的统计对象单位范围不完全相同（有新增或撤销单位），为保持数据的可比性，同时列出统计对象本年和上年数据。

三、有关统计标准的变化说明

（一）关于行业划分。行业划分执行《国民经济行业分类》(GB/T 4754-2017）标准。

（二）关于三次产业划分。2003 年，根据《国民经济行业分类》(GB/T 4754—2002)，国家统计局印发了《国家统计局关于印发〈三次产业划分规定〉的通知》(国统字〔2003〕14 号)。2012 年，根据国家质检总局和国家标准委颁布的《国民经济行业分类》(GB/T 4754—2011)，国家统计局对 2003 年《三次产业划分规定》进行了修订。主要在以下方面作出调整：一是将门类“农、林、牧、渔业”中的“农、林、牧、渔服务业”，“采矿业”中的“开采辅助活动”，“制造业”中的“金属制品、机械和设备修理业”等三个大类一并调整到第三产业。调整后，第一产业为 4 个大类；第二产业为 2 个门类和 36 个大类；第三产业为 15 个门类和 3 个大类。二是明确第三产业即为服务业。

本章 2012 年及以后三次产业的分类执行调整后的划分规定。

Brief Introduction

I. Main Content

Statistics in this chapter include: main indicators for the tertiary industry and their percentages of Beijing's total, main indicators for tertiary industry above designated size, financial status of tertiary industry above designated size as well as logistics industry and exhibition activities.

II. Scope of Statistics

1. The tertiary industry above designated size includes legal entities above designated size in all sectors other than international organizations. Specifically, it includes enterprises in wholesale with annual main business income of RMB 20 million and above, enterprises in retail trade with annual main business income of RMB 5 million and above, star-level hotels and non-star-level enterprises with annual main business income of RMB 2 million and above in accommodation, enterprises in restaurants with annual main business income of RMB 2 million and above, all legal entities under financial regulation and the subordinate industrial activity units as well as the legal entities in finance that are not subject to financial regulation and with annual business income of RMB 5 million and above, and other legal entities engaged in Internet finance business and with annual business income of RMB 5 million and above, all legal entities in real estate development sector.

In 2018, it included enterprises with annual business income of RMB 5 million and above or with period-end employees of 50 and above in resident services, repair and other services, and in culture, sports and entertainment, enterprises with annual business income of RMB 10 million and above or with period-end employees of 50 and above in the rest of the sectors, and legal entities following the accounting system designed for administrative institutions and non-government non-profit organizations and with total annual income of RMB 10 million and above.

In 2019, it included enterprises with annual business income of RMB 5 million and above in resident services, repair and other services, and in culture, sports and entertainment as well as in social works, enterprises with annual business income of RMB 10 million and above in the rest of the sectors, and legal entities in health care sector following the accounting system designed for institutions and non-government non-profit organizations and with total annual income of RMB 20 million and above, and legal entities with total annual income of RMB 10 million and above in the rest of the sectors.

2. Data on logistics industry were calculated based on annual statistical report on financial status and other relevant statistics of legal entities in logistics industry.

3. Statistical scope of MICE industry covers service companies and reception companies holding the exhibitions, in details, including: legal entities and industrial activity units in accommodation sector above designated size in accommodation, venues for exhibitions and sponsors of large exhibitions (with the list provided by Beijing Municipal Bureau of Public Security), together with the above-designated-size units and travel agencies providing various professional services for exhibition activities. As the scope of companies under survey is not completely the same (there are companies newly added and phasing out), data in both the current year and previous year are presented to keep the data comparable.

III. Changes in Relevant Statistical Standards

(I) Classification of Sectors. The standards in the *Classification of National Economic Sectors* (GB/T 4754-2017) have been implemented in the classification of sectors.

(II) Classification of Three Industries. According to the *Classification of National Economic Sectors* (GB/T 4754-2002), the National Bureau of Statistics issued the *Notice of the National Bureau of Statistics on the Issuance of the 'Regulations on Three Industries Classification'* (G.T.Z. [2003] No. 14) in 2003. According to the *Classification of National Economic Sectors* (GB/T 4754-2011) promulgated by the General Administration of Quality Supervision, Inspection and Quarantine of the People's Republic of China and the Standardization Administration of the People's Republic of China, the National Bureau of Statistics revised the *Regulations on Three Industries Classification* of 2003 version. Adjustments were mainly made in the following aspects: Firstly, the "service activities for agriculture, forestry, animal husbandry and fishing" in the category of "agriculture, forestry, animal production and hunting, fishing", the "mining support service activities" in the category of "mining and quarrying", and the "repair of fabricated metal products, machinery and equipment" in the category of "manufacturing" were adjusted to the tertiary industry. After adjustment, the primary industry fell into 4 categories; the secondary industry fell into 2 classes and 36 categories; and the tertiary industry fell into 15 classes and 3 categories. Secondly, the tertiary industry was defined as the service industry.

The classification of three industries since 2012 as mentioned in this chapter has all been subject to the classification provisions after adjustment.

14-1 第三产业主要指标及占全市比重(2000-2019年)

项 目		Item		2000	2001	2002	2003	2004
增加值	(亿元)	Value Added	(100 million yuan)	2174.9	2653.6	3208.2	3726.7	4393.4
占全市比重	(%)	Percentage of the Total	(%)	66.4	68.7	70.9	70.8	70.3
劳动生产率	(元/人)	Overall Labor Productivity	(yuan/person)	65302	78046	89352	94215	90158
相当于全市比例	(%)	Percentage of the Total	(%)	123.3	126.1	129.1	123.6	112.3
从业人员年末人数	(万人)	Year-end Employed Persons	(10000 persons)	338.2	341.8	376.3	414.8	559.8
占全市比重	(%)	Percentage of the Total	(%)	54.6	54.4	55.4	59.0	65.5
固定资产投资	(亿元)	Investment in Fixed Assets	(100 million yuan)	510.3	1367.9	1621.8	1875.4	2112.7
占全市比重	(%)	Percentage of the Total	(%)	39.3	89.3	89.4	86.9	83.6
实际利用外资金额	(亿美元)	Actual Use of Foreign Capital	(USD 100 million)	22.2	12.8	12.5	14.0	19.2
占全市比重	(%)	Percentage of the Total	(%)	90.5	72.4	69.8	65.3	62.4
能源消费总量	(万吨标准煤)	Energy Consumption	(10000 tons of SCE)	1080.9	1196.2	1334.5	1391.0	1638.0
占全市比重	(%)	Percentage of the Total	(%)	26.1	28.3	30.1	29.9	31.9

MAIN INDICATORS OF THE TERTIARY INDUSTRY AND THEIR PERCENTAGES OF BEIJING'S TOTAL (2000-2019)

2005	2006	2007	2008	2009	2010	2011	2012	2013	2014	2015	2016	2017	2018	2019
5155.5	6227.7	7912.8	9175.1	10047.7	11608.1	13491.0	15020.3	16806.5	18333.9	20218.9	22245.7	24711.7	27508.1	29542.5
72.1	74.3	75.9	77.7	77.9	77.6	78.5	79.0	79.5	80.0	81.6	82.3	82.7	83.1	83.5
90091	102203	122898	134512	138876	154363	173084	184434	196326	207269	221046	232634	249274	272980	285674
109.1	109.5	109.8	109.5	106.5	104.7	105.8	105.5	104.4	103.9	104.5	103.5	102.9	102.4	101.4
584.7	634.0	653.7	710.5	736.5	767.5	791.4	837.4	874.7	894.4	935.0	977.5	1005.2	1010.2	1058.1
66.6	68.9	69.3	72.4	73.8	74.4	74.0	75.6	76.7	77.3	78.8	80.1	80.6	81.6	83.1
2405.6	2993.8	3465.8	3434.4	4389.5	4922.3	5101.3	5597.5	6101.7	6681.6	7202.8	7639.0	7958.4		
85.1	88.8	87.4	89.2	90.3	89.6	86.3	86.6	86.8	88.4	90.1	90.3	88.9		
23.0	34.5	40.8	44.4	52.0	56.3	62.4	69.1	70.1	79.3	123.2	123.2	232.0	148.6	148.6
65.2	75.9	80.6	72.9	84.9	88.5	88.5	85.9	82.2	87.7	94.8	94.6	95.4	85.8	85.8
1771.7	1962.8	2198.4	2394.3	2527.3	2654.4	2818.9	2967.0	3109.1	3236.5	3312.6	3414.4	3519.3	3681.4	3762.5
35.1	36.4	38.2	41.4	42.1	41.7	44.1	45.2	46.2	47.4	48.7	49.4	49.6	50.6	51.1

14-2 规模以上第三产业法人单位主要指标(2004-2019年)
MAIN INDICATORS FOR TERTIARY INDUSTRY LEGAL ENTITIES ABOVE DESIGNATED SIZE (2004-2019)

年 份 Year	单位数 (个) Number of Enterprises (unit)	平均用工人数 (万人) Average Number of Employed Persons (10000 persons)	资产总计 (亿元) Total Assets (100 million yuan)	收入合计 (亿元) Total Income (100 million yuan)	应交税金合计 (亿元) Total Tax Payable (100 million yuan)	企业利润总额 (亿元) Total Profits (100 million yuan)
2004	25725	301.4	184985.5	21467.2	908.1	1544.8
2005	23661	323.3	274180.3	24444.6	1004.0	2696.1
2006	24921	340.4	336485.9	29468.7	1376.0	2967.2
2007	25651	373.5	422458.7	38361.8	2360.9	4511.2
2008	34820	443.6	579095.5	47524.3	1855.2	4577.6
2009	36177	472.1	712313.4	55390.3	2560.8	10540.8
2010	36064	487.9	798485.4	69106.8	3122.4	10236.3
2011	36102	509.9	909953.5	79246.0	4018.9	11413.1
2012	36616	545.0	1022849.7	92138.2	4652.8	14248.4
2013	36504	565.2	1093973.1	103398.8	5415.4	18410.6
2014	36361	586.6	1242344.8	110308.2	5998.0	20601.7
2015	32698	616.9	1397969.4	110154.4	6725.2	24752.9
2016	33308	635.5	1583118.8	116751.1	5928.1	23973.9
2017	34055	665.6	1716653.2	131866.5	6239.9	26742.6
2018	32747	664.4	1781671.1	134677.6		23006.8
2019	39736	680.3	1859323.9	151615.5	6211.7	28815.1

注：1.应交税金合计主要包括应交增值税、所得税费用、税金及附加等，下同。
2.2018年，平均用工人数中，金融业为从业人员期末人数；企业利润总额中，金融业为营业利润数据；应交税金合计因部分行业数据缺失，无法计算汇总数据（下表同）。

Note: a) Total tax payable mainly includes VAT payable, income tax expense, tax and surtax, etc, the same bellow.
b) In 2018, in the Average Number of Employed Persons, the data of finance referred to the period-end number of employed persons; and in the Total Profits, the data of finance referred to the operating profit data; in the Total Tax payable, the summary data cannot be calculated due to absence of some in dustry date(same as the following table).

14-3 规模以上第三产业法人单位主要经济指标(2018年)
MAIN INDICATORS FOR TERTIARY INDUSTRY LEGAL ENTITIES ABOVE DESIGNATED SIZE (2018)

项　目	Item	单位数 (个) Number of Enterprises (unit)	平均用工人数 (万人) Average Number of Employed Persons (10000 persons)	资产总计 (亿元) Total Assets (100 million yuan)	收入合计 (亿元) Total Incomes (100 million yuan)	利润总额 (亿元) Total Profits (100 million yuan)
合　计	**Total**	**32747**	**664.4**	**1781671.1**	**134677.6**	**23006.8**
按隶属关系分	**By Affiliation**					
中　央	Central	3733	117.0	1450738.4	52741.1	15209.4
地　方	Local	29014	547.5	330932.7	81936.5	7797.4
按行业分	**By Sector**					
批发和零售业	Wholesale and Retail Trade	6984	71.6	45981.3	57831.9	1500.5
交通运输、仓储和邮政业	Transport, Storage and Post	930	55.2	12448.7	4686.3	398.7
住宿和餐饮业	Accommodation and Restaurants	2189	36.7	1986.9	1086.7	50.6
信息传输、软件和信息技术服务业	Information Transmission,Software and Information Technology Services	3520	91.1	45061.8	11851.4	3331.7
金融业	Financial Intermediation	2412	60.9	1453737.5	24521.8	12308.0
房地产业	Real Estate	3551	51.0	70190.7	5513.1	894.6
租赁和商务服务业	Leasing and Business Services	3919	96.3	107629.8	8775.0	3860.2
科学研究和技术服务业	Scientific Research and Technical Services	3106	57.4	19502.6	7058.5	535.1
水利、环境和公共设施管理业	Management of Water Conservancy, Environment and Public Facilities	538	11.1	4438.1	829.6	19.9
居民服务、修理和其他服务业	Resident Services, Repair and Other Services	451	10.6	237.7	213.5	3.0
教　育	Education	1532	42.5	5722.0	2433.9	9.9
卫生和社会工作	Health Care and Social Works	726	26.8	2042.3	2255.2	-2.7
文化、体育和娱乐业	Culture, Sports and Entertainment	1319	16.2	5880.2	1947.3	177.3
公共管理、社会保障和社会组织	Pulic Administration,Social Security and Social Organizations	1570	36.9	6811.4	5673.4	
按登记注册类型分	**By Registration Type**					
内　资	Domestic Investment Economy	29929	558.4	1709566.9	108443.2	18832.0
港澳台商投资	Hong Kong, Macao and Taiwan-invested Enterprises	1233	56.7	28804.0	12236.7	880.8
外商投资	Foreign Funded Units	1578	49.3	43300.3	13997.7	3294.0

14-4 规模以上第三产业法人单位主要经济指标(2019年)

项 目	Item	单位数 (个) Number of Enter-prises (unit)
合 计	**Total**	**39736**
按隶属关系分	**By Affiliation**	
中 央	Central	3712
地 方	Local	36024
按行业分	**By Sector**	
批发和零售业	Wholesale and Retail Trade	9740
交通运输、仓储和邮政业	Transport, Storage and Post	1015
住宿和餐饮业	Accommodation and Restaurants	3185
信息传输、软件和信息技术服务业	Information Transmission,Software and Information Technology Services	3861
金融业	Financial Intermediation	2344
房地产业	Real Estate	3735
租赁和商务服务业	Leasing and Business Services	5950
科学研究和技术服务业	Scientific Research and Technical Services	3737
水利、环境和公共设施管理业	Management of Water Conservancy, Environment and Public Facilities	665
居民服务、修理和其他服务业	Resident Services, Repair and Other Services	603
教 育	Education	1885
卫生和社会工作	Health Care and Social Works	861
文化、体育和娱乐业	Culture, Sports and Entertainment	1768
公共管理、社会保障和社会组织	Pulic Administration,Social Security and Social Organizations	387
按登记注册类型分	**By Registration Type**	
内 资	Domestic Investment Economy	36610
国 有	State-owned Units	4313
集 体	Collective-owned Units	394
股份合作	Share Holding	231
联 营	Joint Ownership Units	22
有限责任公司	Limited-Liability Corporations	12872
股份有限公司	Share Holding Corporations Ltd.	1269
私 营	Private Units	17022
其 他	Others	487
港澳台商投资	Hong Kong, Macao and Taiwan-invested Enterprises	1382
外商投资	Foreign Funded Units	1744

MAIN INDICATORS FOR TERTIARY INDUSTRY LEGAL ENTITIES ABOVE DESIGNATED SIZE (2019)

平均用工人数 (万人) Average Number of Employed Persons (10000 persons)	资产总计 (亿元) Total Assets (100 million yuan)	收入合计 (亿元) Total Incomes (100 million yuan)	应交税金合计 (亿元) Total Tax (100 million yuan)	利润总额 (亿元) Total Profits (100 million yuan)
680.3	**1859323.9**	**151615.5**	**6211.7**	**28815.1**
122.8	1395755.9	57698.0	2774.5	20806.7
557.5	463568.1	93917.5	3437.2	8008.5
75.4	49814.6	64176.7	860.1	1578.1
60.7	19821.0	6787.9	295.6	622.2
39.6	2118.0	1266.8	48.8	44.7
97.8	49726.8	14774.5	543.0	2275.9
61.8	1503538.8	31052.4	2882.2	18525.8
53.1	73011.6	5872.3	791.3	715.1
106.2	117827.3	9931.3	390.9	4205.4
61.1	22323.5	7828.6	232.7	548.8
12.6	5810.8	926.0	28.3	16.7
11.4	318.4	286.2	12.3	9.1
51.9	5357.6	2825.2	30.8	10.9
29.2	2240.6	2585.1	5.0	-9.8
17.6	6497.4	2356.9	88.8	272.2
1.7	917.5	945.6	1.9	
571.3	1769105.9	122386.1	5217.5	25564.3
105.3	304540.0	10224.9	308.9	2389.7
3.6	2136.1	283.4	17.5	23.3
2.6	736.7	120.2	4.8	2.5
0.2	37.8	12.0	0.7	-0.2
228.3	385426.2	68292.3	2273.4	15245.8
73.1	1048771.0	23193.4	2114.7	7478.9
150.9	26476.9	19604.7	485.7	405.0
7.3	981.2	655.3	11.8	19.1
59.1	36873.5	14355.4	410.4	932.5
49.9	53344.5	14873.9	583.9	2318.3

14-5 按登记注册类型分规模以上第三产业企业财务状况(2019年)

单位：万元

项目	Item	企业单位个数(个) Number of Enterprises (unit)	资产负债		
			资产总计 Total Assets	流动资产合计 Total Current Assets	#应收账款 Accounts Receivable
合计	**Total**	**35855**	**16333281073**	**1834896241**	**186163010**
按隶属关系分	**By Affiliation**				
中央	Central	2565	11748416813	513235663	51156453
地方	Local	33290	4584864260	1321660578	135006557
按登记注册类型分	**By Registration Type**				
内资企业	Domestically-invested Enterprises	32732	15431123311	1540787608	152862208
国有企业	State-owned Enterprises	887	793336770	71913748	2173684
集体企业	Collectively-owned Enterprises	360	21001196	14563633	2690000
股份合作企业	Joint-equity Cooperative Enterprises	231	7366845	5029719	200738
联营企业	Associated Enterprises	21	373931	231945	5284
有限责任公司	Limited-Liability Companies	12866	3854224793	1027284586	95665424
股份有限公司	Companies Limited by Shares	1269	10487709933	233955569	19589299
私营企业	Private Enterprises	17010	264740692	186193619	32480208
其他企业	Others	88	2369151	1614789	57572
港澳台商投资企业	Hong Kong, Macao and Taiwan-invested Enterprises	1381	368728796	147646202	13549431
外商投资企业	Foreign-invested Enterprises	1742	533428966	146462431	19751370

FINANCIAL STATUS OF TERTIARY INDUSTRY ENTERPRISES ABOVE DESIGNATED SIZE BY REGISTRATION TYPE(2019)

(10000 yuan)

固定资产原价 Total Original Value of Fixed Assets	负债合计 Total Liabilities	所有者权益合计 Total Owner's Equity	#实收资本 Paid-up Capital
361961762	**12120474269**	**4212806803**	**1615115416**
180564999	8758289452	2990127361	1065573056
181396763	3362184817	1222679443	549542359
287642403	11531360213	3899763098	1493802258
34992427	569234959	224101811	60531293
4238946	14504251	6496946	651971
1549883	4638886	2727959	374619
129410	185030	188901	228336
157402092	1934995341	1919229452	918625373
74034119	8813440451	1674269482	405640294
14999310	192869641	71871050	107544591
296216	1491655	877496	205782
53601721	254040192	114688604	74920076
20717638	335073864	198355102	46393082

14-5 续表

单位：万元

项目	Item	损益及分配 营业收入 Businesses Income	营业成本 Business Cost	销售费用 Sales Expenses	管理费用 Management Expenses
合计	**Total**	**1436812225**	**940188905**	**67652977**	**68936651**
按隶属关系分	**By Affiliation**				
中央	Central	532042325	289338734	6579383	12490617
地方	Local	904769900	650850171	61073594	56446035
按登记注册类型分	**By Registration Type**				
内资企业	Domestically-invested Enterprises	1144533741	726590080	41474745	49746873
国有企业	State-owned Enterprises	28270765	19244120	873836	2769979
集体企业	Collectively-owned Enterprises	2566324	1769308	153312	424015
股份合作企业	Joint-equity Cooperative Enterprises	1201547	815310	115421	291519
联营企业	Associated Enterprises	117328	84718	10338	22681
有限责任公司	Limited-Liability Companies	682895887	477381015	20974481	26637615
股份有限公司	Companies Limited by Shares	231934213	69424225	3855198	4995445
私营企业	Private Enterprises	195991413	157027191	15324005	14399426
其他企业	Others	1556265	844193	168155	206194
港澳台商投资企业	Hong Kong, Macao and Taiwan-invested Enterprises	143553830	105230952	13788494	10216663
外商投资企业	Foreign-invested Enterprises	148724654	108367874	12389737	8973115

14-5 continued

(10000 yuan)

Profits and Losses			应交税金合计 Total Tax Payable	#税金及附加 Tax and Surtax	#所得税费用 Income Tax Expense
研发费用 R&D Expenses	财务费用 Financial Expenses	利润总额 Total Profits			
20215842	**20610111**	**288151234**	**61872632**	**9011892**	**30759311**
2385480	7238087	208066529	27573506	2091057	18304412
17830361	13372025	80084705	34299126	6920835	12454898
14052321	19145669	255643062	51930545	7444340	26293274
92938	313729	23897305	2861162	649111	900924
2028	73182	233340	174573	72449	50303
2223	6299	25485	48331	16335	14245
325	-1716	-1606	7054	2925	850
7796144	13604287	152457774	22733384	4496614	10689616
2509331	3613027	74789372	21147144	1245507	13510845
3647199	1569724	4050111	4856511	933783	1098485
2135	-32863	191281	102387	27616	28006
4223483	1289215	9325240	4103612	698173	1952022
1940038	175228	23182932	5838475	869380	2514015

14-6 分行业规模以上第三产业企业财务状况(2019年)

单位：万元

项目	Item	企业单位个数(个) Number of Enterprises (unit)	资产负债 资产总计 Total Assets	流动资产合计 Total Current Assets
合　计	**Total**	**35855**	**16333281073**	**1834896241**
批发和零售业	**Wholesale and Retail Trade**	**9740**	**498145827**	**361962051**
批发业	Wholesale	7309	448444819	322477899
零售业	Retail Trade	2431	49701008	39484153
交通运输、仓储和邮政业	**Transport, Storage and Post**	**1014**	**198202758**	**42424841**
铁路运输业	Railway Transport	16	87755497	12755314
道路运输业	Road Transport	492	33244530	8623176
水上运输业	Water Transport	3	43597	16618
航空运输业	Air Transport	32	35316364	6723153
管道运输业	Transport Via Pipelines	2	18534260	724953
多式联运和运输代理业	Multimodal Transport and Transport Agent Service	318	11383628	7186921
装卸搬运和仓储业	Loading, Unloading, Portage and Storage	108	3290713	1672856
邮政业	Post	43	8634169	4721850
住宿和餐饮业	**Accommodation and Restaurants**	**3185**	**21179506**	**10413435**
住宿业	Accommodation	1207	15650198	6825403
餐饮业	Restaurants	1978	5529307	3588032
信息传输、软件和信息技术服务业	**Information Transmission, Software and Information Technology Services**	**3807**	**494721485**	**218879747**
电信、广播电视和卫星传输服务	Telecommunications, Broadcasting, Television and Satellite Transmission Services	274	250788235	63680049
互联网和相关服务	Internet and Related Services	693	73025431	50371898
软件和信息技术服务业	Software and Information Technology Services	2840	170907820	104827801
金融业	**Finance**	**2318**	**12916067678**	**104956616**
货币金融服务	Monetary Financial Services	765	10432728782	30488744
资本市场服务	Capital Market Services	732	717272955	26885809
保险业	Insurance	580	673283792	2101633
其他金融业	Other Financial Services	241	1092782150	45480430

FINANCIAL STATUS OF TERTIARY INDUSTRY ENTERPRISES ABOVE DESIGNATED SIZE(BY SECTOR) (2019)

(10000 yuan)

Assets and Liabilites				
#应收账款 Accounts Receivable	固定资产原价 Total Original Value of Fixed Assets	负债合计 Total Liabilities	所有者权益合计 Total Owner's Equity	#实收资本 Paid-up Capital Capital
186163010	**361961762**	**12120474269**	**4212806803**	**1615115416**
63878196	**19851275**	**351413365**	**146732461**	**81244737**
59502980	14456255	314503787	133941031	73735522
4375216	5395020	36909578	12791430	7509216
9123125	**122922616**	**86376002**	**111826757**	**73560309**
3828044	59339461	30671467	57084029	45691767
1181341	22085873	16861992	16382539	6518287
6640	70706	21480	22117	14655
1401655	19870316	20187887	15128477	4901568
9581	18061945	6142673	12391587	10140759
1437342	502055	6069074	5314554	2307940
212569	1164252	1897279	1393434	1068975
1045952	1828009	4524149	4110020	2916359
479995	**10608450**	**15688995**	**5490511**	**6430262**
207013	9219984	11440409	4209789	4343959
272983	1388466	4248586	1280722	2086303
38658133	**49322028**	**199118783**	**295602702**	**161948806**
5970485	25801472	67076671	183711564	117808014
6171811	10690398	47693211	25332219	13185556
26515838	12830158	84348901	86558919	30955235
4803559	**36254954**	**10226109872**	**2689957806**	**854990848**
2049371	25088431	9189791999	1242936784	269709997
1320254	1928989	274234087	443038867	120279777
301183	7344238	433295567	239988224	115172192
1132751	1893296	328788220	763993930	349828882

14-6　续表 1

单位：万元

项　目	Item	损益及分配 营业收入 Business Income	营业成本 Business Cost	销售费用 Sales Expenses
合　计	**Total**	**1436812225**	**940188905**	**67652977**
批发和零售业	**Wholesale and Retail Trade**	**641767367**	**590237141**	**26660073**
批发业	Wholesale	554362412	514021160	18869913
零售业	Retail Trade	87404955	76215982	7790160
交通运输、仓储和邮政业	**Transport, Storage and Post**	**67874095**	**57505085**	**2655107**
铁路运输业	Railway Transport	16844345	13342882	4878
道路运输业	Road Transport	13821308	14500004	266998
水上运输业	Water Transport	28596	19309	1174
航空运输业	Air Transport	14643951	12243332	676940
管道运输业	Transport Via Pipelines	2875492	1171654	35
多式联运和运输代理业	Multimodal Transport and Transport Agent Service	10562162	9385376	289231
装卸搬运和仓储业	Loading, Unloading, Portage and Storage	1297469	1032861	60546
邮政业	Post	7800772	5809668	1355305
住宿和餐饮业	**Accommodation and Restaurants**	**12667968**	**4972338**	**4633740**
住宿业	Accommodation	4360514	1246227	1321896
餐饮业	Restaurants	8307454	3726111	3311844
信息传输、软件和信息技术服务业	**Information Transmission, Software and Information Technology Services**	**146783111**	**88934633**	**16706108**
电信、广播电视和卫星传输服务	Telecommunications, Broadcasting, Television and Satellite Transmission Services	15076304	10715852	1163369
互联网和相关服务	Internet and Related Services	49626729	32104279	7505747
软件和信息技术服务业	Software and Information Technology Services	82080079	46114502	8036992
金融业	**Finance**	**309918389**	**9414389**	**2032730**
货币金融服务	Monetary Financial Services	115720182	2679361	658205
资本市场服务	Capital Market Services	42401893	725061	307280
保险业	Insurance	74484689	1379581	250415
其他金融业	Other Financial Services	77311626	4630387	816830

14-6 continued 1

(10000 yuan)

Profits and Losses				应交税金合计 Total Tax Payable		
管理费用 Management Expenses	研发费用 R&D Expenses	财务费用 Financial Expenses	利润总额 Total Profits		#税金及附加 Tax and Surtax	#所得税费用 Income Tax Expense
68936651	**20215842**	**20610111**	**288151234**	**61872632**	**9011892**	**30759311**
13403424	**1139051**	**2839688**	**15781042**	**8601158**	**1474930**	**2899934**
10873713	978088	2582994	15006109	7009233	1191594	2547127
2529710	160964	256694	774933	1591925	283336	352808
3253391	**128176**	**1338223**	**6221890**	**2955781**	**189311**	**1960166**
632371	26266	262025	2576477	1213339	42472	785925
827055	45331	326639	172557	367445	45713	134749
3429		211	4372	1937	128	1161
423160	22804	633893	1009005	413077	47291	278972
117143	2266	75540	1838663	627724	18639	547335
562124	24990	17716	528744	117230	7355	81174
133611	3143	5771	87842	41305	10886	18113
554499	3376	16428	4230	173725	16826	112738
2412538	**717**	**191254**	**446525**	**488363**	**133269**	**197908**
1389062	9	157021	215132	317703	117494	102163
1023477	708	34233	231394	170660	15776	95745
15183846	**14505778**	**329034**	**22759218**	**5426450**	**856837**	**1590400**
1376714	859633	90260	13171858	260076	73451	138328
3569397	4126113	-236095	1536313	1653475	399813	486444
10237736	9520032	474870	8051047	3512900	383573	965629
3732258		**899963**	**185258257**	**28820871**	**1186433**	**19182283**
815832		185009	50020273	20636907	796872	13793838
1153457		326401	35602577	4509935	121335	3368963
585910		-6234	29815027	1428683	169715	319101
1177059		394787	69820381	2245346	98511	1700381

14-6 续表 2

单位：万元

项 目	Item	企业单位个数(个) Number of Enterprises (unit)	资产负债 资产总计 Total Assets
房地产业	**Real Estate**	**3720**	**729420924**
租赁和商务服务业	**Renting and Leasing Activities, Business Services**	**5716**	**1169554402**
租赁业	Renting and Leasing	174	13856859
商务服务业	Business Services	5542	1155697543
科学研究和技术服务业	**Scientific Research and Development, Technical Services**	**3230**	**192804793**
研究和试验发展	Research and Experimental Development	301	16583546
专业技术服务业	Professional Technical Services	1616	121173823
科技推广和应用服务业	Technique Generalization and Application Services	1313	55047423
水利、环境和公共设施管理业	**Management of Water Conservancy, Environment and Public Facilities**	**421**	**44628027**
水利管理业	Management of Water Conservancy	14	15879732
生态保护和环境治理业	Ecological Protection and Environmental Control	82	4543601
公共设施管理业	Management of Public Facilities	315	16477125
土地管理业	Management of Land	10	7727569
居民服务、修理和其他服务业	**Resident Services, Repair and Other Services**	**569**	**2850765**
居民服务业	Resident Services	159	1043869
机动车、电子产品和日用产品修理业	Repair of Motor Vehicles, Electronics and Household Appliances	187	1009359
其他服务业	Other Services	223	797536
教 育	**Education**	**356**	**8006701**
卫生和社会工作	**Healthcare and Social Works**	**295**	**3562805**
卫 生	Healthcare	278	3236665
社会工作	Social Works	17	326140
文化、体育和娱乐业	**Culture, Sports and Entertainment**	**1484**	**54135404**
新闻和出版业	Journalism and Publishing	436	16489298
广播、电视、电影和影视录音制作业	Radio Broadcasting, Television, Movies, Videos and Sound Recording	453	29123671
文化艺术业	Culture and Arts	167	2100687
体 育	Sports Activities	155	2712675
娱乐业	Entertainment	273	3709073

14-6 Continued 2

(10000 yuan)

Assets and Liabilites					
流动资产合计 Total Current Assets	#应收账款 Accounts Receivable	固定资产原价 Total Original Value of Fixed Assets	负债合计 Total Liabilities	所有者权益合计 Total Owner's Equity	#实收资本 Paid-up Capital
538850476	**17873389**	**35268281**	**562286850**	**167134073**	**87295061**
384605378	**22113184**	**40559843**	**521262672**	**648291730**	**289576950**
6962794	1031780	7489931	7725084	6131775	3851464
377642584	21081404	33069912	513537588	642159955	285725486
112487454	**22068216**	**17241592**	**101639421**	**91165371**	**41428555**
9035513	1490409	3774983	6450199	10133348	4908371
72455818	14509959	8414464	66699758	54474065	21352263
30996124	6067848	5052145	28489465	26557959	15167921
15052401	**3313739**	**19634074**	**25266939**	**19361089**	**3852955**
1601448	808932	13803979	5620474	10259258	473894
3258476	1233094	545697	2654864	1888737	887754
4711973	997952	5115846	11021167	5455958	1615191
5480505	273762	168552	5970434	1757135	876117
2039155	**479838**	**413664**	**2055957**	**794808**	**745740**
722995	133775	114562	918347	125522	210620
767573	197505	152117	684777	324582	273784
548587	148559	146984	452833	344703	261336
5766357	**314000**	**890835**	**6408423**	**1598278**	**643720**
2276232	**412574**	**1229660**	**3225175**	**337630**	**965678**
2055858	394241	1139042	2988512	248153	844425
220374	18333	90618	236663	89477	121254
35182096	**2645061**	**7764491**	**19621815**	**34513588**	**12431792**
11331132	591752	2481259	5358192	11131106	3275015
18056094	1275358	3478912	7409738	21713932	7669059
1538628	148297	193171	1092419	1008268	418648
1542430	284531	1099787	2860803	-148128	633515
2713812	345123	511362	2900663	808410	435556

14-6 续表 3

单位：万元

项 目	Item	损益及分配 营业收入 Business Income	营业成本 Business Cost
房地产业	**Real Estate**	**58634510**	**38242509**
租赁和商务服务业	**Renting and Leasing Activities, Business Services**	**97311591**	**76223212**
租赁业	Renting and Leasing	2718044	2022835
商务服务业	Business Services	94593547	74200377
科学研究和技术服务业	**Scientific Research and Development, Technical Services**	**64207911**	**48719581**
研究和试验发展	Research and Experimental Development	5014759	3335963
专业技术服务业	Professional Technical Services	41781996	33140500
科技推广和应用服务业	Technique Generalization and Application Services	17411157	12243119
水利、环境和公共设施管理业	**Management of Water Conservancy, Environment and Public Facilities**	**6243664**	**5093355**
水利管理业	Management of Water Conservancy	895597	865466
生态保护和环境治理业	Ecological Protection and Environmental Control	1608373	1161195
公共设施管理业	Management of Public Facilities	3414310	2765741
土地管理业	Management of Land	325385	300953
居民服务、修理和其他服务业	**Resident Services, Repair and Other Services**	**2671858**	**1789562**
居民服务业	Resident Services	661622	348607
机动车、电子产品和日用产品修理业	Repair of Motor Vehicles, Electronics and Household Appliances	1211309	901076
其他服务业	Other Services	798927	539879
教 育	**Education**	**5977555**	**2956036**
卫生和社会工作	**Healthcare and Social Works**	**3258028**	**2367580**
卫 生	Healthcare	3198999	2322842
社会工作	Social Works	59029	44738
文化、体育和娱乐业	**Culture, Sports and Entertainment**	**19496178**	**13733485**
新闻和出版业	Journalism and Publishing	5771848	3439007
广播、电视、电影和影视录音制作业	Radio Broadcasting, Television, Movies, Videos and Sound Recording	9979838	7450335
文化艺术业	Culture and Arts	1009274	726301
体 育	Sports Activities	1199920	1023537
娱乐业	Entertainment	1535299	1094306

14-6 continued 3

(10000 yuan)

Profits and Losses					应交税金合计 Total Tax Payable	#税金及附加 Tax and Surtax	#所得税费用 Income Tax Expense
销售费用 Sales Expenses	管理费用 Manage-ment Expenses	研发费用 R&D Expenses	财务费用 Financial Expenses	利润总额 Total Profits			
2790264	**6150227**	**28951**	**4372013**	**7150897**	**7910973**	**4004324**	**1991780**
5829890	**12927507**	**1403825**	**10186880**	**42053817**	**3874887**	**616406**	**1683178**
127695	238204	35115	211031	68995	179934	16887	55901
5702195	12689303	1368709	9975849	41984822	3694953	599519	1627277
2505787	**6635483**	**2478138**	**393373**	**5488461**	**2255913**	**296191**	**791089**
188728	757128	631956	-22444	622523	206678	40639	82785
1041081	3820147	918491	258693	3677398	1457633	177373	487607
1275978	2058208	927691	157123	1188540	591603	78180	220697
197843	**602953**	**87212**	**227701**	**167455**	**272943**	**45100**	**62753**
5141	58194	8078	131918	-179472	50425	6156	3892
64404	127216	52430	37808	165374	72930	6932	24013
124709	380566	26704	45767	192253	137653	24226	35217
3590	36978		12209	-10700	11936	7787	-370
412378	**388206**	**8274**	**1536**	**90904**	**121488**	**12275**	**32491**
160684	124129	1372	-973	34596	30601	2738	16012
154900	111944	3877	639	37213	50815	5383	12451
96794	152133	3026	1869	19096	40072	4155	4028
1552118	**1038962**	**344144**	**-5780**	**108759**	**250244**	**22172**	**88445**
378871	**574896**	**12074**	**40431**	**-97861**	**42895**	**3834**	**34767**
373056	551338	11763	41430	-85259	41462	3277	34711
5815	23558	312	-999	-12601	1432	557	56
1298067	**2632961**	**79503**	**-204205**	**2721870**	**850666**	**170810**	**244117**
666547	1160040	13011	-69088	1019353	301144	47969	69874
264527	775693	31490	-150650	1802040	409025	95693	116716
79975	152424	8616	-7385	134848	49603	5255	24537
142921	300029	4810	16431	-270934	33959	14086	10549
144098	244775	21576	6487	36564	56936	7807	22441

14-7 物流业活动情况
STATISTICS FOR LOGISTICS

项　目	Item	2019	2018	2019年为2018年% 2019 as % of 2018
物流业务收入　（亿元）	**Business Income of Logistics Sector (100 million yuan)**	**3289.8**	**3046.7**	**108.0**
运输收入	Transportation Income	2480.3	2268.2	109.4
保管收入	Storage Income	717.9	692.1	103.7
一体化物流业务收入	Integrated Logistics Income	91.6	86.5	106.0
社会物流总额　（亿元）	**Total Amount of Social Logistics (100 million yuan)**	**83119.0**	**77720.2**	**106.9**
农产品	Agricultural Products	237.1	250.6	94.6
工业品	Industrial Products	13892.7	13799.3	100.7
进口货物	Imported Goods	23495.7	22303.9	105.3
再生资源	Renewable Resources	78.4	155.1	50.6
外省市流入物品	Goods from Other Provinces and Cities	44948.0	40904.2	109.9
单位与居民物品	Entities and Residents' Goods	467.1	307.2	152.0
物流业从业人员平均人数　（万人）	**Employment in Logistics Sector (10000 persons)**	**46.5**	**46.8**	**99.4**
交通运输、邮政、仓储业	Transportation, Post, Storage	32.3	32.8	98.4
采掘业、制造业、批发和零售业	Excavation, Manufacturing, Wholesale and Retail Trade	14.2	13.9	101.7

14-8 会展业活动情况
STATISTICS FOR MICE INDUSTRY IN BEIJING

项 目		Item		2019	2019年为2018年% 2019 as % of 2018
人员情况		**Employed Persons**			
从业人员平均人数	(万人)	Average Number of Employed Persons	(10000 person)	14.7	108.0
接待设施情况		**Facilities**			
接待场所会议室个数	(个)	Number of Meeting Rooms	(unit)	5265	100.8
#座位数超过500座的会议室		Number of Meeting Rooms with More Than 500 Seats		231	106.0
接待场所会议室使用面积	(万平方米)	Usable Area of Meeting Rooms	(10000 sq.m)	82.2	101.8
接待场所会议室可容纳人数	(万人)	Capacity of Meeting Rooms	(10000 person)	52.0	102.3
会议情况		**Meetings**			
接待会议个数	(万个)	Number of Meetings Held in Beijing	(10000 unit)	23.6	98.5
#国际会议		International Meetings		0.3	78.5
接待会议人数	(万人次)	Number of Meeting Participants	(10000 person-times)	2093.6	99.1
#国际会议		International Meeting Participants		56.1	87.8
展览情况		**Exhibitions**			
接待展览个数	(个)	Number of Exhibitions Held in Beijing	(unit)	865	107.7
#国际展览		International Exhibitions		265	179.1
接待展览累计面积(含室外展览面积)	(万平方米)	Total Exhibition Area (including outdoor exhibition area)	(10000 sq.m)	1083.6	161.3
#国际展览累计面积		International Exhibition Area		349.1	94.7
接待展览观众人数	(万人次)	Number of Exhibition Visitors	(10000 person-times)	1633.1	202.6
#国际展览观众人数		International Exhibition Visitors		828.0	418.0
收入情况		**Revenues**			
会展收入	(亿元)	Total Revenues from MICE Industry	(100 million yuan)	345.4	106.0
#会议收入	(亿元)	Revenues from Meetings	(100 million yuan)	165.7	101.0
#国际会议收入		Revenues from International Meetings		14.2	116.7
展览收入	(亿元)	Revenues from Exhibitions	(100 million yuan)	174.9	110.7
#国际展览收入		Revenues from International Exhibitions		51.4	103.1

注：1.人员情况和收入情况包括会展场馆、限额以上住宿业法人单位和产业活动单位、会展举办单位以及规模以上会议及展览服务业法人单位和旅行社等。
2.接待设施情况、会议情况和展览情况包括会展场馆、限额以上住宿业法人单位和产业活动单位。
3.表中发展速度按可比口径计算。

Note: a) Data on employed persons and revenues cover the MICE venues, legal entities above designated size and industrial activity units in accommodation industry, organizers of MICE, together with the legal entities and travel agencies above designated size in conference and exhibition services industry, etc.
b) Data on facilities, meetings and exhibitions cover the MICE venues, legal entities above designated size and industrial activity units in accommodation industry.
c) Indicators of development rate in the table are calculated in terms of comparable caliber.

主要统计指标解释

物流业务收入 指通过物流业务活动取得的收入。包括企业完成运输、存储、装卸、搬运、包装、流通加工、配送、信息等物流业务取得的收入之和。反映物流相关行业物流活动的总规模。

物流业从业人员 指企业中直接或间接从事物流活动的人数。直接从事物流活动的人员包括在企业中从事运输、配送、装卸搬运、仓储保管等物流活动并取得劳动报酬的从业人员；间接从事物流活动的人员包括在企业中从事物流管理活动并取得劳动报酬的从业人员，包括采购、销售部门的主管人员，但不包括采购、销售部门内部办事人员。

社会物流总额 指第一次进入市内需求领域，产生从供应地向接受地实体流动的物品的价值总额。包括六个方面的内容：进入需求领域的农产品物流总额、工业品物流总额、进口货物物流总额、外省市调入物品物流总额、再生资源物流总额、单位与居民物品物流总额。.

接待会议个数 指报告期内，接待的各种类型会议的个数。包括国际会议和国内会议。

接待国际会议个数 指报告期内，接待的国际会议的个数。国际会议是指在我国境内举办的，与会者来自 3 个或 3 个以上中国大陆以外国家和地区（含港、澳、台地区）的会议、论坛、研讨会、报告会、交流会等。

接待展览个数 指报告期内，接待的各种类型展览的个数。包括国际展览和国内展览。

接待国际展览个数 指报告期内，接待的国际展览的个数。国际展览指中国大陆以外国家和地区（含港、澳、台地区）的参展商参展面积达到该次展出面积 20%以上的展览个数。

Explanatory Notes on Main Statistical Indicators

Business Income of Logistics Sector refers to the income earned from logistics business activities, which is equal to the sum of incomes from such logistics operations completed by enterprises as transportation, storage, loading and unloading, handling, package, circulation and processing, delivery, and information. It reflects the overall scale of logistics activities in logistics related sector.

Employees in Logistics Sector refers to the number of persons directly and indirectly engaged in logistics activities in enterprises. Persons directly engaging in logistics activities are those engaging in logistics activities such as transportation, delivery, loading and unloading, handling, storage and warehouse keeping in enterprises and receiving labor remuneration; persons indirectly engaging in logistics activities are those engaging in management activities in enterprises and receiving labor remuneration, including executives in purchase and sales departments, but excluding clerks in purchase and sales departments.

Total Amount of Social Logistics refers to the total value of goods entering the demand area in the city for the first time and having physical flow from the supply place to the receiving place, consisting of value on six aspects: total logistics amount of agricultural products, total logistics amount of industrial products, total logistics amount of imported goods, total logistics amount of goods transferred from other provinces and cities, total logistics amount of recycled resources, and total logistics amount of corporate and household supplies entering the demand field.

Number of Meeting Held in Beijing refers to the number of various types of conference held in Beijing in the reporting period, including international and domestic conferences.

Number of International Meeting refers to the number of international conferences held in Beijing in the reporting period. International conference means any conference, forum, seminar, report conference, and workshops, etc. held in our country, with participants coming from 3 or more countries and regions (including Hong Kong, Macao and Taiwan) outside Chinese mainland.

Number of Exhibitions Held in Beijing refers to the number of various types of exhibitions held in Beijing in the reporting period, including international and domestic exhibitions.

Number of International Exhibitions Received refers to the number of international exhibitions received in the reporting period. International exhibition means any exhibition with participants from countries and regions (including Hong Kong, Macao and Taiwan) outside Chinese mainland whose exhibition floorage accounts for more than 20% of the exhibition.

15

交通运输邮电业

TRANSPORT, POST AND TELECOMMUNICATON SERVICES

简要说明

一、主要内容

本章资料主要反映北京市交通运输业和邮政电信业发展的基本状况。包括客货运输情况、机动车保有量、邮政电信业务总量等数据。

二、统计调查范围和口径说明

铁路数据统计范围为国家铁路运营情况，不含地方铁路、合资铁路和军用铁路及由厂矿企事业单位自建的铁路专用线和专用铁道；公路里程口径为年末通车里程数，不含在建和未正式投入使用的公路里程；公路运输统计范围包括在北京市注册从事公路货运的全部企事业单位和私人(包括个体联户)的车辆；管道运输资料包括输送原油、成品油、天然气以及其他气体的管线长度、输送能力及完成的运输量；民航运输资料统计范围为各航空公司从事国内运输、港澳台运输、国际运输的定期航班航线条数及里程、运输量，不包括在京运输飞行的外省市及外国航空公司。

邮政电信资料包括邮政和电信运营企业为社会公众提供的各类邮政和电信服务，不含专用网业务资料；民用汽车包括在公安交通管理部门已注册登记领有民用车辆牌照的全部汽车。

Brief Introduction

I. Main Content

Statistics in this chapter mainly show the basic situation of development of transport, post and telecommunication in Beijing, including situation of passenger and freight traffic, number of motor vehicles possessed, and business volume of post and telecommunication services, and so on.

II. Scope of Statistics and Survey and Explanations on Statistical Standards

Scope of statistics for data on railways cover the operation of national railways, excluding local railways, railways built by joint ventures, military railways, and dedicated lines and railways built by factories, mines, enterprises and public institutions. Data on the length of highways refer to the length open to traffic at the year end, excluding those under construction and not put into use. Highway transport statistics cover the vehicles of all enterprises and public institutions as well as individuals (including self-employed) registered in Beijing for highway freight transport. Data on pipeline transport include the length, capacity and completed traffic of pipelines for transport of crude oil, refined oil, natural gas, and other gases. Scope of statistics for data on civil aviation cover the number, mileage, and traffic volume of regular flight lines for domestic transport, transport from and to Hong Kong, Macao and Taiwan, and international transport of different airline companies, excluding non-local and foreign airlines which operate flights in Beijing.

Data on post and telecommunication include those on postal and telecom services offered by post and telecom operators, excluding data on services of dedicated networks. Data on civil automobiles include all vehicles registered with traffic administration and granted license plates.

15-1 交通运输邮电业基本情况(1978-2019年)
TRANSPORT, POST AND TELECOMMUNICATION (1978-2019)

年 份 Year	铁路里程(公里) Railway Mileage (km)	公路里程(公里) Highway Mileage (km)	客运量(万人) Passenger Traffic (10000 persons)				货运量(万吨) Freight Traffic (10000 tons)				
				铁 路 Railway	公 路 Highway	民 航 Civil Aviation		铁 路 Railway	公 路 Highway	民 航 Civil Aviation	管 道 Pipeline
1978	699	6562	4431	2264	2120	47	7394	3370	4023	1	
1979	700	7278	4777	2504	2220	53	7764	3485	4277	2	
1980	707	7487	5285	2762	2465	58	7571	3356	4213	2	
1981	858	7566	5877	2982	2824	71	8546	3046	5498	2	
1982	858	7683	6215	3205	2931	79	9097	3065	5812	2	218
1983	860	8058	6662	3546	3038	78	9403	3152	6016	3	232
1984	864	8271	7273	3877	3287	109	9671	3133	6301	3	234
1985	876	8482	7203	4078	2978	147	8739	3029	5436	4	270
1986	876	8995	7337	4106	3059	172	22121	3030	18794	6	291
1987	876	9103	7763	4418	3117	228	23068	3125	19734	8	201
1988	876	9124	8491	4782	3460	249	24749	3168	21308	9	264
1989	876	9371	7434	4214	3034	186	25184	3144	21767	8	265
1990	876	9648	7480	3770	3490	220	26648	3051	23326	10	262
1991	876	10259	7704	4036	3378	289	26804	2983	23739	11	71
1992	875	10827	8158	4196	3593	369	27707	2912	24700	14	80
1993	875	11260	7607	4374	2781	452	29865	3048	26730	17	70
1994	875	11532	8537	3992	4008	537	30825	3006	27700	19	99
1995	875	11811	8913	4017	4250	646	32184	2974	29087	17	106
1996	922	12084	8801	3650	4395	756	32907	2851	29960	18	78
1997	924	12306	9263	3613	4902	748	32351	2883	29360	20	87
1998	924	12498	11228	3762	6704	762	30127	2563	27490	22	52
1999	997	12825	14866	4201	9878	788	28275	2583	25635	30	27
2000	997	13600	18396	4458	13009	929	30717	2612	28010	35	60
2001	987	13891	22469	4750	16630	1090	30607	2505	28007	38	57
2002	987	14359	28384	5032	22103	1249	30961	2348	28375	44	194
2003	964	14453	30520	4352	24940	1228	30925	2265	28361	45	254
2004	964	14630	49750	5437	41463	2850	31700	1959	29256	73	412
2005	966	14696	60841	5779	51925	3137	32509	1976	30050	77	406
2006	962	20503	12276	6269	2482	3525	33547	1956	30953	89	549
2007	962	20754	20040	6915	9275	3850	20770	1925	17872	98	875
2008	956	20340	128525	7644	117118	3763	21885	1733	18689	93	1369
2009	956	20755	133872	8161	121373	4339	22017	1635	18753	98	1531
2010	956	21114	140663	8903	126130	5630	23712	1572	20184	130	1827
2011	1067	21347	145773	9755	129918	6100	26849	1380	23276	132	2061
2012	1115	21492	149037	10315	132333	6389	28650	1232	24925	134	2359
2013	1116	21673	71056	11588	52481	6988	28294	1078	24651	136	2429
2014	1124	21849	71715	12609	52354	6752	29518	1132	25416	149	2821
2015	1124	21885	69924	12821	49931	7172	23236	1004	19044	158	3030
2016	1103	22026	69292	13380	48040	7872	24099	725	19972	163	3239
2017	1103	22226	67420	13873	44940	8607	23879	704	19374	175	3627
2018	1103	22256	67571	14273	44175	9123	25244	569	20278	177	4221
2019	1205	22366	72148	14755	48151	9241	27338	449	22325	166	4398

注：1．铁路数据为北京市市辖范围，2005年以前来源于北京铁路分局，2005年及以后来源于北京铁路局。

2．从2006年开始，公路里程包括村道数据。

3．2006-2007年公路客运量为持有道路运输经营许可证的客运车辆发生的旅客运输量；从2008年开始，调整为旅游客运、省际客运企业、郊区客运和市郊公交的运输量。2013年公路客运量、公路旅客周转量范围调整为省际客运、旅游客运和郊区客运，市郊公交不再纳入客运量统计。

4．从2007年开始，公路货物运输为营业性运量。2019年，开展了道路货物运输量专项调查，表中2019年公路货运量和公路货物周转量为当年调查数据，下同。

5．民航统计范围为北京地区的民航运输法人单位，不包括在京运输飞行的外省市及外国航空公司。

Note: a) Railway figures are statistics within Beijing's jurisdiction. Figures for years before 2005 were from Beijing Railway Branch, those in and after 2005 were from Beijing Railway Bureau.

b) From 2006, road mileage includes figures of rural roads.

c) In 2006 and 2007, highway passenger traffic referred to passenger traffic of passenger vehicles with road transport operation permit; since 2008, highway passenger traffic has been adjusted to refer to the transportation volume of tourist passenger transport, inter-provincial passenger transport enterprises, suburban passenger transport and suburban public transport. In 2013, the statistical scope of highway passenger traffic and highway passenger turnover was changed to inter-provincial, tourist and suburban passenger transport, and suburban public transport was no longer included in the statistics on passenger traffic.

d) From 2007, highway freight traffic refers to freight for operational purpose. Specific survey on road freight traffic was carried out in 2019; data on highway freight traffic and highway turnover in the table were the survey data of the year, the same below.

e) Civil aviation covers legal entities of civil aviation registered in Beijing, excluding airlines of other provinces and other countries with transport and flight in Beijing.

15-1 续表 1 Continued 1

年份 Year	旅客周转量(万人公里) Total Passenger Turnover (10000 passengers-km)	铁路 Railway	公路 Highway	民航 Civil Aviation	货物周转量(万吨公里) Total Freight Turnover (10000 ton-km)	铁路 Railway	公路 Highway	民航 Civil Aviation	管道 Pipeline
1978			59367				92247		
1979			64033				97616		
1980			73692				93899		
1981			81879				93254		
1982	755815	641550	90092	24173	3451037	3329450	106767	13530	1290
1983	853655	723200	103742	26713	3794223	3666600	110118	16099	1406
1984	968481	821431	113871	33179	4309798	4171789	115740	20896	1373
1985	1089919	936300	109184	44435	4719663	4576400	114156	27437	1670
1986	1133620	496288	119065	518267	2569579	2133836	405645	28281	1817
1987	1281763	534720	133735	613308	2792589	2282106	471393	37966	1124
1988	1503508	588947	141625	772936	2887270	2344684	498391	42612	1583
1989	1216981	521263	122435	573283	2765660	2179878	546022	38194	1566
1990	1198022	467332	132350	598339	2688246	2067402	574635	44662	1547
1991	1383465	506431	139041	737993	2799731	2153176	591187	54929	439
1992	1666810	531574	161735	973501	2938746	2230406	642200	65614	527
1993	1656130	551392	127461	977277	3143512	2301941	767790	73216	565
1994	1906718	547488	180030	1179200	3107722	2303265	725740	78142	575
1995	2076879	508995	234540	1333344	3231034	2393403	762027	74940	663
1996	2219196	459514	250488	1509194	3176234	2311011	784888	79983	352
1997	2272177	477538	261204	1533435	3129097	2263274	769190	96202	431
1998	2419787	505554	304592	1609641	2846652	1952602	783237	110470	343
1999	2701471	579759	400597	1721115	2838857	1929269	754264	155171	153
2000	3139918	627222	527645	1985051	2996414	2001875	826438	167691	410
2001	3462571	677146	529776	2255649	3159848	2167201	826437	165832	378
2002	3961623	642676	603510	2715437	3405498	2213728	835873	195792	160105
2003	3933077	619631	693100	2620346	3620777	2409620	789952	208058	213147
2004	7580057	738956	1582441	5258660	4022791	2571459	822992	270182	358158
2005	8380778	776028	1873754	5730996	4577370	3108137	854944	281672	332617
2006	8254536	890691	791947	6571898	4231243	2625719	885991	335693	383840
2007	9603464	908438	1474249	7220776	4490390	2684862	792883	376074	636572
2008	10419977	902281	2409604	7108091	4542168	2535249	840878	356744	809297
2009	11464758	935596	2677144	7852018	4412317	2293902	878887	355257	884271
2010	13995404	995507	2906492	10093405	5136580	2574567	1015944	482467	1063602
2011	15286501	1086609	3036655	11163237	6169272	3113203	1323259	474856	1257955
2012	15957877	1163833	3047757	11746287	6383052	3076143	1397736	489845	1419328
2013	14987719	1179555	1360831	12447333	6809063	3231824	1561929	491861	1523448
2014	16027249	1356313	1382967	13287969	6728238	2843623	1651938	553661	1679016
2015	17476775	1493106	1301210	14682459	6236947	2247538	1563562	637018	1788829
2016	18893132	1508200	1176740	16208192	6713288	2290438	1613192	671413	2138246
2017	20558450	1537625	993965	18026860	7000530	2464289	1592419	743891	2199932
2018	22199810	1545658	993699	19660453	7806542	2668681	1674068	784179	2679614
2019	22918448	1589007	1047823	20281618	9007714	2575184	2756801	727190	2948539

15-1 续表 2 Continued 2

年 份 Year	机动车保有量（万辆） Possession of Motor Vehicles (10000 units)	#民用汽车 Civil Motor Vehicles	#私人汽车 Private Vehicles	邮电业务总量（亿元） Business Volume of Post and Telecommunications Service (100 million yuan)	年末固定电话用户数（万户） Year-end Number of Fixed Telephone Subscribers (10000 subscribers)	年末移动电话用户数（万户） Year-end Number of Mobile Phone Subscribers (10000 subscribers)	固定电话主线普及率（线/百人） Popularization Rate of Main Line of Fixed Telephones (lines/100 persons)	移动电话普及率（户/百人） Popularization Rate of Mobile Phones (subscribers/100 persons)	固定互联网宽带接入用户数（万户） Subscribers of Broad Band Internet (10000 subscribers)
1978		6.1		2.4	7.3		0.8		
1979		7.0		2.7	7.8		0.9		
1980		8.1		3.0	8.4		0.9		
1981		8.9		3.2	9.2		1.0		
1982		9.3		3.5	9.8		1.1		
1983		9.8		3.9	10.9		1.2		
1984		12.1		4.6	12.1		1.3		
1985		16.0		5.4	13.6		1.4		
1986		18.6		6.2	16.5		1.6		
1987		19.3	0.7	7.1	19.5		1.9		
1988		22.2	1.3	8.4	23.8		2.2		
1989		24.8	2.4	9.8	27.8		2.6		
1990		27.1	2.8	11.9	33.3	0.3	3.1	0.03	
1991		29.7	3.5	15.7	39.5	0.7	3.6	0.1	
1992		34.1	4.9	21.6	48.0	1.2	4.4	0.1	
1993		41.6	6.7	31.1	66.5	3.2	6.0	0.3	
1994		48.1	8.5	41.9	100.4	7.7	8.9	0.7	
1995		58.9	12.8	56.1	150.5	16.9	12.0	1.4	
1996		62.2	17.4	72.9	195.7	31.0	15.5	2.5	
1997		78.4	29.8	93.0	251.2	62.0	20.3	5.0	
1998		89.8	40.7	129.1	313.3	104.2	25.1	8.4	
1999		95.1	44.7	165.9	376.3	186.2	29.9	14.8	
2000	157.8	104.1	49.4	214.7	451.2	347.2	33.1	25.5	
2001	169.9	114.5	62.4	218.3	525.7	629.4	38.0	45.4	
2002	189.9	133.9	81.1	254.0	585.5	919.5	41.1	64.6	
2003	212.4	163.1	107.1	304.0	682.7	1109.0	46.9	76.1	
2004	229.6	187.1	129.8	343.8	847.8	1340.9	56.8	89.8	
2005	258.3	214.6	154.0	413.0	943.5	1459.8	61.3	94.9	228.9
2006	287.6	244.1	181.0	504.6	905.2	1571.1	56.5	98.1	281.2
2007	312.8	277.8	212.1	672.6	914.5	1598.3	54.6	95.4	347.2
2008	350.4	318.1	248.3	800.8	884.9	1616.2	50.0	91.3	382.7
2009	401.9	372.1	300.3	917.5	893.1	1825.4	48.0	98.1	451.7
2010	480.9	452.9	374.4	1108.9	885.6	2129.8	45.1	108.6	545.6
2011	498.3	473.2	389.7	487.9	883.9	2575.9	43.8	127.6	523.4
2012	520.0	495.7	407.5	546.5	883.1	3168.0	42.7	153.1	572.0
2013	543.7	518.9	426.5	652.5	867.6	3373.8	41.0	159.5	534.7
2014	559.1	532.4	437.2	751.1	831.1	4076.2	38.6	189.4	552.7
2015	561.9	535.0	440.3	991.2	784.7	4051.6	36.2	186.7	491.7
2016	571.7	548.4	452.8	1468.6 (667.1)	694.4	3868.7	32.0	178.0	475.5
2017	590.9	563.8	467.2	958.5	649.0	3752.1	29.9	172.9	541.6
2018	608.4	574.6	479.0	1861.0	614.5	4008.8	28.5	186.1	634.7
2019	636.5	590.8	497.4	2759.6	555.4	4019.7	25.8	186.7	688.5

注：1. 邮电业务总量2000年及以前按1990年不变价格计算，2001—2010年按2000年不变价格计算，2011—2016年按2010年不变价格计算，自2017年起，邮政业务量按2010年不变价计算，电信业务量按2015年不变价格计算。表内括号内数据是分别按2010年、2015年不变价格计算。

2. 表内“邮电业务总量”中，邮政业务量的统计范围为中国邮政集团公司北京分公司和中国邮政快递物流股份有限公司北京分公司。

3. 2006—2010年主线普及率和移动电话普及率根据北京市第六次全国人口普查数据进行了修订。

Note: a) Business volume of post and telecommunication service in and before 2000 was calculated at 1990's constant prices; that of 2001-2010 was calculated at 2000's constant prices; that of 2011-2016 was calculated at 2010's constant prices; since 2017, business volume of post service was calculated at 2010's constant prices, and that of telecommunication service was calculated at 2015's constant prices. Data in ( ) in this table were calculated respectively at 2010's and 2015's constant prices.

b) Among the "business volume of post and telecommunication service" in this table, the statistical range of the business volume of post service is China Post Group Beijing Branch and China Postal Express & Logistics Co., Ltd. Beijing Branch.

c) Data of popularization rate of main line and mobile phones for 2006-2010 were adjusted on the basis of the sixth national population census in Beijing.

15-2 社会客货运总量(换算周转量)
PASSENGER AND FREIGHT TRAFFIC (CONVERTED TURNOVER)

单位：万吨公里 (10000 tons-km)

项目	Item	2019	2018	2019年为2018年% 2019 as % of 2018	构成(%) Composition(%)	
					2019	2018
运输总量	**Total**	**12482469.3**	**11184844.0**	**111.6**	**100.0**	**100.0**
铁路	Railway	4164191.2	4214338.9	98.8	33.4	37.7
公路	Highway	2861583.3	1773438.2	161.4	22.9	15.9
民航	Civil Aviation	2508155.9	2517453.1	99.6	20.1	22.5
管道	Pipeline	2948538.8	2679613.9	110.0	23.6	24.0

15-3 运输线路
TRANSPORTATION ROUTES

项目	Item	条数(条) Number (line)		长度(公里) Length (km)	
		2019	2018	2019	2018
铁路	Railway	63	58	1205.3	1103.1
公路	Highway	10327	10271	22365.9	22255.8
民航	Civil Aviation				
#中国国际航空公司	Air China	451	437		
中国新华航空有限责任公司	China Xinhua Airlines	760	685		
管道	Pipeline	29	28	5513.4	5437.9

注：铁路长度为营业里程，管道长度为管输里程。
Note: Railway length refers to operating mileage, and pipeline length refers to transportation mileage.

15-4 铁路、民航主要技术经济指标
MAIN TECHNICAL AND ECONOMIC INDICATORS OF RAILWAY AND CIVIL AVIATION

项目	Item	2019	2018	2019年为2018年% 2019 as % of 2018
铁路	**Railway**			
内燃机车每万吨公里耗柴油 （千克）	Diesel Consumption of Diesel Locomotives per 10 000 Ton-km (kg)	37.1	37.2	99.7
电力机车每万吨公里耗电 （千瓦时）	Electricity Consumption of Electric Locomotives per 10000 Ton-km (kWh)	111.1	110.6	100.5
民航	**Civil Aviation**			
每吨公里耗航空油 （千克）	Aviation-oil Consumption per Ton-km (kg)	0.28	0.27	102.5

15-5 机动车保有量
NUMBER OF CIVIL MOTOR VEHICLES

单位：万辆 (10000 units)

项目	Item	2019	2018	2019年为2018年% 2019 as % of 2018
机动车	**Motor Vehicles**	**636.5**	**608.4**	**104.6**
#民用汽车	Civil Automobiles	590.8	574.6	102.8
#载货汽车	Trucks	47.6	40.0	119.0
载客汽车	Passanger Vehicles	536.7	528.0	101.6
#私人汽车	Private Cars	497.4	479.0	103.8
#轿车	Sedans	303.0	307.1	98.7

资料来源：北京市公安局公安交通管理局。
Source: Beijing Traffic Management Bureau.

15-6 邮电业务主要指标
MAIN INDICATORS OF POST AND TELECOMMUNICATIONS SERVICE

项 目		Item		2019	2018	2019年为2018年% 2019 as % of 2018
邮电业务总量	**(亿元)**	**Business Volume of Post and Telecommunications Service**	**(100 million yuan)**	**2759.6**	**1861.0**	**148.3**
邮政业务量		Post Service		77.6	90.0	86.3
电信业务量		Telecommunications Service		2682.0	1771.0	151.4
邮电业务		**Post and Telecommunications Service**				
函　件	(万件)	Letters	(10000 pcs)	18679.0	21428.5	87.2
包　裹	(万件)	Package	(10000 pcs)	143.9	190.0	75.7
特快专递业务量	(万件)	Express Mail Services	(10000 pcs)	228716.4	220875.6	103.5
汇　兑	(万笔)	Postal Remittance Transac	(10000 pcs)	47.0	85.0	55.3
订销报纸(累计)	(万份)	Newspapers Subscribed and Sold (Accumulative)	(10000 copies)	62662.7	64333.2	97.4
订销杂志(累计)	(万份)	Magazines Subscribed and Sold (Accumulative)	(10000 copies)	2279.6	2506.7	90.9
邮政代理储蓄期末余额	(亿元)	Ending Balance of Postal Agency Savings	(100 million yuan)	1055.3	908.9	116.1
长途电话通话量(固定)	(亿分钟)	Long-distance Calls (Fixed Telephone)	(100 million minutes)	23.6	31.0	75.9
本地电话通话量(固定)	(亿分钟)	Local Calls (Fixed Telephone)	(100 million minutes)	36.3	56.7	64.0
移动电话通话量	(亿分钟)	Calls of Mobile Phones	(100 million minutes)	1081.9	1219.7	88.7
移动短信业务量	(亿条)	Short Message Services	(100 million messages)	1214.9	1156.3	105.1
年末移动电话用户	(万户)	Year-end Mobile Phone Subscribers	(10000 subscribers)	4019.7	4008.8	100.3
年末固定电话用户	(万户)	Year-end Fixed Telephone Subscribers	(10000 subscribers)	555.4	614.5	90.4
长途光缆纤芯长度	(芯公里)	Fiber Core Length of Long-distance Optic Cables	(core-km)	239779	225493	106.3
局用交换机容量	(万门)	Capacity of Office Telephone Exchanges	(10000 units)	1196.9	1216.0	98.4
移动电话交换机容量	(万户)	Capacity of Mobile Phone Exchanges	(10000 subscribers)	8295	6540	126.8
固定电话主线普及率	(线/百人)	Popularization Rate of Main Line of Fixed Telephones	(lines/100 persons)	25.8	28.5	
移动电话普及率	(户/百人)	Popularization Rate of Mobile Phones	(Subscribers/100 persons)	186.7	186.1	
固定互联网宽带接入用户数	(万户)	Subscribers of Broad Band Internet	(10000 subscribers)	688.5	634.7	108.5

注：1.本表邮政业务量的统计范围为中国邮政集团公司北京分公司和中国邮政快递物流股份有限公司北京分公司。
2.邮政业务量执行2010年不变价标准，电信业务量执行2015年不变价标准，同期数据和增速为可比口径数据。
3.特快专递业务量范围为取得快递业务经营许可企业及其备案分支机构。

Note: a) In this table,the statistical range of business volume of post service is China Post Group Beijing Branch and China Postal Ltd.Beijing Branch.
b) The business volume of post service implements the constant-price standard of 2010, and the business volume of telecommunications service implements the constant-price standard of 2015; the data and growth rate for the same period are calculated in terms of comparable items.
c) Enterprises permitted to conduct express delivery businesses and their filed branches are required to submit the business volume of express mail services.

主要统计指标解释

货（客）运量 指在一定时期内，各种运输工具实际运送的货物重量（旅客数量）。是反映运输业为国民经济和人民生活服务的数量指标，也是制定和检查运输生产计划，研究运输发展规模和速度的重要指标。货运按吨计算，客运按人计算。货物不论运输距离长短，货物类别，均按实际重量统计；旅客不论行程远近或票价多少，均按一人一次作为客运量统计。半价票、小孩票也按一人统计。

货物（旅客）周转量 指在一定时期内，由各种运输工具运送的货物（旅客）数量与其相应运输距离的乘积之总和，是反映运输业生产总成果的重要指标，也是编制和检查运输生产计划、计算运输效率、劳动生产率以及核算运输单位的主要基础资料。计算货物周转量通常按发出站与到达站之间的最短距离，也就是计费距离计算。

邮电业务总量 指以货币形式表示的邮政、电信通信企业为社会提供各类邮政、电信通信服务的总数量。计算方法为各类业务的实物量分别乘以相应的不变单价，求出各类业务的货币量加总求得。没有不变单价的业务按其业务收入直接相加。

函件 是指邮政部门为用户传递以书面信息为主的邮件，包括信件、印刷品和邮送广告。

包裹 指符合包裹准寄范围，通过邮政渠道寄递的物品。包括国内普通包裹、国内快递包裹、国际及港澳台包裹。

移动电话用户 指报告期末通过移动电话交换机进入移动电话网的全部电话用户。包括各类签约用户、智能网预付费用户、无线上网卡用户等。

固定电话用户 指在电信企业登记注册，且在报告期末实际已经接入电信企业固定电话网上的全部电话用户（包括局用电话交换机、接入网设备、软交换用户接入设备、无线市话设备）上的全部电话用户。

局用交换机容量 是指安装在本地电信企业内用于接续本地固定电话的电话交换机容量。包括现用和备用的人工或自动交换机（含远端模块）的全部容量，包括接入网设备容量。

移动电话交换机容量 指移动电话交换机根据一定话务模型和交换机处理能力计算出来的最大同时服务用户的数量。

固定电话主线普及率 是指报告期行政区域常住人口中，平均每百人拥有的固定电话主线数。计算公式为：

$$固定电话主线普及率=\frac{电话主线数(本地电话用户)}{行政区域常住人口数}$$

移动电话普及率 是指报告期行政区域常住人口中，平均每百人拥有的移动电话的用户数。计算公式为：

$$移动电话普及率=\frac{移动电话用户总数}{行政区域常住人口数}$$

固定互联网宽带接入用户数 指报告期末在电信企业登记注册，通过 xDSL、FTTx+LAN 以及其他宽带接入方式和普通专线接入公众互联网的用户。

Explanatory Notes on Main Statistical Indicators

Freight (Passenger) Traffic refers to the weight of freight (number of passenger) transported with various means within a specific period of time It is a quantitative measure to show how the transport industry serves the national economy and people's life, and is also an important indicator for preparing and reviewing transport plan and studying the development scale and speed of the transport industry. Freight transport is calculated in tons and passenger traffic is calculated in the number of persons. Regardless of the types or traveling distance of freight, freight transport is calculated in terms of the actual weight of goods; and regardless of the traveling distance or ticket price, passenger traffic is calculated following the principle that one person can be counted only once in one trip. The passenger who travels with a half-price ticket or a child ticket is also calculated as one person.

Freight (Passenger) Turnover refers to the sum of the product of the volume of transported cargo (passengers) multiplied by the transport distance during a certain period of time. This is an important indicator to show the total results of the transport industry, and also serves as main basic data for preparing and reviewing transport plans and measuring transport efficiency, labor productivity and the transport unit. Freight turnover is usually calculated by the shortest distance between the departure station and the arrival station, namely the charging distance.

Business Volume of Post and Telecommunication refers to the total amount of post and telecommunication services, expressed in monetary terms, provided by the post and telecommunication enterprises for the society. Business volume of post and telecommunication is the sum of each service in kind multiplying with its correspondent unit price (constant price). For business without constant price, add their business revenue directly.

Letters mean mails mainly in the form of written information delivered by postal authorities, including letters, prints and delivered advertisements.

Package means articles permitted for mailing, and mailed through postal channels, including domestic regular parcels, domestic express parcels, international parcels, and parcels from and to Hong Kong, Macao and Taiwan.

Mobile Phone Subscribers refer to all users who have been connected with the mobile telephone communication network through the mobile telephone switchboards at the end of the reporting period. Included are various types of subscriber, prepaid users for intelligent network and wireless network card users.

Fixed-line Telephone Subscribers refer to all subscribers who have gone through registration procedures in the telecom companies and have actually been connected to the fixed-line telephone network of telecom companies at the end of the reporting period. Included are all subscribers of office telephone exchanges, access network equipment, soft switch user access equipment, and wireless local telephone equipment.

Capacity of Local Exchanges means the capacity of phone exchangers installed in local telecom companies and used for linking local fixed-line telephones. It is the sum of all capacity of existing and backup manual or automatic exchangers (with far-end modules), including the capacity of network access equipment.

Capacity of Mobile Phone Exchanges means the maximum number of users receiving services simultaneously from mobile phone exchangers, calculated from certain traffic model and exchanger processing capacity.

Popularization Rate of Fixed-line Telephones means the average number of main lines of fixed-line telephones owned per one hundred persons of permanent population in administrative areas in the reporting period. It is calculated with the following formula:

Popularization Rate of Fixed-line Telephones = Number of Main Lines of Telephone (Local Phone Users) / Number of Permanent Population in Administrative Areas

Popularization Rate of Mobile Phones means the average number of mobile phones owned per 100 persons among permanent population in administrative areas in the reporting period. It is calculated with the following formula:

Popularization Rate of Mobile Phones = Total Number of Mobile Phone Users / Permanent Population in Administrative Areas

Subscribers of Broadband Internet means subscribers registered at telecom companies to connect with public Internet through xDSL, FTTx+LAN as well as other broadband connections and general special lines at the end of reporting period.

16

批发和零售业、住宿和餐饮业

WHOLESALE AND RETAIL TRADE, ACCOMMODATION AND RESTAURANTS

简 要 说 明

一、主要内容

本章资料反映北京市商品流通市场发展及批发和零售业、住宿和餐饮业经营情况。包括有社会消费品零售总额，批发和零售业商品购进、销售、库存、商品分类销售情况；住宿业和餐饮业经营情况，限额以上批发和零售业、住宿业和餐饮业财务状况，连锁企业基本情况，商品交易市场基本情况、成交额，北京消费者信心指数。

二、统计范围

社会消费品零售总额指标于1993年、1997年和2003年进行了调整。1993年起不再包括对农民的农业生产资料；1997年起不再包括居民购买住房；2003年起不再包括由各种经济类型的制造业法人企业、产业活动单位直接售给城乡居民（包括本企业职工）和社会集团的商品以及农民对非农业居民的零售额。

限额以上批发和零售业、住宿业和餐饮业统计限额标准：2008年以前，批发业为年销售额2000万元及以上；零售业为年销售额500万元及以上；住宿业为星级饭店和星级以外年营业收入500万元及以上；餐饮业为年营业额200万元及以上。2008年调整后，批发业为年主营业务收入2000万元及以上；零售业为年主营收入500万元及以上；住宿业为星级饭店和星级以外年主营业务收入200万元及以上；餐饮业为年主营业务收入200万元及以上。

北京消费者信心指数调查范围覆盖全市16个区。

三、调查方法

限额以上批发和零售业、住宿和餐饮业单位采用全面调查；连锁企业、商品交易市场采取全数调查；限额以下批发和零售业、住宿和餐饮业法人单位及个体户采用抽样调查。

北京消费者信心指数调查采用计算机辅助电话方式调查，调查对象为居住在北京市半年以上18-65周岁的城乡居民。

四、有关统计标准的变化说明

2010年以前企业大中小型划分执行2003年《统计上大中小型企业划分办法（暂行）》。2011年至2017年大中小微型企业划分标准执行国家统计局《关于统计上大中小微型企业划分办法》（国统字[2011]75号）；自2018年起，执行《统计上大中小微型企业划分办法（2017）》（国统字[2017]213号）。

五、本章中关于历史数据调整的问题

按照国家统计局统一要求和统一方法，本章中1978年至2003年的社会消费品零售总额数据，根据北京市第一次全国经济普查结果，采用“速度推算法”进行了修订，2004年数据为北京市第一次全国经济普查数据；2005-2007年数据根据第二次经济普查结果，采用“趋势离差法”进行了修订，2008年数据为第二次经济普查数据；2009-2012年数据根据第三次经济普查结果进行了修订，2013年数据为第三次经济普查数据；在前三次普查数据修订基础上，1992年-2019年社会消费品零售总额数据根据第四次经济普查结果，采用“趋势离差法”进行了修订，2018年数据为第四次经济普查数据。

Brief Introduction

I. Main Content

Statistics in this chapter show the development of commodity circulation market and the operations of wholesale and retail trades, accommodation and restaurants. Including: total retail sales of consumer goods, commodity purchase, sales and inventory in wholesale and retail trades, and sales of commodities by category; operation situation of accommodation and restaurants; financial status of wholesale, retail, accommodation and restaurants enterprises above designated size; basic situation of chain businesses; basic situation and turnover of commodity transaction markets; and consumer confidence index.

II. Scope of Statistics

Adjustments were made to the indicators of total retail sales of consumer goods in 1993, 1997 and 2003. From 1993, the indicator did not cover agricultural means of production for farmers any longer; from 1997, it did not cover houses bought by residents any longer; from 2003, it did not cover goods sold by corporate manufacturing enterprises and industrial activity entities of various economic types to urban and rural residents (including enterprises' own employees) and social groups as well as retail sales by farmers to non-agricultural residents any longer.

As for standards for wholesale and retail trades, accommodation and restaurants above designated size, before 2008, for wholesale trades, the standard was annual sales of RMB 20 million and above; for retail trades, annual sales of RMB 5 million and above; for accommodation, star-rated hotels and non-star-rated hotels with annual business income of RMB 5 million and above; for restaurants, annual turnover of RMB 2 million and above. After adjustments were made in 2008, the designated size is, for whole sale trades, annual main business income of RMB 20 million and above; for retail trades, annual main business income of RMB 5 million and above; for accommodation, star-rated hotels and non-star-rated hotels with annual main business income of RMB 2 million and above; for restaurants, annual main business income of RMB 2 million and above.

Survey of consumer confidence index covers 16 districts in the City.

III. Methods of Survey

The method of comprehensive survey was used for statistics of wholesale and retail trades, accommodation, and restaurants service enterprises above designated size; complete enumeration was used for chain businesses, and commodity trading markets; sample survey was used for wholesale and retail trades, accommodation, and restaurants corporate enterprises below designated size as well as self-employed businesses.

Statistics on consumer confidence index were obtained through computer-aided phone calls to urban and rural residents aged 18-65 who have been living in Beijing for more than half a year.

IV. Changes in Relevant Statistical Standards

Before 2010, the classification of small, medium and large-sized enterprises should comply with the standards in the *Measures for Statistical Classification of Small, Medium and Large-sized Enterprises (Temporary)* 2003. The classification of micro, small, medium and large-sized enterprises should comply with the standards in the *Measures for Statistical Classification of Micro, Small, Medium and Large-sized Enterprises* (G.T.Z. [2011] No. 75) of the National Bureau of Statistics from 2011 to 2017. Since 2018, the classification has been in line with the standards in the *Measures for Statistical Classification of Micro, Small, Medium and Large-sized Enterprises (2017)* (G.T.Z. [2017] No. 213).

V. Adjustment to Historical Data

In accordance with the unified requirements and methods put forward by the National Bureau of Statistics, data for 1978-2003 on total retail sales of consumer goods were revised with the "speed calculation method" according to the results of the first national economic census in Beijing. Data for 2004 were gathered from the first national economic census in Beijing. Data for 2005-2007 were revised with the "trend deviation method" in accordance with the second economic census results. Data for 2008 were gathered from the second economic census. Data for 2009-2012 were revised in accordance with the third economic census results. Data for 2013 were gathered from the third economic census. On the basis of the previous three revisions of the census data, data for 1992 – 2019 on total retail sales of consumer goods were revised with the "trend deviation method"; and data for 2018 were gathered from the fourth economic census.

16-1 社会消费品零售总额(1978-2019年)
TOTAL RETAIL SALES OF CONSUMER GOODS (1978-2019)

单位：亿元 (100 million yuan)

年 份 Year	社会消费品零售总额 Total Retail Sales of Consumer Goods	#限额以上批发和零售业网上零售额 Online Retail Sales of Wholesale and Retail Enterprises above Designated Size	按商品类别分 By Category of Commodity			
			吃类商品 Food	穿类商品 Clothing	用类商品 Daily use Articles	烧类商品 Fuels
1978	44.2		18.0	8.9	16.0	1.3
1979	53.3		20.8	11.3	19.7	1.5
1980	62.8		24.9	13.4	22.9	1.6
1981	70.7		28.0	14.5	26.5	1.7
1982	75.4		29.7	13.7	30.3	1.7
1983	86.4		34.0	15.7	34.8	1.9
1984	105.8		39.6	18.7	45.2	2.3
1985	134.4		49.6	22.5	59.4	2.9
1986	155.0		60.7	22.8	68.0	3.5
1987	188.9		77.4	27.4	80.2	3.9
1988	256.0		100.6	36.0	114.9	4.5
1989	294.8		119.4	34.9	134.1	6.4
1990	345.1		136.8	45.6	154.6	8.1
1991	408.3		158.2	53.7	187.6	8.8
1992	503.0		193.6	66.9	230.5	12.0
1993	615.8		220.8	96.6	281.8	16.5
1994	778.1		283.5	125.6	349.3	19.7
1995	971.8		406.4	139.4	407.9	18.2
1996	1093.6		428.4	153.2	491.8	20.2
1997	1254.3		449.1	162.5	608.3	34.3
1998	1436.2		401.1	168.4	823.1	43.7
1999	1589.9		419.4	145.4	951.7	73.4
2000	1760.3		459.6	161.8	1050.5	88.4
2001	1958.1		515.7	180.8	1161.1	100.5
2002	2159.9		527.3	179.4	1330.2	123.0
2003	2492.6		563.0	200.8	1587.2	141.7
2004	2883.6		691.1	231.2	1748.7	212.6
2005	3221.4		802.8	269.1	1901.1	248.3
2006	3673.3		873.2	299.4	2172.8	328.0
2007	4307.4		1000.3	341.1	2614.9	351.1
2008	5257.5		1223.0	413.2	3233.4	387.8
2009	6140.0		1344.9	476.9	3928.0	390.2
2010	7273.0		1517.8	552.7	4718.9	483.5
2011	8334.8		1781.6	671.2	5262.8	619.3
2012	9440.2		1916.9	725.3	6140.2	657.8
2013	10382.5		1965.9	733.4	7039.2	644.0
2014	11354.0	1456.9	2027.7	740.1	7937.2	649.0
2015	12271.9	2016.9	2215.5	747.6	8758.8	549.9
2016	13134.9	2049.0	2336.4	764.2	9457.2	577.1
2017	13933.7	2371.4	2468.6	794.9	10069.9	600.4
2018	14422.3	2632.9	2623.1	817.3	10339.9	642.1
2019	15063.7	3366.3	2822.8	811.2	10829.1	600.6

16-2 社会消费品零售总额(2019年)

TOTAL RETAIL SALES OF CONSUMER GOODS(2019)

单位：亿元 (100 million yuan)

项 目	Item	2019	2019年为2018年% 2019 as % of 2018
社会消费品零售总额	**Total Retail Sales of Consumer Goods**	**15063.7**	**104.4**
按商品类别分	**By Category of Commodity**		
吃类商品	Food	2822.8	107.6
穿类商品	Clothing	811.2	99.2
用类商品	Daily Use Articles	10829.1	104.7
烧类商品	Fuels	600.6	93.5
按消费品形态分	**By Form of Consumer Goods**		
餐饮收入	Food and Beverage Income	1225.4	106.2
商品零售	Retail Sales of Commodities	13838.3	104.3

注：表中发展速度按可比口径计算。
Note: Indicators of development rate in the table are calculated in terms of comparable caliber.

16-3 按登记注册类型分限额以上批发和零售企业商品零售额(2018年)

RETAIL SALES OF GOODS IN WHOLESALE AND RETAIL ENTERPRISES ABOVE DESIGNATED SIZE BY REGISTRATION TYPE (2018)

单位：万元 (10000 yuan)

项 目	Item	商品零售额 Retail Sales of Goods	批发业 Wholesale	零售业 Retail Trade
合 计	**Total**	**84886063**	**10049586**	**74836477**
内资企业	Domestic Funded Enterprises	68583053	7583014	61000039
#国 有	State-owned Enterprises	966113	24979	941133
集 体	Collectively-owned Enterprises	303218	11069	292148
股份有限公司	Companies Limited by Shares	8501090	1732929	6768161
港澳台商投资企业	Hong Kong, Macao and Taiwan-invested Enterprises	4590137	410022	4180115
外商投资企业	Foreign-invested Enterprises	11708677	2056550	9652127

注：本表统计范围为限额以上批发和零售业法人单位、产业活动单位和个体经营户(16—4至16—10表同)。
Note: Figures in this table cover legal entities in wholesale and retail trade above designated size, activity entities and individual entities (same as the tablethe from 16-4、16-6 to 16-9).

16-4 按登记注册类型分限额以上批发和零售企业商品零售额(2019年)
RETAIL SALES OF GOODS IN WHOLESALE AND RETAIL ENTERPRISES ABOVE DESIGNATED SIZE BY REGISTRATION TYPE (2019)

单位：万元 (10000 yuan)

项　目	Item	商品零售额 Retail Sales of Goods	批发业 Wholesale	零售业 Retail Trade
合　计	**Total**	**94646764**	**15557103**	**79089661**
内资企业	Domestic Funded Enterprises	72335953	9533172	62802781
#国　有	State-owned Enterprises	1072471	30109	1042362
集　体	Collectively-owned Enterprises	281718	11096	270622
股份有限公司	Companies Limited by Shares	8274277	1484252	6790025
港澳台商投资企业	Hong Kong, Macao and Taiwan-invested Enterprises	8771722	3697010	5074712
外商投资企业	Foreign-invested Enterprises	13537978	2326921	11211057

16-5 限额以上批发和零售业商品购进、销售、库存情况(2018年)
TOTAL VALUE OF PURCHASES, SALES AND INVENTORY IN WHOLESALE AND RETAIL ENTERPRISES ABOVE DESIGNATED SIZE (2018)

单位：万元 (10000 yuan)

项　目	Item	合计 Total Sales	批发业 Wholesale	零售业 Retail
商品购进额	**Total Purchases of Commodities**	**631179348**	**538967727**	**92211621**
商品销售额	**Total Sales of Commodities**	**677531015**	**576081177**	**101449838**
批发额	Wholesale sales	592644952	566031591	26613361
零售额	Retail sales	84886063	10049586	74836477
期末商品库存额	**Inventory (Year-end)**	**57841595**	**49561126**	**8280469**

16-6 限额以上批发和零售业商品购进、销售、库存情况(2019年)
TOTAL VALUE OF PURCHASES, SALES AND INVENTORY IN WHOLESALE AND RETAIL ENTERPRISES ABOVE DESIGNATED SIZE (2019)

单位：万元 (10000 yuan)

项　目	Item	合计 Total Sales	批发业 Wholesale	零售业 Retail
商品购进额	**Total Purchases of Commodities**	**693785485**	**605509651**	**88275834**
商品销售额	**Total Sales of Commodities**	**738919894**	**644166512**	**94753382**
批发额	Wholesale sales	644273129	628609409	15663720
零售额	Retail sales	94646764	15557103	79089661
期末商品库存额	**Inventory (Year-end)**	**65707816**	**57977160**	**7730656**

16-7 限额以上批发和零售业商品销售类值(2018年)
SALES BY CATEGORY FOR WHOLESALE AND RETAIL ENTERPRISES ABOVE DESIGNATED SIZE (2018)

单位：万元 (10000 yuan)

项　目	Item	商品销售额 Total Sales	批发额 Wholesale sales	零售额 Retail sales
合　计	**Total**	**677531015**	**592644952**	**84886063**
粮油、食品类	Cereal, Oil and Food	29691016	22723007	6968009
#粮油类	Cereal and Oil	11657819	10678057	979762
肉禽蛋类	Meat, Poultry and Eggs	4036937	3039354	997584
饮料类	Beverages	4610543	3592303	1018240
烟酒类	Tobacco and Liquor	12000193	10505787	1494406
服装鞋帽、针纺织品类	Clothing, Shoes, Hats and Textiles	11872652	5723832	6148820
#服装类	Clothing	7640288	2766859	4873430
鞋帽类	Shoes and Hats	2365848	1371446	994402
针纺织品类	Knitwear and Textiles	1866516	1585527	280989
化妆品类	Cosmetics	3505927	1619428	1886499
金银珠宝类	Gold, Silver and Jewelry	14783366	11799452	2983915
日用品类	Articles for Daily Use	12397235	8079243	4317992
#儿童玩具类	Children's Toys	1252928	642720	610208
五金、电料类	Hardware and Electrical Materials	1602905	1447077	155828
体育、娱乐用品类	Sports and Recreation Goods	10402922	9037396	1365525
书报杂志类	Newspapers and Magazines	2679549	1787973	891576
电子出版物及音像制品类	E-Journals and Video Products	640296	402537	237760
家用电器和音像器材类	Household Appliances and Audiovisual Products	27939860	22482576	5457283
中西药品类	Traditional Chinese and Western Medicines	20365841	12440776	7925065
#西药类	Western Medicines	13566746	7587325	5979421
中草药及中成药类	Chinese Herbal Medicines and Chinese Patent Medicines	3291753	1497696	1794057
文化办公用品类	Cultural and Office Goods	42091311	34996504	7094807
家具类	Furniture	1228202	234320	993882
通讯器材类	Communication Devices	70079038	59396460	10682578
煤炭及制品类	Coal and Coal Products	34921804	34918176	3628
木材及制品类	Wood and Wooden Products	5045110	5045110	
石油及制品类	Petroleum and Its Products	65189263	59629855	5559408
化工材料及制品类	Raw Chemical Materials	72639677	72639677	
#化肥类	Fertilizer	7511729	7511729	
金属材料类	Metal Materials	85046883	85046883	
建筑及装潢材料类	Building and Decoration Materials	5977076	5624811	352264
机电产品及设备类	Electric-mechanic Products and Equipment	32717659	32288274	429385
#农机类	Agricultural Machinery	647723	647723	
汽车类	Automobiles	80372916	62092736	18280180
种子饲料类	Seed and Feedstuff	2445085	2445085	
棉麻类	Cotton and Hemp	3526819	3526730	89
其他类	Others	23757869	23118945	638924

16–8 限额以上批发和零售业商品销售类值(2019年)
SALES BY CATEGORY FOR WHOLESALE AND RETAIL ENTERPRISES ABOVE DESIGNATED SIZE (2019)

单位：万元 (10000 yuan)

项 目	Item	商品销售额 Total Sales	批发额 Wholesale sales	零售额 Retail sales
合 计	**Total**	**738924996**	**644273129**	**94651867**
粮油、食品类	Cereal, Oil and Food	38548386	30273836	8274550
#粮油类	Cereal and Oil	14340295	13271929	1068365
肉禽蛋类	Meat, Poultry and Eggs	5242025	4020123	1221901
饮料类	Beverages	5362613	4081419	1281195
烟酒类	Tobacco and Liquor	13134178	11188800	1945378
服装鞋帽、针纺织品类	Clothing, Shoes, Hats and Textiles	11840735	5361081	6479655
#服装类	Clothing	7903072	2758450	5144622
鞋帽类	Shoes and Hats	2404750	1334036	1070714
针纺织品类	Knitwear and Textiles	1532913	1268595	264319
化妆品类	Cosmetics	4018546	1856299	2162247
金银珠宝类	Gold, Silver and Jewelry	17095861	14328776	2767085
日用品类	Articles for Daily Use	17540646	11219786	6320860
#儿童玩具类	Children's Toys	2051679	889586	1162093
五金、电料类	Hardware and Electrical Materials	1959902	1752917	206985
体育、娱乐用品类	Sports and Recreation Goods	11704189	10044123	1660066
书报杂志类	Newspapers and Magazines	2823366	1927386	895980
电子出版物及音像制品类	E-Journals and Video Products	975185	622495	352690
家用电器和音像器材类	Household Appliances and Audiovisual Products	34149156	26259734	7889422
中西药品类	Traditional Chinese and Western Medicines	21223132	13053336	8169796
#西药类	Western Medicines	14200361	8060802	6139559
中草药及中成药类	Chinese Herbal Medicines and Chinese Patent Medicines	3289382	1467699	1821683
文化办公用品类	Cultural and Office Goods	43723761	37389423	6334338
家具类	Furniture	1455846	340213	1115633
通讯器材类	Communication Devices	83801054	71215208	12585846
煤炭及制品类	Coal and Coal Products	33776825	33763427	13399
木材及制品类	Wood and Wooden Products	5755384	5755384	
石油及制品类	Petroleum and Its Products	57671153	52410154	5261000
化工材料及制品类	Raw Chemical Materials	71798144	71798144	
#化肥类	Fertilizer	8258765	8258765	
金属材料类	Metal Materials	98940955	98940955	
建筑及装潢材料类	Building and Decoration Materials	5937001	5499013	437988
机电产品及设备类	Electric-mechanic Products and Equipment	33859569	33346754	512815
#农机类	Agricultural Machinery	522407	522407	
汽车类	Automobiles	85632877	67035180	18597697
种子饲料类	Seed and Feedstuff	2745624	2745624	
棉麻类	Cotton and Hemp	3501218	3501008	210
其他类	Others	29949689	28562658	1387031

16−9 限额以上住宿和餐饮业经营情况(2018年)
STATISTICS FOR ACCOMMODATION AND RESTAURANTS ABOVE DESIGNATED SIZE (2018)

项　　目	Item	合　计 Total	住宿业 Accommodation Industry	餐饮业 Catering Industry
客房数　(间)	**Number of Rooms (room)**	**227253**	**221874**	**5379**
床位数　(个)	**Number of Beds (unit)**	**368980**	**359208**	**9772**
餐位数　(位)	**Number of Tables (table)**	**1491551**	**299955**	**1191596**
营业额　(万元)	**Turnover (10000 yuan)**	**12507674**	**5197041**	**7310633**
客房收入	Income from Rooms	2970032	2928380	41652
餐费收入	Income from Money	8161298	1297189	6864109
商品销售额	Sales of Commodities	271380	46352	225028
其他收入	Other Incomes	1104963	925119	179844

注：本表统计范围为限额以上住宿和餐饮业法人单位、产业活动单位和个体经营户。
Note:This table covers legal entities in accommodation and restaurants above designated size, activity entities and individual entities .

16—10 限额以上住宿和餐饮业经营情况(2019年)
STATISTICS FOR ACCOMMODATION AND RESTAURANTS ABOVE DESIGNATED SIZE (2019)

项　　目		Item		合 计 Total	住宿业 Accommodation Industry	餐饮业 Catering Industry
客房数	**(间)**	**Number of Rooms**	**(room)**	**262225**	**254048**	**8177**
床位数	**(个)**	**Number of Beds**	**(unit)**	**416254**	**401759**	**14495**
餐位数	**(位)**	**Number of Tables**	**(table)**	**1731941**	**299598**	**1432343**
营业额	**(万元)**	**Turnover**	**(10000 yuan)**	**14453147**	**5504689**	**8948457**
客房收入		Income from Rooms		3279463	3222846	56617
餐费收入		Income from Money		9564555	1268974	8295581
商品销售额		Sales of Commodities		385499	46320	339179
其他收入		Other Incomes		1223630	966549	257080

注：本表统计范围为限额以上住宿和餐饮业法人单位、产业活动单位和个体经营户。
Note:This table covers legal entities in accommodation and restaurants above designated size, activity entities and individual entities .

16-11 限额以上批发和零售业企业财务状况(2018年)

单位：万元

项目	Item	企业单位个数(个) Number of Enterprises (unit)	资产总计 Total Assets	流动资产合计 Total Current Assets
合　计	**Total**	**6984**	**459812689**	**340945514**
按隶属关系分	**By Affiliation**			
中　央	Central	461	172156598	118742588
地　方	Local	6523	287656090	222202926
按企业登记注册类型分	**By Registration Type**			
内　资	Domestically-invested Enterprises	6418	342674773	249597708
国　有	State-owned Enterprises	125	8644562	7046467
集　体	Collectively-owned Enterprises	53	1021172	543844
股份合作	Joint-equity Cooperative Enterprises	44	193223	172758
联　营	Associate Enterprises	2	3642	3629
有限责任公司	Limited Liability Companies	2538	247100420	182921531
股份有限公司	Companies Limited by Shares	157	40021866	18624509
私　营	Private Enterprises	3496	45681755	40281233
其　他	Other	3	8134	3739
港澳台商投资	Hong Kong, Macao and Taiwan-invested Enterprises	214	42142509	34005519
外商投资	Foreign-invested Enterprises	352	74995407	57342287
按国民经济行业分	**By Sector**			
批发业	Wholesale	5122	411244039	303263110
农、林、牧、渔产品批发	Wholesale of Agriculture, Forestry, Animal Production and Hunting, and Fishing Products	113	26528739	16095125
食品、饮料及烟草制品批发	Wholesale of Foods, Beverage and Tobaccos	505	23780348	18593375
纺织、服装及家庭用品批发	Wholesale of Textile, Clothes and Household Commodities	455	34841507	29718377
文化、体育用品及器材批发	Wholesale of Cultural and Sports Goods and Equipment	257	14362270	9805999
医药及医疗器材批发	Wholesale of Medicine and Medical Devices	728	17969441	15162829
矿产品、建材及化工产品批发	Wholesale of Mineral Products, Building Materials, and Chemical Products	1308	160367665	108335993
机械设备、五金交电及电子产品批发	Wholesale of Mechanical Equipment, Hardware and Electronic Products	1628	105839111	83868426
贸易经纪与代理	Trade Broker and Agent	41	18641110	15720694
其他批发业	Others	87	8913850	5962292
零售业	Retail	1862	48568650	37682404
综合零售	Integrated Retail	191	11035973	6558333
食品、饮料及烟草制品专门零售	Special Retails of Foods, Beverage and Tobacoos	89	988219	740840
纺织、服装及日用品专门零售	Special Retail of Textile, Clothing and Domestic Commodities	164	2294380	1986648
文化、体育用品及器材专门零售	Special Retail of Cultural and Sports Goods and Equipment	119	3040224	2445351
医药及医疗器材专门零售	Special Retail of Medicine and Medical Devices	100	4978970	3052938
汽车、摩托车、零配件和燃料及其他动力销售	Sales of Automobiles, Motorcycles, Accessories, Fuels and Other Power	740	9707240	7659113
家用电器及电子产品专门零售	Special Retail of Household Electrical Appliances and Electronic Products	208	12527334	11822765
五金、家具及室内装修材料专门零售	Special Retail of Hardware, Furniture and Indoor Decoration Materials	55	798253	581038
货摊、无店铺及其他零售业	Stand Retail, Retail Without Shops and Other Retail	196	3198058	2835379
按规模划分	**By Size**			
#大中型企业	Medium and Large-sized Enterprises	3372	394157063	286307050

FINANCIAL STATUS OF WHOLESALE AND RETAIL ENTERPRISES ABOVE DESIGNATED SIZE (2018)

(10000 yuan)

资产负债 Assets and Liabilities						
#应收账款 Accounts Receivable	固定资产原价 Total Original Value of Fixed Assets	负债合计 Total Liabilities	#流动负债合计 Total Current Liabilities	#应付账款 Accounts Payable	所有者权益合计 Total Owner's Equity	#实收资本 Paid-up Capital
57243127	**17439627**	**328636202**	**292813469**	**78560122**	**131176486**	**72778001**
23312090	6470475	115366998	101212894	28569450	56789600	36882338
33931037	10969152	213269204	191600575	49990672	74386886	35895664
48046379	13776452	247242552	218325772	58805700	95432221	57747582
385163	704505	4371623	4310478	495035	4272939	746879
67803	133251	780138	527241	113696	241034	93903
21458	21607	148023	147962	27890	45200	29877
14	155	3203	3203	1227	439	535
35797875	9072223	180945628	164435975	46767212	66154792	46962345
3157392	1634973	22456510	15387395	2754281	17565356	4427635
8615612	2204651	38534776	33511399	8646024	7146979	5485397
1062	5087	2652	2119	336	5482	1012
2938991	1416031	35769755	32636769	7693163	6372753	5780727
6257757	2247144	45623895	41850929	12061259	29371512	9249693
52650274	11999089	291737237	258699669	69311611	119506802	65679097
1856874	420434	18761615	16393071	2082118	7767124	2861485
1787553	1356676	17607652	16706932	2893150	6172697	3058371
1631034	697503	28443659	28192858	6246678	6397847	4087634
1582708	584735	10110824	6801693	1339196	4251446	2635639
5696977	626018	12607325	11843748	5359295	5362116	1896516
18558334	5289139	113039316	93446473	23881330	47328348	35144171
14876519	2729454	70107960	65893160	19223565	35731151	13275783
5775945	131511	15112698	14330334	7381660	3528411	1943060
884331	163619	5946189	5091399	904620	2967662	776438
4592853	5440538	36898965	34113801	9248511	11669684	7098905
171535	2423191	7694543	6539214	1746809	3341431	1918389
37186	283756	455176	447233	140176	533043	196182
393930	283021	1787330	1641887	476281	507050	574833
258815	278642	1931995	1668519	433182	1108228	438870
443094	82677	3522345	3287587	583929	1456626	617360
484950	1619235	7414690	7201133	951159	2292550	1847946
1743908	203175	9396730	8774174	2537966	3130604	589043
39938	108531	610123	587138	177955	188130	224973
1019499	158310	4086034	3966914	2201055	-887977	691308
48366764	14115445	276609909	250294090	69023527	117547155	58653770

16-11 续表

单位：万元

项 目	Item	损 益 营业收入 Business Income	 营业成本 Business Cost	 销售费用 Sales Expenses
合 计	**Total**	**578319035**	**531647994**	**23234979**
按隶属关系分	**By Affiliation**			
中 央	Central	202968465	193893572	3323944
地 方	Local	375350570	337754422	19911034
按企业登记注册类型分	**By Registration Type**			
内 资	Domestically-invested Enterprises	425594248	398363499	13133350
国 有	State-owned Enterprises	11753204	10477919	284651
集 体	Collectively-owned Enterprises	905636	833372	29706
股份合作	Joint-equity Cooperative Enterprises	380803	349530	12126
联 营	Associate Enterprises	16796	16440	408
有限责任公司	Limited Liability Companies	316307743	299171683	8004907
股份有限公司	Companies Limited by Shares	31162853	28529934	1416186
私 营	Private Enterprises	65055667	58973856	3385016
其 他	Other	11547	10766	351
港澳台商投资	Hong Kong, Macao and Taiwan-invested Enterprises	64279334	57886352	3342021
外商投资	Foreign-invested Enterprises	88445453	75398143	6759608
按国民经济行业分	**By Sector**			
批发业	Wholesale	500197339	463849435	16308904
农、林、牧、渔产品批发	Wholesale of Agriculture, Forestry, Animal Production and Hunting, and Fishing Products	15921213	15228767	172881
食品、饮料及烟草制品批发	Wholesale of Foods, Beverage and Tobaccos	28739998	24733080	2187886
纺织、服装及家庭用品批发	Wholesale of Textile, Clothes and Household Commodities	53364632	47772414	3096125
文化、体育用品及器材批发	Wholesale of Cultural and Sports Goods and Equipment	17120181	15306582	966284
医药及医疗器材批发	Wholesale of Medicine and Medical Devices	23105756	19013176	2059289
矿产品、建材及化工产品批发	Wholesale of Mineral Products, Building Materials, and Chemical Products	219584394	213670771	2311360
机械设备、五金交电及电子产品批发	Wholesale of Mechanical Equipment, Hardware and Electronic Products	132094638	118854192	5256914
贸易经纪与代理	Trade Broker and Agent	5385648	4933443	104473
其他批发业	Others	4880879	4337008	153693
零售业	Retail	78121697	67798560	6926075
综合零售	Integrated Retail	13150466	9994466	2149066
食品、饮料及烟草制品专门零售	Special Retails of Foods, Beverage and Tobacoos	1166991	765200	239456
纺织、服装及日用品专门零售	Special Retail of Textile, Clothing and Domestic Commodities	3245287	2126732	863843
文化、体育用品及器材专门零售	Special Retail of Cultural and Sports Goods and Equipment	3498463	2913888	312233
医药及医疗器材专门零售	Special Retail of Medicine and Medical Devices	2782822	2458110	167866
汽车、摩托车、零配件和燃料及其他动力销售	Sales of Automobiles, Motorcycles, Accessories, Fuels and Other Power	23535455	21583063	970009
家用电器及电子产品专门零售	Special Retail of Household Electrical Appliances and Electronic Products	19502030	18077120	1029992
五金、家具及室内装修材料专门零售	Special Retail of Hardware, Furniture and Indoor Decoration Materials	929510	604471	226195
货摊、无店铺及其他零售业	Stand Retail, Retail Without Shops and Other Retail	10310672	9275508	967417
按规模划分	**By Size**			
#大中型企业	Medium and Large-sized Enterprises	504680085	461917642	21325729

注：应交税金合计包括应交增值税、所得税费用和税金及附加。

16-11 Continued

(10000 yuan)

Profits and Losses			应交税金合计			
管理费用 Management Expenses	财务费用 Financial Expenses	利润总额 Total Profits	Total Tax Payable	#税金及附加 Main Tax and Surtax	#所得税费用 Income Tax Expense	#应交增值税 Value Added Tax Payable
11941653	**3080136**	**15004809**	**9812033**	**1353485**	**3353781**	**5104767**
2063148	1332033	5079539	2502921	491125	994341	1017455
9878505	1748103	9925270	7309112	862360	2359440	4087312
6930288	2825848	7676619	5837036	991366	1748896	3096774
231390	-40685	643928	621481	317031	135847	168603
24505	19723	4978	16301	2729	1880	11692
16743	-133	2251	4559	408	818	3333
74	107	-334	990	65	7	918
4182778	2133883	5662375	3651563	478887	1253609	1919067
586268	340051	905363	519812	84352	151098	284362
1888327	372870	457801	1022325	107889	205637	708799
204	33	258	5	5		
2457543	282234	296514	655786	91644	190928	373214
2553822	-27946	7031677	3319210	270475	1413957	1634778
9571179	2714312	13977461	8251715	1079023	3010582	4162110
230735	369351	306042	118198	20159	50826	47213
625800	73823	1317804	1180024	376463	255059	548502
2026374	-7389	902878	551638	63933	126846	360858
445976	220253	-65850	286920	41307	101211	144403
826457	130864	1154879	881464	73869	283497	524098
1646821	1483180	2624551	1446267	197781	535674	712812
3459521	136233	6972863	3540714	289931	1515623	1735160
126710	232366	397815	117546	9288	83290	24967
182784	75631	366479	128946	6291	58558	64097
2370474	365825	1027349	1560318	274462	343198	942657
684398	119906	415394	362137	77638	106982	177518
68135	132	94709	77027	6715	27307	43005
178466	8125	55932	149601	17397	21370	110834
168559	13767	91510	115307	32330	33073	49904
91718	52317	139056	54354	6669	9222	38462
540925	114174	289708	427675	89558	91355	246762
265304	34192	152545	190138	22262	31624	136251
76433	4230	15888	45270	6502	7486	31282
296537	18983	-227394	138810	15392	14779	108639
10737423	2525866	14658456	8904385	1241637	3094341	4568407

Note: Total tax payable includes VAT payable, income tax expense, tax and surtax.

16—12 限额以上批发和零售业企业财务状况(2019年)

单位：万元

项目	Item	企业单位个数(个) Number of Enterprises (unit)	资产总计 Total Assets	流动资产合计 Total Current Assets
合计	**Total**	**9740**	**498145827**	**361962051**
按隶属关系分	**By Affiliation**			
中央	Central	466	187341769	128816563
地方	Local	9274	310804058	233145489
按企业登记注册类型分	**By Registration Type**			
内资	Domestically-invested Enterprises	9072	377183118	271496505
国有	State-owned Enterprises	122	7861405	6229081
集体	Collectively-owned Enterprises	66	1158216	701034
股份合作	Joint-equity Cooperative Enterprises	54	164025	150596
联营	Associate Enterprises	4	151495	122461
有限责任公司	Limited Liability Companies	2694	262163466	191972505
股份有限公司	Companies Limited by Shares	156	49278040	23299158
私营	Private Enterprises	5968	56391940	49012125
其他	Other	8	14531	9545
港澳台商投资	Hong Kong, Macao and Taiwan-invested Enterprises	246	41211925	31174102
外商投资	Foreign-invested Enterprises	422	79750785	59291444
按国民经济行业分	**By Sector**			
批发业	Wholesale	7309	448444819	322477899
农、林、牧、渔产品批发	Wholesale of Agriculture, Forestry, Animal Production and Hunting, and Fishing Products	157	28417003	17525891
食品、饮料及烟草制品批发	Wholesale of Foods, Beverage and Tobaccos	818	29989547	23249465
纺织、服装及家庭用品批发	Wholesale of Textile, Clothes and Household Commodities	618	34443462	27064877
文化、体育用品及器材批发	Wholesale of Cultural and Sports Goods and Equipment	406	15706716	11063658
医药及医疗器材批发	Wholesale of Medicine and Medical Devices	909	25335185	20100682
矿产品、建材及化工产品批发	Wholesale of Mineral Products, Building Materials, and Chemical Products	1847	170058030	110620831
机械设备、五金交电及电子产品批发	Wholesale of Mechanical Equipment, Hardware and Electronic Products	2359	114777346	88848614
贸易经纪与代理	Trade Broker and Agent	62	21185232	17933282
其他批发业	Others	133	8532300	6070600
零售业	Retail	2431	49701008	39484153
综合零售	Integrated Retail	213	11780510	7367954
食品、饮料及烟草制品专门零售	Special Retails of Foods, Beverage and Tobacoos	185	1336672	1062767
纺织、服装及日用品专门零售	Special Retail of Textile, Clothing and Domestic Commodities	220	2447138	2058447
文化、体育用品及器材专门零售	Special Retail of Cultural and Sports Goods and Equipment	169	3448645	2708901
医药及医疗器材专门零售	Special Retail of Medicine and Medical Devices	110	946861	708955
汽车、摩托车、零配件和燃料及其他动力销售	Sales of Automobiles, Motorcycles, Accessories, Fuels and Other Power	855	9930972	7661021
家用电器及电子产品专门零售	Special Retail of Household Electrical Appliances and Electronic Products	257	11126821	10328915
五金、家具及室内装修材料专门零售	Special Retail of Hardware, Furniture and Indoor Decoration Materials	83	897654	622668
货摊、无店铺及其他零售业	Stand Retail, Retail Without Shops and Other Retail	339	7785736	6964525
按规模划分	**By Size**			
#大中型企业	Medium and Large-sized Enterprises	3807	427019259	301815063

FINANCIAL STATUS OF WHOLESALE AND RETAIL ENTERPRISES ABOVE DESIGNATED SIZE (2019)

(10000 yuan)

资产负债 Assets and Liabilities					所有者权益合计 Total Owner's Equity	#实收资本 Paid-up Capital
#应收账款 Accounts Receivable	固定资产原价 Total Original Value of Fixed Assets	负债合计 Total Liabilities	#流动负债合计 Total Current Liabilities	#应付账款 Accounts Payable		
63878196	**19851275**	**351413365**	**314818522**	**85415407**	**146732461**	**81244737**
25888414	6983135	127094967	110337100	30919611	60246803	38704485
37989783	12868140	224318398	204481422	54495796	86485659	42540253
53921333	14934410	269277898	240985213	63924485	107905219	64665819
229685	803262	3840921	3748873	313564	4020484	755438
231557	112140	902307	658838	130309	255908	74058
22967	21011	108872	108778	24279	55153	32130
1616	21369	49615	48904	2699	101880	173560
37221166	9798535	191721659	173058286	48227784	70441806	49002938
3040111	1833254	26795111	19004337	2999091	22482929	6242409
13169463	2339163	45852528	44350510	12222924	10539412	8383832
4768	5676	6884	6687	3836	7647	1455
3001342	2100670	34354623	30363515	9067438	6857301	6144257
6955522	2816196	47780844	43469793	12423483	31969941	10434662
59502980	14456255	314503787	280757309	75792283	133941031	73735522
1859700	408431	20175958	17395425	1995112	8241046	3217509
2220657	1633992	23203749	21788454	3885241	6785798	4559592
1658547	878095	26040729	24930860	6976727	8402732	4721875
1465008	589630	11163955	8240936	1472257	4542761	2826904
6580030	810677	17738269	16753447	6576636	7596916	3018617
21014486	5954760	116796264	99180525	23873991	53261765	36958631
16777346	3855106	76167515	70686176	21531952	38609830	15088325
6917297	147444	16891010	16324792	8331669	4294222	2154225
1009908	178121	6326339	5456696	1148699	2205961	1189844
4375216	5395020	36909578	34061212	9623124	12791430	7509216
298187	1990381	7536201	6977828	1959490	4244309	2101132
77576	305278	697809	681546	229149	638863	241945
370970	321508	1987068	1386384	579553	460069	637311
325521	334601	2193126	2048336	503368	1255518	529703
215232	35854	552768	536556	261752	394094	103373
506795	1667176	7649551	7182483	1008042	2281421	2025245
677264	163245	7903171	7122198	1146846	3223650	563035
65920	119412	639101	622365	139356	258553	275077
1837752	457566	7750783	7503517	3795568	34953	1032396
51541899	16090255	293945062	263790958	72216081	133074196	66206929

16-12 续表

单位：万元

项 目	Item	损益 营业收入 Business Income	损益 营业成本 Business Cost	损益 销售费用 Sales Expenses
合 计	**Total**	**641767367**	**590237141**	**26660073**
按隶属关系分	**By Affiliation**			
中 央	Central	208445310	200332553	3353773
地 方	Local	433322057	389904589	23306301
按企业登记注册类型分	**By Registration Type**			
内 资	Domestically-invested Enterprises	469694931	440579306	14758354
国 有	State-owned Enterprises	9283626	8048510	223314
集 体	Collectively-owned Enterprises	1131550	1058718	28144
股份合作	Joint-equity Cooperative Enterprises	474591	437440	13214
联 营	Associate Enterprises	24179	22094	869
有限责任公司	Limited Liability Companies	333069865	316477826	8344636
股份有限公司	Companies Limited by Shares	37072675	34474403	1432095
私 营	Private Enterprises	88608158	80031197	4715633
其 他	Other	30289	29119	449
港澳台商投资	Hong Kong, Macao and Taiwan-invested Enterprises	72452893	65215909	4218865
外商投资	Foreign-invested Enterprises	99619542	84441926	7682855
按国民经济行业分	**By Sector**			
批发业	Wholesale	554362412	514021160	18869913
农、林、牧、渔产品批发	Wholesale of Agriculture, Forestry, Animal Production and Hunting, and Fishing Products	18559934	17980943	184707
食品、饮料及烟草制品批发	Wholesale of Foods, Beverage and Tobaccos	35075764	30857162	2399926
纺织、服装及家庭用品批发	Wholesale of Textile, Clothes and Household Commodities	63084089	56390994	3734879
文化、体育用品及器材批发	Wholesale of Cultural and Sports Goods and Equipment	17727943	15819661	929995
医药及医疗器材批发	Wholesale of Medicine and Medical Devices	27895693	23221177	2242373
矿产品、建材及化工产品批发	Wholesale of Mineral Products, Building Materials, and Chemical Products	232232263	226035909	2867815
机械设备、五金交电及电子产品批发	Wholesale of Mechanical Equipment, Hardware and Electronic Products	149636405	134727734	6176314
贸易经纪与代理	Trade Broker and Agent	4630688	4138616	111884
其他批发业	Others	5519633	4848965	222021
零售业	Retail	87404955	76215982	7790160
综合零售	Integrated Retail	14073125	10768988	2377336
食品、饮料及烟草制品专门零售	Special Retails of Foods, Beverage and Tobacoos	1796926	1283937	304921
纺织、服装及日用品专门零售	Special Retail of Textile, Clothing and Domestic Commodities	3120233	1937298	912398
文化、体育用品及器材专门零售	Special Retail of Cultural and Sports Goods and Equipment	3805783	3044604	390165
医药及医疗器材专门零售	Special Retail of Medicine and Medical Devices	1345249	1110551	147047
汽车、摩托车、零配件和燃料及其他动力销售	Sales of Automobiles, Motorcycles, Accessories, Fuels and Other Power	23965950	22004983	1062028
家用电器及电子产品专门零售	Special Retail of Household Electrical Appliances and Electronic Products	9417670	8348888	627804
五金、家具及室内装修材料专门零售	Special Retail of Hardware, Furniture and Indoor Decoration Materials	1052866	705256	235728
货摊、无店铺及其他零售业	Stand Retail, Retail Without Shops and Other Retail	28827154	27011478	1732734
按规模划分	**By Size**			
#大中型企业	Medium and Large-sized Enterprises	554247772	508311756	23954982

注：应交税金合计包括应交增值税、所得税费用和税金及附加。

16-12 Continued

(10000 yuan)

Profits and Losses				应交税金合计 Total Tax Payable			
管理费用 Management Expenses	研发费用 R&D Expenses	财务费用 Financial Expenses	利润总额 Total Profits		#税金及附加 Main Tax and Surtax	#所得税费用 Income Tax Expense	#应交增值税 Value Added Tax Payable
13403424	**1139051**	**2839688**	**15781042**	**8601158**	**1474930**	**2899934**	**4226294**
2103844	128874	1083901	4807279	1783212	420384	739547	623281
11299579	1010177	1755787	10973763	6817946	1054546	2160387	3603013
7852164	742107	2664807	8128135	5315183	1150540	1564038	2600605
232097	740	-66944	680303	609704	331342	148360	130001
25521		17995	2346	7774	3161	1380	3233
17737	133	-132	6085	4930	579	1026	3326
3307		-1278	-588	884	226	100	558
4225955	366537	1927361	5289957	2809000	435472	1019507	1354020
573287	85534	429645	1433242	468592	80276	159957	228359
2773578	289161	358117	716714	1414275	299483	233697	881095
683	4	42	77	25	1	12	12
2748655	160913	173203	658278	625781	94279	229081	302420
2802605	236031	1678	6994629	2660195	230111	1106815	1323269
10873713	978088	2582994	15006109	7009233	1191594	2547127	3270512
251468	20800	397387	121082	54741	18157	25806	10778
674769	27682	87885	1133954	1043791	403383	237902	402506
2472663	94122	-47286	1094061	560435	67908	146800	345727
489368	79765	159328	258177	244989	25622	89872	129495
959599	58423	186704	1304532	891592	74694	319674	497223
2265530	90088	1400922	3845466	1447310	340047	516973	590289
3435559	568910	253178	6475384	2533339	246419	1070950	1215970
149145	1309	71867	503134	118754	9049	81284	28421
175614	36989	73010	270321	114283	6315	57867	50102
2529710	160964	256694	774933	1591925	283336	352808	955782
691587	18797	38295	326634	337103	71003	104474	161626
100367	438	2875	105223	78004	6648	30614	40742
240105	4153	13527	8417	134609	15882	20141	98586
207882	3618	10524	170091	137063	37616	36797	62650
58514	464	2318	30940	33930	3285	9914	20731
583048	8927	121612	163396	409031	95151	73667	240213
237059	45131	38678	136714	186714	17785	44756	124173
84790	2165	2444	23571	39134	6254	6731	26150
326359	77271	26422	-190053	236338	29711	25716	180912
11536054	1057719	2373980	14891385	7439705	1182039	2608376	3649290

Note: Total tax payable includes VAT payable, income tax expense, tax and surtax.

16-13 限额以上住宿和餐饮业企业财务状况(2018年)

单位：万元

项　目	Item	企业单位个数(个) Number of Enterprises (unit)	资产总计 Total Assets	流动资产合计 Total Current Assets
合　计	**Total**	**2189**	**19869386**	**9305060**
按隶属关系分	**By Affiliation**			
中　央	Central	148	2053553	653027
地　方	Local	2041	17815833	8652033
按登记注册类型分	**By Registration Type**			
内　资	Domestically-invested Enterprises	2029	13829997	6909462
国　有	State-owned Enterprises	174	2096491	653600
集　体	Collectively-owned Enterprises	44	219847	66294
股份合作	Joint-equity Cooperative Enterprises	40	112373	60290
联　营	Associate Enterprises	2	4727	4265
有限责任公司	Limited Liability Companies	749	8042432	3922192
股份有限公司	Companies Limited by Shares	26	538591	272662
私　营	Private Enterprises	993	2815536	1930158
其　他	Other	1	***	***
港澳台商投资	Hong Kong, Macao and Taiwan-invested Enterprises	94	3972330	1807343
外商投资	Foreign-invested Enterprises	66	2067058	588255
按行业类别分	**By Sector Type**			
住宿业	Accommodation Enterprises	930	15661186	6554843
旅游饭店	Tourism Hotels	523	12727352	5020686
一般旅馆	Common Inns	379	2123786	1020028
民宿服务	Home Lodging Services	2	1237	877
其他住宿业	Other Accommodation Enterprises	26	808810	513252
餐饮业	Restaurants Enterprises	1259	4208200	2750217
正餐服务	Dinner Services	1054	2753646	1838095
快餐服务	Fast Food Services	98	1012834	567677
饮料及冷饮服务	Beverage and Cold Drink Services	24	283560	202850
餐饮配送及外卖送餐服务	Catering Distribution and Delivery Services	44	69661	62352
其他餐饮业	Other Restaurants Enterprises	39	88500	79244

FINANCIAL STATUS OF ACCOMMODATION AND RESTAURANTS ENTERPRISES ABOVE DESIGNATED SIZE (2018)

(10000 yuan)

资产负债 Assets and Liabilities						
#应收账款 Accounts Receivable	固定资产原价 Total Original Value of Fixed Assets	负债合计 Total Liabilities	#流动负债合计 Total Current Liabilities	#应付账款 Accounts Payable	所有者权益合计 Total Owner's Equity	#实收资本 Paid-up Capital
381725	**10599217**	**14534590**	**11017895**	**1024827**	**5334796**	**5422873**
32866	1992420	1145302	771559	36236	908252	804403
348859	8606797	13389288	10246335	988591	4426545	4618470
308215	7643389	11158498	8753036	795544	2671500	3871822
24937	1987867	1056933	745797	41020	1039558	958090
1727	249755	156168	75882	6123	63680	30970
1753	72819	85660	76852	6276	26714	11980
-104	3466	4380	3819	563	346	3922
152493	4436097	6842461	5325392	390604	1199972	2280797
10596	168811	308007	260744	15468	230584	110710
116813	724574	2704889	2264551	335490	110647	475354
***	***	***	***	***	***	***
46127	1958120	2325910	1592280	157674	1646420	1062288
27383	997708	1050183	672579	71610	1016876	488762
175478	9543814	11531196	8224382	431714	4129990	4554168
132436	8654664	9328052	6643932	349257	3399300	3861514
38291	739408	1400253	1163341	71020	723534	626809
43	155	794	794		444	500
4708	149587	802097	416316	11437	6712	65344
206247	1055403	3003394	2793513	593113	1204806	868705
132301	682392	2255427	2081850	398695	498219	644392
24759	301633	510365	482001	128871	502469	153217
12219	50025	129181	121401	20274	154379	28089
13178	10213	41815	41765	17301	27846	16632
23791	11140	66606	66496	27972	21893	26375

16-13 续表

单位：万元

项目	Item	损益 营业收入 Business Income	营业成本 Business Cost	销售费用 Sales Expenses	管理费用 Management Expenses
合计	**Total**	**10867009**	**3901569**	**4097397**	**2148099**
按隶属关系分	**By Affiliation**				
中央	Central	796070	241949	224757	274371
地方	Local	10070939	3659620	3872640	1873729
按登记注册类型分	**By Registration Type**				
内资	Domestically-invested Enterprises	7038286	2578972	2553263	1614767
国有	State-owned Enterprises	695980	158901	231735	276052
集体	Collectively-owned Enterprises	112821	24795	47313	29511
股份合作	Joint-equity Cooperative Enterprises	61797	24502	20868	13335
联营	Associate Enterprises	4581	935	2074	1289
有限责任公司	Limited Liability Companies	3460540	1236368	1211247	837266
股份有限公司	Companies Limited by Shares	210864	67993	86626	45666
私营	Private Enterprises	2491704	1065480	953400	411648
其他	Other	***	***	***	***
港澳台商投资	Hong Kong, Macao and Taiwan-invested Enterprises	2418783	687454	1091083	326150
外商投资	Foreign-invested Enterprises	1409939	635143	453051	207183
按行业类别分	**By Sector Type**				
住宿业	Accommodation Enterprises	4050999	1056578	1228263	1364885
旅游饭店	Tourism Hotels	3136971	823563	904694	1099839
一般旅馆	Common Inns	800071	206464	294981	232183
民宿服务	Home Lodging Services	1648	146	965	558
其他住宿业	Other Accommodation Enterprises	112309	26406	27622	32305
餐饮业	Restaurants Enterprises	6816010	2844990	2869135	783214
正餐服务	Dinner Services	4075878	1715256	1684854	550010
快餐服务	Fast Food Services	2007398	792516	906016	171797
饮料及冷饮服务	Beverage and Cold Drink Services	338725	86138	180358	20188
餐饮配送及外卖送餐服务	Catering Distribution and Delivery Services	143063	101092	24647	14358
其他餐饮业	Other Restaurants Enterprises	250946	149989	73260	26862

注：应交税金合计包括应交增值税、所得税费用和税金及附加。

16–13 continued

(10000 yuan)

Profits and Losses		应交税金合计 Total Tax Payable			
财务费用 Financial Expenses	利润总额 Total Profits		#税金及附加 Tax and Surcharges	#所得税费用 Income Tax Expense	#应交增值税 Value Added Tax Payable
179392	**506289**	**442564**	**118130**	**187038**	**137395**
-3759	33404	59320	22044	18664	18612
183151	472884	383244	96086	168374	118784
129012	143074	288507	74840	91465	122201
1004	22679	46660	15908	12493	18260
-79	9959	6932	911	2772	3249
49	2778	3094	931	741	1423
7	189	313	92	80	142
95406	52266	156594	46003	53988	56604
1101	16576	8578	2106	2967	3504
31523	38628	66336	8890	18426	39019
***	***	***	***	***	***
34740	272449	107074	28530	66738	11806
15640	90765	46984	14760	28835	3389
153845	184399	289350	104630	90275	94446
110194	140802	234298	93149	69638	71511
19231	45611	46362	8009	18579	19773
3	-33	100	5	51	45
24417	-1981	8590	3467	2007	3117
25547	321890	153213	13500	96764	42950
25451	122356	97105	10379	43305	43421
728	144554	29067	1698	37366	-9998
-1051	52542	17413	407	14297	2709
198	2359	3976	362	790	2824
222	79	5653	653	1006	3994

Note: Total tax payable mainly includes VAT payable, income tax expense, tax and surtax.

16–14 限额以上住宿和餐饮业企业财务状况(2019年)

单位：万元

项目	Item	企业单位个数(个) Number of Enterprises (unit)	资产总计 Total Assets	流动资产合计 Total Current Assets
合　计	**Total**	**3185**	**21179506**	**10413435**
按隶属关系分	**By Affiliation**			
中　央	Central	138	2026049	724234
地　方	Local	3047	19153456	9689201
按登记注册类型分	**By Registration Type**			
内　资	Domestically-invested Enterprises	2998	14846800	7818774
国　有	State-owned Enterprises	165	1749142	603021
集　体	Collectively-owned Enterprises	57	221853	65504
股份合作	Joint-equity Cooperative Enterprises	40	103417	51408
联　营	Associate Enterprises	3	8564	6086
有限责任公司	Limited Liability Companies	869	8657148	4336485
股份有限公司	Companies Limited by Shares	23	756267	458690
私　营	Private Enterprises	1841	3350410	2297580
港澳台商投资	Hong Kong, Macao and Taiwan-invested Enterprises	100	4223134	1952411
外商投资	Foreign-invested Enterprises	87	2109571	642251
按行业类别分	**By Sector Type**			
住宿业	Accommodation Enterprises	1207	15650198	6825403
旅游饭店	Tourism Hotels	544	12023791	4890075
一般旅馆	Common Inns	617	2656979	1315129
民宿服务	Home Lodging Services	3	6722	788
其他住宿业	Other Accommodation Enterprises	43	962707	619410
餐饮业	Restaurants Enterprises	1978	5529307	3588032
正餐服务	Dinner Services	1656	3151693	2050012
快餐服务	Fast Food Services	145	1304595	629085
饮料及冷饮服务	Beverage and Cold Drink Services	50	809510	686210
餐饮配送及外卖送餐服务	Catering Distribution and Delivery Services	66	104153	88092
其他餐饮业	Other Restaurants Enterprises	61	159357	134634

FINANCIAL STATUS OF ACCOMMODATION ENTERPRISES ABOVE DESIGNATED SIZE (2019)

(10000 yuan)

资产负债 Assets and Liabilities						
#应收账款 Accounts Receivable	固定资产原价 Total Original Value of Fixed Assets	负债合计 Total Liabilities	#流动负债合计 Total Current Liabilities	#应付账款 Accounts Payable	所有者权益合计 Total Owner's Equity	#实收资本 Paid-up Capital
479995	**10608450**	**15688995**	**11833507**	**1240119**	**5490511**	**6430262**
40743	1966002	1046746	649784	61552	979303	737536
439252	8642448	14642249	11183723	1178568	4511208	5692726
382003	7657652	12144770	9667535	1006945	2702030	4935868
16620	1668505	972994	685174	43738	776148	624099
3334	248034	152329	76298	7716	69523	30201
3662	55748	77540	70982	7385	25876	10911
20	3757	5792	5231	597	2772	6922
190006	4584583	7096300	5554989	509291	1560849	2598749
3539	172837	547629	521467	14065	208638	101564
164822	924187	3292186	2753394	424152	58224	1563422
51466	1869760	2541256	1463644	148087	1681879	961864
46526	1081038	1002969	702328	85087	1106602	532530
207013	9219984	11440409	8063432	482605	4209789	4343959
157571	7881799	8827001	6322636	375341	3196790	3344254
43177	1141709	1734366	1383138	93986	922613	901154
139	149	7942	7942	41	-1220	188
6126	196327	871100	349716	13237	91607	98363
272983	1388466	4248586	3770075	757514	1280722	2086303
156008	932088	2585435	2303138	403650	566258	1801874
29668	340564	741864	560149	145480	562731	146890
23355	72453	708813	698290	136366	100696	67879
25968	22252	66253	64000	23433	37901	25906
37985	21110	146221	144498	48585	13136	43754

16-14 续表

单位：万元

项目	Item	损益 营业收入 Business Income	营业成本 Business Cost	销售费用 Sales Expenses	管理费用 Management Expenses
合　计	**Total**	**12667968**	**4972338**	**4633740**	**2412538**
按隶属关系分	**By Affiliation**				
中　央	Central	814163	255690	221860	260170
地　方	Local	11853805	4716647	4411880	2152368
按登记注册类型分	**By Registration Type**				
内　资	Domestically-invested Enterprises	8526107	3488351	2948502	1866624
国　有	State-owned Enterprises	695124	167342	229288	257127
集　体	Collectively-owned Enterprises	120713	30298	45778	31606
股份合作	Joint-equity Cooperative Enterprises	63826	26489	20484	13038
联　营	Associate Enterprises	6471	1184	2928	1864
有限责任公司	Limited Liability Companies	3922261	1568968	1347423	882831
股份有限公司	Companies Limited by Shares	164026	57984	67768	31755
私　营	Private Enterprises	3553686	1636085	1234835	648404
港澳台商投资	Hong Kong, Macao and Taiwan-invested Enterprises	2580177	787214	1172548	317999
外商投资	Foreign-invested Enterprises	1561684	696773	512690	227915
按行业类别分	**By Sector Type**				
住宿业	Accommodation Enterprises	4360514	1246227	1321896	1389062
旅游饭店	Tourism Hotels	3092434	865422	898711	1041497
一般旅馆	Common Inns	1122373	342593	389526	307101
民宿服务	Home Lodging Services	2303	1112	773	893
其他住宿业	Other Accommodation Enterprises	143405	37101	32887	39572
餐饮业	Restaurants Enterprises	8307454	3726111	3311844	1023477
正餐服务	Dinner Services	4803200	2094157	1900862	696167
快餐服务	Fast Food Services	2342532	1000252	1011038	202355
饮料及冷饮服务	Beverage and Cold Drink Services	577202	233995	285082	54427
餐饮配送及外卖送餐服务	Catering Distribution and Delivery Services	199504	139748	35907	21799
其他餐饮业	Other Restaurants Enterprises	385016	257958	78956	48729

注：应交税金合计包括应交增值税、所得税费用和税金及附加。

16-14 continued

(10000 yuan)

Profits and Losses			应交税金合计 Total Tax Payable			
研发费用 R&D Expenses	财务费用 Financial Expenses	利润总额 Total Profits		#税金及附加 Tax and Surcharges	#所得税费用 Income Tax Expense	#应交增值税 Value Added Tax Payable
717	**191254**	**446525**	**488363**	**133269**	**197908**	**157185**
	-3604	58213	63988	23773	20068	20147
717	194858	388313	424375	109496	177841	137038
329	134191	121069	322876	89375	102269	131232
	1886	26503	50999	17787	13155	20057
3	-25	12720	7253	966	2725	3562
	25	3194	3225	939	799	1487
	73	337	348	96	1	252
82	95907	44848	170424	56226	66254	47944
110	1625	15581	6840	2131	1950	2760
134	34700	17887	83786	11231	17384	55171
373	45840	247445	109606	25315	63631	20660
15	11223	78012	55880	18579	32009	5293
9	157021	215132	317703	117494	102163	98046
7	103813	154584	245367	100207	80044	65116
2	27250	56006	60302	13112	18910	28280
	32	-456	144	10	24	109
	25926	4998	11890	4164	3185	4541
708	34233	231394	170660	15776	95745	59139
381	28286	97008	102872	11667	43019	48186
322	6483	129339	38624	1914	35248	1462
1	-1067	3311	14764	509	15377	-1121
1	229	1920	4782	583	804	3394
4	301	-185	9618	1103	1297	7217

Note: Total tax payable mainly includes VAT payable, income tax expense, tax and surtax.

16-15 连锁企业基本情况(2001-2019年)
STATISTICS FOR CHAIN ENTERPRISES (2001-2019)

年 份 Year	连锁总店(个) Number of General Chain Stores (unit)	门店总数(个) Number of Stores (unit)	从业人员年末人数(人) Year-end Number of Employed Persons (person)	营业面积(平方米) Operating Area (sq.m)	商品销售额(营业额)(万元) Sales of Commodities (Turnover) (10000 yuan)	#零售额 Retail Sales
2001	129	2123	139470	1605808	4831168	2186540
2002	146	3523	109089	2356266	6621975	6487185
2003	153	4519	132030	3405562	8404232	7601221
2004	196	5432	153942	3783507	8603560	8337829
2005	188	5973	166598	4376383	10612658	9507168
2006	205	6730	170007	5546003	11229026	9514297
2007	210	7645	185114	6677266	13890913	11573838
2008	240	8611	223954	6745802	15720473	12954839
2009	240	8928	218024	6995047	17366414	13816796
2010	234	9299	228292	7268786	21329783	16255496
2011	233	9845	280798	7953891	25742536	19507890
2012	220	10014	287975	8339674	26758403	20140433
2013	241	11111	299445	9026207	27834646	21495798
2014	243	11433	279567	9252645	28173728	21100845
2015	238	11942	279596	9238023	30453838	24508274
2016	245	12604	303319	11519137	32375249	27797369
2017	252	13450	316141	11121572	35574270	29557163
2018	277	15603	331018	11394589	38230004	31093369
2019	291	16126	326133	11183441	38223984	32566351

16-16 连锁企业基本情况(按登记注册类型、经营业态分)(2019年)
STATISTICS FOR CHAIN ENTERPRISES (BY REGISTRATION TYPE OF ENTERPRISES AND OPERATION FORMS) (2019)

项目	Item	门店总数(个) Number of Stores (unit)	从业人员年末人数(人) Year-end Number of Employed Persons (person)	营业面积(平方米) Operating Area (sq.m)	商品销售额(营业额)(万元) Sales of Commodities (10000 yuan)	#零售额 Retail Sales
合计	**Total**	**16126**	**326133**	**11183441**	**38223984**	**32566351**
按登记注册类型分	**By Registration Type**					
内资	Domestically-invested Enterprises	9988	170718	8346177	26996957	21664225
国有	State-owned Enterprises	239	4720	111768	448088	382686
集体	Collectively-owned Enterprises	15	463	48780	52671	49253
股份合作	Joint-equity Cooperative Enterprises	3	34	630	750	750
联营	Associated Enterprises	5	13	928	776	776
有限责任公司	Limited Liability Companies	5209	83793	3060907	11959004	9796853
股份有限公司	Companies Limited by Shares	1756	51280	4107313	12344310	9412885
私营	Private Enterprises	2761	30415	1015851	2191358	2021023
其他	Others					
港澳台商投资	Hong Kong, Macao and Taiwan-invested Enterprises	3366	73801	1216540	2935511	2809482
外商投资	Foreign-invested Enterprises	2772	81614	1620724	8291516	8092644
按经营业态分	**By Operation Form**					
零售业态	Retail	9898	159778	8770911	33304526	27847502
便利店	Convenient Stores	2394	9337	321858	805737	757221
折扣店	Discount Stores	5	345	69690	112413	112413
超市	Supermarkets	1529	43411	1860810	5379204	3895773
大型超市	Large Supermarkets	494	37969	2027745	3846505	3727068
仓储会员店	Warehouse Club Stores	5	1522	53462	270812	270812
百货店	Department Stores	102	14156	2547025	3743368	3739715
专业店	Specialty Stores	2504	20967	1094841	7542089	6350091
加油站	Gas Stations	644	5712	308408	5795129	3336116
专卖店	Exclusive Stores	2211	25483	426936	5594352	5443377
家居建材商店	Furniture and Building Material Stores	10	876	60136	214917	214917
餐饮业态	Catering Enterprises	6114	163474	2408130	4804201	4717840
中式正餐	Chinese Dinner	1013	41092	1024046	1555387	1539805
中式快餐	Chinese Fast Food	1738	30479	432631	1116929	1084096
外国风味正餐	Exotic Dinner	823	32504	269330	561892	557509
外国风味快餐	Exotic Fast Food	1378	45505	427182	1098447	1066566
茶馆	Teahouses	5	19	810	270	270
咖啡店	Cafés	1129	13561	251808	461480	459798
其他	Others	28	314	2323	9796	9796
住宿业态	Accommodation Enterprises	114	2881	4400	115258	1009
旅游饭店	Tourism Hotels	26	1012		36150	14
一般旅馆	Common Inns	88	1869	4400	79108	996

16-17 商品交易市场基本情况(2019年)
STATISTICS FOR COMMODITY TRANSACTION MARKETS (2019)

项　　目	Item	市场数量 (个) Number of Markets (unit)	总摊位数 (个) Number of Booths (unit)	成交额 (亿元) Turnover (100 million yuan)
合计	**Total**	**483**	**150047**	**4235.1**
按经营方式分	**By Business Practice**			
批发市场	Wholesale Market	50	42681	3038.2
零售市场	Retail Market	433	107366	1196.9
按经营环境分	**By Business Environment**			
露天式	Open-air	90	37015	2430.6
封闭式	Closed	375	104146	1643.2
其　他	Others	18	8886	161.3

16-18 亿元及以上商品交易市场基本情况(2019年)
STATISTICS FOR COMMODITY TRANSACTION MARKETS OVER RMB 100 MILLION (2019)

项　　目	Item	市场数量 (个) Number of markets (unit)	总摊位数 (个) Number of Booths (unit)	#出租摊位数 Number of Booths on Lease	成交额 (亿元) Turnover (100 million yuan)
合计	**Total**	**92**	**74093**	**63507**	**4157.4**
按经营方式分	**By Business Practice**				
批发市场	Wholesale Market	31	37626	30782	3033.6
零售市场	Retail Market	61	36467	32725	1123.8
按经营环境分	**By Business Environment**				
露天式	Open-air	14	13428	10561	2415.2
封闭式	Closed	73	54246	47095	1584.6
其　他	Others	5	6419	5851	157.7

16-19 商品交易市场经营情况(2019年)
STATISTICS FOR COMMODITY TRANSACTION MARKETS (2019)

项目	Item	市场数量(个) Number of Markets (unit)	出租摊位数(个) Number of Booths (unit)	营业面积(万平方米) Operating Area (10,000 sq.m)	成交额(亿元) Turnover (100 million yuan)
合计	**Total**	**483**	**122467**	**933.0**	**4235.1**
综合市场	**Comprehensive Markets**	**251**	**61921**	**407.7**	**2636.4**
生产资料综合市场	Comprehensive Market of Capital Goods				
工业消费品综合市场	Comprehensive Market of Industrial Consumer Goods	20	4886	16.2	17.7
农产品综合市场	Comprehensive Market of Agricultural Products	159	40633	304.0	2601.4
其他综合市场	Other Comprehensive Markets	72	16402	87.5	17.3
专业市场	**Specialized Markets**	**232**	**60546**	**525.2**	**1598.7**
生产资料市场	**Market of Capital Goods**	**29**	**5473**	**61.5**	**87.5**
木材市场	Timber Market				
建材市场	Building Material Market	25	4850	43.4	43.1
化工材料及制品市场	Chemical Material and Product Market				
金属材料市场	Metal Material Market	3	343	16.4	31.8
机械设备市场	Mechanical Equipment Market				
其他生产资料市场	Other Markets of Capital Goods	1	280	1.7	12.5
农产品市场	**Agricultural Product Market**	**37**	**6697**	**80.1**	**349.4**
粮油市场	Foodstuff and Oil Market	1	52	0.1	0.1
肉禽蛋市场	Meat, Poultry and Egg Market	4	928	2.9	3.5
水产品市场	Aquatic Product Market	6	2180	15.1	102.2
蔬菜市场	Vegetable Market	16	2533	36.5	230.9
干鲜果品市场	Dried and Fresh Fruit Market	2	325	23.6	9.5
其他农产品市场	Other Agricultural Product Markets	8	679	2.0	3.3
食品、饮料及烟酒市场	**Food, Beverage, Tobacco and Wine Market**	**12**	**1409**	**8.7**	**6.4**
食品饮料市场	Food and Beverage Market				
茶叶市场	Tea Market	9	1294	8.1	6.2
其他食品饮料及烟酒市场	Other Food, Beverage, Tobacco and Wine Markets	3	115	0.6	0.2
纺织、服装、鞋帽市场	**Textile, Costume, Shoe and Hat Market**	**32**	**14802**	**58.0**	**37.7**
布料及纺织品市场	Cloth and Textile Market	1	200	0.4	0.4
服装市场	Clothing Market	23	12003	49.5	31.6
鞋帽市场	Shoe and Hat Market				
其他纺织服装鞋帽市场	Other Textile, Costume, Shoe and Cap Markets	8	2599	8.1	5.7
日用品及文化用品市场	**Domestic Commodity and Cultural Article Market**	**10**	**2270**	**8.4**	**5.4**
小商品市场	Small Commodity Market	1	362	0.8	0.4

16-19 续表 Continued

项目	Item	市场数量(个) Number of Markets (unit)	出租摊位数(个) Number of Booths (unit)	营业面积(万平方米) Operating Area (10000 sq.m)	成交额(亿元) Turnover (100 million yuan)
箱包市场	Case and Bag Market				
玩具市场	Toy Market				
文具市场	Stationary Market	1	780	2	1
图书、报刊杂志市场	Book, Newspaper, and Magazine Market	2	231	1.6	2.9
音像制品及电子出版物市场	Audiovisual Product and E-journal Market				
体育用品市场	Sports Good Market				
其他日用品及文化用品市场	Other Domestic Commodity and Cultural Article Market	6	897	4.1	1.5
黄金、珠宝、玉器等首饰市场	**Market of Gold, Jewelry, and Jade**	**13**	**2371**	**11.3**	**12.6**
电器、通讯器材、电子设备市场	**Market of Electrical Appliances, Communication Devices, and Electronic Equipment**	**7**	**3033**	**7.5**	**56.4**
家电市场	Household Appliance Market	1	61	0.6	0.1
通讯器材市场	Communication Device Market	1	240	0.8	0.4
照相、摄像器材市场	Photographic and Camera Shooting Equipment Market	1	211	0.9	2.7
计算机及辅助设备市场	Computer and Supporting Equipment Market	3	1308	3.1	25.7
其他电器、通讯器材、电子设备市场	Other Electrical Appliance, Communication Device and Electronic Equipment Market	1	1213	2	28
医药、医疗用品及器材市场	**Medicine, Medial Article and Equipment Market**				
中药材市场	Chinese Herb Market				
其他医药、医疗用品及器材市场	Other Medicine, Medial Article and Equipment Market				
家具、五金及装饰材料市场	**Furniture, Hardware, and Decoration Material Market**	**47**	**12338**	**173.1**	**153.7**
家具市场	Furniture Market	23	5920	107.3	49.9
装饰材料市场	Decoration Materials Market	12	3965	44.1	94.8
灯具市场	Lamp and Lantern Market	4	600	8.6	1.8
厨具、盥洗设备市场	Kitchen and Washroom Equipment Market				
五金材料市场	Hardware Market	2	354	3.6	3.5
其他装修市场	Other Decoration Market	6	1499	9.5	3.6
汽车、摩托车及零配件市场	**Automobile, Autobike, and Part and Fitting Market**	**18**	**4615**	**85.7**	**880.9**
汽车市场	Automobile Market	11	1815	61.1	829.9
摩托车市场	Autobike Market				
机动车零配件市场	Automobile Part and Fitting Market	7	2800	24.6	51.1
花、鸟、鱼、虫市场	**Flower, Bird, Fish and Insect Market**	**7**	**1190**	**4.6**	**0.7**
花卉市场	Flower Market	5	730	1.7	0.5
鸟市场	Bird Market				
观赏鱼市场	Fish Market	1	110	1.8	0.1
其他花鸟鱼虫市场	Other Flower, Bird, Fish and Insect Market	1	350	1.1	0.1
旧货市场	**Secondhand Goods Market**	**10**	**5873**	**13.6**	**4.7**
古玩、古董、字画市场	Curio, Antique, Calligraphy and Painting Market	7	1576	8.7	0.9
邮票、硬币市场	Stamp and Coin Market	1	887	0.8	0.7
其他旧货市场	Other Secondhand Goods Market	2	3410	4.1	3.2
其他专业市场	**Other Specialized Markets**	**10**	**475**	**12.7**	**3.3**

16-20 北京消费者信心指数(2019年各季度)
BEIJING CONSUMER CONFIDENCE INDEX EACH QUARTER(2019)

项 目	Item	一季度 First Quarter	二季度 Second Quarter	三季度 Third Quarter	四季度 Fourth Quarter
消费者信心指数	**Consumer Confidence Index**	**119.3**	**118.0**	**118.1**	**119.3**
消费者满意指数	**Consumer Satisfaction Index**	**118.5**	**117.2**	**116.9**	**118.5**
就业状况满意指数	Index of Satisfaction with Employment Status	131.0	132.8	133.3	132.5
家庭收入状况满意指数	Index of Satisfaction with Household Income Status	110.4	109.5	109.8	114.2
耐用消费品购买时机满意指数	Index of Satisfaction with Durable Consumer Goods	114.1	109.2	107.7	108.7
消费者预期指数	**Consumer Expectation Index**	**119.9**	**118.5**	**118.9**	**119.8**
就业状况预期指数	Index of Expectation for Employment Status	127.8	127.0	127.9	125.8
家庭收入状况预期指数	Index of Expectation for Household Income Status	111.9	110.0	109.8	113.8

主要统计指标解释

社会消费品零售总额 指企业（单位、个体户）通过交易直接售给个人、社会集团非生产、非经营用的实物商品金额，以及提供餐饮服务所取得的收入金额。个人包括城乡居民和入境人员，社会集团包括机关、社会团体、部队、学校、企事业单位、居委会或村委会等。

批发和零售业单位 指在流通环节从事商品批发活动和零售活动的单位。

商品购进额 指从本企业（单位）以外的单位和个人购进(包括从国外直接进口)作为转卖或加工后转卖的商品金额（含增值税）。本指标反映批发和零售业从国内外市场上购进商品的总量。

商品销售额 指对本企业以外的单位和个人出售的商品金额（包括售给本单位消费用的商品，含增值税）。本指标反映批发和零售业在国内市场上销售商品以及出口商品的总量。

期末商品库存额 对于批发和零售业法人企业和个体经营户，是指取得所有权的全部商品金额（含增值税）；对于批发和零售业产业活动单位，是指期末实际在库且归属法人具有所有权的全部商品金额（含增值税）。这个指标反映批发和零售业的商品库存情况，以及对市场商品供应的保证程度。

连锁总店（总部） 负责连锁企业资源（商号、商誉、经营模式、服务标准、管理模式等）的开发、配置、控制或使用等功能的企业核心管理机构。连锁经营是指经营同类商品或服务，使用统一商号的若干店铺，在同一总店（总部）的管理下，采取统一采购或特许经营等方式,实现规模效益的组织形式，包括直营连锁、特许连锁和自愿连锁三种形式。直营连锁是指连锁店铺由连锁公司全资或控股开设，在总部的直接控制下，开展统一经营的连锁经营形式；特许连锁是指拥有注册商标、企业标志、专利、专有技术等经营资源的企业（特许人），以合同形式将其拥有的经营资源许可其他经营者（被特许人）使用，被特许人按合同约定在统一的经营模式下开展经营，并向特许人支付特许经营费用的连锁经营形式；自愿连锁是指若干个店铺或企业自愿组合起来，在不改变各自资产所有权关系的情况下，以同一个品牌形象面对消费者，以共同进货为纽带开展的连锁经营形式。

连锁门店 在连锁企业经营管理的基础上，按照总店（总部）的指示和服务规范要求，承担日常销售业务的店铺，称连锁门店，包括直营店（控股店）和加盟店。

（1）直营店（控股店） 是指由连锁企业总部投资开设，按连锁经营管理模式，由总部统一管理的店铺。

（2）加盟店 是指在特许连锁中，被特许人获得特许人授权后，使用其商标、商号、经营模式、专利和专有技术等经营资源建立的店铺，也包括自愿连锁的成员店。

门店总数 指该连锁企业所拥有的全部门店（包括直营店和加盟店）数量。其中，总店（如果总公司有门店的话）作为一个直营店处理。此外，有的地区分出控股店，控股店按直营店统计。

餐饮业企业 指在一定场所，专门从事对食物进行现场烹饪、调制，并出售给顾客主要供现场消费服务活动的单位（含法人单位、产业活动单位、个体经营户）。如各种饭馆、中西餐厅、酒馆、茶馆和火车餐车、车站食堂、飞机场餐厅等。

住宿业企业 指有偿为顾客提供临时住宿服务活动的单位（含法人单位、产业活动单位、个体经营户）。如旅游饭店、宾馆、酒店和旅馆、旅店等。

商品交易市场 指经有关部门和组织批准设立，有固定场所、设施，有经营管理部门和监管人员，若干市场经营者入内，常年或实际开业三个月以上，集中、公开、独立地进行生活消费品、生产资料等现货商品交易以及提供相关服务的交易场所，包括各类消费品市场，生产资料市场等。

消费者信心指数 是综合反映并量化消费者对当前经济形势评价和对经济前景、收入水平、收入预期以及消费心理状态的主观感受，是预测经济走势和消费趋向的一个先行指标，是监测经济周期变化不可缺少的依据。消费者信心指数由消费者满意指数和消费者预期指数构成。其中消费者满意指数反映了消费者对当前经济生活的评价；消费者预期指数反映了消费者对未来一段时期经济发展变化的预期。

消费者信心指数值的含义 指数取值介于 0 和 200 之间，100 为指数强弱临界点。指数超过 100，表明消费者信心处于强信心区，数值由 100 趋近 200，表明消费者信心逐渐增强；反之，指数小于 100 时，表示消费者信心处于弱信心区，数值由 100 趋近 0，表明消费者信心逐渐减弱。

Explanatory Notes on Main Statistical Indicators

Total Retail Sales of Consumer Goods refer to the total prices of physical commodities sold by enterprises (entities or self-employed businesses) through transaction directly to individuals and social groups to be used for non-productive and non-operating purposes, combined with the amount of income from provision of food and beverage services. Individuals include urban and rural residents and persons entering China. Social groups include government agencies, social organizations, armies, schools, enterprises and public institutions, residents' committee or villagers' committee, and so on.

Wholesale and Retail Entities refer to entities engaged in commodity wholesale and retail activities in circulation.

Total Purchases of Commodities refer to the total value (VAT included) of purchases (including direct imports from foreign countries) of commodities by the enterprises (entities) from other entities or individuals for the purpose of re-selling, either with or without further processing of the commodities purchased. This indicator is used to show the total value of purchases of retail and wholesale commodities from domestic and overseas markets.

Total Sales of Commodities refer to value of commodities sold by the enterprises to other entities and individuals (including the commodities consumed by the enterprises themselves, VAT included). This indicator is used to show the total value of wholesale and retail commodities sold in domestic markets and exported.

Inventory (year-end) refers to, for corporate enterprises and self-employed businesses in wholesale and retail trades, the value of all commodities with ownership gained (VAT included); for industrial activity entities in wholesale and retail trades, refer to the value of all commodities actually in storage and owned by their legal person at the end of the reference period (VAT included). This indicator shows the commodity inventory in wholesale and retail trades, and to what extent the commodities will be supplied to the market.

General Chain Store (Headquarters) means the core management organization in an enterprise, responsible for the development, deployment, control or use of resources (trade name, goodwill, operating model, service standards and management model, etc.) of the chain enterprise. Chain operation means an organization form in which several stores using unified trade name dealing in the same commodities or providing the same services through uniform purchase or franchise operation under the management of the same general store (headquarters) to achieve benefits of scale. Chain operation falls into direct-sale chain, franchised chain and voluntary chain. Direct-sale chain is a form of chain operation that chain stores are wholly funded or controlled by chain companies, carrying out uniform operation under the direct control of headquarters; franchised chain is a form of chain operation that any enterprise (the franchiser) owning operating resources, such as trademarks, logos, patents and proprietary technologies, authorize such operating resources to any other operator (the franchisee) by contract, and the franchisee operates under uniform operating model as stated in the contract, and pays franchise fees to the franchiser; voluntary chain is a form of chain operation that several stores or enterprises combine together voluntarily to face consumers with the same brand image without changing their own asset ownership relations, and link together through joint purchase.

Chain Stores Based on the operation and management of chain enterprises, stores carrying out daily sales business by following the general store's (headquarters) instruction and required service standards are called chained stores. They include direct-sale stores (controlled stores) and franchised stores.

(1) Direct-sale Stores (Controlled Stores) refer to stores opened with funds from the headquarters of chain enterprises, using the chain operation and management model, and under the uniform management of the headquarters.

(2) Franchised Stores refer to, in franchise chains, stores established after the franchisee is authorized by the franchiser to use its trademark, trade name, operating model, patent and proprietary technologies and other operating resources. Voluntary chain members are also included.

Total Number of Stores refers to the number of all stores owned by the chain enterprises (including direct-sale stores and franchised stores). The general store (if the parent company has stores) is regarded as a direct-sale store. In addition, controlled stores are considered separately in some areas, which are regarded as direct-sale stores.

Restaurants Enterprises refer to entities (including legal entities, industrial activity entities and self-employed businesses) specialized in cooking and seasoning food which is sold to clients for on-site consumption at a specific site, such as various restaurants, Chinese food and Western food restaurants, pubs, teahouses, dining compartments on trains, canteens at railway stations, and restaurants at airports.

Accommodation Enterprises refer to entities (including legal entities, industrial activity entities and self-employed businesses) providing clients with temporary accommodation services, such as tourist hotels, guesthouses, rest houses and inns, for a fee.

Commodity Transaction Markets refer to transaction sites approved by competent authorities and organizations, with fixed places and facilities. There are operation management departments and regulating personnel in the markets, where several operators stay over years or open for over three months, conducting transactions of on-hand commodities such as living consumables and capital goods, and offering relevant services in a concentrated, open and independent manner. Commodity transaction markets include various markets of consumer goods and capital good market, etc.

Consumer Confidence Index is an indicator reflecting and quantifying the consumers' evaluation on current economic situation, and their personal feeling about the economic prospects, income level, income expectation, and psychological state of consumption. It serves as a leading indicator predicting the trend of economy and tendency of consumption, and an essential basis for monitoring the changes in economic cycle. Consumer Confidence Index consists of consumer satisfaction index and consumer expectation index, and the former one reflects consumers' evaluation on current economic life; consumer expectation index reflects consumers' expectation on the development and changes in the economic prospect in the future.

The Meaning of Consumer Confidence Index The index ranges from 0 to 200. 100 represents a critical point between strong and weak confidence. An index greater than 100 indicates the consumers' confidence is strong. An index going toward 200 from 100 shows the consumers' confidence is becoming gradually strong; in contrary, an index smaller than 100 means the consumers' confidence is weak. When the index goes toward 0 from 100, it means the consumers' confidence is weakening gradually.

17

北京统计年鉴2020　BEIJING STATISTICAL YEARBOOK

旅游业
TOURISM

简要说明

一、主要内容

本章资料主要反映国际旅游和国内旅游情况。包括旅游人数及其在京花费情况、星级饭店经营及接待住宿者情况、旅行社接待及出境旅游情况、A 级及以上重点旅游景区活动情况等。

二、调查方法

星级饭店、旅行社、A 级及以上和重点旅游景区有关数据通过全面调查取得。

三、调查范围

1.星级饭店统计范围为有经营活动的星级饭店法人单位、产业活动单位和个体经营户。

2.旅行社统计范围为有经营活动的全部旅行社（其中出境旅游情况统计范围为有特许经营出境旅游业务权的旅行社）。

3.A 级及以上和重点旅游景区统计范围为有经营活动的 A 级及以上和重点旅游景区。

Brief Introduction

I. Main Content and Scope of Statistics

Statistics in this chapter mainly show the situation of tourism and international tourism. Including: statistics for the number and cost of tourists to Beijing, operation and reception of star-rated hotels, reception and outbound tourism made through travel agencies, activities at Level A-or-above key scenic spots, and so on.

II. Methods of Survey

Data concerning star-rated hotels, travel agencies, Level A-or-above key scenic spots were obtained through comprehensive survey.

III. Scope of Survey

1. The scope of statistics on star-rated hotels covers the star-rated hotel legal entities, industrial activity units and self-employed businesses that engage in business activities.

2. The scope of statistics on travel agencies covers all travel agencies that engage in business activities (of which, the scope of statistics for outbound tourism covers the travel agencies that have the franchise to engage in outbound tourism business).

3. The scope of statistics on Level A-or-above key scenic spots covers the Level A-or-above key scenic spots that engage in business activities.

17-1 国际、国内旅游情况(1978-2019年)
STATISTICS FOR INTERNATIONAL AND DOMESTIC TOURISM (1978-2019)

年 份 Year	来京游客人数 (万人次) Number of Tourists to Beijing (10000 person-times)	入境游客 Inbound Tourists	国内游客 Domestic Tourists	国际旅游收入 (亿美元) Revenue from Inbound Tourism (USD 100 million)	国内旅游收入 (亿元) Revenue from Domestic Tourism (100 million yuan)
1978		18.7		1.0	
1979		25.2		0.9	
1980		28.6		1.2	
1981		39.4		1.2	
1982		45.7		1.3	
1983		50.9		1.4	
1984		65.7		2.3	
1985		93.7		3.2	
1986		99.0		4.6	
1987		108.1		5.5	
1988		120.4		6.7	
1989		64.5		4.7	
1990		100.0		6.6	
1991		132.0		8.5	
1992		174.8		10.7	
1993		202.8		12.4	
1994	6913.0	203.0	6710.0	20.1	298.0
1995	6527.0	207.0	6320.0	21.8	352.6
1996	7901.9	218.9	7683.0	22.5	359.6
1997	8450.8	229.8	8221.0	22.5	391.3
1998	8951.5	220.1	8731.4	23.8	424.5
1999	9512.4	252.4	9260.0	25.0	530.0
2000	10468.1	282.1	10186.0	27.7	683.0
2001	11292.8	285.8	11007.0	29.5	887.7
2002	11810.4	310.4	11500.0	31.1	930.0
2003	8885.1	185.1	8700.0	19.0	706.0
2004	12265.5	315.5	11950.0	31.7	1145.0
2005	12862.9	362.9	12500.0	36.2	1300.0
2006	13590.3	390.3	13200.0	40.3	1482.7
2007	14715.5	435.5	14280.0	45.8	1753.6
2008	14560.0	379.0	14181.0	44.6	1907.0
2009	16669.5	412.5	16257.0	43.6	2144.5
2010	18390.1	490.1	17900.0	50.4	2425.1
2011	21404.4	520.4	20884.0	54.2	2864.3
2012	23134.6	500.9	22633.7	51.5	3301.3
2013	25189.0	450.1	24738.8	47.9	3666.3
2014	26149.7	427.5	25722.2	46.1	3997.0
2015	27279.0	420.0	26859.0	46.1	4320.0
2016	28531.5	416.5	28115.0	50.7	4683.0
2017	29746.2	392.6	29353.6	51.3	5122.4
2018	31093.6	400.4	30693.2	55.2	5556.2
2019	32209.9	376.9	31833.0	51.9	5866.2

资料来源：2018年及以前国内游客、国际旅游收入、国内旅游收入来源于北京市文化和旅游局。2019年起，本表数据均来源于北京市文化和旅游局。

Source: Data of Domestic Tourists,Revenue from Inbound Tourism, Revenue from Domestic Tourism were provided by Beijing Municipal Bureau of Culture and Tourism.Since 2019, all data in this table were from Beijing Municipal Bureau of Culture and Tourism.

17-2 按客源地分入境游客人数(1978-2019年)
NUMBER OF INBOUND TOURISTS BY COUNTRY/REGION (1978-2019)

单位：万人次 (10000 person-times)

年份 Year	入境游客人数 Number of Inbound Tourists	港澳台同胞 Hong Kong, Macao and Taiwan Tourists	#中国香港 Hong Kong, China	外国人 Foreigner	#日本 Japan	#韩国 Korea	#美国 United States	#英国 United Kingdom	#法国 France	#德国 Germany	#俄罗斯 Russia
1978	18.7	3.3		15.4							
1979	25.2	4.1		21.1							
1980	28.6	5.8		21.7	6.0		3.7	1.3	0.9	0.9	
1981	39.4	6.8		31.3	5.3		3.8	1.1	1.1	1.0	
1982	45.7	8.2		35.9	8.2		6.6	1.3	1.3	1.4	
1983	50.9	8.9		39.7	10.0		9.4	1.5	1.5	1.7	0.1
1984	65.7	10.0		52.1	17.2		12.5	2.3	2.1	2.5	0.1
1985	93.7	13.6		74.0	27.6		14.8	3.9	3.2	4.0	0.2
1986	99.0	15.8		79.0	25.5		14.7	4.1	3.1	4.6	0.3
1987	108.1	21.8		81.7	26.3		16.5	4.5	4.3	5.1	0.3
1988	120.4	28.8		86.5	27.8		16.7	4.2	4.2	5.4	0.7
1989	64.5	16.6		46.0	12.2		7.3	2.4	2.1	3.3	1.0
1990	100.0	34.7	11.4	63.8	18.2		8.6	2.9	2.0	4.0	1.5
1991	132.0	38.2	17.6	91.4	27.6	4.3	9.5	4.3	3.7	6.0	3.5
1992	174.8	51.2	24.6	120.5	37.6	5.6	12.3	4.4	6.6	9.4	5.1
1993	202.8	52.8	29.4	145.0	39.3	7.3	14.3	5.3	6.9	12.0	7.7
1994	203.0	39.4	25.7	160.0	41.1	12.7	15.4	5.4	6.7	9.7	4.9
1995	207.0	36.3	25.4	166.5	42.4	17.3	17.4	5.8	6.2	8.8	6.2
1996	218.9	38.6	25.5	176.2	43.0	18.0	18.5	7.5	6.6	10.0	6.9
1997	229.8	40.3	26.3	186.9	43.0	19.4	21.7	9.0	6.5	9.1	6.5
1998	220.1	39.1	25.0	178.2	43.5	8.2	23.2	8.8	6.9	11.3	6.2
1999	252.4	44.1	26.5	205.0	45.6	19.2	24.1	8.8	7.9	10.5	4.6
2000	282.1	44.1	25.0	238.0	54.3	27.8	31.1	9.7	9.6	12.1	3.9
2001	285.8	45.9	26.9	239.9	50.7	32.7	33.1	11.1	10.2	12.3	4.9
2002	310.4	43.9	25.5	266.5	56.5	38.0	37.4	12.9	11.3	12.2	5.2
2003	185.1	32.4	21.7	152.7	29.2	24.5	19.4	8.1	5.5	6.3	5.2
2004	315.5	47.4	27.7	268.1	52.3	42.4	37.4	11.8	11.1	11.5	8.2
2005	362.9	51.3	31.4	311.6	45.0	45.3	46.5	13.9	13.6	14.6	9.7
2006	390.3	52.0	30.3	338.3	50.6	42.4	49.8	14.8	14.2	15.3	15.0
2007	435.5	52.9	31.3	382.6	58.8	44.4	60.3	17.0	16.4	17.5	18.3
2008	379.0	43.3	28.1	335.7	40.0	35.3	53.8	17.5	14.5	16.0	17.9
2009	412.5	69.6	44.4	342.9	46.2	35.2	57.9	16.3	12.9	16.8	15.0
2010	490.1	68.4	40.3	421.6	52.6	50.6	70.0	16.8	14.3	20.1	19.0
2011	520.4	73.0	43.4	447.4	51.0	53.4	78.9	18.8	15.0	22.2	20.5
2012	500.9	66.5	37.6	434.4	43.7	44.2	75.1	18.5	15.1	24.5	20.0
2013	450.1	62.5	35.4	387.6	24.9	37.7	74.7	17.5	13.4	23.0	16.7
2014	427.5	62.0	34.2	365.5	24.9	38.7	71.5	16.9	13.4	22.6	13.7
2015	420.0	62.4	34.9	357.6	25.8	41.6	69.4	17.2	15.3	21.2	10.3
2016	416.5	61.8	35.3	354.8	24.8	37.9	70.3	18.3	13.2	20.6	9.5
2017	392.6	60.6	34.4	332.0	24.2	23.5	67.3	16.5	12.3	19.4	9.3
2018	400.4	60.6	34.8	339.8	24.9	24.8	72.0	15.9	12.7	19.4	8.7
2019	376.9	56.2	32.2	320.7	24.7	24.2	62.9	15.3	12.0	19.8	9.6

注：1．1980—1999年的入境游客人数由外国游客、港澳台游客、华侨三部分组成，2000年及以后华侨包括在外国游客内。
2．1990—1999年香港游客人数为香港、澳门合计。

资料来源：2019年起，本表数据来源于北京市文化和旅游局。

Note: a) Number of inbound tourists in 1980-1999 consisted of foreign visitors, visitors from Hong Kong, Macao and Taiwan, and overseas Chinese. Overseas Chinese were included in the number of foreign visitors in and after 2000.
b) Tourists from Hong Kong in 1990-1999 were the total number of tourists from Hong Kong and Macao.

Source:Since 2019, all data in this table were from Beijing Municipal Bureau of Culture and Tourism.

17–3 来京游客人数
NUMBER OF TOURISTS TO BEIJING

单位：万人次 (10000 person-times)

项　　目	Item	2019	2018	2019年为2018年% 2019 as % of 2018
合　　计	**Total**	**32209.9**	**31093.6**	**103.6**
国内游客人数	**Number of Domestic Tourists**	**31833.0**	**30693.2**	**103.7**
外地来京游客	Tourists to Beijing from Outside Beijing	19267.0	18976.2	101.5
本市游客	Local Tourists	12566.0	11717.0	107.2
入境游客人数	**Number of Inbound Tourists**	**376.9**	**400.4**	**94.1**
港澳台同胞	Hong Kong, Macao and Taiwan Tourists	56.2	60.6	92.7
中国香港	Hong Kong, China	32.2	34.8	92.5
中国澳门	Macao, China	1.8	1.6	110.9
中国台湾	Taiwan, China	22.2	24.2	91.8
外国人	Foreigners	320.7	339.8	94.4
亚　洲	Asia	112.5	114.3	98.4
#日　本	Japan	24.7	24.9	99.4
韩　国	Korea	24.2	24.8	97.8
菲律宾	Philippines	3.1	2.6	117.8
印度尼西亚	Indonesia	4.5	5.0	90.5
马来西亚	Malaysia	8.2	8.7	94.1
新加坡	Singapore	12.7	12.3	103.4
泰　国	Thailand	5.7	7.5	76.4
印　度	India	7.5	6.8	111.1
蒙　古	Mongolia	2.9	3.1	93.2
美　洲	America	83.0	97.0	85.6
#美　国	United States	62.9	72.0	87.4
加拿大	Canada	10.0	15.2	66.0
欧　洲	Europe	99.6	101.2	98.4
#英　国	United Kingdom	15.3	15.9	96.0
法　国	France	12.0	12.7	94.8
德　国	Germany	19.8	19.4	101.9
意大利	Italy	6.9	6.5	105.9
西班牙	Spain	4.5	4.8	94.3
瑞　典	Sweden	2.7	3.0	89.6
瑞　士	Switzerland	3.0	3.2	94.2
俄罗斯	Russia	9.6	8.7	109.8
大洋洲	Oceania	16.6	17.4	95.5
#澳大利亚	Australia	14.1	15.0	94.0
新西兰	New Zealand	2.2	2.0	111.1
非　洲	Africa	7.4	8.4	87.8
其　他	Others	1.6	1.5	107.6

资料来源：2018年及以前，“国内游客人数”相关资料来自北京市文化和旅游局。2019年起，本表数据均来自北京市文化和旅游局。
Source: In and before 2018, data related to Number of Domestic Tourists were provided by Beijing Municipal Bureau of Culture and Tourism. Since 2019, all data in this table are provided by Beijing Municipal Bureau of Culture and Tourism.

17-4 在京旅游花费构成情况(2005-2019年)
COMPOSITION OF EXPENDITURES FOR TOURISM IN BEIJING (2005-2019)

单位：% (%)

项目	Item	2005	2006	2007	2008	2009	2010	2011	2012	2013	2014	2015	2016	2017	2018	2019
入境游客花费构成	**Compositition of Expenditures for Inbound Tourists**	**100.0**	**100.0**	**100.0**	**100.0**	**100.0**	**100.0**	**100.0**	**100.0**	**100.0**	**100.0**	**100.0**	**100.0**	**100.0**	**100.0**	**100.0**
长途交通费	Long-distance Transportation Expenses	35.3	30.0	29.0	31.1	37.4	28.1	26.4	28.0	26.9	27.0	36.8	38.3	37.7	27.2	28.4
民航	Air	30.9	29.6	24.4	25.3	27.1	19.8	20.5	22.3	21.2	21.4	30.8	38.0	37.1	26.2	27.6
铁路	Railway	1.1	0.3	3.0	3.6	5.5	5.3	3.4	3.3	3.7	3.6	3.2	0.2	0.4	0.6	0.6
公路	Highway	3.3	0.1	1.6	2.2	4.8	3.0	2.5	2.4	2.0	2.0	2.7	0.1	0.2	0.3	0.2
市内交通费	Local Transportation Expenses	1.1	1.7	2.6	2.4	2.7	3.4	3.5	3.5	2.5	2.6	2.4	2.5	1.4	3.0	4.0
住宿	Accommodation	17.3	32.0	16.9	16.4	14.5	14.4	15.5	16.5	16.9	16.7	12.8	18.3	14.4	19.0	19.0
餐饮	Restaurants	9.2	11.7	8.7	8.7	7.5	8.7	6.8	7.4	7.3	7.4	6.2	11.4	6.8	8.2	9.4
购物	Shopping	19.9	15.9	22.5	19.1	20.4	25.1	25.3	23.5	27.6	26.7	19.9	18.5	27.6	26.0	24.5
邮电通讯	Post and Telecommunications	3.4	0.8	2.7	3.8	2.7	3.2	2.0	2.2	1.7	1.7	2.4	0.2	0.6	0.7	0.4
景区游览	Scenic Spot Sightseeing	4.7	2.3	4.2	4.8	3.9	4.7	4.2	5.0	4.2	4.3	3.3	4.2	2.4	3.9	4.5
文化娱乐	Culture and Entertainment	4.6	3.2	5.0	4.5	4.6	5.0	6.0	5.4	3.8	4.0	4.2	4.6	2.1	2.3	1.4
其他	Others	4.5	2.4	8.4	9.2	6.3	7.4	10.3	8.5	9.1	9.6	12.1	2.0	7.0	9.7	8.3
外地来京游客花费构成	**Compositition of Expenditures for Tourists from Outside Beijing**	**100.0**	**100.0**	**100.0**	**100.0**	**100.0**	**100.0**	**100.0**	**100.0**	**100.0**	**100.0**	**100.0**	**100.0**	**100.0**	**100.0**	**100.0**
长途交通费	Long-distance Transportation Expenses	12.8	15.1	16.3	15.4	12.9	12.8	13.5	15.5	17.0	17.6	17.0	15.8	14.3	12.4	11.8
民航	Air		8.0	9.2	9.1	6.6	6.0	6.2	7.7	7.5	7.1	7.4	7.5	6.2	4.7	4.8
铁路	Railway		6.1	6.4	4.5	1.3	5.8	6.9	7.5	9.1	10.2	9.3	8.0	7.3	6.4	5.8
公路	Highway		1.1	0.7	1.8	5.0	1.0	0.3	0.3	0.4	0.3	0.3	0.3	0.8	1.4	1.2
市内交通费	Local Transportation Expenses	5.7	5.1	5.5	5.6	4.9	5.0	4.5	4.0	3.8	3.8	4.0	3.9	4.1	3.9	4.2
住宿	Accommodation	17.2	14.9	17.3	15.1	17.7	19.6	20.0	19.8	19.5	20.2	18.7	17.8	19.0	18.8	19.1
餐饮	Restaurants	19.8	18.7	20.5	23.2	21.8	20.2	20.9	21.4	21.4	22.1	22.1	22.8	22.2	21.6	21.1
购物	Shopping	24.1	22.2	25.8	32.7	34.5	34.5	34.3	32.1	30.9	28.2	30.2	31.3	31.2	32.4	31.8
邮电通讯	Post and Telecommunications	1.0	1.2	1.8	1.0	0.6	0.5	0.3	0.2	0.2	0.3	0.3	0.2	0.2	0.2	0.2
景区游览	Scenic Spot Sightseeing	9.1	9.5	7.2	4.5	6.1	6.2	5.7	6.1	6.6	6.5	6.2	6.6	7.3	8.0	9.2
文化娱乐	Culture and Entertainment	3.1	2.5	1.9	1.6	1.2	1.0	0.8	0.7	0.5	0.6	0.7	0.9	1.2	1.9	2.0
其他	Others	7.1	10.8	3.7	0.9	0.3	0.2	0.1	0.1	0.1	0.7	0.8	0.7	0.6	0.8	0.8

资料来源：北京市文化和旅游局。
Source: Beijing Municipal Bureau of Culture and Tourism.

17-5 星级饭店接待及经营情况(1995-2019年)

RECEPTION AND OPERATION OF STAR-RATED HOTELS (1995-2019)

年 份 Year	企业个数(个) Number of Enterprises (unit)	接待住宿人数(万人次) Tourists Received (10000 person-time)	接待住宿人天数(万人天) Persons-Day Received (10000 person-day)	出租率(%) Renting Rate (%)	平均房价(元/间天) Average Prices (yuan/room.day)	营业收入(万元) Business Income (10000 yuan)	利润总额(万元) Total Profits (10000 yuan)	从业人员平均人数(人) Average Number of Employed Persons (person)
1995	191	484.6	1843.4	67.0	491	1136136	188095	98535
1996	207	485.3	1691.6	63.0	483	1132827	153145	94352
1997	235	541.8	1801.4	59.0	463	1145884	104918	103255
1998	262	605.0	1867.7	55.0	397	1038991	-24239	104391
1999	263	681.5	1918.6	57.0	352	970907	22383	103827
2000	294	854.5	2830.6	61.0	394	1099739	30661	96115
2001	363	1038.5	3191.7	62.0	384	1202746	50466	105792
2002	390	1071.2	2437.6	62.0	392	1307094	27212	107091
2003	441	1007.4	2497.2	52.0	389	1227956	-33471	105994
2004	464	1270.8	2798.9	65.0	409	1654198	117541	107386
2005	594	1543.6	3227.5	62.0	425	1851166	154283	126817
2006	597	1578.5	3284.5	61.3	460	2055300	194460	126430
2007	638	1664.2	3403.6	60.2	494	2369964	219891	129523
2008	694	1566.1	3206.6	52.0	605	2504849	232746	130609
2009	815	1827.3	3652.8	49.2	430	2261411	-76121	134159
2010	729	2125.4	4173.5	56.4	450	2607769	79464	130050
2011	598	2111.1	4119.6	59.9	482	2853358	162374	128609
2012	612	2101.0	4085.2	60.0	523	3031116	179495	122379
2013	614	1958.8	3769.5	58.4	530	2727974	111669	112512
2014	581	1940.3	3664.6	57.6	513	2568185	12499	99258
2015	528	2008.6	3790.7	60.6	520	2576003	52866	92606
2016	523	2017.1	3704.0	62.6	533	2614497	274585	84868
2017	519	1926.8	3580.6	64.8	572	2575127	297712	76603
2018	419	1902.8	3549.5	66.9	597	2759567	286677	74410
2019	395	1817.4	3320.7	69.8	560	2747721	284366	69399

注：1．表中企业个数为全市星级宾馆饭店数，其余指标1995—1999年为涉外饭店数据，2000年及以后为星级宾馆饭店数据。
　　2．从2011年开始北京市文化和旅游局每年对全市星级饭店进行重新评定，对未达标饭店取消星级。
资料来源：2019年起“出租率”“平均房价”数据来自北京市文化和旅游局。

Note: a) Number of Enterprises refer to the number of star-rated hotels in Beijing, Other indicators covered hotels for foreign tourists for 1995-1999, and star-rated hotels after 2000.
b) From 2011, Beijing Municipal Burean of Culture and Tourism reevalutaed star-rated hotels across the city , and cancelled the rating of hotels that did not meet the standard.

Source:Data related to Renting Rate and Average Prices were provided by Beijing Municipal Bureau of Cultuer and Tourism Since 2019.

17-6 星级饭店出租率和平均房价
RENTING RATE AND AVERAGE PRICES OF STAR-RATED HOTELS

项 目	Item	出租率(%) Renting Rate (%)		平均房价(元/间天) Average Prices (yuan/room.day)	
		2019	2018	2019	2018
合 计	**Total**	**69.8**	**66.9**	**560**	**597**
五 星	5-Star	71.0	69.6	910	877
四 星	4-Star	69.0	69.6	559	543
三 星	3-Star	62.7	63.4	437	419
二星及以下	2-Star and below	60.5	58.8	379	327

资料来源：2019年起“出租率”“平均房价”数据来自北京市文化和旅游局。
Source:Data related to Renting Rate and Average Prices were provided by Beijing Municipal Bureau of Cultuer and Tourism Since 2019.

17-7 星级饭店经营情况
OPERATION OF STAR-RATED HOTELS

项 目	Item	企业个数(个) Number of Enterprises (unit)		营业收入(万元) Business Income (10000 yuan)		利润总额(万元) Total Profits (10000 yuan)		从业人员平均人数(人) Average Number of Employed Persons (person)	
		2019	2018	2019	2018	2019	2018	2019	2018
合 计	**Total**	**395**	**419**	**2747721**	**2759567**	**284366**	**286677**	**69399**	**74410**
四星、五星合计	**Hotels of 4 and 5 Star Grade**	**174**	**180**	**2163066**	**2180846**	**276386**	**284997**	**50538**	**53755**
五 星	5-Star	62	67	1280297	1302281	176246	181206	25947	27908
四 星	4-Star	112	113	882769	878565	100140	103791	24591	25847
一星至三星合计	**Hotels of 1 to 3-Star Grade**	**221**	**239**	**584656**	**578721**	**7980**	**1680**	**18861**	**20655**
三 星	3-Star	156	164	502809	483057	994	-2668	16228	17366
二星及以下	2-Star and below	65	75	81846	95664	6986	4348	2633	3289

17-8 星级饭店接待住宿者情况(按住宿者类别分)
TOURSITS RECEIVED BY STAR-RATED HOTELS (BY TYPE OF TOURISTS)

项　目	Item	接待量 Tourists Received 2019	2018	2019年为2018年% 2019 as % of 2018
接待住宿人数　（万人次）	**Tourists Received　(10000 person-times)**	**1817.4**	**1902.8**	**95.5**
国内住宿者	Domestic Tourists	1639.9	1693.2	96.9
外国人	Foreigners	155.3	182.5	85.1
香港同胞	Compatriots from Hong Kong, China	12.9	15.4	83.7
澳门同胞	Compatriots from Macao, China	0.7	0.8	95.1
台湾同胞	Compatriots from Taiwan, China	8.6	10.9	78.5
接待住宿人天数　（万人天）	**Persons-day Received (10000 persons-day)**	**3320.7**	**3549.5**	**93.6**
国内住宿者	Domestic Tourists	2958.6	3124.9	94.7
外国人	Foreigners	317.8	368.5	86.2
香港同胞	Compatriots from Hong Kong, China	24.7	31.6	78.2
澳门同胞	Compatriots from Macao, China	1.7	1.7	99.9
台湾同胞	Compatriots from Taiwan, China	17.9	22.9	78.2

17-9 星级饭店接待住宿者情况(按饭店星级分)
TOURSITS RECEIVED BY STAR-RATED HOTELS (BY STAR RATING)

单位：万人次　　(10000 person-times)

项　目	Item	接待量 Tourists Received 2019	2018	2019年为2018年% 2019 as % of 2018
接待住宿人数	**Tourists Received**	**1817.4**	**1902.8**	**95.5**
五星级	5-Star	578.8	626.3	92.4
四星级	4-Star	649.0	662.0	98.0
三星级	3-Star	450.2	472.8	95.2
二星级及以下	2-Star and below	139.4	141.8	98.3
接待入境住宿人数	**Inbound Tourists Received**	**177.5**	**209.6**	**84.7**
五星级	5-Star	99.1	122.9	80.6
四星级	4-Star	65.2	72.3	90.2
三星级	3-Star	9.8	10.9	89.6
二星级及以下	2-Star and below	3.5	3.5	99.7

17-10 旅行社接待及经营情况(1990-2019年)
RECEPTION AND OPERATION OF TRAVEL AGENCIES (1990-2019)

年份 Year	企业个数(个) Number of Enterprises (unit)	外联(组团)人数(万人次) Number of Inbound Tourists (Organized) (10000 person-times)	接待人数(万人次) Tourists Received (10000 person-times)	国内居民出境人数(万人次) Number of Outbound Chinese Tourists (10000 person-times)	营业收入(万元) Business Income (10000 yuan)	利润总额(万元) Total Profits (10000 yuan)	从业人员平均人数(人) Average Number of Employed Persons (person)
1990		32.5	54.7				
1991		53.3	69.1				
1992		61.2	100.7				
1993		71.3	103.6				
1994		84.1	91.0	1.0			
1995	100	85.7	87.4	1.2	290987.9	107654.6	
1996	105	88.0	78.6	2.7	351634.7	13520.8	
1997	110	87.3	76.0	3.8	386254.1	16009.6	
1998	131	85.0	69.0	6.6	387562.7	21319.9	
1999	120	103.1	92.9	11.1	485678.8	26572.0	
2000	127	123.7	101.0	13.7	576244.6	28744.7	6280
2001	140	143.4	130.1	21.9	700529.0	18682.5	8259
2002	151	179.4	176.3	28.5	823551.0	23362.0	9350
2003	147	80.2	82.4	31.9	553787.0	-11829.0	8382
2004	147	274.8	252.6	51.4	1059989.0	11444.0	7760
2005	147	308.4	278.2	51.7	1316063.0	10240.0	8752
2006	147	343.9	315.7	79.2	1610265.0	7012.0	8659
2007	189	424.1	377.9	100.2	2101874.5	28409.2	11597
2008	245	359.6	310.1	102.0	2166898.1	18121.6	14369
2009	265	370.6	306.6	84.9	2134058.8	5904.6	15262
2010	819	538.1	542.2	149.6	3517099.4	22636.2	21454
2011	919	593.9	552.3	184.3	4436713.3	20879.2	23871
2012	1021	684.5	519.1	272.5	5415692.9	35274.4	28022
2013	1147	661.3	441.6	331.0	6103603.4	64177.5	31694
2014	1243	628.0	427.0	410.2	6989125.4	27881.7	33591
2015	1238	655.5	468.0	533.1	8355826.3	-17132.1	37780
2016	1162	667.9	466.8	571.3	8788779.0	-29589.9	40812
2017	1139	573.0	422.3	511.5	8819738.7	122815.9	37952
2018	1192	544.5	377.8	510.9	9439120.6	590.2	37660
2019	1440	635.8	455.7	484.5	10394925.9	-6714.6	39779

注：本表2009年及以前为国际旅行社口径，从2010年起调整为全部旅行社口径。
Note: Figures in this table refer to international travel agencies in and before 2009, and all travel agencies after 2010.

17-11 旅行社外联(组团)及接待情况
TOURISTS GROUPED (ORGANIZED) AND RECEIVED BY TRAVEL AGENCIES

项目	Item	2019	2018	2019年为2018年% 2019 as % of 2018
外联(组团)人数 (万人次)	**Tourists Grouped (Organized) (10000 person-times)**	**635.8**	**544.5**	**116.8**
国内旅游者	Domestic Tourists	524.6	451.6	116.2
港澳同胞	Compatriots from Hong Kong and Macao, China	3.1	4.1	75.6
台湾同胞	Compatriots from Taiwan, China	5.0	4.2	120.7
外国人	Foreigners	103.0	84.6	121.8
接待人数 (万人次)	**Tourists Received (10000 person-times)**	**455.7**	**377.8**	**120.6**
国内旅游者	Domestic Tourists	359.5	273.4	131.5
港澳同胞	Compatriots from Hong Kong and Macao, China	4.3	5.6	77.3
台湾同胞	Compatriots from Taiwan, China	3.8	3.9	98.5
外国人	Foreigners	88.1	94.9	92.8
外联(组团)人天数(万人天)	**Persons-day of Tourists Grouped (Organized) (10000 persons-day)**	**3046.5**	**2184.2**	**139.5**
国内旅游者	Domestic Tourists	2551.0	1716.1	148.7
港澳同胞	Compatriots from Hong Kong and Macao, China	13.0	20.0	65.1
台湾同胞	Compatriots from Taiwan, China	25.4	22.5	112.9
外国人	Foreigners	457.0	425.6	107.4
接待人天数 (万人天)	**Persons-day of Tourists Received (10000 persons-day)**	**1833.9**	**1465.8**	**125.1**
国内旅游者	Domestic Tourists	1439.9	1044.4	137.9
港澳同胞	Compatriots from Hong Kong and Macao, China	20.6	27.9	73.9
台湾同胞	Compatriots from Taiwan, China	17.1	18.9	90.3
外国人	Foreigners	356.3	374.6	95.1

17-12 旅行社组织国内居民出境旅游情况
OUTBOUND CHINESE TOURISTS ORGANIZED BY TRAVEL AGENCIES

单位：万人次 (10000 person-times)

项 目	Item	2019	2018	2019年为2018年% 2019 as % of 2018
旅行社个数(个)	**Number of Travel Agencies (unit)**	**517**	**426**	**121.4**
国内居民出境人数	**Number of Outbound Chinese Tourists**	**484.5**	**510.9**	**94.8**
前往国别及地区	**Countries and Regions of Destination**			
#中国香港	Hong Kong, China	10.5	12.0	87.0
中国澳门	Macao, China	11.4	10.6	106.9
中国台湾	Taiwan, China	4.9	4.6	107.8
泰 国	Thailand	50.8	73.9	68.8
新加坡	Singapore	13.1	10.3	126.8
马来西亚	Malaysia	11.9	11.7	101.7
菲律宾	Philippines	11.2	17.1	65.6
韩 国	Korea	20.7	20.3	102.0
日 本	Japan	95.6	82.2	116.3
澳大利亚	Australia	15.6	8.9	174.2
新西兰	New Zealand	6.4	4.9	128.6

注：1. 国内居民出境人数统计中，游客一次出境旅游去往多个国家及地区的，只统计一次，不重复统计。
2. 前往国别及地区统计中，游客一次出境旅游去往多个国家及地区的，分别计入前往国家及地区。

Note: a) In the statistics for number of outbound Chinese tourists, if a tourist went to several countries and regions, is counted only once, which has not been calculated repeatedly.
b) In the statistics for "countries and regions of destination", if a tourist went to several countries and regions, he/she would be included in each country and region.

17-13 旅行社经营情况
OPERATION OF TRAVEL SERVICES

单位：万元 (10000 yuan)

项　目	Item	2019	2018	2019年为2018年% 2019 as % of 2018
企业个数 (个)	Number of Enterprises (unit)	1440	1192	120.8
营业收入	Business Income	10394926	9439121	110.1
营业成本	Business Cost	9661304	8823907	109.5
营业费用	Business Expenses	413295	392141	105.4
营业税金及附加	Business Tax and Surtax	9177	8604	106.7
管理费用	Management Expenses	346818	303186	114.4
营业利润	Business Profits	-12941	-21967	
利润总额	Total Profits	-6715	590	
从业人员平均人数 (人)	Average Number of Employed Persons (person)	39779	37660	105.6

17-14 A级及以上和重点旅游景区活动情况
STATISTICS FOR KEY SIGHT SPOTS ABOVE GRADE A

项　目	Item	2019	2018	2019年为2018年% 2019 as % of 2018
A级及以上和重点旅游景区数 (个)	Number of Key Sight Spots Above Grade (unit)	244	247	98.8
收入合计 (万元)	Total Income (10000 yuan)	882511	867894	101.7
门票收入	Ticket Income	523709	503235	104.1
商品销售收入	Commodity Sales	30904	29946	103.2
其他收入	Other Income	327899	334714	98.0
接待人数 (万人次)	Tourists Received (10000 person-times)	31772	31131	102.1
#入境旅游者人数	Inbound Tourists	681	753	90.4

主要统计指标解释

入境游客 指来中国（大陆）观光、度假、探亲访友、就医疗养、购物、参加会议或从事经济、文化、体育、宗教活动，且在中国（大陆）的旅游住宿设施内至少停留一夜的外国人、港澳台同胞等游客。入境游客不包括以下人员：(1) 应邀来华访问的政府部长以上官员及其随行人员；(2) 外国驻华使领馆官员、外交人员以及随行的家庭服务人员和受赡养者；(3) 常住中国（大陆）一年以上的外国专家、留学生、记者、商务机构人员等；(4) 乘坐国际航班过境不需要通过护照检查进入中国（大陆）口岸的中转旅客；(5) 边境地区往来的边民；(6) 回大陆定居的港澳台同胞；(7) 已在中国（大陆）定居的外国人和原已出境又返回在中国（大陆）定居的外国侨民；(8) 归国的中国（大陆）出国人员。

国内游客 指中国（大陆）居民离开惯常居住地在境内其他地方的旅游住宿设施内至少停留一夜，最长不超过 12 个月的国内游客。

国际旅游收入 指入境游客在中国（大陆）境内旅行、游览过程中用于交通、参观游览、住宿、餐饮、购物、娱乐等全部花费。

国内旅游收入 指国内游客在国内旅行、游览过程中用于交通、参观游览、住宿、餐饮、购物、娱乐等全部花费。

外联（组团）入境旅游者人数 指报告期内旅行社自组外联的入境旅游者人数，反映旅行社对外招徕的能力。旅行社按以下要求统计外联人数：入境游客不论其停留时间多少、旅游线路长短，只统计一次；旅行社只统计本社自组外联团的实到人数，不包括非本社外联、仅由本社接受委托办理签证的人数。

接待入境旅游者人数 指报告期内本旅行社派地陪接待的入境人数。

出境旅游总人数 指中国（大陆）公民因公或因私出境前往其他国家、中国香港特别行政区、澳门特别行政区和台湾省观光、度假、探亲访友、就医疗养、购物、参加会议或从事经济、文化、体育、宗教活动的人数。统计时，出境游客按每出境一次统计 1 人次。

Explanatory Notes on Main Statistical Indicators

Inbound Tourists refer to tourists from foreign countries, Hong Kong, Macao and Taiwan to (mainland of) China for sightseeing, holidays, visiting relatives and friends, medical service and rehabilitation, shopping, conferences, or economic, cultural, sports and religious activities, and staying in a tour accommodation facility in (the mainland of) China for at least one night. They do not include: (1) officials above the rank of governmental ministers, and their accompanying persons who visit China upon invitation; (2) officials in foreign embassies and consulates in China, diplomatic personnel, and their accompanying family service personnel and dependents; (3) foreign experts, students, reporters, and personnel in business institutions who have been in (the mainland of) China for more than one year; (4) transit passengers via (the mainland of) China by international flights without passport checking; (5) people living on the frontiers who pass through borders; (6) compatriots from Hong Kong, Macao and Taiwan who settle down in the mainland of China; (7) Foreigners that have settled down in China and foreign nationals that have left the country and then come back to settle down in (the mainland of) China; (8) Chinese (mainland) people who have gone abroad and returned to China.

Domestic Tourists refer to domestic visitors as residents in (the mainland of) China who leave their regular dwelling places to stay at least one night and at most 12 months in a travel accommodation facility of other domestic places.

Revenue from Inbound Tourism means the total spending of inbound tourists on traffic, tour, accommodation, restaurants, shopping, entertainment and so on during their tour and travel in (the mainland of) China.

Revenue from Domestic Tourism means the total spending of domestic tourists on traffic, tour, accommodation, restaurants, shopping and entertainment, and so on during their tour and travel in China.

Number of Inbound Tourists Organized by Travel Agencies means the number of inbound tourists organized by travel agencies in the reporting period. It shows the capacity of travel agencies in attracting inbound tourists; travel agencies shall count the tourists organized as follows: an inbound tourist is regarded as one visit regardless of the duration and distance of the tour; only the actual tourists organized by travel agencies are included. Those organized by other travel agencies or those who have visa submitted by the travel agencies are not included.

Number of Inbound Tourists Received means the number of inbound tourists received by local guides dispatched by travel agencies in the reporting period.

Total Number of Outbound Tourists means the number of citizens from (the mainland of) China who visit other countries, Hong Kong Special Administrative Region of PRC, Macao Special Administrative Region of PRC, and Taiwan for sightseeing, holiday, visiting relatives and friends, medical service and rehabilitation, shopping, conferences, or economic, cultural, sport and religious activities for official or private purpose. One visit is calculated as one person-time.

18

金融业
FINANCE

简要说明

主要内容

本章资料主要包括金融机构信贷收支情况、证券市场交易情况、保险业务情况、上市公司基本情况。

Brief Introduction

Main Content

Statistics in this chapter mainly consist of the balance of credit for financial institutions, transactions in securities market, insurance business, and basic information of listed companies.

18-1 北京市金融机构(含外资)存贷款余额(1978-2019年)
DEPOSIT AND LOAN BALANCE OF FINANCIAL INSTITUTIONS (INCLUDING FOREIGN BANKS) (1978-2019)

单位：亿元 (100 million yuan)

年份 Year	金融机构本外币存款余额 Balance of Savings Deposit in Domestic and Foreign Currencies in Financial Institutions	#人民币存款 RMB Deposits	金融机构本外币存款 Deposits in Domestic and Foreign Currencies in Financial Institutions					
			中资金融机构存款合计 Total Deposits in Chinese Financial Institutions	#人民币存款 RMB Deposits	#外汇(亿美元) Foreign Exchange (USD 100 million)	外资银行存款合计 Total Deposits in Foreign-funded Financial Bank	#人民币存款 RMB Deposits	#外汇(亿美元) Foreign Exchange (USD 100 million)
1978				114.7				
1979				139.1				
1980				168.0				
1981				220.5				
1982				279.2				
1983				321.3				
1984				375.5				
1985				411.0				
1986				508.8				
1987				610.8				
1988				609.9				
1989				717.6				
1990				893.9				
1991				1244.1				
1992				1528.3				
1993				1873.1				
1994				2677.3				
1995				3527.2				
1996				4378.9				
1997				5228.0				
1998				6666.8				
1999				8267.2				
2000	11526.0		11461.8	9759.8	205.6			…
2001	14109.2		14042.1	12223.4	219.8			7.3
2002	17438.4		17369.9	15392.7	238.9			8.3
2003	20476.0		20398.2	18321.9	250.9			9.4
2004	23781.3	21625.9	23679.3	21625.9	248.1			12.3
2005	28969.9	26785.9	28800.9	26731.3	256.4		54.6	14.2
2006	33793.3	31313.8	33484.1	31179.2	295.2		134.5	22.4
2007	37700.3	35369.7	37087.5	35014.1	283.8		355.6	35.2
2008	43980.7	42107.6	43094.4	41500.0	233.3	886.3	607.5	40.8
2009	56960.1	54275.5	55804.8	53428.8	348.0	1155.3	846.6	45.2
2010	66584.6	64453.9	64897.6	63025.2	282.7	1687.0	1428.7	39.0
2011	75001.9	72655.4	73018.9	70985.1	322.8	1983.1	1670.3	49.6
2012	84837.3	81389.6	82615.9	79620.6	476.5	2221.4	1769.1	72.0
2013	91660.5	87990.6	89187.4	85897.2	539.6	2473.1	2093.4	62.3
2014	100095.5	95370.5	97645.9	93326.0	706.0	2449.6	2044.5	66.2
2015	128573.0	123767.4	126164.8	121878.9	660.0	2461.0	1941.3	80.0
2016	138408.9	132791.9	135510.3	130648.0	700.9	2933.1	2178.5	108.8
2017	144086.0	137952.1	141013.6	135501.4	843.6	3155.7	2534.0	95.1
2018	157092.2	150430.4	154237.3	148136.3	888.9	2960.6	2399.8	81.7
2019	171062.3	164349.5	168238.8	162063.9	885.1	2931.3	2393.4	77.1

资料来源：中国人民银行营业管理部。
Source: Operations Office of People's Bank of China.

18-1 续表 Continued

单位：亿元 (100 million yuan)

年 份 Year	金融机构本外币贷款余额 Balance of Loans in Domestic and Foreign Currencies in Financial Institutions	#人民币贷款 RMB Loans	#中长期贷款 Medium-term &Long-term Loans	金融机构本外币贷款 Loans in Domestic and Foreign Currencies in Financial Institutions					
				中资金融机构贷款合计 Total Loans in Chinese Financial Institutions	#人民币贷款 RMB Loans	#外汇(亿美元) Foreign Exchange (USD 100 million)	外资银行贷款合计 Total Loans in Foreign-funded Financial Bank	#人民币贷款 RMB Loans	#外汇(亿美元) Foreign Exchange (USD 100 million)
1978					53.9				
1979					74.2				
1980					87.3				
1981					91.3				
1982					109.1				
1983					149.5				
1984					174.3				
1985					249.8				
1986					299.2				
1987					346.1				
1988					415.7				
1989					487.1				
1990					573.1				
1991					735.8				
1992					894.7				
1993					1128.1				
1994					1429.0				
1995					1779.1				
1996					2082.8				
1997					2720.7				
1998					3326.6				
1999					4007.8				
2000	6407.9		3106.7	6306.3	6008.2	27.7			9.0
2001	7612.2		3797.3	7514.9	7202.9	37.4			10.8
2002	9704.3		5026.9	9602.6	9230.8	44.9			12.1
2003	12057.7		6352.0	11884.4	11314.7	68.8			20.9
2004	13577.7		7506.4	13312.3	12600.2	86.0			32.0
2005	15335.5		8632.4	14996.6	13792.2	149.2		42.3	36.8
2006	18131.6	15632.7	11142.8	17631.7	15486.9	274.7		145.8	45.4
2007	19861.5	17812.5	12217.6	19053.9	17360.2	231.9	807.5	452.3	48.6
2008	23010.7	19985.0	14688.9	22160.5	19431.1	399.4	850.2	554.0	43.3
2009	31052.9	25421.8	21163.8	30151.6	24805.1	783.0	901.3	616.7	41.7
2010	36479.6	29563.8	26180.2	35352.0	28748.1	997.2	1127.6	815.6	47.1
2011	39660.5	33367.0	24886.3	38410.3	32434.6	948.4	1250.2	932.5	50.4
2012	43189.5	36441.3	26333.5	41839.8	35441.7	1017.9	1349.7	999.6	55.7
2013	47880.9	40506.7	28171.7	46539.5	39557.5	1145.2	1341.4	949.2	64.3
2014	53650.6	45458.7	30882.3	52254.3	44438.8	1277.3	1396.2	1019.9	61.5
2015	58559.4	50559.5	33671.3	57281.2	49530.8	1193.6	1994.3	1676.9	48.9
2016	63739.4	56618.9	37471.3	62492.2	55553.2	1000.3	2005.9	1725.8	40.4
2017	69556.2	63382.5	42001.7	68091.3	62132.4	911.9	2275.3	1945.2	50.5
2018	70483.7	66767.0	42948.9	69071.1	65520.3	517.4	1865.9	1641.2	32.7
2019	76875.6	73575.9	42861.7	75336.5	72177.0	452.9	1744.6	1589.7	22.2

18-2 北京市金融机构(含外资)本外币信贷收支情况(2019年)
BALANCE OF CREDIT IN DOMESTIC AND FOREIGN CURRENCIES FOR FINANCIAL INSTITUTIONS (INCLUDING FOREIGN BANKS)(2019)

单位：亿元，汇率：6.9762 (100 million yuan ,at an exchange rate of 6.9762)

项目	Item	余额 Balance	比年初增减额(+、-) Increase or Decrease than the Beginning of the Year
各项存款	**Total Deposits**	**171062.3**	**13922.4**
#人民币存款	RMB Deposits	164349.5	13874.7
境内存款	Domestic Deposits	168960.7	13800.1
住户存款	Resident Deposits	38865.0	4804.1
非金融企业存款	Non-financial Corporate Deposits	60346.2	3547.8
机关团体存款	General Government Deposits	40362.0	2115.0
财政性存款	Fiscal Deposits	1572.1	-110.1
非银行业金融机构存款	Deposits of Non-banking Financial Institutions	27815.3	3443.4
境外存款	Overseas Deposits	2101.6	122.3
各项贷款	**Total Loans**	**76875.6**	**6232.9**
#人民币贷款	RMB Loans	73575.9	6653.5
境内贷款	Domestic Loans	75273.8	6818.5
住户贷款	Resident Loans	19116.8	1115.7
非金融企业及机关团体贷款	Loans of Non-financial Companies and Organizations	55530.9	5520.7
非银行业金融机构贷款	Loans of Non-banking Financial Institutions	626.1	182.1
境外贷款	Overseas Loans	1601.8	-585.6

资料来源：中国人民银行营业管理部。
Source: Operations Office of People's Bank of China.

18-3 北京市中资金融机构本外币信贷收支情况(2019年)
BALANCE OF CREDIT IN DOMESTIC AND FOREIGN CURRENCIES FOR DOMESTICALLY-FUNDED FINANCIAL INSTITUTIONS(2019)

单位：亿元，汇率：6.9762 (100 million yuan ,at an exchange rate of 6.9762)

项　目	Item	余　额 Balance	比年初增减额(+、-) Increase or Decrease than Year-beginning
各项存款	**Total Deposits**	**168238.8**	**13954.2**
#人民币存款	RMB Deposits	162063.9	13883.2
境内存款	Domestic Deposits	166376.9	13834.1
住户存款	Resident Deposits	38541.3	4777.4
非金融企业存款	Non-financial Corporate Deposits	58118.9	3560.4
机关团体存款	General Government Deposits	40361.7	2115.0
财政性存款	Fiscal Deposits	1572.1	-110.1
非银行业金融机构存款	Deposits of Non-banking Financial Institutions	27782.9	3491.3
境外存款	Overseas Deposits	1861.9	120.1
各项贷款	**Total Loans**	**75336.5**	**6106.4**
#人民币贷款	RMB Loans	72177.0	6501.3
境内贷款	Domestic Loans	73806.8	6689.1
住户贷款	Resident Loans	18885.9	1100.7
非金融企业及机关团体贷款	Loans of Non-financial Companies and Organizations	54294.8	5406.3
非银行业金融机构贷款	Loans of Non-banking Financial Institutions	626.1	182.1
境外贷款	Overseas Loans	1529.7	-582.7

资料来源：中国人民银行营业管理部。
Source: Operations Office of People's Bank of China.

18-4 银行、保险系统机构及人员(2019年)
INSTITUTIONS AND PERSONNEL OF BANKING AND INSURANCE SYSTEMS (2019)

项　　目	Item	银行系统 Banking System		保险系统 Insurance System	
		机　构(个) Institutions (unit)	人　员(人) Personnel (person)	机　构(个) Institutions (unit)	人　员(人) Personnel (person)
合　计	**Total**	**3767**	**201410**	**715**	**207783**
东 城 区	Dongcheng District	272	18499	74	32695
西 城 区	Xicheng District	396	82039	81	37111
朝 阳 区	Chaoyang District	834	24315	150	50973
丰 台 区	Fengtai District	327	16777	41	6324
石景山区	Shijingshan District	117	8209	22	5830
海 淀 区	Haidian District	650	29409	54	15203
门头沟区	Mentougou District	58	1593	10	871
房 山 区	Fangshan District	123	2115	39	7156
通 州 区	Tongzhou District	168	3244	43	9686
顺 义 区	Shunyi District	153	3137	36	9092
昌 平 区	Changping District	166	3047	40	9562
大 兴 区	Daxing District	203	4070	34	5204
怀 柔 区	Huairou District	88	1321	21	4478
平 谷 区	Pinggu District	79	1252	32	4963
密 云 区	Miyun District	82	1410	23	5689
延 庆 区	Yanqing District	51	973	15	2946

注：1．本表口径为在北京地区经营的银行、保险公司的总行(总公司)、分行(分公司)及所属分支机构。
　　2．保险系统人员构成中含营销员。

Note: a) Figures in this table cover the headquarters (head offices), branches banks (branch companies) and subsidiaries of banks and insurance companies operating in Beijing.
b) Personnel of insurance system includes marketing personnel.

18–5 上市公司基本情况(1993–2019年)
LISTED COMPANIES (1993-2019)

年 份 Year	年末上市公司(家) Companies Listed by Year-end (unit)	上市公司总股本(万股) Total Equity of Listed Companies (10000 Shares)	股票首发数量(万股) Initial Public Offering Shares (10000 Shares)	首发募集资金(亿元) Funds Raised Through IPO (10000 yuan)	增发募集资金(亿元) Funds Raised Through Right Offerings (10000 yuan)	配股募集资金(亿元) Funds Raised Through Seasoned Equity Offerings (10000 yuan)
1993	3	24592	3924	58.0		28.8
1994	7	124038	20300	11.7		0.5
1995	7	133309				3.8
1996	13	198956	29763	12.8		1.9
1997	26	470026	80200	52.2		7.0
1998	33	723561	52750	32.9		20.2
1999	43	1439894	121242	63.0	10.8	10.7
2000	54	2015049	156000	143.5	22.2	46.0
2001	63	9764783	345500	191.6		17.0
2002	68	11929954	23800	16.8	14.9	
2003	74	11493598	373600	188.7	2.8	2.2
2004	83	12553074	21300	16.7	28.4	7.1
2005	83	13159721			3.1	
2006	92	58156652	2667911	1073.4	79.4	
2007	104	86151941	2428976	2433.3	304.7	12.1
2008	109	90486962	698853	546.9	502.0	63.8
2009	126	97911881	2179290	1154.2	430.7	
2010	165	137726461	3481552	1298.3	348.7	777.0
2011	194	143088054	420483	462.0	661.7	175.6
2012	217	146788089	211752	191.4	436.2	69.1
2013	219	151694399			183.9	32.5
2014	235	214359521	67787	74.9	1319.0	4.9
2015	264	225020500	532142	312.5	1423.3	
2016	281	232028500	149046	130.3	1859.3	49.4
2017	306	240045300	224743	127.0	1281.4	7.7
2018	316	255999835	266223	127.3	1963.8	10.7
2019	346	269765900	1222741	686.7	924.0	

注：1. 本表数据按注册地统计。
2. 1995年、2005年和2013年无新股发行。
资料来源：中国证券监督管理委员会北京证监局。
Note: a) Statistics in this table are counted in terms of registered area.
b) There were no shares issued in 1995, 2005 and 2013.
Source: Beijing Regulatory Bureau of China Securities Regulatory Commission.

18-6 证券市场交易情况(2000-2019年)
STATISTICS FOR TRADING IN SECURITIES MARKETS (2000-2019)

单位：亿元 (100 million yuan)

年 份 Year	证券市场交易额 Trading Volume of Securities Market	#股票交易 Stock Trading	#基金交易 Fund Trading
2000	14727.2	9546.2	376.2
2001	12734.2	6473.1	401.2
2002	12827.0	4504.4	269.4
2003	24703.7	5492.9	152.3
2004	22169.4	7290.1	100.2
2005	12930.0	5352.1	69.1
2006	22639.7	15233.3	353.4
2007	92468.8	76476.3	1512.4
2008	71281.5	49581.7	734.0
2009	119975.9	95815.6	1229.3
2010	129495.2	100366.0	1354.0
2011	148956.4	80737.8	2028.9
2012	190779.0	62644.5	2413.6
2013	318274.3	92020.5	3732.5
2014	450773.4	138493.4	10557.4
2015	918064.8	453359.2	32363.6
2016	859649.2	208613.3	31085.7
2017	1000257.0	194744.7	22105.7
2018	911465.7	149887.0	25144.4
2019	946425.6	185027.5	25041.5

注：本表数据来源于上海证券交易所和深圳证券交易所公布的分地区数据。
Note: Data in this table are derived from the regional data published by Shanghai Stock Exchange and Shenzhen Stock Exchange.

18-7 保险业务情况(1997-2019年)
INSURANCE BUSINESS (1997-2019)

单位：亿元 (100 million yuan)

年 份 Year	原保险 保费收入 Premium Income of Original Insurance	人身险 Life Insurance	财产险 Property Insurance	赔付 支 出 Compensation Expenses	人身险 Life Insurance	财产险 Property Insurance
1997	102.5					
1998	88.6					
1999	91.8			29.9		
2000	93.4			28.4		
2001	141.3			32.0		
2002	234.1			46.9		
2003	282.5			48.0		
2004	279.3			55.3		
2005	498.2			75.4		
2006	411.5	327.2	84.4	84.0	45.1	38.9
2007	498.1	386.3	111.8	135.4	85.7	49.7
2008	585.9	451.8	134.1	188.9	121.0	67.9
2009	697.6	533.2	164.4	196.0	110.6	85.4
2010	966.5	754.2	212.3	199.7	105.9	93.7
2011	820.9	588.4	232.6	232.8	113.8	119.0
2012	923.1	656.1	267.0	286.2	133.9	152.3
2013	994.4	706.4	288.0	318.2	152.9	165.3
2014	1207.2	892.5	314.8	407.2	224.6	182.7
2015	1403.9	1059.2	344.7	506.6	300.0	206.6
2016	1839.0	1469.7	369.2	596.6	367.3	229.3
2017	1973.2	1568.8	404.4	577.7	365.3	212.5
2018	1793.3	1370.7	422.7	629.4	383.5	245.9
2019	2076.5	1621.6	454.8	719.0	449.6	269.3

资料来源：中国保险监督管理委员会北京监管局。
Source: Beijing Regulatory Bureau of China Insurance Regulatory Commission.

18−8 保险业务情况
STATISTICS FOR INSURANCE BUSINESS

单位：亿元 (100 million yuan)

项　　目	Item	原保险保费收入 Premium Income of Original Insurance		赔付支出 Compensation Expenses	
		2019	2018	2019	2018
合　　计	**Total**	**2076.5**	**1793.3**	**719.0**	**629.4**
人身险业务小计	**Subtotal of Life Insurance**	**1621.6**	**1370.7**	**449.6**	**383.5**
人寿保险	Life Insurance	1162.6	990.3	320.4	273.4
非分红产品	Non-participating Products	599.0	481.1	129.4	54.4
分红产品	Participating Products	559.1	505.2	190.0	218.0
投资连接产品	Investment-linked Products	0.4	0.4	0.1	0.1
万能产品	Universal Products	4.1	3.6	0.9	1.0
意外伤害保险	Accident Insurance	58.3	64.5	14.7	16.5
健康保险	Health Insurance	400.7	315.9	114.5	93.6
财产险业务小计	**Subtotal of Property Insurance**	**454.8**	**422.7**	**269.3**	**245.9**
#企业财产保险	Enterprise Property Insurance	42.5	39.2	17.2	23.2
家庭财产保险	Household Property Insurance	7.3	6.1	3.6	2.3
机动车辆及第三者责任保险	Motor Vehicle and Third Party Liability Insurance	268.2	271.9	171.0	170.2
货物运输保险	Freight Transport Insurance	11.7	11.4	4.4	5.2
责任保险	Liability Insurance	53.8	45.1	25.8	22.5
工程险	Construction Insurance	11.4	8.7	4.7	3.9

资料来源：中国保险监督管理委员会北京监管局。
Source: Beijing Regulatory Bureau of China Insurance Regulatory Commission.

主要统计指标解释

存款 企业、机关、团体或居民根据可以收回的原则，把货币资金存入银行或其他信用机构保管并取得一定利息的一种信用活动形式。根据存款对象的不同可划分为非金融企业存款、财政性存款、机关团体存款、住户存款、非银行金融机构存款等科目。它是银行信贷资金的主要来源。

贷款 银行或其他信用机构根据必须归还的原则，按一定利率，为企业、个人等提供资金的一种信用活动形式。我国银行贷款分为短期贷款、中长期贷款、委托及信托类贷款、其他类贷款等。

原保险保费收入 是指保险企业确认的原保险合同保费收入。是投保人根据保险合同的有关规定，为被保险人取得因约定危险事故发生所造成的经济损失补偿（或给付）权利，付给保险人的代价。包括财产险和人身险收入。

保险赔付支出 公司按保险合同约定支付给被保险人（或受益人）的赔款、保险金、给付等。包括赔款支出、死伤医疗给付、满期给付和年金给付。

股票交易额 在统计期末北京地区证券营业部在上海证券交易所和深圳证券交易所的股票交易金额。

基金交易额 在统计期末北京地区证券营业部在上海证券交易所和深圳证券交易所的基金交易金额。

Explanatory Notes on Main Statistical Indicators

Deposit is a form of credit activity that enterprises, public institutions, groups or residents save their money, on a reclaimable basis, in banks or other credit institutions and receive certain interest. In terms of depositors, there are non-financial enterprise deposit, fiscal deposit, government agency deposit, household deposit, non-bank financial institution deposit and so on, which constitute a main source of bank funds for extending credit.

Loan is a form of credit activity that banks or other credit institutions provide funds which must be repaid for enterprise and individuals at a given interest rate. In China, bank loans are classified as short-, medium-, and long-term loans, entrusted and trust loans, and others.

Premium Income means the income of insurance premium of original insurance contracts confirmed by insurance companies. It is the price paid by policy holders to the insurer for the right to receive compensation (claim settlement) for any economic loss caused by agreed dangerous accidents pursuant to relevant provisions in the insurance contract. There are property insurance and life insurance incomes.

Insurance Indemnity Payments refer to indemnity, insurance money, and claim settlement, etc. paid by the insurance company to the insurant (or beneficiary) as agreed in the insurance contract, including indemnity payment, claim settlement for medical costs of death and injury, maturity payment and annuity payment.

Stock Market Turnover means the transaction amount of stocks traded by Beijing securities sales departments in Shanghai Stock Exchange and Shenzhen Stock Exchange, by the end of the statistical period.

Funds Turnover means the transaction amount of funds traded by Beijing securities sales departments in Shanghai Stock Exchange and Shenzhen Stock Exchange, by the end of the statistical period.

19

科 技
SCIENCE AND TECHNOLOGY

简要说明

一、主要内容

本章资料主要包括研究与试验发展（R&D）人员情况，研究与试验发展（R&D）经费情况，研究与试验发展（R&D）项目（课题）情况，研究机构情况，规模以上工业企业 R&D 活动基本情况，限额以上信息传输、软件和信息技术服务业企业研究与试验发展(R&D)活动基本情况，规模以上高技术制造业主要科技指标，高等学校科技活动情况、研究与开发机构研发活动、专利申请及授权情况等。

二、统计范围

国民经济中研究与试验发展（R&D）活动相对密集行业的法人单位，主要数据包括：农、林、牧、渔业，采矿业，制造业，电力、热力、燃气及水的生产和供应业，建筑业，交通运输、仓储和邮政业，信息传输、软件和信息技术服务业，金融业，租赁和商务服务业，科学研究和技术服务业，水利、环境和公共设施管理业，教育，卫生和社会工作，文化、体育和娱乐业，公共管理、社会保障和社会组织等。

三、有关统计标准的变化说明

（一）关于行业划分。2017 年及以前执行《国民经济行业分类》（GB/T 4754–2011）标准，2018 年起执行《国民经济行业分类》（GB/T 4754—2017）标准。

（二）关于三次产业划分。2003 年，根据《国民经济行业分类》（GB/T 4754—2002），国家统计局印发了《国家统计局关于印发〈三次产业划分规定〉的通知》（国统字〔2003〕14 号）。2012 年，根据国家质检总局和国家标准委颁布的《国民经济行业分类》（GB/T 4754—2011），国家统计局对 2003 年《三次产业划分规定》进行了修订。主要在以下方面作出调整：一是将门类“农、林、牧、渔业”中的“农、林、牧、渔服务业”，“采矿业”中的“开采辅助活动”，“制造业”中的“金属制品、机械和设备修理业”等三个大类一并调整到第三产业。调整后，第一产业为 4 个大类；第二产业为 2 个门类和 36 个大类；第三产业为 15 个门类和 3 个大类。二是明确第三产业即为服务业。

本章 2012 年及以后三次产业的分类执行调整后的划分规定。

（三）关于高技术制造业。根据国家统计局《关于印发高技术产业（制造业）分类（2013）的通知》（国统字〔2013〕55 号），本分类在《高技术产业统计分类目录》（国统字〔2002〕33 号）的基础上修订完成，采用了原分类的基本结构框架。自 2013 年开始执行此标准。

Brief Introduction

I. Main Content

Statistics in this chapter mainly consist of the situation of R&D personnel, R&D funds, R&D projects (tasks), research institutions, basic information on R&D activities of industrial enterprises above designated size, basic information on R&D activities of information transmission, software and information technology service enterprises above designated size, major science and technology indicators of high-tech manufacturing above designated size, scientific and technological activities of colleges and universities, R&D activities of research and development institutions, patent application and licensing, etc.

II. Scope of Statistics

Included in this chapter are the corporate entities in sectors with relatively intensive R&D activities in national economy, such as agriculture, forestry, animal production and hunting, fishing, mining, manufacturing, generation and distribution of electricity, heating, gas and water, construction, transport, storage and post, scientific research and development, technology services, information transmission, software and information technology services, finance, renting and leasing activities and business services, management of water conservancy, environment and public facilities, education, healthcare and social works, culture, sports and entertainment, public administration, social security and social organizations, etc.

III. Changes in Relevant Statistical Standards

(I) Classification of Sectors. The standards in the *Classification of National Economic Sectors* (GB/T 4754-2011) were implemented before 2017. The standards in the *Classification of National Economic Sectors (GB/T 4754-2017) are implemented since 2018.*

(II) Classification of Three Industries. According to the *Classification of National Economic Sectors* (GB/T 4754-2002), the National Bureau of Statistics issued the *Notice of the National Bureau of Statistics on the Issuance of the 'Regulations on Three Industries Classification'* (G.T.Z. [2003] No. 14) in 2003. According to the *Classification of National Economic Sectors* (GB/T 4754-2011) promulgated by the General Administration of Quality Supervision, Inspection and Quarantine of the People's Republic of China and the Standardization Administration of the People's Republic of China, the National Bureau of Statistics revised the *Regulations on Three Industries Classification* of 2003 version in 2012. Adjustments were mainly made in the following aspects: Firstly, the "service activities for agriculture, forestry, animal husbandry and fishing" in the category of "agriculture, forestry, animal production and hunting, fishing", the "mining support service activities" in the category of "mining and quarrying", and the "repair of fabricated metal products, machinery and equipment" in the category of "manufacturing" were adjusted to the tertiary industry. After adjustment, the primary industry fell into 4 categories; the secondary industry fell into 2 classes and 36 categories; and the tertiary industry fell into 15 classes and 3 categories. Secondly, the tertiary industry was defined as the service industry.

The classification of three industries since 2012 as mentioned in this chapter has all been subject to the classification provisions after adjustment.

(III) High-tech Manufacturing. According to the *Circular of National Bureau of Statistics on Printing and Issuing the Classification of High-tech Industry (Manufacturing) 2013* (G.T.Z. [2013] No. 55). This Classification is revised on the basis of *Classified Catalog of High-tech Industry Statistics* (G.T.Z. [2002] No. 33), following the structure of the original classification. The standard has been put in place since 2013.

19-1 科技活动及专利情况(1985-2019年)
SCIENCE AND TECHNOLOGY ACTIVITIES AND PATENTS (1985-2019)

年 份 Year	科技活动人员(人) Personnel Engaged in Science and Technology Activities (person)	研究与试验发展(R&D)人员折合全时当量(人年) Full-time Equivalent of R&D Professionals (person-year)	研究与试验发展(R&D)经费内部支出(万元) Internal R&D Expenditures (10000 yuan)	研究与试验发展(R&D)经费内部支出相当于地区生产总值比例(%) Internal R&D Expenditures as Percentage of GDP (%)
1985				
1986				
1987				
1988				
1989				
1990				
1991	228167			
1992	247525			
1993	252811			
1994	240386			
1995	252232			
1996	265552	84793	418614	2.32
1997	273161	84913	532257	2.54
1998	237127	86602	861138	3.58
1999	229584	85740	938437	3.46
2000	261113	98723	1557011	4.85
2001	240609	95255	1711696	4.54
2002	257326	114919	2195402	4.99
2003	270921	110358	2562518	5.02
2004	301202	152132	3169064	5.14
2005	383153	177765	3795450	5.31
2006	382756	168875	4329878	5.21
2007	450331	204668	5270591	5.23
2008	450147	200080	6200983	5.44
2009	529985	191779	6686351	5.38
2010	529811	193718	8218234	5.69
2011	605980	217255	9366440	5.63
2012	651003	235493	10633640	5.59
2013	681346	242175	11850469	5.61
2014	726792	245384	12687953	5.53
2015	747461	245728	13840231	5.59
2016	810195	253337	14845762	5.49
2017		269835	15796512	5.29
2018		267338	18707701	5.65
2019		313986	22335870	6.31

注：表中2012-2018年研究与试验发展(R&D)经费内部支出相当于地区生产总值的比例根据北京市全国第四次经济普查结果进行了修订。
资料来源：北京市统计局、北京市科学技术委员会、北京市教育委员会、北京市经济和信息化局、北京市知识产权局。
Note: Data on the internal R&D expenditures as percentage of GDP in this table have been revised in accordance with the results of the fourth national economic census in Beijing.
Source: Beijing Municipal Bureau of Statistics, Beijing Municipal Science & Technology Commission, Beijing Municipal Commission of Education, Beijing Municipal Bureau of Economy and Information Technology, Beijing Municipal Intellectual Property Office.

19-1 续表 Continued

年 份 Year	专 利 申请量 (件) Patent Applications (unit)	发 明 Inventions	实用新型 Utility Models	外观设计 Industrial Designs	PCT国际 专 利 申请量 (件) PCT International Patent Applications (unit)	专 利 授权量 (件) Patents Granted (unit)	发 明 Inventions	实用新型 Utility Models	外观设计 Industrial Designs	国内专利 有效量 (件) Domestic Patents in Force (unit)	#发明 专利 Invention Patents	万人发明 专 利 拥有量 (件) Invention Patent Ownership per 10,000 Persons (unit)
1985	1540	754	720	66								
1986	1692	535	1091	66		491	43	408	40			
1987	2425	523	1796	106		776	102	630	44			
1988	3342	702	2494	146		1376	169	1147	60			
1989	3344	742	2408	194		1789	207	1497	85			
1990	4284	830	3214	240		2268	216	1932	120			
1991	4624	1023	3324	277		2369	263	1917	189			
1992	6316	1340	4493	483		3265	312	2724	229			
1993	6972	1483	4931	558		5806	530	4780	496			
1994	6852	1506	4666	680		3914	368	3245	301			
1995	6362	1252	4372	738		4025	328	3169	528			
1996	6595	1441	4255	899		3295	246	2563	486			
1997	6313	1678	3667	968		3327	281	2340	706			
1998	6321	1754	3444	1123		3800	309	2522	969			
1999	7723	2062	4045	1616		5829	573	3948	1308			
2000	10344	3409	4984	1951		5905	1074	3463	1368			
2001	12174	4984	5114	2076		6246	946	3600	1700			
2002	13842	5785	5920	2137		6345	1061	3721	1563			
2003	17003	7833	6665	2505		8248	2261	4244	1743			
2004	18402	8608	6321	3473		9005	3216	3956	1833			
2005	22572	12102	6940	3530		10100	3476	4498	2126		12102	8
2006	26555	14226	8200	4129		11238	3864	5490	1884	36645	13319	8
2007	31680	18763	8819	4098		14954	4824	7364	2766	43584	18421	11
2008	43508	28394	11157	3957		17747	6478	8776	2493	55771	20329	12
2009	50236	29326	15424	5486		22921	9157	10141	3623	71076	28774	16
2010	57296	33466	18637	5193	1272	33511	11209	16579	5723	100623	38996	20
2011	77955	45057	26615	6283	1862	40888	15880	19628	5380	131255	52522	26
2012	92305	52720	32609	6976	2705	50511	20140	24672	5699	170516	69554	34
2013	123336	67554	47586	8196	2981	62671	20695	36301	5675	219243	85434	41
2014	138111	78129	48228	11754	3606	74661	23237	44071	7353	274667	103638	49
2015	156312	88930	53243	14139	4490	94031	35308	45773	12950	344916	133040	62
2016	177497	97424	61361	18712	6651	102323	41425	45376	15522	417666	166722	77
2017	185928	99167	68400	18361	5069	106948	46091	46011	14846	494941	205320	95
2018	211212	117664	70507	23041	6527	123496	46978	59219	17299	569929	241282	112
2019	226113	129930	73021	23162	7165	131716	53127	58393	20196	653053	284288	132

注：按照国家知识产权局相关要求，2016年起对专利相关数据的统计范围进行调整(下同)。
Note: According to relevant requirements of the State Intellectural Property Office, the statistical range of patent-related data was adjusted since 2016.(the same below)

19-2 研究与试验发展(R&D)人员情况

项目	Item	研究与试验发展(R&D)人员(人) R&D Personnel (person)		#本科及以上学历 Bachelor Degree or above	
		2019	2018	2019	2018
合计	**Total**	**464178**	**397034**	**405053**	**341202**
按执行部门分	**By Executive Department**				
企业	Enterprises	195706	175868	163921	142910
工业企业	Industrial Enterprises	65486	69095	48632	51312
非工业企业	Non-industrial Enterprises	130220	106773	115289	91598
科研机构	Scientific Research Institutions	125390	121093	112225	108502
高等学校	Institutions of Higher Education	128146	85855	119757	81519
事业单位	Public Institutions	14936	14218	9150	8271
按行业门类分	**By Sector**				
#制造业	Manufacturing	61135	65433	46106	49347
信息传输、软件和信息技术服务业	Information Transmission, Software and Information Technology Services	71733	58273	55286	44912
科学研究和技术服务业	Scientific Research and Development, Technical Services	176845	164157	159212	148460
教育	Education	128146	85855	119757	81519

资料来源：北京市统计局、北京市科学技术委员会、北京市教育委员会、北京市经济和信息化局。

STATISTICS FOR RESEARCH AND EXPERIMENTAL DEVELOPMENT PERSONNEL

研究与试验发展(R&D)人员折合全时当量(人年) Full-time Equivalent of R&D Professionals (person-year)		基础研究 Basic Research		应用研究 Applied Research		试验发展 Experimental Development	
2019	2018	2019	2018	2019	2018	2019	2018
313986	**267338**	**63478**	**50048**	**92521**	**70880**	**158059**	**146431**
134115	116679	1624	590	12329	4658	120233	111450
44241	46929	73	136	3618	1568	40562	45226
89874	69750	1551	454	8711	3090	79671	66225
108309	105812	33287	32360	41612	41372	33410	32080
63119	36546	26590	15316	34154	20350	2375	881
8443	8302	1978	1782	4425	4501	2041	2020
40515	44887	73	136	3381	1531	37073	43220
52865	40256	53	14	2600	235	50212	40007
141104	132692	36149	34037	49784	46892	55226	51781
63119	36546	26590	15316	34154	20350	2375	881

Source: Beijing Municipal Bureau of Statistics, Beijing Municipal Science & Technology Commission, Beijing Municipal Commission of Education, Beijing Municipal Bureau of Economy and Information Technology.

19-3 研究与试验发展(R&D)经费情况

单位：万元

项 目	Item	研究与试验发展(R&D)经费内部支出 Internal R&D Expenditures		按活动类型分 Group by Type of Activity 基础研究 Basic Research	
		2019	2018	2019	2018
合 计	**Total**	**22335870**	**18707701**	**3554523**	**2777757**
按执行部门分	**By Executive Department**				
企 业	Enterprises	9081986	7805000	64012	18447
工业企业	Industrial Enterprises	2851859	2740103	2994	5659
非工业企业	Non-industrial Enterprises	6230127	5064898	61018	12788
科研机构	Scientific Research Institutions	9942383	8282682	2373530	1817717
高等学校	Institutions of Higher Education	2808088	2154934	1022847	850556
事业单位	Public Institutions	503413	465085	94134	91037
按行业门类分	**By Sector**				
#制造业	Manufacturing	2767739	2660339	2994	5659
信息传输、软件和信息技术服务业	Information Transmission, Software and Information Technology Services	4074575	3406527	1227	207
科学研究和技术服务业	Scientific Research and Development, Technical Services	11822238	9829105	2517498	1914171
教 育	Education	2808088	2154934	1022847	850556

注：表中2018年数据根据北京市第四次全国经济普查结果进行了修订。
资料来源：北京市统计局、北京市科学技术委员会、北京市教育委员会、北京市经济和信息局。

RESEARCH AND EXPERIMENTAL DEVELOPMENT FUNDS

(10000 yuan)

应用研究 Applied Research		试验发展 Experimental Development		按支出用途分 Group by Purpose of Payment			
				日常性支出 Routine Expenses		#人员劳务费 Labor Cost	
2019	2018	2019	2018	2019	2018	2019	2018
5638952	**4128265**	**13142395**	**11801679**	**19741453**	**16013736**	**8461480**	**6597387**
589825	282716	8428149	7503837	8787589	7019942	5289644	3960287
187250	77697	2661615	2656746	2719498	2604423	1168794	1212296
402575	205019	5766534	4847091	6068091	4415520	4120850	2747991
3250456	2581324	4318396	3883640	8152361	6775679	2433036	2099199
1568146	1113950	217095	190428	2427556	1876720	575512	409152
230525	150275	178755	223774	373948	341394	163288	128750
181969	76448	2582776	2578233	2640550	2525758	1133274	1186863
177937	20569	3895411	3385752	4013449	2835237	3079774	2777186
3619636	2852153	5685104	5062781	9852908	8128632	3356852	2661933
1568146	1113950	217095	190428	2427556	1876720	575512	409152

Note: Data of 2018 in the table has been revised in accordance with the results of the fourth national economic census in Beijing.
Source: Beijing Municipal Bureau of Statistics, Beijing Municipal Science & Technology Commission, Beijing Municipal Commission of Education, Beijing Municipal Bureau of Economy and Information Technology.

19-3 续表

单位：万元

项　目	Item	资产性支出 Expenditures for Assets 2019	2018	#仪器和设备 Instruments and Equipment 2019	2018
合　计	**Total**	**2594417**	**2693965**	**1798149**	**2122830**
按执行部门分	**By Executive Department**				
企　业	Enterprises	294397	785058	237774	761378
工业企业	Industrial Enterprises	132361	135680	128617	132970
非工业企业	Non-industrial Enterprises	162036	649378	109157	628408
科研机构	Scientific Research Institutions	1790022	1507002	1148597	1040703
高等学校	Institutions of Higher Education	380533	278214	297189	241442
事业单位	Public Institutions	129466	123691	114589	79307
按行业门类分	**By Sector**				
#制造业	Manufacturing	127189	134581	124276	131901
信息传输、软件和信息技术服务业	Information Transmission, Software and Information Technology Services	61126	571291	44600	558045
科学研究和技术服务业	Scientific Research and Development, Technical Services	1969330	1700473	1311370	1182653
教　育	Education	380533	278214	297189	241442

19-3 continued

(10000 yuan)

按资金来源分 Group by Fund Source							
政府资金 Governmental Funds		企业资金 Enterprise Funds		国外资金 Foreign Funds		其他资金 Others	
2019	2018	2019	2018	2019	2018	2019	2018
10692236	**9205698**	**9867574**	**8304423**	**76534**	**130992**	**1699526**	**1066588**
328940	329287	8742048	7287979	9326	75492	1671	112242
193114	199809	2658745	2457672		11604		71018
135826	129478	6083304	4830308	9326	63888	1671	41224
8245340	6981944	341006	401152	24936	20997	1331100	878590
1674471	1495161	775680	607720	41024	33527	316913	18526
443485	399307	8839	7572	1248	976	49842	57230
182358	192649	2585381	2386089		10583		71018
14222	30744	4060315	3313921		34994	37	26869
8780728	7453780	1625850	1378448	33498	49558	1382162	947320
1674471	1495161	775680	607720	41024	33527	316913	18526

19-4 规模以上工业企业研究与试验发展(R&D)活动基本情况 (2018年)

项目	Item	有研究与试验发展(R&D)活动的企业数(个) Enterprises with R&D Activities (unit)	研究与试验发展(R&D)人员(人) R&D Personnel (person)	研究与试验发展(R&D)人员折合全时当量(人年) Full-time Equivalent of R&D Personnel (person-year)	研究与试验发展(R&D)经费内部支出(万元) Internal R&D Expenditures (10000 yuan)
合计	**Total**	**1127**	**69095**	**46929**	**2740103**
按企业规模分	**By Size of Enterprise**				
#大中型企业	Medium and Large-sized	345	50786	34950	2144187
按隶属关系分	**By Affiliation**				
中央	Central	130	15180	10787	649256
地方	Local	997	53915	36143	2090847
按登记注册类型分	**By Registration Type**				
内资企业	Domestically-invested Enterprises	928	55135	37261	2035458
#国有企业	State-owned Enterprises	13	2198	1567	29237
港澳台商投资企业	Hong Kong, Macao and Taiwan-invested Enterprises	56	4164	2730	233784
外商投资企业	Foreign-invested Enterprises	143	9796	6937	470862
按重点产业分	**By Key Sector**				
#高技术制造业	High-tech Manufacturing	466	30389	21991	1341957

BASIC INFORMATION ON RESEARCH AND EXPERIMENTAL DEVELOPMENT ACTIVITIES OF INDUSTRIAL ENTERPRISES ABOVE DESIGNATED SIZE (2018)

政府资金 Governmental Funds	企业资金 Enterprise Funds	国外资金 Foreign Funds	其他资金 Others	专利申请数(件) Patent Applications (unit)	#发明专利 Inventions	新产品产值(万元) Output Value of New Products (10000 yuan)	新产品销售收入(万元) Sales Income of New Products (10000 yuan)	#出口 Exports
199809	**2457672**	**11604**	**71018**	**20655**	**10386**	**43017071**	**41366175**	**5354562**
163306	1901031	10317	69532	14302	7794	35106760	33433682	4848522
104534	479578	1770	63373	3357	2285	5090522	5213837	164629
95274	1978094	9834	7645	17298	8101	30444046	36152338	5189933
185759	1779782	4515	65402	16250	8142	23229138	23047131	1220183
9352	19050	173	662	455	346	490485	499808	394
2989	230304	404	87	2304	1640	12598024	11351459	2908266
11061	447586	6686	5529	2101	604	7189908	6967586	1226113
122444	1153680			7796	5013	21822203	20280793	4245496

19-5 规模以上工业企业研究与试验发展(R&D)活动基本情况(2019年)

项　目	Item	有研究与试验发展(R&D)活动的企业数(个) Enterprises with R&D Activities (unit)	研究与试验发展(R&D)人　员(人) R&D Personnel (person)	研究与试验发展(R&D)人员折合全时当量(人年) Full-time Equivalent of R&D Personnel (person-year)	研究与试验发展(R&D)经费内部支出(万元) Internal R&D Expenditures (10000 yuan)
合　计	**Total**	**1127**	**65486**	**44241**	**2851859**
按企业规模分	**By Size of Enterprise**				
#大中型企业	Medium and Large-sized	332	48364	32745	2223305
按隶属关系分	**By Affiliation**				
中　央	Central	120	14738	11348	702302
地　方	Local	1007	50748	32893	2149557
按登记注册类型分	**By Registration Type**				
内资企业	Domestically-invested Enterprises	936	52643	34156	2174414
#国有企业	State-owned Enterprises	15	990	622	43159
港澳台商投资企业	Hong Kong, Macao and Taiwan-invested Enterprises	54	3557	2834	248332
外商投资企业	Foreign-invested Enterprises	137	9286	7251	429113
按重点产业分	**By Key Sector**				
#高技术制造业	High-tech Manufacturing	477	277004	20692	1473136

BASIC INFORMATION ON RESEARCH AND EXPERIMENTAL DEVELOPMENT ACTIVITIES OF INDUSTRIAL ENTERPRISES ABOVE DESIGNATED SIZE (2019)

					专利		新产品	
	政府资金 Governmental Funds	企业资金 Enterprise Funds	国外资金 Foreign Funds	其他资金 Others	申请数(件) Patent Applications (unit)	#发明专利 Inventions	销售收入(万元) Sales Income of New Products (10000 yuan)	#出口 Exports
	193114	**2658745**			**22552**	**11543**	**52201988**	**7067372**
	149630	2073675			15829	9015	43043023	6387116
	100585	601717			4390	3117	5973452	90376
	92530	2057027			18162	8426	46228537	6976996
	159078	2015336			17032	8574	24929366	1690029
	5591	37569			526	404	149921	
	1148	247184			3039	2039	15414318	4472165
	32889	396224			2481	930	11858305	905179
	97152	1375984			9619	6332	21893124	5575617

19-6 规模以上工业企业研究与试验发展(R&D)及相关活动情况(按行业分)(2018年)

项目	Item	有研究与试验发展(R&D)活动的企业数 Enterprises with R&D Activities	研究与试验发展(R&D)人员(人) R&D Personnel (person)
合计	**Total**	**1127**	**69095**
采矿业	**Mining and Quarrying**	**7**	**2623**
煤炭开采和洗选业	Mining and Washing of Coal	1	***
石油和天然气开采业	Extraction of Petroleum and Natural Gas	2	***
黑色金属矿采选业	Mining and Processing of Ferrous Metal Ores	1	***
有色金属矿采选业	Mining and Processing of Non-Ferrous Metal Ores		
非金属矿采选业	Mining and Processing of Nonmetal Ores		
开采专业及辅助性活动	Mining Support Service Activities	3	***
其他采矿业	Mining of Other Ores		
制造业	**Manufacturing**	**1108**	**65433**
农副食品加工业	Processing of Food from Agriculture Products	26	922
食品制造业	Manufacture of Foods	28	1113
酒、饮料和精制茶制造业	Manufacture of Wine, Beverage and Refined Tea	6	781
烟草制品业	Manufacture of Cigarettes and Tobacco	1	***
纺织业	Manufacture of Textile	5	67
纺织服装、服饰业	Manufacture of Textile Wearing Apparel and Ornament	4	41
皮革、毛皮、羽毛及其制品和制鞋业	Manufacture of Leather, Fur, Feather and Its Products, and Footwear		
木材加工和木、竹、藤、棕、草制品业	Processing of Timbers, Manufacture of Wood, Bamboo, Rattan, Palm, and Straw Products		
家具制造业	Manufacture of Furniture	3	***
造纸和纸制品业	Manufacture of Paper and Paper Products	7	69
印刷和记录媒介复制业	Printing, Reproduction of Recording Media	17	680
文教、工美、体育和娱乐用品制造业	Manufacture of Articles for Culture,Education, Artwork, Sport and Entertainment Activities	5	99
石油、煤炭及其他燃料加工业	Processing of Petroleum, Coal and Other Fuels Nuclear Fuel	6	82
化学原料和化学制品制造业	Manufacture of Raw Chemical Materials and Chemical Products	52	1398
医药制造业	Manufacture of Medicines	127	7261
化学纤维制造业	Manufacture of Chemical Fibers	1	***
橡胶和塑料制品业	Manufacture of Rubber and Plastics Products	24	831
非金属矿物制品业	Manufacture of Non-Metallic Mineral Products	42	2151
黑色金属冶炼和压延加工业	Smelting and Pressing of Ferrous Metals	3	***
有色金属冶炼和压延加工业	Smelting and Pressing of Non-Ferrous Metals	10	659
金属制品业	Manufacture of Fabricated Metal Products	27	739
通用设备制造业	Manufacture of General-Purpose Machinery	87	4163
专用设备制造业	Manufacture of Special-Purpose Machinery	167	6571
汽车制造业	Manufacture of Motor Vehicles	56	9561
铁路、船舶、航空航天和其他运输设备制造业	Manufacture of Railway Locomotives, Building of Ships and Boats, Manufacture of Air and Spacecrafts and Other Transportation Equipment	46	6171
电气机械和器材制造业	Manufacture of Electrical Machinery and Equipment	104	4521
计算机、通信和其他电子设备制造业	Manufacture of Computers, Communication Equipment and Other Electronic Equipment	150	12938
仪器仪表制造业	Manufacture of Measuring Instruments and Meters	92	3081
其他制造业	Other Manufacturing	6	716
废弃资源综合利用业	Recycling and Disposal of Waste	2	***
金属制品、机械和设备修理业	Repair of Fabricated Metal Products, Machinery and Equipment	4	153
电力、热力、燃气及水的生产和供应业	**Production and Distribution of Electricity, Heating Power, Gas and Water**	**12**	**1039**
电力、热力生产和供应业	Production and Distribution of Electricity and Heating Power	6	373
燃气生产和供应业	Production and Distribution of Gas	1	***
水的生产和供应业	Production and Distribution of Water	5	179

STATISTICS FOR RESEARCH AND EXPERIMENTAL DEVELOPMENT AND RELATED ACTIVITIES OF INDUSTRIAL ENTERPRISES ABOVE ESIGNATED SIZE (BY SECTOR) (2018)

研究与试验发展(R&D)人员折合全时当量(人年) Full-time Equivalent of R&D Personnel (person-year)	研究与试验发展(R&D)经费内部支出(万元) Internal R&D Expenditures (10000 yuan)					专利申请数(件) Applications Patents (unit)		新产品产值(万元) Output Value of New Products (10000 yuan)	新产品销售收入(万元) Sales Income of New Products (10000 yuan)	
		政府资金 Governmental Funds	企业资金 Enterprise Funds	国外资金 Foreign Funds	其他资金 Others		#发明专利 Inventions			#出口 Exports
46929	**2740103**	**199809**	**2457672**	**11604**	**71018**	**20655**	**10386**	**43017071**	**41366175**	**5354562**
1363	**52507**	**5838**	**45648**	**1021**		**449**	**247**		**4001**	
***	***		***			***	***			
***	***	***	***			***	***			
***	***	***	***	***		***	***			
***	***	***	***			***	***		***	
44887	**2660339**	**192649**	**2386089**	**10583**	**71018**	**19322**	**9638**	**43006617**	**41352269**	**5354562**
556	19481	1055	18426			196	65	374438	363741	9783
713	35354	868	34212	274		99	60	283385	283237	16327
295	13483	28	13450	5		31	7	335921	323544	1502
***	***		***	***		***	***	***	***	
22	2026		2026			66	23	35276	37346	12826
23	395		395			47	20	218317	199977	11822
***	***		***			***	***	***	***	***
55	2007		2007			46	4	47699	86710	20653
306	8670	182	8488			111	40	248917	247475	2647
78	1975		1975			93	9	25651	37225	20
61	1640	178	1462			14	14	161711	351261	
999	44162	5405	38639	118		279	232	607253	701200	12825
4927	286445	13895	270235	1340	976	559	417	2957918	2581068	30176
***	***		***			***	***	***	***	
489	23169	49	23033		87	117	20	165019	167610	11159
1181	61463	1989	59391	84		788	323	1804828	1786402	91411
***	***		***			***	***	***	***	
363	20737	2113	18624			140	118	424476	406161	35660
353	19272	448	18825			389	90	455935	520703	39200
2842	133061	5879	125902	1178	102	688	251	2269460	2257620	497566
4402	301587	12838	277577	5925	5247	2717	1286	3025783	2746373	371749
6963	431458	8790	422393	82	193	3964	1402	6277447	6110864	23141
4610	244666	36637	152666		55362	811	552	2100781	2018123	18880
2717	177548	10127	166862	559		1622	842	3259666	3345907	72810
9595	650867	67494	581871	233	1268	4708	3364	16475034	15288238	4043463
2253	92774	3329	88459	613	374	867	321	1024702	1041965	26591
552	45741	21337	16995		7410	187	115	153637	141810	2721
***	***		***			***	***	***	***	
49	3265	11	3254			44	9	45618	45618	
680	**27257**	**1321**	**25936**			**884**	**501**	**10454**	**9905**	
193	4624	30	4595			680	423			
***	***		***			***	***			
105	3667	1291	2376			95	39	10454	9905	

19－7 规模以上工业企业研究与试验发展(R&D)及相关活动情况(按行业分)(2019年)

项 目	Item	有研究与试验发展(R&D)活动的企业数(个) Enterprises with R&D Activities (unit)	研究与试验发展(R&D)人员(人) R&D Personnel (person)
合 计	**Total**	**1127**	**65486**
采矿业	**Mining and Quarrying**	**7**	**1668**
煤炭开采和洗选业	Mining and Washing of Coal		
石油和天然气开采业	Extraction of Petroleum and Natural Gas	2	***
黑色金属矿采选业	Mining and Processing of Ferrous Metal Ores	1	***
有色金属矿采选业	Mining and Processing of Non-Ferrous Metal Ores		
非金属矿采选业	Mining and Processing of Nonmetal Ores		
开采专业及辅助性活动	Mining Support Service Activities	4	826
其他采矿业	Mining of Other Ores		
制造业	**Manufacturing**	**1108**	**61135**
农副食品加工业	Processing of Food from Agriculture Products	19	525
食品制造业	Manufacture of Foods	21	1067
酒、饮料和精制茶制造业	Manufacture of Wine, Beverage and Refined Tea	10	1364
烟草制品业	Manufacture of Cigarettes and Tobacco	1	***
纺织业	Manufacture of Textile	4	81
纺织服装、服饰业	Manufacture of Textile Wearing Apparel and Ornament	6	202
皮革、毛皮、羽毛及其制品和制鞋业	Manufacture of Leather, Fur, Feather and Its Products, and Footwear		
木材加工和木、竹、藤、棕、草制品业	Processing of Timbers, Manufacture of Wood, Bamboo, Rattan, Palm, and Straw Products		
家具制造业	Manufacture of Furniture	3	***
造纸和纸制品业	Manufacture of Paper and Paper Products	7	128
印刷和记录媒介复制业	Printing, Reproduction of Recording Media	18	708
文教、工美、体育和娱乐用品制造业	Manufacture of Articles for Culture,Education, Artwork, Sport and Entertainment Activities	6	55
石油、煤炭及其他燃料加工业	Processing of Petroleum, Coal and Other Fuels Nuclear Fuel	5	113
化学原料和化学制品制造业	Manufacture of Raw Chemical Materials and Chemical Products	54	1398
医药制造业	Manufacture of Medicines	126	6643
化学纤维制造业	Manufacture of Chemical Fibers		
橡胶和塑料制品业	Manufacture of Rubber and Plastics Products	17	265
非金属矿物制品业	Manufacture of Non-Metallic Mineral Products	47	1476
黑色金属冶炼和压延加工业	Smelting and Pressing of Ferrous Metals	2	***
有色金属冶炼和压延加工业	Smelting and Pressing of Non-Ferrous Metals	10	296
金属制品业	Manufacture of Fabricated Metal Products	34	1256
通用设备制造业	Manufacture of General-Purpose Machinery	98	4388
专用设备制造业	Manufacture of Special-Purpose Machinery	181	7618
汽车制造业	Manufacture of Motor Vehicles	44	9338
铁路、船舶、航空航天和其他运输设备制造业	Manufacture of Railway Locomotives, Building of Ships and Boats, Manufacture of Air and Spacecrafts and Other Transportation Equipment	42	3559
电气机械和器材制造业	Manufacture of Electrical Machinery and Equipment	92	4519
计算机、通信和其他电子设备制造业	Manufacture of Computers, Communication Equipment and Other Electronic Equipment	146	11931
仪器仪表制造业	Manufacture of Measuring Instruments and Meters	101	2819
其他制造业	Other Manufacturing	6	842
废弃资源综合利用业	Recycling and Disposal of Waste	2	***
金属制品、机械和设备修理业	Repair of Fabricated Metal Products, Machinery and Equipment	6	309
电力、热力、燃气及水的生产和供应业	**Production and Distribution of Electricity, Heating Power, Gas and Water**	**12**	**2683**
电力、热力生产和供应业	Production and Distribution of Electricity and Heating Power	7	1878
燃气生产和供应业	Production and Distribution of Gas	1	***
水的生产和供应业	Production and Distribution of Water	4	186

STATISTICS FOR RESEARCH AND EXPERIMENTAL DEVELOPMENT AND RELATED ACTIVITIES OF INDUSTRIAL ENTERPRISES ABOVE ESIGNATED SIZE (BY SECTOR) (2019)

研究与试验发展(R&D)人员折合全时当量(人年) Full-time Equivalent of R&D Personnel (person-year)	研究与试验发展(R&D)经费内部支出(万元) Internal R&D Expenditures (10000 yuan)	政府资金 Governmental Funds	企业资金 Enterprise Funds	国外资金 Foreign Funds	其他资金 Others	专利申请数(件) Applications Patents (unit)	#发明专利 Inventions	新产品销售收入(万元) Sales Income of New Products (10000 yuan)	#出口 Exports
44241	**2851859**	**193114**	**2658745**			**22552**	**11543**	**52201988**	**7067372**
1155	**53161**	**9282**	**43879**			**345**	**264**	**49**	
***	***	***	***			***	***		
***	***	***	***			***	***		
411	16352	662	15690			72	43	49	
40515	**2767739**	**182358**	**2585381**			**21295**	**10697**	**48853647**	**7067372**
428	16195	587	15608			208	57	421274	7677
696	31203	669	30534			164	69	352234	11996
503	18868	100	18768			123	11	321986	3377
***	***		***			***	***	***	
47	2489		2489			25	15	40897	14888
70	8741		8741			81	16	274270	72088
								9101	
***	***		***			***	***	***	***
108	2430		2430			15	7	57072	37598
279	11429		11429			185	75	465316	2772
40	1535	3	1532			83	13	81549	
82	3478	…	3478			10	6	350794	
936	40335	234	40101			244	149	526106	12747
5164	326776	12657	314119			786	542	2963093	40138
						6	6	7736	3925
179	13147	24	13123			130	35	139026	8876
1102	64814	1562	63252			710	311	1621675	35740
***	***		***			***	***	***	
124	12035	1872	10164			118	107	343464	26985
780	34458	11341	23117			704	340	960857	58398
3001	133746	7744	126002			896	272	2379952	449044
5211	288731	18084	270648			2747	1229	3124080	385697
3402	438566	18725	419841			4172	1244	10793794	451666
3025	262049	16701	245348			1007	641	1834865	16702
3283	183744	4039	179705			1260	566	3385941	63098
9219	715354	58658	656695			5881	4325	16668058	5324186
1892	105214	9082	96131			1123	441	1153736	34254
715	39555	20274	19281			224	151	310726	4874
***	***		***			***	***	***	
81	6166	2	6165			59	4	60443	
2571	**30959**	**1474**	**29484**			**912**	**582**	**3348293**	
1778	8953	3	8950			736	491	33	
***	***		***			***	***	***	
174	4925	1472	3454			90	45	9218	

19-8 规模以上高技术制造业研究与试验发展(R&D)及相关活动情况

项　目	Item	R&D人员折合全时当量(人年) Full-time Equivalent of R&D Personnel (person-year) 2019	2018
高技术制造业	**High-tech Manufacturing**	**20692**	**21991**
医药制造业	**Manufacture of Medicines**	**5165**	**4927**
#化学药品制造	Manufacture of Chemical Medicine	1897	1850
生物药品制造	Manufacture of Biological Medicine and Biochemical Chemical Products	2170	1607
航空、航天器及设备制造业	**Manufacture of Aircrafts and Spacecrafts**	**2691**	**3506**
#航空航天器修理	Repair of Air and Spacecrafts	62	42
电子及通信设备制造业	**Manufacture of Electronic Equipment and Communication Equipment**	**8308**	**8430**
#通信设备制造、雷达及配套设备	Manufacture of Communication Equipment	4787	3817
电子器件制造	Manufacture of Electronic Appliances	1885	2323
电子元件及电子专用设备制造	Manufacture of Electronic Components	611	751
其他电子设备制造	Manufacture of Other Electronic Equipment	475	980
计算机及办公设备制造业	**Manufacture of Computers and Office Equipments**	**1052**	**1373**
#计算机整机制造	Manufacture of Entired Computer	120	192
医疗仪器设备及仪器仪表制造业	**Manufacture of Medical Equipments and Meters**	**3476**	**3755**
医疗仪器设备及器械制造	Manufacture of Medical Equipment and Appliances	1583	1501
通用仪器仪表制造	Manufacture of Measuring Instrument and Meter	1169	1402

STATISTICS FOR RESEARCH AND EXPERIMENTAL DEVELOPMENT AND RELATED ACTIVITIES OF HIGH-TECH MANUFACTURING ABOVE DESIGNATER SIZE

R&D经费支出 (亿元) R&D Expenditures (100 million yuan)		新产品销售收入 (亿元) Sales Income of New Products (100 million yuan)		专利申请数 (件) Patent Applications (unit)		#发明专利 Inventions	
2019	2018	2019	2018	2019	2018	2019	2018
1473136	**1341957**	**21893124**	**20280793**	**9619**	**7796**	**6332**	**5013**
326776	**286445**	**2963093**	**2581068**	**786**	**559**	**542**	**417**
144930	130285	1149961	1008462	375	212	302	165
133744	74407	1152170	669591	215	210	161	167
232184	**183016**	**411335**	**751200**	**746**	**571**	**530**	**420**
3722	1580	1698		43	42	3	7
632354	**583541**	**14509296**	**13110686**	**3993**	**3253**	**2895**	**2132**
298479	205028	9611129	8868515	1100	721	940	538
212370	184656	2154661	1981666	1597	1233	1227	895
31371	30123	1141024	797127	265	209	132	117
60492	123582	1084572	790015	719	612	472	379
92167	**84917**	**2329504**	**2395578**	**2070**	**1709**	**1500**	**1325**
35795	30180	1649950	1715228	1904	1559	1421	1252
189655	**204038**	**1678447**	**1428787**	**2024**	**1665**	**865**	**680**
84442	111264	524710	386822	901	798	424	359
54171	51542	774475	813604	808	520	309	209

19-9 限额以上信息传输、软件和信息技术服务业企业研究与试验发展(R&D)及相关活动情况(2018年)

项目	Item	有研究与试验发展(R&D)活动的企业数(个) Enterprises with R&D Activities (unit)	研究与试验发展(R&D)人员(人) R&D Personnel (person)	研究与试验发展(R&D)人员折合全时当量(人年) Full-time Equivalent of R&D Personnel (person-year)
合计	**Total**	**219**	**58273**	**40256**
按隶属关系分	**By Affiliation**			
中央	Central	19	1814	684
地方	Local	200	56459	39572
按登记注册类型分	**By Registration Type**			
内资企业	Domestically-invested Enterprises	180	35984	23563
#国有企业	State-owned Enterprises	1	***	***
港澳台商投资企业	Hong Kong, Macao and Taiwan-invested Enterprises	21	10466	6073
外商投资企业	Foreign-invested Enterprises	18	11823	10620
按行业分	**By Sector**			
电信、广播电视和卫星传输服务	Telecommunications, Broadcasting, Television and Satellite Transmission Services	14	10931	10605
互联网和相关服务	Internet and Related Services	41	17028	11720
软件和信息技术服务业	Software and Information Technology Services	164	30314	17931

STATISTICS FOR RESEARCH AND EXPERIMENTAL DEVELOPMENT AND RELATED ACTIVITIES OF INFORMATION TRANSMISSIOM, SOFTWARE AND INFORMATION TECHNICIAL SERVICE ENTERPRISES ABOVE DESIGNATED SIZE (2018)

研究与试验发展(R&D)经费内部支出(万元) Internal R&D Expenditures (10000 yuan)	政府资金 Govern-mental Funds	企业资金 Enterprise Funds	国外资金 Foreign Funds	其他资金 Others	专利申请数(件) Patent Applications (unit)	#发明专利 Inventions
3406527	**30744**	**3313921**	**34994**	**26869**	**41765**	**31290**
71900	2407	66983	197	2314	1337	1221
3334627	28338	3246939	34797	24554	40428	30069
1731611	28830	1687321	1847	13613	28333	21934
***	***				***	***
880390	1640	873636	20	5094	7258	4724
794526	275	752964	33126	8161	6174	4632
696544	1326	673944	18960	2314	2544	2400
1552920	237	1547097	252	5335	10143	7489
1157063	29182	1092880	15781	19220	29078	21401

19-10 限额以上信息传输、软件和信息技术服务业企业研究与试验发展(R&D)及相关活动情况(2019年)

项　目	Item	有研究与试验发展(R&D)活动的企业数(个) Enterprises with R&D Activities (unit)	研究与试验发展(R&D)人员(人) R&D Personnel (person)	研究与试验发展(R&D)人员折合全时当量(人年) Full-time Equivalent of R&D Personnel (person-year)
合　计	**Total**	**587**	**71733**	**52865**
按隶属关系分	**By Affiliation**			
中　央	Central	50	2849	2087
地　方	Local	537	68884	50778
按登记注册类型分	**By Registration Type**			
内资企业	Domestically-invested Enterprises	506	44569	30761
#国有企业	State-owned Enterprises	1	***	***
港澳台商投资企业	Hong Kong, Macao and Taiwan-invested Enterprises	41	16215	13020
外商投资企业	Foreign-invested Enterprises	40	10949	9084
按行业分	**By Sector**			
电信、广播电视和卫星传输服务	Telecommunications, Broadcasting, Television and Satellite Transmission Services	31	9354	8453
互联网和相关服务	Internet and Related Services	104	22148	17413
软件和信息技术服务业	Software and Information Technology Services	452	40231	26999

STATISTICS FOR RESEARCH AND EXPERIMENTAL DEVELOPMENT AND RELATED ACTIVITIES OF INFORMATION TRANSMISSIOM, SOFTWARE AND INFORMATION TECHNICIAL SERVICE ENTERPRISES ABOVE DESIGNATED SIZE (2019)

研究与试验发展(R&D)经费内部支出(万元) Internal R&D Expenditures (10000 yuan)	政府资金 Govern-mental Funds	企业资金 Enterprise Funds	其他资金 Others	专利申请数(件) Patent Applications (unit)	#发明专利 Inventions
4074575	**14222**	**4060315**	**37**	**53480**	**38658**
156487	3255	153232		2155	1863
3918088	10967	3907084		51325	36795
2242754	11429	2231287	37	35876	25522
***	***	***		***	***
1127988	848	1127140		11220	7809
703834	1945	701888		6384	5327
722164	834	721330		3271	3038
1688038	160	1687878		14426	9885
1664374	13229	1651108	37	35783	25735

19-11 研究与开发机构研究与试验发展(R&D)及相关活动情况 (2007-2019年)

项　目		Item		2007
研究与开发机构基本情况		**Basic Information on R&D Institutions**		
机构数	(个)	Number	(unit)	265
中　央		Central		221
地　方		Local		44
研究与试验发展(R&D)投入情况		**R&D Input**		
R&D人员	(万人)	R&D Personnel	(10000 persons)	4.6
按隶属关系分		By Affiliation		
中　央		Central		4.4
地　方		Local		0.2
R&D人员折合全时当量	(万人年)	Full-time Equivalent of R&D Personnel	(10000 persons-year)	3.8
基础研究		Basic Research		1.2
应用研究		Applied Research		1.6
试验发展		Experimental Development		1.0
R&D经费内部支出	(亿元)	Internal R&D Expenditures	(100 million yuan)	103.1
按隶属关系分		By Affiliation		
中　央		Central		99.0
地　方		Local		4.1
按活动类型分		By Type of Activity		
基础研究		Basic Research		26.4
应用研究		Applied Research		45.2
试验发展		Experimental Development		31.5
按资金来源分		By Source of Funds		
政府资金		Governmental Funds		88.6
企业资金		Enterprise Funds		3.2
境外资金		Foreign Funds		1.3
其他资金		Others		10.0
研究与试验发展(R&D)项目(课题)情况		**R&D Projects (Tasks)**		
R&D项目(课题)数	(项)	Number of R&D Projects (Tasks)	(unit)	15079
R&D项目(课题)人员折合全时当量	(万人年)	Full-time Equivalent of R&D Personnel	(10000 persons-year)	2.2
R&D项目(课题)经费内部支出	(亿元)	Internal R&D Expenditures	(100 million yuan)	57.1
科技产出及成果情况		**Science & Technology Output and Achievement**		
发表科技论文	(篇)	Published Articles on Science and Technology	(unit)	37232
#国外发表		Published Abroad		9005
出版科技著作	(种)	Published Writings on Science and Technology	(sort)	1489
专利申请数	(件)	Number of Patents Applications	(unit)	1993
#发明专利		Invention Patents		1784
专利授权数	(件)	Number of Patents Granted	(unit)	985
#发明专利		Invention Patents		752

注：研究与开发机构统计范围为北京市政府部门所属的科学研究与技术开发机构、科技情报与文献机构。
资料来源：北京市科学技术委员会。

STATISTICS FOR RESEARCH AND EXPERIMENTAL DEVELOPMENT AND RELATED ACTIVITIES IN RESEARCH AND DEVELOPMENT INSTITUTIONS (2007-2019)

2008	2009	2010	2011	2012	2013	2014	2015	2016	2017	2018	2019
266	275	281	280	288	287	299	296	303	300	292	291
225	228	231	231	238	237	248	245	254	250	242	242
41	47	50	49	50	50	51	51	49	50	50	49
4.8	5.2	5.7	5.9	6.3	6.6	6.6	6.8	6.9	7.4	7.3	7.8
4.5	4.9	5.4	5.6	5.9	6.2	6.2	6.3	6.4	6.9	6.8	7.3
0.3	0.3	0.3	0.3	0.4	0.4	0.4	0.5	0.5	0.5	0.5	0.5
3.9	4.2	4.6	4.7	5.3	5.5	5.5	5.6	5.6	5.9	6.0	6.2
1.3	1.4	1.5	1.6	1.8	1.9	2.0	2.1	2.5	2.4	2.6	2.7
1.6	1.7	2.0	2.1	2.2	2.3	2.3	2.2	2.2	2.7	2.6	2.6
1.0	1.1	1.1	1.0	1.3	1.3	1.2	1.3	0.9	0.8	0.8	0.9
123.8	150.3	187.0	195.1	222.0	246.8	271.2	295.6	301.5	329.1	373.0	457.3
117.4	143.9	178.9	185.1	211.5	236.3	253.6	277.0	280.4	309.2	351.3	435.7
6.4	6.4	8.1	10.0	10.5	10.5	17.6	18.6	21.1	19.9	21.7	21.6
28.3	39.2	49.9	58.5	65.1	73.6	86.5	96.8	109.1	130.2	156.9	191.6
49.0	61.5	78.0	84.0	92.0	102.2	108.9	120.5	131.3	146.4	157.8	201.2
46.5	49.6	59.1	52.6	64.9	71.0	75.8	78.3	61.1	52.5	58.3	64.5
106.6	126.3	164.4	168.0	192.6	220.0	244.6	266.3	262.1	289.6	317.9	398.2
4.0	4.4	3.6	6.6	6.5	8.2	8.2	12.1	16.1	16.7	22.7	24.1
1.8	2.0	1.5	2.5	1.5	1.9	1.8	2.0	1.7	2.2	2.1	2.5
11.4	17.6	17.5	18.0	21.4	16.7	16.6	15.2	21.6	20.6	30.3	32.5
16383	17816	19545	20333	22842	23949	25550	26762	26998	31749	32133	35308
2.3	3.8	4.1	4.3	4.9	5.0	5.0	5.0	4.7	5.0	5.1	5.2
70.9	87.1	107.2	115.0	142.7	156.8	161.0	173.5	162.0	189.3	215.3	234.2
37149	39380	39384	41442	44218	45509	48040	48734	49517	49346	50178	55304
9184	12011	11696	13361	14003	17216	17905	18915	19800	21687	23176	26998
1636	1873	1601	1828	1670	1921	2058	2261	2453	2164	2461	2143
2488	3182	3879	4880	5456	6192	6004	6464	6657	7141	7574	9069
2119	2772	3450	4373	4798	5144	5115	5164	5543	5779	6059	7147
1146	1574	1879	2260	3251	3646	3932	4702	5522	5449	5319	6377
922	1299	1455	1756	2635	2763	3001	3529	4184	4246	3767	4479

Note: R&D institutions cover scientific research and technological development institutions, scientific and technological information institutions subordinate to government authorities of Beijing.
Source: Beijing Municipal Science & Technology Commission.

19-12 高等学校研究与试验发展(R&D)及相关活动情况
STATISTICS FOR RESEARCH AND EXPERIMENTAL DEVELOPMENT AND RELATED ACTIVITIES IN COLLEGES & UNIVERSITIES

项目		Item		2019	2018
高等学校基本情况		**Basic Information of Colleges & Universities**			
学校数	(个)	Number of Colleges and Universities	(unit)	116	119
#理工农医		Colleges & Universities of Science, Engineering, Agriculture, Medical Science		74	73
#人文社科		Colleges & Universities of Arts and Social Sciences		88	92
研究与试验发展(R&D)机构数	(个)	Number of R&D Institutions	(unit)	1124	
研究与试验发展(R&D)投入情况		**R&D Input**			
R&D人员	(万人)	R&D Personnel	(10000 person)	12.81	8.59
R&D人员折合全时当量	(万人年)	Full-time Equivalent of R&D Personnel	(10000 persons-year)	6.31	3.65
基础研究		Basic Research		2.66	1.53
应用研究		Applied Research		3.42	2.03
试验发展		Experimental Development		0.24	0.09
R&D经费内部支出	(亿元)	Internal R&D Expenditures	(100 million yuan)	280.81	215.49
按活动类型分		By Type of Activity			
基础研究		Basic Research		102.28	85.06
应用研究		Applied Research		156.81	111.39
试验发展		Experimental Development		21.71	19.04
按资金来源分		By Source of Funds			
#政府资金		Governmental Funds		198.18	149.52
企业资金		Enterprise Funds		75.61	60.77
研究与试验发展(R&D)项目(课题)情况		**R&D Projects (Tasks)**			
R&D项目(课题)数	(项)	Number of R&D Projects (Tasks)	(unit)	115571	105930
R&D项目(课题)人员折合全时当量	(万人年)	Full-time Equivalent of R&D Personnel	(10000 persons-year)	6.31	3.65
R&D项目(课题)经费内部支出	(亿元)	Internal R&D Expenditures	(100 million yuan)	205.60	163.30
科技产出及成果情况		**Science & Technology Output and Achievement**			
发表科技论文	(篇)	Published Articles on Science and Technology	(unit)	131118	129562
#国外发表		Published Abroad		58870	
出版科技著作	(种)	Published Writings on Science and Technology	(Sort)	4567	4617
专利申请数	(件)	Number of Patent Applications	(unit)	19848	17479
#发明专利		Invention Patents		16799	14550
专利授权数	(件)	Number of Patents Granted	(unit)	13617	11318
#发明专利		Invention Patents	(unit)	10232	8506

资料来源：北京市教育委员会。
Source: Beijing Municipal Commission of Education.

19−13 科学技术协会及所属学会工作情况(2019)
STATISTICS FOR SCIENCE AND TECHNOLOGY ASSOCIATION AND SUBORDINATE INSTITUTES (2019)

项 目		Item		合计 Total	市科协 Municipal Science and Technology Association	市级学会 Institutes at Municipal Level
基本情况		**Basic Information**				
机构数	(个)	Number of Institutions	(unit)	185	1	184
机关从业人员	(人)	Number of Employed Persons in the Institutions	(person)	1115	53	1062
学术交流活动		**Academic Exchange Activities**				
国内学术会议	(次)	Domestic Academic Meetings	(time)	911	9	902
参加人数	(人次)	Number of Participants	(person-time)	188937	1325	187612
交流论文	(篇)	Number of Papers Exchagned	(unit)	19696	54	19642
境内国际学术会议	(次)	Domestically-held International Academic Meetings	(time)	52	3	49
参加人数	(人次)	Number of Participants	(person-time)	19061	1315	17746
交流论文	(篇)	Number of Papers Exchagned	(unit)	3488	26	3462
港澳台地区学术会议	(次)	Academic Meetings Held in Kong Kong,Macao and Taiwan	(time)	6	2	4
参加人数	(人次)	Number of Participants	(person-time)	842	410	432
交流论文	(篇)	Number of Papers Exchagned	(unit)	101	33	68
科技期刊		**Science and Technology Journals**				
主办科技期刊种数	(种)	Types of Science and Technology Journals Sponsored	(sort)	24	1	23
科技期刊总印数	(万册)	Number of Total Printings of Science and Technology Journals	(10000 copies)	834130	203630	630500
科技期刊发表论文数	(篇)	Papers Published on Science and Technology Journals	(unit)	5582	240	5342
科普活动		**Activities to Popularize Scientific Knowledge**				
举办科普宣讲活动	(次)	Scientific Knowledge Lectures	(time)	2642	332	2310
播放科技广播、影视节目	(分钟)	Playing Radio, Films and TV Programs on Science and Technology	(minute)	4652	420	4232
举办实用技术培训	(次)	Holding Practical Technology Trainings	(time)	265	64	201
推广新技术、新品种	(项)	Promoting New Technologies and New Varieties	(unit)	111		111
参加活动科技人员总数	(人次)	Participating in Science and Technology Personnel	(person-time)	25581	389	25192
参加活动的学会、协会、研究会	(个次)	Participating in Socieities, Associations and Research Institutes	(unit-time)	428	6	422
科技传播		**Science and Technology Dissemination**				
主办科技报纸种数	(种)	Types of Science and Technology Newspaper Sponsored	(sort)	2		2
制作科普挂图种数	(种)	Types of Scientific Knowlede Flip Charts Produced	(sort)	43	8	35
制作科技广播、影视节目套数	(套)	Science and Technology Raido, Films and TV Programs Produced	(unit)	301	52	249
制作科普动漫作品套数	(套)	Scientific Knowledge Animation Works Produced	(unit)	14	8	6
主办科技网站	(个)	Science and Technology Websites Sponsored	(unit)	52	9	43
科技开放与交流		**Science and Technology Opening-up and Exchange**				
加入国际民间科技组织	(个)	International Cilvilian Science and Technology Organizations Joined	(unit)	27	1	26
参加国外科技活动人数	(人次)	Number of Persons Participating in Foreign Science and Technology Activities	(person-time)	419	90	329
参加港澳台地区科技活动人数	(人次)	Number of Persons Participating in Science and Technology Activities in Hong Kong, Macao and Taiwan	(person-time)	317	20	297
接待国外专家学者	(人次)	Foreign Experts and Scholars Received	(person-time)	639	325	314
接待港澳台地区专家学者	(人次)	Experts and Scholars from Kong Kong, Macao and Taiwan Received	(person-time)	473	253	220
科技服务		**Science and Technology Service**				
提供决策咨询报告	(篇)	Providing Policy-making Consulting Reports	(unit)	86	18	68
举办决策咨询活动	(次)	Holding Policy-making Consulting Activities	(time)	130	10	120

注：本表统计范围为北京市科学技术协会所属学会、研究会。
资料来源：北京市科学技术协会。
Note: Figures in this table cover societies and research institutes affiliated with Beijing Association for Science & Technology.
Source: Beijing Association for Science & Technology.

19－14 技术合同成交情况(1990－2019年)
STATISTICS FOR CONCLUSION OF TECHNOLOGICAL CONTRACTS (1990-2019)

年 份 Year	合同数(项) Number of Contracts (unit)	技术合同成交总额(亿元) Total Volume of Transaction of Technological Contracts (100 million yuan)	#技术交易额 Total Volume of Transaction of Technology	#流向外省市 Flowing to Other Provinces and Municipalities	#流向天津和河北 Flowing to Other Tianjin and Hebei	实现合同总金额(亿元) Total Volume of Transaction Achieved in Contracts (100 million yuan)	#技术交易实现金额 Amount of Technological Transactions Achieved
1990	18588	20.3	10.5			15.4	8.4
1991	18547	22.4	13.1			15.3	9.1
1992	23395	31.3	22.2			20.0	14.4
1993	20461	35.6	25.6			24.9	17.6
1994	15220	37.2	26.9			26.9	20.4
1995	16347	41.2	32.2			28.4	22.3
1996	14850	45.8	39.2			29.6	25.4
1997	13866	54.3	48.1			31.1	27.8
1998	20724	81.6	73.9			42.1	37.6
1999	20711	92.2	88.5			43.6	41.0
2000	21270	140.3	126.3	65.5		60.3	56.3
2001	23921	191.0	164.8	85.4		97.6	93.0
2002	27037	221.1	181.0	100.4		101.9	97.2
2003	32173	265.5	226.8	132.4		119.9	113.9
2004	35478	331.8	294.3	165.8		148.7	143.4
2005	37505	434.4	350.4	204.9		201.4	180.6
2006	51575	697.3	572.6	325.3		349.5	319.7
2007	50972	882.6	660.3	407.4		418.1	353.5
2008	52742	1027.2	778.1	487.0		406.2	375.0
2009	49938	1236.2	906.9	498.2		516.8	452.9
2010	50847	1579.5	1066.7	654.8		536.0	505.6
2011	53552	1890.3	1268.3	635.9		580.4	563.3
2012	59969	2458.5	2048.6	1385.0		739.8	707.0
2013	62743	2851.2	2252.4	1615.9		684.0	659.3
2014	67278	3136.0	2531.5	1722.0		708.2	675.1
2015	72272	3452.6	2767.8	1878.7	111.5	1229.7	1206.9
2016	74965	3940.8	2919.3	1997.2	154.7	749.2	717.0
2017	81266	4485.3	3703.9	2327.3	203.5	889.0	853.0
2018	82486	4957.8	4069.5	3014.9	227.4	986.2	889.5
2019	83171	5695.3	4389.0	2866.9	282.8	1075.7	1006.1

资料来源：北京技术市场管理办公室。
Source: Beijing Technical Market Management Office.

19−15 技术合同成交情况
CONCLUSION OF TECHNICAL CONTRACTS

项　目	Item	合同数(项) Number of Contracts (unit)		成交额(亿元) Volume of Transaction (100 million yuan)	
		2019	2018	2019	2018
合　计	**Total**	**83171**	**82486**	**5695.3**	**4957.8**
按合同类别分类	**By Type of Contract**				
技术开发合同	Technological Development	25390	26599	945.8	959.0
技术转让合同	Technology Transfer	1951	1799	684.7	212.0
技术咨询合同	Technical Consultation	4176	4336	43.9	40.1
技术服务合同	Technical Service	51654	49752	4021.0	3746.7
按合同卖方类别分类	**By Type of Seller**				
机关法人	Government Organisations				
事业法人	Public Institutions	12816	13695	173.3	183.7
社团法人	Mass Organisations	9	13	0.1	0.2
企业法人	Enterprises	70079	68541	5509.0	4768.2
自然人	Natural Persons	27	24	0.6	0.4
其他组织	Other Organizations	240	213	12.3	5.4
按合同买方类别分类	**By Type of Buyer**				
机关法人	Government Organisations	6268	6321	549.8	330.1
事业法人	Public Institutions	16691	16228	321.0	321.5
社团法人	Mass Organisations	933	981	25.3	27.1
企业法人	Enterprises	58040	57391	4763.3	4227.7
自然人	Natural Persons	377	445	3.0	2.5
其他组织	Other Organizations	862	1120	32.8	48.9
按服务社会经济目标分类	**By Social and Economic Service Objectives**				
环境保护、生态建设及污染防治	Environmental Protection, Ecological Development and Pollution Control	2808	2598	699.6	757.8
能源生产、分配和合理利用	Energy Production, Allocation and Reasonable Utilization	5834	5137	826.0	632.0
卫生事业发展	Health Services	2615	2578	110.8	73.2
教育事业发展	Education Development	6048	5269	64.7	64.8
基础设施以及城市和农村规划	Infrastructure and Rural and Urban Planning	3902	5899	1084.1	1229.7
社会发展和社会服务	Social Development and Social Services	36928	36104	1558.3	1240.0
地球和大气层的探索与利用	Exploration and Utilization Of The Earth and Atmosphere	117	72	2.0	0.8
民用空间探测及开发	Private Space Exploration and Development	289	388	5.3	11.2
农林牧渔业发展	Development in Agriculture, Forestry, Animal Production and Hunting, Fishing	1521	2000	14.4	24.9
工商业发展	Industrial and Commercial Development	3950	4026	116.2	139.0
非定向研究	Non-Directional Research	3138	2592	61.2	83.9
其他民用目标	Other Civilian Target	11346	10388	959.6	523.1
国防	National Defense	4675	5435	192.9	177.4
按技术流向分类	**By Spread Area of Technology**				
流向本市	To Beijing	34158	33836	2077.7	1219.5
#天津流入	From Tianjin	2340	2129	82.0	84.5
河北流入	From Hebei	787	574	37.1	16.6
流向外省市	To Other Provinces and Municipalities	47897	47454	2866.9	3014.9
#流向天津	To Tianjin	1815	1748	68.6	33.6
流向河北	To Hebei	3093	3119	214.2	193.8
技术出口	Exports	1116	1196	750.7	723.4

资料来源：北京技术市场管理办公室。
Source: Beijing Technical Market Management Office.

19–16 科技成果及获奖情况(2001–2019年)
STATISTICS FOR SCIENTIFIC AND TECHNOLOGICAL ACHIEVEMENTS AND AWARDS (2001-2019)

单位：项 (unit)

年 份 Year	科技成果登记数 Registered Number of Scientific and Technological Achievements	#国家技术发明奖 National Awards of Technical Invention	#国家科学技术进步奖 National Awards of Scientific and Technological Advancement
2001	326	1	38
2002	275	5	48
2003	468	5	52
2004	976	6	43
2005	1018	8	52
2006	1002	12	64
2007	1010	9	44
2008	1016	13	42
2009	1023	11	54
2010	1030	11	53
2011	1035	5	56
2012	1040	22	53
2013	1043	19	38
2014	1042	15	49
2015	1045	17	42
2016	728	10	47
2017	844	23	40
2018	863	16	40
2019	766	11	42

资料来源：北京市科学技术委员会。
Source: Beijing Municipal Science & Technology Commission.

19-17 专利申请及授权情况
APPLICATIONS AND GRANTING OF PATENTS

单位：件 (unit)

项 目	Item	申请量 Patent Applications		授权量 Patents Granted	
		2019	2018	2019	2018
合 计	**Total**	**226113**	**211212**	**131716**	**123496**
按种类分	**By Type**				
发 明	Inventions	129930	117664	53127	46978
实用新型	Utility Models	73021	70507	58393	59219
外观设计	Industrial Designs	23162	23041	20196	17299
按对象分	**By Applicant**				
工矿企业	Industrial and Mining Enterprises	162948	150385	96946	93222
大专院校	Universities & Colleges	22213	20008	12147	9892
科研单位	Scientific Research Institutes	20511	18527	12296	9734
机关团体	Government Organizations	4873	4185	3002	1969
个 人	Individuals	15568	18107	7325	8679

资料来源：北京市知识产权局。
Source: Beijing Intellectual Property Office.

19-18 有效发明专利情况
STATISTICS FOR VALID INVENTION PATENTS

单位：件 (unit)

项 目	Item	2019	2018
合 计	**Total**	**284288**	**241282**
按对象分	**By Applicant**		
工矿企业	Industrial and Mininig Enterprises	183557	152901
大专院校	Universities & Colleges	43769	37815
科研单位	Scientific Research Institutes	45862	39901
机关团体	Government Organizations	3362	2848
个 人	Individuals	7738	7817

资料来源：北京市知识产权局。
Source: Beijing Intellectual Property Office.

主要统计指标解释

科技活动人员 指报告年度调查单位直接从事科技活动、以及从事科技活动管理和为科技活动提供直接服务的人员。直接从事科技活动人员包括：在单位办的研究室、实验室、技术开发中心及中试车间（基地）等机构中从事科技活动的人员；虽不在上述机构工作，但编入科技活动项目（课题）组的人员等。从事科技活动管理和为科技活动提供直接服务的人员包括：与科技活动相关的行政管理人员，以及直接为科技活动提供资料文献、材料供应、设备维护等服务的人员。

研究与试验发展（R&D） 指在科学技术领域，为增加知识总量、以及运用这些知识去创造新的应用而进行的系统的创造性的活动，包括基础研究、应用研究、试验发展三类活动。

研究与试验发展（R&D）人员 指单位内部从事基础研究、应用研究和试验发展三类活动的人员。包括直接参加上述三类项目活动的人员以及这三类项目的管理人员和直接服务人员。为研发活动提供直接服务的人员包括直接为研发活动提供资料文献、材料供应、设备维护等服务的人员。

研究与试验发展（R&D）人员折合全时当量 是国际上通用的、用于比较科技人力投入的指标。指 R&D 全时人员（全年从事 R&D 活动累积工作时间占全部工作时间的 90% 及以上人员）工作量与非全时人员按实际工作时间折算的工作量之和。

研究与试验发展（R&D）内部支出 指调查单位在报告年度用于内部开展 R&D 活动（基础研究、应用研究和试验发展）的实际支出。包括用于 R&D 项目（课题）活动的直接支出，以及间接用于 R&D 活动的管理费、服务费、与 R&D 有关的基本建设支出以及外协加工费等，不包括生产性活动支出、归还贷款支出以及与外单位合作或委托外单位进行 R&D 活动而转拨给对方的经费支出。

专利 是专利权的简称，是对发明人的发明创造经审查合格后，由专利局依据专利法授予发明人和设计人对该项发明创造享有的专有权。包括发明、实用新型和外观设计。

发明专利 指专利法及其实施细则所称的发明，指对产品、方法或者改进所提出的新的技术方案。

实用新型专利 指专利法及其实施细则所称的实用新型，指对产品的形状、构造或者其结合所提出的适于实用的新的技术方案。

外观设计专利 指专利法及其实施细则所称的外观设计，指对产品的形状、图案、色彩或者其结合所做出的富有美感并适于工业上应用的新设计。

Explanatory Notes on Main Statistical Indicators

Personnel Engaged in Science and Technology Activities refer to persons directly engaged in science and technology activities as well as persons engaged in science and technology management and persons offering direct services to science and technology activities in the surveyed entities in the reporting year. Persons directly engaged in science and technology activities include: persons engaged in science and technology activities in such institutions as research labs of entities, laboratories, technical development centers and middle-stage test workshops (bases); persons not working in the above-mentioned institutions but included in the science and technology activity project (task) team, etc. Persons engaged in science and technology management and persons offering direct services for science and technology activities include administrative staff related to science and technology activities, as well as persons directly providing information and literature, supply of materials, equipment maintenance and other services.

R&D refers to systematic and creative activities in the field of science and technology to increase the total knowledge, and apply such knowledge to create new applications, including three kinds of activities, i.e. basic research, applied research, and experimental development.

R&D Personnel refer to persons in the surveyed entities who are engaged in three kinds of activities, i.e. basic research, applied research and experimental development. They include those who participate in the above-mentioned three kinds of activities directly, research management personnel and persons directly serving these activities. Persons providing direct services include those who provide information and literature, supply of materials, equipment maintenance and other services.

Full-Time Equivalent of R&D Personnel is an indicator globally used to compare input of scientific talents. It refers to the sum of workload of full-time R&D personnel (the personnel whose accumulative annual working time involved in R&D activities takes 90% and above of the whole working time) plus the workload of non-full time personnel that is equivalent of the actual working time.

Internal R&D Expenditure means the actual disbursement of investigated entities on internal R&D activities (basic research, applied research, and experimental development) in the reporting year, including direct spending on R&D project (task) activities, and management expenses and service fees indirectly spent on R&D activities, R&D related basic construction expense and external assisting processing charges, etc., excluding production-based activity expense, loan repayment expense and fund transferred to external institution cooperated or entrusted to conduct R&D activities.

Patent is the abbreviation of patent right, referring to the exclusive right granted by patent authorities upon examination and approval of inventions and creations to the inventors and designers with regard to the invention, including inventions, utility models and industrial designs.

Invention means the invention mentioned in the Patent Law and its detailed rules for implementation, i.e. the new technological solutions presented for the product, methodology, or improvement.

Utility Model means the utility model mentioned in the Patent Law and its detailed rules for implementation, i.e. the new practical technological solutions presented for the product shape, structure, color or combination.

Industrial Design means the industrial design mentioned in the Patent Law and its detailed rules for implementation, i.e. new designs of product shape, pattern, color or combination which are aesthetic and suitable for industrial applications.

20

北京统计年鉴2020　BEIJING STATISTICAL YEARBOOK

教育
EDUCATION

简要说明

主要内容

教育统计资料包括高等教育（研究生教育、普通本专科教育、成人本专科教育、其他各类高等学历教育）、中等教育(高中阶段、初中阶段)、小学教育、学前教育、特殊教育(盲聋哑和弱智儿童学校等)、工读学校等资料。主要指标包括学校数、在校学生数、招生数、毕业生数、教职工数、专任教师数等内容。

Brief Introduction

Main Content

Educational statistics include those for higher education (postgraduate education, undergraduate and junior college education, undergraduate and junior college education for adults, and other kinds of higher education for diplomas); secondary education (senior high school, junior high school); primary education; preschool education; special education (schools for the blind, deaf and mute, and mentally handicapped children, etc.); work-study schools for delinquent children. Main indicators include the number of schools, number of student enrollment, number of new enrollment, number of graduates, number of teachers and staff, and number of full-time teachers, etc.

20-1 教育基本情况(1978-2019年)
BASIC STATISTICS FOR EDUCATION (1978-2019)

年 份 Year	全市各类学校数(个) Total Number of Various Schools (unit)	#普通高等学校 General Institutions of Higher Education	#中等教育 Secondary Education	#普通高中 Regular Senior Secondary Schools	#小学教育 Primary Schools	全市各类学校在校学生数(人) Enrolled Students in Various Schools (person)	#普通本专科 Regular Undergraduates and College Students	#中等教育 Secondary Education	#普通高中 Regular Senior Secondary Schools	#小学教育 Primary Schools
1978		35			4666		48618		415612	937336
1979		48			4534		55073		299974	968723
1980		50			4485		83032		312188	951763
1981		51			4445		98044		175180	900350
1982		51			4381		93878		92401	854516
1983		54			4269		90894		88657	838078
1984		57			4168		102962		110916	763204
1985		61			4059		122791		119876	733605
1986		66			3995		129647		109862	749101
1987		67			3875		136694		109023	777982
1988		67			3793		145134		108106	850577
1989		67			3703		141625		110745	934696
1990		67			3611		139646		100669	995831
1991	8496	67	1168	282	3482	2142085	136940	565357	93728	1013268
1992	8052	67	1150	279	3306	2194268	139978	617847	82894	1001762
1993	7789	66	1145	280	3190	2266932	158906	679821	78261	1022166
1994	7574	67	1150	280	3035	2348406	175203	758310	86584	1024503
1995	7158	65	1170	286	2867	2380096	182173	834903	102522	1007301
1996	7121	65	1189	296	2780	2388002	189953	881912	118476	999740
1997	6858	65	1181	288	2696	2361438	195842	887644	133461	977323
1998	6456	63	1190	282	2511	2325043	212984	895042	145966	919531
1999	5807	64	1182	275	2352	2297673	234033	931029	161473	836655
2000	5458	59	1159	302	2169	2299433	282585	972930	179002	743109
2001	4873	61	1111	289	1960	2297107	340284	988985	194283	664443
2002	4447	62	998	325	1824	2294947	398573	984117	220667	594241
2003	4158	74	977	329	1652	2299416	458898	968035	250959	546530
2004	3971	77	945	338	1504	2291594	500245	919178	274803	516042
2005	3782	79	917	335	1403	2264004	536724	859132	278358	494482
2006	3751	82	888	335	1310	2910228	554702	799074	259414	473275
2007	3593	83	863	328	1235	3195763	567875	839038	243818	666617
2008	3508	82	838	325	1202	3208704	575639	782866	219163	659500
2009	3425	88	804	305	1160	3214354	577154	740396	203477	647101
2010	3330	89	779	289	1104	3299555	577828	727741	198415	653255
2011	3367	89	769	290	1090	3426025	578633	711130	195072	680457
2012	3314	91	760	289	1081	3568273	581844	732224	193505	718655
2013	3439	89	757	291	1093	3736003	589234	706713	187586	789276
2014	3437	89	766	306	1040	3774868	594614	651443	177554	821152
2015	3454	90	768	306	996	3734245	593448	587112	169412	850321
2016	3524	91	767	305	984	3733544	588389	552468	163130	868417
2017	3556	92	766	304	984	3861492	580663	522658	163977	875849
2018	3585	92	757	309	970	4083211	581133	525434	155478	913216
2019	3640	93	765	318	941	4124862	585971	538096	152857	941614

注：1. 从2007年开始，普通中学、小学、工读学校、特殊教育、学前教育在校学生数包括外省市户口借读学生。
2. 1991-2005年，中等教育为普通中等学校口径，包括普通中专、技工学校、职业中学、普通中学和工读学校；2006年起，包括普通中专、成人中专、技工学校、职业高中和普通中学。

资料来源：北京市教育委员会。

Note: a) From 2007, enrolled students in general high schools, primary schools, work-study schools for delinquent children, special education schools, and pre-school education included those from outside Beijing and studying in Beijing on temporary basis.

b) In 1991-2005, general middle schools included technical secondary schools, technician training schools, vocational schools, general high schools, and work-study schools. In and after 2006, middle schools included technical secondary schools, technical secondary schools for adults, technician training schools, vocational senior high schools and general high schools.

Source: Beijing Municipal Education Commission.

20-1 续表 1 Continued 1

年 份 Year	全 市 各类学校 招生数(人) New Enrollment in Various Schools (person)	#普通本专科 Regular Undergraduates and College Students	#中等教育 Secondary Education	#普通高中 Regular Senior Secondary Schools	#小学教育 Primary Schools	全 市 各类学校 毕业生数(人) Number of Graduates in Various Schools (person)	#普通本专科 Regular Undergraduates and College Students
1978		17445		161288	199076		10881
1979		15848		160340	154809		8585
1980		17972		131961	138751		8233
1981		17921		54296	121744		2289
1982		21936		35212	104357		25753
1983		27988		40282	96028		31009
1984		31805		47068	103482		20110
1985		40670		35265	135048		21442
1986		35390		27863	160513		26953
1987		41163		41186	156954		34894
1988		42187		35429	184516		33066
1989		33557		33254	184609		35863
1990		36275		30596	161742		36171
1991	571685	37700	205107	28589	148300	487740	37702
1992	622142	41517	232765	25790	157145	520787	37075
1993	651729	52205	242274	26275	175853	526982	32888
1994	704933	51884	287642	34704	186315	528199	34855
1995	691972	52868	308786	40803	168903	554690	45094
1996	628772	55269	289612	42603	156898	575969	46471
1997	581091	56884	289719	49566	124231	584120	49973
1998	581786	62264	308157	52956	100415	600662	49322
1999	603332	78354	320731	56998	94358	603027	49936
2000	635328	99397	324862	65890	92002	604900	51556
2001	641432	116344	313257	69195	91230	617889	55831
2002	671956	128320	326835	84679	86406	624329	67621
2003	662877	143483	302071	94894	82631	610826	83816
2004	635842	147298	271396	93519	73577	614137	99637
2005	630515	156124	259133	88605	71020	622974	117367
2006	851808	154969	234524	76375	73138	787596	132488
2007	927144	156222	252709	71590	109203	851126	138834
2008	938891	157238	236714	68397	110440	832585	149459
2009	962648	158992	240937	65983	102414	865025	152336
2010	1002141	155228	238954	65649	113728	834340	150156
2011	1050131	157543	243754	64146	132719	838521	151277
2012	1108574	162042	254790	63381	141738	881804	152980
2013	1182301	163081	239010	59983	165807	923050	148689
2014	1113688	160056	202434	55184	153249	937209	147023
2015	1091756	152741	186517	56743	145876	961180	152118
2016	1115515	154715	180881	53544	145274	924267	153005
2017	1248003	153028	181936	53755	157559	939184	152990
2018	1286509	155784	172981	47355	184339	940336	146654
2019	1196902	156820	190366	51403	182873	1018835	144645

20-1 续表 2 Continued 2

年 份 Year	#中等教育 Secondary Education	#普通高中 Regular Senior Secondary Schools	#小 学 教 育 Primary Schools	专任教师数（人） Full-time Teachers (person)	平均每一专任教师负担学生数(人) Average Number of Students Instructed by a Full-time Teacher(person) 普通中学 General Middle Schools	小 学 Primary Schools
1978		174899	151950		19.9	20.7
1979		239813	114047		16.1	21.3
1980		145501	144025		14.8	21.7
1981		170992	162306		13.4	19.7
1982		111153	135562		12.3	19.5
1983			95919		11.5	19.6
1984		24498	169251		13.2	18.2
1985		24720	156035		13.9	17.4
1986		36942	138350		14.1	17.3
1987		43589	121599		12.8	16.8
1988		36127	105948		11.4	17.6
1989		29267	97208		11.0	19.1
1990		40369	102782		10.1	18.6
1991		34428	132544	168485	10.5	18.0
1992		32471	156306	169249	11.3	17.4
1993		27428	157838	170361	12.1	17.4
1994		24112	184566	175025	13.1	16.9
1995		23353	183894	176591	13.6	16.5
1996		25170	162030	178006	13.7	16.1
1997		33010	146023	179080	13.2	15.7
1998		39683	156194	178210	12.8	14.9
1999		40660	175656	175496	13.2	13.7
2000		47569	185059	167040	14.1	12.8
2001		51263	167076	168080	14.3	12.1
2002		51180	156683	166490	14.2	11.2
2003		56601	123580	166510	13.7	11.0
2004		66556	100139	172055	12.9	10.6
2005		73260	93486	174589	11.8	10.3
2006	290047	78037	90799	191365	10.8	9.8
2007	272651	78408	112332	195568	11.5	13.8
2008	262871	78468	112268	199114	10.9	13.5
2009	253067	70132	110730	203825	10.0	13.0
2010	233837	62305	102971	206602	10.2	13.2
2011	223955	58275	101678	199789	9.8	13.4
2012	224938	55657	109492	204812	9.7	13.7
2013	240225	58072	111839	216463	9.5	14.4
2014	229640	57773	112819	225165	9.0	14.4
2015	205795	57738	103893	226043	8.4	14.3
2016	182511	52841	111481	231251	7.9	14.0
2017	168125	49685	125938	236346	7.7	13.6
2018	158863	51065	124610	241719	7.9	13.9
2019	157545	50390	138968	248239	8.2	13.8

20-2　幼儿园基本情况(1978-2019年)
BASIC STATISTICS FOR KINDERGARTENS (1978-2019)

单位：人　　　　(person)

年　份 Year	园数(所) Number of Kindergartens (unit)	班数(个) Number of Classes (unit)	离园人数 Children Leaving	入园人数 Children Entering	在园人数 Children Enrollment	教职工数 Teachers and Staff	#专任教师 Full-time Teachers
1978	5074				235923	39982	8369
1979	4623				237037	40424	8777
1980	3991				219407	38475	7765
1981	3888				233089	38832	8814
1982	3849				254458	42663	9271
1983	1999				306975	48666	8234
1984	3682				295427	47721	9499
1985	2955				316024	47033	10523
1986	3503				342824	52654	12690
1987	3732				364011	54211	14449
1988	3563				354367	52105	14705
1989	3509				344394	50280	17208
1990	3798				372555	49587	17972
1991	3761		133788	172884	402699	49472	18788
1992	3510		158740	181299	404779	48007	18513
1993	3369		165963	170580	372368	44741	18114
1994	3301		113652	167267	352979	42118	17413
1995	3024		103355	148272	315277	38549	16084
1996	3056		135376	112449	271752	33586	14792
1997	2892		110345	95140	253478	32811	14596
1998	2662		99279	93819	245046	30362	13841
1999	2180		91996	89463	237055	29367	13216
2000	2047		85301	91724	229012	27257	12595
2001	1719	8259	85842	87892	217521	26106	12479
2002	1540	8494	79447	91092	213794	25402	12127
2003	1430	7733	76879	86465	199390	26324	13056
2004	1422	8087	71677	86672	205532	28326	14208
2005	1358	8148	71926	83485	202301	28026	14813
2006	1361	8051	70400	68299	197546	28958	15632
2007	1306	8132	70681	83969	214423	30465	17013
2008	1266	8382	72119	85938	226681	32535	18176
2009	1253	9036	65684	89761	247778	34973	17952
2010	1245	9883	68135	105048	276994	37227	21677
2011	1305	11213	76790	115539	311417	44458	24170
2012	1266	11882	79131	115248	331524	48080	26330
2013	1384	12580	88322	128106	348681	53049	28806
2014	1426	13245	96478	133977	364954	57950	31692
2015	1487	14098	101928	149042	394121	61903	34040
2016	1570	14913	99626	152769	416982	65806	36071
2017	1604	15810	105651	177354	445535	69100	37903
2018	1657	16176	117102	165130	450645	71686	38867
2019	1733	16934	118178	168166	467595	79777	41187

资料来源：北京市教育委员会。
Source: Beijing Municipal Education Commission.

20-3 各类学校基本情况
BASIC STATISTICS FOR VARIOUS SCHOOLS

单位：人 (person)

项目	Item	校数(所) Number of Schools (unit)		教职工数 Teachers and Staff		#专任教师 Full-time Teachers	
		2019	2018	2019	2018	2019	2018
合计	**Total**	**3640**	**3585**	**394425**	**382107**	**248239**	**241719**
高等教育	**Higher Education**	**175**	**174**	**147629**	**146141**	**71206**	**70491**
研究生培养机构(不计校数)	Institutions Providing Postgraduate Programs (Number of Schools Not Counted)	(147)	(147)			-64853.0	(60298)
高等学校	Institutions of Higer Education	(59)	(59)			-53999.0	(49867)
科研机构	Research Institutes	(88)	(88)			-10854.0	(10431)
普通高等学校	General Institutions of Higher Education	93	92	141372	139435	68685	67755
成人高等学校	Adult Institutions of Higher Education	18	18	3259	3298	1376	1424
民办的其他高等教育机构	Privately-funded Institutions of Higher Education	64	64	2998	3408	1145	1312
中等教育	**Secondary Education**	**765**	**757**	**103598**	**101653**	**78901**	**76662**
高中阶段教育	Senior Secondary Education	429	422	103598	101653	54956	53494
普通高中	General Middle Schools	318	309	91277	88974	47326	45730
中等职业教育	Secondary Vocational Schools	111	113	12321	12679	7630	7764
普通中专	General Technical Secondary Schools	29	29	3242	3232	1825	1823
成人中专	Technical Secondary Schools for Adults	11	11	563	573	277	286
职业高中	Vocational Senior High Schools	44	46	5517	5702	3917	4038
技工学校	Technician Training Schools	27	27	2999	3172	1611	1617
初中阶段教育	Junior Secondary Education	336	335			23945	23168
小学教育	**Primary Schools**	**941**	**970**	**61934**	**61138**	**55758**	**54531**
工读学校	**Work-Study Schools for Delinquent Children**	**6**	**6**	**253**	**263**	**194**	**202**
特殊教育	**Special Education**	**20**	**21**	**1234**	**1226**	**993**	**966**
学前教育	**Pre-school Education**	**1733**	**1657**	**79777**	**71686**	**41187**	**38867**

注：1. 普通高中的教职工数中包含普通初中的教职工数。
2. 表中带( )数据不计入“校数”的合计数据中。
资料来源：北京市教育委员会。
Note: a) Number of "Teachers and Staff" in general senior high schools includes those in general junior high schools.
b) In this table data with ( ) were not be calculated in the total number of schools.
Source: Beijing Municipal Education Commission.

20-3 续表 Continued

单位：人 (person)

项目	Item	毕业生数 Graduates 2019	毕业生数 Graduates 2018	招生数 New Enrollment 2019	招生数 New Enrollment 2018	在校学生数 Total Enrollment 2019	在校学生数 Total Enrollment 2018
合 计	**Total**	**1018835**	**940336**	**1196902**	**1286509**	**4124862**	**4083211**
高等教育	**Higher Education**	**602554**	**538102**	**654285**	**762872**	**2170144**	**2187006**
研究生	Postgraduates	91874	86622	123938	117154	360621	335983
高等学校	Institutions of Higher Education	87259	82311	118034	111185	341717	317903
科研机构	Scientific Research Institutions	4615	4311	5904	5969	18904	18080
普通本专科	General Undergraduates and College Students	144645	146654	156820	155784	585971	581133
中央部委属高校	Under Central Ministries and Commissions	73832	73843	81432	80786	322730	317752
市属高校	Under Municipal Government	70813	72811	75388	74998	263241	263381
公办高校	Public Colleges and Universities	54683	56538	58922	59508	206208	205928
民办高校	Privately-funded Colleges and Universities	16130	16273	16466	15490	57033	57453
成人本专科	Adult Undergraduates and College Students	58535	59573	47601	54558	129736	144097
成人高等学校	Adult Institutions of Higher Education	4485	4900	5274	5746	11444	11628
普通高等学校	General Institutions of Higher Education	54050	54673	42327	48812	118292	132469
在职人员攻读	Employees Enrolled in Graduate Programes						
硕士学位	Leading to Master Degrees					21362	37243
网络本专科生	Students Enrolled in Internet-based Courses	307500	245253	325926	435376	1072454	1088550
中等教育	**Secondary Education**	**157545**	**158863**	**190366**	**172981**	**538096**	**525434**
高中阶段教育	Senior Secondary	84201	88605	72968	71997	229374	246463
普通高中	General Middle Schools	50390	51065	51403	47355	152857	155478
#北京市户籍	Registered Residents of Beijing	47135	48093	46930	43463	141451	144216
中等职业教育	Secondary Vocational Schools	33811	37540	21565	24642	76517	90985
普通中专	General Technical Secondary Schools	12707	12695	8271	7869	29951	35094
成人中专	Technical Secondary Schools for Adults	6970	8193	1274	4056	11240	18649
职业高中	Vocational High Schools	3262	5149	3033	2448	8165	8556
技工学校	Technical Schools	10872	11503	8987	10269	27161	28686
初中阶段教育	Junior Secondary Education	73344	70258	117398	100984	308722	278971
#北京市户籍	Registered Residents of Beijing	60075	55662	92505	75935	245561	212999
小学教育	**Primary Education**	**138968**	**124610**	**182873**	**184339**	**941614**	**913216**
#北京市户籍	Registered Residents of Beijing	91456	75510	136722	136599	683799	636628
工读学校	**Work-study School for Delinquent Children**	**204**	**205**	**186**	**189**	**451**	**503**
特殊教育	**Special Education Schools**	**1386**	**1454**	**1026**	**998**	**6962**	**6407**
学前教育	**Preschool Education**	**118178**	**117102**	**168166**	**165130**	**467595**	**450645**

20-4 高等教育学生情况(2019年) STATISTICS FOR STUDENTS IN INSTITUTIONS OF HIGHER EDUCATION (2019)

单位：人 (person)

项目	Item	毕(结)业生人数 Number of Graduates	招生数 New Enrollment	在校学生数 Total Enrollment
普通本科、专科生	General Undergraduates and Junior College Students	144645	156820	585971
专科	Enrolled in Specialized Courses Education	26008	27504	73977
本科	Enrolled in Full Undergraduate Courses	118637	129316	511994
成人本科、专科生	Adult Undergraduates and Junior College Students	58535	47601	129736
专科	Enrolled in Specialized Courses Education	23429	14804	36726
本科	Enrolled in Full Undergraduate Courses	35106	32797	93010
网络本科、专科生	Students Enrolled in Internet-based Courses	307500	325926	1072454
专科	Enrolled in Specialized Courses	204321	165358	600952
本科	Enrolled in Full Undergraduate Courses	103179	160568	471502
研究生	Postgraduates	91874	123938	360621
硕士	Master Degree	76149	99623	259811
博士	Doctor Degree	15725	24315	100810
在职人员攻读硕士学位	Employees Enrolled in Graduate Programes Leading to Master Degrees			21362
自考助学班	Classes for Self-Learning Programs	33		166
普通预科生	College Preparatory Courses			1391
研究生课程进修班	Postgraduate Courses for Advanced Study			
进修及培训	In-Service Training Courses	1247741		
留学生	Overseas Students	26187	29987	50760

资料来源：北京市教育委员会。
Source: Beijing Municipal Education Commission.

20-5 普通高等学校本专科基本情况(2019年) BASIC STATISTICS FOR GENERAL INSTITUTIONS OF HIGHER EDUCATION (2019)

单位：人 (person)

项目	Item	校数(所) Number of Schools (unit)	毕业生数 Graduates	招生数 New Enrollment	在校学生数 Total Enrollment	教职工数 Teachers and Staff	#专任教师 Full-time Teachers
合计	**Total**	**93**	**144645**	**156820**	**585971**	**141372**	**68685**
#女生	Females		88838	92660	335752	69935	31726
综合大学	Comprehensive Universities	5	18657	18990	71115	24037	10495
理工院校	Science and Engineering	31	57395	62698	235501	55335	27818
农业院校	Agriculture	3	5907	6427	23110	4454	2720
林业院校	Forestry	1	3027	3329	13449	1994	1258
医药院校	Medicine	4	3919	5157	19364	16443	3465
师范院校	Teacher Training	2	5084	6207	22244	5583	3711
语文院校	Literature	10	11416	11886	44630	7787	4530
财经院校	Finance and Economics	16	18884	20833	74330	10893	6563
政法院校	Politics and Law	8	9898	9793	36935	6244	2970
体育院校	Physical Culture	3	2983	3366	12824	1762	1187
艺术院校	Art	9	4770	5285	21137	4997	2843
民族院校	Minorities Colleges	1	2705	2849	11332	1843	1125

资料来源：北京市教育委员会。
Source: Beijing Municipal Education Commission.

20–6 普通高校分学科研究生情况(2019年)
STATISTICS FOR POSTGRADUATES BY SUBJECT OF STUDY OF GENERAL INSTITUTIONS OF HIGHER EDUCATION (2019)

单位：人 (person)

项 目	Item	毕业生 Graduates			招生数 New Enrollment			在校学生数 Student Enrollment		
		合计 Total	硕士 Master Degree	博士 Doctor Degree	合计 Total	硕士 Master Degree	博士 Doctor Degree	合计 Total	硕士 Master Degree	博士 Doctor Degree
合 计	**Total**	**87259**	**72635**	**14624**	**118034**	**95211**	**22823**	**341717**	**247146**	**94571**
#女 生	Females	45930	40070	5860	61742	51845	9897	170829	131954	38875
学术型学位	**Academic Degree**	**48185**	**34249**	**13936**	**61286**	**40167**	**21119**	**201855**	**111881**	**89974**
哲 学	Philosophy	590	396	194	633	392	241	2260	1177	1083
经济学	Economics	2949	2343	606	3407	2373	1034	10604	6109	4495
法 学	Law	4378	3592	786	5559	4115	1444	16732	10725	6007
教育学	Education	1571	1290	281	1977	1502	475	6384	4412	1972
文 学	Literature	3423	2858	565	3788	2936	852	12212	8495	3717
历史学	History	565	399	166	666	418	248	2390	1260	1130
理 学	Science	7294	3685	3609	10388	5510	4878	35271	15121	20150
工 学	Engineering	18657	13322	5335	24013	15682	8331	81824	44813	37011
农 学	Agriculture	1122	710	412	1499	915	584	4619	2212	2407
医 学	Medicine	2229	1325	904	3027	1647	1380	8926	4673	4253
军事学	Military	8	6	2				10	1	9
管理学	Management	4123	3297	826	4754	3544	1210	15592	9351	6241
艺术学	Art	1276	1026	250	1575	1133	442	5031	3532	1499
专业学位	**Professional Degree**	**39074**	**38386**	**688**	**56748**	**55044**	**1704**	**139862**	**135265**	**4597**

资料来源：北京市教育委员会。
Source: Beijing Municipal Education Commission.

20-7 高等教育外国留学生情况(2019年)
STATISTICS FOR FOREIGN STUDENTS STUDYING IN BEIJING FOR HIGHER EDUCATION (2019)

单位：人 (person)

项目	Item	毕(结)业生数 Graduates	授予学位人数 Number of Students Conferred with Degree	招生数 New Enrollment	在校学生数 Total Enrollment
合计	**Total**	**26187**	**6385**	**29987**	**50760**
#女生	Females	12788	2830	14750	22990
按学历划分	**By Educational Background**				
专科	Enrolled in Specialized Courses	680	612	1095	4756
本科	Enrolled in Full Undergraduate Courses	3137	2910	4192	9524
硕士	Master Degree	3532	2863	5230	15512
博士	Doctor Degree	130		88	225
培训	Training	18708		19382	20743
按地区划分	**By Region**				
亚洲	Asia	13562	3934	15343	28956
非洲	Africa	2220	1103	2952	5910
欧洲	Europe	6354	801	7068	9413
北美洲	North America	2960	349	3307	4435
南美洲	South America	477	126	581	1028
大洋洲	Oceania	614	72	736	1018
按经费来源	**By Source of Funds**				
国际组织资助	From International Organizations	199	191	214	466
中国政府资助	From Chinese Government	6373	2920	8276	17929
本国政府资助	From the Government of the Students' Home Country	280	118	176	411
学校间交换	Interscholastic Exchange	3731	188	4276	5041
自费	Self Funding	15604	2968	17045	26913

资料来源：北京市教育委员会。
Source: Beijing Municipal Education Commission.

20–8　普通中专分科情况(2019年)
BASIC STATISTICS FOR SPECIALIZED SECONDARY SCHOOLS BY MAJOR (2019)

单位：人 (person)

项　目	Item	毕业生数 Graduates	招生数 New Enrollment	在校学生数 Total Enrollment
合　计	**Total**	**12707**	**8271**	**29951**
#女　生	Females	5982	3925	14135
按类别分	**By Category**			
农林牧渔类	Agriculture, Forestry, Animal Production and Hunting, Fishing	114	61	169
资源环境类	Resources and Environment	35		
能源与新能源类	Energy and New Energy	53		
土木水利类	Construction and Water Conservancy	538	176	658
加工制造类	Processing and Manufacturing	716	109	472
石油化工类	Petroleum and Chemicals			
轻纺食品类	Light Industry, Textile and Foods	100		91
交通运输类	Transportation	2325	1049	4304
信息技术类	IT	804	352	1589
医药卫生类	Medicine and Health	1721	1437	4830
休闲保健类	Recreation and Healthcare			
财经商贸类	Finance, Business and Trade	1586	634	2492
旅游服务类	Tourism Services	195	68	296
文化艺术类	Culture and Arts	1424	1289	6131
体育与健身	Sports and Fitness	362	322	1120
教育类	Education	1099	1214	3392
司法服务类	Judicial Services	188	101	387
公共管理与服务类	Public Management and Services	219	109	413
其　他	Others	1228	1350	3607

资料来源：北京市教育委员会。
Source: Beijing Municipal Education Commission.

20−9 职业高中分科情况(2019年)
BASIC STATISTICS FOR VOCATIONAL SCHOOLS BY MAJOR (2019)

单位：人 (person)

项　目	Item	毕业生数 Graduates	招生数 New Enrollment	在校学生数 Total Enrollment
合　计	**Total**	**3262**	**3033**	**8165**
#女　生	Females	1524	1377	3594
按类别分	**By Category**			
农林牧渔类	Agriculture, Forestry, Animal Production and Hunting, Fishing	31	43	93
资源环境类	Resources and Environment		5	13
能源与新能源类	Energy and New Energy		10	40
土木水利类	Construction and Water Conservancy	17	20	47
加工制造类	Processing and Manufacturing	41	30	123
石油化工类	Petroleum and Chemicals			
轻纺食品类	Light Industry, Textile and Foods	22	22	76
交通运输类	Transportation	515	487	1261
信息技术类	IT	502	525	1416
医药卫生类	Medicine and Health	85	49	119
休闲保健类	Recreation and Healthcare	25	14	35
财经商贸类	Finance, Business and Trade	451	305	851
旅游服务类	Tourism Services	409	267	743
文化艺术类	Culture and Arts	329	416	1176
体育与健身	Sports and Fitness	19	33	65
教育类	Education	711	762	1997
司法服务类	Judicial Services	40		
公共管理与服务类	Public Management and Services	65	35	97
其　他	Others		10	13

资料来源：北京市教育委员会。
Source: Beijing Municipal Education Commission.

20-10　校外教育情况(2019年)
STATISTICS FOR AFTER-SCHOOL EDUCATION (2019)

单位：人　　(person)

项　目	Item	单位数(个) Number of Organizations(unit)	活动小组数(个) Activity Groups(unit)	参加小组学生数 Participating Students	教职工人数 Teachers and Staff	#专任教师数 Full-time Teachers	兼职教师数 Part-time Teachers
合　计	**Total**	**58**	**8256**	**515933**	**2151**	**1399**	**1006**
少年宫	Children's Palaces	21	6104	180837	1460	904	563
少年科技馆	Children's Scientific Museums	9	468	111641	268	207	73
少年之家	Children's Homes	27	1668	209455	396	262	370
少年活动站	Children's Clubs	1	16	14000	27	26	

资料来源：北京市教育委员会。
Source: Beijing Municipal Education Commission.

20-11　幼儿园基本情况(2019年)
STATISTICS FOR KINDERGARTENS (2019)

单位：人　　(person)

项　目	Item	总计 Total	#女 Females	城区 In City	镇区 In Counties and Towns	乡村 In Villages
园　数　(所)	Number of Kindergartens　(unit)	1733		1357	148	228
班　数　(个)	Number of Classes　(unit)	16934		14117	1550	1267
在园幼儿数	Children Enrollment	467595	226517	393853	42762	30980
教职工数	Teachers and Staff	79777	72418	68965	6165	4647
#园　长	Headmasters	2681	2562	2197	229	255
专任教师	Full-time Teachers	41187	40250	35442	3276	2469
卫生保健人员	Health Workers	3808	3765	3339	283	186

资料来源：北京市教育委员会。
Source: Beijing Municipal Education Commission.

20-12 高等教育自学考试情况
STATISTICS FOR HIGHER EDUCATION SELF-STUDY EXAMINATION

项目		Item		2019	2018
报考人次	(人次)	Number of Registered Person-times	(person-time)	127326	150981
报考科次	(科次)	Number of Registered Subject-times	(person-time)	382453	500731
发出专科毕业证书	(个)	Number of Junior College Diplomas Issued	(unit)	2876	3692
发出本科毕业证书	(个)	Number of General College Diplomas Issued	(unit)	4095	3446
开考专业	(个)	Number of Majors Examined	(unit)	66	81

资料来源：北京市教育委员会。
Source: Beijing Municipal Education Commission.

20-13 特殊教育情况(2019年)
STATISTICS FOR SPECIAL EDUCATION (2019)

单位：人 (person)

项目	Item	毕业生 Graduates	招生数 New Enrollment	在校学生数 Total Enrollment
合　计	**Total**	**1386**	**1026**	**6962**
#女　生	Females	453	364	2382
特殊教育学校	Special Education Schools	415	431	2791
小学附设特教班	Special Classes Attached to Primary Schools	15	8	72
小学随班就读	Studying in Primary Schools	432	163	2297
普通(职业)初中随班就读	Studying in General Junior Secondary (Vocational) Classes	518	424	1757

资料来源：北京市教育委员会。
Source: Beijing Municipal Education Commission.

20-14 职业技术培训机构基本情况(2019年)
BASIC STATISTICS FOR VOCATIONAL AND TECHNICAL TRAINING INSTITUTIONS(2019)

项目	Item	学校数(所) Schools (unit)	教学班(点、个) Teaching Classes (site,unit)	结业生数(人次) Students Completing Courses (person-time)	#女性 Females
合计	**Total**	**3188**	**39979**	**2423238**	**1250483**
#少数民族	National Miniorities			10011	5945
按培训机构分	**By Training Institution**				
职工技术培训学校(机构)	**Technical Training Schools (Institutions) for Employees**	**22**	**378**	**23192**	**11670**
教育部门和集体办	Run by Education Authorities and Collectively-run	4	194	11967	8726
其他部门办	Run by Other Authorities	1	16	1562	301
民办	Privately-funded	17	168	9663	2643
农村成人文化技术培训学校(机构)	**Cultural and Technical Training Schools (Institutions) for Rural Adults**	**1874**	**8541**	**638483**	**420698**
#教育部门和集体办	Run by Education Authorities and Collectively-run	1874	8541	638483	420698
县办	Run by Counties	3	29	8758	6070
乡办	Run by Townships	146	5308	482281	295412
村办	Run by Villages	1725	3204	147444	119216
其他培训机构(含社会培训机构)	**Other Training Institutions (Including Social Training Institutions)**	**1292**	**31060**	**1761563**	**818115**
教育部门和集体办	Run by Education Authorities and Collectively-run	59	73	62315	38707
其他部门办	Run by Other Authorities	146	165	542795	168899
民办	Privately-funded	1085	30804	1156313	610409
中外合作办		2	18	140	100
按培训形式分	**Group by Form of Training**				
#资格证书培训	Qualification Certificate Training			206691	112864
岗位证书培训	Job Post Certificate Training			213624	122529

资料来源：北京市教育委员会、北京市人力资源和社会保障局。
Source: Beijing Municipal Education Commission, Beijing Municipal Human Resources and Social Security Bureau.

20-14 续表 Continued

单位：人 (person)

项目	Item	注册学生数 Student Enrollment	#女性 Females	教职工数 Teachers and Staff	#专任教师 Full-time Teachers	聘请校外教师 External Teachers Retained
合计	**Total**	**2729282**	**1294341**	**48329**	**20425**	**14326**
#少数民族	National Miniorities	13750	7155	297	141	140
按培训机构分	**By Training Institution**					
职工技术培训学校(机构)	**Technical Training Schools (Institutions) for Employees**	**24166**	**9313**	**636**	**422**	**295**
教育部门和集体办	Run by Education Authorities and Collectively-run	8917	6009	281	216	170
其他部门办	Run by Other Authorities	1562	301	7	5	18
民办	Privately-funded	13687	3003	348	201	107
农村成人文化技术培训学校(机构)	**Cultural and Technical Training Schools (Institutions) for Rural Adults**	**507926**	**220999**	**1341**	**502**	**1943**
#教育部门和集体办	Run by Education Authorities and Collectively-run	507926	220999	1341	502	1943
县办	Run by Counties	8589	6008	54	39	71
乡办	Run by Townships	384081	138420	612	428	1413
村办	Run by Villages	115256	76571	675	35	459
其他培训机构(含社会培训机构)	**Other Training Institutions (Including Social Training Institutions)**	**2197190**	**1064029**	**46352**	**19501**	**12088**
教育部门和集体办	Run by Education Authorities and Collectively-run	91417	44376	2718	873	897
其他部门办	Run by Other Authorities	615219	179649	15834	5309	5057
民办	Privately-funded	1490414	839904	27787	13317	6132
中外合作办		140	100	13	2	2
按培训形式分	**Group by Form of Training**					
#资格证书培训	Qualification Certificate Training					
岗位证书培训	Job Post Certificate Training					

20—15 民办教育基本情况(2019年)
STATSTICS FOR PRIVATELY-FUNDED EDUCATION (2019)

单位：人 (person)

项 目	Item	校数(所) Number of Schools (unit)	毕业生数 Graduates	招生数 New Enrollment	在校学生数 Total Enrollment	教职工数 Teachers and Staff	#专任教师 Full-time Teachers	兼任教师数 Part-time Teachers
合 计	**Total**	**1016**	**73848**	**100289**	**306669**	**58821**	**28379**	**3266**
民办高等教育	**Privately-funded Higher Education**	**80**	**16130**	**16466**	**57033**	**8706**	**3849**	**3039**
普通高校	General Institutions of Higher Education	16	16130	16466	57033	5708	2704	1896
民办高等教育机构	Other Privately-funded Higher Education Institutions	64				2998	1145	1143
民办中等教育	**Privately-funded Secondary Education**	**118**	**8669**	**11654**	**32764**	**14184**	**8408**	**189**
高中阶段教育	Senior High School Education	90	2493	2117	7460	14184	8408	189
民办普通高中	Privately-funded Senior High Schools	71	1657	1864	6465	13508	8081	30
民办中等职业教育	Privately-funded Secondary Vocational Education	19	836	253	995	676	327	159
初中阶段教育	Junior High School Education	28	6176	9537	25304			
民办小学	**Privately-funded Primary Schools**	**53**	**8219**	**8371**	**44380**	**1826**	**1255**	**5**
民办幼儿园	**Privately-funded Kindergartens**	**765**	**40830**	**63798**	**172492**	**34105**	**14867**	**33**

资料来源：北京市教育委员会。
Source: Beijing Municipal Education Commission.

20—16 高校办学条件(2019年)
SCHOOL CONDITIONS OF HIGHER EDUCATION INSTITUTIONS (2019)

项 目	Item	合计 Total	中央 Central	市属市管 Municipal
普通高校	**General Institutions of Higher Education**			
校舍建筑面积 (平方米)	Building Area (sq.m)	42196067	29818153	12377914
占地面积 (平方米)	Floor Space (sq.m)	48200893	31690608	16510284
图 书 (万册)	Books (10000 volumes)	11830	7516	4315
固定资产总值 (万元)	Total Value of Fixed Assets (10000 yuan)	19640081	14080200	5559881
#科学科研仪器设备值	Value of Scientific Research Instruments and Equipment	6753572	4738597	2014975
成人高校	**Institutions of Higher Education for Adults**			
校舍建筑面积 (平方米)	Building Area (sq.m)	793790	334430	459360
占地面积 (平方米)	Floor Space (sq.m)	1334692	472830	861862
图 书 (万册)	Books (10000 volumes)	228	59	169
固定资产总值 (万元)	Total Value of Fixed Assets (10000 yuan)	291143	183126	108017
#科学科研仪器设备值	Value of Scientific Research Instruments and Equipment	40065	5740	34326

资料来源：北京市教育委员会。
Source: Beijing Municipal Education Commission.

20-17 基础教育办学条件(2019年)
SCHOOL CONDITIONS OF BASIC EDUCATION (2019)

单位：平方米 (sq.m)

项目	Item	普通中学 General Middle Schools	小学 Primary Schools
学校占地面积	Floor Space	25694055	14432738
校舍建筑面积	Building Area	15357825	7590879
#当年新增	Newly Added in the Year	509115	266538
#危房面积	Area of Dangerous Buildings		3168
教学及辅助用房	Teaching and Auxiliary Houses	5714008	3521760
普通教室	Classrooms	3261896	2711389
实验室	Laboratories	928256	219769
图书室	Libraries	417886	189044
微机室	Computer Rooms	226918	147261
语音室	Language Labs	44530	18573
体育馆	Gymnasiums	834522	235723
行政办公用房	Administrative Houses	1653029	900123
生活用房	Houses for Life	4256176	1334462
其他用房	Houses for Other Purposes	3734612	1834533
计算机 (台)	Computers (unit)	363493	262809
图书藏量 (册)	Books Collections (volume)	31157056	27695662
电子图书藏量 (册)	E-book Collections (volumes)	7997750	3952896

资料来源：北京市教育委员会。
Source: Beijing Municipal Education Commission.

20-18 非本市户籍、外国籍学生情况(2019年)
STATISTICS FOR STUDENTS FROM OTHER PROVINCES, MUNICIPALITIES AND AUTONOMOUS REGIONS ALONG WITH OTHER COUNTRIES (2019)

单位：人 (person)

项目	Item	非本市户籍学生数 Students from Other Provinces, Municipalities and Autonomous Regions	#民办学校 Privately-funded Schools	外国籍学生数 Overseas Students	#民办学校 Privately-funded Education
合计	**Total**	**461105**	**102876**	**5780**	**2339**
普通中学	General Middle Schools	74567	10875	1434	246
初中	Junior Secondary Schools	63161	10345	709	198
高中	Senior Secondary Schools	11406	530	725	48
中等职业教育	Vocational Secondary Schools	14072	218	358	
小学	Primary Schools	257815	26650	2077	591
特殊教育	Special Education Schools	344		1	
幼儿园	Kindergartens	114307	65133	1910	1502

资料来源：北京市教育委员会。
Source: Beijing Municipal Education Commission.

20–19　教育经费情况（2014–2018年）
STATISTICS FOR EDUCATIONAL FUNDS (2014-2018)

单位：万元 (10000 yuan)

年份 Year	合计 Total	国家财政性教育经费 Government Appropriation for Education	#一般公共预算教育经费 General Public Budget for Education	民办学校中举办者投入 Funds from Runners of Private Schools	社会捐赠经费 Funds from Social Donations	事业收入 Income from Undertakings	#学费 Tuition Fees	其他教育经费 Other Educational Funds
2014	10937374	9683641	7584873	10529	10431	1048953	833849	183820
2015	11171250	9810774	8474342	10685	9624	1177133	925848	163034
2016	11934724	10491718	8822890	9261	10879	1299205	1034188	123662
2017	12512746	10863394	9557007	6368	9341	1478756	1201615	154888
2018	13525400	11661674	10207229	8711	6503	1651516	1331358	196996

资料来源：北京市教育委员会。
Source: Beijing Municipal Education Commission.

20–20　生均一般公共预算教育事业费支出和公用经费支出情况
AVERAGE GENERAL PUBLIC BUDGET FOR EDUCATIONAL EXPENSES AND PUBLIC EXPENDITURE

单位：元 (yuan)

项目	Item	2018	2017	2018年为2017年% 2018 as % of 2017
生均一般公共预算教育事业费支出	**Average General Public Budget Educational Expenses**			
幼儿园	Kindergartens	36841.48	32012.80	115.1
普通小学	Regular Primary Schools	31375.64	30016.78	104.5
普通初中	Regular Junior Secondary Schools	59768.35	57636.12	103.7
普通高中	Regular Senior Secondary Schools	66083.69	61409.06	107.6
中等职业学校	Secondary Vocational Schools	53861.27	53256.01	101.1
普通高等学校	General Institutions of Higher Education	58805.03	63805.40	92.2
生均一般公共预算公用经费支出	**Average General Public Budget Public Expenditure**			
幼儿园	Kindergartens	15488.29	13159.54	117.7
普通小学	Regular Primary Schools	11092.22	10855.08	102.2
普通初中	Regular Junior Secondary Schools	21603.57	21282.49	101.5
普通高中	Regular Senior Secondary Schools	22721.41	21677.24	104.8
中等职业学校	Secondary Vocational Schools	21712.91	25370.60	85.6
普通高等学校	General Institutions of Higher Education	26795.81	32126.86	83.4

资料来源：北京市教育委员会。
Source: Beijing Municipal Education Commission.

主要统计指标解释

研究生培养机构 指经国家批准按国家计划招收和培养硕士、博士和其他研究生的高等学校和科学研究机构。

普通高等学校 指按国家规定的设置标准和审批程序批准举办的，通过国家统一招生考试，招收高中毕业生为主要培养对象，实施高等教育的全日制大学、独立设置的学院和高等专科学校、短期职业大学。

成人高等学校 指按国家规定的设置标准和审批程序批准举办的，通过全国成人高等教育统一招生考试，招收具有高中毕业或同等学历的人员为主要培养对象，利用函授、业余、脱产等多种形式对其实施高等学历教育的学校。包括：职工高等学校、农民高等学校、管理干部学院、教育学院、独立函授学院、广播电视大学和其他机构。

高等教育机构 指经省、自治区、直辖市教育行政部门审批并颁发办学许可证，不具有颁发学历文凭资格的实施高等教育的单位。

民办学校 指经有关主管部门批准，公民个人、社会团体及其他社会组织等利用非国家财政性教育经费，面向社会举办的学校及其他教育机构。

学历文凭考试机构 经教育行政部门专门批准，进行全日制高等教育的民办其他高等教育机构。

专科教育 应当使学生掌握本专业必备的基础理论、专门应用技术知识，具有从事本专业实际工作的基本技能和技术应用能力。全日制专科教育的基本修业年限为二至三年。

本科教育 应当使学生比较系统地掌握本学科、专业必需的基础理论、基本知识，掌握本专业必要的基本技能、方法和相关知识，具有从事本专业实际工作和研究工作的初步能力。全日制本科教育的基本修业年限为四至五年。

硕士研究生教育 应当使学生掌握本学科坚实的基础理论、系统的专业知识，掌握相应的技能、方法和相关知识，具有从事本专业实际工作和科学研究工作的能力。硕士研究生教育的基本修业年限为二至三年。

博士研究生教育 应当使学生掌握本学科坚实宽广的基础理论、系统深入的专业知识、相应的技能和方法，具有独立从事本学科创造性科学研究工作和实际工作的能力。博士研究生教育的基本修业年限为三至四年。

网络学生 指经教育部批准的现代远程教育试点学校设立的网络教育学院，基于互联网上实施高等学历教育所招收的普通和成人本科、专科学生。

在职人员攻读硕士学位学生 指经国务院学位委员会批准的，为提高在职人员业务水平，通过攻读硕士学位入学全国联考所招收的学生。培养的学生只有学位没有学历。

外国留学生 指接受来中国学习的外籍学生。

毕业生数 指上学年度内，具有学籍的学生学完教学计划规定的全部课程，考试及格，取得毕业证书，实际毕业的学生数。不包括结业生和肄业生数。

招生数 指新学年开始时，按照国家计划实际招收入学的新生数。不包括留级生和复读学生数。

在校学生数 指学年初开学以后，具有学籍的注册学生数。

结业生数 指具有学籍的学生学习期满，有一门以上主要课程(包括毕业论文或毕业设计)不及格或其他方面不合格，未予毕业而发给结业证书的学生数。不包括短训班和单科结业学生。

教职工数 指在学校(机构)工作并由学校(机构)支付工资的教职工人数。教职工数包括校本部教职工、科研机构人员、校办企业职工、其他附设机构人员。

专任教师 指主要从事教育工作的人员。包括临时（一年以内）调去帮助做其他工作的教学人员。不包括调离教学岗位，担任行政领导工作或其他工作的原教学人员；不包括兼任教师和代课教师。

特殊教育学校 指具备适应残疾儿童少年学习、康复、生活特点的场所和设施，招收盲聋哑、智力残疾及其他有特殊需要的儿童少年实施普通初等、普通中等或中等职业教育的独立设置学校。包括盲人学校、聋人学校、弱智学校、其他特殊教育学校。

学校占地面积 指学校校园内的土地面积，不包括校园外学校拥有的农场、林场及校办工厂等的土地面积。

校舍建筑面积 指产权归学校所有，已经使用的各种用房的建筑面积。不包括尚未竣工的在建工程和借用、租用的房舍或临时搭用的棚舍。

危房面积 指年久失修、结构构件受到严重损坏，有倒塌危险，经房管部门鉴定属于危房的面积。

Explanatory Notes on Main Statistical Indicators

Institutions Providing Postgraduate Programs refer to colleges and universities, research institutions recruiting and educating postgraduates of master's degree, doctor's degree and other degree upon approval by the government and under the State plan.

Regular Institutions of Higher Education refer to educational establishments set up according to the state's establishment standards and examination and approval procedures, recruiting graduates from senior secondary schools as the main target by National Matriculation Test. They include full-time universities, independent colleges and higher professional schools, short-term vocational colleges.

Adult Institutions of Higher Education refer to educational establishments, set up in line with the state's establishment standards and examination and approval procedures, recruiting personnel with senior high school or equivalent educational diploma through national college entrance test for adults, and providing higher education courses in many forms including correspondence, spare-time, or full-time teaching for adults. Institutions of higher learning for adults include schools of higher education for staff and workers, schools of higher education for farmers, colleges for management cadres, pedagogical colleges, independent correspondence colleges, Radio and TV universities and other educational establishments.

Higher Education Institutions refer to institutions offering higher education upon examination and approval by administrative departments in charge of education in provinces, autonomous regions and municipalities, with an education license, which are not eligible for conferring diploma.

Civilian-run Schools refer to schools and other educational institutions run by individuals, social groups and other social organizations upon approval by relevant competent authorities, by using educational funds not from state revenues.

Diploma Test Institutions refer to other civilian-run higher education institutions offering full-time higher education upon special approval by educational administration.

Secondary Technical Education shall enable students to understand necessary basic theories and special knowledge on applied technologies of a specialty, have basic skills and technical application ability for practice of the specialty. Full-time secondary technical education offers a basic study term of 2-3 years.

Undergraduate Education shall enable students to understand necessary basic theories and knowledge of a subject or specialty, have necessary basic skills, methodology and relevant knowledge of the specialty, and have preliminary skills for practical work and research of the specialty. Full-time undergraduate education offers a basic study term of 4-5 years.

Master's-degree Postgraduate Education shall enable students to understand solid basic theories, systematic professional knowledge of a subject, have relevant skills, methodology and relevant knowledge of the specialty, and have the ability for practical work and research of the specialty. Master's-degree postgraduate education offers a basic study term of 2-3 years.

Doctor's-degree Postgraduate Education shall enable students to understand solid and extensive basic theories, systematic and in-depth professional knowledge, relevant skills and methodology of a subject, have the ability for independent creative research and practical work of the specialty. Doctor's-degree postgraduate education offers a basic study term of 3-4 years.

Online Students refer to students for Internet-based higher education for diplomas for general undergraduate courses, undergraduate courses for adults, and secondary technical courses, recruited in online education colleges opened in schools as modern remote education pilots approved by the Ministry of Education.

Employees Enrolled in Graduate Programs for Master's Degree refer to students recruited through national entrance examination for studies of Master's degree approved by the Academic Degree Commission of the State Council, in order to improve the practical skills of on-the-job personnel. Graduated students will be conferred academic degree only, without academic credentials.

Foreign Students Studying in China refers to foreign students who study in China.

Number of Graduates means the number of enrolled students who are actually graduated after passing all exams and receiving a diploma upon completing all courses stated in the teaching plan within the last academic year. This does not include the number of students completing all courses with any one course not passed, and students not completing all courses or discontinuing their schooling.

Number of New Enrollment refers to the number of students actually recruited at the beginning of a new academic year in line with State plan, excluding the number of students failing to go up to the next grade and those resuming their interrupted studies.

Number of Student Enrollment means the number of students enrolled after the beginning of a new academic year.

Number of Students Completing Courses means the number of enrolled students completing their schooling with one and more courses not passed (including the graduation paper or graduation design) or other aspects not passed, who are not granted for graduation and awarded a certificate of completion, excluding the number of students completing short-term training courses and single-subject programs.

Number of Teachers and Staff means the number of teachers and staff working in and paid by schools (institutions). It includes the number of teachers and staff in the principal campus, in research institutions, school-run enterprises and other subsidiaries.

Full-time Teachers refer to personnel mainly engaged in teaching, including persons temporarily (within one year) transferred to other jobs, excluding persons transferred from teaching to administrative leadership or other jobs; excluding part-time teachers and teachers taking over a class for absent teachers.

Schools for Special Education refer to the independently set up schools with such characteristics as being suitable for learning, rehabilitation and life of disabled children and adolescents that enroll the blind, deaf and mute children and adolescents as well as those with mentally disabilities or other special needs to offer general primary, general secondary or secondary vocational education. They include schools for the blind, schools for the deaf, schools for the mentally disabled and other special education schools.

Area of Land Occupied by School means the area of land within campus, excluding the area of land occupied by farms, forest farms and school-run factories that are owned by the school but are outside the schoolyard.

Floor Space of Schoolhouse refers to the building area of various houses of which the property right is owned by the school and which have been used, excluding houses not completed and under construction, borrowed and rented, or temporarily built sheds and houses.

Area of Dilapidated Houses refers to the area of those houses that have not been repaired for many years, have seriously damaged components, are at the risk of collapse, and are identified by the house administration authority as dilapidated houses.

21

卫生及社会服务
HEALTH CARE AND SOCIAL SERVICES

简 要 说 明

主要内容

本章资料主要反映卫生、社会服务、残疾人事业的发展情况。

卫生部分统计资料主要包括卫生总费用、医疗卫生机构、卫生技术人员、床位数，医院工作情况，主要疾病死亡原因及构成，全市主要健康指标等情况。

社会服务部分统计资料主要包括基层社会工作、收养性单位、社会救助、婚姻登记情况。

残疾人统计资料主要包括残疾人康复、教育、就业、社会保障、就业和维权援助情况。

Brief Introduction

Main Content

Statistics in this chapter mainly show the development of health, social services and undertakings for disabled people.

Statistics for health mainly include the total health expenditures, the number of medical and health institutions, number of medical technical personnel, number of ward beds, works of hospitals, major causes of death and composition, main health indicators of Beijing, and so on.

Statistics for social services mainly consist of grass-roots social work, adoption institutions, social relief, and marriage registration.

Statistics for disabled persons mainly include information on rehabilitation, education, employment, social security, employment and aid for right protection of disabled persons.

21-1 卫生事业基本情况(1978-2019年)

年 份 Year	医疗卫生机构(个) Medical and Health Institutions (unit)	#医 院 Hospitals	#疾病预防控制中心(防疫站) Centers for Disease Control and Prevention	#妇幼保健院(所、站) Maternity and Child Care Centers (Stations)	#社区卫生服务中心(站) Community Health Services Centers (Stations)
1978	3263	125	22	15	
1979	3614	124	22	17	
1980	3818	129	22	19	
1981	4135	139	22	19	
1982	4389	149	22	18	
1983	4312	149	22	19	
1984	4173	160	22	18	
1985	4248	188	22	18	
1986	4483	198	22	20	
1987	4744	222	22	19	
1988	4342	266	22	17	
1989	4398	284	22	17	
1990	4953	325	22	17	
1991	4970	337	22	17	
1992	4868	345	22	16	
1993	4962	364	32	16	
1994	4958	387	33	16	
1995	4955	387	33	15	
1996	6470	405	33	13	
1997	6577	435	33	13	
1998	5723	449	32	11	
1999	5990	460	32	8	
2000	6176	458	30	8	
2001	5969	458	30	9	
2002	4998	461	24	19	35
2003	5075	459	29	19	36
2004	7236	503	29	19	43
2005	7536	519	28	18	93
2006	7640	541	28	18	90
2007	9023	535	31	18	1126
2008	9647	537	31	19	1282
2009	9717	522	31	19	1395
2010	9511	550	31	19	1587
2011	9699	569	32	19	1744
2012	9974	608	32	19	1897
2013	10141	647	32	19	1926
2014	10265	672	32	19	1958
2015	10425	701	30	19	1979
2016	10637	713	29	20	1997
2017	10986	732	28	20	2066
2018	11100	736	29	21	2079
2019	11340	745	29	19	2075

注：1．2010年及以前，本表中所有数据都不包含村卫生室及驻京部队医院情况。2011年开始，包含村卫生室情况。2012年开始，除床位数外均包含驻京部队医院数据，下同。

2．2010年开始，原卫生院数据并入到社区卫生服务中心(站)等其他卫生机构。

资料来源：北京市卫生健康委员会。

BASIC STATISTICS ON HEALTH CARE (1978-2019)

医疗卫生机构人员(人) Employed Persons in Medical and Health Institutions (person)	#卫生技术人员 Medical Technical Personnel	#执业(助理)医师 Certified (Assistant) Physicians	#注册护士 Registered Nurses
90174	65943	28435	16085
97942	72131	31842	17398
102601	74753	34365	17492
110774	81183	37886	20025
114420	83843	39385	20389
119222	86593	41216	21181
124664	89362	42112	22286
127771	90831	42216	23782
132865	94433	43403	25383
142556	101829	46007	27786
145362	105237	48216	30250
150062	108108	49361	32056
156304	111614	50934	34565
161103	114342	52309	35714
164213	115825	53254	36768
165170	116173	53906	36687
164867	116818	53865	36608
164436	115967	54114	36719
164981	116849	54091	37712
167090	119256	54909	38630
162609	115976	51902	38883
161823	116597	52646	39625
160258	115510	51570	39900
158185	115935	52100	40537
144021	109564	47236	38879
148406	112212	47887	39912
157157	116905	49283	41547
161432	120170	50913	42897
170586	127193	53084	45647
186290	139478	55156	50926
197765	150134	58904	55348
212086	160695	62578	61634
223694	171328	66165	67332
235708	181938	69749	72812
276654	219714	82192	95202
294012	229720	85819	100652
304990	242923	89590	106167
321151	256531	96445	114294
330777	264850	100878	117760
346255	276969	105732	123158
351765	281686	109376	123589
369139	297259	115771	131314

Note: a) In and before 2010, figures in this table did not include village health clinics and hospitals of troops stationed in Beijing. From 2011, figures included village health clinics. From 2012,figures in this table include troops stationed in Beijing with the bed number excluded. stationed in Beijing, the same below.

b) From 2010, data on health centers were incorporated into other health institutions such as community health service centers (stations).

Source: Beijing Municipal Health Commission.

21-1 续表 Continued

年 份 Year	医疗机构实有床位数(张) Beds in Medical Institutions (unit)	#医 院 Hospitals	每千户籍人口执业(助理)医师数(人) Certified (Assistant) Doctors per 1000 Registered Population (person)	每千户籍人口注册护士数(人) Registered Nurses per 1000 Registered Population (person)	每千户籍人口医院床位数(张) Ward Beds per 1000 Registered Population (unit)	每千常住人口执业(助理)医师数(人) Certified (Assistant) Doctors per 1000 Permanent Population (person)	每千常住人口注册护士数(人) Registered Nurses per 1000 Permanent Population (person)	每千常住人口医院床位数(张) Ward Beds per 1000 Permanent Population (unit)
1978	29767	23668	3.35	1.89	2.79			
1979	30231	24092	3.66	1.87	2.77			
1980	32453	25770	3.88	1.97	2.91			
1981	33666	26934	4.20	2.20	2.99			
1982	34574	28209	4.30	2.23	3.07			
1983	35987	29612	4.40	2.26	3.17			
1984	38580	31933	4.40	2.33	3.38			
1985	41603	35166	4.44	2.48	3.67			
1986	43956	38133	4.47	3.72	3.93			
1987	47538	41178	4.66	2.81	4.17			
1988	53078	45334	4.82	3.02	4.53			
1989	55623	48558	4.83	3.14	4.76			
1990	59036	51860	4.93	3.35	5.02			
1991	61744	54888	5.03	3.44	5.28			
1992	63230	55858	5.10	3.52	5.35			
1993	65621	58605	5.13	3.49	5.58			
1994	67112	60661	5.07	3.45	5.71			
1995	66925	60337	5.06	3.43	5.64			
1996	66760	60997	5.02	3.50	5.66			
1997	67946	61865	5.06	3.56	5.70			
1998	69095	63144	4.76	3.56	5.79			
1999	69465	63660	4.79	3.60	5.79			
2000	71245	65138	4.66	3.60	5.88			
2001	73053	66537	4.64	3.61	5.93			
2002	75188	67750	4.18	3.44	5.96			
2003	74298	66990	4.21	3.51	5.83			
2004	77359	69850	4.25	3.60	6.01	3.30	2.78	
2005	79067	72329	4.32	3.66	6.13	3.31	2.79	
2006	81440	74762	4.41	3.84	6.24	3.36	2.89	6.77
2007	83736	76915	4.53	4.19	6.34	3.38	3.12	4.71
2008	86196	79089	4.78	4.50	6.43	3.48	3.27	4.67
2009	90100	82471	5.00	4.94	6.62	3.57	3.51	4.70
2010	92871	85935	5.24	5.35	6.83	3.37	3.43	4.38
2011	94735	87596	5.46	5.70	6.85	3.46	3.61	4.34
2012	100167	92610	6.33	7.34	7.14	3.97	4.60	4.48
2013	104034	96558	6.52	7.65	7.34	4.06	4.76	4.57
2014	109789	102851	6.72	7.96	7.71	4.16	4.93	4.78
2015	111555	104644	7.17	8.50	7.78	4.44	5.27	4.82
2016	116963	110021	7.40	8.64	8.07	4.64	5.42	5.06
2017	120557	113576	7.78	9.06	8.36	4.87	5.67	5.23
2018	123508	116279	7.95	8.98	8.45	5.08	5.74	5.40
2019	127111	119574	8.28	9.40	8.56	5.38	6.10	5.55

21-2 卫生总费用(2000-2018年)
TOTAL HEALTH EXPENDITURES (2000-2018)

年份 Year	卫生总费用(亿元) Total Health Expenditures (100 million yuan)	政府卫生支出 Health Expenditures by Governments		社会卫生支出 Social Health Expenditures		个人现金卫生支出 Health Expenditures in Cash by Individuals	
		绝对数(亿元) Absolute Number (100 million yuan)	占卫生总费用比重(%) As % of Total (%)	绝对数(亿元) Absolute Number (100 million yuan)	占卫生总费用比重(%) As % of Total (%)	绝对数(亿元) Absolute Number (100 million yuan)	占卫生总费用比重(%) As % of Total (%)
2000	166.7	34.7	20.8	61.8	37.1	70.3	42.1
2001	201.1	45.3	22.5	73.2	36.4	82.7	41.1
2002	262.4	48.5	18.5	99.6	38.0	114.2	43.5
2003	314.2	65.8	20.9	132.0	42.0	116.3	37.0
2004	357.2	69.4	19.4	150.7	42.2	137.1	38.4
2005	432.8	85.7	19.8	187.8	43.4	159.2	36.8
2006	497.4	115.9	23.3	208.0	41.8	173.5	34.9
2007	523.2	142.0	27.2	212.0	40.5	169.2	32.3
2008	668.5	180.0	26.9	271.3	40.6	217.3	32.5
2009	689.6	201.1	29.2	296.3	43.0	192.2	27.9
2010	814.7	226.8	27.8	385.1	47.3	202.8	24.9
2011	977.3	275.5	28.2	453.2	46.4	248.6	25.4
2012	1190.0	320.4	26.9	601.0	50.5	268.7	22.6
2013	1349.6	356.4	26.4	717.8	53.2	275.5	20.4
2014	1594.6	394.4	24.7	890.6	55.9	309.7	19.4
2015	1834.8	445.8	24.3	1069.9	58.3	319.1	17.4
2016	2049.0	468.0	22.8	1247.2	60.9	333.8	16.3
2017	2193.8	507.4	23.1	1327.4	60.5	359.0	16.4
2018	2500.8	580.0	23.2	1530.0	61.2	390.9	15.6

资料来源：北京市卫生健康委员会。
Source: Beijing Municipal Health Commission.

21-3 医疗卫生机构基本情况
BASIC STATISTICS FOR MEDICAL AND HEALTH CARE INSTITUTIONS

项目	Item	2019	2018	构成(%) Composition (%)	
				2019	2018
机构数 (个)	**Number of Institutions (unit)**	**11340**	**11100**	**100.0**	**100.0**
#医院	Hospitals	745	736	6.6	6.6
社区卫生服务中心(站)	Health Service Centers (Stations) for Community	2075	2079	18.3	18.7
门诊部	Outpatient Departments	1355	1268	11.9	11.4
妇幼保健院(所、站)	Maternity and Child Care Hospitals	19	21	0.2	0.2
疾病预防控制中心(防疫站)	Disease Prevention and Control Center (Epidemic Prevention Station)	29	29	0.3	0.3
专科疾病防治院(所、站)	Specific Disease Prevention and Cure Centers	25	26	0.2	0.2
诊所、卫生所、医务室、护理站	Clinics, Health Centers, Infirmaries, Nursing Stations	4300	4132	37.9	37.2
床位数 (张)	**Number of Beds (unit)**	**127111**	**123508**	**100.0**	**100.0**
#医院	Hospitals	119574	116279	94.1	94.1
社区卫生服务中心(站)	Health Service Centers (Stations) for Community	4879	4774	3.8	3.9
妇幼保健院(所、站)	Maternity and Child Care Hospitals	2049	2021	1.6	1.6
专科疾病防治院(所、站)	Specific Disease Prevention and Cure Centers	609	434	0.5	0.4
卫生技术人员数 (人)	**Number of Medical Technical Personnel (person)**	**297259**	**281686**	**100.0**	**100.0**
#医院	Hospitals	215470	206209	72.5	73.2
社区卫生服务中心(站)	Health Service Centers (Stations) for Community	32818	30970	11.0	11.0
妇幼保健院(所、站)	Maternity and Child Care Hospitals	5845	5646	2.0	2.0
专科疾病防治院(所、站)	Specific Disease Prevention and Cure Centers	703	555	0.2	0.2
#执业(助理)医师	Certified Doctors	115771	109376	38.9	38.8
注册护士	Registered Nurses	131314	123589	44.2	43.9

注：本表数据除床位数外均包含驻京部队医院数据。
资料来源：北京市卫生健康委员会。
Note: Figures in this table include troops stationed in Beijing with the bed number excluded.
Source: Beijing Municipal Health Commission.

21-4 医院基本情况(2019年)
BASIC STATISTICS ON HOSPITALS (2019)

项目	Item	医院数 (个) Hospitals (unit)	床位数 (张) Beds (unit)	职工人数 (人) Employed Persons (person)	#卫生技术人员 Medical Technical Personnel	#执业医师 Certified Doctors	#中医 Doctors of Traditional Chinese Medicine
合计	**Total**	**745**	**119574**	**262588**	**215470**	**76414**	**12490**
按隶属关系分	**By Affiliation**						
#市属	Municipal	30	25007	51734	42707	14568	957
区属	Districts	96	32200	57749	47446	17088	4006
按专业分	**By Specialty**						
#综合医院	General Hospitals	291	65129	160747	136410	48530	2240
中医医院	Hospital Specialized in Traditional Chinese Medicine	177	15115	31410	24999	10324	7334
中西医结合医院	Hospitals Combining Western Medicine with Traditional Chinese Medicine	44	10184	15558	12776	4734	2041
民族医院	Nationality Hospitals	3	220	381	275	103	73
口腔医院	Stomatology Hospitals	35	707	6176	4754	1813	9
眼科医院	Ophthalmology Hospitals	14	589	1151	707	211	9
肿瘤医院	Tumor Hospitals	10	4324	6740	5224	1521	48
心血管病医院	Hospitals for Cardiovascular Diseases	2	1374	3604	3097	780	12
胸科医院	Thorax Hospitals	1	638	865	694	188	4
妇(产)科医院	Hospitals for Gynecology and Obstetrics	19	1413	5402	3746	1178	30
儿童医院	Children's Hospitals	11	2347	5979	4831	1679	107
精神病医院	Psychiatric Hospital	24	7907	6324	4602	1077	63
传染病医院	Infectious Disease Hospitals	3	1636	3305	2716	885	43
骨科医院	Hospitals of Orthopedics	9	966	1526	1183	408	86
整形外科医院	Orthopaedics Hospitals	1	328	838	568	224	
其他专科医院	Other Specialized Hospitals	35	2744	4939	3428	1059	170
护理院	Nursing Hospitals	10	220	192	122	28	2

注：本表数据除床位数外均包括驻京部队数据。
资料来源：北京市卫生健康委员会。
Note: Figures in this table include troops stationed in Beijing with the bed number excluded.
Source: Beijing Municipal Health Commission.

21-4 续表 Continued

单位：人 (person)

项 目	Item	#执业助理医师 Certified Assistant Doctors	#中医 Doctors of Traditional Chinese Medicine	#注册护士 Registered Nurses	#药师(士) Pharmacists (Assistant Pharmacists)	#影像技师(士) Image Technicians (Assistant Technicians)	#检验师(士) Laboratorians (Assistant Laboratorians)
合 计	**Total**	**1974**	**479**	**104874**	**9529**	**3467**	**5876**
按隶属关系分	**By Affiliation**						
#市 级	Municipal	157	6	20460	1952	815	1338
区 级	Districts	372	47	22088	2699	703	1568
按专业分	**By Specialty**						
综合医院	General Hospitals	735	98	69405	4916	1980	3335
中医医院	Hospital Specialized in Traditional Chinese Medicine	403	248	9491	2255	464	815
中西医结合医院	Hospitals Combining Western Medicine with Traditional Chinese Medicine	192	70	5884	787	189	402
民族医院	Nationality Hospitals	17	12	116	22	6	4
口腔医院	Stomatology Hospitals	144		2155	51	93	33
眼科医院	Ophthalmology Hospitals	14	1	345	38	6	24
肿瘤医院	Tumor Hospitals	30	1	2475	197	216	127
心血管病医院	Hospitals for Cardiovascular Diseases	1		1724	63	56	56
胸科医院	Thorax Hospitals			404	30	29	24
妇(产)科医院	Hospitals for Gynecology and Obstetrics	49	2	1979	147	42	211
儿童医院	Children's Hospitals	30	5	2109	231	93	255
精神病医院	Psychiatric Hospitals	62	3	2593	227	38	129
传染病医院	Infectious Disease Hospitals	3		1292	138	48	129
骨科医院	Hospitals of Orthopedics	27	8	582	57	30	35
整形外科医院	Orthopaedics Hospitals			275	13	7	10
其他专科医院	Other Specialized Hospitals	147	16	1561	136	76	110
护理院	Nursing Hospitals	3	2	38	4	1	2

21−5 医院工作情况(2019年)
WORKS OF HOSPITALS (2019)

项目	Item	诊疗人次数(千人次) Patients Treated (1000 person times)	#门诊 Out-patients	健康检查人数(千人次) Health Check (1000 person times)	平均开放病床数(张) Beds in Use (unit)	入院人数(千人次) In-patients (1000 person times)	出院人数(千人次) Discharged Patients (1000 person times)
合计	**Total**	**172091.1**	**144317.8**	**3961.9**	**115191**	**3691.1**	**4208.4**
#综合医院	General Hospitals	110790.9	85615.9	2846.8	64185	2407.3	2924.7
中医医院	Hospital Specialized in Traditional Chinese Medicine	30150.3	29278.4	419.3	14172	310.6	309.1
中西医结合医院	Hospitals Combining Western Medicine with Traditional Chinese Medicine	9339.3	8720.0	402.2	10024	183.9	186.8
民族医院	Nationality Hospitals	121.2	121.2		181	2.4	2.4
口腔医院	Stomatology Hospitals	3572.6	3417.1	0.9	464	10.6	10.6
眼科医院	Ophthalmology Hospitals	342.2	337.8	25.7	587	20.0	19.9
肿瘤医院	Tumor Hospitals	1904.7	1874.2	115.6	3623	244.8	244.7
心血管病医院	Hospitals for Cardiovascular Diseases	813.1	781.0	4.0	1374	76.5	76.3
胸科医院	Thorax Hospitals	281.1	276.0		630	17.0	17.0
妇(产)科医院	Hospitals for Gynecology and Obstetrics	2314.7	2243.2	2.2	1352	69.3	69.2
儿童医院	Children's Hospitals	6223.6	5663.9	13.5	2137	148.6	147.3
精神病医院	Psychiatric Hospitals	1762.8	1747.5	6.8	7583	25.2	25.2
传染病医院	Infectious Disease Hospitals	1538.4	1437.5	0.9	1635	54.4	54.3
骨科医院	Hospitals of Orthopedics	588.9	570.7	17.6	966	20.9	20.8
整形外科医院	Orthopaedics Hospitals	209.6	200.0	0.2	328	12.1	12.0
其他专科医院	Other Specialized Hospitals	978.8	902.7	22.1	2470	36.6	36.4
护理院	Nursing Centers	0.2	0.2		161	0.3	0.1

资料来源：北京市卫生健康委员会。
Source: Beijing Municipal Health Commission.

21-5 续表 Continued

项 目	Item	病死率 (%) Case Fatality Rate (%)	病床周转次数 (次) Turnover Beds (time)	病床使用率 (%) Utilization Rate of Beds (%)	出院者平均住院日 (日) Average Hospitalization Period (day)
合 计	**Total**	**1.0**	**32.0**	**82.6**	**8.6**
#综合医院	General Hospitals	1.0	37.4	85.0	8.2
中医医院	Hospital Specialized in Traditional Chinese Medicine	1.4	21.8	69.7	11.4
中西医结合医院	Hospitals Combining Western Medicine with Traditional Chinese Medicine	3.1	18.6	79.5	14.7
民族医院	Nationality Hospitals	0.9	13.5	60.0	16.2
口腔医院	Stomatology Hospitals		22.8	46.7	7.5
眼科医院	Ophthalmology Hospitals		33.9	30.6	3.1
肿瘤医院	Tumor Hospitals	0.2	67.5	91.8	5.5
心血管病医院	Hospitals for Cardiovascular Diseases	0.2	55.6	94.6	6.2
胸科医院	Thorax Hospitals	0.4	27.0	92.1	12.7
妇(产)科医院	Hospitals for Gynecology and Obstetrics	…	51.2	57.4	4.1
儿童医院	Children's Hospitals	0.1	68.9	113.2	5.5
精神病医院	Psychiatric Hospital	0.6	3.3	99.3	79.1
传染病医院	Infectious Disease Hospitals	1.6	33.2	93.9	10.3
骨科医院	Hospitals of Orthopedics	1.6	21.5	83.9	13.9
整形外科医院	Orthopaedics Hospitals		36.7	76.7	5.0
其他专科医院	Other Specialized Hospitals	3.2	14.7	66.3	14.2
护理院	Nursing Centers	18.7	0.8	52.6	58.7

21-6 居民前十位死因顺位、死亡率及构成(2019年)
DEATH RATE AND COMPOSITION OF 10 MAJOR DISEASES (2019)

顺位 No.	死因名称	Cause of Death	死亡率(1/10万) Death Rate (1/100 thousands)	构成(%) Composition (%)
	全市	**Total**		
1	恶性肿瘤	Malignant Tumour	185.6	26.5
2	心脏病	Heart Disease	183.2	26.2
3	脑血管病	Cerebrovasular Disease	128.3	18.3
4	呼吸系统疾病	Disease of the Respiratory System	65.6	9.4
5	损伤和中毒	Trauma and Toxicosis	30.4	4.3
6	内分泌、营养、代谢及免疫疾病	Endocrine, Nutrition, Metabolite and Immunity Disease	22.5	3.2
7	消化系统疾病	Disease of the Digestive System	19.4	2.8
8	神经系统疾病	Neurological Disease	10.2	1.5
9	泌尿生殖系统疾病	Disease of the Genitourinary System	5.7	0.8
10	传染病	Infectious Disease	4.5	0.7
	男性	**Male**		
1	恶性肿瘤	Malignant Tumour	221.1	27.8
2	心脏病	Heart Disease	193.8	24.3
3	脑血管病	Cerebrovasular Disease	148.4	18.6
4	呼吸系统疾病	Disease of the Respiratory System	78.3	9.8
5	损伤和中毒	Trauma and Toxicosis	35.7	4.5
6	内分泌、营养、代谢及免疫疾病	Endocrine, Nutrition, Metabolite and Immunity Disease	23.1	2.9
7	消化系统疾病	Disease of the Digestive System	22.5	2.8
8	神经系统疾病	Neurological Disease	11.8	1.5
9	传染病	Infectious Disease	6.0	0.8
10	泌尿生殖系统疾病	Disease of the Genitourinary System	5.9	0.7
	女性	**Female**	172.7	28.5
1	心脏病	Heart Disease	150.4	24.8
2	恶性肿瘤	Malignant Tumour	108.5	17.9
3	脑血管病	Cerebrovasular Disease	53.1	8.8
4	呼吸系统疾病	Disease of the Respiratory System	25.2	4.2
5	损伤和中毒	Trauma and Toxicosis	22.0	3.6
6	内分泌、营养、代谢及免疫疾病	Endocrine, Nutrition, Metabolite and Immunity Disease	16.3	2.7
7	消化系统疾病	Disease of the Digestive System	8.6	1.4
8	神经系统疾病	Neurological Disease	5.5	0.9
9	泌尿生殖系统疾病	Disease of the Genitourinary System	4.8	0.8
10	精神障碍	Mental Disorders		

资料来源：北京市卫生健康委员会。
Source: Beijing Municipal Health Commission.

21-7 主要健康指标情况(1978-2019年)
MAJOR HEALTH INDICATIONS(1978-2019)

年 份 Year	婴 儿 死亡率 (‰) Infant Mortality (‰)	新生儿 死亡率 (‰) Newborn Baby Mortality (‰)	孕产妇 死亡率 (1/10万) Pregnant & Lying-in Women Mortality (1/100000)	甲乙类传染 病发病率 (1/10万) Incidence Rate of Catogory A and B Epidemics (1/100000)
1978	17.11	12.21	31.00	
1979	16.97	10.08	34.70	1584.25
1980	14.79	10.24	26.30	2165.23
1981	13.84	9.22	48.50	2225.71
1982	12.97	8.02	24.50	2193.16
1983	13.79	8.78	28.10	1904.55
1984	10.98	7.78	16.80	1666.68
1985	13.94	10.41	22.90	1335.23
1986	16.05	12.13	30.50	1120.19
1987	15.56	11.08	26.60	826.51
1988	14.98	10.48	24.80	640.98
1989	14.96	10.53	34.50	547.61
1990	11.66	8.49	25.00	509.55
1991	12.46	8.56	24.00	448.23
1992	12.12	8.93	30.10	385.98
1993	10.38	7.21	16.50	356.66
1994	10.93	7.29	18.94	374.31
1995	11.45	7.52	22.27	309.99
1996	10.05	6.97	15.32	340.24
1997	9.45	6.36	23.69	294.41
1998	7.58	5.53	10.46	306.37
1999	7.95	5.94	17.53	308.10
2000	5.36	3.70	9.70	301.19
2001	6.01	4.05	11.71	276.85
2002	5.56	3.70	15.12	282.95
2003	5.89	3.83	15.60	228.00
2004	4.61	3.49	15.19	408.03
2005	4.35	3.29	15.91	445.91
2006	4.66	3.42	7.87	448.70
2007	3.89	2.65	16.74	421.02
2008	3.70	2.45	18.52	312.99
2009	3.49	2.47	14.55	339.89
2010	3.29	2.06	12.14	268.99
2011	2.84	1.88	9.09	226.76
2012	2.87	1.91	6.05	174.45
2013	2.33	1.52	9.45	155.87
2014	2.33	1.46	7.19	165.49
2015	2.42	1.52	8.69	150.86
2016	2.21	1.48	10.83	138.00
2017	2.29	1.45	8.17	139.60
2018	2.15	1.26	10.64	131.50
2019	1.99	1.21	2.96	139.80

资料来源：北京市卫生健康委员会。
Source: Beijing Municipal Health Commission.

21−8 基层社会工作情况
STATISTICS FOR GRASSROOT SOCIAL WORK

项　　目		Item		2019	2018	2019年为208年% 2019 as % of 2018
社区服务机构数	(个)	Number of Service Facilities in Urban Communities	(unit)	12128	11895	102.0
#社区服务中心	(个)	Community Service Centers	(unit)	204	203	100.5
城市便民利民服务网点数	(个)	Number of Urban Convenient Service Outlets	(unit)	5454	5456	100.0

资料来源：中共北京市委社会工作委员会北京市民政局。
Source: Social Work Committee of Beijing Municipal Committee of the Communist Party of China Beijing Municipal Civil Affairs Bureau.

21−9 收养性单位情况(2019年)
STATISTICS ON ADOPTING INSTITUTIONS (2019)

项　目		Item		合计 In Total	#社会福利院 Social Welfare Institutions	#儿童福利院 Children's Welfare Institutions	#福利类精神病院和医院 Welfare Mental Hospitals and Hospitals	#养老公寓机构 Urban Elderly Care Agencies	#农村特困养老机构 Rural Elderly Care Agencies
单位数	(个)	Institutions	(unit)	591	10	10	1	545	5
职工人数	(人)	Employed Persons	(person)	20175	1130	543	54	17823	46
床位数	(张)	Beds	(unit)	115476	4585	2518	52	103674	304
年末在院人数	(人)	Persons Received	(person)	50337	2617	1206	23	43962	74
#自　费		Self-supported		41906	1806		23	40035	42

资料来源：中共北京市委社会工作委员会北京市民政局。
Source: Social Work Committee of Beijing Municipal Committee of the Communist Party of China Beijing Municipal Civil Affairs Bureau.

21-10 婚姻登记(1981-2019年)
BASIC STATISTICS FOR MARRIAGE AND DIVORCE REGISTRATIONS (1981-2019)

年份 Year	结婚对数(对) Registered Marriages (couple)	#涉外及华侨、港澳台居民登记结婚对数 Registered Marriages with Foreigners and Overseas Chinese and Citizens of Hong Kong, Macao and Taiwan (couple)	初婚人数(人) Number of First Marriage (person)	离婚对数(对) Registered Divorces (couple)	#民政部门登记离婚对数 Divorces Registered in the Civil Affair Department (couple)
1981	200352		389936	5170	1780
1982	141253		261851	5359	1581
1983	117976		227676	5322	1465
1984	113362		217649	5654	1387
1985	134462		258255	5874	1746
1986	143105		274634	7541	2474
1987	149952		267424	8916	3218
1988	113333		212544	10664	4198
1989	103829		188287	12515	5174
1990	92988		169510	14748	5791
1991	91979		165752	15287	6483
1992	89095		158241	15567	6477
1993	89938		160127	17829	7589
1994	90379		160793	19928	8327
1995	85511		148722	20160	8096
1996	86803		146666	20716	8225
1997	84208		144040	22257	8628
1998	85534		146750	23708	9381
1999	83312		141740	23922	8502
2000	80212		136500	26616	6384
2001	79385	873	133259	27683	5425
2002	76136	606	126371	27691	5810
2003	93526	761	158729	30637	10142
2004	126436	974	214443	32657	21013
2005	96956	937	158736	34244	23991
2006	171286	1172	294223	35505	24954
2007	117926	991	193387	36622	26432
2008	147516	1165	246309	37619	27277
2009	181771	1176	305803	41299	29998
2010	138104	1085	222269	43970	32595
2011	173238	1260	288406	43521	32999
2012	174114	1242	287436	48575	38243
2013	163676	1070	251636	64610	54536
2014	170027	1149	253774	65623	56192
2015	166018	1018	229546	82195	73000
2016	166207	1012	200750	105806	97583
2017	151454	916	179316	80697	72964
2018	137818	847	169157	74349	66616
2019	128959	754	141528	84027	76358

注：离婚对数包括在民政部门登记的对数和经法院调离和判离的对数。
资料来源：中共北京市委社会工作委员会北京市民政局、北京市高级人民法院。
Note: Registered divorces include those registered in the civil affair department and those mediated and judged in courts.
Source: Social Work Committee of Beijing Municipal Committee of the Communist Party of China Beijing Municipal Civil Affairs Bureau, and The People's High Court of Beijing.

21－11 婚姻登记情况
BASIC STATISTICS ON MARRIAGE AND DIVORCE REGISTRATIONS

项 目		Item		2019	2018	2019年为2018年% 2019 as % of 2018
登记结婚对数	**(对)**	**Registered Marriages**	**(couple)**	**128959**	**137818**	**93.6**
按婚前状况分		**By Pre-marriage Status**				
初婚人数	(人)	First Marriages	(person)	141528	169157	83.7
再婚人数	(人)	Remarriages	(person)	116390	106479	109.3
#女 性		Females		57306	51902	110.4
按居住地分		**By Place of Residence**				
内地居民登记结婚对数	(对)	Registered Marriages in Mainland	(couple)	128205	136971	93.6
涉外及华侨、港澳台居民登记结婚对数	(对)	Registered Marriages with Foreigners and Overseas Chinese and Citizens of Hong Kong, Macao and Taiwan	(couple)	754	847	89.0
内地居民	(人)	Mainland Residents	(person)	735	767	95.8
#女 性		Females		489	541	90.4
香港居民	(人)	Hong Kong Residents	(person)	59	47	125.5
澳门居民	(人)	Macao Residents	(person)	6	6	100.0
台湾居民	(人)	Taiwan Residents	(person)	100	120	83.3
华 侨	(人)	Overseas Chinese	(person)	9	13	69.2
外国人	(人)	Foreigners	(person)	599	741	80.8
离婚登记对数	**(对)**	**Registered Divorces**	**(couple)**	**76358**	**66616**	**114.6**
内地居民登记离婚对数	(对)	Registered Divorces in Mainland	(couple)	76102	66391	114.6
涉外及华侨、港澳台居民登记离婚对数	(对)	Registered Divorces with Foreigners and Overseas Chinese and Citizens of Hong Kong, Macao and Taiwan	(couple)	256	225	113.8

注：离婚对数不含法院调离和判离数。
资料来源：中共北京市委社会工作委员会北京市民政局。
Note: Number of registered divorces excludes the divorces mediated and ruled by courts.
Source: Social Work Committee of Beijing Municipal Committee of the Communist Party of China Beijing Municipal Civil Affairs Bureau.

21－12 残疾人事业基本情况
BASIC INFORMATION OF UNDERTAKINGS FOR DISABLED PERSONS

项目		Item		2019	2018
康复		**Rehabilitation**			
0－6岁残疾儿童享受康复政策人数	(人)	Number of Disabled Children of 0 to 6 Years Old Enjoying Rehabilitation Policies	(person)	1561	1420
7－15岁残疾儿童少年享受康复政策人数	(人)	Number of Disabled Children and Teenagers of 7 to15 Years Old Enjoying Rehabilitation Policies	(person)	1093	3062
残疾人接受辅助器具服务人数	(人)	Number of Disabled Persons With Assistive Devices	(person)	260501	198838
精神残疾人接受免费服药人数	(人)	Number of Mentally Disabled Persons Receiving Free		53050	36076
培训		**Training**			
职业教育与培训机构数(残联认定)	(个)	Number of Vocational Education and Training Institutions (recognized by China Disabled Persons' Federation)	(unit)	53	53
职业技能培训人数	(人次)	Number of Persons Receiving Vocational Skill Training	(person-time)	4272	5921
就业		**Employment**			
盲人按摩		Massage by Persons with Visual Disability			
保健按摩机构	(家)	Healthcare Massage Institutions	(unit)	401	434
医疗按摩机构	(家)	Medical Massage Institutions	(unit)	2	3
保健按摩员培训人次	(人次)	Massage Therapists Training	(person-time)	296	153
医疗按摩员培训人次	(人次)	Keep-fit Massager Training	(person-time)	428	119
扶贫		**Poverty Alleviation**			
扶持农村残疾人数	(人)	Number of Disabled Persons Supported in Rural Areas	(person)	1058	1054
社会保障		**Social Security**			
已纳入最低生活保障范围人数	(人)	Covered by the Basic Living System	(person)	34192	33941
享受困难残疾人生活补贴人数	(人)	Number of Persons Enjoying Subsistence Allowance for Disabled Persons with Difficulties	(person)	120621	124272
享受重度残疾人护理补贴人数	(人)	Number of Persons Enjoying Severe Disability Nursing Subsidy	(person)	203650	202157
参加城乡居民养老保险残疾人数	(人)	Number of Disabled Persons Insured by Urban Resident Pension Insurance	(person)	59075	70007
参加城乡居民医疗保险残疾人数	(人)	Number of Disabled Persons Insured by Urban Resident		210842	181263
残联组织建设		**Organization Building of Disabled Persons' Federation**			
残疾人工作者数	(人)	Workers for Disabled Persons	(person)	1305	1280
维权援助					
维权信访咨询件数	(件)	Right Protection Letters, Visits and Consulting	(case)	31123	30705
维权法律服务件数	(件)	Right Protection Legal Aid	(case)	1476	1698

资料来源：北京市残疾人联合会。
Source: Social Work Committee of Beijing Municipal Committee of the Communist Party of China Beijing Municipal Civil Affairs Bureau.

21-13 救助情况
STATISTICS ON ASSISTANCE

单位：人 (person)

项目	Item	人数 Number of Persons 2019	2018	2019年为2018年% 2019 as % of 2018
社会救助对象总人数	**Total Number of Persons Receiving Social Relief**	**109742**	**110651**	**99.2**
城市居民最低生活保障人数	Number of Persons Receiving Subsistence Allowances in Urban Areas	65423	67325	97.2
农村居民最低生活保障人数	Number of Persons Receiving Subsistence Allowances in Rural Areas	37671	37691	99.9
农村五保供养人数	Rural Residents Enjoying Five Guarantees	5338	4599	116.1
#农村集中五保供养人数	Collective Rural Residents Enjoying Five Guarantees	1587	1608	98.7
城市特困集中供养人数	Collective Urban Poor Residents Enjoying Special Subsidies	600	441	136.1
城市特困分散供养人数	Scattered Urban Poor Residents Enjoying Special Subsidies	710	595	119.3

注：“农村居民最低生活保障人数”不含“农村五保供养人数”。
资料来源：中共北京市委社会工作委员会北京市民政局。
Note: Number of persons receiving subsistence allowances in rural areas excludes Rural Residents Enjoying the Five Guarantees.
Source: Social Work Committee of Beijing Municipal Committee of the Communist Party of China Beijing Municipal Civil Affairs Bureau.

主要统计指标解释

卫 生

医疗卫生机构 指从卫生行政部门取得《医疗机构执业许可证》，或从民政、工商行政、机构编制管理部门取得法人单位登记证书，为社会提供医疗保健、疾病控制、卫生监督服务或从事医学科研和医学在职培训等工作的单位。

卫生技术人员 指由医疗卫生机构支付工资的全部固定职工和合同制职工中现任职务为卫生技术工作的专业人员，不包括从事管理工作的人员。

执业（助理）医师和注册护士 指领取（助理）医师执业证书和注册护士证书的人员，不包括从事管理工作的医师和护士。

死亡率（死因死亡率） 是指某种原因（如疾病）所致的死亡人数占户籍人口比重。

婴儿死亡率 指某地区一年内每 1000 名活产婴儿与未满 1 岁的婴儿死亡人数之比。婴儿死亡率可以衡量一个国家或地区经济文化、居民健康状况和卫生保健事业发展情况，同时也是人口平均期望寿命研究的重要内容。

新生儿死亡率 指年内新生儿死亡数与活产数之比，一般以千分率表示。新生儿死亡指出生至 28 天以内（即 0-27 天）死亡人数。

孕产妇死亡率 指某年某地每十万活产中的孕产妇死亡比例。同婴儿死亡率一样，孕产妇死亡率是评价某一地区社会发展状况的重要指标，它的高低与社会经济状况、孕产妇社会环境及卫生保健服务有直接的联系。

社会服务

社会救助对象总人数 指在报告期末生活在当地规定的最低生活保障线以下的家庭人员及国家规定由民政部门救济的特殊人员和 60 年代精简退职老职工救济人员等。

社区服务机构数 指报告期末社区服务站、社区服务中心、其它社区服务设施的总和。

Explanatory Notes on Main Statistical Indicators

Health

Medical and Health **Institutions** refer to institutions granted with *License for Medical Institution* by the health administration authority, or granted with certificate of corporate unit by the civil affair, administration for industry and commerce, management authority of institutional organization, and providing medical service and healthcare, disease control, health supervision service or carrying out medical research and education, and so on.

Medical Technical Personnel refer to all fixed employees and of contract-based employees, professional personnel in health technology, who receive pays from medical and health institutions, excluding personnel engaged in management.

Certified（Assistant） Doctors and Registered Nurses refer to personnel who have received a physician practicing certificate（Assistant） and certified nurse certificate, excluding physicians and nurses engaged in management.

Mortality (Cause-specific Death Rate) means the proportion of persons dead due to certain cause (such as disease) in the permanent population.

Infant Mortality means the rate of dead infants under 1 year old to 1,000 live infants in an area in a year. Infant death rate measures the development of economy, culture, citizen health and health care in a country or region. It is also an important component of study on average life expectancy of population.

Neonatal Mortality Rate refers to the rate of dead newborn babies to live births in a year, generally expressed in permillage. Death toll of newborns refers to the number of newborns that died within 28 days after birth (i.e. 0-27 days).

Pregnant and Lying-in Women Mortality refers to the rate of dead pregnant and lying-in women to 100,000 live pregnant and lying-in women in an area in a year. This is an important indicator to evaluate the social development status in an area. The figure of this indicator is directly related to the social and economic status, social environment and health care service for pregnant and lying-in women.

Social Services

Total Number of Persons Receiving Social Relief refer to the number of family members living under the minimum living standard provided by local governments, special persons receiving relief by civil affair authorities in line with national regulations, as well as employed persons retired because of streamlining in the 1960s, at the end of the reporting period.

Number of Service Facilities in Urban Communities refers to the total number of community service stations, service centers, and other service facilities, by the end of reporting period.

22

文化和体育
CULTURE AND SPORTS

简要说明

一、主要内容

本章资料主要反映文化、体育发展情况。

文化部分主要包括公共图书馆、文化馆、档案馆、博物馆、广播、电影、电视、新闻出版以及文化产业发展等情况。

体育部分主要包括体育场地情况、运动员和裁判员情况、运动员获奖情况以及体育彩票等。

二、统计范围

文化产业资料根据规模以上文化产业法人单位有关资料测算取得，包括企业法人和事业法人。

三、有关统计标准的变化说明

关于文化产业。执行国家统计局印发的《文化及相关产业分类（2018)》。

Brief Introduction

I. Main Content

Statistics in this chapter mainly show the development of culture and sports.

Cultural statistics mainly include the situation of public libraries, cultural centers, archives, museums, broadcast, films, television and press, and the development of cultural industry, etc.

Sports statistics mainly include sports venues, athletes and referees, awards received by athletes and sports lottery tickets, etc.

II. Scope of Statistics

Data on cultural industry are calculated and obtained based on related data of legal entities of the cultural industry above designated size, including legal bodies of enterprise and legal bodies of public institutial.

III. Changes in Relevant Statistical Standards

Cultural Industry. The *Classification of Cultural and Related Industries (2018)* issued by the National Bureau of Statistics is implemented.

22-1 图书馆、文化馆、档案馆情况(1978-2019年)
LIBRARIES, CULTURAL CENTERS AND ARCHIVES (1978-2019)

年份 Year	公共图书馆 Public Libraries				群众艺术馆、文化馆 Mass Art Centers, Cultural Centers		档案馆 Archiving Institutions			
	个数 (个) Number (unit)	总藏数 (万册、万件) Total Collections (10000 volumes)	建筑面积 (万平方米) Building Area (10000 sq.m)	书刊文献外借人次 (万人次) Person-times Borrowing Books, Magazines, and Documents (10000 person-times)	个数 (个) Number (unit)	组织文艺活动 (次) Art Activities Organized (times)	个数 (个) Number (unit)	建筑面积 (平方米) Building Area (sq.m)	利用档案资料人次 (万人次) Person-times of Using Files (10000 person-times)	案卷 (万卷件) Records (10000 rolls)
1978	18	1423		168.5	19	516				
1979	21	1502		173.7	19	1033				
1980	20	1606	1.8	210.4	19	778				
1981	21	1614	1.9	211.0	19	1131				
1982	21	1676	2.0	228.4	20	1334				
1983	21	1733	1.9	243.0	20	1015				
1984	22	1824	2.3	223.7	22	489				
1985	22	1860	3.0	219.9	23	469				
1986	23	1874	6.0	219.9	23	883				
1987	23	1959	20.6	169.8	23	1067	20	10695	1.30	86.1
1988	23	2050	23.4	300.4	23	647	20	21472	1.46	116.0
1989	23	2128	24.5		23	1411	20	31280	1.48	156.3
1990	23	2205	25.0		23	1429	20	23618	2.51	167.4
1991	23	2281	25.3		23	1128	20	33491	3.24	177.5
1992	23	2397	25.4	147.0	23	978	20	35950	2.64	181.3
1993	23	2461	25.5	212.0	23	764	20	37650	1.73	192.4
1994	23	2548	23.8	383.8	23	1034	20	42641	1.50	192.4
1995	23	2629	24.1	139.3	23	1127	20	65489	1.42	204.1
1996	22	2652	25.3	145.6	23	2277	20	62994	3.03	223.7
1997	23	2789	25.7	188.0	23	1875	20	64147	2.69	227.4
1998	24	2848	25.6	189.0	23	2554	20	67759	2.71	240.8
1999	24	2934	26.4	607.0	23	1490	20	72597	2.52	259.5
2000	26	3020	27.0	283.0	23	1809	20	72596	3.01	278.3
2001	26	3133	31.4	287.7	23	1822	20	72730	4.17	297.0
2002	26	3248	30.7	337.5	20	1817	20	72946	4.53	328.4
2003	26	3355	30.9	334.8	20	2023	20	81519	6.27	359.0
2004	26	3451	30.9	405.0	22	1826	20	83162	7.03	379.1
2005	26	3626	31.7	480.0	22	3697	20	84656	6.97	404.7
2006	25	3776	31.0	515.0	21	2200	20	93773	10.59	436.7
2007	25	3940	31.5	479.0	21	4752	20	93463	9.51	461.7
2008	25	4100	33.4	450.0	20	3007	20	97605	9.00	495.7
2009	25	4368	41.9	471.0	20	3470	20	97605	9.88	523.8
2010	25	4613	42.4	441.0	20	3564	18	97611	13.45	558.0
2011	25	5049	42.1	333.0	20	3401	18	97976	12.30	582.9
2012	25	5556	47.6	317.0	20	3848	18	98879	12.37	602.5
2013	25	5316	48.4	325.0	20	4769	18	101896	23.85	636.1
2014	25	5601	52.7	407.0	20	2158	18	98220	22.18	697.9
2015	25	5943	52.4	438.0	20	2587	18	96256	14.90	733.2
2016	25	6229	55.3	549.0	21	3417	18	119930	21.95	764.7
2017	24	6528	57.8	431.0	20	3431	18	123401	19.99	827.7
2018	24	6777	57.6	503.0	20	3278	18	122722	15.04	867.5
2019	24	7048	57.6	480.0	20	3182	18	212864	14.83	910.0

注：1.1978—1981年，群众艺术馆、文化馆数据不包括群众艺术馆。
2.2019年，北京市档案馆新馆建成，故表中档案馆建筑面积较往年增加较多，下同。
资料来源：北京市文化和旅游局、国家图书馆、北京市档案局。

Note: a) In 1978-1981, the data of mass art centers and cultural centers didn't include those of mass art centers.
b) The new Beijing Municipal Archives was completed in 2019. Therefore, the building area of archives in the table was increased more than that in previous years, the same below.

Source: Beijing Municipal Bureau of Culture and Tourism, National Library of China, and Beijing Municipal Bureau of Archives.

22-2 博物馆情况(1982—2019年)
STATISTICS FOR MUSEUMS (1982-2019)

年份 Year	全市按行业管理登记的博物馆数(个) Museums Registered by Industry Administration (unit)	文物藏品数(万件) Cultural Relic Collections (10000 units)	博物馆及其他文物保护机构(文物局系统内) Museums and Other Cultural Relic Protection and Administration Organizations (under the jurisdiction of Beijing Municipal Administration of Cultural Heritage) 个数(个) Number (unit)	#博物馆 Museums	文物藏品数(万件) Cultural Relic Collections (10000 units)	#一级品(件) Grade-I Collections (unit)	参观人次(万人次) Visitors (10000 person-times)
1982			28		8.4	294	9.7
1983			29		4.0		58.0
1984							
1985			32		9.0		20.0
1986			39	7	21.0		905.0
1987							
1988			42	11	21.0		1098.0
1989			46	12	14.0		992.0
1990							
1991			46	12	11.7	2901	6629.1
1992							
1993			50	16	17.4	479	2423.4
1994			51	17	16.7	447	955.0
1995			51	17	16.7	447	2100.3
1996			51	17	18.0	443	2009.3
1997			54	24	18.2	443	935.8
1998			56	26	18.3	387	697.8
1999			54	26	18.5	374	5641.8
2000			53	25	18.2	367	702.7
2001			58	26	17.3	366	99.1
2002			48	27	20.1	716	170.8
2003			55	27	112.4	716	119.2
2004			66	31	370.4	656	599.9
2005			73	34	115.1	620	1370.9
2006			70	33	115.5	643	1416.7
2007			69	34	113.5	439	1493.0
2008	148	331	71	37	116.0	678	1368.4
2009	151	331	76	40	117.0	722	1647.9
2010	156	332	79	41	117.0	725	1712.1
2011	162	430	78	41	117.0	852	1373.4
2012	165	430	78	41	117.0	903	1887.9
2013	167	430	78	41	117.0	903	1760.0
2014	171	430	78	41	128.0	891	1848.0
2015	173	430	77	40	126.0	931	2069.1
2016	178	430	79	43	128.0	960	1994.3
2017	179	430	78	43	128.0	1160	2362.7
2018	179	463	78	43	128.0	1144	2383.5
2019	183	463	78	43	129.0	1167	2530.8

资料来源：北京市文物局。
Source: Beijing Municipal Administration of Cultural Heritage.

22-3 博物馆及其他文物保护管理机构情况(2019年)
STATISTICS FOR MUSEUMS AND OTHER CULTURAL RELIC PROTECTION AND ADMINISTRATION ORGANIZATIONS (2019)

项目	Item	合计 Total	市属 Under the Jurisdiction of the City	区属 Under the Jurisdiction of the District
全市按行业管理登记的博物馆	**Museums Registered by Industry Administration**			
博物馆数 (个)	Museums (unit)	183	45	44
#正常开放的博物馆数	Museums Normally Open	161	40	43
#免费开放的博物馆数	Museums Open for Free	84	25	25
文物藏品数 (万件)	Cultural Relic Collections (10000 units)	462.5		
参观人次 (万人次)	Visitors (10000 person-times)	8000		
文物古迹个数 (处)	Cultural Relics and Historical Sites (unit)	3665		
文物拍卖机构数 (个)	Organizations of Cultural Relic Auctions (unit)	191		
举办文物艺术品拍卖场次 (场)	Cultural Relic Auctions (time)	815		
文物拍卖标的数 (件、套)	Auction Targets (unit)	176869		
文物拍卖标的成交金额 (亿元)	Turnover of Cultural Relic Auctions (100 million yuan)	177.0		
文物局系统内博物馆及文物保护管理机构 (个)	**Museums and Cultural Relic Protection and Administration Organizations under the Municipal Administration of Cultural Heritage (unit)**	**78**	**28**	**50**
#博物馆	Museums	43	18	25
博物馆按类别分	Grouped by Category			
综合性	Comprehensive	16	5	11
历史性	Historical	19	10	9
艺术性	Art	2	2	
自然科技类	Natural Science	2		2
其他类	Others	4	1	3
从业人员 (人)	Employment (person)	3960	1283	2677
文物藏品数 (万件)	Cultural Relic Collections (10000 units)	129	123	6
#一级品 (件)	Grade-I Collections (unit)	1167	697	470
参观人次 (万人次)	Visitors (10000 person-times)	2530.8	403.5	2127.3
本年收入 (万元)	Revenues in the Year (10000 yuan)	304958	126950	178008
#财政收入	Fiscal Revenue	173885	77514	96371
门票收入	Ticket Revenue	57539	599	56940
本年支出 (万元)	Expenditures in the Year (10000 yuan)	291904	125195	166709

注：全市博物馆数为北京地区按行业管理登记的博物馆数。
资料来源：北京市文物局。
Note: Number of museums in the city means the number of museums registered by industrial administration in Beijing.
Source: Beijing Municipal Administration of Cultural Heritage.

22-4 公共图书馆(2019年)
PUBLIC LIBRARIES (2019)

项目	Item	合计 Total	中央属 Under Central Jurisdiction	市属 Under the Jurisdiction of the City	区属 Under the Jurisdiction of the District
个数 (个)	Number (unit)	24	1	1	22
从业人员 (人)	Employed Persons (person)	2629	1411	350	868
总藏数 (万册、万件)	Total Collections (10000 volumes)	7048	4036	906	2106
#图书	Books	4356	1550	758	2048
建筑面积 (万平方米)	Building Area (10000 sq.m)	57.6	27.8	9.4	20.4
阅览座席 (个)	Seating Capacity of Reading Roo (unit)	20937	5427	3317	12193
总流通人次 (万人次)	Total Number of Visitors (10000 person-times)	2546	577	539	1430
#书刊文献外借人次	Person-times Borrowing Books, Magazines and Documents	480	35	39	406
书刊文献外借册次 (万册次)	Volume-times of Borrowed Books, Magazines and Documents (10000 volunme-times)	1328	62	196	1070

资料来源：北京市文化和旅游局、国家图书馆。
Source: Beijing Municipal Bureau of Culture and Tourism, and National Library of China.

22-5 群众艺术馆、文化馆和文化站情况(2019年)
STATISTICS FOR MASS ART CENTERS, CULTURAL CENTERS AND CULTURAL STATIONS(2019)

项目	Item	合计 Total	群众艺术馆 Mass Art Centers	文化馆 Cultural Centers	文化站 Cultural Stations
个数 (个)	Number (unit)	354	1	19	334
从业人员 (人)	Employed Persons (person)	3437	52	863	2522
举办展览个数 (个)	Exhibitions Held (unit)	1826	1	332	1493
组织文艺活动 (次)	Art Activities Organized (times)	47132	60	3122	43950

资料来源：北京市文化和旅游局。
Source: Beijing Municipal Bureau of Culture and Tourism.

22-6 档案事业基本情况(2019年)
STATISTICS FOR ARCHIVING INSTITUTIONS (2019)

项 目		Item		合 计 Total	市 属 Under the Jurisdiction of the City	区 属 Under the Jurisdiction of the District
档案馆个数	(个)	**Number of Archives**	(unit)	**18**	**2**	**16**
建筑面积	(平方米)	**Building Areas**	(sq.m)	**212864**	**125650**	**87214**
馆藏档案情况		**Files Colllected in Archives**				
全 宗	(个)	Full Archives	(unit)	3545	978	2567
案 卷	(万卷件)	Records	(10000 rolls)	910.0	334.6	575.4
建国前档案		Files Prior to the Foundation of PRC		100.7	98.8	1.9
建国后档案		Files After the Foundation of PRC		809.3	235.7	573.5
录音、录像、影片档案	(盘)	Tape, Video, and Film Files	(piece)	49416	35293	14123
照片档案	(张)	Photo Files	(disc)	798779	357139	441640
缩微胶片	(万幅)	Microfiches	(10000 rolls)	5552	5502	50
档案利用情况		**File Utilization**				
本年利用档案人次	(人次)	Person-times Using Files in the Year	(person-times)	146776	12378	134398
本年利用档案	(万卷件次)	Files Used in the Year	(10000 roll.times)	26.7	9.0	17.7
本年利用现行文件和资料册次	(册次)	Existing Documents and Data Books Used in the Year	(volume-times)	2432	289	2143
本年利用现行文件和资料人次	(人次)	Person-times Using Existing Documents and Data in the Year	(person-times)	1562	110	1452

资料来源：北京市档案局。
Source: Beijing Municipal Bureau of Archives.

22-7 电影、电视、广播电台情况(1978-2019年)

年 份 Year	电 影 Films			电 视 TVs		
	放映场次 (万场次) Show Times (10000 Times)	观影人次 (万人次) Person-times Watching Film (10000 Person-times)	票房收入 (亿元) Ticket Revenue (100 million yuan)	公共电视节目套数 (套) Number of Public TV Programs (unit)	平均每日电视节目播出时间 (小时) Average Daily Hours of TV Programs (hour)	电视综合覆盖率 (%) Comprehensive Coverage Rate of TVs (%)
1978	31.9	29924.1				
1979	35.5	34626.0				
1980	33.1	31189.5		1	4.3	
1981	31.9	30067.0		1	5.5	100.00
1982	32.8	28743.5		1	6.9	91.00
1983	30.1	27345.5		1	7.1	90.00
1984	27.8	23966.7		1	7.2	98.00
1985	23.0	18875.0		1	7.5	98.00
1986	20.6	15904.4		2	19.1	98.00
1987	19.0	13517.7		2	13.6	98.00
1988	19.2	13269.4		2	19.4	98.00
1989	21.5	14492.6		4	25.4	98.00
1990	20.7	12771.2		4	29.4	98.00
1991	21.3	12558.3		4	27.8	98.00
1992	22.1	11587.4		6	45.0	98.00
1993	11.9	5369.8		7	58.2	98.00
1994	10.6	2166.5	0.5	9	77.8	98.30
1995	9.2	1598.6	0.9	12	98.4	98.30
1996	11.5	1644.1	1.1	12	101.0	98.81
1997	12.6	1742.3	1.2	12	111.0	99.12
1998	12.3	1443.5	1.3	12	110.7	99.60
1999	11.7	964.7		12	118.4	99.80
2000	12.2	873.2		12	122.5	99.80
2001	12.6	804.7	0.9	16	200.2	99.91
2002	12.3	827.4	1.1	18	329.4	99.82
2003	11.8	683.0	1.4	19	259.3	99.90
2004	18.1	814.4	1.9	24	244.2	99.50
2005	22.6	873.8	2.3	25	329.8	99.99
2006	28.0	1221.0	3.0	25	294.2	99.99
2007	38.0	1711.0	3.7	25	309.1	99.99
2008	46.8	1767.3	5.4	24	309.1	99.99
2009	62.4	2451.5	8.2	26	319.1	99.99
2010	74.3	2923.3	11.8	26	319.2	99.99
2011	97.4	3235.9	13.5	25	334.2	100.00
2012	120.0	3954.6	16.2	26	343.7	100.00
2013	137.8	4288.5	18.6	26	347.9	100.00
2014	162.8	5281.3	22.9	26	344.0	100.00
2015	198.1	7212.7	31.6	26	351.1	100.00
2016	228.5	6926.7	30.3	26	360.3	100.00
2017	273.9	7701.7	34.0	26	360.5	100.00
2018	309.6	7645.3	35.0	26	375.7	100.00
2019	356.2	7634.1	36.1	26	353.5	100.00

注：自2019年起，原“电视节目套数”更名为“公共电视节目套数”，原“广播节目套数”更名为“公共广播节目套数”。
资料来源：北京市电影局、北京市广播电视局。

STATISTICS FOR FILMS, TELEVISIONS, AND BROADCASTING STATIONS (1978-2019)

电　视 TVs				广播电台 Broadcasting Stations		
农村电视综合覆盖率 (%) Comprehensive Coverage Rate of TVs in Rural Area (%)	无线电视综合覆盖率 (%) Comprehensive Coverage Rate of Wireless TVs (%)	有线电视用户数 (万户) Number of Cable TV Subscnbers (10000 households)	有线电视入户率 (%) Access Rate of Cable TVs (%)	公共广播节目套　数 (套) Number of Public Radio Programs (set)	平均每日广播节目播出时间 (小时) Average Daily Show Hours of Radio Programs (hour)	广　播综合覆盖率 (%) Comprehensive Coverage Rate of Broadcast (%)
				4	56.1	
				4	57.2	100.00
				4	59.4	98.00
				5	62.0	98.00
				5	73.7	98.00
				5	65.9	98.00
				5	66.2	98.00
				6	68.8	98.00
				6	76.3	98.00
				7	78.7	98.00
				7	77.9	98.00
				7	77.9	98.00
				10	94.8	98.00
				12	134.8	98.00
		52.71		12	134.9	98.00
		82.21		13	148.3	91.00
		182.97		13	150.3	96.97
		202.75		15	156.1	98.44
		230.97		16	174.7	99.98
		165.78	43.24	16	178.2	99.96
		175.71	45.80	16	188.9	97.7
		205.95	51.76	16	192.4	99.91
		231.24	57.05	16	197.4	99.88
		243.00	58.39	16	197.9	99.91
	97.57	265.50	62.09	16	229.6	100.00
	99.99	282.00	64.12	17	281.9	100.00
99.97	94.90	319.58	70.75	17	282.9	100.00
99.97	93.13	345.06	74.43	17	288.9	99.98
99.97	93.19	383.13	81.00	17	297.4	99.98
99.97	94.38	413.50	85.90	18	316.6	99.99
99.97	98.72	448.12	91.68	18	324.8	99.99
100.00	99.74	475.92	95.90	18	329.6	100.00
100.00	99.75	495.70	99.13	25	471.7	100.00
100.00	99.75	524.59	103.00	25	473.6	100.00
100.00	99.75	551.57	106.85	25	472.6	100.00
100.00	99.75	569.13	108.88	25	470.4	100.00
100.00	99.75	580.42	109.66	26	493.6	100.00
100.00	99.81	586.83	109.04	26	496.3	100.00
100.00	99.81	594.55	109.48	26	496.2	100.00
100.00	100	598.92	109.12	26	499.6	100.00

Note: Since 2019, the original Number of TV Programs has been changed to Number of Public TV Programs, and the original Number of Radio Programs has been changed to Number of Public Radio Programs.
Source: Beijing Municipal Bureau of Film, Beijing Municipal Radio and Television Bureau.

22-8 电影、电视剧制作情况
STATISTICS FOR PRODUCTION OF FILMS AND TV PLAYS

项 目	Item	2019 全国 National Total	2019 北京 Beijing	2019 占全国比重(%) As % of National Total	2018 全国 National Total	2018 北京 Beijing	2018 占全国比重(%) As % of National Total
生产电影 (部)	Feature Films (piece)	1037	310	29.9	1082	410	37.9
制作电视剧 (部)	TV Plays (piece)	254	67	26.4	323	55	17.0
(集)	(episode)	10650	2843	26.7	13726	2503	18.2

资料来源：北京市电影局、北京市广播电视局。
Source: Beijing Municipal Bureau of Film, Beijing Municipal Radio and Television Bureau.

22-9 电影放映单位情况
STATISTICS FOR MOVIE PROJECTION ORGANIZATIONS

项 目	Item	2019	2018
放映单位数 (个)	Number of Projection Organizations (unit)	256	238
总银幕数 (块)	Total Screens (piece)	1836	1675
放映场次 (万场次)	Show Times (10000 times)	356.2	309.6
观影人次 (万人次)	Audience (10000 person-times)	7634.1	7645.3
票房收入 (亿元)	Ticket Revenues (100million yuan)	36.1	35.0

资料来源：北京市电影局。
Source: Beijing Municipal Bureau of Film.

22-10 电视台情况
STATISTICS FOR TELEVISION STATIONS

项目	Item	2019		2018	
		中央 Central	地方 Local	中央 Central	地方 Local
基本情况	**Basic Statistics**				
电视台 (座)	Television Stations (unit)	1	1	1	1
公共电视节目套数 (套)	Number of Public Programs (unit)	34	26	30	26
全年公共电视节目播出时间 (小时)	Annual Broadcast Time of Public Programs (hour)	281168	129028	241474	137139
播放节目情况	**Shows of TV Programs**				
新闻咨询类节目 (小时)	News and Consulting Programs (hour)	72665	22719	70479	27693
专题服务类节目 (小时)	Special Service Programs (hour)	95957	39317	76732	48338
综艺益智类节目 (小时)	Entertainment and Education Programs (hour)	38874	6548	38019	6789
影视剧类节目 (小时)	Movie and TV Play Programs (hour)	62832	29626	50404	28413
广告类节目 (小时)	Commercial Programs (hour)	8558	13793	5739	11842
其他类节目 (小时)	Other Programs (hour)	2252	17024	100	14064

注：电视台数不包括区电视台。
资料来源：北京市广播电视局、国家广播电视总局。
Note: Number of television stations excludes TV stations of districts.
Source:Beijing Municipal Radio and Television Bureau, National Radio and Television Administration.

22-11 广播电台情况
STATISTICS FOR BROADCASTING STATIONS

项目	Item	2019		2018	
		中央 Central	地方 Local	中央 Central	地方 Local
基本情况	**Basic Statistics**				
电台数 (座)	Number of Broadcasting Stations (unit)	2	1	2	1
公共广播节目套数 (套)	Number of Public Programs (unit)	23	26	23	26
全年公共广播节目播出时间 (小时)	Annual Broadcast Time of Public Programs (hour)	180781	182343	179752	181098
播放节目情况	**Shows of Radio Programs**				
新闻咨询类节目 (小时)	News and Consulting Programs (hour)	40623	18201	43631	18263
专题服务类节目 (小时)	Special Service Programs (hour)	65263	37070	61226	36411
综艺类节目 (小时)	Entertainment and Education Programs (hour)	50294	97280	44272	93176
广播剧类节目 (小时)	Radio Plays (hour)	1879	6754	2585	6633
广告类节目 (小时)	Commercial Programs (hour)	9103	16421	8933	14047
其他类节目 (小时)	Other Programs (hour)	13619	6617	19105	12538

注：1.广播电台数不包括区电台。
2.公共节目套数中含县级广播电视台的广播节目套数。
资料来源：北京市广播电视局、国家广播电视总局。
Note: a) Number of broadcasting stations excluded those of districts.
b) Public programs included broadcast programs of radio stations at county levels.
Source: Beijing Municipal Radio and Television Bureau, National Radio and Television Administration.

22-12 广播电视综合覆盖率(2019年)
COMPREHENSIVE COVERAGE RATE OF BROADCASTS AND TELEVISIONS (2019)

项　目	Item	2019
广播综合覆盖率 (%)	Comprehensive Coverage Rate of Broadcasts (%)	100.0
农村广播综合覆盖率 (%)	Comprehensive Coverage Rate of Broadcasts in Rural Areas (%)	100.0
无线广播综合覆盖率 (%)	Comprehensive Coverage Rate of Radios (%)	100.0
电视综合覆盖率 (%)	Comprehensive Coverage Rate of Televisions (%)	100.0
农村电视综合覆盖率 (%)	Comprehensive Coverage Rate of Televisions in Rural Areas (%)	100.0
无线电视综合覆盖率 (%)	Comprehensive Coverage Rate of Wireless Televisions (%)	100.0
有线电视入户率 (%)	Access Rate of Wire Broadcasting and Cable TVs (%)	109.1
有线电视用户数 (万户)	Subscribers of Cable TVs (10000 households)	598.9
#高清电视实际用户数	Subscribers of High-definition Interactive Digital Televisions	550.1
付费电视用户数	Subscribers of Pay TVs	106.2
农村有线广播电视实际用户数	Subscribers of Wire Broadcasting and Cable TVs in Rural Areas	91.4

资料来源：北京市广播电视局。
Source: Beijing Municipal Radio and Television Bureau.

22-13 报纸、期刊、图书出版情况(1978-2018年)
NEWSPAPER, JOURNAL AND BOOK PUBLICATIONS (1978-2018)

年 份 Year	报纸出版 Newspaper Publications				期刊出版 Journal Publications				图书出版 Books Publications		
	种 数 (种) Types (kind)	平均期印数 (万份) Average Printed Copies Per Issue (10000 copies)	总印数 (亿份) Total Printed Copies (100 million copies)	总印张 (亿印张) Total Sheets Printed (100 million pieces)	种 数 (种) Types (kind)	平均期印数 (万册) Average Printed Copies Per Issue (10000 copies)	总印数 (亿册) Total Printed Copies (100 million copies)	总印张 (亿印张) Total Sheets Printed (100 million pieces)	种 数 (种) Types (kind)	总印数 (亿册、亿张) Total Sheets Printed (100 million copies)	总印张 (亿印张) Total Sheets Printed (100 million pieces)
1978	11		68.5		468		4.5		5253	5.1	
1979	16		81.6		697		5.9		6723	5.9	
1980	41		84.5		839		5.8		9534	6.3	
1981	55		83.1		886		6.7		11139	7.8	
1982	57		78.3		882		6.7		13862	8.7	
1983	61		79.9		940		6.8		14384	8.5	
1984	73		83.0		987		7.9		15636	8.4	
1985	99		86.0		1098		8.2		17178	9.0	
1986	126		82.0		1206		8.0		19362	5.8	
1987	129		86.0		1409		8.2		21843	6.9	
1988	151		87.0		1514		8.2		23689	7.3	
1989	161		66.0		1580		6.2		25980	6.3	
1990	148		68.0		1415		5.9		27345	6.2	
1991	157		76.7		1499		6.8		29609	7.1	
1992	164	3886	81.4	88.4	1594	6043	7.8	22.3	31320	7.8	58.7
1993	170	3965	81.7	87.7	1597	6037	7.8	22.4	34393	8.6	71.0
1994	233	3759	70.0	92.6	1854	5328	6.3	19.1	38498	8.3	71.7
1995	240	3823	72.9	108.3	1884	5018	6.4	19.6	38819	8.3	70.2
1996	242		70.5		2129		6.1		41572	9.5	
1997	242	3624	71.8	122.2	2162	5396	6.6	22.9	45775	9.9	78.6
1998	247	3561	71.7	130.0	2274	5797	7.3	26.5	50155	11.0	86.1
1999	247	3520	71.7	144.7	2273	6116	8.0	35.2	54783	11.3	93.4
2000	240	3343	68.7	149.6	2352	5909	7.9	33.0	57821	9.6	93.0
2001	243	3339	69.4	153.2	2374	5761	8.1	32.6	63928	10.3	105.1
2002	247	3364	71.0	169.9	2377	5708	8.2	34.3	73836	12.2	127.5
2003	250	3393	72.5	190.4	2382	5702	8.2	34.3	85244	13.8	140.8
2004	253	3405	70.4	206.5	2791	5233	8.0	35.5	98312	15.2	157.2
2005	255	3169	66.2	227.2	2809	4957	7.7	40.8	108152	17.1	180.5
2006	256	3651	74.0	240.4	2809	5077	8.3	47.4	113232	17.2	186.1
2007	256	3454	73.1	218.6	2809	5340	9.2	54.2	125412	18.7	195.3
2008	259	3328	73.2	241.3	2898	5392	9.4	55.4	136284	20.8	220.0
2009	260	3232	71.6	232.5	3030	5373	9.7	59.4	144211	21.0	220.2
2010	262	3406	77.5	275.6	3063	5519	10.0	69.6	155209	21.5	251.2
2011	254	3453	83.1	293.7	3044	5991	10.2	76.7	167942	22.6	243.1
2012	257	3725	89.5	300.2	3064	5940	10.3	76.7	179634	22.5	250.7
2013	254	3737	91.7	298.2	3053	6094	10.4	78.0	192137	24.0	269.5
2014	256	3550	89.9	289.3	3123	5867	10.0	74.0	194259	23.6	258.7
2015	253	3389	87.4	267.5	3168	5539	9.3	68.0	205992	24.5	271.0
2016	252	3297	86.0	259.3	3221	5471	9.1	63.2	213413	26.9	286.8
2017	249	3215	83.9	249.7	3242	5325	8.6	57.1	217765	26.7	294.3
2018	247	3120	83.1	239.9	3244	5299	8.1	55.1	220632	29.7	327.1

注：1991年及以前，报纸、期刊、图书为出版数；1992年及以后均为总印数。
资料来源：北京市新闻出版局。
Note: Figures on newspaper, journals and books in and before 1991 were figures of publications; after 1992, they were total sheet printed.
Source: Beijing Municipal Press and Publication Bureau.

22-14 报纸出版情况
NEWSPAPER PUBLICATION

项目	Item	种数(种) Types of Publications (kind)		平均期印数(万份) Average Printed Copies Per Issue (10000 copies)		总印数(亿份) Total Printed Copies (100 million copies)		总印张(亿印张) Total Sheets Printed (100 million pieces)	
		2018	2017	2018	2017	2018	2017	2018	2017
合 计	**Total**	**247**	**249**	**3120.4**	**3214.6**	**83.1**	**83.9**	**239.9**	**249.7**
#综合报	Comprehensive	31	32	1187.1	1198.6	41.6	41.7	146.3	146.2
专业报	Professional	176	176	1428.1	1462.7	33.5	33.7	77.1	85.8

资料来源：北京市新闻出版局。
Source: Beijing Municipal Press and Publication Bureau.

22-15 期刊出版情况
JOURNAL PUBLICATION

项目	Item	种数(种) Types of Publications (kind)		平均期印数(万册) Average Printed Copies Per Issue (10000 copies)		总印数(亿册) Total Printed Copies (100 million copies)		总印张(亿印张) Total Sheets Printed (100 million pieces)	
		2018	2017	2018	2017	2018	2017	2018	2017
合 计	**Total**	**3244**	**3242**	**5299**	**5325**	**8.1**	**8.6**	**55.1**	**57.1**
综 合	Comprehensive	67	68	91	95	0.2	0.2	1.4	1.5
哲学、社会科学	Philosophy and Social Sciences	984	982	3785	3632	5.8	5.9	31.5	31.4
自然科学技术	Natural Sciences and Technology	1647	1645	802	896	1.0	1.2	13.3	13.5
文化、教育	Culture and Education	391	391	480	552	0.9	1.0	7.1	8.6
文学、艺术	Literature and Art	155	156	140	149	0.3	0.3	1.8	2.0

资料来源：北京市新闻出版局。
Source: Beijing Municipal Press and Publication Bureau.

22-16 图书出版情况
BOOK PUBLICATION

项目	Item	出版图书种数合计(种) Types of Publications (kind) 2018	2017	#新书 New Publications 2018	2017	总印数(万册、万张) Total Printed Copies (10000 volumes, 10000 pieces) 2018	2017	总印张(万印张) Total Sheets Printed (10000 print sheets) 2018	2017
合计	**Total**	**220632**	**217765**	**107011**	**109685**	**296694**	**267395**	**3271432**	**2943054**
书籍合计	**Books**	**220505**	**217640**	**106958**	**109608**	**294512**	**265695**	**3262811**	**2936146**
马列主义、毛泽东思想	Maxism, Leninism, Mao Zedong Thought	644	494	419	312	2332	978	41104	16246
哲学	Philosophy	5983	5908	3703	3656	4742	4203	67462	59545
社会科学总论	General Social Sciences	3658	3377	1870	1748	2202	1804	35924	28638
政治、法律	Politics and Law	13907	13536	9683	9446	25314	16416	306062	219615
军事	Military Science	806	871	540	649	459	466	6301	6219
经济	Economics	25155	24943	13634	14114	14026	11979	224770	199505
文化、科学、教育、体育	Culture, Science, Education and Sports	43780	45386	17682	18338	154893	149145	1261917	1230943
语言、文字	Languages	11933	12288	3911	4428	17531	16108	242936	227567
文学	Literature	19553	18168	12664	12264	26515	21597	341783	270275
艺术	Art	9953	9477	5398	5952	6790	6733	63743	61688
历史、地理	History and Geography	9595	9092	5868	5781	8036	6858	119633	108181
自然科学总论	General Natural Sciences	470	400	241	219	279	318	3972	3459
数学科学、化学	Mathematics and Chemistry	6701	6648	1733	1796	3256	2801	54872	49443
天文学、物理科学	Astronomy and Physics	1930	1962	1211	1358	819	724	10261	10818
生物科学	Biology	2342	2025	1013	922	1319	1010	19375	15100
医药、卫生	Medicine and Healthcare	14974	14263	7555	7593	7972	7165	157931	137927
农业科学	Agricultural Sciences	3535	3617	1913	2017	1093	1143	13333	13539
工业技术	Industrial Technologies	37591	37083	13640	14566	12956	12357	237702	226999
交通运输	Transportation	4195	4506	1793	2027	1770	1948	24943	26986
航空、航天	Aeronautics and Aerospace	528	420	329	258	129	104	1771	1544
环境科学	Environmental Sciences	1841	1708	1096	1044	738	510	11370	6268
综合性图书	General Books	1431	1468	1062	1120	1341	1326	15647	15642
图片及小件印品合计	**Pictures and Small Printed Publications**	**127**	**125**	**53**	**77**	**2182**	**1700**	**8621**	**6908**

资料来源：北京市新闻出版局。
Source: Beijing Municipal Press and Publication Bureau.

22-17 录音制品出版情况
PUBLICATION OF AUDIO PRODUCTS

项目 Item	录音带 Audio-tapes				激光唱盘 CDs				高密度激光唱盘及其他 DVDs-A and Others			
	种数(种) Types (kind)		数量(万盒) Number (10000 cassettes)		种数(种) Types (kind)		数量(万张) Number (10000 pieces)		种数(种) Types (kind)		数量(万张) Number (10000 pieces)	
	2018	2017	2018	2017	2018	2017	2018	2017	2018	2017	2018	2017
合　计 Total	**584**	**678**	**5301.1**	**5607.4**	**2155**	**2266**	**7422.2**	**6202.7**	**209**	**484**	**50.2**	**630.9**
#市　属 Municipal	15	76	1.5	10.8	196	139	90.2	92.5	18	19	12.6	23.5

资料来源：北京市新闻出版局。
Source: Beijing Municipal Press and Publication Bureau.

22-18 录像制品出版情况
PUBLICATION OF VIDEO PRODUCTS

项目 Item	录像带 Videotapes				激光视盘 VCDs				高密度激光视盘 DVD-Vs			
	种数(种) Types (kind)		数量(万盒) Number (10000 cassettes)		种数(种) Kind (kind)		数量(万张) Number (10000 pieces)		种数(种) Types (kind)		数量(万张) Number (10000 pieces)	
	2018	2017	2018	2017	2018	2017	2018	2017	2018	2017	2018	2017
合　计 Total	**121**	**99**	**20.1**	**18.8**	**261**	**349**	**1084.8**	**1030.8**	**2072**	**2028**	**2431.0**	**2108.0**
#市　属 Municipal	2	3		…					177	125	49.7	27.7

资料来源：北京市新闻出版局。
Source: Beijing Municipal Press and Publication Bureau.

22-19 电子出版物出版情况(2018年)
PUBLICATION OF E-PUBLICATIONS (2018)

项目 Item	只读光盘 CD-ROMs		交互式光盘及其他 CD-Is and Others		高密度只读光盘 DVD-ROMs	
	种数(种) Types (kind)	数量(万盒) Number (10000 cassettes)	种数(种) Types (kind)	数量(万张) Number (10000 pieces)	种数(种) Types (kind)	数量(万张) Number (10000 pieces)
合　计 Total	**3165**	**17192.9**	**252**	**203.1**	**1707**	**2270.6**
#市　属 Municipal	45	43.6			96	1.0

资料来源：北京市新闻出版局。
Source: Beijing Municipal Press and Publication Bureau.

22−20 引进版权量情况
NUMBER OF IMPORTED COPYRIGHTS

单位：件 (set)

项　目	Item	2018	2017
引进版权量	**Number of Imported Copyrights**	**9216**	**9488**
软件和电子出版物	Softwares and E-Publications	114	113
图　书	Books	9102	9375

资料来源：北京市新闻出版局。
Source: Beijing Municipal Press and Publication Bureau.

22−21 主要年份文化产业增加值情况(2004−2018年)
ADDED VALUE OF CULTURAL INDUSTRY IN MAIN YEARS (2004−2018)

年　份 Year	增加值 (亿元) Added Value (100 million yuan)	占地区生产总值比重 (%) As % of GDP (%)
2004	398.3	6.4
2008	681.6	5.8
2011	1358.7	7.9
2012	1569.4	8.2
2013	1754.2	8.3
2014	1937.2	8.5
2015	2081.4	8.4
2016	2217.4	8.2
2017	2723.5	9.1
2018	3075.1	9.3

注：1.2004−2012年文化产业增加值仅包括法人单位数据，2013年及以后为包括个体经营户在内的全口径数据。
2.本表数据根据北京市第四次全国经济普查进行了修订。

Note: a) The figures on the added value of cultural industry for 2004 to 2012 included the data of legal entities only; and figures for and after 2013 were those of full coverage including data of self-employed businesses.
b) The data in this table have been revised in accordance with the fourth national economic census in Beijing.

22-22 规模以上文化产业企业经营情况(2013-2019年)
OPERATION OF CULTURAL INDUSTRY ENTERPRISES ABOVE DESIGNATED SIZE (2013-2019)

年 份 Year	企业单位数 (个) Number of Enterprises (unit)	平均用工人数 (万人) Average Number of Employed Persons (10000 persons)	资产总计 (亿元) Total Assets (100 million yuan)	营业收入 (亿元) Business Income (100 million yuan)	利润总额 (亿元) Total Profits (100 million yuan)
2013	3981	41.6	5731.0	5155.2	390.2
2014	3820	47.8	7937.9	6876.9	495.6
2015	3418	47.4	9419.6	7548.1	550.8
2016	3539	48.1	10870.2	8195.4	530.5
2017	3994	54.1	13887.9	9586.0	802.9
2018	3887	53.5	16579.0	10963.0	852.7
2019	4831	54.8	19020.3	12997.3	739.1

22-23 规模以上文化产业法人单位基本情况(2018年)
STATISTICS OF CULTURAL INDUSTRY ABOVE DESIGNATED SIZE (2018)

项 目	Item	资产总计 (亿元) Total Assets (100 million yuan)	收入合计 (亿元) Total Income (100 million yuan)	平均用工人数 (万人) Average Number of Employed Persons (10000 persons)
合 计	**Total**	**19123.3**	**11835.7**	**61.5**
文化核心领域	**Core Fields of Culture**	**17345.9**	**10334.9**	**50.8**
新闻信息服务	News and Information Service	5674.3	3177.6	16.3
内容创作生产	Content Creation and Production	4110.6	1880.9	14.4
创意设计服务	Creative Design Service	2531.5	2959.3	10.7
文化传播渠道	Culture Transmission Channel	2973.7	2178.3	6.5
文化投资运营	Cultural Investment and Operation	1671.0	29.6	0.2
文化娱乐休闲服务	Cultural, Entertainment and Recreational Service	384.9	109.2	2.7
文化相关领域	**Culture-related Fields**	**1777.4**	**1500.8**	**10.8**
文化辅助生产和中介服务	Cultural Auxiliary Production and Intermediary Service	1171.0	756.8	8.7
文化装备生产	Cultural Equipment Production	276.8	173.2	1.0
文化消费终端生产	Cultural Consumption Terminal Production	329.5	570.8	1.1

22-24 规模以上文化产业法人单位基本情况(2019年)
STATISTICS OF CULTURAL INDUSTRY ABOVE DESIGNATED SIZE (2019)

项 目	Item	资产总计(亿元) Total Assets (100 million yuan)	收入合计(亿元) Total Income (100 million yuan)	平均用工人数(万人) Average Number of Employed Persons (10000 persons)
合 计	**Total**	**20198.0**	**13544.3**	**61.8**
文化核心领域	**Core Fields of Culture**	**18267.9**	**11972.6**	**50.7**
新闻信息服务	News and Information Service	5083.4	3353.3	13.0
内容创作生产	Content Creation and Production	4705.2	2080.5	15.4
创意设计服务	Creative Design Service	2827.4	3466.0	11.4
文化传播渠道	Culture Transmission Channel	3391.8	2919.4	8.0
文化投资运营	Cultural Investment and Operation	1854.1	32.3	0.3
文化娱乐休闲服务	Cultural, Entertainment and Recreational Service	406.0	121.2	2.7
文化相关领域	**Culture-related Fields**	**1930.1**	**1571.6**	**11.0**
文化辅助生产和中介服务	Cultural Auxiliary Production and Intermediary Service	1352.5	865.3	9.2
文化装备生产	Cultural Equipment Production	279.8	140.7	1.0
文化消费终端生产	Cultural Consumption Terminal Production	297.8	565.7	0.8

22-25 主要年份体育场地情况
SITUATION OF THE GYMNASIUMS AND STADIUMS IN MAIN YEARS

单位：个 (unit)

年 份 Year	合 计 Total	#体育场 Stadiums	#体育馆 Gymnasiums	#游泳场馆 Natatoriums	#室 内 Indoor	#各种训练房 Exercise Rooms
1950	19	1				2
1955	61	1		2	2	10
1960	124	2		4	3	19
1970	188	2	2	8	3	24
1975	234	3	2	11	4	28
1980	293	3	2	12	4	32
1985	405	4	2	20	8	54
1990	780	12	12	49	26	153
1995	1381	18	18	88	56	291
2000	2815	35	24	214	161	863
2001	3500	42	27	283	216	1101
2002	4176	57	33	334	263	1358
2003	6100	93	36	443	371	1729
2004	6104	93	36	443	371	1729
2005	6112	93	36	446	374	1731
2006	6122	93	36	446	374	1734
2007	6146	94	37	446	374	1736
2008	6149	94	37	446	374	1739
2009	6149	94	37	446	374	1739
2010	6151	94	37	446	374	1741
2011	6151	94	37	446	374	1741
2012	6156	94	37	447	375	1742
2013	20075	131	70	590	548	2836

注：自2013年开始，体育场地数据不再按年度进行统计，年度数据可参考第六次全国体育场地普查数据(普查时点为2013年12月31日)，最新数据将于第七次体育场地普查结束后更新。

资料来源：北京市体育局。

Note: The data on gymnasiums and stadiums were not analyzed by year since 2013; for annual data, please refer to the data of the six thnational census on gymnasiums and stadiums (date of census: December 31st, 2013). The latest data shall be updated after the end of the seventh national census on gymnasiums and stadiums.

Source: BeiJing Municipal Bureau of Sports.

22−26 运动员、裁判员情况
ATHLETES AND REFEREES

单位：人 (person)

项 目	Item	2019	#女 性 Females	2018	#女 性 Females
分等级运动员发展人数	**Number of Graded Athletes**	**2530**	**956**	**2003**	**753**
国际级运动健将	World-class Athletes	12	6	3	3
国家级运动健将	National Grade Athletes	205	97	128	46
一 级	First Grade Athletes	914	410	631	267
二 级	Second Grade Athletes	1399	443	1241	437
分等级裁判员发展人数	**Number of Graded Referees**	**1491**	**480**	**891**	**237**
一 级	First Grade Referees	196	48	400	108
二 级	Second Grade Referees	1295	432	491	129

资料来源：北京市体育局。
Source: BeiJing Municipal Bureau of Sports.

22−27 运动员获奖牌情况(2019年)
STATISTICS FOR MEDALS WON (2019)

单位：块 (piece)

项 目	Item	金 牌 Gold	银 牌 Silver	铜 牌 Copper
合 计	**Total**	**71**	**66**	**64**
国际比赛	International Competitions	17	10	11
国内比赛	Domestic Competitions	54	56	53

资料来源：北京市体育局。
Source: BeiJing Municipal Bureau of Sports.

22−28 体育彩票
SPORTS LOTTERY

项 目	Item	2019	2018
电脑体育彩票销售点数 (个)	Number of Computer Sports Lottery Tickets Sold (unit)	2777	2618
体育彩票发行额 (万元)	Circulation of Sports Lottery (10000 yuan)	731884	782200
体育彩票公益金提取额 (万元)	Public Welfare Funds Drawn from Sports Lottery (10000 yuan)	194306	198097

资料来源：北京市体育局。
Source: BeiJing Municipal Bureau of Sports.

主要统计指标解释

文　化

公共图书馆藏书　指各级文化部门举办的面向社会服务的独立的图书馆（不包括文化馆的图书室，也不包括文化系统以外的图书馆）藏书数量。

广播综合覆盖率　根据国家广电总局制定的《广播电视人口覆盖率统计技术标准和方法》进行统计调查的，在对象区内能接收到广播节目的覆盖人口数占本行政区域内人口总数的比率。

农村广播综合覆盖率　根据国家广电总局制定的《广播电视人口覆盖率统计技术标准和方法》进行统计调查的，在对象区内能接收到广播节目的农村人口数占本行政区域内农村人口总数的比率。农村是指经国家批准设立的乡镇人民政府的乡和农村建制镇所辖区，不包括县政府驻地镇。

无线广播综合覆盖率　根据国家广电总局制定的《广播电视人口覆盖率统计技术标准和方法》进行统计调查的，在对象区内能接收到用中、短波、调频等无线传输技术发射转播的广播节目的人口数占本行政区域内人口总数的比率。包括中央、省、地市、县四级无线广播综合覆盖人口。

电视综合覆盖率　根据国家广电总局制定的《广播电视人口覆盖率统计技术标准和方法》进行统计调查的，在对象区内能接收到电视节目的人口数占本行政区域内人口总数的比率，包括中央、省、地市、县电视节目综合覆盖人口。

农村电视综合覆盖率　根据国家广电总局制定的《广播电视人口覆盖率统计技术标准和方法》进行统计调查的，在对象区内能接收到电视节目的农村人口数占本行政区域内农村人口总数的比率，包括中央、省、地市、县电视节目综合覆盖农村人口。农村是指经国家批准设立的乡镇人民政府的乡和农村建制镇所辖区，不包括县政府驻地镇。

无线电视综合覆盖率　根据国家广电总局制定的《广播电视人口覆盖率统计技术标准和方法》进行统计调查的，在对象区内能接收到用中、短波、调频等无线传输技术发射转播的电视节目的人口数占本行政区域内人口总数的比率。包括中央、省、地市、县四级无线电视综合覆盖人口。

有线电视入户率　指通过广播电视有线传输网收看电视节目的家庭用户数（包括接收模拟信号和接收数字信号的有线电视用户数，不包括宾馆、单位、写字楼等集体用户）与本行政区域内总户数的比率。

有线电视用户数　指通过广播电视有线传输网收看数字信号电视节目的家庭用户数。

付费电视用户数　指通过广播电视有线传输网收看数字信号的电视节目，并交纳收看费的有线电视家庭用户数。

体　育

体育场地　指专门用于体育训练、比赛和健身活动的，有一定投资的公益性或经营性体育建筑设施，包括必要的附属功能用房。

等级运动员人数　指经考核正式批准授予等级运动员称号的人数。运动员等级分为国际级运动健将、国家级运动健将、一级运动员、二级运动员、三级运动员、少年级运动员。

等级裁判员人数　指经考核正式批准授予等级裁判员称号的人数。裁判员等级分为国际级裁判、国家级裁判、一级裁判、二级裁判、三级裁判。

运动员获奖牌情况　指当年北京市运动员在世界比赛、亚洲比赛、全国比赛中获得金、银、铜牌的数量。

Explanatory Notes on Main Statistical Indicators

Culture

Collection of Books in Public Libraries means the number of books collected in independent libraries open to the public and run by all-level cultural bodies (excluding book rooms in culture centers, and books collected in libraries not included in the cultural system).

Comprehensive Coverage Rate of Broadcast means the share of population who can receive broadcasting programs in the target area, calculated in line with *Statistical Standard and Method on Television and Radio Coverage of Population* established by the State Administration of Broadcasting, Film and Television, of the total population in the administrative area.

Comprehensive Coverage Rate of Broadcast in Rural Area means the share of rural population who can receive broadcasting programs in the target area, calculated in line with *Statistical Standard and Method on Television and Radio Coverage of Population* established by the National Administration of Broadcasting, Film and Television, of the total rural population in the administrative area. Rural area means villages of towns with people's governments approved by the State and areas under the jurisdiction of rural towns with organizational system, excluding towns where people's governments of counties are located.

Comprehensive Coverage Rate of Radio means the share of population who can receive broadcasting programs transmitted with short-wave, medium-wave, FM and other radio transmission technologies in the target area, calculated in line with *Statistical Standard and Method on Television and Radio Coverage of Population* established by the National Administration of Broadcasting, Film and Television, of the total population in the administrative area, including the population covered by broadcasting programs from central, provincial, prefectural cities and county radio stations.

Comprehensive Coverage Rate of TV means the share of population who can receive TV programs in the target area, calculated in line with *Statistical Standard and Method on Television and Radio Coverage of Population* established by the National Administration of Broadcasting, Film and Television, of the total population in the administrative area, including the population covered by TV programs from central, provincial, prefectural cities and county TV stations.

Comprehensive Coverage Rate of TV in Rural Area means the share of rural population who can receive TV programs in the target area, calculated in line with *Statistical Standard and Method on Television and Radio Coverage of Population* established by the National Administration of Broadcasting, Film and Television, of the total rural population in the administrative area, including the population covered by TV programs from central, provincial, prefectural cities and county TV stations. Rural area means villages of towns with people's governments approved by the State and areas under the jurisdiction of rural towns with organizational system, excluding towns where people's governments of counties are located.

Comprehensive Coverage Rate of Wireless TV means the share of population who can receive TV programs transmitted with short-wave, medium-wave, FM and other radio transmission technologies in the target area, calculated in line with *Statistical Standard and Method on Television and Radio Coverage of Population* established by the National Administration of Broadcasting, Film and Television, of the total population in the administrative area, including the population covered by radio television programs from central, provincial, prefectural cities and county TV stations.

Access Rate of CATV refers to the percentage of households which can watch television programs by cable broadcasting and television transmission network (including cable TV households receiving analog signals and digital signals, excluding collective subscribers such as hotels, companies and entities, office buildings), to the total households in the administrative area).

Number of Cable Subscribers means the number of households watching digital-signal TV programs through the TV and radio cable transmission network.

Number of Pay TV Subscribers means the number of cable TV households watching digital-signal TV programs through the TV and radio cable transmission network and paying fees for watching.

Sports

Sports Venues refer to sports building facilities for public welfare or operating purpose, specially used for sports training, games and fitness activities, and with certain investment.

Number of Graded Athletes means the number of athletes formally granted with the title of graded athlete upon examination. Grades of athletes include international master sportsman, national maser sportsman, grade-I athlete, grade-II athlete, grade-III athlete and juvenile athlete.

Number of Graded Referees means the number of referees formally granted with the title of graded referees upon examination. Grades of referees include international referee, national referee, grade-I referee, grade-II referee and grade-III referee.

Medals Won by Athletes mean the number of gold, silver and copper medals won by athletes of Beijing in world games, Asian games and national games.

23

北京统计年鉴2020　BEIJING STATISTICAL YEARBOOK

公共管理、社会保障和社会组织

PUBLIC MANAGEMENT, SOCIAL SECURITY AND SOCIAL ORGANIZATION

简要说明

主要内容

本章资料主要包括社会活动参与、公检法司、社会保障、妇女及儿童发展规划监测情况等。

1.社会活动参与部分主要包括历届北京市人大代表和政协委员人数及议案情况、妇联组织和工会组织等情况。

2.公检法司部分主要包括公安机关、法院、检察院的收案、结案情况，交通事故、火灾、安全生产情况，以及司法局提供的律师、公证、调解工作等情况。

3.社会保障部分主要包括社会保障相关待遇标准和参加社会保障情况。

4.妇女与儿童发展规划监测资料主要包括妇女参与决策和管理、就业、教育、健康、法律保护等情况，儿童的健康、教育、法律保护社会生活环境等情况。

Brief Introduction

Main Content

Statistics in this chapter mainly consist of statistics for social activity participation, public security institutions, procuratorates, courts, judicial authorities, social security, women and children development planning and monitoring.

1. Statistics for social activity participation mainly consist of the numbers of deputies and proposals at people's congress and political consulting conferences of Beijing in previous years, women's federation and organizations and labor unions.

2.Statistics for public security institutions, procuratorates, courts, and judicial authorities cover the cases accepted and settled by public security organs, courts and procuratorates, the statistics on traffic accidents, fires and safe production, and the information on lawyers, notary, mediation provided by juridical bureaus.

3. Statistics for social security mainly consist of the social security benefits level and the social security participation.

4.Supervision data on women and children development are composed of women's participation in decision making and management, employment, education, health, legal protection, and so on; children's health, education, legal protection, social living environment, etc.

23-1 历届北京市人代会代表人数性别构成及议案、建议数
NUMBER AND SEX COMPOSITION OF DEPUTIES、NUMBERS OF PROPOSALS AND SUGGESTIONS OF ALL THE PREVIOUS BEIJING MUNICIPAL PEOPLE'S CONGRESS

项 目 Item	代表人数 (人) Number of Deputies (person)	女 性 Females	男 性 Males	性别比例(%) Sex Percentage (%) 女 性 Females	男 性 Males	议案立案数 (件) Number of Proposals on Record (case)	建议数 (件) Suggestions (case)
第 一 届 1st	564	106	458	18.8	81.2		
第 二 届 2nd	619	142	477	22.9	77.1		
第 三 届 3rd	618	162	456	26.2	73.8		
第 四 届 4th	745	202	543	27.1	72.9		
第 五 届 5th	751	203	548	27.0	73.0		
第 七 届 7th	1195	325	870	27.1	72.9		
第 八 届 8th	973	252	721	25.9	74.1	55	6644
第 九 届 9th	880	217	663	24.7	75.3	86	7921
第 十 届 10th	885	224	661	25.3	74.7	156	7281
第十一届 11th	763	197	566	25.8	74.2	166	9717
第十二届 12th	762	235	527	30.8	69.2	276	9859
第十三届 13th	771	236	535	30.6	69.4	153	7576
第十四届 14th	771	257	514	33.3	66.7	157	6136
第十五届 15th	771	296	475	38.4	61.6	156	2176

注：1. 北京市人大常委会是经北京市七届三次人民代表大会选举成立的，故一至七届人代会无议案及建议数。
2. 代表人数为届首选举数，议案立案数及建议数均为本届五年会上及平时议案立案及建议的合计数。
资料来源：北京市人民代表大会常务委员会。
Note: a) Standing Committee of Beijing People's Congress was established upon election at the 3rd Session of Beijing 7th People's Congress. As a result, there were no proposals and suggestions at the 1st-7th People's Congresses.
b) Deputies were those first elected for that term. Number of proposals on record and suggestions included those at the meeting of the term and/or at ordinary times.
Source: Standing Committee of Beijing Municipal People's Congress (BMPC).

23-2 历届北京市政协会委员人数及提案立案数
NUMBER OF MEMBERS AND PROPOSALS OF ALL THE PREVIOUS BEIJING CPPCC

届别 Term	起止年月 Beginning-ending Month	委员人数(人) Number of Members (person)	女性 Females	男性 Males	提案立案数(件) Number of Proposals on Record (case)
第一届 1st	1955.04-1959.09	270	40	230	37
第二届 2nd	1959.09-1962.12	463	84	379	13
第三届 3rd	1962.12-1965.09	519	92	427	884
第四届 4th	1965.09-1977.11	529	88	441	23
第五届 5th	1977.11-1983.03	779	161	618	1610
第六届 6th	1983.03-1988.01	766	168	598	3122
第七届 7th	1988.01-1993.01	703	179	524	4276
第八届 8th	1993.01-1998.01	740	185	555	4975
第九届 9th	1998.01-2003.01	782	203	579	6240
第十届 10th	2003.01-2008.01	824	226	598	6871
第十一届 11th	2008.01-2013.01	737	233	504	5354
第十二届 12th	2013.01-2018.01	758	237	521	5410
第十三届 13th	2018.01-2019.12	758	239	519	2174

资料来源：中国人民政治协商会议北京市委员会。
Source: The Chinese People's Political Consultative Conference Beijing Committe.

23-3 公安、法院、检察院收案、结案情况(2005-2019年)
CASES ACCEPTED AND SETTLED BY PUBLIC SECURITY DEPARTMENTS, COURTS AND PROCURATORATES (2005-2019)

项目	Item	2005	2006	2007	2008	2009	2010
公安机关办理案件	**Cases Handled by Public Security Departments**						
侦破刑事案件	**Criminal Cases Detected by Public Security Departments**						
立案 (起)	Cases Put on File (case)	107988	120554	127446	90045	98750	104327
破案 (起)	Cases Settled (case)	59035	66399	74232	63294	71950	80401
法院办理案件	**Cases Handled by Courts**						
刑事案件收、结案情况	**Criminal Cases Accepted and Settled in Courts**						
收案 (件)	Cases Accepted (case)	17488	17725	19592	20024	18819	19824
结案 (件)	Cases Settled (case)	17624	17701	19536	20004	18773	19870
婚姻家庭、继承纠纷案件	**Marriage and Inheritance Dispute**						
收、结案情况	**Cases Accepted and Settled in Courts**						
收案 (件)	Cases Accepted (case)	26739	27860	28089	30402	33056	36799
结案 (件)	Cases Settled (case)	27002	27845	27916	29499	32902	37160
合同纠纷案件	**Contract Dispute Cases Accepted and**						
收、结案情况	**Settled in Courts**						
收案 (件)	Cases Accepted (case)	133534	141485	135099	144948	153766	148655
结案 (件)	Cases Settled (case)	135612	141439	134829	140512	152128	153130
权属、侵权纠纷及其他	**Ownership, Infringement Dispute and Other**						
民事案件收、结案情况	**Civil Cases Accepted and Settled in Courts**						
收案 (件)	Cases Accepted (case)	42690	44890	46892	53864	58057	64379
结案 (件)	Cases Settled (case)	43166	45005	46372	51668	57135	65763
检察机关办理案件	**Cases Handled by Procuratorial Organs**						
审查逮捕案件	**Arrest Cases to Be Examined and Approved**						
收案 (件)	Cases Accepted (case)	17441	18137	19126	16584	17593	18060
结案 (件)	Cases Settled (case)	16398	16795	17210	16562	17606	17946
审查起诉案件	**Cases of prosecution to be reviewed and made**						
收案 (件)	Cases Accepted (case)	19672	19869	21462	20137	20453	20982
结案 (件)	Cases Settled (case)	17899	18517	20394	19047	19989	19825

资料来源：北京市公安局、北京市人民检察院、北京市高级人民法院。
Source: Beijing Municipal Bureau of Public Security, the People's Procuratorate of Beijing, and the People's High Court of Beijing.

23-3 续表 Continued

项目	Item	2011	2012	2013	2014	2015	2016	2017	2018	2019
公安机关办理案件	**Cases Handled by Public Security Departments**									
侦破刑事案件	**Criminal Cases Detected by Public Security Departments**									
立案 (起)	Cases Put on File (case)	142835	145724	140498	153334	174374	150312	140250	138696	138291
破案 (起)	Cases Settled (case)	89156	101776	112594	122383	115807	65376	64002	74857	81755
法院办理案件	**Cases Handled by Courts**									
刑事案件收、结案情况	**Criminal Cases Accepted and Settled in Courts**									
收案 (件)	Cases Accepted (case)	19574	22168	19109	20556	19980	16737	18584	17091	20320
结案 (件)	Cases Settled (case)	19423	22084	19012	20357	19667	16905	18628	17062	19582
婚姻家庭、继承纠纷案件 收、结案情况	**Marriage and Inheritance Disputes Cases Accepted and Settled in Courts**									
收案 (件)	Cases Accepted (case)	35251	35418	37347	39390	43869	43141	50467	52675	49077
结案 (件)	Cases Settled (case)	35149	35201	35296	38565	40436	43606	51800	52950	49402
合同纠纷案件 收、结案情况	**Contract Dispute Cases Accepted and Settled in Courts**									
收案 (件)	Cases Accepted (case)	144433	145017	149237	162893	237850	253456	279287	347240	343861
结案 (件)	Cases Settled (case)	144766	143153	141642	155472	207012	255852	285872	346884	338714
权属、侵权纠纷及其他 民事案件收、结案情况	**Ownership, Infringement Dispute and Other Civil Cases Accepted and Settled in Courts**									
收案 (件)	Cases Accepted (case)	65972	62736	64747	69541	85554	100574	114284	109296	119759
结案 (件)	Cases Settled (case)	66405	62235	61688	67444	76644	100399	115125	110443	118326
检察机关办理案件	**Cases Handled by Procuratorial Organs**									
审查逮捕案件	**Arrest Cases to Be Examined and Approved**									
收案 (件)	Cases Accepted (case)	18279	18563	16861	16594	14880	14307	16651	17359	19995
结案 (件)	Cases Settled (case)	18208	18644	16860	16606	14840	14265	16663	17318	19992
审查起诉案件	**Cases of prosecution to be reviewed and made**									
收案 (件)	Cases Accepted (case)	20986	23553	21798	22251	20181	18786	21039	20311	24023
结案 (件)	Cases Settled (case)	20293	21980	20684	22455	19935	18361	20807	19688	22825

23-4 刑事案件情况
STATISTICS FOR CRIMINAL CASES

单位：起 (case)

项　目	Item	2019	2018	2019年为2018年% 2019 as % of 2018
刑事案件	**Criminal Cases**			
立　案	Cases Registered	138291	138696	99.7
破　案	Cases Settled	81755	74857	109.2

资料来源：北京市公安局。
Source: Beijing Municipal Bureau of Public Security.

23-5 检察机关办理各类案件情况(2019年)
STATISTICS FOR CASES HANDLED BY PROCURATORIAL ORGANS (2019)

项　目	Item	受案(受理) Cases Accepted		审结案合计 Cases Settled	
		件 Case	人 Person	件 Case	人 Person
审查逮捕案件	**Arrests to Be Examined and Approved**	**19995**	**28699**	**19992**	**28666**
批准逮捕	Approved			13287	17726
不批准逮捕	Disapproved			6705	10940
审查起诉案件	**Prosecution to Be Reviewed and Made**	**24023**	**32433**	**22825**	**29560**
起　诉	Prosecuted			19659	25084
不起诉	Non-prosecution			3102	4392
附条件不起诉	Conditional Non-prosecution			64	84
举报案件	**Reported Cases**	**958**		**773**	
控告案件	**Complaints**	**7064**		**6103**	
申诉案件	**Appeal Cases**	**14347**		**12334**	
民事检察案件	**Civil Cases**	**2943**		**2989**	
行政检察案件	**Administrative Cases**	**1107**		**1112**	

资料来源：北京市人民检察院。
Source: The People's Procuratorate of Beijing.

23-6 法院行政案件收、结案情况(2019年)
STATISTICS FOR ADMINISTRATIVE CASES ACCEPTED AND SETTLED BY COURT (2019)

单位：件 (case)

项目	Item	收案 Cases Accepted	结案 Cases Settled	#判决 Judgment	#裁定 Mediation
合计	**Total**	**28702**	**31016**	**21291**	**9720**
公安	Public Security	1282	1221	417	803
资源	Resources	1127	1199	337	862
城建	City Construction	1674	1660	468	1190
工商	Industry and Commerce	901	917	337	580
专利	Patents	1623	1183	896	287
劳动和社会保障	Labor and Social Security	471	457	240	217
教育	Education	75	76	19	57
其他	Others	21549	24303	18577	5724

注：法院行政案件收结案为一审审结数。
资料来源：北京市高级人民法院。
Note: The statistics for administrative cases accepted and settled by court refer to the number of concluded cases at the first trial.
Source: The People's High Court of Beijing.

23-7 法院刑事案件收、结案情况(2019年)
STATISTICS FOR CRIMINAL CASES ACCEPTED AND SETTLED BY COURT (2019)

项目	Item	收案(件) Cases Accepted (case)	结案(件) Cases Settled (case)	判决发生法律效力 Judgment with Legal Forces: 件数(件) Number of Cases (case)	人数(人) Number of Persons(person)
合计	**Total**	**20320**	**19582**	**18952**	**23357**
#危害公共安全罪	Offences against Public Security	5500	5424	5239	5314
破坏社会主义市场经济秩序罪	Offences against the Socialist Market Economy Order	2026	1776	1716	2832
侵犯公民人身权利、民主权利罪	Offences against Civil Personal Rights and Democratic Rights	2983	2924	2801	3330
侵犯财产罪	Offences against Property	5955	5695	5551	6858
妨害社会管理秩序罪	Offences against Social Administration	3591	3514	3423	4764
危害国防利益罪	Offences against National Defense Interest	24	23	24	29
贪污贿赂罪	Crimes of Corruption and Bribery	224	211	181	207
渎职罪	Crimes of Misconduct in Office	13	9	12	17

注：法院刑事案件收结案为一审审结数。
资料来源：北京市高级人民法院。
Note: The statistics for criminal cases accepted and settled by court refer to the number of concluded cases at the first trial.
Source: The People's High Court of Beijing.

23-8 法院婚姻家庭、继承纠纷案件收、结案情况(2019年)
STATISTICS FOR MARRIAGE AND FAMILY AND INHERITANCE DISPUTE CASES ACCEPTED AND SETTLED BY COURT (2019)

单位：件 (case)

项 目	Item	收 案 Cases Accepted	结 案 Cases Settled	#判 决 Judgment	#调 解 Mediation
合 计	**Total**	**49077**	**49402**	**12015**	**20129**
婚姻家庭纠纷	**Marriage and Family Disputes**	**32060**	**32407**	**9016**	**11555**
离 婚	Divorces	17169	17412	5540	5024
同居关系	Cohabitation	300	293	82	115
抚养、扶养关系纠纷	Child-support Disputes	1364	1362	285	730
抚育费纠纷	Child-support Payment Disputes	1482	1503	605	434
赡养纠纷	Support Disputes	1188	1162	427	313
分家析产	Family Property Division	6438	6511	880	3698
其 他	Others	4119	4164	1197	1241
继承纠纷	**Inheritance Disputes**	**17017**	**16995**	**2999**	**8574**
法定继承	Legal Inheritance	9803	9865	1282	5793
遗嘱继承	Testamentary Inheritance	1464	1485	550	459
其 他	Others	5750	5645	1167	2322

注：法院婚姻家庭、继承纠纷案件收、结案为一审审结案数。
资料来源：北京市高级人民法院。
Note: The statistics for marriage and family and inheritance dispute cases accepted and settled by court refer to the number of concluded cases at the first trial.
Source: Higher People's Court of Beijing Municipality.

23-9 法院合同纠纷案件收、结案情况(2019年)
STATISTICS FOR CONTRACT CASES ACCEPTED AND SETTLED BY COURT (2019)

单位：件 (case)

项目	Item	收案 Cases Accepted	结案 Cases Settled	#判决 Judgment	#调解 Mediation
合计	**Total**	**343861**	**338714**	**128011**	**52463**
#买卖合同纠纷	Trade Contracts	36149	36837	12401	7368
房地产开发经营	Real Estate Development & Operation				
合同纠纷	Contracts	58	68	35	4
供电、水、气、热力	Electricity, Water, Gas, Heating				
合同纠纷	Supply contracts	27985	28245	2247	4174
借款合同纠纷	Loan Contracts	93754	91227	46221	13185
租赁合同纠纷	Lease Contracts	24703	24386	9062	4513
建设工程合同纠纷	Construction Contracts	8419	7944	2935	1769
承揽合同纠纷	Contracts for Hire of Work	3985	3799	1265	945
运输合同纠纷	Transportation Contracts	1263	1188	549	250
农村承包合同纠纷	Rural Contracts	2271	2208	1348	170
劳务合同纠纷	Labor Contracts	10296	9905	3033	2570
服务合同纠纷	Service Contracts	56573	55727	9106	7905
其他	Others	78405	77180	39809	9610

注：法院合同纠纷案件收结案为一审审结数。
资料来源：北京市高级人民法院。
Note: The statistics for contract cases accepted and settled by court refer to the number of concluded cases at the first trial.
Source: Higher People's Court of Beijing Municipality.

23-10 法院权属、侵权纠纷及其他民事案件收、结案情况(2019年)
STATISTICS FOR OWNERSHIP, TORTIOUS DISPUTES AND OTHER CIVIL CASES ACCEPTED AND SETTLED BY COURT (2019)

单位：件 (case)

项目	Item	收案 Cases Accepted	结案 Cases Settled	#判决 Judgment	#调解 Mediation
合计	**Total**	**119759**	**118326**	**34714**	**17442**
所有权及与所有权相关权利纠纷	Ownership and Related Rights	21446	21273	7058	4311
票据、证券权益纠纷	Bill and Securities Rights	1355	1353	253	114
股东权纠纷	Shareholder's Rights	3585	3341	1369	365
不正当竞争纠纷	Unfair Competition	661	599	215	59
人身权纠纷	Personal Rights	14340	14338	5023	2461
特殊侵权纠纷	Special Infringements	21897	21326	10453	5164
适用特别程序案件	Special-poceeding Cases	2119	2020	1514	10
其他	Others	54356	54076	8829	4958

注：法院权属、侵权纠纷及其他民事案件收、结案为一审审结数。
资料来源：北京市高级人民法院。
Note: The statistics for ownership, tortious disputes and other civil cases accepted and settled by court refer to the number of concluded cases at the first trial.
Source: The People's High Court of Beijing.

23-11 离婚、青少年刑事案犯情况
STATISTICS FOR DIVORCE AND JUVENILE CRIMINAL CASES

项目	Item	2019	2018
婚姻家庭纠纷案件数(结案) (件)	Marriage and Family Disputes (Closed) (case)	32407	36170
#离婚案件数	Divorce Cases	17412	19132
#调离案件数	Cases of Divorce Reconciled	4850	5253
判离案件数	Cases of Divorce Judged	2584	2480
青少年罪犯人数 (人)	Teenager Offenders (person)	2834	2803
14周岁以上不满16周岁罪犯人数	Teenager Offenders 14-16	20	30
16周岁以上不满18周岁罪犯人数	Teenager Offenders 16-18	212	218
18周岁以上不满25周岁罪犯人数	Teenager Offenders 18-25	2602	2555
青少年刑事案犯占全部刑事案犯的比重 (%)	Teenager Criminal Offenders as % of Total Criminal Offenders (%)	12.2	16.6

注：婚姻家庭纠纷案件数为一审审结数。
资料来源：北京市高级人民法院。
Note: The number of marriage and family disputes refers to the number of concluded cases at the first trial.
Source: The People's High Court of Beijing.

23-12 律师工作
STATISTICS FOR LAWYERS

项　目	Item	2019	2018	2019年为2018年% 2019 as % of 2018
律师事务所 （个）	Law Firms (unit)	2735	2466	110.9
执业律师 （人）	Number of Practicing Lawyers (person)	34907	32134	108.6
专职律师	Full-time Lawyers (person)	31621	29457	107.3
兼职律师	Part-time Lawyers (person)	1051	930	113.0
公司律师	Company Lawyers (person)	624	520	120.0
公职律师	Government Lawyers (person)	1225	1191	102.9
法律援助律师	Legal Aid Lawyers (person)	386	36	1072.2
担任法律顾问 （家）	Legal Counsel (unit)	43436	33131	131.1
民事诉讼代理 （件）	Civil Case Litigation Agencies (case)	175792	142176	123.6
行政诉讼代理 （件）	Administrative Case Litigation Agencies (case)	21527	18201	118.3
刑事诉讼辩护及代理 （件）	Criminal Case Litigation Agencies (case)	21557	17705	121.8
非诉讼法律事务 （件）	Off-court Cases (case)	184534	166195	111.0

资料来源：北京市司法局。
Source: Beijing Municipal Bureau of Justice.

23-13 调解工作
MEDIATION

项　目	Item	2019	2018	2019年为2018年% 2019 as % of 2018
人民调解委员会个数 （个）	People's Mediation Committees (unit)	7625	7749	98.4
调解员人数 （万人）	Mediators (10000 persons)	4.6	6.0	76.5
调解各类纠纷件数 （万件）	Disputes Mediated (10000 cases)	23.6	22.1	106.5
#调解各类纠纷成功件数	Disputes Mediated Successfully	20.5	18.6	110.6
人民调解组织排查纠纷 （次）	Disputes Investigated by People's Mediation Organization (times)	350528	107015	327.6
预防纠纷 （件）	Disputes Prevented (case)	23053	20922	110.2

资料来源：北京市司法局。
Source: Beijing Municipal Bureau of Justice.

23-14 公证工作
NOTARIZATIONS

项　　目		Item		2019	2018	2019年为2018年% 2019 as % of 2018
公证机构个数	(个)	Notary Offices	(unit)	25	25	100.0
执业公证员人数	(人)	Certified Notaries	(person)	416	392	106.1
总办证数	(件)	Certificates Issued	(case)	745372	775253	96.1
国内公证业务		Domestic Notarial Services		417048	425916	97.9
涉外公证业务		Foreign-Relatesd Notarial Documments		323187	344142	93.9
涉港澳公证业务		Hong Kong, Macao Affairs		2754	2688	102.5
涉台公证业务		Naiwan Notarial Services		2383	2507	95.1

资料来源：北京市司法局。
Source: Beijing Municipal Bureau of Justice.

23-15 法律援助工作情况
STATISTICS FOR LEGAL AID

项　　目		Item		2019	2018	2019年为2018年% 2019 as % of 2018
法律援助机构个数	(个)	Number of Legal Aid Agencies	(unit)	17	17	100.0
法律援助机构人员数	(人)	Number of Legal Aid Persons	(person)	110	109	100.9
承办民事法律援助案件数	(件)	Civil Cases Aided	(case)	26988	27087	99.6
承办刑事法律援助案件数	(件)	Criminal Cases Aided	(case)	10547	10079	104.6
承办行政法律援助案件数	(件)	Administrative Cases Aided	(case)	90	144	62.5
法律援助机构接待咨询人次	(万人次)	Consultations by Legal Aid Agencies	(10000 person-times)	44.0	35.5	124.1
得到法律援助机构援助的妇女人数	(人次)	Females Receiving Aids from Legal Aid Agencies	(person-times)	9969	17080	58.4
得到法律援助机构援助的未成年人数	(人次)	Juveniles Receiving Aids from Legal Aid Agencies	(person-times)	1024	1569	65.3

资料来源：北京市司法局。
Source: Beijing Municiapl Bureau of Justice.

23-16 司法鉴定工作情况
STATISTICS FOR JUDICIAL APPRAISAL

项　　目		Item		2019	2018
司法鉴定机构个数	（个）	Judicial Appraisal Organizations	(unit)	126	116
司法鉴定人员数	（人）	Judicial Appraisal Personnel	(person)	1774	1684
司法鉴定业务量	（件）	Judicial Appraisal Cases Proceeded	(case)	92334	86601

注：本表中司法鉴定机构数为北京市司法局审核登记的全部司法鉴定机构个数。
资料来源：北京市司法局。
Note: In the table, the number of judicial appraisal organizations is the number of all judicial appraisal organizations approved by and registered with Beijing Municipal Bureau of Justice.
Source: Beijing Municipal Bureau of Justice.

23-17 消防建设情况(1996-2019年)
STATISTICS FOR FIRECONTROL (1996-2019)

年　份 Year	消防站数（支） Number of Fire Stations (unit)	消防站消防车辆数（辆） Number of Fire-fighting Vehicles of Fire Station (unit)	企业专职消防队队数（支） Number of Full-time Fire Brigades in Enterprises (unit)	企业专职消防队人数（人） Persons of Full-time Fire-fighters in Enterprises (person)
1996	36	180	101	1865
1997	38	190	104	1885
1998	41	210	108	1993
1999	44	236	120	2447
2000	47	259	120	2447
2001	50	266	120	2447
2002	52	296	112	2228
2003	56	303	112	2147
2004	57	381	120	2477
2005	57	342	120	2477
2006	64	357	109	2269
2007	69	401	109	2269
2008	77	558	109	2269
2009	86	572	109	2269
2010	91	664	109	2269
2011	98	604	87	1766
2012	107	670	76	1405
2013	122	735	76	1405
2014	125	799	76	1405
2015	134	858	78	1410
2016	143	916	65	1307
2017	145	924	65	1307
2018	211	1066	65	1307
2019	250	1177	65	1307

资料来源：2017年及以前数据来源于北京市公安局消防局，2018年起数据来源于北京市消防总队。
Source: Data for and before 2017 were from Fire Department of Beijing Municipal Bureau of Public Security. Data since 2018 are from Beijing Fire Corps.

23－18 火灾及损失
FIRE ACCIDENTS AND LOSSES

项　目	Item	火灾起数(起) Fire Accidents (time) 2019	2018	直接经济损失(万元) Direct Economic Losses (10000 yuan) 2019	2018
火灾起数　（起）	**Fire Accidents　(case)**	**3040**	**3293**	**7175.2**	**3646.6**
特别重大火灾	Extraordinarily Serious				
重大火灾	Serious				
较大火灾	Big Fire	3	2	2907.1	51.8
一般火灾	Relatively Big Fire	3037	3291	4268.2	3594.8
起火原因	**Cause of Fire**				
电　气	Electricity and Gas	1370	1260	2142.3	2266.7
生产作业	Violation of Operation	108	148	3142.0	136.1
生活用火不慎	Carelessness in Fire Use	410	407	198.9	235.9
吸　烟	Smoking	60	97	54.9	33.6
玩　火	Fire Playing	13	19	7.7	46.9
自　燃	Spontaneous Combustion	89	104	120.9	206.1
雷　击	Thunderstroke	1	1	2.5	0.1
静　电	Static	2		14.0	
放　火	Incendiarism	74	98	423.1	193.7
其　他	Others	913	1159	1069.1	527.5
受伤人数　（人）	**Number of Injuries　(person)**	**29**	**14**		
死亡人数　（人）	**Number of Deaths　(person)**	**27**	**32**		

资料来源：北京市消防总队。
Source:Beijing Fire Corps.

23－19 交通事故及损失
STATISTICS FOR TRAFFIC ACCIDENTS AND LOSSES

项　目		Item		2019	2018	2019年为2018年% 2019 as % of 2018
交通事故		**Traffic Accidents**				
交通事故发生数	(起)	Number of Traffic Accidents	(case)	3110	3255	95.5
受伤人数	(人)	Number of Injuries	(person)	2789	2809	99.3
死亡人数	(人)	Number of Deaths	(person)	1258	1298	96.9
机动车事故		**Motor Vehicle Accidents**				
机动车事故发生数	(起)	Number of Motor Vehicle Accidents	(case)	2414	2670	90.4
受伤人数	(人)	Number of Injuries	(person)	2181	2398	91.0
死亡人数	(人)	Number of Deaths	(person)	1033	1106	93.4
直接经济损失	**(万元)**	**Direct Economic Losses**	**(10000 yuan)**	**3528.0**	**3519.6**	**100.2**
每万辆机动车死亡人数	**(人)**	**Persons Died Per 10000 Motor Vehicles**	**(person)**	**1.98**	**2.13**	

资料来源：北京市公安局公安交通管理局。
Source: Beijing Municipal Bureau of Traffic Management.

23-20 安全生产情况
STATISTICS FOR SAFE PRODUCTION

项目	Item	2019	2018
亿元地区生产总值安全生产事故死亡率 (人/亿元)	Death Rate of Work Accidents Per 100 Million Yuan GDP (person/100 million yuan)	0.013	0.017
工矿商贸企业从业人员10万人生产安全事故死亡率 (人/10万人)	Death Rate of Work Accidents in the Mining, Commercial and Trade Industries Per 100000 Persons (1/100000)	0.72	0.84
道路交通万车死亡率 (人/万车)	Road Traffic Death Rate Per 10000 Vehicles (person/10000 vehicles)	1.98	2.13
食品安全监督抽检合格率 (%)	Up-to -standard Rate of Food Security Supervision Spot Checks (%)	98.85	98.99
#重点食品安全监督抽检合格率	Up-to-standard Rate of Key Foods Security Supervision Spot Checks	98.89	98.69
药品抽验合格率 (%)	Up-to-standard Rate of Drug Spot Checks (%)	100.00	99.78

资料来源：北京市市场监督管理局、北京市公安局公安交通管理局、北京市应急管理局。
Source: Beijing Municipal Administration of Market Supervision, Beijing Traffic Management Bureau, Beijing Emergency Management Bureau.

23-21 地震应急避难场所情况
EMERGENT EARTHQUAKE REFUGES

项目	Item	2019	2018
地震应急避难场所累计个数 (个)	Total Number of Emergent Earthquake Refuges (unit)	165	169
地震应急避难场所累计面积 (万平方米)	Total Area of Emergent Earthquake Refuges (10000 sq.m)	2298	2203

资料来源：北京市地震局。
Source: Beijing Municipal Bureau of Earthquake.

23–22 社会保障相关待遇标准(1994–2019年)
LEVEL ON SOCIAL SECURITY BENEFITS (1994-2019)

单位：元/月 (yuan/month)

年份 Year	标准 Standard	职工最低工资 Minimum Wages of Employed Persons	失业保险金最低标准 Minimum Unemployment Insurance	城乡最低生活保障标准 Minimum Subsistence Allowance for Urban and Rural Residents
1994		210		
1995		240	174	
1996		270	189	170
1997		290	203	190
1998		310	217	200
1999年第一次	First-time in 1999	320	224	210
1999年第二次	Second-time in 1999	400	291	273
2000		412	300	280
2001		435	305	285
2002		465	326	290
2003		465	326	290
2004年第一次	First-time in 2004	495		
2004年第二次	Second-time in 2004	545	347	290
2005		580	382	300
2006		640	392	310
2007		730	422	330
2008		800	502	390
2009		800	562	410
2010		960	632	430
2011		1160	782	500
2012		1260	842	520
2013		1400	892	580
2014		1560	1012	650
2015		1720	1122	710
2016		1890	1212	800
2017		2000	1292	900
2018		2120	1536	1000
2019		2200	1706	1100

注：表中2017年及以前“城乡最低生活保障标准”数据为“城市居民最低生活保障标准”数据。

资料来源：城乡最低生活保障标准由中共北京市委社会工作委员会北京市民政局提供，其他资料由北京市人力资源和社会保障局提供。

Note: Data on minimum subsistence allowance for urban and rural residents of 2017 and before in this table refer to the data of minimum subsistence allowance for urban residents.

Source: Data on minimum subsistence allowance for urban and rural residents are provided by Social Work Committee of Beijing Municipal Committee of the Communist Party of China Beijing Municipal Civil Affairs Bureau, other data are provided by Beijing Municipal Human Resources and Social Security Bureau.

23-23 参加社会保障情况(1995-2019年)

单位：万人

年 份 Year	参加企业职工基本养老保险人数 Enterprise Employed Persons Participating in Basic Pension Insurance	参加职工基本医疗保险人数 Staff and Workers Participating in Basic Medical Care Insurance	参加失业保险人数 Employed Persons Participating in Unemployment Insurance	参加工伤保险人数 Employed Persons Participating in Work-related Injury Insurance	参加生育保险人数 Employed Persons Participating in Maternity Insurance
1995	261.1		219.8		
1996	252.0		214.5		
1997	264.3		214.0		
1998	359.2		222.9		
1999	379.0		289.0		
2000	391.6		287.8	212.0	
2001	425.9	210.2	287.2	212.7	
2002	436.2	353.8	299.5	221.0	
2003	448.5	436.1	306.6	242.9	
2004	460.0	484.0	308.0	259.0	
2005	520.0	574.8	394.6	328.9	226.1
2006	604.1	679.5	482.2	465.3	263.3
2007	671.7	783.0	535.3	609.2	290.6
2008	758.1	871.0	614.3	666.5	324.1
2009	827.7	938.4	675.7	747.1	346.8
2010	982.5	1063.7	774.2	823.8	372.2
2011	1091.9	1188.0	881.0	862.4	395.3
2012	1206.4	1279.7	1006.7	897.2	844.7
2013	1311.3	1354.8	1025.1	920.3	883.2
2014	1392.6	1431.3	1057.1	961.0	915.6
2015	1424.2	1475.7	1082.3	1020.1	941.6
2016	1459.1	1517.6	1117.5	1060.2	981.0
2017	1514.3	1569.2	1170.2	1117.9	1035.2
2018	1591.5	1628.9	1240.7	1187.0	1104.0
2019	1651.6	1682.5	1294.8	1242.2	1156.4

注：1．2001年开始设置基本医疗保险指标，以前年份为大病统筹，2000年参加大病统筹人数为232.6万人。
2．参加城乡居民基本医疗保险人数2017年及以前数据为参加城镇居民基本医疗保险人数，下同。
3．从2006年起，农村居民最低生活保障人数不含农村五保供养人员。

资料来源：城市居民最低生活保障人数和农村居民最低生活保障人数来源于中共北京市委社会工作委员会北京市民政局，其他资料来源于北京市人力资源和社会保障局、北京市医疗保障局。

SOCIAL SECURITY PARTICIPATION (1995-2019)

(10000 persons)

参加城乡居民基本养老保障人数 Residents Participating in Urban and Rural Basic Pension Security	参加城乡居民基本医疗保险人数 Residents Participating in Urban and Rural Basic Medical Care	参加新型农村合作医疗人数 Residents Participating in New-type Rural Cooperative Medical Care	城市居民最低生活保障人数 Residents Receiving Subsistence Allowances in Urban Areas	农村居民最低生活保障人数 Residents Receiving Subsistence Allowances in Rural Areas
			0.9	
			0.9	
			2.8	
			4.3	1.2
			6.7	1.6
			7.8	1.8
			12.0	5.4
			16.1	6.7
		234.0	16.1	7.5
		250.4	15.5	7.8
		261.0	15.2	7.1
		268.5	14.8	7.8
		272.5	14.5	7.9
		274.9	14.7	8.0
	143.7	278.5	13.7	7.7
	159.8	276.8	11.7	7.0
	151.9	267.5	11.0	6.3
	160.1	254.4	10.4	6.0
	173.0	242.6	8.9	5.1
	181.0	223.9	8.5	4.9
215.7	191.2	211.9	8.2	4.7
213.1	202.2	186.9	7.8	4.4
209.0	392.2		6.7	3.8
204.7	400.1		6.5	3.8

Note: a) The basic medical care indicator was set from 2001. Before that it was called general healthcare program for major diseases which cover 2.326 million people in 2000.

b) Figures on residents participating in urban and rural basic medical care in and before 2017 referred to that of residents participating in urban basic medical care, the same below.

c) Residents receiving subsistence allowance in rural areas excluded rural persons enjoying five guarantees from 2006.

Source: Figures on residents receiving subsistence allowances in urban areas and residents receiving subsistence allowances in rural areas are from Social Work Committee of Beijing Municipal Committee of the Communist Party of China Beijing Municipal Civil Affairs Bureau; other data are from Beijing Municipal Human Resources and Social Security Bureau and Beijing Municipal Medical Insurance Bureau.

23-24 城镇职工参加社会保险情况(2019年)
PARTICIPATION OF EMPLOYED PERSONS FOR SOCIAL SECURITY INSURANCE PROGRAMS IN THE URBAN AREA (2019)

项目	Item	参加企业职工基本养老保险 Participation of Basic Pension Insurance for Enterprise Employed Persons		参加职工基本医疗保险 Participation of Basic Medical Insurance for Employed Persons	
		单位个数(个) Number of Entities (unit)	人数(人) Number of Persons (person)	单位个数(个) Number of Entities (unit)	人数(人) Number of Persons (person)
合计	**Total**	**684740**	**16516233**	**628929**	**16825174**
按登记注册类型分	**By Registration Type**				
国有	State-owned	6392	1907489	5599	1974100
集体	Collectively-owned	6089	226789	4932	217728
其他	Others	672259	14381955	618398	14633346
按隶属关系划分	**By Affiliation**				
中央单位	Central	7515	1967430	6523	1911504
地方单位	Local	677225	14548803	622406	14913670

资料来源：北京市人力资源和社会保障局、北京市医疗保障局。
Source: Beijing Municipal Human Resources and Social Security Bureau, Beijing Municipal Medical Insurance Bureau.

23-24 续表 Continued

项目	Item	参加失业保险 Unemployment Insurance		参加工伤保险 Industrial Injury Insurance		参加生育保险 Maternity Insurance	
		单位个数(个) Number of Entities (unit)	人数(人) Number of Persons (person)	单位个数(个) Number of Entities (unit)	人数(人) Number of Persons (person)	单位个数(个) Number of Entities (unit)	人数(人) Number of Persons (person)
合计	**Total**	**677542**	**12947809**	**694477**	**12422459**	**675312**	**11563511**
按登记注册类型分	**By Registration Type**						
国有	State-owned	18227	2087635	19179	2243833	6241	983440
集体	Collectively-owned	5475	110380	5666	118201	5769	105248
其他	Others	653840	10749794	669632	10060425	663302	10474823
按隶属关系划分	**By Affiliation**						
中央单位	Central	7157	1558064	7525	1534221	7221	1285942
地方单位	Local	670385	11389745	686952	10888238	668091	10277569

资料来源：北京市人力资源和社会保障局、北京市医疗保障局。
Source: Beijing Municipal Human Resources and Social Security Bureau, Beijing Municipal Medical Insurance Bureau.

23-25 城乡居民参加社会保险情况(2010-2019年)

PARTICIPATION OF RURAL AND URBAN RESIDENTS FOR SOCIAL SECURITY INSURANCE PROGRAMS (2010-2019)

单位：万人 (10000 persons)

年 份 Year	参加城乡居民基本养老保障人数 Residents Participating in Urban and Rural Basic Pension Security	参加城乡居民基本医疗保险人数 Residents Participating in Urban and Rural Basic Medical Care Insurance	学生儿童 Students and Children	无保障老人 Unguaranteed Aged Persons	无业居民 Unemployed Residents
2010		143.7	121.3	17.7	4.7
2011		159.8	135.5	19.1	5.3
2012		151.9	128.6	18.5	4.8
2013		160.1	137.5	18.8	3.7
2014		173.0	149.8	19.7	3.6
2015		181.0	157.7	19.8	3.4
2016	215.7	191.2	168.0	19.9	3.3
2017	213.1	202.2	179.2	19.9	3.2
2018	209.0	392.2	221.9	111.8	58.6
2019	204.7	400.1	232.5	114.3	53.3

资料来源：北京市人力资源和社会保障局、北京市医疗保障局。
Source: Beijing Municipal Human Resources and Social Security Bureau, Beijing Municipal Medical Insurance Bureau.

23-26 妇联组织状况

STATISTICS FOR WOMEN'S FEDERATIONS AND ORGANIZATIONS

单位：个，人 (unit,person)

项 目	Item	2019	2018	2019年为2018年% 2019 as % of 2018
妇联组织状况	**Status of Women's Federations and Organizations**			
区妇联数	Number of Women's Federations in Districts	16	16	100.0
乡、镇妇联组织数	Number of Women's Federations in Townships	180	181	99.4
街道妇联组织数	Number of Women's Federations in Subdistricts	153	149	102.7
社区妇联组织数	Number of Women's Federations in Communities	3171	2957	107.2
村妇联组织数	Number of Women's Federations in Villages	3645	3702	98.5
妇联干部状况	**Status of Cadres in Women's Federation**			
区妇联干部数	Cadres in Women's Federations in Districts	315	312	101.0
乡、镇、街道妇联干部数	Cadres in Women's Federations in Townships, Towns and Subdistricts	641	333	192.5
各类妇女联谊组织数	**Women's Sodalities**	**37**	**34**	**108.8**

资料来源：北京市妇女联合会。
Source: Beijing Women's Federation.

23–27 工会组织建设情况(2019年)
STATISTICS FOR LABOR UNIONS (2019)

项　目	Item	基层工会组织（个）Grassroot Labor Unions (unit)	职工人数（人）Number of Employed Persons (person)	会员人数（人）Number of Members (person)
合　计	**Total**	**32302**	**4491479**	**4174500**
按单位类别划分	**By Registration Type**			
国有企业	State-owned Enterprises	1231	560909	539393
集体企业	Collectively-owned Enterprises	1431	144219	136349
股份合作企业	Joint-equity Cooperative Enterprises	392	51266	45379
联营企业	Associated Enterprises	33	2441	2332
国有独资公司	Solely State-owned Enterprises	566	170923	162822
其他有限责任公司	Other Limited-Liability Companies	11248	1095784	978730
国有控股公司	State-holding Companies	361	248697	245768
其他股份有限公司	Other Holding Companies	933	190425	158063
私营企业	Private Enterprises	5528	453849	394760
其他内资企业	Other Domestically-invested Enterprises	64	5872	5577
港澳台商投资企业	Hong Kong, Macao and Taiwan-invested Enterprises	346	81288	73256
外商投资企业	Foreign-invested Enterprises	797	241061	216811
事业单位	Public Institutions	4087	629648	610641
机关	Governmental Agencies and Organizations	1453	264706	262729
其他	Other	3832	350391	341890
按系统分	**By System**			
工业国防工会	Labor Unions for Industry and National Defence	713	281946	267524
工　业	Industry	699	272246	257869
国　防	National Defence	14	9700	9655
建筑工会	Construction	1346	523612	405879
本　市	Local	460	212435	205093
市　外	Non-local	886	311177	200786
服务业工会	Services	663	238211	220866
交通运输工会	Transportation	222	258936	257011
政法卫文工会	Politics, Law, Health Care and Culture	275	119224	117388
教育工会	Education	59	120963	115295
金融工会	Finance	51	129980	129894
市直机关工会	Institutions under Direct Municipal Leadership	400	46255	45251
区工会	Labor Unions in Districts and Counties	28573	2772352	2615392

资料来源：北京市总工会。
Source: Beijing Federation of Labor Unions.

23-28 北京市妇女发展规划监测统计资料
SUPERVISORY STATISTICS ON WOMEN DEVELOPMENT PROGRAMS OF BEIJING

项目		Item		2019	2018
城镇单位就业人员数	(万人)	Employed Persons in Urban Entites	(10000 persons)	791.3	819.3
#女性		Females		333.3	338.6
城镇登记失业人员总数	(万人)	Urban Registered Unemployment	(10000 persons)	23.7	23.9
#女性		Females		9.6	9.6
城镇登记失业人员就业人数	(万人)	Employed Persons from Urban Registered Unemployment	(10000 persons)	15.6	15.1
#女性		Females		6.2	6.1
参加基本养老保险人数	(万人)	Number of Participants in Basic Pension Insurance	(10000 persons)	1651.6	1591.5
#女性		Females		746.2	719.3
参加基本医疗保险人数	(万人)	Number of Participants in Basic Medical Insurance	(10000 persons)	1682.5	1628.9
#女性		Females		777.0	751.2
参加失业保险人数	(万人)	Number of Participants in Unemployment Insurance	(10000 persons)	1294.8	1240.7
#女性		Females		569.1	546.6
参加工伤保险人数	(万人)	Number of Participants in Work Injury Insurance	(10000 persons)	1242.2	1187.0
#女性		Females		534.9	507.5
城乡居民养老保险参保人数	(万人)	Number of Urban and Rural Residents Participating in Basic Pension Insurance for Urban and Rural Residents	(10000 persons)	204.7	209.0
#女性		Females		114.5	117.1
市人大女代表领衔提出的议案数	(件)	Number of Proposals Put Forward by Women Deputies of Beijing Municipal People's Congress(BMPC)	(case)	218	27
市政协女委员提出的提案数	(件)	Number of Proposals Put Forward by Women Deputies of Beijing Committee of Chinese People's Political Consultative Conference	(case)	509	437
普通高校在校学生人数	(万人)	Enrollment in Institutions of Higher Education	(10000 persons)	58.6	58.1
#女性		Females		29.8	29.8
在读研究生人数	(万人)	Number of Enrolled Postgraduates	(10000 persons)	36.1	33.6
#女性		Females		18.0	16.6
成人本专科在校生人数	(万人)	Enrollment of Technical Higher and Secondary Education for Adults	(10000 persons)	13.0	14.4
#女性		Females		6.8	7.9
妇科病普查率	(%)	Rate of Gynaopathy General Surveys	(%)	84.6	82.8
高危孕产妇住院分娩率	(%)	Birth-giving Rate of High-risk Lying-in Women in Hospitals	(%)	100.0	100.0
抓获刑事作案成员中女性比例	(%)	Share of Females in Criminal Suspects Captured	(%)	18.6	16.2
得到法律援助机构援助的妇女人数	(人)	Number of Women Receiving Aids from Law Aid Institutions	(person)	9969	17080

资料来源：北京市统计局、北京市人力资源和社会保障局、北京市医疗保障局、北京市人民代表大会常务委员会、中国人民政治协商会议北京市委员会、北京市教育委员会、北京市卫生健康委员会、北京市公安局、北京市司法局。

Source: Beijing Municipal Bureau of Statistics, Beijing Municipal Human Resources and Social Security Bureau, Beijing Municipal Medical Insurance Bureau,Standing Committee of Beijing Municipal People's Congress (BMPC), Beijing Municipal Education Commission, Beijing Municipal Health Commission,Beijing Municipal Bureau of Public Security,Beijing Municipal Bureau of Justice.

23-29 北京市儿童发展规划监测统计资料
SUPERVISORY STATISTICS FOR CHILDREN DEVELOPMENT IN BEIJING

项　目		Item		2019	2018
婚前医学检查率	(%)	Rate of Premarital Medical Checks	(%)	19.55	16.50
新生儿遗传代谢性疾病筛查率	(%)	Screening Rate of Genic Metabolic Diseases for Newborn	(%)	100.37	99.62
出生缺陷监测率	(%)	Monitoring Rate of Birth Deficiencies	(%)	100.0	100.0
新生儿听力筛查率	(%)	Screening Rate of Hearing for Newborns	(%)	97.08	98.33
出生缺陷发生率	(‰)	Rate of Birth Deficiencies	(‰)	19.25	19.36
7岁以下儿童保健管理率	(%)	Rate of Health Management for Children Under 7 Years Old	(%)	98.89	98.83
0-6个月婴儿纯母乳喂养率	(%)	Rate of Exclusive Breast Breeding for Infants of 0-6 Months	(%)	72.93	73.32
婴儿死亡率	(‰)	Mortality Rate of Infants	(‰)	1.99	2.15
5岁以下儿童死亡率	(‰)	Mortality Rate of Children below 5 Years Old	(‰)	2.53	2.69
儿童肥胖率(0-6岁)	(%)	Rate of Obesity for Children of 0-6 Years Old	(%)	3.49	3.61
儿童龋齿率(0-6岁)	(%)	Rate of Decayed Teeth for Children of 0-6 Years Old	(%)	20.64	19.73
卡介苗疫苗接种率	(%)	Rate of Inoculation of BCG Vaccines	(%)	98.64	99.38
脊髓灰质炎疫苗接种率	(%)	Rate of Inoculation of Poliomyelities Polio Vaccines	(%)	99.90	99.58
百白破疫苗接种率	(%)	Rate of Inoculation of Pertussis, Diphtheria and Tetanus Vaccines	(%)	99.91	99.68
含麻疹成分疫苗接种率	(%)	Rate of Inoculation of Vaccines with Measle Ingredients	(%)	99.91	99.64
孕产妇系统管理率	(%)	Rate of Systematic Management for Pregnant and Lying-in	(%)	91.67	97.48
孕产妇健康教育普及率	(%)	Popularization Rate of Health Education for Pregnant and Lying-in Women	(%)	99.93	99.97
孕产妇住院分娩率	(%)	Birth-giving Rate of Pregnant and Lying-in Women in Hospital	(%)	100.0	100.0
孕产妇死亡率	(1/10万)	Mortality Rate of Pregnant and Lying-in Women	(1/100000)	2.96	10.64

资料来源：北京市卫生健康委员会。
Source:Beijing Municipal Health Commission.

主要统计指标解释

参加企业职工基本养老保险人数 指报告期末按照国家法律、法规和有关政策规定参加企业职工基本养老保险并在社保经办机构已建立缴费记录档案的职工人数，包括中断缴费但未终止养老保险关系的职工人数和参加基本养老保险的离休、退休和退职人员的人数。不包括只登记未建立缴费记录档案的人数。

参加基本医疗保险人数 指报告期末按国家有关规定参加基本医疗保险的人数。包括参加保险的职工人数和退休人员数。

参加失业保险人数 指报告期末按照国家法律、法规和有关政策规定参加了失业保险的城镇企业事业单位的职工及地方政府规定参加失业保险的其他人员的人数。参加失业保险人数为参加失业保险的职工人数。

参加工伤保险人数 指报告期末参加工伤保险的职工人数。

参加生育保险人数 指报告期末参加生育保险的职工人数。

参加农村新型合作医疗人数 指截止报告期末乡镇已参加农村新型合作医疗的总人数。农村新型合作医疗制度是由政府组织、引导、支持，农民自愿参加，集体、个人和政府多方筹资，以大病统筹为主的农民医疗互助共济制度。

城市居民最低生活保障人数 指报告期末家庭平均收入在当地规定的最低生活保障线以下的城镇居民数。包括“三无”对象、失业人员和在职、下岗、退休人员等。

农村居民最低生活保障人数 指报告期末在建立农村最低生活保障制度的地区，得到当地政府或集体给予最低生活保障的农业人口家庭人数。

律师 指受聘参加律师事务所工作，提任法律顾问、刑（民）事代理人、刑事辩护人，办理非诉讼事件、解答法律询问，代写法律事务文书等主要从事律师业务的专职法律工作者和兼职律师。

公证人员 指在国家公证机关依法办理公证事务的司法人员。包括公证员、助理公证员和在公证处工作的其他人员。

调解人员 指人民调解委员会担负调解民间一般民事纠纷和轻微违法行为所引起的纠纷的工作人员。包括调解委员会的委员和调解小组调解员。

地震应急避难场所 指适用于地震等自然灾害，也适用于其他事件应急状态下，供居民紧急疏散的公园、公共绿地、城市广场、体育场、学校运动场等场地数量。

Explanatory Notes on Main Statistical Indicators

Participation of Basic Pension Insurance for Enterprise Employed Persons refers to the number of employed persons participating in basic pension insurance and keeping insurance premium payment records with social security organizations in accordance with provisions in national laws, rules and relevant policies at the end of reporting period, including the number of employed persons suspending the payment of insurance premium without terminating the pension insurance relation as well as retired employed persons participating in basic endowment insurance, excluding the number of persons only registered but having no insurance premium payment records.

Number of People Participating in Basic Medical Care Insurance refers to the number of persons participating in basic medical care insurance programs at the end of the reporting period in accordance with relevant national regulations, including the number of employed persons and retired persons participating in the insurance.

Number of People Participating in Unemployment Insurance refers to the number of employed persons in urban enterprises and public institutions participating in unemployment insurance programs at the end of the reporting period in accordance with provisions in national laws, rules and relevant policies, as well as other persons specified by local governments to participate in unemployment insurance. The number of persons participating in unemployment insurance program is the number of employees who participate in unemployment insurance.

Number of People Participating in Work-related Injury Insurance refers to the number of employed persons participating in work-related injury insurance programs at the end of the reporting period.

Number of People Participating in Maternity Insurance refers to the number of employed persons participating in maternity insurance programs at the end of the reporting period.

Number of People Participating in New-type Rural Cooperative Medical Care refers to the total number of rural residents who have participated in the new-type rural cooperative medical care programs at the end of the reporting period. The new-type rural medical care system is a system of mutual aid in medical care for rural residents that is organized, guided and supported by the government, in which the rural residents voluntarily participate. It is a system of multi-party financing by collective entities, individuals and the government, and is mainly based on social pooling for serious disease.

Number of Residents Receiving Subsistence Allowances in Urban Areas refers to the number of urban residents whose average family income is below locally provided minimum living standard at the end of the reporting period, including elderly persons, minors, psychotic patients and disables who have no statutory guardian, no fixed pocketbook, no labor ability, unemployed persons, on-the-job persons, laid-off persons, and retired persons, etc.

Number of Residents Receiving Subsistence Allowances in Rural Areas refers to the number of persons in agricultural families covered by subsistence allowances of local government or collective entities in an area where rural minimum living standard guarantee system is established, at the end of reporting period.

Lawyer refers to a full-time legal worker and part-time lawyer joining a law firm, serving as a legal consultant, criminal (civil) proxy, criminal counsel, handling non-lawsuit events, answering legal questions, writing legal documents for others, and other lawyer business.

Notary refers to any judicial person handling notarization matters in national notarization agencies according to laws, including notaries, assistant notaries, and other personnel working in notarization offices.

Mediator refer to working personnel responsible for mediating general civil disputes as well as disputes caused by slightly illegal acts in any people's mediation committee, including members of people's mediation committees and mediators of mediation teams.

Emergent Earthquake Refuges refer to the number of parks, public green land, city squares, gyms, school playgrounds for residents' emergent evacuation in the event of natural disasters such as earthquake, and under the condition of other emergent events.

24

北京统计年鉴2020　BEIJING STATISTICAL YEARBOOK

开发区
DEVELOPMENT ZONES

简要说明

一、主要内容

本章资料主要反映北京市开发区基本情况，招商、入资、投资、生产情况，重点介绍了北京经济技术开发区和中关村国家自主创新示范区的主要情况。

二、统计范围

根据 2012 年《国务院关于同意调整中关村国家自主创新示范区空间规模和布局的批复》，自 2013 年起，中关村国家自主创新示范区的统计范围在原有的海淀园、丰台园、昌平园、电子城科技园、亦庄园、德胜园、雍和园、石景山园、通州园和大兴生物医药产业基地的基础上，增加了平谷园、门头沟园、顺义园、房山园、密云园、怀柔园和延庆园七个园区。同时，“电子城科技园”更名为“朝阳园”；“德胜园”更名为“西城园”；“雍和园”更名为“东城园”。

中关村国家自主创新示范区亦庄园在中关村国家自主创新示范区与北京经济技术开发区中为重叠部分。

Brief Introduction

I. Main Content

Statistics in this chapter mainly show the basic condition of development zones in Beijing, the business invitation, capital contribution, investment, and production status. This chapter mainly focuses on the situation of Beijing Economic-Technological Development Area, and Zhongguancun National Independent Innovation Demonstration Zone.

II. Notes on Changes in This Chapter

According to the Official Reply of the State Council on Approving the Adjustment of Spatial Scale and Layout of Zhongguancun National Innovation Demonstration Area issued in 2012, the statistic scope of Zhongguancun Area has been enlarged to include Pinggu Sub-park, Mentougou Sub-park, Shunyi Sub-park, Fangshan Sub-park, Miyun Sub-park, Huairou Sub-park and Yanqing Sub-park to supplement Haidian Sub-park, Fengtai Sub-park, Changping Sub-park, Electronic Park, Yizhuang Sub-park, Deshengyuan Sub-park, Yonghe Sub-park, Shijingshan Sub-park, Tongzhou Sub-park and Daxing Ecological Sub-park Pharmaceutical Base. At the same time, Electronic Park is changed into Chaoyang Sub-park, Deshengyuan Sub-park into Xicheng Sub-park and Yonghe Sub-park into Dongcheng Sub-park.

Data of Zhongguancun Yizhuang Sub-park is counted in both Zhongguancun National Independent Innovation Demonstration Zone and Beijing Economic-Technological Development Area.

24-1 开发区基本情况(2019年)
STATISTICS ON DEVELOPMENT ZONES (2019)

项 目		Item		国家级 National	市 级 Municipal
开发区个数	(个)	Number of Development Zones	(unit)	3	16
区规划总面积	(公顷)	Total Planned Area of Development Zones	(hectare)	45682.9	10462.0
累计已开发土地面积	(公顷)	Accumulated Area of Developed Land	(hectare)	33236.9	7791.3
累计已供应土地面积	(公顷)	Accumulated Area of Supplied Land	(hectare)	30439.5	6086.1
累计已建成城镇建设用地面积	(公顷)	Accumulated Area of Land for Urban Development	(hectare)	26399.5	5657.0
累计招商项目企业个数	(个)	Accumulated Number of Enterprises of Business Inviting Programs	(unit)	85067	33098
累计招商项目总投资	(亿元)	Accumulative Total Investment of Business Inviting	(100 million yuan)	37931.7	9266.0
累计招商项目注册资本	(亿元)	Accumulative Registered Capital of Business Inviting Programs	(100 million yuan)	35937.6	9523.6
#三资企业		Three Kinds of Foreign-funded Enterprises		4122.3	805.9
累计招商项目合同外资金额	(亿美元)	Accumulative Contracted Foreign Capital of Business Inviting Programs	(USD 100 million)	478.8	72.5
累计招商项目外商实际投资	(亿美元)	Accumulated Actual Foreign Investment of Business Inviting Programs	(USD 100 million)	368.2	67.9
总收入	(亿元)	Total Revenue	(100 million yuan)	73700.0	10171.4
工业总产值(当年价格)	(亿元)	Gross Output Value of Industry (at current prices)	(100 million yuan)	12692.2	1942.6
利润总额	(亿元)	Total Profits	(100 million yuan)	4369.1	887.7
应缴税金	(亿元)	Total Taxes Payable	(100 million yuan)	2134.0	303.7

注：1．本表中的开发区包括国家级及北京市级开发区，下同。
2．表内“累计”指自开始至年末的累计数。
3．本表市级开发区“总收入”“工业总产值(当年价格)”“利润总额”和“应缴税金”数据的统计范围为注册在开发区内的规模(限额)以上法人单位。

Note: a) Development zones in this table include those at national level and Beijing municipal,the same below.
b) Accumulative data in this table refer to the accumulation from the beginning to the end of this year.
c) The statistical scope of total revenue, gross output value of industry (at current prices), total profits and total taxes payable of municipal-level development zones in this table cover legal entities above designated size that are registered in the development zones.

24–2 开发区土地开发情况(2019年)
LAND EXPLOITATION OF DEVELOPMENT ZONES(2019)

单位：公顷 (hectare)

名　称	Item	规划总面积 Total Planned Area	累计已开发土地面积 Accumulated Area of Developed Land	累计已供应土地面积 Accumulated Area of Supplied Land	累计已建成城镇建设用地 Accumulated Area of Land for Urban Development
国家级开发区	**State-level Development Zone**	**45682.9**	**33236.9**	**30439.5**	**26399.5**
北京经济技术开发区	Beijing Economic-Technological Development Area	5960.0	5114.6	4407.4	3956.8
中关村国家自主创新示范区	Zhongguancun National Independent Innovation Demonstration Zone	41854.3	30450.8	25708.5	24862.2
海 淀 园	Haidian Sub-park	17430.6	14176.4	13906.2	13428.7
丰 台 园	Fengtai Sub-park	818.0	470.0	426.2	415.2
昌 平 园	Changping Sub-park	5140.3	2742.8	2492.7	1954.2
朝 阳 园	Chaoyang Sub-park	2610.0	1471.9	1447.1	1067.4
亦 庄 园	Yizhuang Sub-park	2678.0	2678.0		2678.0
西 城 园	Xicheng Sub-park	1000.0	1000.0	1000.0	1000.0
东 城 园	Dongcheng Sub-park	603.0	288.8		288.8
石景山园	Shijingshan Sub-park	1334.0	400.0	400.0	133.4
通 州 园	Tongzhou Sub-park	3434.6	2323.4	1973.9	1284.6
大 兴 园	Daxing Sub-park	1124.7	710.2	573.4	354.5
平 谷 园	PingGu Sub-park	508.0	227.7	103.4	85.2
门头沟园	MenTouGou Sub-park	189.0	120.0	120.0	
房 山 园	FangShan Sub-park	1572.6	1204.7	1145.2	747.9
顺 义 园	ShunYi Sub-park	1208.5	912.4	599.5	412.2
密 云 园	MiYun Sub-park	1000.8	699.3	607.0	462.4
怀 柔 园	HuaiRou Sub-park	711.0	693.1	664.3	359.2
延 庆 园	YanQing Sub-park	491.2	332.3	249.6	190.6
北京天竺综合保税区	Beijing Tianzhu Bonded Area	546.6	349.5	323.7	258.5
市级开发区	**Municipal-level Development Zone**	**10462.0**	**7791.3**	**6086.1**	**5657.0**
北京石龙经济开发区	Shilong Economic Development Zone	189.0	120.0	120.0	
北京良乡经济开发区	Liangxiang Economic Development Zone	240.9	136.1	132.7	117.4
北京大兴经济开发区	Daxing Economic Development Zone	416.0	394.6	394.6	377.6
北京通州经济开发区	Tongzhou Economic Development Zone	1947.6	770.7	750.5	637.3
北京雁栖经济开发区	Yanqi Economic Development Zone	1096.0	1096.0	722.2	637.6
北京兴谷经济开发区	Xinggu Economic Development Zone	503.2	571.7	421.6	596.0
北京密云经济开发区	Miyun Economic Development Zone	1249.5	1249.5	1000.4	910.0
北京八达岭经济开发区	Badaling Economic Development Zone	491.2	332.3	249.6	190.6
北京永乐经济开发区	Yongle Economic Development Zone	459.8	219.3	137.1	137.1
北京延庆经济开发区	Yanqing Economic Development Zone				
北京昌平小汤山工业园区	Changping Xiaotangshan Industrial Park	257.3	23.5	23.5	45.3
北京采育经济开发区	Caiyu Economic Development Zone	355.0	327.1	319.7	285.0
北京房山工业园区	Fangshan Industrial Park	218.5	159.5	150.7	122.8
北京马坊工业园区	Mafang Bonded Area Industrial Park	345.6	202.5	140.4	114.7
北京临空经济核心区	Beijing Airport Economic Core Area	1360.4	1245.9	700.0	662.5
北京顺义科技创新产业功能区	Beijing Shunyi Science and Technology Innovation Industry Functional Area	1332.0	942.6	823.2	823.2

注：1.中关村国家自主创新示范区亦庄园数据在中关村国家自主创新示范区与北京经济技术开发区中为重叠部分。
2.北京八达岭经济开发区包括北京延庆经济开发区数据。
3.表内“累计”指自开始至年末的累计数。

Note: a) Data on Yizhuang Sub-park of Zhongguancun National Independent Innovation Demonstration Zone are overlapped in Zhongguancun National Independent Innovation Demonstration Zone and Beijing Economic and Technological Development Area.
b) The data on Badaling Economic Development Zone include the data on Yanqing Economic Development Zone.
c) "Accumulated" in this table refers to the accumulation from the beginning to the end of the year.

24-3 开发区招商、入资情况(2019年)

名 称	Item	招商项目企业个数(个) Number of Enterprises Involved in Business Inviting Programs (unit)
国家级开发区	**State-level Development Zone**	**85067**
北京经济技术开发区	Beijing Economic-Technological Development Area	25894
中关村国家自主创新示范区	Zhongguancun National Independent Innovation Demonstration Zone	59645
海 淀 园	Haidian Sub-park	29985
丰 台 园	Fengtai Sub-park	12506
昌 平 园	Changping Sub-park	4813
朝 阳 园	Chaoyang Sub-park	2212
亦 庄 园	Yizhuang Sub-park	1013
西 城 园	Xicheng Sub-park	842
东 城 园	Dongcheng Sub-park	2630
石景山园	Shijingshan Sub-park	3163
通 州 园	Tongzhou Sub-park	526
大 兴 园	Daxing Sub-park	176
平 谷 园	PingGu Sub-park	245
门头沟园	MenTouGou Sub-park	278
房 山 园	FangShan Sub-park	340
顺 义 园	ShunYi Sub-park	577
密 云 园	MiYun Sub-park	159
怀 柔 园	HuaiRou Sub-park	180
延 庆 园	YanQing Sub-park	
北京天竺综合保税区	Beijing Tianzhu Bonded Area	541
市级开发区	**Municipal-level Development Zone**	**33098**
北京石龙经济开发区	Shilong Economic Development Zone	12963
北京良乡经济开发区	Liangxiang Economic Development Zone	80
北京大兴经济开发区	Daxing Economic Development Zone	6451
北京通州经济开发区	Tongzhou Economic Development Zone	89
北京雁栖经济开发区	Yanqi Economic Development Zone	1846
北京兴谷经济开发区	Xinggu Economic Development Zone	309
北京密云经济开发区	Miyun Economic Development Zone	264
北京八达岭经济开发区	Badaling Economic Development Zone	4533
北京永乐经济开发区	Yongle Economic Development Zone	105
北京延庆经济开发区	Yanqing Economic Development Zone	
北京昌平小汤山工业园区	Changping Xiaotangshan Industrial Park	78
大兴采育经济开发区	Caiyu Economic Development Zone	60
北京房山工业园区	Fangshan Industrial Park	31
北京马坊工业园区	Mafang Industrial Park	74
北京临空经济核心区	Beijing Airport Economic Core Area	4196
北京顺义科技创新产业功能区	Beijing Shunyi Science and Technology Innovation Industry Functional Area	2019

注：1.中关村国家自主创新示范区亦庄园数据在中关村国家自主创新示范区与北京经济技术开发区中为重叠部分。
2.北京八达岭经济开发区包括北京延庆经济开发区数据。

STATISTICS FOR BUSINESS INVITATION AND INVESTMENT IN DEVELOPMENT ZONES (2019)

自开始至报告期累计 Accumulative Number from Beginning				
项目 总投资（万元） Total Investment (10000 yuan)	注册资本（万元） Registered Capital (10000 yuan)	#三资企业 Foreign-funded Enterprises	合同外资金额（万美元） Contracted Foreign Capital (USD 10000)	外商实际投资（万美元） Actual Foreign Investment (USD 10000)
379317353	**359375553**	**41222585**	**4788499**	**3681627**
123388094	109425175	15870740	1250093	929947
270165561	259510664	29105406	3739593	2948240
112521384	111457514	15118621	2318375	1589377
34164448	34164448	280043	31449	39149
37317242	35584584	1445788	130311	130311
14324805	14324805	2674358	198253	198253
19313689	11580571	4549870	365887	357421
26250679	26250679	1394145	202094	202094
2762313	2762313	123787	3293	3142
7708725	7708725	282751	98447	39080
2639197	1893754	417077	24307	24307
428013	409549	29833	7542	7092
529249	524333	14450	7431	4732
1910950	1910950	172327	21996	14925
394955	1794946	280108	75	1451
8132060	7710525	2280745	326375	328115
917400	1129433	41504	3759	8791
850453	303535			
5077387	2020284	796309	164700	160861
92659656	**95236495**	**8059095**	**724724**	**679252**
10160559	10160559	168487	22478	6497
258102	156970	17730	1532	1532
11949236	11470724	228830	10675	9491
2996539	868049	274346	40360	37198
3441444	1162850	460489	240471	252780
1006291	433564	271453	67455	67185
3140671	629041	131210	24807	62206
9960770	11595228	2946	6220	6880
454817	162766	2623		1850
52800	34731	6242	989	655
854874	425256	39998	3409	3409
389755	143024			
314517	314517	88321		
47679281	47679281	3246511	306329	229569
	9999935	3119909		

Note: a) Data on Yizhuang Sub-park of Zhongguancun Demonstration Zone are overlapped in Zhongguancun National Innovation Demonstration Zone and Beijing Economic and Technological Development Area.

b) The data on Badaling Economic Development Zone include the data on Yanqing Economic Development Zone.

24-4 开发区生产情况(2019年)
PRODUCTION OF DEVELOPMENT ZONES (2019)

名称	Item	自年初累计 Accumulative Number from Year-beginning 总收入(万元) Total Revenue (10000 yuan)	利润总额(万元) Total Profits (10000 yuan)
国家级开发区	**State-level Development Zone**	**736999704**	**43690751**
北京经济技术开发区	Beijing Economic-Technological Development Area	131441149	6697334
中关村国家自主创新示范区	Zhongguancun National Independent Innovation Demonstration Zone	664221790	41826039
海淀园	Haidian Sub-park	274594303	14550106
丰台园	Fengtai Sub-park	62728342	3871145
昌平园	Changping Sub-park	45700100	2581634
朝阳园	Chaoyang Sub-park	68890057	4247909
亦庄园	Yizhuang Sub-park	62801499	5198590
西城园	Xicheng Sub-park	33711680	3129427
东城园	Dongcheng Sub-park	30365751	2462112
石景山园	Shijingshan Sub-park	26131947	3097585
通州园	Tongzhou Sub-park	9482538	480349
大兴园	Daxing Sub-park	8541829	556718
平谷园	PingGu Sub-park	1710799	26301
门头沟园	MenTouGou Sub-park	3651255	117200
房山园	FangShan Sub-park	5044805	132959
顺义园	ShunYi Sub-park	19615168	1234212
密云园	MiYun Sub-park	4060496	-224237
怀柔园	HuaiRou Sub-park	5741853	338388
延庆园	YanQing Sub-park	1449369	25642
北京天竺综合保税区	Beijing Tianzhu Bonded Area	4138264	365968
市级开发区	**Municipal-level Development Zone**	**101713531**	**8877050**
北京石龙经济开发区	Shilong Economic Development Zone	10175791	-498576
北京良乡经济开发区	Liangxiang Economic Development Zone	3164955	81999
北京大兴经济开发区	Daxing Economic Development Zone	3573514	134820
北京通州经济开发区	Tongzhou Economic Development Zone	1818724	318654
北京雁栖经济开发区	Yanqi Economic Development Zone	4452046	449800
北京兴谷经济开发区	Xinggu Economic Development Zone	2052348	56201
北京密云经济开发区	Miyun Economic Development Zone	4146341	255575
北京八达岭经济开发区	Badaling Economic Development Zone	2185593	121792
北京永乐经济开发区	Yongle Economic Development Zone	101485	-4300
北京延庆经济开发区	Yanqing Economic Development Zone	8353652	2996510
北京昌平小汤山工业园区	Changping Xiaotangshan Industrial Park	45108	346
大兴采育经济开发区	Caiyu Economic Development Zone	2121866	180827
北京房山工业园区	Fangshan Industrial Park	688468	32948
北京马坊工业园区	Mafang Industrial Park	366317	4254
北京临空经济核心区	Beijing Airport Economic Core Area	45354288	3902418
北京顺义科技创新产业功能区	Beijing Shunyi Science and Technology Innovation Industry Functional Area	13113034	843781

注：1.中关村国家自主创新示范区亦庄园数据在中关村国家自主创新示范区与北京经济技术开发区中为重叠部分。
2.北京经济技术开发区、市级各开发区“总收入”“利润总额”指标的统计范围为规模(限额)以上法人单位。

Note: a) Data on Yizhuang Sub-park of Zhongguancun Demonstration Zone are overlapped in Zhongguancun National Innovation Demonstration Zone and Beijing Economic and Technological Development Area.
b) The statistical scope of total revenue and total profits for Beijing Economic-Technological Development Area and other municipal-level development zones covers legal entities above designated size.

24-5 北京经济技术开发区主要经济指标
MAIN ECONOMIC INDICATORS FOR BEIJING ECONOMIC-TECHNOLOGICAL DEVELOPMENT AREA

项　目		Item		2019	2018	2019年为2018年% 2019 as % of 2018
规划面积	(公顷)	Area Planned	(hectare)	5960.0	5960.0	100.0
开发区生产总值	(亿元)	Gross Output Value	(100 million yuan)	1932.8	1793.5	108.9
工业总产值		Gross Output Value of Industry				
（当年价格）	(亿元)	(at current prices)	(100 million yuan)	4125.2	3713.7	111.1
#高新技术企业		High and New Technology Enterprises		3431.4	3171.8	108.2
销售(营业)收入	(亿元)	Sales(Business)Revenue	(100 million yuan)	13372.0	11049.8	121.0
利润总额	(亿元)	Total Profits	(100 million yuan)	665.4	631.1	105.4
进出口总值	(亿美元)	Total Value of Imports and Exports	(USD 100 million)	195.8	192.9	101.5
出　口		Exports		57.3	63.5	90.3
进　口		Imports		138.5	129.4	107.0
一般公共预算收入	(亿元)	General Public Budget Revenue	(100 million yuan)	270.0	257.3	104.9
一般公共预算支出	(亿元)	General Public Budget Expenditure	(100 million yuan)	226.9	205.7	110.3
实际利用外资	(亿美元)	Actual Use of Foreign Capital	(USD 100 million)	5.6	5.4	104.1
固定资产投资增速	(%)	Growth Rate of Fixed Assets Investment	(%)	-6.6	-6.4	
从业人员期末人数	(人)	Number of Employed Persons	(person)	376819	348075	108.3
从业人员工资总额	(亿元)	Total Wages of Employed Persons	(100 million yuan)	532.5	452.4	117.7

注：工业总产值(当年价格)、销售(营业)收入和利润总额指标的统计范围是规模(限额)以上法人单位。
资料来源：北京经济技术开发区社会发展局、调查队。
Note: The statistical scope of gross output value of industry (at current prices), sales (business) revenue and total profits covers legal entities above designated size.
Source: Social Development Bureau and Survey Team of Beijing Economic-Technological Development Area.

24-6 中关村国家自主创新示范区企业经营及科技活动情况(2008-2019年)
OPERATING ACTIVITIES AND SCIENCE ACTIVITIES OF ENTERPRISES IN ZHONGGUANCUN NATIONAL INNOVATION DEMONSTRATION ZONE (2008-2019)

项目	Item	2008	2009	2010	2011	2012
总收入 (亿元)	**Total Revenue (100 million yuan)**	**10222.4**	**13004.6**	**15940.2**	**19646.0**	**25025.0**
技术收入	Technological Revenue	1693.4	2093.6	2478.3	2845.9	3403.1
产品销售收入	Products Sales Revenue	5229.2	5923.6	6889.6	7809.4	8741.2
#新产品销售收入	Sales Revenue of New Products	3327.0	3203.7	3949.2	3405.1	3352.1
商品销售收入	Commodity Sales Revenue	2398.9	3689.4	5032.2	7161.9	10077.4
其他收入	Other Revenues	900.9	1298.0	1540.1	1828.9	2803.4
实缴税费总额 (亿元)	**Total Tax Paid (100 million yuan)**	**504.0**	**658.7**	**767.2**	**925.8**	**1445.8**
利润总额 (亿元)	**Total Profits (100 million yuan)**	**726.3**	**1122.4**	**1298.9**	**1533.9**	**1788.6**
专利情况	**Statistics on Patents**					
当年专利申请数 (件)	Number of Patents Applied in the Year (unit)	17219	17226	18515	24894	34192
期末有效发明专利数 (件)	Number of Patents in Force at the End of the Period (unit)	9836	11611	13988	15232	23198
当年专利授权数 (件)	Number of Patents Licensed in the Year (unit)	9050	10512	13151	12951	17969

24-6 续表 Continued

项目	Item	2013	2014	2015	2016	2017	2018	2019
总收入 (亿元)	**Total Revenue (100 million yuan)**	**30497.4**	**36057.6**	**40811.9**	**46047.6**	**53025.8**	**58830.9**	**66422.2**
技术收入	Technological Revenue	4032.4	4837.7	6623.6	7580.4	9369.6	11174.3	13450.8
产品销售收入	Products Sales Revenue	10788.4	12474.2	13300.0	14752.5	15934.2	17058.7	19085.2
#新产品销售收入	Sales Revenue of New Products	4070.4	4614.8	4397.5	4565.6	5097.3	4834.9	6430.1
商品销售收入	Commodity Sales Revenue	11339.6	12832.6	13339.5	14522.4	16406.1	17878.0	20253.9
其他收入	Other Revenues	4337.0	5913.1	7548.9	9192.3	11315.9	12719.9	13632.3
实缴税费总额 (亿元)	**Total Tax Paid (100 million yuan)**	**1506.6**	**1857.6**	**2038.1**	**2314.1**	**2598.4**	**2842.0**	**2597.1**
利润总额 (亿元)	**Total Profits (100 million yuan)**	**2264.8**	**3031.5**	**3404.5**	**3732.5**	**4321.1**	**4413.3**	**4182.6**
专利情况	**Statistics on Patents**							
当年专利申请数 (件)	Number of Patents Applied in the Year (unit)	44275	55009	68944	74923	86419	102717	115198
期末有效发明专利数 (件)	Number of Patents in Force at the End of the Perio (unit)	35000	44870	63171	82890	114469	141486	170772
当年专利授权数 (件)	Number of Patents Licensed in the Year (unit)	22308	25065	32327	37629	46046	56374	61221

24–7 中关村国家自主创新示范区企业经营活动情况
OPERATING ACTIVITIES OF ENTERPRISES IN ZHONGGUANCUN NATIONAL INDEPENDENT INNOVATION DEMONSTRATION ZONE

单位：亿元 (100 million yuan)

项　目	Item	2019	2018
工业总产值(当年价格)	Gross Output Value of Industry (at current prices)	11886.7	11129.1
总收入	Total Revenue	66422.2	58830.9
技术收入	Technological Revenue	13450.8	11174.3
产品销售收入	Products Sales Revenue	19085.2	17058.7
#新产品销售收入	Sales Revenue of New Products	6430.1	4834.9
商品销售收入	Commodity Sales Revenue	20253.9	17878.0
其他收入	Other Revenues	13632.3	12719.9
利润总额	Total Profits	4182.6	4413.3
实缴税费总额	Total Tax Paid	2597.1	2842.0
#增值税	Value Added Tax	1248.3	1387.5
所得税	Corporate Income Tax	812.2	911.4
减免税总额	Reduced and Exempted Tax	680.0	604.9
#增值税	Value Added Tax	249.4	237.9
所得税	Corporate Income Tax	419.2	361.2
应交增值税	Value Added Tax Payable	996.2	921.5
出口总额	Foreign Exchange Created by Export	2507.3	2088.4

24-8 中关村国家自主创新示范区企业研发活动情况
SCIENTIFIC ACTIVITIES OF ENTERPRISES IN ZHONGGUANCUN NATIONAL INNOVATION DEMONSTRATION ZONE

项目	Item	2019	2018
研究开发活动情况	**Statistics on Research and Development Activities**		
研究开发人员合计 (人)	Total Number of Research and Development Personnel (person)	863167	784720
#全职人员	Full-time Personnel	805295	736800
研究开发费用合计 (亿元)	Total Research and Development Costs (100 million yuan)	3400.1	2749.4
#人员人工费用	Labor Cost	1899.0	1520.0
委托外部研究开发费用 (亿元)	Costs of Research and Development Conducted by External Units Entrusted (100 million yuan)	310.5	205.3
#委托境外机构	Entrusted Overseas Institution	12.4	8.1
研究开发产出情况	**Research and Development Output**		
专利情况	**Statistics on Patents**		
当年专利申请申请数 (件)	Number of Patents Applied (case)	115198	102717
#发明专利	Invention Patents	70760	64946
期末有效发明专利数 (件)	Number of Patents in Force at the End of the Period (case)	170772	141486
当年专利授权数 (件)	Number of Patent Licensed (case)	61221	56374
论文、著作情况	**Statistics on Papers and Writings**		
发表科技论文 (篇)	Number of Published Scientific Papers (unit)	21120	15818
技术改造和技术获取情况	**Technical Rennovation and Acquisition**		
技术改造经费支出 (亿元)	Expenditures on Technical Rennovation (100 million yuan)	21.3	25.4
引进境外技术经费支出 (亿元)	Expenditures on Introduction of Foreign Technologies (100 million yuan)	16.2	11.7
引进境外技术的消化吸收经费支出 (亿元)	Expenditures on Absorption of Imported Technologies (100 million yuan)	0.7	1.1
购买境内技术经费支出 (亿元)	Expenditures on Purchasing Domestic Technologies (100 million yuan)	18.2	19.9

24—9 中关村国家自主创新示范区企业人力资源情况
HUMAN RESOURCES OF ENTERPRISES IN ZHONGGUANCUN NATIONAL INNOVATION DEMONSTRATION ZONE

单位：人 (person)

项　目	Item	2019	2018
从业人员年末人数	**Number of Employeed Persons at the Year End**	**2809570**	**2720575**
#留学归国人员	Returned Students Studying Abroad	47452	39752
#在岗长期职工	On-the-post Long-term Employed Persons	2575807	2522450
按文化程度分	**By Educational Background**		
#博士及以上	Doctor Degree and Above	30997	29104
#留学归国人员	Returned Students Studying Abroad	3385	3620
硕　士	Masters	346195	319508
#留学归国人员	Returned Students Studying Abroad	34009	28815
大　本	Undergraduates	1303770	1208263
大　专	Junior College	572457	562514
按年龄分	**By Age**		
#29岁及以下	Age 29 and Below	1035612	1049508
30—39岁	30-39	1151555	1085404
40—49岁	40-49	426348	400601
从业人员平均人数	**Average Number of Empolyed Persons**	**2816811**	**2726229**

24—10 中关村国家自主创新示范区企业财务状况
FINANCIAL STATUS OF ENTERPRISES IN ZHONGGUANCUN NATIONAL INNOVATION DEMONSTRATION ZONE

单位：亿元 (100 million yuan)

项　目	Item	2019	2018
资产总计	Total Assets	137046.6	129695.8
流动资产合计	Total Current Assets	72090.2	74571.6
累计折旧	Accumulative Depreciation	7332.4	6617.2
负债合计	Total Liabilities	79892.6	74001.2
所有者权益合计	Total Owner's Equity	57153.9	55694.6
实收资本	Paid-up Capital	32900.4	25913.0
利润总额	Total Profits	4182.6	4413.3

主要统计指标解释

已开发土地面积 指在规划范围内达到“七通一平”标准的，具备进行房屋建筑物施工或出让条件的土地面积。

已供应土地面积 指开发区内通过各种方式获得土地使用权的土地面积，包括出让、划拨、租赁等。

已建成城镇建设用地面积 截至报告期，已经建设并通过竣工验收的国有建设用地。包括已建成的住宅用地、工矿仓储用地、多功能用地、交通运输用地、商服用地、公共管理与公共服务用地，以及其他城镇建设用地等。海关特殊监管区域的已建成城镇建设用地包括现状围网范围内已建成的城镇建设用地，及开发区四至范围与围网范围间的海关专属办公用地。

累计招商项目企业个数 指自开始至报告期末累计招商入区，并经工商管理机关注册取得法人营业执照的企业个数。

累计招商项目总投资 指自开始至报告期末累计批准的合同（章程）规定的投资总额。

累计招商项目注册资本 指自开始至报告期末累计为设立经营企业在工商行政管理机关注册的资本总额。

累计招商项目合同外资金额 指自开始至报告期末累计批准的合同（章程）中，外商和港、澳、台商的出资额。

累计招商项目外商实际投资 指自开始至报告期末累计按合同规定的外方和港、澳、台方以现金、实物、工业产权及专有技术的计价实缴资本投资额。

总收入 指企业全年的生产产品销售收入、技术性收入和与本企业产品相关的商品的销售收入、其它收入等各种收入的总和，总收入等于主营业务收入加上其他业务收入。总收入应按不含增值税的价格计算，不包括补贴收入、营业外收入、投资收益。

出口总额 指出售给外贸部门或直接出售给外商的产品、商品、技术或服务的总金额。包括来料加工装配出口，境外技术合同实现金额及在国内以外汇计价的商品出售和技术服务的总额等。

留学归国人员 指出国学习，取得学位的归国人员。

Explanatory Notes on Main Statistical Indicators

Area of Developed Land refers to the area of land that meets the standard of "seven connections and one leveling" and is qualified for construction or sale.

Area of Supplied Land refers to the area of land whose right of use is acquired in the development zones by various means including sale, transfer, and lease.

Area of Land for Urban Development refers to state-owned construction land that has already gone through construction and acceptance check by the end of the reporting period. It includes land for complete residential buildings, land for industrial, mining and storage use, multi-functional land, land for transportation, land for commercial services, land for public administration and services and other lands for urban development. Land for urban development under special administration of customs includes urban development land completed inside the current seine and land for office buildings of customs inside the development zones and between the seines.

Accumulated Number of Enterprises Involved in Business Inviting Programs refers to the total number of enterprises invited to development zones and awarded with business licenses for legal persons from the administration for industry and commerce from the beginning to the end of the reporting period.

Accumulative Investment of Business Inviting Programs refers to the total investment of contracts (articles of incorporation) approved from the beginning to the end of the reporting period.

Accumulative Registered Capital of Business Inviting Programs refers to the total capital registered with the administration for industry and commerce for the purpose of establishment of operating enterprises from the beginning to the end of the reporting period.

Accumulative Contracted Foreign Capital of Business Inviting Programs refers to the cumulative capital contribution of investors from foreign countries, Hong Kong, Macao and Taiwan as approved in contracts (articles of incorporation) from the beginning to the end of the reporting period.

Accumulative Actual Foreign Investment of Business Inviting Programs refers to the cumulative amount of paid-up capital investment from foreign countries, Hong Kong, Macao and Taiwan made in cash, in physical material, industrial property right and proprietary technology, as stated in contracts, from the beginning to the end of the reporting period.

Total Revenue refers to the sum of income earned by enterprises from sales of their own products, technological income, and income from selling commodities related to their own products, and other income. Total revenue is the sum of main business income and other business income. Total revenue shall be calculated at VAT-excluded prices, and exclude subsidies, non-operating income and return on investment across the year.

Total Exports refers to the total amount of products or commodities sold to foreign trade organizations or directly sold to foreign traders. It includes the value of export of investor's raw materials processed, the value of technical contracts completed at home and abroad, and the total value of domestic commodity sales and technical services measured in foreign currency.

Returned Students Studying Abroad refer to persons who have come home after studying abroad and been conferred with academic degrees.